THE AMERICAN CIRCUS

Susan Weber
Kenneth L. Ames
Matthew Wittmann
Editors

THE AMERICAN CIRCUS

**Published by the
Bard Graduate Center:
Decorative Arts,
Design History,
Material Culture/
New York; and
by Yale University
Press/New Haven
and London**

Rachel Adams
Brenda Assael
Leon Botstein
Ellen Butler Donovan
Fred Dahlinger, Jr.
Janet M. Davis
Rodney Huey
Jennifer Lemmer Posey
Eugene W. Metcalf
Brett Mizelle
Susan Nance
Gregory J. Renoff
Kory W. Rogers
Paul Stirton
Peta Tait
Susan Weber
Matthew Wittmann

Project coordinator: Matthew Wittmann
Project assistant: Ann Marguerite Tartsinis
Coordinator of catalogue photography:
Alexis Mucha
Copy editor: Mary Christian
Catalogue and jacket design: Barbara Glauber,
Florian Brożek, Azusa Kobayashi,
and Greg Skiano/Heavy Meta, New York
Catalogue production, London: Sally Salvesen
Printed and bound: Conti Tipocolor Spa, Italy

Chief Curator and Executive Editor of
Exhibition Publications, Bard Graduate Center:
Nina Stritzler-Levine

Library of Congress
Cataloging-in-Publication Data
The American Circus / Susan Weber.
pages cm
Includes bibliographical references and index.
ISBN 978-0-300-18539-3
1. Circus—United States. I. Weber, Susan,
1954– editor of compilation.
GV1803.A44 2012
791.30973—dc23
2012001063

Front cover: Frederick Whitman Glasier. Frank "Slivers" Oakley, ca. 1903. Photograph. Collection of the John and Mable Ringling Museum of Art, Glasier Glass Plate Negative Collection, 1183

Back cover: "Acrobats and Jugglers and Their Wonderful Feats," illustration from *A Peep at the Circus* (New York: McLoughlin Brothers, 1887). Chromolithograph. Baldwin Library of Historical Children's Literature, University of Florida

Frontispiece: Detail of Frederick Whitman Glasier. "Mademoiselle Omega" Gertrude Dewar, 1908. Photograph. Collection of the John and Mable Ringling Museum of Art, Glasier Glass Plate Negative Collection, 0071

Page 6: Detail of Acrobats on Horseback, 1870. Stock poster, woodcut carved by Joseph Morse, printed by Warren, Johnson & Co., Buffalo. Library of Congress Prints and Photographs Division

Page 436: Frederick Whitman Glasier. Clown with 3 equestrians, ca. 1903. Photograph. Collection of the John and Mable Ringling Museum of Art, Glasier Glass Plate Negative Collection, 1194

The American Circus is made possible
in part with support from the
Mr. and Mrs. Raymond J. Horowitz
Foundation for the Arts

Contents

About the Contributors

Rachel Adams is Professor of English and American Studies at Columbia University. She is the author of *Sideshow U.S.A.: Freaks and the American Cultural Imagination* and *Continental Divides: Remapping the Cultures of North America*, both published by the University of Chicago Press. She is finishing a memoir on raising a child with a disability, forthcoming by Yale University Press.

Kenneth L. Ames has been a professor at the Bard Graduate Center since 1996. His course offerings focus on the decorative arts and material culture of the United States and Western Europe during the last four centuries. He has written extensively on museology, folk art, historical household furnishings, and other classes of objects. His most recent publication is *American Christmas Cards 1900–1960,* a catalogue accompanying a BGC Focus Gallery exhibition in 2011. Current interests include social class and taste and the material aspects of travel and tourism.

Brenda Assael has spent most of her career as Lecturer in Modern British History at Swansea University in the United Kingdom. She is the author of *The Circus and Victorian Society*, as well as numerous articles that explore the intersection of performance and Victorian society and culture. She is currently at work on a monograph on the restaurant in nineteenth-century London and is a McMicken Scholar in the College of Arts and Sciences at the University of Cincinnati as well as a Fellow of the Royal Historical Society (London).

Leon Botstein has been President of Bard College since 1975. He is also Music Director of the American Symphony Orchestra; Artistic Director, Summerscape and Bard Music Festivals; Conductor Laureate, Jerusalem Symphony Orchestra, where he served as Music Director from 2003 to 2010; and editor of *The Musical Quarterly*. Forthcoming publications include a sequel to his book *Jefferson's Children: Education and the Promise of American Culture*; the Tanner Lectures on the *History of Listening*; and an anthology of his essays in German. Published works include *The Compleat Brahms*; *Jews and the City of Vienna, 1870–1938*; *Judentum und Modernität: Essays zur Rolle der Juden in der Deutschen und Österreichischen Kultur, 1848–1938.*

Fred Dahlinger Jr. is Curator of Circus History at the John and Mable Ringling Museum of Art in Sarasota, Florida, a campus of Florida State University. His publication credits include over seventy articles and three books, including *Badger State Showmen*, co-authored with Stuart Thayer. He served as History Consultant for the NEH-supported exhibit and book *The Amazing American Circus Poster* and Contributing Editor for *The Circus 1850–1970*. Dahlinger was recently named the editor and publisher of *Bandwagon*, the bimonthly journal of the Circus Historical Society.

Janet M. Davis is Associate Professor of American Studies, History, and Women's and Gender Studies at the University of Texas at Austin. She is the author of *The Circus Age: Culture and Society under the American Big Top*, winner of a Choice Outstanding Academic Title Award and the Robert W. Hamilton Book Award, as well as a finalist for the George Freedley Memorial Award from the Theatre Library Association. Davis is also the editor of *Circus Queen and Tinker Bell: The Life of Tiny Kline*, by Tiny Kline.

Ellen Butler Donovan is a professor of English at Middle Tennessee State University, where she teaches courses in children's and adolescent literature. She focuses on nineteenth-century children's literature in her research and has presented her findings on the role of the circus in children's literature at several academic conferences. Her current projects include scholarly articles on Nathaniel Hawthorne, James Otis, and the circus picture books of the McLoughlin Brothers.

Rodney Huey worked in the circus industry for two decades, serving as Vice President of Public Relations for Feld Entertainment, Inc., parent company of Ringling Bros. and Barnum & Bailey Circus. He supervised the circus's national public relations and publicity campaigns, and was actively involved with Clown College. He earned a PhD in cultural studies from George Mason University in 2006, writing his dissertation on the construction of the American circus clown. He is the editor of *The International Guide to the Circus*, a media guide of circus terminology.

Eugene W. Metcalf is a professor of American and interdisciplinary studies at Miami University, Ohio. A specialist in American material culture and the cultural politics of American art, he is the author of numerous articles and books and has worked with many art museums creating exhibitions that expand the understanding and appreciation of visual expressions that fall outside commonly accepted Western aesthetic traditions. Most recently, he was coeditor of *Gee's Bend: The Architecture of the Quilt* and *Hard Truths: The Art of Thornton Dial*, catalogues accompanying nationally touring exhibitions organized respectively by the Museum of Fine Arts, Houston, and the Indianapolis Museum of Art.

Brett Mizelle is Professor of History and Director of the American Studies Program at California State University, Long Beach.

His publications include the book *PIG*, a history of the global human-pig relationship, as well as articles, book chapters, and reviews in the fields of nineteenth-century American history and the history of human–animal relationships. He is also a cofounder and current editor of the H-Animal Discussion Network and the recipient of the Humane Society of the United States' Animals and Society Course Award for his university course, "Animals in American Culture."

Susan Nance is a historian of communication and live entertainment. She is Associate Professor at the University of Guelph in Guelph, Ontario, and affiliated faculty of the Campbell Centre for the Study of Animal Welfare. She received her PhD from the University of California, Berkeley, in 2003 and has since published on the histories of parades, civic festivals, and the business of tourism, including *How the Arabian Nights Inspired the American Dream, 1790–1935.* Nance's most recent work, *Entertaining Elephants: Animal Agency and Business Demands in the American Circus,* documents the lives and labors of nineteenth-century circus elephants.

Jennifer Lemmer Posey is Assistant Curator at the Circus Museum with the John and Mable Ringling Museum of Art, Sarasota, Florida, where she has worked since 2002. She received her BA from New College of Florida in 1998 and earned her MA from Florida State University in 2006. Her studies have focused on the history of American art with an emphasis on folk and untrained artists. Posey has published essays on the history of circus spectacles, circus wardrobe, and posters.

Gregory J. Renoff, whose PhD in American History is from Brandeis University, is an associate professor of history at Drury University in Springfield, Missouri, where he has taught since 2003, focusing on the American Civil War, the Vietnam War, and African American History, among other subjects. He is the author of *The Big Tent: The Traveling Circus in Georgia, 1820–1930.*

Kory W. Rogers is Curator of Design Arts at the Shelburne Museum, Shelburne, Vermont. In 2009 he supervised the renovation and reinstallation of Shelburne's Circus Building, which houses the 524-foot-long Roy Arnold miniature circus parade model and the 3,500-piece Kirk Bros. Circus, as well as a selection of circus posters and other related ephemera. In 2010 he organized the exhibition *Circus Day in America,* followed by *Behind the Lens, Under the Big Top: The Photography of Elliot Fenander* in 2011.

Paul Stirton is an associate professor at the Bard Graduate Center in New York. Formerly Senior Lecturer in the History of Art at the University of Glasgow, he was educated at the University of Edinburgh and the Courtauld Institute of Art in the University of London. He is the author of many books and articles on aspects of British and Hungarian art and design, including *"Is Mr Ruskin Living Too Long?": Selected Writings of E. W. Godwin on Victorian Architecture, Design and Culture* (with Juliet Kinchin). He is the editor of *West 86th: A Journal of Decorative Arts, Design History, and Material Culture.*

Peta Tait is Professor of Theatre and Drama at La Trobe University, Australia. Her research focuses on the practice and theory of theater, drama, body-based arts, and performance, and in relation to cultural languages of emotion. She publishes articles and books on circus performance including contemporary new circus. Her recent publications include *Wild and Dangerous Performances: Animals, Emotions, Circus*; *Circus Bodies: Cultural Identity in Aerial Performance*; *Performing Emotions: Gender, Bodies, Spaces*; and *Body Show/s: Australian Viewings of Live Performance,* for which she served as editor.

Susan Weber is Founder and Director of the Bard Graduate Center: Decorative Arts, Design History, Material Culture, New York. She is the author of *The Secular Furniture of E. W. Godwin* and editor of the catalogue *E. W. Godwin: Aesthetic Movement Architect and Designer.* She has co-authored and edited numerous exhibition catalogues, including *Thomas Jeckyll: Architect and Designer*; *Castellani and Italian Archaeological Jewelry*; and *James "Athenian" Stuart: 1713–1788: The Rediscovery of Antiquity.* Currently she is working on the catalogue and exhibition *William Kent, 1685–1748: Designing Georgian Britain,* scheduled for 2013. Weber's many awards include Soane Foundation Honors from Sir John Soane's Museum Foundation (2010), the Philip C. Johnson Award of the Society of Architectural Historians (2005), and the National Arts Club Gold Medal Award (1997).

Matthew Wittmann is a curatorial fellow at the Bard Graduate Center, where he organized the exhibition *Circus and the City: New York, 1793–2010* and authored its catalogue. A graduate of the Program in American Culture at the University of Michigan, his dissertation on the transnational history of U.S. entertainers who traveled around the Pacific in the nineteenth century is currently being revised for publication.

INTRODUCTION

THE CIRCUS IN AMERICA

KENNETH L. AMES

This book is offered as a contribution to the study of the circus in America. It brings together seventeen essays to explore critical aspects of the circus as it developed in the United States from the late eighteenth century to the twentieth. The focus on this country acknowledges that the circus enjoyed exceptional popularity here and that the cultural environment of modernizing America gave the circus dimension and form it did not take elsewhere. In the early nineteenth century the American circus was a modestly scaled entertainment that differed little from its European parents. Over subsequent decades it gradually expanded and evolved, coming to be recognized abroad as a distinctly American variation on an international theme. By the end of the century, the once-modest circus had become the Greatest Show on Earth, created in America and a major manifestation of American cultural values.

A few basic facts about the circus are worth remembering. The name *circus* comes from ancient Rome and refers to a place or building, rather than an activity. The various acrobatic and animal acts and displays associated with the circus have ancient origins. Circuses flourished in given geographic locations, but exhibiting sense of place was not the point. On the contrary, they have typically made allusions to international, cosmopolitan, and exotic performers, animals, and music, even if those claims were fraudulent. The modern circus was the product of an age of increasing mobility, which enabled it to become a global phenomenon. American conditions shaped the circus that evolved here in important ways but the American circus was never narrowly about America. The circus provided entertainment but it was, in the end, primarily a business.

At its height, the circus was a highly complex, multifaceted enterprise. Embodying the idea of anthology or compendium popular in the nineteenth century, the circus presented a living collection of

Fig. 1. Jacob J. Gayer. Two small boys gaze at a circus billboard in Ohio, 1931. Photograph. © Jacob J. Gayer/National Geographic Society/Corbis

visual entertainments, mostly physical and sensational, intended to dazzle and amaze. Although circus promoters traded on the difference and distance of their product from the quotidian world, the circus shared corporate organizational structure and practice and, indeed, became a prominent exemplar of that emerging business model. And, in truth, the circus was a more representative and influential agent of American culture and values than its one-day performances, calculated otherness, and apparent apartness might suggest. Although perhaps not immediately obvious, there are few significant strands of American life that the circus did not touch or reference in some way.

The structure of this book is shaped by subject matter and, to a lesser degree, by chronology. The first chapter sketches out the broad contours of circus history in this country. The next two examine the circus as commercial entertainment within national and transnational contexts. Following chapters concentrate on individual aspects of the circus, starting with advertising, then turning to music, tents, the display and treatment of animals,

performed identities, and circus spectacles. Two chapters step back to study representation of the circus in children's literature and within the world of toys. The penultimate essay returns to the circus of Depression-era America and the role of the WPA. A final piece provides destabilizing perspectives on the freak show of the past and on disability today.

We make no claim to examine every feature of the circus, for the subject is simply too rich. The essays here explore much of the most important terrain, offering refinements to conventional understandings of the circus as well as fresh, sometimes surprising information and insights. Some of the essays focus sharply on certain details or episodes, while others take a wider purview, attentive to the reciprocal relationship of the circus to the larger society and culture. What was American about the American circus? What does the circus reveal about the world that sustained it? What did the circus contribute to subsequent popular culture and entertainment? How might we understand the circus today? These and other questions animate the essays that follow. Taken together, they provide a rich interpretive account of the once-prominent composite artifact known as the circus.

Janet M. Davis opens this album of circus essays by examining the characteristics that came to distinguish the American version of this imported cultural form: immense size, capacity for novelty and innovation, and itinerancy. Admiration of bigness pervaded the modernizing world but Americans seemed particularly drawn to it. Davis links American gigantism to the land itself, concurrent national expansion, and industrial maturation. Core components of the Gilded Age circus had pre-industrial origins, but nineteenth-century industrial and capitalist practices and the high value attached to bigness helped to repackage, reframe, and expand

Fig. 2. Frederick W. Glasier. Equestrienne on horseback, ca. 1903. Photograph. Collection of the John and Mable Ringling Museum of Art Archives, Glasier Glass Plate Negative Collection, 0063

the circus into an iconic popular entertainment that dominated its era.

Davis argues that the immensity of the American continent was critical to the development of the circus as an itinerant form of entertainment. It is no surprise that the history of the circus has a near parallel in the history of the railroad. The railroad defined American cities and communities: where rail went, cities grew and commerce flourished; where it did not, stagnation and decline ensued. The newly settled Midwest became home to national railway hubs and to what eventually became some of the nation's most prominent circuses. Then, where rail went, so went the circus.

But before the railroad, the American circus was a smattering of smallish operations concen-

Fig. 3. W. W. Cole's Great Circus, Menagerie & Congress of Living Wonders, ca. 1882. Poster, printed by the Strobridge Lithographing Company, Cincinnati. Collection of the John and Mable Ringling Museum of Art, Tibbals Collection, ht2004396

trated on the East Coast. Matthew Wittmann shows that even in its infancy, the circus in this country had already adopted an "almost exclusively itinerant mode." Mobility enabled these traveling shows to take advantage of market opportunities in the dispersed settlement patterns of the early republic, expand throughout the North American continent, then follow trade routes to the Caribbean. This transnational movement of circus companies and performers early on made the American circus a distinctly cosmopolitan enterprise.

It was more often form than content that distinguished American circuses. Performers and acts were more or less interchangeable from one circus or one country to another but the mobile structure that characterized American circuses was continually refined and perfected, benefiting from the experience of national and international travel and exposure. While not always recognized as such, the American circus was among this country's early successful export products, along with minstrel shows, furniture, clocks, and firearms. American

Fig. 4. Circus parade, ca. 1891. Stock poster, printed by Calvert Lith. Co., Detroit. Library of Congress Prints and Photographs Division

show managers were adept and adventurous at this form of entrepreneurship, finding profitable markets in Central and South America and, after the California Gold Rush, on the West Coast and beyond, in Hawaii, Australia, and even Japan.

Wittmann argues that failing to understand the circus as transnational leads to seriously flawed understanding. Brenda Assael likewise cautions against narrowly nationalist readings by showing how American and British circuses of the late nineteenth century became partners in what she calls "the cultural project of imperial display and celebration." Interchange between British and American circuses had a long history, which meant that many American circus performers found ready employment in Britain. American shows also routinely toured the country. By the late nineteenth century, some of these had become immense in scale and popularity. Although resistance to these massive entertainment invasions from the U.S. might have been expected, Assael argues that they were readily integrated into Britain's dynamic and evolving circus market. Rather than threatening the local circus industry, traveling American circuses generated greater public enthusiasm for the genre. Furthermore, British and American circus performances and spectacles of the era were ideologically united, displaying "a shared commitment to an imperial reading of the world."

It is intriguing to think about the circus growing larger over time and ritually occupying, if only for a day or two, cities and towns across America and around the world. This peculiarly nomadic habit posed many challenges, especially in logistics, supply, and the need for publicity. There was no point in bringing a circus to town if no one knew about it. Advertising took two forms, advance and immediate. The key vehicle for advance publicity was the canonical circus poster, familiar then and now to mil-

lions of people. Circus posters are among the most important printing accomplishments of the nineteenth century and the most common surviving artifacts of the great age of the circus. Paul Stirton's discussion of these colorful graphics confronts the curious truth that despite these apparent qualifications, circus posters are largely absent from art-historical studies of posters. Apparently the features that enhanced their power as advertising also eliminated them from consideration as art. Stirton's close and even-handed examination of the design and fabrication of circus posters illuminates some of the reasons for their success as advertising as well as for resistance to acknowledging them as art today. Stirton also describes the meticulously scheduled and systematized process of posting advertising for upcoming shows. For better or worse, the development of advertising as a sophisticated part of marketing—and a prominent and intrusive presence on the landscape—owes much to the American circus of the nineteenth century.

Call posters tools or call them weapons; Kory Rogers is inclined to the second definition. He describes one late-nineteenth-century poster war, the evidence of which was discovered on the walls of a Colchester, Vermont, house in 1991 and is now preserved at the Shelburne Museum. It was common practice for poster crews to blanket prominent surfaces with advance notices of their coming show. But what if billposters for another circus had beaten them to it? No problem. Cover their posters with your own, as was done to this Colchester house in 1883, when billposters for Adam Forepaugh plastered over advertisements for John B. Doris. This find is compelling testimony to the rough-and-tumble competition of the circus business.

Once a circus was in town, the second phase of advertising came into play. This was the circus parade. Gregory Renoff sketches the rise and fall of this "living, moving advertisement" for the circus that, in the case of the largest concerns, became a spectacular entertainment in its own right. Festive and celebratory circus parades cost spectators nothing but captured their attention, offering a preview of what awaited inside the big top. Seasoned circus observers learned to judge the circus by its parade, rather than by its less reliable posters.

But circus parades eventually collided with changing urban conditions. As cities became more populous, more complex, and more congested, the circus parade went from being an exciting enhancement of daily life to an annoying interruption. What seemed a good idea in the 1870s was already a nuisance in some of the larger cities by the 1890s. And so by the 1920s, circus parades were largely a thing of the past. But they never entirely disappeared. One of America's most famous modern holiday parades is directly descended from the circus parade and still retains some of its features.

Can there be a parade without music? In the circus parade, music was provided by uniformed musicians who traveled in a gaudily decorated bandwagon, and sometimes also by an ear-splitting calliope, audible miles away. Musicians may have constituted only one unit in a parade but music was essential to the parade and to the entire circus. Music provided continuity from the circus parade to performance to after-show. It defined and shaped audience experience by framing, coloring, underlining, and punctuating the visual, it unified and integrated a jumble of otherwise incoherent and unrelated performances.

Leon Botstein introduces his account of circus music with Igor Stravinsky's 1942 *Circus Polka,* a composition hardly typical of traditional circus fare. The distinctly modern sound and structure of Stravinsky's piece seemed out of place at the circus and underlined an increasing gulf between circus music and classical or "serious" music. But in the earlier years, circus bands routinely played popular symphonic repertoire and gave many their first exposure to classical music. In fact, as Botstein notes, "the expansion of classical music in America occurred during the great age of the traveling circus," yet another instance of mutually advantageous cultural symbiosis.

Botstein shows that there is much to be learned from close study of the uses of music within the circus. He also reminds us that certain practices developed within that context have outlived their origins. One noteworthy feature of circus music was that it was continuous, providing an aural landscape or backdrop to a changing sequence of performances. That model passed into the cinema and, much diluted, eventually into such banal contexts as elevators and shopping malls, where it is as easily ignored as not. Clearly, a good deal has been lost in the transition.

Music was part of circuses everywhere but tents stood out as typically American. The pattern of itinerancy adopted early on required ready venues for performance. Rather than relying on the haphazard—and limiting—process of locating suitable structures in each town, from 1825 onward American circuses began to take tents on tour with them, thereby guaranteeing themselves a place to perform. As the circus grew larger, so did tents. Fred Dahlinger, Jr., provides an authoritative account of the adoption and development of these portable weather-resistant arenas. He maintains that adopting tents was "the single most important action taken in the history of the American circus."

Like the circus itself, tents date to antiquity. The needs of the nineteenth-century circus provided an impetus for reviving and improving this ancient form. Enlargement of the area covered and refinements to material and construction were largely the result of anonymous collaborative and cumulative effort. Designers of tents learned on the field, while some ideas may have been transferred from the example of sailing craft, where manipulation of broad expanses of canvas, wooden poles, and ropes and hawsers had long before attained considerable sophistication.

Not surprisingly, the addiction to immensity affected circus tents. The size of the tent and the number of spectators who could gather under its top became attractions in their own right, bragged about in advertising and materially affecting audience experience. As impressive as the tent itself were the processes of erecting it and then taking it down, refined to an art form of speed and efficiency. Over time, the circus tent came to emblematize the magical and ephemeral aspect of the circus, here today but gone tomorrow, off to a new venue down the line.

Itinerancy and tents were generally recognized as American contributions to the circus. Susan Nance proposes that we should add elephants to that list. Exotic and immense, these strange-looking and dangerous animals brought prestige and customers to circuses. One elephant was good; ten were better. However, by today's standards, the treatment of its animals was one of the least admirable features of the American circus. From acquisition, to containment and training, to final disposition, the biographies of circus elephants have few high points. Elephants were conscripted and unpaid laborers and performers. But they were liabilities as much as assets, as they were expensive to feed, difficult to control, and generally unpredictable. Nance sketches out the broad outlines of the history of cir-

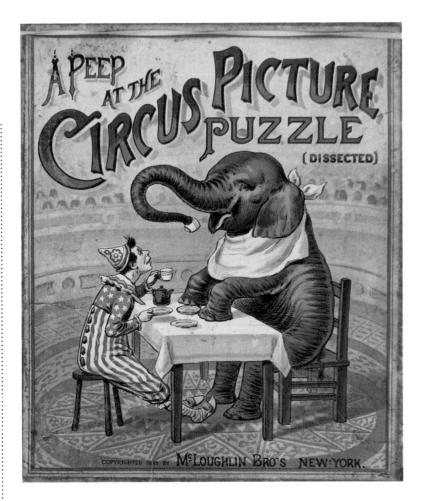

cus elephants. It is difficult to imagine that a more extensive account would make the story much more attractive. The short life of that most famous circus elephant, Jumbo, and his abrupt and violent end, were all too typical.

Animals had been a part of the circus since at least the late eighteenth century. Just about any animal large enough to be seen from a distance and capable of being coaxed or coerced into obeying was potential circus material. Brett Mizelle's chapter examines two animals particularly prominent within the circus: horses and big cats. Unlike elephants, horses could not be considered curiosities, as they were ubiquitous work animals in both urban and rural areas. But they were large, strong, and from earliest antiquity through the nineteenth century had been integrated into displays of human power and mastery. Mizelle describes how

Fig. 5. A Peep at the Circus picture puzzle, 1887. Printed paper, cardboard, McLoughlin Bros., New York. Courtesy of The Strong, Rochester, New York, 107.4230

the familiar horse became "the cornerstone of the modern circus." The trick lay in making the ordinary extraordinary, in transforming the familiar human-horse relationship into something marvelous. Circuses adopted two strategies: multiplying the number of horses under human direction and introducing increasingly challenging acrobatic feats while riding horses full tilt around the arena. That these strategies attracted customers is amply borne out by prominent depictions of both on circus posters.

Fig. 6. "Federal Theatre's Great 3-Ring Circus," 1937. Flyer. Somers Historical Society

Big cats were another matter, however. Like horses, they were large and strong but they were also carnivorous and decidedly dangerous. So-called liberty horses could perform without rider or leads, but who would let big cats run loose under the big top? Lions and tigers had to be contained and subdued. Brute force or the semblance thereof often became part of the big-cat act. In fact, most human-animal performances in one way or another asserted the dominion of humankind over the rest of the animal world, a stance that for many years found widespread approbation throughout American society.

But if one were to enact the ritual of human domination of big cats, what would be an appropriate costume? Circus performers must be costumed and costumes don't just happen. They are selected for effect, for affect, to frame and shape spectator experience and interpretation. Peta Tait argues that costumes are aspects of the "fabricated performance identity" of circus people. These exploit cultural conventions and assumptions and structure spectator reading of performance. And in the circus, all is performance, all is pretend. For people who worked in the cages with the big cats, Tait identifies two characters that were rich in cultural baggage: the military officer and the big-game hunter. The extent to which such roles were fabricated is neatly illustrated by the case of Louis Roth, who was born in Hungary, fled that country to avoid conscription, yet performed with the big cats in the attire of a French army general.

If the performed identities of humans working with big cats were normative and authoritative, Rodney Huey shows that the performed roles of clowns were antinormative and even anticultural. Clowns invert or subvert cultural norms and cultural rules, resisting most of the categories that structure conventional polite society and violating social and cultural expectations. But because cultures often have quite specific meanings, clowns are less likely to be internationally interchangeable than other performers. This raises intriguing questions about the tramp clown, known elsewhere but generally considered an American specialty. Why this might have been so is a matter well worth pondering.

On the other hand, the grand theatrical and processional spectacles, known as specs, that reached their apogee around 1900 played to enormous crowds around the world. Jennifer Lemmer Posey's account shows that subject matter was sometimes historical, sometimes biblical, sometimes flagrantly nationalistic or imperialistic, and sometimes just plain fluff. Specs were multisensory extravaganzas that did not require a moral or a narrative, but they had to dazzle—and they did, using casts of hundreds, extravagant costumes, and lavish displays of movement, color, and sound.

Specs were further evidence of the prevailing penchant for enormity. The larger the circus company, the larger the spec typically promoted as "on a scale of magnificence and grandeur never before attempted," or in other such hyperbole. The enticing depictions of *Jerusalem and the Crusades, Columbus and the Discovery of America*, and *Nero, or the Destruction of Rome* on posters confirm that these were designed to exhilarate and exhaust audiences with tidal waves of sensory immersion.

But if all were mere gratuitous sensory stimulation, was the circus appropriate for children? Two chapters examine reverberations of the circus in the world of American childhood. Ellen Butler Donovan explores representations of the circus in children's literature while Eugene Metcalf analyzes the nature and meaning of circus toys. Perhaps not

surprisingly, the two genres reveal opposing perspectives on the circus.

Donovan notes that the circus is a familiar presence in books and articles written for children. Oddly enough, however, the circus most frequently depicted is the small, wagon-drawn show common before the advent of the large and complex railroad circus. In other words, the circus for children is the circus in its childhood. The predominant viewpoint in literature is middle-class and male. Writings about nineteenth-century boyhood tend to view the circus nostalgically, recalling the wonder and excitement of the circus's arrival in town. In fiction for children, on the other hand, ambivalence is more typical. As Donovan observes, "children's literature teeters unsteadily between depictions of fascination and glamour of the circus and portrayals of deception, evil, and abuse." The circus and what Donovan calls "the pastoral ideal of childhood" were both products of the nineteenth century; yet many authors thought that the circus posed a serious threat to that ideal. Paradoxically, while the circus became a vehicle for expressing anxieties about childhood, it was also recognized that only in childhood were its "unabashed pleasures" fully enjoyed.

But that meant a likely market for circus toys. Eugene Metcalf reminds us of the emergence of an increasingly consumption-oriented society in the late nineteenth century and of the new varieties of toys that began to appear. These, he argues, became instruments of escape, fantasy, and play. Some allowed children (boys, primarily) to play at manipulating their own miniature circus worlds. Increasingly manufactured in the United States, circus toys reflected and promoted ideologies and cultural assumptions of the day. Toys replicated aspects of the circus in miniature but miniaturization implies control, on the one hand, and falsification on the other. A toy elephant may have referenced Jumbo, but it was an abstracted, denatured, and deceptively unthreatening evocation.

Circus toys presented a different perspective on the circus than that generally expressed in literature. Cautionary tales for youth tended to look at abuses behind the scenes while toys ignored that part of the circus to focus on performance. Both acknowledged in different ways that the emergence of the circus and formulation of a conception of innocent and uncorrupted childhood were products of the same age. Metcalf notes that although the circus was emphatically an adult creation, its performance,

Fig. 7. Main Entrance for the Ringling Bros. & Barnum and Bailey Circus, 1924. Collection of the John and Mable Ringling Museum of Art, Tibbals Collection, ht0001228

if not its inner workings, "represented a place far beyond the real world of adults," rather like the fantasy world of Peter Pan.

The final two essays return to the circus in an age of decline and reinvention. Susan Weber offers a finely detailed portrait of the WPA Circus in New York, a tale touching on scores of circus biographies but also fundamentally a depressing account of the circus as a pale reflection of its earlier self. Even before the miseries and mass unemployment of the Great Depression, the circus had shown ample evidence of decline. WPA involvement gave employment to a considerable body of people with circus experience and brightened the lives of city children, many of whom had little familiarity with the circus or other unaffordable pleasures. Depression slid on to war and when that ended, culture and society had changed so significantly that there was little room for the old-fashioned circus. It might be argued that the most noteworthy outcomes of the WPA Circus were the subsequent careers of actors Nick Cravat and Burt Lancaster. Both prospered in the film industry, with Lancaster starring in the circus-themed *Trapeze* in 1956.

Cravat and Lancaster were admired for their acrobatic prowess. Their achievement rests on their considerable and demonstrable ability. But what of people with disability? People with congenital deformities were once exhibited in what were called "freak shows." In our final essay, Rachel Adams reviews the history of the freak show as an adjunct to the circus but turns from the past to the present to focus on the people with disabilities depicted in Richard Butchins's film *The Last American Freak Show*. The performers make a living by exhibiting themselves and flaunting, rather than trying to conceal, their differences. The film reveals the loneliness and marginalization that come with disability, as well as the very real difficulties disabled people have in making a living. The film poses questions about the place of people with disabilities within the circus and, more broadly, within modern society, where evidence of lingering prejudice is easily found.

It was that most American of circus entrepreneurs, crafty Connecticut Yankee Phineas T. Barnum, who is credited with introducing the freak show, which Butchins calls "a truly American art form." The claim for art is open to debate but it certainly is American, and that truth neatly problematizes the notion of Americanization that ties these essays together. Americanization involved, in the end, a complex web of interrelated factors of unequal importance and merit. Increasing American involvement in the transnational circus industry shaped the form it took at the high point of its popularity. But like so many other stories of achievement and success, more may be due to fortuitous circumstances than to individual genius. The circus and the conditions of rapidly modernizing America were right for each other and so the two rose in tandem. But America continued to change while the circus could not. Perhaps, in the end, the great success of the circus was little more than historical coincidence, albeit with glorious results.

Rachel Adams's essay brings us into close contact with real people struggling with serious limitations and suffering and forces confrontation with difficult social issues. It raises points that are not easy to read and think about. This provocative and unsettling piece is, as the expression goes, a hard act to follow, and so, with it the book ends. But pondering the complicated story of the circus goes on.

Frenzeny & Tavernier

①

^{THE} CIRCUS AMERICANIZED

JANET M. DAVIS

During the week of Christmas 1897, Barnum & Bailey's Greatest Show on Earth descended upon London. Several of the largest ships on the Atlantic Transport Line carried sections of the gargantuan circus across the ocean. Just one of those vessels, a retrofitted cattle ship, the *Massachusetts*, had a load line of 8,000 tons, ferrying twenty-six elephants, hundreds of horses and ponies, lions, seals, leopards, deer, cattle, yak, zebus, tigers, camels, the celebrity chimpanzee Johanna, 224 workmen, thirty performers, and scores of agents and managers (*fig. 1.1*).[1] The Barnum & Bailey circus program proudly described how the Olympia theater had been essentially rebuilt to accommodate this massive American circus, which contained over a thousand performers in its opening spectacle alone: "Huge iron columns, sixty-five feet high, have replaced the wooden ones formerly there; additional seating capacity has been provided; three big equestrian rings, two platforms,

a hippodrome race track, and mammoth stage 365 feet long, where the military drama will be produced, have all been newly built. The Palmarium [an adjacent, semicircular building] has been refitted also and now resembles a veritable jungle" (*fig. 1.2*).[2] A press release in the *New York Times* reported: "A large and eager crowd assembled outside of the entrance to the Olympia four hours before the doors were opened on the first day."[3]

The three-ring circus remained at the Olympia until April 1898. Its voluminous canvas tents, poles, guy lines, and the rest of its "housing supplies" were scheduled to arrive in England by ship in early spring 1898. Thereafter, the circus hit the rails, touring the British Isles and Europe for the next five years under canvas and in permanent buildings. Barnum & Bailey traveled on four trains containing sixty-one specially built railroad cars (*fig. 1.3*). According to circus press agents, continental audiences were enthralled by the show's equipment and logistics: "The characteristically American equip-

◀ *Detail of fig. 1.28.* Frenzeny and Tavernier, "The Circus Coming into Town," cover of *Harper's Weekly*, October 4, 1873. HarpWeek, LLC

ment of the show everywhere elicited the greatest interest. The railway cars, the patent couplers, electric plant, organization, methods, scheme of unloading and reloading and other matters which are so familiar in this country, were in these foreign countries wondered at and admired."[4]

Indeed, the tenting supplies were voluminous. Barnum & Bailey's cavernous canvas big top could hold 15,000 people, and like the retrofitted Olympia theater, could accommodate a thousand performers and scores of animals swirling in constant kinetic motion across three rings, two stages, an outer hippodrome track, and in the vertical aerial space above the ground. Additional tents housed other parts of the show, such as the menagerie and sideshow, as well as stables and dining and dressing tents. Barnum & Bailey's street parade was so magnificently satisfying for some audiences that they mistook it for the whole show. The British impresario E. H. Bostock observed how his own circus and menagerie business at the Glasgow Olympia theater profited from this misperception as country folk streamed to his Glasgow Zoo once Barnum & Bailey's parade was over.[5]

British audiences had not seen anything like this before: Barnum & Bailey's circus was a virtual universe compared to the native tenting shows, per-

manent circus amphitheaters, and portable wooden buildings that dotted the landscape. The largest British tenting show, Powell and Clarke's circus, could hold approximately 7,000 people in the 1880s—a true canvas monster compared to the majority of British circuses, which took place in relatively compact permanent circus buildings. The traditional circus venues in the mold of the seminal Astley's Amphitheatre typically accommodated between 2,000 to 3,000 spectators, whereas family-based, one-ring caravan shows dating from the early nineteenth century held about 1,000 to 1,500 people. Even in comparison to the elaborately ornamented pillars, columns, billowing folds of chintz, velvet, flags, and flying Cupids that graced the grand circus buildings at Birmingham, Leicester, Liverpool, London, and Leeds, Barnum & Bailey's circus was an unparalleled sensory feast.[6]

Yet many British showmen saw nothing original about the monstrous American circus, and belittled it as bloated, vapid, and derivative. Participating in a long tradition of European criticism that dismissed the originality of American cultural productions and social institutions, "Lord" George Sanger sniffed that even the signature giantism of the American circus was blatantly imitative, pointing to his own brief adoption of three rings in

▲ *Fig. 1.1.* "P. T. Barnum's Greatest Show on Earth, & The Great London Circus Combined with Sanger's Royal British Menagerie & Grand International Allied Shows," 1882. Poster, printed by the Strobridge Lithographing Company, Cincinnati. Cincinnati Art Museum, Gift of the Strobridge Lithographing Company, 1965.686.76

1860: "There is nothing that American showmen have ever done that Englishmen have not done first and done better.... I mention these things just to show that in the matter of exhibitions, in spite of tall talk, America has always followed, but never led, the Old Country."[7]

Despite Sanger's misgivings, the American railroad circus was hardly a gaudy copy of its trans-Atlantic ancestors. Although it employed considerable talent from Europe and Britain and contained readily identifiable elements of older Continental entertainments such as the menagerie, melodrama, trick riding, ballet, pony races, acrobatics, and pantomime, the American railroad circus cohered them into an innovative—rather than imitative—amusement. Its cultural syncretism made it uniquely American. Moreover, it endlessly reinvented itself, adding and subtracting popular features from other cultural forms to remain novel and salable. Transformed by the nation's peculiar historical contingencies of geography, demography, expansionism, and technological modernization, the circus became an iconic American popular entertainment during the nineteenth century. Its itinerancy, bigness, and endless capacity for novelty and reinvention made it American.

This essay suggests that the evolution of the circus into a distinctly American popular form was inextricably tied to national expansion and industrial maturation. This symbiotic relationship might seem curious because the circus was powered by preindustrial muscle, defined by its coordinated performances of animal and human athleticism in a ring. But industrial steam and locomotive power remade the circus, making it gigantic, itinerant, intricately organized, and able to travel coast to coast (*fig. 1.4*). During the nineteenth century, internal improvements and new technologies like the duck canvas tent and proliferating railroad networks

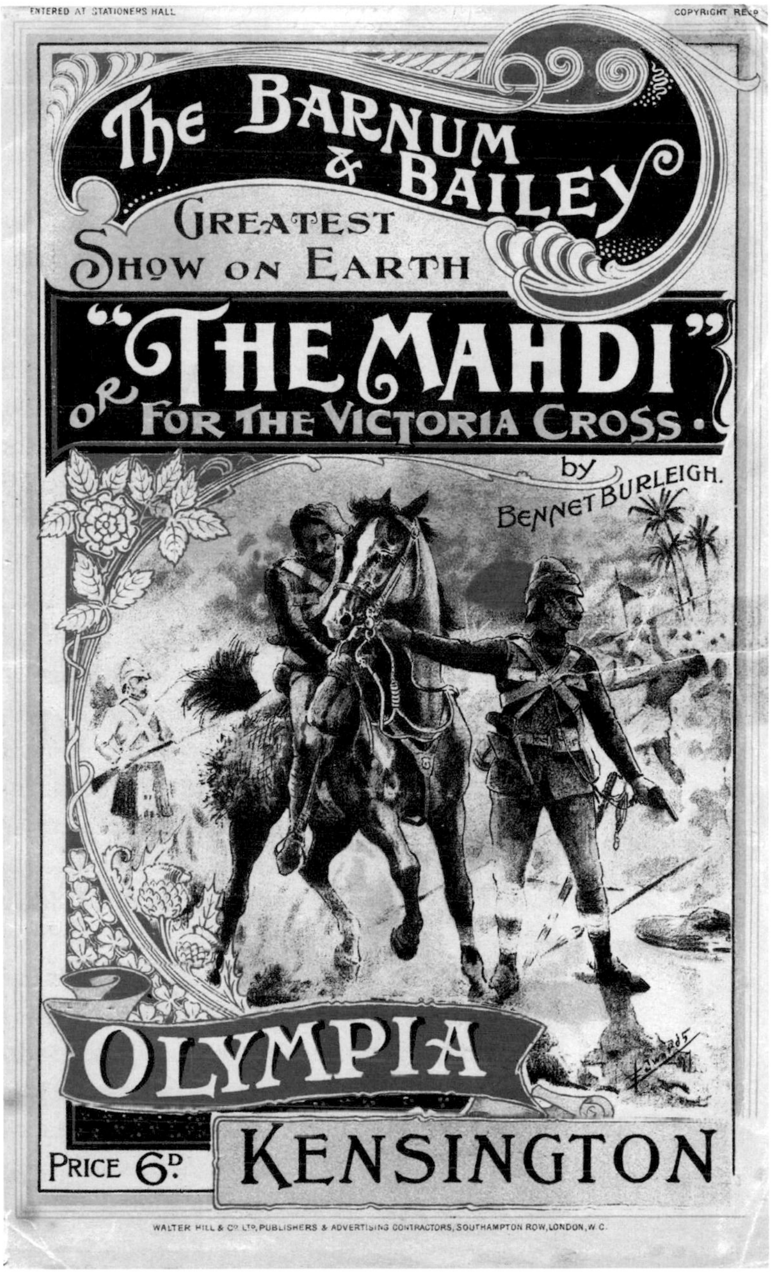

Fig. 1.2. *"The Mahdi" or for the Victoria Cross*, 1898. Program, published by Walter Hill & Co. Ltd, London. Circus World Museum, CWi-2365

Fig. 1.3. "In the railway yards," Train car being unloaded from the steamer in Hamburg, 1900. Photograph. McCaddon Collection of the Barnum & Bailey Circus, box 27; Department of Rare Books and Special Collections, Princeton University Library

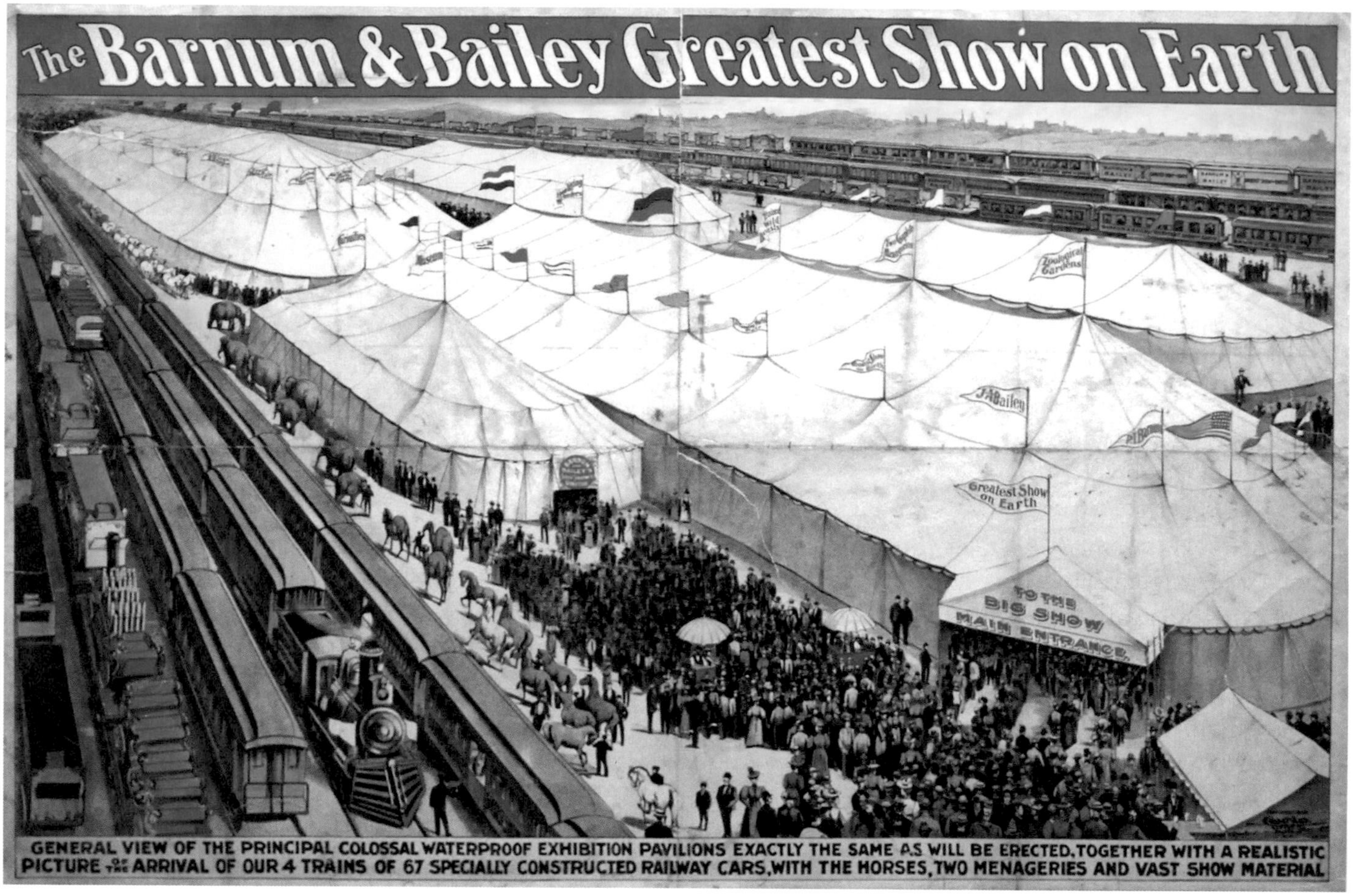
The Barnum & Bailey Greatest Show on Earth
J.A.Bailey
Greatest Show on Earth
TO THE BIG SHOW MAIN ENTRANCE
GENERAL VIEW OF THE PRINCIPAL COLOSSAL WATERPROOF EXHIBITION PAVILIONS EXACTLY THE SAME AS WILL BE ERECTED, TOGETHER WITH A REALISTIC PICTURE OF THE ARRIVAL OF OUR 4 TRAINS OF 67 SPECIALLY CONSTRUCTED RAILWAY CARS, WITH THE HORSES, TWO MENAGERIES AND VAST SHOW MATERIAL

made this metamorphosis possible, transforming the circus into a movable canvas city. In short, these developments made the circus modern and peculiarly American. More broadly put, the railroad circus was an important part of the wider transnational growth of "Americanization," or the proliferation of U.S. mass culture and consumer products around the globe. Americanization was an economic and cultural process that was integrally tied to what historian Alan Trachtenberg calls "incorporation": the symbiotic growth of combination and monopoly formation, managerial capitalism, standardization, assembly-line production, mass markets, and mass cultural forms during the Gilded Age.[8] Furthermore, historians Robert Rydell and Rob Kroes contend that Americanized cultural forms such as film were generally wedded to "production techniques that seemed to follow an industrial rather than an artistic logic."[9] The sprawling, routinized, and systematized circus Americanized fully embodied the cultural and economic contours of incorporation.

This essay also contends that the nation's frontier geography and demographics helped transform the circus into a uniquely Americanized cultural form. As a cultural imaginary, the frontier nurtured exceptionalist myths and symbols regarding the nation's representative republican government, which complemented the circus's rhetorical emphasis on providing accessible entertainment for all classes "at little cost." In 1893 historian Frederick Jackson Turner transformed the frontier into a theory of history, arguing that it had served as a laboratory for American democracy, as well as a safety valve for restless migrants and immigrants. Now that the U.S. Census Department had declared that there was no longer a distinct line between frontier and settle-

▲ *Fig. 1.4.* The Barnum & Bailey Greatest Show on Earth, ca. 1894. Poster, printed by the Courier Company, Buffalo. Circus World Museum

ment in 1893, Turner surmised that a new stage of American history had begun.[10]

The railroad became the ideal medium for the circus in a frontier society with scattershot settlement patterns on its periphery. Railroad companies gave the largest American circuses substantial discounts, which enabled them to transport thousands of people, animals, and supplies with more efficiency and speed than any other kind of transportation. By contrast, in Great Britain, distances between towns were significantly smaller than in the United States, which militated against the need for circuses to move by rail (the Bertram Mills circus was one of only a handful of shows that traveled by railroad from 1933 to 1955). In addition, the scarcity of other established entertainment forms in American agricultural and frontier communities such as stationary theaters, menageries, and periodic religious and commercial fairs meant that U.S. consumers were hungry for entertainment—much like colonial residents in Australia, another frontier society whose circuses became highly mobile as they expanded

into new areas of settlement in the mid-nineteenth century.[11] As a result, the American circus became a totalizing institution, defined by myriad features: its complex advertising system, its compelling impresario narratives of rags-to-riches and moral-free agency, its patriotic content, and its salable respectability, thus making it a harbinger of modern American mass culture.

The Arrival of the European Circus in the New Republic

The earliest circuses in the New Republic, however, could hardly be called American. All hailed from Great Britain and Europe. When the Scottish trick rider John Bill Ricketts first brought the circus to the New Republic from Great Britain, the giant American railroad shows of the future would have been incomprehensible. Landing in 1792 at Philadelphia, the nation's largest city, Ricketts opened a riding school. On April 3, 1793, Ricketts and his fellow troupers made their debut performance and brought the key elements of the British circus into a circular arena for the first time on American soil: acrobatic riding, pantomime, clowning, tumbling, rope dancing, and animal tricks (*fig. 1.5*). Showing in both enclosed and open wooden arenas at major urban centers along the eastern seaboard, Ricketts's show attracted hefty crowds and the patronage of distinguished Americans, including President George Washington. The popularity of the circus was such that it attracted so-called "knotholers," those who were unable or unwilling to buy a ticket and gained their name because they opted to squint at the action through a knothole on a wall or ceiling.[12] Despite robust attendance, Ricketts faced precarious conditions in the "howling wilderness"

Fig. 1.5. "Mr. Ricketts the Equestrian Hero," 1796. Etching. The Historical Society of Pennsylvania, Bb 96 R424

of North America. Arenas frequently burned to the ground and travel was difficult on the rocky, deeply rutted paths that passed for roads. Competition also stiffened in 1796 with the arrival of the Swedish impresario Philip Lailson, who quickly became Ricketts's chief rival. A year later, Lailson presented the first circus street parade in America as a way to draw attention away from Ricketts.[13] After Ricketts's circus building in Philadelphia burned yet again in late 1799, he became so frustrated that he quit the United States altogether in search of new markets in the West Indies. While traveling home to Britain, he was lost at sea.[14]

Aspects of Early Americanization: The Canvas Tent and the Menagerie

On the frontier margins of American society, showmen hunted relentlessly for new markets during the early national period and antebellum era. In a volatile economy wracked by cyclical financial panics and hobbled by crude transportation networks, this was no easy task. During his brief life, Joshua Purdy Brown, a scrappy and innovative impresario from Somers, New York, added an essential Americanizing element to the circus that also expanded its market reach on the frontier: the canvas tent. John Bill Ricketts had performed in a roofless canvas sidewall arena in 1795 at Hartford, Connecticut, and menagerie owners regularly used sidewall arenas after 1810; however, Brown's enclosed portable performance site marked a new era in circus history. On November 22, 1825, the *Delaware Gazette* printed an advertisement for a "pavilion circus,"

Pavilion Circus.

THE Proprietors of the Pavilion Circus respectfully inform the public that they will give

Equestrian Exhibitions;

This evening, (Tuesday, November 22.) in the Circus, at the Cross Keys Tavern, kept by Mr. Vandever, on the Kennet road, when will be brought forward a variety of new and interesting performances.

If the weather should prove favourable, there will be a performance to-morrow evening, (Wednesday) otherwise this evening will be the last.

Doors open at half past 6. Performance will commence at 7 o'clock. Admittance—Box, 50 cents : Pit, 25 cents. Children under 12 years of age, half price. Tickets to be had at the bar of Mr. *Smith's* Hotel, and at the Circus.

Nov. 22—1t

shown under the auspices of Brown and his partner Lewis Bailey, which would offer "equestrian exhibitions" at the Cross Keys Tavern on Kennett Road (*fig. 1.6*). The tavern's location outside the Wilmington city limits allowed circuses and menageries to show there without censure from the town's Quaker leaders, who flatly refused showmen entry into Wilmington proper as part of their objection to public amusements.[15] The advertisement's prosaic verbiage made no reference to the innovative character of this new "pavilion circus."

The adoption of the tent quickly transformed the daily rhythms and reach of the American circus, creating a new standard of ritual one-day show stops that likely began with regularity on May 29, 1826, in Bedford, Virginia.[16] Still, the tent itself did not single-handedly cause these changes. It simply enabled American showmen to capitalize on the uniqueness of the nation's vast frontier marketplace. In densely populated British and European industrial societies, the tenting show was the exception, rather than the norm. Here, the evolution of the British circus underscores the unique trajectory of the tenting show in the United States. Because of the explosive growth of industrial centers in the nineteenth century, British showmen opted to perform at established urban amphitheaters. Distances between stationary theaters from town to town were so small that it made little sense to incur the additional labor and structural costs of tent travel. Britain's consistently damp, cool climate also made the permanent circus building a more attractive alternative to the chilly tent, particularly during the winter months, a time when American shows typically took a hiatus and individual acts sought work in sunnier climes or performed in winter shows that more closely resembled European circuses.[17] Owing to its long historical nexus with the theater, the British circus was

◄ *Fig. 1.6.* J. Purdy Brown Circus advertisement from the *Delaware Gazette,* Nov. 22, 1825. Courtesy of the Delaware Historical Society

a familiar, stationary artifact of daily life, a cultural form that was, in the words of historian Brenda Assael, "just around the corner."[18] By contrast, the virtually wholesale adoption of the tent fueled a degree of mobility in the American circus that was hitherto unknown. Showmen could set up, perform, tear down, and move on in the course of a day. As the circus historian Stuart Thayer puts it, "No longer was [a showman] confined to cities, the population of which guaranteed a large enough patronage to support the cost of a wooden arena. Almost no potential audience was too small for him."[19]

New capital demands for equipment and labor associated with tenting shows made constant movement a necessity in the United States. While tenting showmen no longer incurred the considerable upfront costs of constructing a wooden circus building, they now had to purchase wagons, horses, and the services of trained teamsters. More significantly, they also had to provide room and board for animals, performers, musicians, other personnel, as well as paying for the upkeep of the horses that moved the show. Thayer argues that these ongoing expenses dictated the necessity for profitable one-day stands.[20]

Transportation costs accelerated when Joshua Purdy Brown—ever the innovator—added another defining feature of the circus Americanized to his show in 1828: the animal menagerie. On March 1, 1828, Brown's sub-company, managed by his cousin Benjamin Brown, left Charleston, South Carolina, with the Boston caravan menagerie in tow, an outfit that also had been playing Charleston. Over the next year, the circus and menagerie slowly plodded north together, moving roughly fifteen miles per day by horse and wagon. The show offered dual admission: fifty cents for both, or twenty-five cents for just the menagerie.[21] Although menageries more often operated independently during this era, the combination presaged the eventual incorporation of menageries into the touring circus by midcentury.

The menagerie performed invaluable social and cultural work at the American circus. The wedding of these two amusements helped enterprising showmen escape censure from local Protestant clergy and politicians who deemed the circus immoral for its display of the seminude athletic body, as well as its sneaky thieves and pickpockets who prowled around the show grounds. For these reasons, Vermont and Connecticut banned the circus outright during the antebellum era.[22] Composed variously of exotic felines, monkeys, an occasional elephant, kangaroo, llama, camel, gnu, sloth, bear, or rhinoceros before the Civil War, the antebellum circus menagerie provided showmen with living proof that their

Fig. 1.7. "Grand Exhibition of Living Animals," ca. 1818. Poster, printed by J. B. Butler, Pittsburgh. © Shelburne Museum, Shelburne, Vermont, Gift of Harry T. Peters Sr. Family, 1959, 1959-67.117

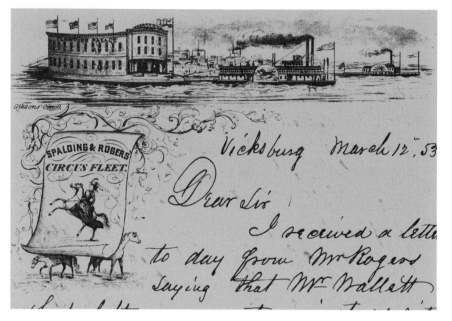

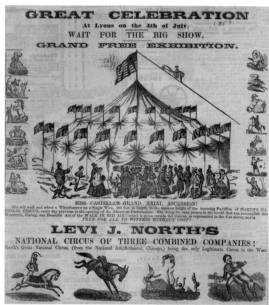

circuses could entertain and educate (*fig. 1.7*). The circus historian Fred Dahlinger notes that this imperative transformed the American circus's physical and moral geography: showmen quickly realized that separating the big top and the menagerie into two tents was good for business. Those who were uncomfortable with the big top's scantily clad human bodies and its often rowdy crowds could simply avoid it altogether.[23] The menagerie thus helped expand the moral frontiers of the circus to audiences that had previously shunned it.

River Highways and the Expansion of the American Circus to the Middle West

The rise of elaborate tenting circuses with menageries during the 1820s and 1830s chronicled a developing nation on the move. Showmen such as Joshua Purdy Brown, Jeremiah P. Fogg, Samuel P. Stickney, Aaron Turner, Levi North, and Seth B. Howes followed the waves of settlement westward. In the 1820s and 1830s, the "West" encompassed a range of country that included Kentucky and the territories created by the Northwest Ordinances (1784–87)—Ohio, Indiana, Illinois, Michigan, and Wisconsin. Showmen readily used new transportation arteries like the Cumberland Gap Road (also known as the National Road) and the Erie Canal (1825) to reach far-flung new markets starving for popular entertainment. Horses powered circus travel on terrestrial roadways and along the Erie Canal, where horses or mules pulled passenger boats through the dredged shallow channel of what historian Carol Sheriff called the "artificial river."[24]

The advent of steam power accelerated the demographic expansion of the nation, as well as the scale and reach of the circus. River cities became important circus destinations. After Robert Fulton invented the steamboat in 1807, this technology hastened the growth of sprawling river palaces that were able to accommodate over a thousand spectators at a performance—a significant structural foundation for the uniquely American giantism of the railroad era after the Civil War. Antebellum frontier cities on the Ohio River were major circus sites. Between 1834 and 1860, Cincinnati had 184 circus days (including indoor winter show dates), more than any other city in the nation. Louisville, Kentucky, also on the Ohio River, was a distant second at ninety shows. During this period, Cincinnati was the only city in the United States to have a dedicated circus column in a local

Fig. 1.8. Spalding & Rogers' Circus Fleet letterhead, 1853. Circus World Museum, CWi-2327

Fig. 1.9. "Great Celebration at Lyons on the Fourth of July," 1857. Levi J. North's National Circus of Three Combined Companies. July 4th engagement in Lyons, Illinois. Unknown newspaper advertisement. Circus World Museum, CWi-2336

newspaper. Shows steamed their way from Pittsburgh to New Orleans through the interconnected river network, chugging up and down the Ohio and Mississippi Rivers, and playing circus-hungry Cincinnati coming and going (*fig. 1.8*). Owing to the popularity of the Queen City as a circus hot spot, auxiliary circus industries thrived there in the antebellum era: wagon makers, shipbuilders, lithographers (the Strobridge Company, in particular), and cage builders. Yet the prominence of the circus in Cincinnati was fleeting. With the decline of the steamship and rise of the railroad during the Civil War, Cincinnati became just another show date for circuses by the end of the nineteenth century.[25]

Nonetheless, the geography of the Middle West permanently influenced the development of the American circus. Abundant, inexpensive, grassy pastureland and a convenient convergence of river systems that served as a gateway to the trans-Mississippi West made the region attractive to enterprising showmen from the East. In 1847, Edmund and Jeremiah Mabie became the first eastern showmen to purchase and build permanent circus quarters in the Middle West. They relocated from Putnam County, New York, to Delavan, Wisconsin Territory, so that they could tour Missouri, Iowa, and Illinois early in the season, thus avoiding direct competition with other eastern circuses, which would not reach the region until later in the summer (*fig. 1.9*). After the Civil War, a generation of midwestern showmen permanently reoriented the center of the American circus industry away from the East, including Dan Castello, William Cameron (W. C.) Coup, the Gollmar brothers, and most famously, the Wisconsin and Iowa–born Ringling brothers—whose outfit grew from a puny wagon company in the early 1880s to the biggest railroad show in the business in 1907.[26]

The Railroad and the Maturation of the Transcontinental Americanized Circus

The railroad Americanized the circus more thoroughly than any other technology. Still, this transformation was rife with growing pains. From the 1830s to the 1860s, the first railroad circuses were noticeably smaller than contemporary overland wagon shows—much to the disappointment of paying customers who wanted to see something novel (*fig. 1.10*). These early railroad shows generally contained no menagerie, sideshow, or street parade. They contended with a tangle of irregular track gauge. Some of the earliest railroad shows were known as "gilley" productions because laborers had to transport the show stock by hand from the rail yard to the show grounds. As a result, these first railroad shows typically were skeletal operations. Moreover, railroad companies typically demanded that circus proprietors pay for their expenditures all at once, a difficult proposition that magnified the precarious position of these experimental showmen. As a result, before the 1870s, the term "railroad circus" was an insult. It was also a warning to any smart audience member that he or she would likely be disappointed by a bare-bones show that would pale in comparison to the wide diversity of animals and acts on contemporary wagon circuses, the biggest of which was P. T. Barnum's Great Traveling World's Fair of 1871 (*fig. 1.11*).

This all changed in the 1870s. Although overland wagon shows were still common, a handful of circuses became behemoth railroad shows, a development that ultimately redefined the American circus. The standardization of train track and gauge and the transcontinental expansion of the railroad hastened this departure. The ceremonial hammering of the golden spike at Promontory Summit, Utah, which

fused the Union Pacific and Central Pacific Railroads into the world's longest continuous railroad, set the spectacular tone. On May 10, 1869, Governor Leland Stanford of California used a silver maul wrapped with telegraph wire to tap the wire-laden golden spike, a gentle hammer pat that triggered an instantaneous, transcontinental flow of information: urban alarms across the nation blared in unison to huge cheering crowds, many singing "The Star-Spangled Banner," as fire-alarm telegraphs received the signal from Promontory Summit; New York City and San Francisco officials had attached telegraph wires to cannons on the shores of the Atlantic and Pacific Oceans; as the signal pulsed, the cannons fired mightily into the sea—a show of American technological power to the world. In the words of historian David Haward Bain, "For all intents and purposes the entire nation was now connected in one great electrical current."[27] To make material sense of this unfathomable enormity, Americans used a circus animal as a metaphor for the transcontinental railroad: "the elephant" served as shorthand for the railroad during its construction and operation.[28]

At the time of this raucous national celebration, the circus impresario Dan Castello was showing in Omaha, the eastern terminus of the Union Pacific Railroad. His partner James M. Nixon urged him to take the show all the way to California on the new transcontinental railroad. With ten cages, a bandwagon, two elephants, and two camels (and journeying overland from Cheyenne to Denver because the transcontinental railroad was not routed there), Castello was the first circus showman to travel coast to coast in a single season. The tour was one of the most lucrative circus tours in history: Castello earned 1,000 dollars per day for thirty-one straight days in rough, entertainment-hungry frontier regions (even in Laramie, Wyoming, where two

Fig. 1.10. "Look Out for the Locomotive! Spalding & Rogers' New Railroad Circus," 1856. Herald, printed by "Times" Job Press J. H. & F. F. Farwell, Boston. McCaddon Collection of the Barnum & Bailey Circus, box 685 folder 10; Department of Rare Books and Special Collections, Princeton University Library

bandits were publicly hanged on the show's opening day). Castello also pocketed a quick 60,000 dollars profit when he and his partners sold the majority of the show in California at the end of the season.[29] In 1872, the impresario W. C. Coup unleashed the potential for even greater efficiency and profitability on the rails when he introduced his new flatcar and wagon design, which now enabled laborers to roll fully loaded circus wagons on and off the train. With these innovations in place, Coup and his partner P. T. Barnum transformed the Great Traveling World's Fair into a mammoth railroad outfit that ushered in a new era. Several other showmen quickly followed suit over the next two decades, including James Bailey, Adam Forepaugh, the Sells brothers, the Ringling brothers, and W. W. Cole—reportedly

the first showman to become a millionaire solely from his circus operations.[30]

The business historian Alfred Chandler argues that the advent of the railroad catalyzed the rise of big business—the institutional signature of America's transformation from a rural, agrarian, commercial economy into an urban, industrial one. Because its success depended on speed, efficiency, and standardization across transcontinental space and time, the railroad and to a lesser extent its predecessor, the telegraph, necessitated an increasingly complex managerial system to supervise its far-flung operations. The railroad's unprecedented building costs and fixed expenses likewise gave rise to another artifact of American modernization: the investment banker.[31] As a testament to the influence

Fig. 1.11. "P. T. Barnum's Great Traveling Moral Exposition of the Wonder World," 1871. Courier, printed by Wynkoop & Hellerbeck, Steam Book and Job Printers, New York. Circus World Museum, CWi-2328

of the railroad companies, they unilaterally divided the United States into time zones in 1883 without seeking the validating stamp of federal legislation, thus standardizing the nation's sense of time into the readily familiar Pacific, Mountain, Central, and Eastern time zones.

The managerial complexity and specialized division of labor within the American railroad circus after 1872 validated Chandler's key insights concerning the relationship between the railroad and big business. Circus management positions proliferated in this new age of speedy transcontinental rail-road travel to facilitate the quick and seamless movement of people, animals, equipment, and information: general managers, general contractors, railroad contractors, general agents, foreign agents, press agents, opposition agents (who studied the movement, marketing strategy, and content of equally mobile rival shows), a legal team, and a host of bosses who oversaw entire circus departments, in addition to specialized teams of billposters, laborers, animal handlers, and secondary performers. Inspired by the success of Coup's inventive railroad car design, other financially secure showmen purchased—rather than leased—their own specially designed cars.[32] Showmen and their routing team performed extensive market research to choose the most potentially profitable routes, using multiple indices to determine where to show, factory productivity, weather conditions, crop reports, construction starts, and the presence of summer resorts. Once showmen determined their route, specially trained managers, most notably the general contractor, negotiated a potentially bewildering number of logistical turns: securing licenses, pricing deals with railroad companies, local contracts for animal feed, liverymen (local drivers), meat, water, fuel, eggs, milk, and other supplies.[33] The general contractor was the first circus worker to cover the route, and he made written arrangements for virtually everything that the outfit needed.[34]

A Colorful Riot in Advance of the Show: The Circus Poster

Months in advance of what audiences across the nation called "Circus Day," an explosion of vivid posters told audiences that the show was coming. Storefronts, walls, barns, and geographical land-

Fig. 1.12. "P. T. Barnum's One and Only Greatest Show on Earth," 1879. Poster, printed by the Courier Company, Buffalo. Circus World Museum, CWi-2333

marks were all probable targets for mummification—with approximately two to six complimentary tickets, or comps, as a form of payment to the property owner for the privilege of advertising there. Press agents also gave local media, law enforcement, and politicians comps as a way to generate positive press and to provide additional surveillance on Circus Day.

The circus poster was a key artifact of Americanization, a visual icon of big business that embodied a specialized labor process in its manufacturing and distribution, and a critical form of communication in a far-flung frontier society.[35] Its combination of extravagant verbosity and elaborate images made it a crossroads cultural form, still firmly planted in the print age (or, what historian Warren Susman termed "a culture that had taken form under Bible and dictionary"), as well as heralding the ascendancy of poet Vachel Lindsay's "hieroglyphic civilization" saturated in visual media.[36] The print age dominated the earliest black-and-white posters, which were replete with verbiage and bore a striking resemblance to theater playbills. The showman Richard Sands likely developed the first American poster to use two colors from woodblocks or type in the early 1840s. By the 1870s, American printers were making stock circus posters using up to six

Fig. 1.13. "W. W. Cole's New 9 Shows Consolidated. The New and Novel Act of Two Ladies Riding in One Ring at the Same Time," 1882. Poster, printed by the Strobridge Lithographing Company, Cincinnati. Cincinnati Art Museum, Gift of the Strobridge Lithographing Company, 1965.685.1

colors from woodblocks (*fig. 1.12*). Lithography on limestone plates and, later, metal plates and offset printing, further refined the circus poster into an intricate form of ephemeral art.[37] Machine-produced by the thousands, the speed of the industrial production process was heightened by the use of stock reproducible images of big-top performances, spectacles, panoramic views of the menagerie and sideshow, and sweeping scenes of a show's arrival at the rail yard. Lithograph companies also produced specialized posters of individual celebrity animals, performers, and showmen (*fig. 1.13*). The complexity of design and content demanded deliberate viewing, thus beckoning pedestrians to scrutinize these images at close range. Intended for sustained inspection via foot or horseback, the circus poster bore little resemblance to its successors on modern highways, which convey a single word, corporate logo, or image to be digested at seventy miles per hour.

The circus poster was a visual sign of American giantism. It was also a manifestation of the railroad circus's distinctive specialized labor process. Billposters pasted a minimum of 5,000 circus posters in each town on the route, often months in advance of the actual show.[38] In large cities, the number of posters was even greater. In New York City, the Barnum & Bailey circus usually played for an entire month at Madison Square Garden and in nearby Brooklyn, which necessitated mammoth paper supplies: in 1893 the circus plastered 27,110 sheets in

New York City, 9,525 on the railways and 8,186 additional bills in surrounding cities.[39]

Billposters traveled the route with other members of the advance team on separate trains to secure the arrangements in each town and to mark the territory for the upcoming circus. Writing for *McClure's Magazine* in 1894, the journalist Charles Theodore Murray chronicled his observations for the wider public after riding shotgun alongside the advance team with Barnum & Bailey that season. He described a disciplined system of planning and advertising that would debunk any mention of a three-ring circus as a metaphor for chaos. Barnum & Bailey had four separate advertising cars that followed each other a week or two apart on the same route (*fig. 1.14*). According to Murray, each car cost 1,000 dollars per week to operate, and each typically had eight to eleven billposters, a boss-billposter, several lithographers, a manager, and, on occasion, an advance press agent, who solidified the advertising arrangements with local newspapers.[40]

In brief, the first car, also known as the "skirmishing," or "opposition" car, served as a troubleshooter. The advance men riding there made certain that competing shows, collectively called the "opposition," did not steal a previously arranged date, or sabotage earlier transportation contracts made soon after circus managers had determined the route for the upcoming season. The second car focused primarily on posting the bills and arranging newspaper

Fig. 1.14. Frederick Whitman Glasier. Barnum & Bailey Advance Car #1, 1903. Photograph. Collection of the John and Mable Ringling Museum of Art, Glasier Glass Plate Negative Collection, 1307

Fig. 1.15. Frederick Whitman Glasier. Barnum & Bailey billposters, Brockton, Massachusetts, 1906. Photograph. Collection of the John and Mable Ringling Museum of Art, Glasier Glass Plate Negative Collection, 1320

Fig. 1.16. "Barnum Imitates 4-Paw," 1884. Herald. Circus World Museum, CWi-2330

publicity for the show. As an audacious demonstration of Forepaugh's reach in 1891, the agents Geoffrey Robinson and Whiting Allen posted bills for the circus atop Pike's Peak at an elevation of 14,441 feet.[41]

The third and fourth cars made certain that the posters remained visible, finalized outstanding contracts and provisions, as well as generating publicity within a fifty-mile periphery of the show site. Car number four publicized the upcoming production along the rural periphery, so even the most isolated audiences felt the circus's reach. Called the "excursion" car, car number four traveled all of the railroad routes in a fifty-mile circumference around the circus stop. The billposters on this car covered this area with bills advertising special train schedules and excursion rates. The manager of the excursion car verified the arrangements for special rail ticket prices and travel times that had been made earlier by the excursion agent, who worked directly with railroad officials to make special travel arrangements for circus audiences.[42] Within a week or two of the production date, the last car finalized the arrangements and billing work done by the previous cars and also quickly remedied any gaps in presswork or billposting.[43] After this final car finished all remaining business, the circus was ready to come to town.

The billposter team transformed the landscape, claimed it for the circus, and moved on. In so doing, the American circus was a pioneer of modern advertising. In 1896, for example, the Ringling Bros. contracted 128,000 dollars for posters alone.[44] A turn-of-the-century trade publication, *Billboard Advertising,* observed that the circus was the first U.S. business to master the use of the poster. Indeed, the circus transformed this disposable art form into spectacle. Some shows transformed individual posters into puzzle pieces that formed a single giant banner when pasted together (sometimes as many as thirty-two individual posters), thus comprising an overwhelming visual narrative of a show's spectacular offerings (*fig. 1.15*).[45]

Billposters were also important policing agents on subsequent phases of the advance. Retracing the route, they checked to see if bills had been defaced, destroyed by rain, or covered by a rival or another advertiser. When competing showmen covered or destroyed the posters, the situation could become ugly. Barnum and Forepaugh challenged each other in a brutal

Gillespie White-Washing Forepaugh's Elephant, Tiny, Renamed "Light of Asia"

BARNUM IMITATES 4-PAW

FOREPAUGH HAS BEEN IMITATING BARNUM for years. For once BARNUM will imitate FOREPAUGH.

BARNUM has had an elephant artificially colored and will show in his parade

FREE

AT EASTON THURS., MAY **15**

A WHITE ELEPHANT JUST LIKE FOREPAUGH'S WHITE-WASHED ONE

WAIT FOR BARNUM AND JUMBO!

SO BIG·SO BEWILDERINGLY GORGEOUS·SO MAGNIFICENT IT CANNOT BE PICTURED DESCRIBED. GIVEN ABSOLUTELY FREE UPON THE PUBLIC STREETS AT 10 O'CLOCK A.M.

"sticker war" in the 1870s and 1880s, thus mirroring (on a smaller scale) the cutthroat business practices of John D. Rockefeller, Andrew Carnegie, J. P. Morgan, and other Gilded Age robber barons. Barnum and Forepaugh's respective press agents slandered each other's show in the combative, florid world of the penny press, where new typesetting and paper-making technologies had brought down the price of newspapers steadily since the 1830s (*fig. 1.16*). Both circuses attempted to thwart the other by performing in locales where the other was slated to show. Teams of billposters routinely tore down the posters belonging to the "opposition," and posted bills advertising their own show instead. These "sticker wars" heightened the hostility between Forepaugh and Barnum, and even—on occasion—led to brawls. According to

Louis E. Cooke, a press agent for both shows during his long career: "The competition between Forepaugh and the Barnum, Bailey & Hutchinson shows was terrific. Extraordinary salaries were offered and paid to agents, performers, and everyone else who might possibly be of advantage to either concern. Heated arguments and demands often arose. Hostile sentiment prevailed. Rivalry ran rampant with close opposition at nearly every exhibition stand."[46] In 1882 tensions became so fierce that the two showmen agreed to divide their routes temporarily, alternating where they showed—a practice that other proprietors followed when relations became rough in subsequent decades.[47]

Circus posters visually documented showmen as Gilded Age capitalists. Impresarios frequently

Fig. 1.17. "Ringling Brothers' Big Million Dollar Free Street Show and Big New Parade," 1904. Poster, printed by the Courier Company, Buffalo. Collection of the John and Mable Ringling Museum of Art, Tibbals Collection, ht2001291

branded posters with their physical likeness appearing alongside the grand, baroque title of their circus, which, in turn, chronicled the rise of new circus monopolies—from P. T. Barnum's Great Traveling World's Fair in 1871, to Barnum & Bailey's Greatest Show on Earth in 1880, and finally, Ringling Bros. and Barnum & Bailey Combined Shows in 1919. As a whole, circus mergers, in conjunction with other factors like competition from new media, helped shrink the total number of shows from approximately ninety-eight in 1903 to thirteen in 1956.[48] The five Ringling Bros. circus partners frequently appeared on their signature poster logo in a row, each sporting a heavy brown moustache and a stand-up collar, which rendered them virtually identical and instantly recognizable across the nation (*fig. 1.17*). Owing to the show's familiarity, audiences often referred to the circus in shorthand: "the five brothers in a row," or simply, "the five moustaches."[49]

The circus poster also chronicled the power and prestige of big money. Posters contained a shower of superlatives, describing a vast menagerie of exotic animals, enormous "herds and droves," a thousand-fold cast appearing in the grand opening spectacle, scores of mile-long railroad cars, the use of expensive new technology like the electric light, the bicycle, or the automobile, the procurement of the most accomplished and famous international performers, the financial solvency to offer luxurious accommodations for premier artists like Lillian Leitzel, and omnipresent ledgers of prodigious daily expenses. For instance, a poster for the Adam Forepaugh circus depicted the showman as a fortress of a man, standing confidently with hands in pockets over a frightened group of rivals (including P. T. Barnum and James A. Bailey) scampering to safety. The poster proclaimed: "A Giant Among the Pigmys, Towers Above His Rivals. Adam Forepaugh, America's Most Successful Show-

Fig. 1.18. "Adam Forepaugh: A Giant Among the Pigmys," ca. 1882. Poster, printed by the Strobridge Lithographing Company, Cincinnati. Collection of the John and Mable Ringling Museum of Art, Tibbals Collection, ht2000399

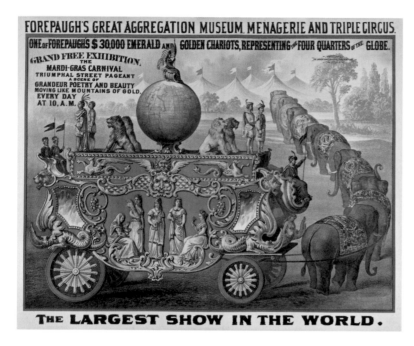

1250 Characters on a Stage Space Bigger than 100 Theatres" (*fig. 1.20*).

A Moral, Instructive Show: Rags to Riches, Feminine Pulchritude, and Patriotic Spectacle at the Americanized Circus

The posters' display of wealth and numerical superiority provided a vivid doppelgänger for another common theme of Americanization: the bootstraps narrative of the circus capitalist. The biggest players in the Gilded Age circus industry such as Barnum, Bailey, Forepaugh, and the Ringling brothers trumpeted their rise from modest means as evidence of their industry, thrift, and sobriety—in essence, showing their audiences that their shows were respectable institutions, run by men of unimpeachable character. Barnum was born to modest means, while the five Ringling brothers (and their three other siblings) struggled to survive as the children of an itinerant immigrant German harness maker. Forepaugh was a scrappy butcher's apprentice as a boy. He grew up to become a horse dealer and got rich making lucrative Union Army cavalry contracts during the Civil War. He entered the circus business by accident when a broke showman paid him in exotic animals. James Bailey ran away to the circus from an abusive home as a boy and rose through the ranks over the years. In repeated iterations of self-invention in his autobiographies and prescriptive, how-to books, such as *Thirty Years of Hustling* and *The Art of Money Getting*, Barnum stressed how perseverance and strong moral fiber led to his success (in spite of book titles that suggested otherwise). In 1825, his insolvent father, Philo, died when Barnum, the oldest of five children, was fifteen years old, leaving his mother nothing to support the family: "I was obliged to get trusted for

man" (*fig. 1.18*). Another Forepaugh poster illustrated one of the circus's many lavish "$30,000.00 Emerald and Golden Chariots . . . Moving Like Mountains of Gold Everyday at 10:00 AM" (*fig. 1.19*). The Ringling Bros. similarly sought to impress the public with a poster that delineated their "Big Million Dollar" street parade (*see fig. 11.7*) and Barnum & Bailey hyped gargantuan spectacles such as *Cleopatra* in 1912: a "Dazzling World Story Tremendously Told by

▲ Fig. 1.19. "Forepaugh's Great Aggregation, Museum, Menagerie and Triple Circus," ca. 1880. Poster, printed by the Strobridge Lithographing Company, Cincinnati. Collection of the John and Mable Ringling Museum of Art, Tibbals Collection, ht2000400

▲ Fig. 1.20. "Barnum & Bailey's New Superb Spectacle *Cleopatra*," 1912. Poster, printed by the Strobridge Lithographing Company, Cincinnati. Collection of the John and Mable Ringling Museum of Art, Tibbals Collection, ht2000313

the pair of shoes I wore to my father's funeral. I literally began the world with nothing, and was barefooted at that."[50] Barnum flatly rejected luck in favor of pluck: "There is no such thing in the world as luck. There never was a man who could go out in the morning and find a purse full of gold in the street to-day, and another to-morrow, and so on, day after day. He may do so once in his life; but so far as mere luck is concerned, he is as liable to lose it as to find it."[51]

Alfred T. Ringling used his family's hardscrabble history to validate the high moral character of the circus in *Life Story of the Ringling Brothers* (*fig. 1.21*). The Ringlings proudly advertised their circus as a "New School of American Showmen," a "Sunday School" entertainment that forever changed the circus business (even though P. T. Barnum made similar claims of pioneering propriety): "[T]he

Ringling brothers have transformed the nature of the circus so materially, that to-day it bears a far different relation to the world than it did twenty years ago. At that time it was not unusual to see a horde of dishonest, greedy, and rapacious camp-followers like vampires infesting the routes of traveling shows."[52] Published in 1900 just as the Ringling Bros. Circus was poised to become the largest in the nation (while Barnum & Bailey toured Europe in a state of relative distraction about the U.S. circus market), *Life Story of the Ringling Brothers* chronicled a threadbare childhood in Baraboo, Wisconsin, and McGregor, Iowa. The boys loved to play "circus" for their siblings and playmates, using straight pins as currency. As teenagers, they put together a regional wagon show, The Ringling Brothers' Classic and Comic Concert Company, which dodged brawls,

Fig. 1.21. "Ringling Bros., Monarchs of the Circus World," 1901. Poster, printed by the Courier Company, Buffalo. Fred D. Pfening III Collection

blizzards, and bad business as the brothers rolled across Wisconsin, working relentlessly "like beavers."[53] According to their *Life Story*, early hardship taught them well: they were frugal, cooperative, and so deeply loyal to one another that each brother worked without a contract in his respective part of the show. They prohibited liquor and gambling on the show grounds, thus earning their "Sunday school" stripes: "But they knew not the meaning of the word 'fail,' and by ignoring the power of difficulties, and by a constant determination to overcome them, they vanquished misfortune and often made a disadvantage turn to their favor."[54] Circus posters gave visual form to the grinding toil and determination in the *Life Story of the Ringling Brothers* with images of backbreaking "early trials" like chopping down trees

juxtaposed with later measures of success: thirty elephants, a massive big top, and an opulent parade. Lest any viewer miss the poster's visual chronicle of upward mobility, the copy triumphantly proclaimed: "Starting without a Dollar They Have Built Up the Largest Show in the World."

These rags-to-riches impresario narratives represented an essential aspect of Americanization. With the hard-won success and the ostensible moral integrity of the showman in full view on the circus poster, press release, and autobiography, Gilded Age proprietors made claims for the educative power of their circuses that translated the co-ordinated display of animal and human bodies into spectacles of discipline and virtue. Like their antebellum predecessors, Gilded Age showmen high-

Fig. 1.22. Equestriennes, 1891. Poster, printed by the United States Printing Co. © Shelburne Museum, Shelburne, Vermont, Gift of Harry T. Peters Sr. Family, 1959, 1959-67.104

lighted the instructive power of the menagerie as a way to validate their shows as wholesome. In the media blitz that preceded the arrival of the circus, press agents placed stories in local newspapers (in exchange for "comps" to the show) about individual animals—such as the sacrificial goodness of Barnum's late elephant, Jumbo, who died in 1885 after reportedly saving the lives of a beloved elephant friend, Tom Thumb, and his keeper, Mathew Scott, by pushing them out of the path of an oncoming train. Press releases also focused on the romantic lives of animals, such as Barnum & Bailey's faux chimpanzee couple, Johanna and Chiko, in 1893.[55] These animals were readily recognizable to audiences months ahead of the show because they were common poster subjects, featured individually, like Jumbo, or in vast, menagerie panoramas, such as Johanna and Chiko.

Women performers were keystones of moral rectitude in the showman's universe of respectable entertainments during the Gilded Age and Progressive Era. Although female performers had worked at the American circus since its inception in the early republic, late-eighteenth- and early-nineteenth-century show bills downplayed the presence of women because Protestant ministers and social reformers were often hostile to public displays of the female body. Yet in the Gilded Age, women performers became a critical part of defining the American railroad circus as respectable. Clad in corseted leotards and tights, acrobatic and equestrian women (like animals) were prominent poster subjects (*fig. 1.22*). By the standards of the day, these performers were nearly nude, and thus, one might assume, vulnerable to censure in an era of escalating Comstockian purity and anti-vice reform because they roamed the nation in scant costuming, performing for pay in front of thousands each day.[56]

However, showmen used several effective strategies to blunt potential protest against female performers who might otherwise be targeted. For one, the advance team ferried press releases to local newspapers that included stories about the domestic propriety of individual circus women—in addition to billing thousands of titillating posters of kinetic and scantily clad female bodies. These nuggets of "news" (verbatim in each town along the route and published in local newspapers in exchange for comp tickets to the show) breathlessly described proper young ballet girls quitting the circus for marriage to upstanding young men; acrobats and equestriennes who loved to cook and embroider; and young women who lived under the careful eyes of parents and brothers on the show. Showmen also publicized gender-specific appearance and conduct rules that women performers were contractually obliged to obey: women were required to return to the sleeping car "at a reasonable hour"; to avoid "male companions" when off duty; they were prohibited "at all times and places" from engaging in "flirting and boisterous conduct"; they were forbidden from stopping at hotels "at any time"; and they had to be "neat and modest in appearance," and to avoid "dress in a flashy, loud style." Ringling Bros. management described such policies as a critical part of maintaining order

Fig. 1.23. Frederick Whitman Glasier. "Mademoiselle Omega" Gertrude Dewar, 1908. Photograph. Collection of the John and Mable Ringling Museum of Art, Glasier Glass Plate Negative Collection, 0071

within the traveling community: "It is intended to protect the girls in every possible way. Good order and good behavior are necessary if you are to be comfortable and happy."[57] As a final strategy, showmen also contextualized the physical labor of the circus woman as an exemplary aspect of the contemporary physical culture movement. As accomplished—but womanly—athletes, circus women were paragons of wholesome physical beauty (*fig. 1.23*).

Nonetheless, a dialectics of sexual titillation and propriety fueled representations of female performers at the American railroad circus. Amplifying the images of virtual female nudity on the posters themselves, press agents reminded audiences that female performers wore tights—fully in view—under their short skirts. Showmen's strategies to contain the subversive potential of the female circus body were also racially inflected. While press agents used the rhetoric of domesticity to characterize European American performers, they presented women of color as fierce, immodest, mannish, or animal-human hybrids. Commonly advertised in the aggregate—"Dahomey Savages; Ubangi Savages; the Giraffe-Neck Women of Burma"; and so on—women of color generally performed at the sideshow, or as part of an ephemeral feature of Barnum & Bailey's

circus in the 1890s, the Grand Ethnological Congress of Strange and Savage Tribes, where exotic people performed next to animals from their homelands in popular performances of evolutionary theory and contemporary racial hierarchy (*fig. 1.24*). Marketed with references to bare skin—akin to representations of European American female circus bodies—women of color were also billed as educationally illuminating "specimens" of their respective races.[58]

Race, gender, and Americanization collided in the most fully formed narrative of the railroad circus: the patriotic spectacle. In advance of the show, press agents blanketed future audiences with information about these sprawling dramatic reenactments of historical and contemporary events. The grand entry spec, or spectacle, opened the big-top program immediately after the musical overture ended. Circuses had occasionally included historical pageants and reenactments since the antebellum era, but the railroad facilitated a cast of over a thousand starting in the 1890s. Spectacles like Barnum & Bailey's 500,000-dollar production *Columbus and the Discovery of America* (1892), and Adam Forepaugh's 1776, *Historic Scenes and Battles of the American Revolution* (1893), recreated American history in teleological terms, as the inevitable march

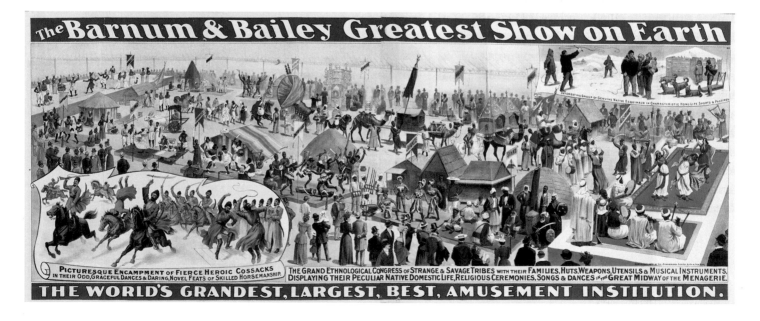

of European American civilization and democratic institutions. With superlative verbosity, the Forepaugh program proclaimed, "The Revolution made us a nation destined to be the very greatest of all the earth, consequently it is the principal and primal event in our history."[59] The musical overture preceding these specs framed the ideological narrative with a mix of popular marches, familiar operatic tunes, and plantation melodies.

Plantation music influenced the cultural meanings of these spectacles with its nostalgic evocation of a tranquil southern society with white supremacist hierarchies firmly in place, and its elision of the Civil War. Because the largest railroad circuses traveled nationally, they avoided regionally fractious representations of the nation's past, and thus virtually ignored the Civil War as a spec subject. The showman Yankee Robinson reenacted *au courant* scenes from Civil War battles during the war itself in 1862 and 1863, but in subsequent decades, the Sells Brothers circus was the only show to recreate a Civil War battle in a brief demonstration of an artillery race in 1887 from the Battle of Shiloh. The Civil War fleetingly reappeared as part of a uniformed pageant featuring American veterans of every war, which opened the Adam Forepaugh & Sells Brothers circus in 1905.[60] In an era of escalating racial violence, Jim Crow disenfranchisement, and segregation (in which black southern circus audiences entered the show from separate openings in the tent), other parts of American culture recast the Civil War and Reconstruction in racist terms. These representations included Thomas Dixon's popular Ku Klux Klan trilogy (1905–7); the rise of the Dunning School of Civil War–era historiography at Columbia University (under the aegis of William Archibald Dunning), which indicted the freedmen and their white northern allies, rather than white southern terrorism, for

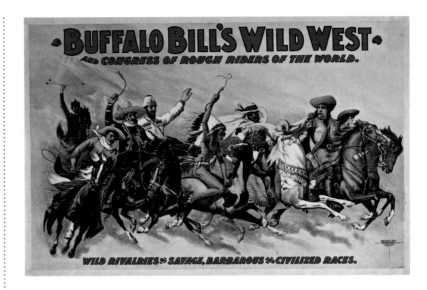

the failures of Reconstruction and the rise of Jim Crow; and the success of D. W. Griffith's blockbuster feature film *The Birth of a Nation* which brought Dixon's Klan trilogy to movie palaces throughout the nation in 1915.[61]

American railroad circus spectacles heralded a unified, patriotic vision of the nation and its place in the world. Specifically, Native American performers and the Spanish-American War provided showmen with frontier narratives of continental and overseas expansion, couched in exceptionalist language of manifest destiny and American progress. In collaboration with William F. "Buffalo Bill" Cody, Gordon W. "Pawnee Bill" Lillie, and other proprietors of the Wild West show, a distinctive entertainment that overlapped with the circus in terms of its content and common financial investors, circus showmen created spectacles of Native American cultural life that reified Indian cultural practices (to the chagrin of assimilation-minded reformers), but also provided a justification for conquest and uplift in the age of the Indian Wars (*fig. 1.25*). Additionally, circus and Wild West show posters provided visual

narratives of ideological continuity between the Indian Wars and overseas empire building: captioned with "Wild Rivalries of Savage, Barbarous and Civilized Races," a poster for Buffalo Bill's Wild West depicted a thundering, transnational panoply of "savage" people of color on horseback (including a muscular, tattooed, virtually nude Native American man with open mouth) alongside Cody and possibly Annie Oakley. Such images extended the logic of European American racial hierarchies, manifest destiny, and nation building from the continental theater of the Indian Wars to the global stage.

During the Spanish-American War era, American railroad shows capitalized on battle scenes, diplomacy, and the new territories now under U.S. control as topical sources of novelty, in addition to burnishing the circus's patriotic credentials. Spectacles showcased the nation's growing influence on the world stage and its ability to lead and enlighten its territorial subjects, including Filipinos, Hawaiians, Guamanians, Samoans, and Puerto Ricans. On its European tour, Barnum & Bailey promulgated the United States' rising international stature in *America's Great Naval Victory at Santiago* (fig. 1.26); Adam Forepaugh & Sells Brothers celebrated U.S. control of the Canal Zone in *Panama; or, the Portals*

of the Sea; or, the Stars and Stripes (1905); and Barnum & Bailey staged *Peace, America's Immortal Triumph*, (1906), which reenacted President Theodore Roosevelt's successful mediation of the Portsmouth Treaty in 1905 that ended the Russo-Japanese War. Circuses enhanced their authority as sources of up-to-date information about U.S. expansionism with displays of animals from the American empire, such as a Philippine boa constrictor named after the Filipino nationalist Emilio Aguinaldo, at the Ringling Bros. Circus, or a male and female pair of "midget cattle" at the Adam Forepaugh Shows from the island of Upolu, Samoa, an Oceana island neighbor of American Samoa.[62]

Circuses supplied local newspapers with a steady stream of press releases that chronicled patriotic activities and feeling on the show. For example, after President McKinley was assassinated in 1901, the *Los Angeles Times* reported that the Ringling Bros. Circus canceled its afternoon show to participate in a public memorial service for the slain president:

Deep down in the breasts of even the clowns and the sideshow freaks is a well-spring of patriotism.... The Ringling Bros., although at great loss to themselves, with commendable respect for the government to which they owe allegiance, and the great body of American people from which they derive their patronage, cut out their afternoon performance yesterday, in order that their employees might join with the public generally in doing honor to the foremost American of his time.... With true loyalty to the Stars and Stripes, and with profoundest reverence and respect for the dead President, they joined in holding a memorial service that, in sincerity and devotion, was exceeded by none of the many remarkable outpourings of grief and reverence the land over.[63]

Fig. 1.26. "The Barnum & Bailey Greatest Show on Earth, *America's Great Naval Victory at Santiago*," 1899. Poster, printed by the Strobridge Lithographing Company, Cincinnati. Circus World Museum, CWi-2312

By canceling the performance in order to honor the late president, the show advertised the purity of its larger purpose: to appear patriotic, self-sacrificing, and honorable—a far cry from the crass, profit-minded hustle of the modern show business. Yet at the same time, the show used the somber occasion as an opportunity to advertise itself as a source of mirth with references to the "well-spring of patriotism" in "even" its cast of clowns and freaks.

American showmen eagerly publicized their patriotic credentials with endorsements from the U.S. military. Army officers periodically rode with railroad circuses to study their organization and transportation techniques: hauling roughly 1,200 people, animals, tents, and supplies across the country, day after day, railroad shows possessed a degree of social order in intimate quarters that was just as impressively disciplined as their scripted canvas performances.[64] During Barnum & Bailey's European tour (1897–1902), German army officers also looked to the show's logistical system as a model for its own operations, a fact that circus press agents quickly reported to American newspapers: "So great was the satisfaction in Germany with the portable hotel carried by the circus, that the identical scheme was adopted for the use of the national army when in the field."[65] Readily identified from within the United States and from without, the circus's logistical specialization was a defining element of Americanization.

Circus Day: An American Ritual

Audience members were equally fascinated by circus logistics. Just as the German and American military had observed, Circus Day was an efficient spectacle of labor and physical movement in which the process of erection and disassembly was an essential part of

Fig. 1.27. Frederick Whitman Glasier. *Barnum & Bailey Circus Day,* 1903. Photograph. Collection of the John and Mable Ringling Museum of Art, Glasier Glass Plate Negative Collection, 0890

Fig. 1.28. Frenzeny and Tavernier, "The Circus Coming into Town," cover of *Harper's Weekly*, October 4, 1873. HarpWeek, LLC

the show. Dedicated audience members awakened before dawn to witness the arrival of the first of four trains carrying the show. Photographers captured these scenes of hundreds, even thousands of townspeople, crowding the rail yard to watch a virtual army of laborers roll the wagons off the rails, aided by elephants and horses, moving the collapsible canvas city, piece by piece, wagon by wagon, to the lot (*fig. 1.27*). Spread over approximately nine acres on the show grounds, the syncopated rhythms of sledging the stakes into the ground and raising the tent poles were punctuated by workmen singing sea shanties and animals bawling and growling. Later that morning, thousands of residents and rural visitors quit work and school (cancelled for Circus Day), crowding Main Street to watch the free parade wend slowly through town—gilded wagons, horses, calliope, en-

caged snarling felines, camels, elephants, a band, forty-horse hitch, and scores of performers (*fig. 1.28*). Newspapers across the country, from Monroe, Wisconsin, to Waxahachie, Texas, reported the presence of anywhere from 10,000 to 20,000 people in town.[66] The circus typically performed twice per stop—in the afternoon and evening. Audiences milled inside the sideshow tent, usually paying an extra dime to see the assemblage of giantesses, thin men, fat ladies, armless men, bearded ladies, "missing links," and tattooed people. The menagerie tent attached to the big top afforded opportunities for close inspection of caged animals before the big show (*fig. 1.29*). The live circus band signaled audiences to hurry in to the big top, lest they miss the show. On three rings, two raised stages, and an outer hippodrome track, roughly 10,000 to 15,000 spectators witnessed twenty to twenty-five acts during the show in a kinetic buzz of constant movement that was carefully scripted to music (*fig. 1.30*). While audiences watched the action inside the big top, workmen began the process of disassembly outside, readying the circus for its next journey. Enterprising showmen induced audiences to pay extra cash for an "aftershow concert," to watch the final teardown, in conjunction with some other performance piece, such as a Wild West display of fancy horsemanship and marksmanship.[67] The writer and critic William Dean Howells found such giant "city circuses" overwhelming: "We

▲ *Fig. 1.29.* Frederick Whitman Glasier. Menagerie tent of the Ringling Bros. Circus, 1905. Photograph. Collection of the John and Mable Ringling Museum of Art, Glasier Glass Plate Negative Collection, 0986 and 0987

◀ *Fig. 1.30.* Interior view of crowd and performance at Ringling Bros. and Barnum & Bailey Circus, ca. 1922–38. Photograph. Collection of the John and Mable Ringling Museum of Art, Tibbals Collection, ht0003264

are all accustomed, in the gross and foolish superfluity of these city circuses, to see no feat quite through, but to turn our greedy eyes at the most important instant in the hope of greater wonders in another ring. We have four or five clowns, in as many varieties of grotesque costume, as well as a lady clown in befitting dress; but we hear none of them speak."[68]

Audience members responded to the all-encompassing sensory whirlwind of the railroad circus in oppositional ways. In contrast to the seamless spectacle of specialized human, elephant, and equine labor that created the canvas city on Circus Day, some spectators used the occasion for lawlessness. Thefts, for one, were common. For instance, on November 9, 1900, the Terrell (Texas) *Times-Star* reported that during the Ringling Bros. evening performance, thieves were busy: "A sneak thief entered the palatial home of W. B. Martin Wednesday evening while the inmates were attending the circus and stole a gold watch belonging to Mrs. F. L. Irvine and three gold rings. Entrance to the building was gained by knocking out a window pane."[69] Circus Day was also an occasion for other forms of social chaos, such as vandalism, drunkenness, and voyeurism. Occasionally, transgression slid into mayhem with ritualized fights between families bearing old grudges, or violence that erupted among the thousands of strangers in town.

Circus Day violence was often the product of racial inequality, thus representing yet another facet of Americanization. Circus route books (a daily diary published at the end of the season) documented acts of racist violence on Circus Day.[70] African American circus workers were particularly vulnerable. On June 15, 1920, a Circus Day crowd became a murderous mob in Duluth, Minnesota. After the John Robinson circus performed the night before, local police arrested and jailed six black roustabouts ac-cused of sexually assaulting a young white woman, whose male friend told police that the six workingmen had held up the pair at gunpoint behind the big top after the evening performance. The circus moved on to its next show stop at Virginia, Minnesota, without offering any support for the imperiled employees—roustabouts, after all, were expendable labor, poorly paid, and hired and fired throughout the season. Within hours, Duluth authorities had hunted down and arrested four other African American roustabouts at the Robinson show.

News of the allegations exploded across the region, fanned by sensational reportage in area newspapers. The next evening, a white mob (estimates ran as high as 10,000 people) stormed the Duluth city jail with bricks, rails, and bats, shattering windows and destroying doors, meeting little resistance from local police. The mob dragged three of the men—Elias Clayton, Elmer Jackson, and Isaac McGhie—outside, held a mock trial, beat them to death, and lynched them from a light pole on the corner of First Street and Second Avenue East. The murders received national attention. The *New York Times* reported a scene of "frenzy," "revelry," and "blood lust": "The crowd which 'attended' the hanging bee was like a crowd attending a carnival. Giggling boys and girls looked skyward today where the bodies of the negroes swung during the hours before daylight. The police, restored to authority by the mob itself after the purpose of the lynch law 'court' had been accomplished, cut down the bodies at dawn."[71] Just as quickly as it had formed, the mob vanished. In the aftermath of the murders, the remaining jailed defendants staunchly maintained their innocence. Based on flimsy evidence, one of the accused, Max Mason, was convicted of rape and served four years in prison before receiving a pardon on condition that he leave the state. Three white men served prison

time for riot. The murders prompted passage of a Minnesota state anti-lynching law in 1921. No one, however, was ever convicted for the murder of the three circus workers.[72]

The horrifying chain of events in Duluth, Minnesota, underscored the fundamental contradictions of the circus Americanized. The big top's omnipresence in rural and urban markets alike was founded upon comforting narratives of democratic inclusion and social leveling. As a way to validate the circus's accessible, democratic appeal, press agents freely advertised the economic mobility of its rags-to-riches proprietors and star performers, in conjunction with its ability to offer educational (and titillating) novelty and excitement to "all classes at little cost." According to the *Arkansas Democrat* in 1898: "Ringling Bros.' circus represents, in its best aspect, this peculiar American institution. It began like thousands of successful enterprises in this liberty-loving land in a small and unpretentious way, but its progress has been nothing short of marvel-

ous."[73] However, the circus Americanized also reinforced a status quo of exclusion and inequality with its performances of racial hierarchy under the big top and sideshow, as well as the volatile conduct of its massive, pushing crowds on Circus Day. As a cultural ritual that brought thousands of people together, cheek and jowl, the railroad circus brought to the surface long-standing social and cultural forms of inequality that were at the very center of the American experience.

The rise of new media such as film, radio, and television, as well as transportation technologies like the car and airplane, eventually displaced the railroad circus as an authoritative portal to the wider world. At the turn of the twentieth century, the circus Americanized was becoming so big that its chief architect, James A. Bailey, wished to escape it. In anticipation of the resurgence of the one-ring show a hundred years later, Bailey envisioned a new, exclusive circus centered on individual artistry, rather than scripted chaos for the masses. Inspired

Fig. 1.31. Bill Bailey. "Ringling Bros. and Barnum & Bailey Circus: *Let Freedom Ring,*" 1943. Poster. Collection of the John and Mable Ringling Museum of Art, Tibbals Collection, ht2001725

by the small circuses he saw in opera houses and fancy circus buildings while touring Europe, Bailey privately bemoaned the Greatest Show on Earth in its current form:

> The circus delux must be a place of beauty and thrills...No more meaningless advertising street parades...No more cheap side shows, or concerts, or peddling of toy balloons and other cheap articles to the annoyance of patrons. No more menagerie of drowsy animals in narrow cages, dimly lighted...The New Circus will be in smaller tents, water proof, more compact, comfortably seated...Reserved numbered chairs and private box seats may be purchased by diagram from one to two weeks in advance, so patrons may avoid the pushing crowds.[74]

Bailey died in 1906, before he could realize his vision of a new "circus delux," but the gargantuan railroad circus itself was slowly folding under its own weight. The morning parade was the first casualty. As shows escalated in size at the turn of the twentieth century, railroad logistics became increasingly tricky. The rising numbers of trains for haulage created difficulties in getting each train to the next destination on time. By the 1920s, the parade had all but vanished.[75] Other features like spectacles of current events, the ethnological congress, and (eventually) the sideshow and menagerie followed. In order to cut labor costs after a bitter unionizing drive with the Teamsters and the workingmen, Ringling Bros. and Barnum & Bailey abandoned the canvas big top permanently in 1956, in favor of performing at indoor arenas. A key feature of the biggest circus Americanized had vanished. And in 2006, the Ringling show opted to run its three units—Red, Blue, and Gold—without three rings and fewer animals, in fa-

vor of new video projections and greater pyrotechnical pizzazz. Critics characterized the revised show as "the ringless brothers circus."[76]

Despite the disappearance of key physical features of Americanization at the nation's largest circus, the ideological significance of the circus Americanized remains (*fig. 1.31*). On the eve of the American-led invasion of Iraq in 2003, the producer and chief executive officer of the Ringling Bros. and Barnum & Bailey Circus, Kenneth Feld, reported that attendance had climbed by fifteen percent overall in the last two years and had spiked after September 11, 2001. He noted that at recent shows in Virginia, "we played to full houses of military families and got letters of thanks from the commanders."[77] In 2009, at the height of the most serious economic downturn since the Great Depression, attendance figures at Ringling Bros. and Barnum & Bailey climbed steadily. According to Thomas J. Crangle, an event-marketing consultant based in Las Vegas, "For many families now a trip to Disney World is out of the question, but a drive to Ringling can give the kids a vacation for an afternoon." Likewise, Kenneth Feld characterized his circus as "the nation's entertainment security blanket....We are the Wal-Mart of the entertainment business, affordable for everyone."[78] In the end, the distinctive, overwhelming physical presence of the circus Americanized has long past. However, its ability to repackage the world into an accessible, patriotic spectacle of domesticated exoticism and danger, as well as its comforting narratives of social pluralism, remain a defining feature of American culture.

1 "Circus Animals Aboard," *New York Times*, Nov. 12, 1897, www.nytimes.com (accessed Oct. 18, 2010).

2 "The Mahdi or for the Victoria Cross," Barnum & Bailey's Greatest Show on Earth, show program (London: Walter Hill, 1898), 41, Program Collection, Robert Parkinson Research Library, Circus World Museum, Baraboo, Wisconsin (hereafter CWM).

3 "Barnum's in London," *New York Times*, Jan. 16, 1898, www.nytimes.com (accessed Oct. 18, 2010).

4 "Greatest Show to Return," *New York Times*, Dec. 22, 1901, www.nytimes.com (accessed Oct. 18, 2010).

5 E. H. Bostock, *Menageries, Circuses and Theatres* (New York: Frederick A. Stokes Company, 1928), 157, Harry Ransom Center for the Humanities, Austin, Texas (hereafter HRC).

6 George Speaight, *History of the Circus* (London: Tantivy Press, 1980), 42–45; Helen Stoddart, *Rings of Desire: Circus History and Representation* (Manchester: Manchester University Press, 2000), 39–43.

7 "Lord" George Sanger, *Seventy Years a Showman* (London: J. M. Dent & Sons, 1926 [1910]), 232–33; British circus books reinforced Sanger's argument by bolstering British ideals of bourgeois respectability and cultural purity—vis-à-vis the Americans. According to the anthropologist Yoram Carmeli, "[T]he bourgeois notion of Britishness and British history, as reified and authenticated through circus, revolved, in part, around a rejection of the 'contaminating' influence of Americanization which undercut the cultural hegemony of traditional upper classes." Yoram S. Carmeli, "The Invention of Circus and Bourgeois Hegemony: A Glance at British Circus Books," *Journal of Popular Culture* 29, no. 1 (Summer 1995), 216. European political philosophers likewise participated in this tradition, dismissing America's "home-grown" democratic traditions as imitative. Hannah Arendt, for example, characterized the United States as a tabula rasa for "the founding of new settlements which adopted the legal and political institutions of the mother country." See Hannah Arendt, *The Origins of Totalitarianism* (New York: Harcourt Brace Jovanovich, 1973), 186.

8 Alan Trachtenberg, *The Incorporation of America: Culture and Society in the Gilded Age* (New York: Hill and Wang, 1982).

9 Robert W. Rydell and Rob Kroes, *Buffalo Bill in Bologna: The Americanization of the World, 1869–1922* (Chicago: University of Chicago Press, 2005), 119.

10 Frederick Jackson Turner, "The Significance of the Frontier in American History," *Report of the American Historical Association for 1893*, 199–227.

11 See Mark St. Leon, "Circus & Nation: A Critical Inquiry into Circus in Its Australian Setting, 1847–2006, from the Perspectives of Society, Enterprise, and Culture" (diss. University of Sydney, Australia, 2006); also see Mark St. Leon, *Circus: The Australian Story* (Melbourne: Melbourne Books, 2011).

12 Stuart Thayer, *Annals of the American Circus*, combined edition (Seattle: Dauven and Thayer, 2000), 6.

13 Ibid., 8.

14 Ibid., 12.

15 Ibid., 75; Robert C. Allen, *Horrible Prettiness: Burlesque and American Culture* (Chapel Hill: University of North Carolina Press, 1991), 47–48.

16 Thayer, *Annals of the American Circus*, 77.

17 Brenda Assael, *The Circus and Victorian Society* (Charlottesville: University of Virginia Press, 2005), 27.

18 Ibid., 8.

19 Thayer, *Annals of the American Circus*, 75.

20 Ibid., 76.

21 Ibid., 76, 99.

22 Thayer, "The Anti-Circus Laws in Connecticut, 1773–1840," *Bandwagon* 20 (Jan.–Feb. 1976), 18; "Legislating the Shows: Vermont, 1824–1933," *Bandwagon* 25 (July–Aug. 1981), 20; Janet M. Davis, *The Circus Age: Culture and Society under the American Big Top* (Chapel Hill: University of North Carolina Press, 2002), 17.

23 See the essay by Fred Dahlinger in this volume.

24 On canal horses, see Carol Sheriff, *The Artificial River: The Erie Canal and the Paradox of Progress, 1817–1862* (New York: Hill and Wang, 1996), 4, 141.

25 Stuart L. Thayer, "The Steamboat, the Circus, and Cincinnati," in *The Amazing American Circus Poster: The Strobridge Lithographing Company*, ed. Kristin Spangenberg and Deborah W. Walk (Cincinnati and Sarasota: Cincinnati Art Museum and the John and Mable Ringling Museum of Art, 2011), 11–13.

26 For a detailed history of Wisconsin's showmen see Fred Dahlinger, Jr. and Stuart Thayer, *Badger State Showmen: A History of Wisconsin's Circus Heritage* (Madison: Grote Publishing, 1998).

27 David Haward Bain, *Empire Express: Building the First Transcontinental Railroad* (New York: Viking, 1999), 663–72, quote from 664.

28 Stephen Ambrose, *Nothing Like It in the World: The Men Who Built the Transcontinental Railroad, 1863–1869* (New York: Simon and Schuster, 2000), 101.

29 William L. Slout, *Olympians of the Sawdust Circle: A Biographical Dictionary of the Nineteenth-Century American Circus* (San Bernardino, CA: Borgo Press, 1998), 46–47.

30 Ibid., 54; Dahlinger and Thayer, *Badger State Showmen*, 34.

31 Alfred Dupont Chandler, *The Visible Hand: The Managerial Revolution in American Business* (Cambridge, MA: Belknap Press, 1977); and Alfred Dupont Chandler, ed., *The Railroads: The Nation's First Big Business. Sources and Readings* (New York: Harcourt, 1965).

32 Fred Dahlinger, Jr., *Show Trains of the 20th Century* (Hudson, WI: Iconografix, 2000), 4.

33 Davis, *Circus Age*, 42–43; for John Ringling's marketing strategy used in press releases see "Charms of Circus Draws Big Crowd," unidentified newspaper clipping, Monroe, WI, Aug, 18, 1899, Newspaper Collection, CWM.

34 Charles Theodore Murray, "In Advance of the Circus." *McClure's Magazine*, Aug. 1894, 253; Circus Scrapbook Collection, MWEZ+N.C.6312, Billy Rose Theatre Collection, New York Public Library for the Performing Arts, in Davis, *Circus Age*, 43.

35 On circus posters see, Kristin Spangenberg and Deborah W. Walk, eds. *The Amazing American Circus Poster: The Strobridge Lithographing Company*. (Cincinnati and Sarasota: Cincinnati Art Museum and the John and Mable Ringling Museum of Art, 2011).

36 Warren I. Susman, *Culture as History: The Transformation of American Society in the Twentieth Century* (New York: Pantheon Books, 1985), 110–11.

37 Don B. Wilmeth and Edwin Martin, *Mud Show: American Tent Circus Life* (Albuquerque: University of New Mexico Press, 1988), 14; Speaight, *History of the Circus*, 124–25.

38 "The Barnum & Bailey Official Route Book," season of 1893 (Buffalo: Harvey L. Watkins, 1893): 24–25, Route Book Collection, CWM, quoted in Davis, *Circus Age*, 44.

39 "The Barnum & Bailey Official Route Book," season of 1893, 28–29, quoted in ibid., 42.

40 Murray, "In Advance of the Circus," 252, quoted in ibid., 43.

41 F. B. Hutchinson, "Official Route Book of the Adam Forepaugh Shows," season 1894 (Buffalo: Courier Co., 1894), 45, Route Book Collection, CWM, quoted in ibid., 44.

42 Murray, "In Advance of the Circus," 260; "Beneath White Tents, A Route Book of Ringling Bros.' World's Greatest Shows, Season 1894," 35, Program Collection, CWM, quoted in ibid., 46.

43 Murray, "In Advance of the Circus," 260, quoted in ibid., 46.

44 *Billboard*, Dec. 1, 1897, 9, quoted in ibid., 45.

45 "Billing Like a Circus," *Billboard Advertising*, Sept. 1, 1896, quoted in ibid., 45.

46 Louis E. Cooke, "Reminiscences of a Showman," *Newark Evening Star*, July 1, 1915, Newspaper Collection, CWM.

47 Dahlinger and Thayer, *Badger State Showmen*, 83, quoted in Davis, *Circus Age*, 250, note 23.

48 Marcello Truzzi, "The Decline of the American Circus: The Shrinkage of an Institution," in Marcello Truzzi, ed., *Sociology and Everyday Life* (Englewood Cliffs, NJ: Prentice-Hall, 1968), 315–16, quoted in ibid., 229.

49 On "the five brothers in a row," see Jerry Apps, *Ringlingville USA: The Stupendous Story of Seven*

Siblings and Their Stunning Circus Success (Madison: Wisconsin Historical Society Press, 2005), 70.

50 P. T. Barnum, *Thirty Years of Hustling: Or, How to Get On* (Rutland, IL: C. C. Thompson, 1890), 171; see also P. T. Barnum, *Struggles and Triumphs: or, Forty Years' Recollections of P. T. Barnum* (Hartford, CT: J. B. Burr, 1869), 39. The verbatim quote appears in both texts.

51 P. T. Barnum, *Thirty Years of Hustling*, 67–68.

52 Alfred T. Ringling, *Life Story of the Ringling Brothers* (Chicago: R. R. Donnelley & Sons, 1900), 18.

53 Ibid., 173.

54 Ibid., 204.

55 See Davis, *Circus Age*, 155–57.

56 In 1873 Anthony Comstock pressed successfully for legislation prohibiting lewd literature, images, and birth control information and devices in the U.S. Mail. In his subsequent capacity as Special Agent and Postal Inspector for the U.S. Post Office, Comstock personally inspected and censored lewd images of the body in popular periodicals, burlesque, dime museum, the nascent film industry, anatomy textbooks, and physical culture shows. Comstock and his allies created surveillance organizations, such as the New York Society for the Suppression of Vice, to prevent improper activities in dance halls, ice cream parlors, amusement parks, and "cheap nickel dumps." See Helen Lefkowitz Horowitz, *Rereading Sex: Battles over Sexual Knowledge and Suppression in Nineteenth-Century America* (New York: Knopf, 2002); Andrea Friedman, *Prurient Interests: Gender, Democracy, and Obscenity in New York City, 1909–1945* (New York: Columbia University Press, 2000); Nicola Beisel, *Imperiled Innocents: Anthony Comstock and Family Reproduction in Victorian America* (Princeton: Princeton University Press, 1997); Harvey Green, *Fit for America: Health, Fitness, Sport and American Society* (Baltimore: Johns Hopkins University Press, 1986).

57 See Davis, *Circus Age*, 99–107. Specifically, see Ringling Bros. circus work contract for Kathy Edwards, October 1912; "Suggestions and Rules Employees Ringling Bros.," issued by Charles Ringling, early 1900s; Ringling Bros., circus work contract for Miss Lulu Welsh, 1912; all from Archival Collections, Work Contracts, CWM.

58 See ibid., 118–38.

59 "The Adam Forepaugh Shows Program" (Buffalo: Courier Co., 1893), Circus Programs, box 12, folder 7, Joseph T. McCaddon Collection, Princeton University Library, quoted in ibid., 202.

60 See ibid., 200.

61 For a concise summary of the Dunning School, see Eric Foner, *Reconstruction: America's Unfinished Revolution, 1863–1877* (New York: Harper and Row, 1988).

62 "Pair of Midget Cattle (Male and Female) from Upolu or Samoa," Adam Forepaugh Shows, n.d., Howard Tibbals Collection, the John and Mable Ringling Museum of Art, Sarasota; ibid., 224.

63 "The Circus Annual, A Route Book of Ringling Bros. World's Greatest Shows," season 1901 (Chicago: Central Printing and Engraving Co., 1901), 81, Route Book Collection, CWM.

64 Davis, *Circus Age*, 78–79.

65 "Greatest Show to Return," *New York Times*, Dec. 22, 1901, www.nytimes.com (accessed Oct. 18, 2010).

66 "Charms of Circus Draws Big Crowd," unidentified newspaper clipping, Monroe, WI, Aug. 18, 1899, Newspaper Collection, CWM; "The Circus," *Waxahachie Daily Light*, Waxahachie, TX, Nov. 2, 1898, 1, Dolph Briscoe Center for American History, University of Texas at Austin (hereafter CAH).

67 See Davis, *Circus Age*, 1–7.

68 William Dean Howells, *Literature and Life* (New York: Harper and Brothers, 1902), 125.

69 News blurb, Terrell (Texas) *Times-Star*, Nov. 9, 1900, 5, CAH.

70 See Davis, *Circus Age*, 224, 292.

71 "Move to Punish Duluth Lynchers," *New York Times*, June 17, 1920, www.nytimes.com (accessed Oct. 27, 2010).

72 "Duluth Lynchings Online Resource," http://collections.mnhs.org/duluthlynchings/html/lynchings.htm (accessed Oct. 27, 2010).

73 "Big Day To-Morrow," *Arkansas Democrat*, Oct. 17, 1898, CAH.

74 Joseph T. McCaddon, "The New Circus," July 17, 1935, Correspondence, box 10, folder 7, Joseph T. McCaddon Collection, Princeton University Library, quoted in Davis, *Circus Age*, 56.

75 See the essays by Fred Dahlinger, Jr. and Gregory Renoff in this volume.

76 Glenn Collins, "Circus Flies o'er Troubles with Greatest of Ease," *New York Times*, March 24, 2009, www.nytimes.com (accessed June 23, 2010).

77 Glenn Collins, "Running Away to the Circus: In Anxious Times Get Thrills and Catharsis," *New York Times*, March 19, 2003, www.nytimes.com (accessed June 23, 2010).

78 Collins, "Circus Flies o'er Troubles with Greatest of Ease."

② THE TRANSNATIONAL HISTORY OF THE EARLY AMERICAN CIRCUS

MATTHEW WITTMANN

Although the development of the circus in the United States during the late eighteenth and early nineteenth centuries was an uncommonly transnational affair, its history has largely been delimited by national boundaries. A better understanding of the evolution of the early American circus requires a broader framework, one that emphasizes how transnational circulations animated the incipient industry. The circus in the United States was initially dominated by European entertainers and impresarios. However, the pattern shifted in the 1820s and 1830s with the ascendance of native-born showmen and performers, and the circus developed in a distinctively American fashion, defined by its cultural syncretism and, most significantly, by the almost exclusively itinerant mode that was adopted. This, combined with the robust domestic market, paved the way for the success of the American circus abroad.

After a brief review of its international roots and dynamic growth in United States, this essay focuses on the contemporaneous emergence and export of a recognizably American form of the circus in the late 1820s. In the decades that followed, the transnational scope of American circus activity extended throughout the hemisphere, across the Atlantic, and eventually into the Pacific. Tracing this transnational trajectory offers new insights into the antebellum U.S. entertainment industry and the broader circulatory patterns it influenced. American showmen skillfully adapted the cosmopolitan cultural form of the circus for both domestic and foreign audiences. Their success was an early indicator of the extraordinary reach and appeal of U.S. popular culture.

Before the spring of 1793, when English equestrian John Bill Ricketts opened the first circus in Philadelphia, commercial entertainment in the United States was limited to a few venues in urban centers and a small number of touring shows of acrobats, musicians, and other performers, as well as

◀ *Detail of fig. 2.21.* "Scene at Melbourne, Australia, Feb. 14, 1877," ca. 1881. Poster, printed by the Strobridge Lithographing Company, Cincinnati. Collection of the John and Mable Ringling Museum of Art, Tibbals Collection, ht2004494

sundry scientific and animal exhibitions. By the mid-nineteenth century, many of these entertainments were integrated into circus repertories or museums, both variegated forms of popular culture.[1] While little is known about early itinerant entertainers in the United States, most of them came from abroad, principally from the British Isles.[2] In the same vein, nearly all of the initial circus managers and performers also came from overseas.

The English equestrian John Bill Ricketts formed his pioneering circus company from a motley crew of European performers, augmenting it with American apprentices and talent, most notably acrobat and dancer John Durang.[3] Four years after Ricketts's arrival in 1792, a rival Swedish equestrian, Philip Lailson, opened a circus in Boston with a company of fourteen performers whose surnames betray a mix of French, German, Irish, and Italian backgrounds.[4] Ricketts and Lailson toured the principal American cities over the next few years, but following their departure in 1800, and despite efforts by some of their performers and local entrepreneurs, there was a lull in circus activity.[5]

This lasted until the arrival of Victor Pepin and Jean Breschard in 1807. Pepin was born in Albany but moved to France with his father at a young age. He returned to the United States in partnership with Breschard and they advertised themselves as the "First Riding Masters of the Academies of Paris" when they debuted in Boston in late December.[6] Over the next decade, Pepin, Breschard, and the Italian equestrian Cayetano Mariotini were the principal circus impresarios in the United States, culling together performers from prior companies, some American-born talent, and occasional newcomers from abroad. In November 1816 James West, a celebrated equestrian with the Royal Circus in London, landed in New York with a large circus company that performed widely and profitably throughout the growing nation.[7]

The evident success of these foreign managers prompted native impresarios to try their luck in the circus business. The most notable of these were New York City's most prominent theatrical entrepreneurs, Stephen Price and Edmund Simpson, who jointly managed the tony Park Theatre.[8] When James West's circus opened on Broadway in February 1822 for an extended season, Price and Simpson set about conniving ways to dispatch the unwanted competition. After luring Sam Tatnall, who was the first distinguished American-born equestrian, away from West, they set him to breaking horses in a lot behind the Park Theatre and spread rumors about building their own arena. West agreed to sell his operation, which included a stud of horses and circus properties in several other cities, for a "handsome fortune."[9] As the Park Theatre opened its fall season in 1822, Price and Simpson sent their new circus company to Philadelphia, where it was joined by James Hunter, a recent arrival from Astley's Amphitheatre in London. Hunter was the first rider in the United States to perform on what advertisements described as "a horse in a rude state of nature"—bareback—and this novelty, coupled with his graceful style, made him a star.[10] He was also the first foreign circus performer specifically contracted for an American tour, and his success ensured that even as American showmen took over the business, they would continue to recruit international talent to enrich receipts.[11]

In 1824, the appearance of the first American-born circus proprietor, James W. Bancker, marked the beginning of a transformation in the circus business in the United States.[12] The number of circuses increased exponentially, from just two in 1822 to some seventeen companies six years later.[13] Moreover, by the late 1820s all of the early European impresarios had either retired or moved on, leaving the field to ascendant American showmen such as Aaron Turner, George F. Bailey, and Rufus Welch.[14] Although foreign performers continued to be featured in American circuses, there was a proliferation of native-born talent. But it was not simply the growing number of shows or personnel changes that heralded the arrival of the American circus.

The most significant development was J. Purdy Brown and Lewis Bailey's use of a canvas tent or "pavilion" during their 1826 season.[15] The tent altered almost every aspect of the circus industry in the United States, from the character of the performances to the circus's logistics and financing. The advantages were readily apparent, and the innovation was adopted so swiftly that a decade after its introduction, every American circus was performing under canvas, with the exception of a few remaining permanent venues in New York City and other urban centers.[16] Tents were more cost effective than the structures that circuses had typically relied upon and, most importantly, they offered an unprecedented degree of mobility. The shift to canvas was transformative for the American circus, as it vastly expanded its audience throughout the nation and beyond.

The rise of native-born showmen occurred amid a surge of cultural nationalism in the United States. The burgeoning show trade drew on vibrant vernacular forms, and the new types of commercial entertainment were intimately connected to issues of national identity.[17] James Fenimore Cooper, Edwin Forrest, and a cohort of other popular writers, performers, and artists were intent on demonstrating that the United States was not a cultural backwater. They were part of a broad effort to celebrate a uniquely American culture in the arts, incorporating patriotic themes and vernacular characters such as the Yankee, the backwoodsman, and the minstrel. The circus was a particularly democratic form of entertainment, and its promoters shaped the content to ensure it had mass appeal in the "era of the common man."[18]

Overlapping demographic, geographic, and economic developments also provided expanding audiences for the new American circuses. In just two generations the population of the United States more than tripled. It exploded from five million at the turn of the century to over seventeen million in 1840, pushing westward through the Ohio River Valley and beyond the Mississippi. These new markets in cities, towns, and provincial backwaters welcomed the kind of traveling entertainment that the new mobile circus business offered. The decades bracketed by the Panic of 1819 and the Panic of 1837 were also economically prosperous, encouraging a wave of entrepreneurs to try to make their fortune with a touring show.

American showmen dominated the related business of traveling menageries. The profits realized from the first elephants drove the expansion of animal exhibitions, and by the 1820s, a dozen or so menageries—ever larger and more exotic—toured the country. Their mobility assured almost limitless audiences, and a great variety of animals was supplied by a transnational network of European dealers and Yankee traders. At the center of the menagerie business was a loose confederation of showmen from New York's Westchester and Putnam Counties who were inspired by the profits that an enterprising local farmer named Hachaliah Bailey garnered from touring the elephant Betty (also called Old Bet). The circus and the menagerie were initially distinct forms of entertainment that were more often seen separately but in the 1830s this group played a defining role in the evolution of the American circus by combining the two.[19]

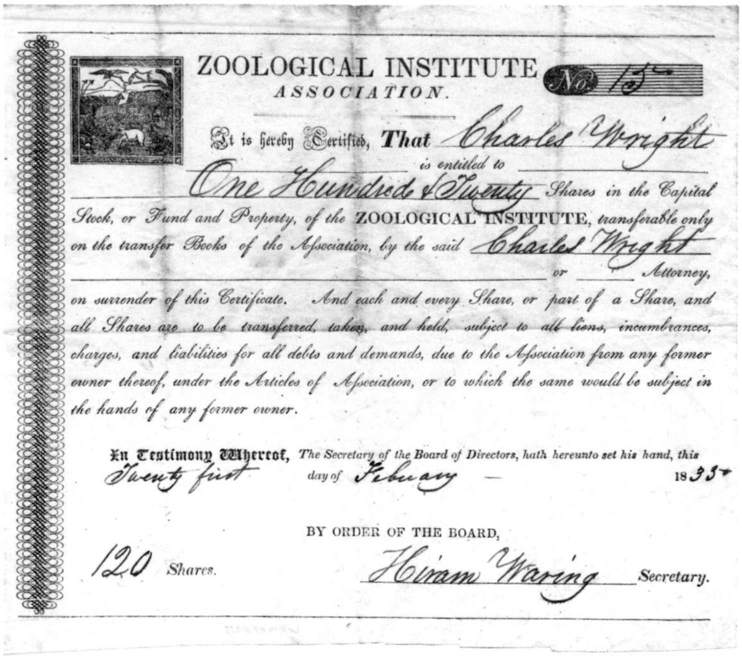

ZOOLOGICAL INSTITUTE
ASSOCIATION.
No. 15

It is hereby Certified, That Charles Wright is entitled to One Hundred & Twenty Shares in the Capital Stock, or Fund and Property, of the ZOOLOGICAL INSTITUTE, transferable only on the transfer Books of the Association, by the said Charles Wright or Attorney, on surrender of this Certificate. And each and every Share, or part of a Share, and all Shares are to be transferred, taken, and held, subject to all liens, incumbrances, charges, and liabilities for all debts and demands, due to the Association from any former owner thereof, under the Articles of Association, or to which the same would be subject in the hands of any former owner.

In Testimony Whereof, The Secretary of the Board of Directors, hath hereunto set his hand, this Twenty first day of Febuary 1835.

BY ORDER OF THE BOARD,

120 Shares. Hiram Waring Secretary.

The spectacular growth and merger of the circus and menagerie business played a formative role in the rise of U.S. culture industries and was a dimension of an ongoing and intersecting set of social, economic, and technological developments that historians have characterized as the "market revolution."[20] Perhaps the best example of this dynamic was the Zoological Institute, a capital stock company created in January 1835 by a group of showmen and investors in Somers, New York. The conglomeration combined the resources of some dozen menageries and three circuses, whose appraised value in conjunction with cash raised from issuing stock gave the corporation $329,325 in total capital (*fig. 2.1*). A board of directors was put in charge of apportioning resources and proscribing routes for its constituent units, which included circus and menagerie combinations, and the Zoological Institute managed thirteen of the twenty shows that toured the United States during the 1835 season. As a purveyor of popular entertainment, it was unprecedented in its size and organization. Despite its initial success, the association foundered amid the Panic of 1837, but it stands as a good example of the ways American showmen capitalized on a robust market.[21]

Most important for this essay was how the growth and consolidation of the circus business enabled shows to become much more active in markets abroad. While the early history of the circus in the United States was largely about European management and absorbing foreign influences, there was a definite shift in initiative around 1830. As the industry burgeoned and the American circus evolved into its own distinctive form, its proprietors and performers became increasingly assertive both at home and abroad. Touring overseas demanded mobility and capital. The manner in which the circus developed in the United States ensured that American showmen had both. Initially, the expanding field of American circus activity was oriented toward the Atlantic world, extending from the Canadian provinces to the Caribbean and to Central and South America. By the mid-1830s American performers were starring in European circuses, but the established competition for the most part discouraged full American companies from venturing across the Atlantic. But the American circus flourished in markets that lacked comparable forms of popular entertainment. This was made abundantly clear in the wake of the California Gold Rush, when American showmen quickly moved in to capitalize on the emerging cultural markets of the Pacific world. By the mid-nineteenth century, when the American circus reached maturity, it was a global enterprise.

The career of Benjamin Brown in many ways epitomized the history of the early American circus. Brown was born in 1799 and, like so many of his fellow showmen, hailed from Westchester County. After working a variety of odd jobs, he entered the show trade in 1823 with his brother Christopher, managing a menagerie owned by Hachaliah Bailey, whose major attractions were an elephant known as Little Bet and a lion. Following a dispute over

▲ *Fig. 2.1.* Charles Wright's stock certificate for 120 shares of the Zoological Institute Association, 1835. Somers Historical Society

money at the end of the 1825 season, Brown left the concern to serve as an equestrian manager for a circus owned by his uncle, J. Purdy Brown, during its watershed 1826 season under canvas. By the following year he was managing a small circus in partnership with Christopher and another brother, Herschel, on a circuit through Virginia and the Carolinas. During the 1828 season, the Brown brothers' circus traveled in tandem with a menagerie owned by Charles Wright, debuting the kind of combination that became standard among American circuses over the next decade.[22] They continued to tour the southern states for the next two years, but the itinerant entertainment business was booming and competition was proving increasingly stiff.[23]

In the winter of 1830 the Brown brothers tried their luck abroad with a tour through the Caribbean. They were neither the first circus nor even the first American showmen to tour there. It is important to note how the initial American circuses touring abroad did so through already established transnational entertainment circuits. Star European performers and theatrical companies who toured the United States often also visited the principal Canadian and Caribbean cities and ports. Ricketts, Lailson, Pepin, and other European managers took their circus companies to Canada, the West Indies, Mexico, and Cuba during or after their time in the United States. In late 1826 Samuel McCracken took the Albany Circus Company to Jamaica for a season, inaugurating a pattern whereby American circuses traveled south to escape the slow winter months in the United States.[24] American showmen also began to explore new routes and what were ostensibly more marginal markets. In 1829–30 a circus managed by Eman Handy and Rufus Welch toured through Cuba, St. Thomas, Cartagena (Colombia), and other locales.[25]

The dispersed nature of this American circus activity and scanty newspaper coverage makes these early efforts difficult to trace, but it is clear from U.S. sources that the pace and scope of overseas touring was expanding rapidly. It was in this context that the small circus managed by Benjamin Brown and his brothers departed Charleston in 1830 for their initial venture overseas. Although their precise route remains unclear, they stayed abroad for fifteen months, a duration that suggests that the tour was a successful one.[26] Their first stop was Saint-Pierre, Martinique, where a handbill for the Cirque Olympique, as they called it, offered a glimpse at the makeup of the company (*fig. 2.2*). Although all three Brown brothers traveled with the show, Benjamin was the

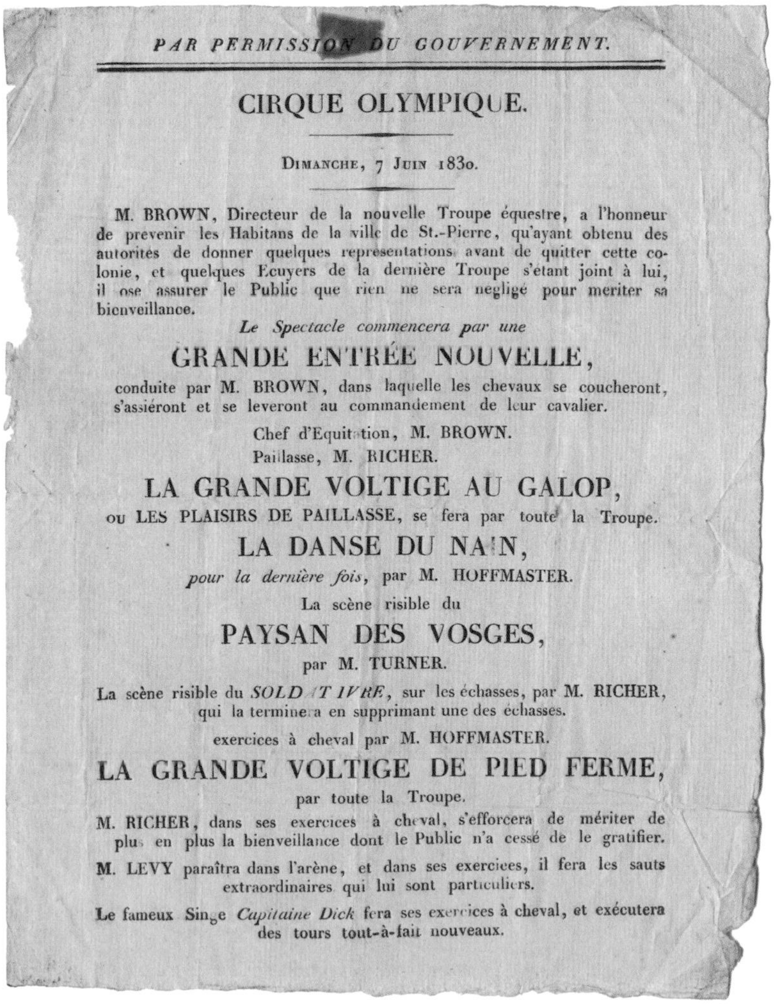

PAR PERMISSION DU GOUVERNEMENT.

CIRQUE OLYMPIQUE.

DIMANCHE, 7 JUIN 1830.

M. BROWN, Directeur de la nouvelle Troupe équestre, a l'honneur de prevenir les Habitans de la ville de St.-Pierre, qu'ayant obtenu des autorites de donner quelques representations avant de quitter cette colonie, et quelques Ecuyers de la dernière Troupe s'étant joint à lui, il ose assurer le Public que rien ne sera negligé pour meriter sa bienveillance.

Le Spectacle commencera par une

GRANDE ENTRÉE NOUVELLE,

conduite par M. BROWN, dans laquelle les chevaux se coucheront, s'assiéront et se leveront au commandement de leur cavalier.

Chef d'Equitation, M. BROWN.

Paillasse, M. RICHER.

LA GRANDE VOLTIGE AU GALOP,

ou LES PLAISIRS DE PAILLASSE, se fera par toute la Troupe.

LA DANSE DU NAIN,

pour la dernière fois, par M. HOFFMASTER.

La scène risible du

PAYSAN DES VOSGES,

par M. TURNER.

La scène risible du *SOLDAT IVRE*, sur les échasses, par M. RICHER, qui la terminera en supprimant une des échasses.

exercices à cheval par M. HOFFMASTER.

LA GRANDE VOLTIGE DE PIED FERME,

par toute la Troupe.

M. RICHER, dans ses exercices à cheval, s'efforcera de mériter de plus en plus la bienveillance dont le Public n'a cessé de le gratifier.

M. LEVY paraîtra dans l'arène, et dans ses exercices, il fera les sauts extraordinaires qui lui sont particuliers.

Le fameux Singe *Capitaine Dick* fera ses exercices à cheval, et exécutera des tours tout-à-fait nouveaux.

Fig. 2.2. "Cirque Olympique." Handbill for June 7, 1830, performance in St.-Pierre, Martinique. William L. Clements Library, University of Michigan, Benjamin F. Brown Collection only one to appear in the performance, serving as the ringmaster and appearing in a limited role as an equestrian. The principal rider was Napoleon Turner; three younger riders or apprentices—Andrew Levi or Levy, Frederick Hoffmaster, and a Master George—supported him.[27] Jean Richer served as the clown and they traveled with six horses. The accompanying menagerie featured a lion, a "Brazilian tiger" (a jaguar) and a dozen monkeys, one of which, billed as Kapitein Dick, appeared in the ring as a riding act (*fig. 2.3*). A bill of lading from Berbice, Guyana, lists a "pavilion spar," which indicated that they performed under canvas, although this might not have been necessary everywhere they traveled.[28]

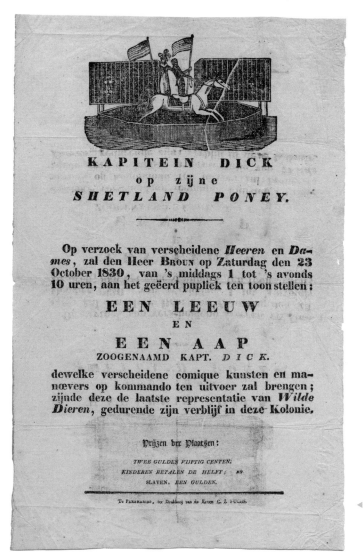

KAPITEIN DICK
op zijne
SHETLAND PONEY.

Op verzoek van verscheidene *Heeren* en *Dames*, zal den Heer Broun op Zaturdag den **23 October 1830**, van 's middags 1 tot 's avonds 10 uren, aan het geëerd publiek ten toon stellen:

EEN LEEUW
EN
EEN AAP
ZOOGENAAMD KAPT. *DICK*.

dewelke verscheidene comique kunsten en manœvers op kommando ten uitvoer zal brengen; zijnde deze de laatste representatie van *Wilde Dieren*, gedurende zijn verblijf in deze Kolonie.

Prijzen der Plaatsen:

TWEE GULDEN FIJFTIG CENTEN;
KINDEREN BETALEN DE HELFT; en
SLAVEN, EEN GULDEN.

Te Paramaribo, ter Drukkerij van de Erven C. J. Fuchs.

A final piece of property carried by the company was a hot-air balloon, a novelty used to generate publicity for the show.[29]

Though the company was rather small, published programs from the Caribbean tour indicate that the entertainment offered was in line with other circuses of that era. A poster billing the show as the Royal Pavilion Circus in Barbados detailed a typical performance, which began with a "Grand New Entry" of costumed horses and riders that went through a variety of coordinated routines (*fig. 2.4*). This was followed by an equestrian act by the apprentice Master Hoffmaster, and then the whole company returned to the ring for a display of "running vaulting." This consisted of equestrians leaping from the ground onto moving horses, while the clown Monsieur Richer mocked the performers, battled with the ringmaster, and generally kept the audience entertained. Next up was the principal rider Turner, who presented "The Dashing Horseman," during which he changed costume and struck poses as his horse galloped around the ring. After a turn by the trained horse Kitty Clover, there was a "scene riding" display by Richer called "The Dying Moor," which was a pantomime of a battle scene.[30]

The entire company again returned to the ring for a presentation of acrobatics billed as "Ground and Lofty Tumbling," followed by a second principal riding act by Master Levi. As the horse galloped at full speed around the ring, he stood on the animal's back and leapt through balloons, which were simply paper-covered hoops that made for a more dramatic display. Years later Benjamin Brown recalled the act:

> The biggest card in my show was a boy named Levi, a Jew. He was a wonderful rider. We had a piece of canvas twelve feet wide, then a hoop eighteen inches in diameter covered with paper, a

Fig. 2.3. "Kapitein Dick." Poster for performance in Paramaribo, Suriname, October 23, 1830; printed by C. J. Fuchs, Paramaribo. William L. Clements Library, University of Michigan, Benjamin F. Brown Collection

balloon it was called, and Levi held in his hand a hoop nine and a half inches in diameter. He'd jump over that banner, through the balloon and through the little hoop, all at the same time. That was called a big feat in those days.[31]

For the finale, the company presented a traditional comic piece called "The Hunted Tailor, or, Billy Button's Unfortunate Journey to Bredford," in which a hurried man struggles to ride a recalcitrant mount.[32] While there is little evidence about how the circus was received, it was certainly a respectable show as it was patronized by colonial officials such as Sir Benjamin d'Urban in Demarary and Sir James Frederick in Bridgetown. Moreover, the duration of the tour and their approximately month-long stays in each location suggest that audiences were satisfied and that it was a profitable venture for the Brown brothers.

Letters and ephemera indicate that at the very least they visited the islands of Martinique, Jamaica, and Barbados and continental ports in Honduras, Suriname, and Guyana before returning to the United States in March 1831. Although they were not the first circus to tour the Caribbean, their travels were much more extensive than prior efforts and the tent seems to have afforded a great deal of flexibility in terms of potential venues. The tour also demonstrated how American circuses were able to move through linguistic and cultural barriers that hampered other forms of entertainment. The Brown brothers took their Pavilion Circus through Pennsylvania and Virginia during the 1831 touring season in the United States and then returned to the West Indies in the winter of 1832.

The winter sojourn south became a frequent pattern for American circuses and standout individual performers as the relative proximity of

Caribbean markets offered opportunities to generate income when the weather or business in the United States was poor.[33] But the islands were also targeted more intensively as the decade progressed. Cuba proved to be a particularly attractive locale. For a tour there in 1837, Joseph D. Palmer organized a large troupe of twenty performers and staff, which included a translator, an advertising agent, six equestrians led by George J. Cadwalader, and the famous tattooed man, James P. O'Connell.[34] The company opened in Havana on June 1, 1837, and toured Cuba for the better part of a year, including a run through the inland towns under canvas.

Fig. 2.4. Royal Pavilion Circus. Poster for performance in Bridgetown, Barbados, July 22, 1830, printed by the Mercury Office, Bridgetown. William L. Clements Library, University of Michigan, Benjamin F. Brown Collection

Although it was seemingly a financial success, dissension between Palmer and the performers led to Cadwalader being defrauded out of almost a year's salary. The company was twice stricken with yellow fever, underscoring some of the risks that performers could face touring abroad.[35] Even so, American circuses continued to extend their field of activity within the hemisphere. The American equestrian Charles Laforest, for one, established a successful circus in Buenos Aires during 1834–35, and other companies were frequenting major South American ports by the late 1830s[36]

Following his time in the Caribbean, Benjamin Brown returned to the United States and worked in the circus and menagerie business as a ringmaster, horse trainer, and manager. Brown embarked on the most adventurous passage of his transnational career in 1838 as an agent for the large menagerie conglomeration of June, Titus & Avengine. He was dis-patched to Africa in an effort to secure some novel attractions for the show, including giraffes, or "camel leopards," as they were then known. Rival showman Rufus Welch and his partners imported two of the unusual-looking animals in June 1838, and they proved an extremely popular feature.[37] After securing letters of safe conduct with the help of the American consul George Gliddon in Cairo, Brown organized a party of over a hundred men for an expedition up the Nile and into the Nubian Desert in early 1839. He spent a year in the hinterlands gathering animals, including four juvenile giraffes, and judging by a sketch made in Cairo, was well adapted to local ways (*fig. 2.5*).

Brown transported his haul to London, where the animals were variously shipped to the United States or sold off to British buyers. Isaac Van Amburgh, the American animal trainer who was also in the employ of June, Titus & Avengine, was then

Fig. 2.5. Benjamin F. Brown in Egypt, 1839. Pencil on paper. William L. Clements Library, University of Michigan, Benjamin F. Brown Collection

starring in Britain, and Brown stayed on to manage him. Over the next few years he looked after the conglomeration's interests there and managed a variety of American performers and companies on British tours.[38] His career aptly illustrated the extent to which the circus business, strung together by a transnational network of agents, performers, and touring shows, had become a global enterprise and the increasingly prominent role that Americans were playing within it.

Benjamin Brown's story also offers a useful pivot on which to turn to the transatlantic dimensions of the expansive American circus industry in the 1830s and 1840s. Given their relative geographic proximity and a general lack of competition, the transnational markets in the colonies and countries south of the United States were frequently exploited by American showmen. Cracking into established European markets was a much trickier proposition. Nevertheless, a broad array of American entertainers, ranging from groups such as the Hutchinson Family Singers and the Virginia Minstrels to singular performers such as T. D. Rice and General Tom Thumb found success touring Great Britain during this era.[39] While there were a few isolated examples of individual American performers in British and continental circuses before the 1830s, the first American circus performers to become stars across the Atlantic were Levi North and Isaac Van Amburgh.[40] North, born on Long Island in 1816, served his apprenticeship with Quick and Mead's Circus, then toured Cuba in 1829 with the aforementioned Welch & Handy show and rose to prominence as a principal rider for J. Purdy Brown's circus during the early 1830s. Regarded as the father of American equestrianism and known as the North Star, he was an excellent overall athlete and the first performer to throw a somersault on moving horseback, a feat he initially accomplished in England with Batty's Circus in 1839.[41]

North had left the United States with the clown Joe Blackburn, who was celebrated as "the American Grimaldi," when the circus business crashed amid the Panic of 1837. Despite the rapid development of the industry in the United States, Astley's Amphitheatre in London remained the center of the transatlantic circus world and North was intent on proving his skill on its famous boards. After much haggling with manager Andrew Ducrow over terms, Blackburn and North debuted at Astley's on June 30, 1838.

As North needed time to adjust to a new horse, his initial appearances were confined to vaulting, which generically included two distinct acts. In the first, performers ran down a specially constructed wooden ramp that ended with a crude trampoline or springboard from which they leaped into the air over animals or other obstacles, impressing the audience with the height and distance of their jumps.[42] The other act utilized a short springboard rather like a diving board that the performer would bounce up and down upon while performing acrobatic feats. North was adept at somersaulting on this short springboard, and his performance simply consisted of doing as many consecutive backward somersaults as possible. In a letter to his family soon after their debut, Blackburn described the scene:

> We made our appearance at Astley's Amphitheatre two weeks since in the vaulting—North, as the American champion, vaulting against Mr. Price, the champion of all Europe, having two spring boards in the ring at once, and two parties, American and English, with the colors of each country on the heads of their horses; myself playing clown to the American party. You may

well imagine my feelings the first night, as well as North. I must say I was frightened dreadfully; not for myself, but for North. I thought he would be so excited that he might get beat; but the trial came, and such a brilliant audience I never had the honor of making a bow to before.... When the finish of the vaulting came, the Champion of England (Price) went on to do his row of somersets, and only threw twenty. Then came the applause; they were certain North could not beat it; but the little Yankee went on and beat him scandalously, doing thirty-three. Such a shout I never heard; I thought the house would come down. If I ever felt well, it was just about that time.... So you see Uncle Sam is ably represented, for we have truly astonished the natives. North rides next week, and they will be more astonished then, for they have no rider to compete with him in this country; and I think I can beat any of them playing clown.[43]

The letter captures the intense cultural nationalism that inflected the era's popular entertainment, and, though undoubtedly somewhat biased, North, Blackburn, and the wave of other American circus performers that followed were clearly having an impact in Britain. The vaulting competition between North and Price was essentially a matter of endurance, as each man in turn would perform a continuous string of "somersets" until they either missed a landing or became exhausted. Their rivalry drew huge crowds over the month that followed and North won every evening except, ironically, on July 4th.[44]

A financial dispute with Ducrow eventually led Blackburn and North to join another circus managed by William Batty, but North's popularity was unabated as his riding created a sensation. In early April 1839, North became the first performer to throw a somersault on a moving horse when the circus was at Henley, and even a reluctant British press was forced to acknowledge that he was "without exception the most graceful and accomplished rider of the day. There are none that we have seen who can approach him."[45] Over the next few years, North would shuttle back and forth across the Atlantic, appearing with a variety of prominent shows on both sides of the ocean. In the summer of 1845 he starred in Paris at the famed Cirque-Olympique established by the Franconi family and performed by royal command before King Louis-Philippe (*fig. 2.6*).[46]

The same week in 1838 that Levi North was making his debut at Astley's, a menagerie under the management of Lewis B. Titus departed New York in what was perhaps the boldest effort yet to break into the British market. The star of what was billed as the "Mammoth American Menagerie" was Isaac Van Amburgh, the young animal trainer who was gaining renown for his daring exploits with wild

Fig. 2.6. Alexandre Lacauchie. "Levi J. North as he appeared before Louis-Philippe, King of the French, and the Royal Family," 1845. Lithograph, printed by J. Rigo et Cie, Paris. © Shelburne Museum, Shelburne, Vermont, 1959-67.49

Fig. 2.7. Sir Edwin Henry Landseer. *Isaac van Amburgh and His Animals*, 1839. Oil on canvas. The Royal Collection © 2011, Her Majesty Queen Elizabeth II, RCIN 406346

beasts.[47] Like North, Van Amburgh made his debut at Astley's Amphitheatre, where two massive wooden cages containing a mix of lions, tigers, and leopards were placed in the arena. He entered the first cage and after some playful fondling with the big cats, proceeded with his act. He pried open the mouth of one lion with his hands and rode about on the animal's back. The leopards were more exuberant, and one perched on his head and shoulders while the others leapt over his extended arm. Van Amburgh, who wore a plain white tunic and held only a small whip, gave the appearance of complete mastery over the animals as he went through a series of routines. One of the highlights was when he maneuvered the lion into a prone position and placed his head in the animal's mouth. For the finale, he made real the biblical phrase that "the lion shall lie down with the lamb," and casually reposed among the seemingly dangerous cats with a young lamb.[48]

Although Van Amburgh was not the first wild animal trainer to perform these sorts of feats, he did so with a fearlessness and command that inspired widespread admiration. He proved so popular that he starred in a series of dramatic vehicles at the Theatre Royal in Drury Lane, where Queen Victoria came to see him on a number of occasions. She was fascinated by his mastery of the animals, writing in her journal, "It's quite beautiful to see, and makes me wish I could do the same!"[49] When the noted painter Sir Edwin Landseer began a large canvas depicting Van Amburgh lying with the lamb, Queen Victoria visited his studio and arranged to purchase the work (*fig. 2.7*). Though critics Charles Dickens and William Macready sneered, his thrilling performances and the seal of royal approval ensured that he was a sensation in London.[50] In the summer of 1839, Van Amburgh crossed the channel and his dramatic displays likewise captivated Parisian audiences.[51] Despite his evident success, Benjamin Brown lamented that he was "too big of a fool" to take full advantage of the opportunities he was presented with in Europe.[52]

Levi North and Isaac Van Amburgh heralded the arrival of a veritable wave of American talent in the decade that followed. But perhaps the greatest impact was made by the first complete American circus company to cross the Atlantic, which arrived under the management of Richard Sands in 1842. Sands was a versatile performer and appeared in a wide variety of equestrian acts during the tour, in-

cluding an impressive Roman riding act on four horses (*fig.2.8*). He was also a very capable manager and his "Great American Circus Company" introduced a number of novel features to British audiences. The most notable was simply its setup, namely a canvas tent. When the show opened in Liverpool in early March 1842, a local newspaper marveled at the "splendid and novel Pavilion, made after an entirely new style, with the most costly interior decorations and appointments forming at once a magnificent spacious Roman Amphitheatre and Arena of the Arts, the whole of which is erected in a few hours; and capable of holding several thousand persons."[53] The Sands company also advertised the show with a daily parade that featured two dozen caparisoned horses and a colorful wagon with a full brass band drawn by a team of eight cream-colored horses (*fig. 2.9*). The show itself featured a typical mix of circus acts and Levi North, by then a star on both sides of the Atlantic, was the principal rider during its first season in Britain (*fig. 2.10*).

While the performances ostensibly differed little from a traditional circus, the musical entr'actes by blackface minstrels were a novelty that garnered

Fig. 2.8. T. C. Wilson. "Mr. R. Sands, in His Principal Acts as He Appeared at the Royal English Opera House," London, 1843. Lithograph, printed by G. Webb & Co. Lith., London. Circus World Museum, CWi-2299A

Fig. 2.9. R. Sand's American Circus Band Carriage in London, ca. 1842. Color lithograph. Collection of the John and Mable Ringling Museum of Art, Tibbals Collection, ht2004429

widespread notice. At different times, two of the most important early American minstrels, Joel Walker Sweeney and Daniel Emmett, performed with the company and their effect was electric (*fig. 2.11*). Joseph Cave, an Englishman who became one of the country's leading minstrels, recalled years later that Sweeney's playing was such that "I shall never forget how my ears tingled and my mouth watered when I heard the tum, tum, tum of that blessed banjo."[54] Though blackface minstrelsy had first been introduced by T. D. Rice a decade earlier, the popularity of minstrel shows surged in the 1840s and ultimately made a lasting impact on British popular music.[55]

After a successful inaugural season, Sands joined forces with Van Amburgh and presented a combined show in 1843 that also involved Benjamin Brown. Reinforcements from the United States were brought in for the following season, and the show's success abroad was a point that Sands exaggeratedly capitalized on for publicity when the circus returned to the United States (*fig. 2.12*).[56] Sands & Co.'s American Circus appeared in a mix of permanent venues and tents during its extended time abroad and two of the leading contemporary British circuses, Batty's and Cooke's, were soon experimenting with tents. A London correspondent for the *Spirit of the Times* reported that William Batty learned about managing a show under canvas from Benjamin Brown. The correspondent opined "there is no man living who understands every branch of business connected with an extensive Circus establishment so well as Mr. Brown," but in the end the American-style tent show was simply not well suited for British conditions.[57]

Transnational relationships were necessarily reciprocal, and one of the most significant developments that emerged out of Van Amburgh and

Sands's time abroad was the ornate circus parade wagons they introduced when the returned to New York. In England they had witnessed spectacular parades by Edwin Hughes's circus that featured

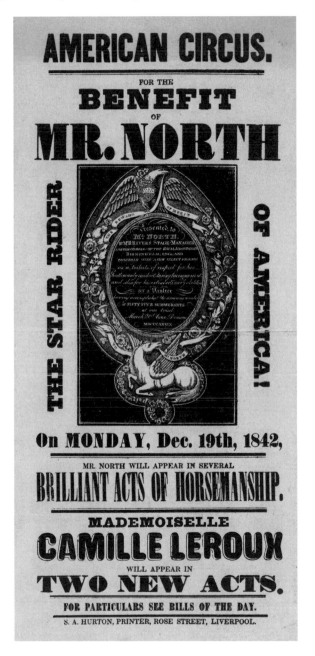

Fig. 2.10. "American Circus. For the Benefit of Mr. North," December 19, 1842. Broadside, printed by S. A. Hurton, Liverpool. Collection of the John and Mable Ringling Museum of Art, SN1549.223.51

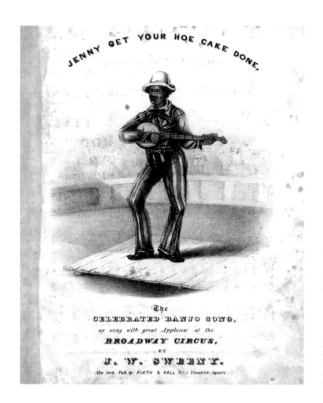

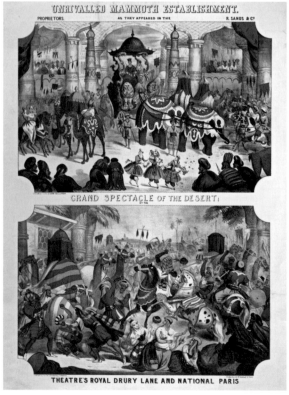

elaborately carved and gilded wagons, most notably his "Burmese Imperial Carriage," which was brightly decorated with large wooden animals and pulled by two elephants. In April 1846 Sands and Van Amburgh jointly opened their season in New York City with a procession of 150 horses and 50 carriages, highlighted by a dazzling new "Triumphal Car" that was more or less a copy of Hughes's design.[58] Other shows were quick to follow suit and the use of decorative parade wagons became a characteristic feature of the American circus.[59]

While Richards Sands was the first American showman to cross the Atlantic with a complete circus, his success abroad ensured that others soon followed. In 1843 Rufus Welch chartered a ship and took a company on an extended tour of the Mediterranean ports, playing at Cadiz, Gibraltar, Malacca, Algiers, the Balearic Islands, and Genoa.[60] Still, outside of France, American circuses largely eschewed the Continent, though standout individual performers were often featured in European circuses. Britain remained the most important destination for American showmen and British historian George Speaight described Sands as the vanguard of an "American Invasion."[61] The strength of the domestic market in the United States meant that the foremost American circuses were much larger and better capitalized than many of their European counterparts. When Howes & Cushing's Great United States Circus arrived in Liverpool in 1857, the British press marveled at the size of the "stupendous moveable circus," and its tents and transport "excited upmost astonishment" among the public.[62] Among the most noted features were a troupe of Native American performers and the Apollonicon, a musical chariot that housed an organ and was drawn by forty cream-colored horses (*fig. 2.13*). The show was so big that it was split into separate units

Fig. 2.11. "'Jenny Get Your Hoe Cake Done,' The Celebrated Banjo Song as Sung with Great Applause at the Broadway Circus By J. W. Sweeney with the Broadway Circus in New York." Sheet music (New York: Firth & Hall, 1840). Lester S. Levy Collection of Sheet Music, box 020, item 020.003; Department of Rare Books and Manuscripts, Sheridan Libraries, Johns Hopkins University

Fig. 2.12. "Unrivalled Mammoth Establishment as They Appeared in the Grand Spectacle of the Desert at the Theatre Royal Drury Lane and National Paris," ca. 1845. Poster, G. Webb & Co. Lith., London, reprinted by G. & W. Endicott, New York. Collection of the John and Mable Ringling Museum of Art, Tibbals Collection, ht2004431

and the managers refreshed their talent during their seven-year sojourn through a combination of local performers and new personnel brought over from the United States.[63] What Howes & Cushing's circus made clear was that the terms of the transnational relationship that animated the American circus were shifting. American showmen were among the most influential players in a circus business that was now a global enterprise, a point perhaps best substantiated by looking at how they exploited the opportunities that opened up around the Pacific in the wake of the California Gold Rush.

The pioneer of the American circus in the Pacific was Joseph Andrew Rowe (*fig. 2.14*). He was born in North Carolina in 1819 and, after being orphaned at a young age, joined Asa T. Smith's circus as an apprentice, becoming a proficient equestrian. By the time he was eighteen and in line with the southward expansion of American circus activity, he was touring the Caribbean in partnership with Mariano Perez, an acrobat and tightrope dancer. Rowe afterward put together a "small but good performing company" in New Orleans and in 1846 em-

barked on a tour through Cuba and Central America. Driven by "a continual thirst to see this portion of America" and the fact that the untapped markets of South America invariably received the show "with delight and astonishment," Rowe traveled overland through Colombia, Ecuador, and Peru.[64] By May 1849 the company was performing in Lima as news about the gold findings filtered down the Pacific Coast. They packed up and headed north immediately, however the crush of gold-seekers was such that it took the troupe almost five months to secure passage on a ship to California. On October 12, 1849, the company finally arrived in San Francisco on board the bark *Tasso*, and just over two weeks later Rowe's Olympic Circus made its debut in a hastily constructed amphitheater.

The demographic and economic boom that accompanied the California Gold Rush created lucrative markets for U.S. entertainers in California and facilitated access to the emerging cultural markets of the larger Pacific world. The enterprising Rowe was among the earliest entertainers to arrive in San Francisco, but also possessed the where-

Fig. 2.13. Ebenezer Landells. "The Apollonicon, or Great Musical Chariot. From the United States." From *Illustrated London News*, September 12, 1857. Picture Collection, The New York Public Library, Astor, Lenox and Tilden Foundations

withal to recognize opportunities opening up farther afield.[65] Rowe was the manager and principal rider of the small company and his wife, Eliza, was an equestrienne in the show. W. H. Foley performed as both a clown and rider while a Master Rafael served as Rowe's apprentice. Signor and Signora Levero, rope-dancers and acrobats, supplemented the equestrian acts.

Although a rather small company by contemporary standards, on November 1, 1849 they debuted to "frequent and uproarious bursts of applause" from the amusement-starved public of San Francisco, who proved willing to pay three dollars for a ticket

to see the show. The *Alta California* described it as a "comfortably fitted up" amphitheater that accommodated fifteen hundred people. The show featured a typical mix of equestrianism, clowning, and acrobatics. The reviewer was particularly excited about the female performers, praising the "pleasing merit" of Mrs. Rowe's riding and "the fearlessness and grace" of Signora Levero on the slack rope.[66] Despite the company's initial success, Foley abruptly left the circus after a month in a dispute over salary and soon after opened a rival amphitheater.[67] Over the next several months, "Rowe's and Foley's circuses would divide the patronage of the community; each of the producers would make his spurt, would be obliged, before long, to close down, and would then manage to work up a reopening."[68] Apparently conceding defeat, in December 1850 Rowe packed up his circus and embarked for Honolulu.

Honolulu was a bustling port that was a center of transpacific commerce and home to a relatively large native and *haole* (foreign) population of merchants, missionaries, and sailors. Rowe arrived there in late December and opened his circus in a specially constructed pavilion on January 10, 1851. His was the first circus to grace the islands. An illustrated broadside produced for the occasion shows that it began with a "Grand Waltz and Star Entree," which culminated in a dance number starring the horse Adonis. The apprentice Master Rafael followed with leaping and vaulting and the first part of the performance was brought to a close by Rowe in a scenic riding act billed as "Montezuma and His Wild Charger." A similar display opened the second part of the show as Walter Howard appeared in a riding act called "Red Man of the Woods" and then Henry Ellsler, a "French Herculean and Gymnastic Professor," performed assorted "feats of strength." In the principal riding act, Rowe represented three different characters: "first,

Fig. 2.14. Lewis J. Stinson. Joseph Andrew Rowe, ca. 1873. Carte-de-visite. Museum of Performance & Design, San Francisco, 110609.001

a Pantaloon; second, an athletic combatant Gladiator; third, the Flight of Mercury." The show concluded with the traditional comic afterpiece "Billy Button's Unfortunate Journey to Branford." Although no individual act was specified, Dave Long served as the clown throughout the proceedings and Howard doubled as the ringmaster.[69]

Honolulu's main newspaper, the *Polynesian*, did not publish a review of the show; this reflected concerns by community members and the Protestant missionaries in particular, about the morality of this kind of popular entertainment.[70] Yet it was plainly a great success as a broadside for the performance four days later noted that Rowe was erecting private boxes for families. A copy of this broadside has some contemporary notations in pencil by Emma Rooke that indicate the royal family was in attendance as one reads: "I walked with the King into His box, Mother & John followed and then the boys Lot, Alex, & Bil[l], the band struck up 'God Save the King.'" (*fig. 2.15*).[71] That Rowe was able to secure royal patronage was significant as it essentially legitimized the new circus as a respectable form of entertainment. The broadside did warn that "an efficient police will be in attendance to preserve order," which suggests there might have been some rowdiness at the debut performance, but this was hardly surprising given that sailors were likely a large part of the audience. Although Rowe was successful in establishing the circus as a popular form of entertainment in the islands, reservations remained. When his erstwhile protégé W. H. Foley arrived in Honolulu with a company the following year, his application to open a circus was denied by the Privy Council due to petitions from concerned residents.[72]

These continuing struggles over popular entertainment in the Hawaiian Kingdom seemed to

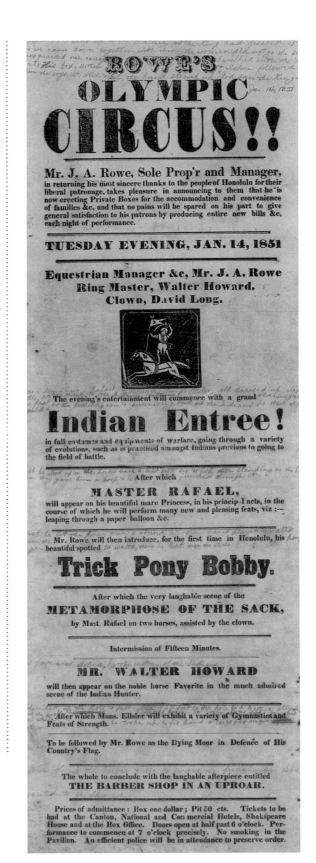

Fig. 2.15. Rowe's Olympic Circus. Broadside for January 14, 1851, performance in Honolulu. Hawai'i State Archives

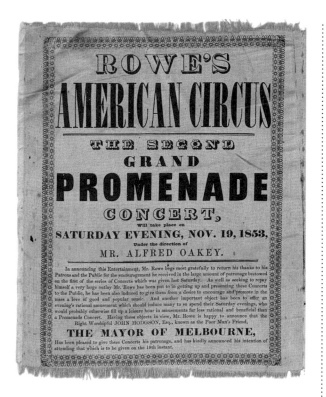

have little impact on Rowe's show, which was buoyed by royal support and extremely popular with *kanaka* or ordinary Hawaiians. In mid-March a correspondent for the *Alta California* reported that the circus was "quite the rage here," as it "happened to hit the fancy of the Kanakas, who are all hard riders." The letter moreover suggested that Rowe was clearing the exorbitant sum of "$1200 to $1400 a night," and these impressive earnings kept Rowe in the islands for eleven months.[73]

The collection of broadsides advertising Rowe's Olympic Circus in the Hawai'i State Archives, several of which include annotations by Emma Rooke, offer insights about the versatility and character of the performances. Rooke was particularly taken with the "Indian Entrée" by Rafael and the Rowes, which featured the elegantly costumed performers "riding around as fast as they possibly

can" and "screaming out as Indians do." In February, Mrs. Rowe debuted her solo riding act and the trick ponies Bobby and Billy were introduced. Walter Howard performed a spectacular-sounding "Grand Trampolening" act in early March that involved "somerseting over 8 horses, and through a *Fire Balloon*." Comments scribbled on a broadside for a March 21 performance also underscored the dangers performers faced. Master Rafael fell off his horse three times in the course of his principal riding act and Walter Howard fell hard doing his Spanish Reaper routine when the horse "went too fast." He attempted it a second time, fell off again, and was unable to continue.[74]

In May and June, the company visited the islands of Maui and Hawaii and reinforcements were brought in from California for the fall season as news of the Victorian gold rush in Australia started to float across the Pacific.[75] Rowe, seemingly ever well attuned to new opportunities, quickly made plans to make the long journey to Melbourne. He purchased a 200-ton brig, the *General Worth*, and advertised a grand farewell benefit for the evening of December 6. A broadside celebrating the occasion contained an interesting mix of Hawaiian and English text and was an apt indication of the way Rowe had effectively fashioned his circus to appeal to a transnational audience.[76] After a successful finale, the company departed for Tahiti on December 12, 1851.[77]

The Society Islands had become a French protectorate in 1842 and the circus set up in the port of Papeete. Rowe later described it as a "very poore place," but the company was apparently graciously received as they performed there for several weeks before continuing on to Australia.[78] They encountered a violent storm soon after leaving Tahiti and were forced to put into port at Auckland for repairs. Though largely by accident, Rowe's circus was the

Fig. 2.16. "Rowe's American Circus, The Second Grand Promenade Concert," November 19, 1853. Silk souvenir program; printed at the Argus Office, Melbourne. By permission of the National Library of Australia

first to visit New Zealand and gave a series of performances there before embarking for Victoria and the goldfields.[79]

When Rowe reached Melbourne in May 1852, he found that the circus was already well established in the Australian colonies. Launceston, Hobart, and Sydney all possessed amphitheaters, though they only hosted circuses intermittently. More pointedly, he had been preempted by John Sullivan Noble, an American circus manager and performer who had brought a small company to Australia in 1851 via Rio de Janeiro and Cape Town. Noble visited Adelaide and Sydney, and then took his Olympic Circus to Melbourne in February 1852 as its population exploded amid the gold rush.[80] Rowe auctioned off the *General Worth* and made plans to construct a canvas-roofed amphitheater, but ran into trouble as the City Magistrates were reluctant to grant a license for another circus. In the ensuing controversy, the Melbourne press sided with Rowe and the application was eventually granted. On the evening of June 28, 1852, Rowe's American Circus opened to an overflowing house.[81]

Even with the "glories of Astley's fresh in our memories," the reviewer for the *Argus* newspaper was impressed with the new circus, and left wondering why "opposition should ever had been offered to Mr. Rowe." Mrs. Rowe was feted as an "elegant and accomplished equestrian," and the clown Yeamans "succeeded throughout the evening in keeping the audience in roars of laughter." The greatest praise was reserved for Master Raphael, who was described as "jumping though hoops, leaping over garters, and standing on his head as if it were the easiest thing imaginable."[82] It was a wild success and for the next two-and-a-half years Rowe's circus was a premiere attraction in the booming city. The well-appointed amphitheater accommodated upward of a thousand people and the boom times allowed Rowe to maintain inflated prices.

During that time, the performances were kept fresh through frequent changes in the program and personnel. Rowe courted a wide public by reserving Thursday evenings for families and by giving liberally to many charitable causes. The amphitheater also hosted civic meetings, theatrical performances, and a series of "Grand Promenade Concerts" by local favorites like the soprano Madame Sara Flower, the "Australian Nightingale" (*fig. 2.16*).[83] The net result was that Rowe made an unprecedented amount of money for a circus manager, despite some intermittent competition. He further buttressed his business by constructing a large building on a neighboring lot that served as an "American bar, supper, oyster, and refreshment" house.[84]

In early 1854 Rowe returned to California to invest in property and engage new talent, leaving his wife Eliza in charge of the circus. It continued to prosper despite a challenge from a company led by W. H. Foley, whose Cirque National boasted an elephant and camels.[85] In San Francisco, Rowe told the press that he had cleared 40,000 pounds over the last year and a half and promptly spent 56,000 dollars on a ranch and other properties near Los Angeles.[86] He arrived back in Melbourne in October only to auction off the horses and properties a week later, and the *Argus* bemoaned that Rowe left "a gap which will with difficulty be filled up."[87] Joseph Andrew Rowe and Eliza returned to California reputedly laden with "over $100,000 in cash and numerous chests of treasure."[88]

The exceptional profits Rowe reaped in Melbourne were due to a combination of factors. First and foremost, his success was owed to his uncanny ability at finding and exploiting new cultural markets. Melbourne was the most remunerative of a long

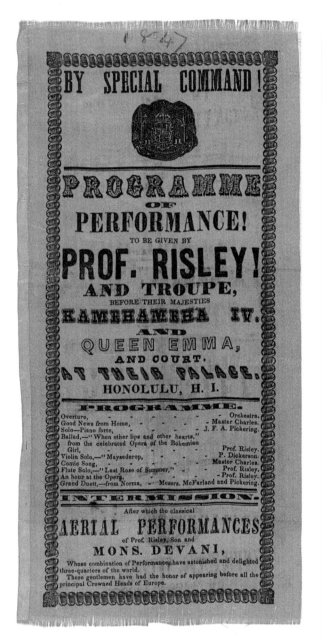

he endeared himself to the public by holding frequent benefits for a variety of local charities and benevolent institutions.[90] In short, Rowe was an effective entrepreneur and showman, and his spectacular success in Melbourne was abetted by the gold-fueled economy, in which commercial entertainment flourished.

Rowe was the first in a parade of American showmen that brought progressively larger and more grandiose circus companies to tour around the Pacific during the nineteenth century. They were part of a diverse mix of international circus performers and managers who plied the Pacific show trade, including luminaries like the French equestrian Louis Soullier and the Italian Giuseppe Chiarini.[91] One of the most fascinating figures that followed in Rowe's wake was Richard Risley Carlisle, popularly known as Professor Risley. Risley was an excellent all-around athlete and gymnast, but what made him famous was his foot-juggling ability. Using his feet to manipulate various objects while on his back, he performed both on the ground and on horseback. Risley's major innovation was to juggle young assistants who were invariably referred to as his sons. The boys flipped between his hands and feet in quick succession, among other feats. The highlight of the act was when the boys rolled tightly up into a ball and were rapidly spun about and repeatedly launched into the air. It was an act that would prove popular the world over.

Risley first appeared with a circus in 1841, and pursued a peripatetic career that took him through the Caribbean and then to Britain, where he joined the influx of American talent in the 1840s.[92] After his initial success in London in 1843, Risley visited principal European cities such as Paris, Brussels, and Rome, even traveling as far as St. Petersburg and Moscow. The French critic Théophile Gautier de-

line of successful moves that were only possible because of the mobility and efficiency of Rowe's operation. Rowe went to great lengths to ensure that his show was seen as a respectable one and was consistently able to secure elite patronage.[89] He also maintained good relations with the local press and

Fig. 2.17. "By Special Command! Programme of Performance! To be Given by Prof. Risley! and Troupe," 1857. Silk souvenir program. Harvard Theatre Collection, Houghton Library, Harvard University scribed an 1844 performance at the Théâtre de la Porte Saint-Martin in Paris:

> There appears a great devil of a genie, perfectly constructed, with magnificent pectorals, muscular arms, but without the enormities of professional strongmen; he is costumed exactly as his children, whom he throws at once some twenty-five feet in the air, as something of a warming-up or preparatory exercises. Then he lies on his back . . . [and] begins a series of *tours de force* the more incredible in that they betray not the least effort, nor the least fatigue, nor the least hesitation. The two adorable gamins, successively or together, climb to the assault of their father, who receives them on the palms of his hands, the soles of his feet, launches them, returns them, throws them, passes them from right to left, holds them in the air, lets them go, picks them up with as much ease as an Indian juggler maneuvers his copper balls.[93]

As Gautier makes clear, Risley was a tremendously skilled performer and earned a fortune abroad before returning to the United States in 1847.[94]

Risley traveled to the Pacific Coast in 1855 and opened in San Francisco with a small company that also featured contortionist Mons. Devani, the "Indian Rubber Man"; rider A. V. Caldwell; and the Coroni family of rope-dancers.[95] His transpacific adventures began in the fall of 1857, when a pared-down version of the Risley Troupe performed in a "Tri-Colored Pavilion" at Honolulu. Risley carried an autograph book that included the signatures and testimonials from several American presidents and European personages that one local newspaper thought was "a sufficient passport, it might be imagined, to any audience in the theatre-going world." A silk souvenir program produced for the troupe's command performance before King Kamehameha IV and Queen Emma bragged that he had "astonished and delighted three-quarters of the world" and their royal signatures were undoubtedly added to his book (*fig. 2.17*).[96]

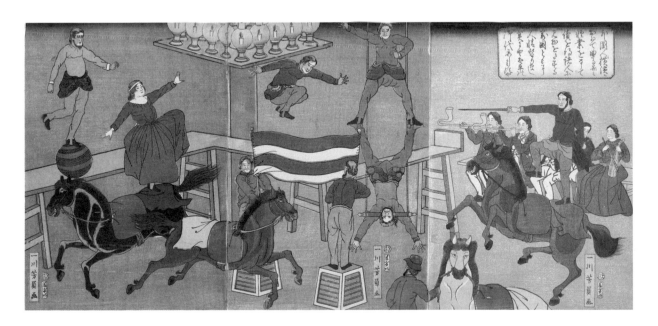

▲ *Fig. 2.18*. Utagawa Yoshikazu, Untitled (*Circus in Yokohama*), April 1864. Triptych of polychrome woodblock prints; ink and color on paper. The Metropolitan Museum of Art, Bequest of William S. Lieberman, 2005 (2007.49.176a–c)

Following Rowe's path, Risley next traveled to Australia via Tahiti and New Zealand. A reviewer there effused that his graceful "acrobatisms" were "undoubtedly superior to anything of the kind which has been exhibited in the colony."[97] After touring through Australia, he tried his hand at prospecting, but failing at that he put together a small circus company and headed to India and the Far East, visiting Singapore, Manila, Hong Kong, and Shanghai over the course of the early 1860s.

Risley landed in Yokohama, Japan, in March 1864 with a company of ten performers and eight horses. They erected a tent on a vacant lot in the area where foreign residents were quartered. On March 28 the first performance of an American circus in Japan was presented to an audience of about 250 native and 200 Western viewers.[98] The show included a pair of Italian acrobats; Miss Lizzie Gordon, equestrienne; Mr. Eugene, dog act; La Petite Cerito, dancer; and a somersaulting rider, Mr. Rooney. The occasion was documented in a beautiful woodblock print by Utagawa Yoshikazu that depicts the various acts (*fig. 2.18*). Unfortunately for Risley, he was unable to present his show anywhere else in Japan as the authorities were strongly opposed to foreign entertainment and the company disbanded in May. Risley found life in Japan amenable enough to stay for the next few years. He went on to pursue a variety of idiosyncratic projects that ranged from importing a herd of dairy cows to building and managing the Royal Olympic Theatre in Yokohama, which on occasion hosted exhibitions featuring Japanese performers.[99]

Risley eventually decided to organize a Japanese troupe for an overseas tour and enlisted the U.S. consul George Fisher and American trader De Witt Clinton Brower to obtain the necessary permissions from the reluctant Japanese government and provide the financial backing for the venture. In December 1866 the eighteen performers were issued the first Japanese passports and they embarked with Risley for San Francisco. The Imperial Japanese Troupe made a sensational tour across the United States and then went on to Europe, where they competed with a grand Cirque American that was organized by a syndicate of American showmen to play at the Exposition Universelle in Paris.[100] The company was so successful that it led to court battles over the profits and prompted an "international scramble" for Japanese performers.[101] Risley thus not only introduced the American circus to Japan, but also inaugurated a cultural exchange that introduced Japanese performers to the world.

The amount of capital and level of organization that was required for the tour by Risley's Japanese troupe demonstrated just how powerful and far-reaching the U.S. entertainment industry was in the 1860s. Although the Civil War initially dampened business, the tenting season of 1863 was likely the most profitable one in circus history to date. With the South closed off and competition in the North intensified, a number of circuses elected to tour abroad. The owners of the largest American circus at the time, Dr. Gilbert R. Spalding and Charles J. Rogers, purchased a ship, renamed their show Spalding & Rogers Ocean Circus, and spent most of the war overseas in South America and the Caribbean.[102] Despite the terrible cost of the conflict, the growth of the rail network and the postwar economic boom spurred the development of the massive American railroad circuses that dominated the late nineteenth-century entertainment industry.[103]

One of the best examples of the ongoing expansion of the American circus industry was the Pacific tour undertaken by Cooper, Bailey & Co.'s Great International Allied Shows, which was the first large-scale railroad circus to travel overseas. The show departed San Francisco in November 1876 and returned to New York City two years later, after an extended tour that was concentrated in Australia but also visited the Dutch East Indies, New Zealand, and South America. The show was run by James A. Bailey, the most outstanding American circus manager of his day. Cooper, Bailey & Co.'s show was an enormous operation that during the 1876 season employed a staff of over 125 personnel and included a full menagerie; hundreds of horses; and tons of advertising paper, properties, and equipment.[104] The evolution of the circus toward these massive touring shows was, in Janet Davis's characterization, a "cultural metonym for national expansion."[105] Cooper, Bailey & Co.'s tour was similarly an expression of the growing power of the United States in the Pacific.

The circus arrived in San Francisco in the fall of 1876, and Bailey charted a steamship at the reported cost of 17,000 dollars to convey the circus across the Pacific.[106] Cooper, Bailey & Co.'s Great

▲ *Fig. 2.19.* Cooper, Bailey & Co.'s Circus, City Park, Sydney, Australia, December 1876. Photograph. McCaddon Collection of the Barnum & Bailey Circus, box 14 folder 4; Department of Rare Books and Special Collections, Princeton University Library

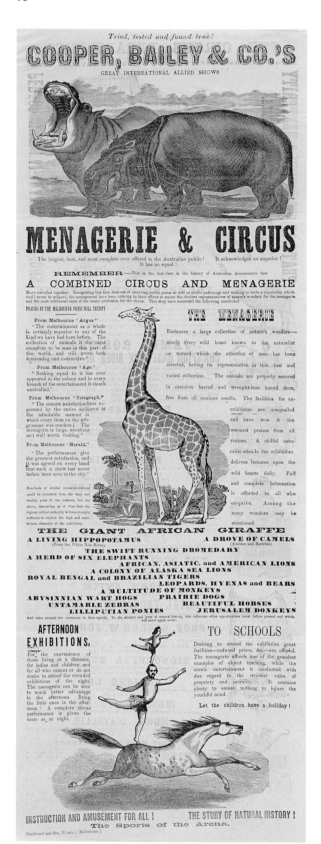

Fig. 2.20. "Cooper, Bailey & Co.'s Great International Allied Shows, Menagerie & Circus," 1877. Herald, printed by Charlwood and Son, Melbourne. McCaddon Collection of the Barnum & Bailey Circus, box 20; Department of Rare Books and Special Collections, Princeton University Library

International Allied Shows debuted in Sydney on December 18, 1876 under a massive main tent that was 500 feet long and 125 feet across and utilized a 150-foot main pole. There were two rings for performances and the seating accommodated upward of 6,000 people (*fig. 2.19*). Among the novelties the show introduced to Australian audiences was an extensive menagerie featuring a giraffe, a hippopotamus, and a herd of six elephants, a "museum of curiosities," and a sideshow. All of these attractions were housed in separate tents. The advertising also "astonished the people" as press agent W. C. Crowley reported, continuing, "they are not used to long billboards covered with hug[e] and highly-colored posters, nor have they seen many lithographs."[107] In Sydney alone, twenty-five thousand heralds detail-

ing the show's varied acts were distributed (*fig. 2.20*). The star performer was James Robinson, legitimately billed as the "Champion Rider of the World," and a large roster of equestrians, acrobats, clowns, and specialty performers like the "French Samson" Mademoiselle D'Atalie, who fired a heavy cannon balanced on her shoulders.

After an auspicious six weeks in Sydney, the circus traveled by steamer to Victoria. The Cooper, Bailey & Co.'s show was so large that it was only able to travel by steamship or railroad and the logistics, size, and efficiency of the operation consistently inspired awe, if not always admiration from its Australian audiences. A lithograph celebrating the arrival of the circus in Melbourne provides an idealized glimpse of the scene with a heading that

Fig. 2.21. "Scene at Melbourne, Australia, Feb. 14th 1877," ca. 1881. Poster, printed by the Strobridge Lithographing Company, Cincinnati. Collection of the John and Mable Ringling Museum of Art, Tibbals Collection, ht2004494

boasted it was: "[t]he only show that ever had the nerve, brains, and capital to make a grand tour of the world" (*fig. 2.21*). The show gave two performances per day, except Sunday, for the next four weeks, and averaged a stunning 4,000 dollars per day in receipts.[108] The inaugural season in Australia was a very profitable one, and Bailey triumphantly returned to New York to recruit new talent while the circus was split into separate units, with a pared-down company traveling as far as Batavia in the Dutch East Indies.[109]

Bailey returned with reinforcements in October 1877, and following a second successful season in Australia, he toured through New Zealand and chartered a ship for Peru, departing Auckland in early May. Although the circus ran into some difficul-

Fig. 2.22. "Cooper Bailey & Co.'s Great International Allied Shows," 1879. Poster, printed by the Strobridge Lithography Company, Cincinnati. Discovery Museum and Planetarium, Bridgeport, Connecticut

ties in South America, a further reduced company visited its principal ports and then arrived in New York City in December 1878. Bailey used the proceeds from his extended overseas tour to purchase the Howes' Great London Circus and fielded the best-equipped show in the country for the 1879 season, complete with electric lights and advertising that puffed the show's overseas adventures.[110] A spectacular four-sheet poster produced that year depicted the route of the tour and overlaid the show's myriad attractions on a brightly colored globe. The poster reflected the enormous size of the contemporary railroad American circus, and the burgeoning globalization of U.S. mass culture (*fig. 2.22*).

The 1876–78 Cooper, Bailey, & Co.'s Great International Allied Shows' tour represented the apogee of the transnational history of the early American circus. Over the preceding half-century, American showmen had transformed the circus and re-exported it to the world. Donald Sassoon postulated that the United States became a powerful exporter of culture because from the beginning "the production of culture was seen as an industrial enterprise" and a vast and diverse domestic market ensured that U.S. cultural forms were both scaled and tested for global consumption.[111] This observation certainly rings true in terms of the circus industry in the United States, which absorbed manifold influences and developed in an innovative fashion guided by the demands of a geographically dispersed and diverse audience. The itinerant mode and exceptional capitalization of American circuses ensured that shows were well prepared to circulate abroad and these travels threw into sharp relief what was distinctive about the American circus.

Perhaps the most remarkable aspect of the larger transnational circus business was its dynamism. At one moment it might serve as a forum for cultural exchange, at another a channel for cultural nationalism. Ultimately, the extraordinary development of the circus in the United States over the course of the nineteenth century and the progressively ambitious efforts of American showmen abroad influenced popular entertainment around the globe and prefigured the ascendance of U.S. mass culture in the twentieth century.

1 Peter Benes, "Itinerant Entertainers in New England and New York, 1687–1830," in *Itinerancy in New England and New York* (Boston: Boston University, 1986), 112–30; Richardson Wright, *Hawkers and Walkers in Early America* (Philadelphia: J. B. Lippincott, 1927).

2 Theater was the most established form of entertainment in the United States at the turn of the nineteenth century, but here again plays and talent were generally imported. Hugh F. Rankin, *The Theater in Colonial America* (Chapel Hill: University of North Carolina Press, 1965); Don B. Wilmeth and C. W. E. Bigsby, eds., *The Cambridge History of American Theatre, Volume One: Beginnings to 1870* (Cambridge: Cambridge University Press, 1998).

3 James S. Moy, "Entertainments at John B. Ricketts's Circus, 1793–1800," *Educational Theater Journal* 30, no. 2 (May 1978), 186–202. Durang was a versatile performer and celebrated dancer whose memoir provides a vivid picture of Ricketts and the early circus in the U.S. Alan Seymour Downer, ed., *The Memoir of John Durang, American Actor, 1785–1816* (Pittsburgh: University of Pittsburgh Press, 1966).

4 Of course surnames and the wide use of pseudonyms in the circus meant that names were often adopted by entrepreneurial design rather than by actual birth, but enough is known about the more prominent performers to establish that there was a diverse mix of nationalities involved. See William L. Slout, *Olympians of the Sawdust Circle: A Biographical Dictionary of the Nineteenth-Century American Circus* (San Bernardino, CA: Borgo Press, 1998).

5 For the authoritative account of the activities of Ricketts, Lailson, and other early American circuses, see Stuart Thayer, *Annals of the American Circus, 1793–1860* (Seattle: Dauven and Thayer, 2001). Also see R. W. G. Vail, *Random Notes on the History of the Early American Circus* (Worcester, MA: American Antiquarian Society, 1934). T. Alston Brown published an occasionally erroneous but still useful serialized history of the American circus in the *New York Clipper* between Dec. 20, 1860 and Feb. 9, 1861, "A Complete History of the Amphitheatre and Circus from Its Earliest Date to 1861," edited and republished by William L. Slout as *Amphitheatres and Circuses: A History from Their Earliest Date to 1861, with Sketches of Some of the Principal Performers* (San Bernadino, CA: Borgo Press, 1994).

6 Stuart Thayer, "Victor Pepin's Genealogy," *Bandwagon* 36, no. 3 (May–June 1992), 31.

7 Thayer, *Annals*, 19, 39–52.

8 Price was a well-to-do lawyer and the first noteworthy American theatrical producer. Edmund Simpson was a British actor who started as the stage manager at the Park Theatre in 1810 and by 1821 was its acting manager: Don B. Wilmeth, *The Cambridge Guide to American Theatre* (Cambridge: Cambridge University Press, 1996).

9 Joe Cowell, *Thirty Years Passed among the Players in England and America* (New York: Harper & Brothers, 1844), 64. As part of the deal, West was barred from opening a circus in the United States. He returned to London and used the proceeds to enter into a long-running partnership with the famed equestrian Andrew Ducrow at Astley's Circus: A. H. Saxon, *The Life and Art of Andrew Ducrow & the Romantic Age of the English Circus* (Hamden, CT: Archon Books, 1978).

10 Only the most skilled equestrians were able to perform the assorted poses and acrobatics that principal riding demanded bareback. More commonly, performers used modified saddles or a riding pad, which afforded better footing and also allowed the more skilled riders to perform feats that would be difficult, if not impossible, to execute bareback. Stuart Thayer, *The Performers: A History of Circus Acts* (Seattle: Dauven and Thayer, 2005), 65–75.

11 This was hardly a surprising move for Price and Simpson given that they have generally been credited with establishing the "star system" in the United States, which centered on importing English talent for American tours: Simon Williams, "European Actors and the Star System in the American Theatre, 1752–1870," in *The Cambridge History of American Theatre, Volume One: Beginnings to 1870* (Cambridge: Cambridge University Press, 1998), 303–37.

12 Bancker's New York Circus seems to have been the first to use the term, *circus* as a noun to designate the traveling troupe. In earlier usage of the term, *circus* referred to the building, with "equestrian company" or some like combination being used to describe the actual troupe. Thayer, *Annals*, 66.

13 Ibid., 95.

14 The only major European circus that subsequently attempted a full-fledged U.S. tour in the nineteenth century was directed by Thomas Taplin Cooke, scion of the famous English circus family. He arrived in 1836 with a large company of performers and after opening in New York, visited Boston, Philadelphia, and Baltimore. Judging by contemporary accounts, it was an impressive show, but a calamitous fire in Baltimore killed most of the horses and the deleterious effects of the Panic of 1837 doomed the venture. T. Allston Brown, *Amphitheatres and Circuses*, 9–11.

15 The "pavilion" was first advertised for a performance in Wilmington, Delaware in late November 1825, but it was not until the following spring that Brown and Bailey used it regularly: Thayer, *Annals*, 75–77.

16 See the essay by Fred Dahlinger, Jr. in this volume.

17 For the seminal studies of the relationship between early American vernacular and commercial cultural forms, see Constance Rourke, *American Humor: A Study of the National Character* (New York: Harcourt, Brace and Company, 1931); *Roots of American Culture, and Other Essays* (New York: Harcourt, Brace, and World, 1942).

18 For an excellent analysis of this dynamic in a theatrical context, see, Bruce A. McConachie, *Melodramatic Formations: American Theatre and Society, 1820–1870* (Iowa City: University of Iowa Press, 1992).

19 Richard W. Flint, "American Showmen and European Dealers: Commerce in Wild Animals in Nineteenth-Century America," in *New Worlds, New Animals: From Menagerie to Zoological Park in the Nineteenth Century*, ed. R. J. Hoage and William A. Deiss (Baltimore: Johns Hopkins University Press, 1996), 97–108; Peter Benes, "To the Curious: Bird and Animal Exhibitions in New England, 1716–1825," in *New England's Creatures, 1400–1900* (Boston: Boston University, 1995), 147–63; Brett Mizelle, "'I Have Brought My Pig to a Fine Market': Animals, Their Exhibitors, and Market Culture in the Early Republic," in *Cultural Change and the Market Revolution in America, 1789–1860*, ed. Scott C. Martin (Lanham, MD: Rowan & Littlefield, 2005), 181–216; Terry Ariano, "Beasts and Ballyhoo, The Menagerie Men of Somers," *Bandwagon* 49, no. 1 (Jan.–Feb. 2005), 23–30.

20 Charles Grier Sellers, *The Market Revolution: Jacksonian America, 1815–1846* (New York: Oxford University Press, 1991); James W. Cook, "The Return of the Culture Industry," in *The Cultural Turn in U.S. History: Past, Present, and Future*, ed. James W. Cook, Lawrence B. Glickman, and Michael O'Malley (Chicago: University of Chicago Press, 2008), 291–317.

21 Richard W. Flint, "Entrepreneurial and Cultural Aspects of the Early-Nineteenth-Century Circus and Menagerie Business," in *Itinerancy in New England and New York*, ed. Peter Benes (Boston: Boston University, 1986), 131–49; Terry Ariano, "Beasts and Ballyhoo." In his early autobiography, Barnum implies that the Zoological Institute was something of a fraud, intended to dupe unwary investors. He derailed a competing bid by some "speculators" for the American Museum in 1841 by reminding the public of its failure. While there might be some truth to his claim, the Panic of 1837 had a devastating impact on the entertainment industry in general and this was undoubtedly the primary reason for its demise. *Life of Barnum* (New York: Redfield, 1855), 219–20.

22 In 1829, Charles Wright was the first American advertised as entering a cage with a lion: Stuart Thayer, "'The Keeper Will Enter the Cage': Early American Wild Animal Trainers," *Bandwagon* 26, no. 6 (Nov.–Dec. 1982), 38–40.

23 The details of Brown's early career were gleaned from a fascinating newspaper interview given toward the end of his life: "The Oldest of Showmen," *New York*

Sun, July 6, 1879, 5. Also, see Stuart Thayer, "The Oldest of Showmen: The Career of Benjamin F. Brown of Somers, New York," *Bandwagon* 50, no. 5 (Sept.–Oct. 2006), 10–16.

24 Thayer, *Annals*, 90.

25 Richard W. Flint, "Rufus Welch: America's Pioneer Circus Showman," *Bandwagon* 50, no. 5 (Sept.–Oct. 1970), 4–11. For a lively account of the tour as later related by Levi North, a young rider with the circus, to the press agent and historian Charles H. Day, see "The Eventful Career of Levi J. North," *New York Clipper*, March 6, 1880, 393.

26 Most of the source material for this account of the Brown brothers' Caribbean tour was derived from papers in the Benjamin F. Brown Collection at the William L. Clements Library at the University of Michigan.

27 Apprentices were children or young adults who traveled with the show and were trained in the circus arts in a kind of indentured servitude. Becoming a successful performer required training from an early age and they were popular with managers because they were essentially unpaid labor and thus provided a cost-effective way of filling out programs. A litany of great performers, including James Robinson, James Nixon, and Tony Pastor, were brought up in this manner after coming to the circus from broken homes or through being orphaned. Although apprentices gained valuable skills, because of their vulnerable position and the dangerous nature of the work, they were sometimes abused and the turnover rate was high. One of the more fascinating documents in the Benjamin F. Brown Collection is a contract signed in Barbados on July 28, 1830, between Frederick Hoffmaster and B. F. Brown & Co. that ended his apprenticeship and enlisted him as a full-fledged member of the troupe. It stipulated a salary of thirty dollars per month, included board and laundry, and allotted him one-third of the gross profit from his benefits, which were performances set aside to honor and remunerate individual performers. On apprentices in general, see Thayer, *The Performers*, 15–20.

28 "Contract between Robert Temple and Co. and Benjamin Brown for the transport of Brown's circus from Paramaribo to Berbice," Nov. 19, 1830, Benjamin F. Brown Collection, William L. Clements Library, The University of Michigan.

29 Balloon ascensions were a novelty that provided circuses a way of generating publicity. Originating in France, Jean-Pierre Blanchard brought the practice of ballooning to the United States in 1793. On their use in the American circus, see Bob Parkinson, "Circus Balloon Ascensions," *Bandwagon* 5, no. 2 (Sept.–Oct. 1964), 3–6.

30 "Scene riding" was a staple of the nineteenth-century circus. The performer rode around the ring and went through various exercises as one of a number of stock characters, such as the Dying Moor, the Roman Gladiator, or the Indian Hunter: Thayer, *The Performers*, 47–51.

31 "Oldest of Showmen," *New York Sun*.

32 Popularly known as "Billy Button's Ride to Brentford," this piece was first featured at Astley's in the 1770s and remained a standard with the circus for well over a century: George Speaight, *A History of the Circus* (London: Tantivy Press, 1980), 24.

33 According to circus historian C. G. Sturtevant, "So great was the demand for the Yankee Circus for over a period of years nearly all performers of reputation accepted engagements during the winter with these shows for at least one trip." "When the American Circus Went Abroad," *White Tops* 12 (Nov.–Dec. 1939), 5.

34 O'Connell was an Irish sailor who was shipwrecked on the Pacific island of Ponphei in the late 1820s and acquired a full-body tattoo during his time as a castaway. He made his way to New York in 1832 and was among the first circus "freaks": *A Residence of Eleven Years in New Holland and the Caroline Islands: Being the Adventures of James F. O'Connell, Edited from His Verbal Narration* (Boston: B. B. Mussey, 1836).

35 This account of the tour of Cuba was derived from the memoirs of equestrian John H. Glenroy, who was an apprentice to Cadwalader. Glenroy subsequently made a representative southern or winter tour with a circus under the direction of Alvah Mann. A ship was chartered for the company of fifteen performers, departing New York City in October 1843. Their extensive itinerary included week- or two-week-long visits to Suriname, Guyana, Demerara, Trinidad, Grenada, Barbados, St. Vincent, St. Lucia, St. Thomas, St. Croix, and Puerto Rico, returning to the United States in April 1844 in time for the summer season. John H. Glenroy (narrator) and Stephen Stanley Stanford (compiler), *Ins and Outs of Circus Life, or, Forty-Two Years Travel of John H. Glenroy, Bareback Rider, through United States, Canada, South America and Cuba* (Boston: M. M. Wing & Co., 1885), 43–53.

36 Raúl H. Castagnino, *El Circo Criollo: Datos Y Documentos Para Su Historia, 1757–1924* (Buenos Aires: Lajouane, 1953), 25–28.

37 Flint, "Rufus Welch," 6–7.

38 "Oldest of Showmen," *New York Sun*.

39 Dale Cockrell, ed. *Excelsior: Journals of the Hutchinson Family Singers* (Stuyvesant: Pendragon Press, 1989); W. T. Lhamon, *Jump Jim Crow: Lost Plays, Lyrics, and Street Prose of the First Atlantic Popular Culture* (Boston: Harvard University Press, 2003); James W. Cook, ed. *The Colossal P. T. Barnum Reader* (Urbana:

University of Illinois Press, 2005); Sarah Meer, *Uncle Tom Mania: Slavery, Minstrelsy, and Transatlantic Culture in the 1850s* (Athens: University of Georgia Press, 2005).

40 George Speaight credited two Catabaw "Indian Chiefs" that appeared at Astley's in 1796 as the first American performers in a European circus. He also noted that the first "white American circus artiste" was likely a woman who rode with William Southby's circus company in Spain in 1816. As there are doubts about whether a Mr. Blackmore who performed at Astley's as the "young American," was indeed from the United States, credit for the first American performer to receive star billing in Britain goes to equestrian Benjamin Stickney, who debuted at Astley's in September 1830: Speaight, *History of the Circus*, 103–4.

41 Day, "The Eventful Career of Levi J. North." Speaight, *History of the Circus*, 54.

42 Thayer, *The Performers*, 25–30. Also see Steven Gossard, "Frank Gardner and the Great Leapers," *Bandwagon* 34, no. 4 (July–Aug. 1990), 12–25.

43 The letter, dated July 18 and addressed to his parents, was printed in the *Baltimore Sun*, Sept. 4, 1838. Other details about Blackburn and North's adventures abroad were culled from a serialized article that appeared in the *New York Clipper* in February 1879 under the elaborate heading: "A Clown's Log, Extracts from the Diary of the Late Joseph Blackburn, Chronicling Incidents of Travel with Circuses in the United States and England Forty Years Ago, with His Opinions of and Allusions to Professionals of the Period." The circus agent and historian Charles H. Day compiled and added commentary to excerpts that were taken from eleven "passbooks" written in pencil by Blackburn that were then in Levi North's possession. Although the originals have been lost, Day's series was usefully collected and republished with additional material and commentary by William L. Slout as *Joe Blackburn's A Clown's Log* (San Bernardino, CA: Borgo Press, 1993).

44 Part of the appeal of the display was alluded to elsewhere in Blackburn's letter, when he noted that it inspired "pretty heavy betting all over the house every night."

45 *The* (London) *Times*, June 5, 1839, quoted in Speaight, *History of the Circus*, 64. When North returned to the United States in 1840, he commanded the unheard-of salary of 350 dollars a week with Welch & Mann's Circus: Thayer, *Annals*, 189.

46 Day, "The Eventful Career of Levi J. North."

47 Hyatt Frost, *A Biographical Sketch of I. A. Van Amburgh: And an Illustrated and Descriptive History of the Animals Contained in this Mammoth Menagerie and Great Moral Exhibition* (New York: Samuel Booth, 1862); Joanne Joys, *The Wild Animal Trainer*

in America (Boulder, CO: Pruett, 1983) and Joanne Joys, "The Wild Things," PhD diss., Bowling Green University, 2011.

48 *The* (London) *Times*, Aug. 24, 1838; *Bell's Life* (London), Aug. 26, 1838.

49 Quoted in George Rowell, *Queen Victoria Goes to the Theatre* (London: P. Elek, 1978), 4.

50 Stanley Weintraub, *Victorian Yankees at Queen Victoria's Court: American Encounters with Victoria and Albert* (Newark: University of Delaware Press, 2011), 18–22.

51 *Le Figaro*, Aug. 22, 1839; "Van Amburgh in Paris," *Spirit of the Times*, Sept. 28, 1839, 360.

52 Among other things, Brown's wife described him as a "a perfect boor in society": "Oldest of Showmen," *New York Sun*, 5.

53 *Liverpool Mercury*, March 8, 1842, quoted in Speaight, *History of the Circus*, 43. While tents had traditionally been used by itinerant entertainers and on fairgrounds, Speaight notes that this was the first "substantial use of a tent for circuses in England."

54 Quoted in Philip F. Gura and James F. Bollman, *America's Instrument: The Banjo in the Nineteenth Century* (Chapel Hill: University of North Carolina Press, 1999), 35. On the intersection of blackface minstrelsy and the circus in the United States, see Stuart Thayer, "The Circus Roots of Negro Minstrelsy," *Bandwagon* 40, no. 6 (Nov.–Dec. 1996), 43–45.

55 Michael Pickering, *Blackface Minstrelsy in Britain* (Aldershot, England and Burlington, VT: Ashgate, 2008). Also see the essay by Brenda Assael in this volume.

56 This poster was one of several that Sands simply had the New York firm G. & W. Endicott reprint when he returned to the United States. It was originally produced by G. Webb and Co., Lith. in London for the spectacle *The Desert; or, the Imaun's Daughter*, which was performed at Drury Lane in 1847 and featured the circus of Edwin Hughes. A. H. Saxon, *Enter Foot and Horse: A History of Hippodrama in England and France* (New Haven: Yale University Press, 1968), 110–11.

57 *Spirit of the Times*, July 26, 1845, 250.

58 The occasion was commemorated in a well-known print by Nathaniel Currier.

59 The American circus parade further expanded in the 1860s and 1870s when Seth B. Howes returned from his British tours with even larger and more ornate tableau wagons. Stuart Thayer, "Parade Wagons 1847," *Bandwagon* 42, no. 2 (March–April 1998), 2–3. George Speaight, "The Origin of the Circus Parade Wagon," *Bandwagon* 21, no. 6 (Nov.–Dec. 1977), 37–39; Richard E. Conover, "The European Influence on the American Circus Parade," *Bandwagon* 5, no. 4 (Jul.–Aug. 1961), 3–9; Fred Dahlinger, Jr., "The

Barnum & London New York Tableaus," *Bandwagon* 30, no. 1 (Jan.–Feb., 1986), 26–28.

60 Louis E. Cooke, "Reminiscences of a Showman," *Newark Evening Star*, Oct. 28, 1915, 12; Flint, "Rufus Welch," 6–7.

61 Speaight, *History of the Circus*, 103–8.

62 *The Era* (London), May 3, 1857, 10.

63 David Fitzroy, *Myers' American Circus* (Prestwich: D. Fitzroy, 2002); Thomas Frost, *Circus Life and Circus Celebrities* (London: Chatto and Windus, 1881), 204–5; Sturtevant, "When the American Circus Went Abroad," 4.

64 Albert Dressler, ed., *California's Pioneer Circus: Memoirs and Personal Correspondence Relative to the Circus Business through the Gold Country in the 50's* (San Francisco: H. S. Crocker, 1926), 1–6.

65 On the early amusement business in San Francisco, see George Rupert MacMinn, *The Theater of the Golden Era in California* (Caldwell, ID: Caxton, 1941); Helene Koon, *Gold Rush Performers: A Biographical Dictionary of Actors, Singers, Dancers, Musicians, Circus Performers and Minstrel Players in America's Far West, 1848 to 1869* (Jefferson, NC: McFarland, 1994).

66 *Alta California* (San Francisco), Nov. 1, 1849.

67 Foley claimed he could not live on a salary of 1200 dollars a month. While this might sound like exaggeration, the Gold Rush prices of goods and services in San Francisco were wildly out of control. Rowe was able to charge three dollars for a ticket that anywhere else in the United States would have cost twenty-five cents: Lawrence Estevan, ed., *San Francisco Theatre Research* 1 (1938), 85–86. For comparison, the two leading actors in a dramatic company in Sacramento at the time were receiving 275 dollars a week: John H. McCabe, "Historical Essay on the Drama in California," in *First Annual of the Territorial Pioneers* (San Francisco: W. M. Hinton & Co., 1877), 73–76.

68 MacMinn, *Theater of the Golden Era*, 474.

69 "Rowe's Olympic Circus," Jan. 10, 1851, Broadside Collection, M-485, Hawai'i State Archives.

70 Helen P. Hoyt, "Theatre in Hawaii–1778–1840," *Annual Report of the Hawaiian Historical Society* (1960), 7–18; on debates about popular entertainments in Honolulu, also see Gavan Daws, *Shoal of Time: A History of the Hawaiian Islands* (New York: Macmillan, 1968), 162–67.

71 The king was Kamehameha III (1813–1854) while Alex (Alexander Liholiho), Lot (Lot Kapauaiwa), and Bill (William Lunalilo) were respectively the next three rulers of the Hawaiian Kingdom. Emma married Alexander Liholiho and was queen from 1856 to 1863 during his reign as Kamehameha IV (1854–63).

72 Privy Council, Aug. 29, 1852, Hawai'i State Archives.

73 *Alta California*, (San Francisco), March 31, 1851, 5.

74 "Rowe's Olympic Circus," Jan. 14, March 6 and 21, 1851, Broadside Collection, M-485, Hawai'i State Archives. Emma Rooke's notations quoted from Jan. 14 and March 21.

75 Dressler, *California's Pioneer Circus*, 13.

76 "Rowe's Olympic Circus," Dec. 6, 1851, Broadside Collection, M-485, Hawai'i State Archives.

77 *Polynesian*, Dec. 13, 1851.

78 J. A. Rowe to John Center, Feb. 7, 1858, republished in Dressler, *California's Pioneer Circus*, 92–93.

79 *New Zealander* (Auckland), March 24, 27 and April 17, 1852.

80 Although circuses had been seen elsewhere in Australia, Noble was "the originator of circus entertainments in Victoria": Mark St. Leon, *The Circus in Australia: Its Origins and Development to 1856*, vol. 1 of *The Circus in Australia* (Penshurst, NSW: Mark St. Leon, 2005), 208. For a valuable general history on the subject, see Mark St. Leon, *Spangles & Sawdust: The Circus in Australia* (Richmond: Greenhouse Publications, 1983). On Melbourne's spectacular growth see Jill Roe, *Marvellous Melbourne: The Emergence of an Australian City* (Sydney: Hicks Smith & Sons, 1974).

81 *Argus*, June 3, 9, and 28, 1852; E. Daniel Potts and Annette Potts, *Young America and Australian Gold: Americans and the Gold Rush of the 1850s* (St. Lucia: University of Queensland Press, 1974), 148–49. It is unclear whether Noble and Rowe came to some sort of agreement or if he was simply unwilling or unable to compete with the new circus, but Noble's company departed a few weeks after Rowe's arrival.

82 *Argus*, June 29, 1852.

83 Ibid., July 9, 1853, and Nov. 14, 1853.

84 It was known as the "The Crystal Palace Refreshment Saloon." *Argus*, Aug. 8, 1853.

85 Foley refitted a venue known as Salle de Valentino and opened there on July 3. After a promising start, business slackened and Foley took his company to the gold diggings. *Argus*, July 3, 4, and Aug. 5, 1854.

86 Potts and Potts, *Young America and Australian Gold*, 149; Dressler, *California's Pioneer Circus*, 21–22.

87 *Argus*, Oct. 14, 1854. Rowe did not bring any new circus performers back from as planned, but the actors Edwin Booth, David Anderson, and Laura Keene arrived on the same vessel, which suggests that word of lucrative opportunities in Melbourne were circulating in the entertainment world. Ibid., Oct. 16, 1854.

88 Dressler, *California's Pioneer Circus*, 15.

89 Rowe prohibited smoking and employed a "strong body of police" to deal with disturbances. Lieutenant-Governor Charles La Trobe attended the circus soon after it opened and the *Argus* announced that it was "pleased to see entertainments of this nature conducted in such a manner that His Excellency and

the better classes of society can patronize them." Quoted in Estevan, *San Francisco Theatre Research*, 1 (1938), 96.

90 When Chiarini's Circus, for whom Rowe had been working as an agent, abruptly discharged and stranded him in Melbourne years later, a weekly paper published an appeal for funds, noting, "When it is remembered that with one exception Mr. Rowe contributed the largest sum ever given by any single individual to the Melbourne Hospital, it will be confessed that he has some preferent claim upon the public of this metropolis." *Australasian*, June 28, 1873.

91 Rowe came out of retirement in 1856 and formed a new circus in an attempt to recreate his earlier success in California and across the Pacific. He followed the same route as before, but the venture foundered in Australia. For more about Rowe and other U.S. entertainers that toured around the nineteenth-century Pacific, see Matthew Wittmann, "Empire of Culture: U.S. Entertainers and the Making of the Pacific Circuit," PhD diss., University of Michigan, 2010. On American circuses in Australia specifically, see Mark St. Leon, *The American Century, 1851–1950*, vol. 3 of *The Circus in Australia* (Penshurst, NSW: Mark St. Leon, 2007), 215–38.

92 Risley was part of the aforementioned company that Alvah Mann took on a winter Caribbean tour in 1843 (see note 35). In 1844 a correspondent to the *Spirit of the Times* noted that it was "somewhat singular that the two most popular objects of attraction in England at the present moment are American . . . namely, the beautiful and classical performances of the Risley's" and "the tiny but symmetrical and interesting Tom Thumb." April 27, 1844, 100.

93 Translated by and quoted in Marian Hannah Winter, "Theatre of Marvels," *Dance Index* 7, nos. 1–2 (Jan.–Feb. 1948), 26–28.

94 Risley was an inveterate gambler and made and lost several fortunes over the course of his career. *The Era* (London), June 21, 1874, 12; Aya Mihara and Stuart Thayer, "Richard Risley Carlisle, Man in Motion," *Bandwagon* 41, no. 1 (Jan.–Feb. 1997), 12–14.

95 Thayer, *Annals*, 385.

96 *Pacific Commercial Advertiser* (Honolulu), Nov. 26 and Dec. 17, 1857, Jan. 7, 1858.

97 *Daily Southern Cross* (Auckland), May 11, 1858, 3; *Argus* (Melbourne), Oct. 12, 1858, 5.

98 *Japan Herald*, March 24, 1864.

99 *Japan Times Daily Advertiser*, Oct. 3, 1865; Mihara and Thayer, "Richard Risley Carlisle," 14.

100 The Cirque American was a large and talented company organized by several prominent American showman to take advantage of the crowds at the World's Fair in Paris. Difficulties with local authorities prevented them from erecting a planned wood and iron pavilion on the Champs-Élysées, but they were able to perform at the Théâtre du Prince Impérial. Star equestrian James Robinson wrote a letter to the agent Frank Rivers that declared: "I am now able to let you know what the Frenchmen think of an American circus. They are stunned, although they dislike to own it." *New York Clipper*, June 22, 1867, 86; William L. Slout, "The Recycling of the Dan Rice Paris Pavilion Circus," *Bandwagon* 42, no. 3 (May–June 1998), 13–21.

101 George Fischer filed a lawsuit against the other involved parties in March 1868. The court proceedings revealed that the troupe made over 100,000 dollars in just over fourteen months: *New York Herald*, March 12, 1868, 8; *New York Clipper*, March 21, 1868, 398. Aya Mihara has published a series of articles documenting the tour, including a fascinating translation of a diary kept by one of the performers: "Professor Risley and Japanese Acrobats: Selections from the Diary of Hirohachi Takana," *Nineteenth Century Theatre* 18, nos. 1–2 (1990), 62–74. On the "international scramble," see David C. Sissons, "Japanese Acrobatic Troupes Touring Australasia, 1867–1900," *Australasian Drama Studies* 35 (Oct. 1999), 73–107.

102 William L. Slout, *Clowns and Cannons: The American Circus during the Civil War* (San Bernardino, CA: Borgo Press, 1997).

103 Janet M. Davis, *The Circus Age: Culture and Society under the American Big Top* (Chapel Hill: University of North Carolina Press, 2002).

104 W. G. Crowley (compiler), *Route of Cooper, Bailey & Co's Great International, Ten Allied Shows in One, During the Season of 1876* (San Francisco: Francis & Valentine, Printers, 1876).

105 Davis, *Circus Age*, 12.

106 Joseph T. McCaddon, Bailey's brother-in-law, was the wardrobe manager on the Australian tour and later wrote an unpublished biography about him that included a detailed account of the tour: McCaddon ms., 14, Joseph T. McCaddon Collection, Bridgeport (CT) Public Library. For a full account of the Australian tour, see Mark St. Leon, "Cooper, Bailey & Co. Great International Allied Shows: The Australian Tours, 1876–78," *Bandwagon* 36, nos. 5–6 (Sept.–Oct. and Nov.–Dec. 1992), 17–30 and 36–47.

107 Crowley went on to claim, "When these things appeared, the police had to clear the sidewalks because the people stopped to gaze at them so much." *New York Clipper*, Jan. 27, 1877, 351.

108 "Cash book, Cooper and Bailey, Australia and South America tours, 1876–1877–1878," McCaddon Collection of the Barnum and Bailey Circus, box 45, folder 8; Department of Rare Books and Special Collections, Princeton University Library.

109 While much of the property, animals, and personnel was sent to winter quarters in Sydney, a small company under the sideshow manager George Middleton planned to tour through the Far East and India, but turned back after poor business and illness in the Dutch East Indies. W. G. Crowley (compiler), *The Australian Tour of Cooper, Bailey & Co's Great International Allied Shows* (Brisbane: Thorne & Greenwell, 1877); George Middleton, *Circus Memoirs: Reminiscences of George Middleton as Told to and Written by His Wife* (Los Angeles: G. Rice & Sonsa, 1913), 40–41.

110 *New York Clipper*, Dec. 21, 1878, 31. Bailey's only real rival by 1880 was P. T. Barnum's Greatest Show on Earth, but after just one season of competition the two men agreed to combine their operations. Interestingly enough, their original plan was not to combine the shows, but to simultaneously operate one circus in the United States and another abroad. William L. Slout, *A Royal Coupling: The Historic Marriage of Barnum and Bailey* (San Bernardino, CA: Borgo Press, 2000), 205–8.

111 Sassoon argues that "the US domestic-consumer base was already culturally fragmented in a way that approximated the global one (126)." "On Cultural Markets," *New Left Review* 17 (Sept.–Oct. 2002), 114.

3

THE AMERICAN CIRCUS IN VICTORIAN BRITAIN

BRENDA ASSAEL

The circus in Britain experienced its heyday in the nineteenth century when small and large troupes traipsed up and down the kingdom touring villages, towns, and large cities. Americans always had a role to play, contributing to small and large companies alike. This article explores the impact that Americans had on the circus in Britain. Its predominant focus is on the influence of P. T. Barnum's Greatest Show on Earth, which first went to Britain in 1889 and then in 1897–99. The scale and extravagance of Barnum's shows had a dramatic effect on the development of the British circus. However, this article insists on placing Barnum's British tours within a broader and more complex interrelationship between the British and American circus. Americans had already been present in the British circus world even before 1889 and Barnum's company had extensive commercial ties with British companies and personnel. Taking a more nuanced approach to Barnum's British tours illuminates the way the circus served as an example of both commercial and cultural hybridity between the United States and Britain at the end of the nineteenth century. Recognizing the complexity of the circus's relationship to the nation-state underlines the messiness of transnational cultural exchange at this time more generally, particularly since British circus culture operated not merely in a national, but also in an imperial, rubric. In the circus, as in other areas, America became Britain's copartner in the cultural project of imperial display and celebration.

Fourteen years before the arrival of the Greatest Show on Earth, the journalist and political radical Thomas Frost published his survey of *Circus Life and Circus Celebrities* (1875). Looking back over the previous half century, Frost was at pains to draw his readers' attention to the close relationship between the American and British circus. Citing famous performers from America in British companies and famous British companies that toured

America, he said the interchange of circus performers between the two countries had existed almost as long as circuses themselves.[1] The circus was, in his eyes, a truly transnational operation, one that depended on an international pool of talent and the free market that enabled the relatively uninhibited movement of labor.

British circuses in the mid-nineteenth century were keen to incorporate American performers who were both specialized and exotic. A particular contribution made by American performers in the British circus took the form of minstrelsy, a phenomenon that could be seen as early as the 1840s. In some cases troupes like the American Comic Operatic Company, which performed at the Circus Royal in Hull in 1843, went by such names in order to heighten their exotic and "genuine" allure. The company promised a grand Ethiopian entertainment, including "a variety of new songs, refrains, dances, odd sayings, etc."[2] The intermingling of "American" and "Ethiopian" nationalities was seen elsewhere. Nearly two years later at Astley's Amphitheatre in London, which was the premier venue for circus entertainment, the Southern American Minstrels featured prominently in the circus's posters promising the appearance of "Messrs. Woolcot, Robbins, Parker and Ring in their American Nationalities and Ethiopian Entertainment" (*fig. 3.1*).[3] In contrast to whites (who may have been British or American), black artists were conceived as culturally monolithic, their identities constructed by the advertisers who promoted them. "American" and "Ethiopian" were merely nationalities that were imposed on them and could change to suit the market and popular taste. Their homogenous exoticism was made explicit by a band of American–Ethiopian serenaders who promised to present the Dundee public in the 1860s with miscellaneous "negro vagaries and strange sayings."[4] The appeal of such artists was not their genuine identity as blacks (of whatever national description) but their ability to parody manners and physical traits of the race they professed to represent.[5]

The performance of blackness had particular appeal to the Victorians, who were fascinated by both the reinforcement and confusion of racial distinctions.[6] By playing Jim Crow and performing ditties like "Stop dat Knocking" or "Black-eyed Susan" with "bones" and banjoes as instruments, they fed a mania for live ethnographic displays. When "white niggers," that is, white performers whose faces were painted black, appeared, the power relations embedded in the display were subverted as racial categories were inverted.[7] One female member from a troupe of Christy Minstrels described to the diarist Arthur Munby the ease with which she managed this act of racial switching: "It takes us half an hour to colour, sir . . . another half hour to wash it off." With their makeup removed, Munby's interviewee revealed, "we're mostly English, but one or two are American," suggesting a kind of international fellowship of racial impersonation.[8] Describing the way in which the minstrel catered to the British public's taste in this regard, the Reverend Haweis said, "English fun is mixed up with negro humour."[9]

Whereas in America minstrel song and dance addressed issues about slavery and plantation life, in Britain this artistic form spoke to an altogether different set of concerns related to imperialism, civilization, and, to some extent, racial fantasy. After observing the Christy Minstrels, Munby recalled "a grown woman with black face and bosom and unctuous arms playing elegantly upon that highly civilized instrument [the piano]." Meanwhile, those around her played the violin and "bones," while, "curious[ly]," others sang sweetly and tenderly, suggesting that their constructed outward vulgarity clashed with their inner refinement.[10] This juxtaposition of low and high, unnatural and natural, black and white, therefore had meaning that went above and beyond mere curiosity or innocent fun. Rather, it fulfilled a desire to invert characteristics of "civilized" peoples in order to affirm British civility and the benefits of the nation's civilizing project. Spectators were therefore implicated as subjects of power along with the black performers, who were subjects to that power and therefore unequal in this exercise, in which meaning was created from representation.

The presence of American performers in the British circus was not confined to minstrelsy. Other performers who specialized in more routine circus acts found employment as well, a fact borne out from the evidence of census returns. Censuses were held every ten years in Britain and their main value for social historians has been in providing information about the settled population. However, sometimes the census was recorded at the very same time that a circus was touring in a particular town, providing us with otherwise unrecoverable data about where circus performers were born and what their age and marital status was. Census records from Crewkerne in Somerset in 1871, for instance, reveal that while the majority of performers in the Powell, Footit, and Clarke's circus were British born, there was present among the troupe a thirty-eight-year-old tightrope artist from France, but also a thirty-five-year-old female performer from New York City.[11] Seven years later, the troupe then in Cork and renamed Powell and Clarke's Paragon Circus had another employee from New York City, an equestrian called Wilson, who was listed as commanding a tidy sum of four pounds for one week's work, according to the company's receipt book.[12] Wilson's earnings reflected not only the high status of equestrians among all circus

▶ *Fig. 3.1.* "Astley's," December 30, 1844. Playbill. Astley's Files, © Victoria and Albert Museum, London

Assael

performers, but perhaps also the value attached to American performers like himself. These two Americans performing in British troupes were not exceptional. Among the thirty-two troupes traveling in Britain in this period, there were at least sixty-eight American artists. So apparently ubiquitous were they that a correspondent for the *Era*, an entertainment and sporting weekly, warned that the profession is "overstocked" and counseled artists in America hungry for work in Britain to make other plans because the market for them was so saturated.[13]

In addition to these individuals in British companies, there were also American companies from the midcentury point that toured Britain. In 1859, Myers' Great American Circus offered "extraordinary equestrian galas during the Whitsun Holidays!" at the Pavilion Theatre in London's Whitechapel Road (*fig. 3.2*). The Great United States Circus that toured in 1857 impressed contemporaries with its procession of carriages driven by forty cream-colored horses. It also featured a large troupe of artists that included Bedouin Arabs "whose feats of eccentric agility are truly outstanding" and "a tribe of North American Indians … who excite the wonder of the country folks by their strange costume and manners."[14] However, it would be unwise to assume at this point that Americans had cornered the market in large-scale performances. Domestic circuses remained competitive into the next two decades in terms of scale and spectacle. For example, in the same year that the Great United States Circus toured, and several months earlier, Messrs. Cooke's traveling circus also had a procession of forty horses being driven by William Henry Cooke, who was both manager and highly accomplished equestrian performer.[15] Clearly if American circuses were to compete, they had to raise the bar higher in scale and spectacle.

In this regard the arrival of P. T. Barnum and James Bailey's Greatest Show on Earth in 1889 marked a turning point in the history of the circus in Britain (*fig. 3.3*). It consisted of "a thousand of the rarest shows from everywhere" with 1,200 employees and 380 superb horses. According to the show's posters, the cost of opening the show at London's Olympia Theatre was 500,000 dollars, although one writer from the *Era* felt obliged to introduce a note of skepticism, estimating the cost in the region of 60,000 pounds (approximately 288,000 dollars, a figure significantly less) (*fig. 3.4*).[16]

Under Barnum's majestic arena, there were three full-size rings and between each ring there was a full-size stage.[17] In addition, there was a menagerie and sideshow. After the presentation of various specialized acts that included juggling, contortionism, and traditional races around the hippodrome track, the Greatest Show on Earth concluded with the drama *Nero; or, the Destruction of Rome*, by producer and director Imre Kiralfy (*fig. 3.5*). It was a unique event by British circus standards, although it had an affinity with a tradition of equestrian spectacle commonly found in amphitheaters across Britain since the previous century.[18] A musical score was specially written for the piece by the Milanese composer Angelo Venanzi, who conducted it in person. *Nero* had numerous tableaux, hundreds of participants including several hundred ballet girls, and ended with the consumption of Rome by fire.[19] Posters claimed that this exhibition cost 75,000 dollars in scenery alone. Barnum's lavish show at Olympia lasted from six until midnight, at least for those who were committed to getting their money's worth. Many did, leading one *Era* reviewer to note that the show rendered patrons "weary and worn, [as they] walked home—and so unseemly was the hour, and so few and far

TRIUMPHAL.

between the conveyances, that a good many of them *had* to walk."[20]

Such quibbles aside, the press response to the show was extremely positive, not to say fulsome. Indeed, Barnum expressed a general satisfaction about the press reviews of his show. So impressed was he with a review of the show in the London

Fig. 3.3. *Funny Folks*: *The Comic Companion to the Newspaper*, November 16, 1889. McCaddon Collection of the Barnum & Bailey Circus, box 31, folder 9; Department of Rare Books and Special Collections, Princeton University Library

Times that he wrote to a friend in January 1890 that "money could not have purchased it."[21] He also delighted in the fact that "the lesser branches of the press & all shades of the people from crown to cabin are unanimous in praise of the pluck & enterprise [of the show]."[22] Besides royals like the Prince and Princess of Wales and the King of Greece, prominent political and diplomatic figures attended opening night at Olympia including Lord Randolph Churchill, Lord Rosebery, Henry White (Secretary of the U.S. Legation), General John C. New (U.S. Consul-General), and William Gladstone and his wife (*fig. 3.6*).[23] The toast of the town, Barnum was honored at a banquet at the Hotel Victoria two days before, an affair that was presided over by the Earl of Kilmorey and attended by about two hundred friends.[24] Journalist George Augustus Sala made the opening toast, equating Barnum with great historical figures: "Mr Barnum ... had had predecessors. When Julius Caesar crossed the Rubicon was not that a show? Was not Alexander the Great a showman? ... But their shows were the shedding of blood, and with all the misery, and wretchedness, and sinfulness of war." But Barnum's was "eminently pacific and instructive." Barnum replied that "for more than half a century he had done his best to elevate and refine public amusements."[25]

Almost ten years later, Barnum's circus came back, but without Barnum, who died in 1891. This time, it did more than just perform at Olympia in London for sixteen weeks. Now under the exclusive management of James Bailey (who kept Barnum's name in the circus's title), the show stayed in Britain for two years between 1897 and 1899. It performed at Olympia during the winter season 1897–98 and 1898–99 (running from December to early April). It then toured throughout the provinces, as was customary for most circuses in Britain, during the spring seasons (running from April to November) in 1898 and 1899. Special excursion trains took daytrippers from nearby towns and the countryside to see Barnum's show. During the 1898 tour, when Barnum's performed in Liverpool, for example, a

▲ *Fig. 3.4*. Detail of "P. T. Barnum's Greatest Show on Earth, Exhibiting Only at the Olympia in London," 1889. Poster. Mander and Mitchenson Collection, University of Bristol/ArenaPAL

▲ *Fig. 3.5*. "Barnum & Bailey's Greatest Show on Earth, Excursions from Everywhere," ca. 1889–90. Poster, printed by the Strobridge Lithographing Company, Cincinnati. Collection of the John and Mable Ringling Museum of Art, Tibbals Collection, ht2000126

city that boasted several local circuses, including the long-established Hengler's, "incoming trains were crowded, and even river luggage boats had to be requisitioned in order to convey the multitudes from the Cheshire side of the Mersey."[26] An extraordinary number of people must have experienced the 1898 tour given that the company visited 71 cities and towns over a period of 186 days and gave 362 performances. It traveled 2,976 miles, the longest journey lasting 208 miles while the shortest was only 5 (*fig. 3.7*).[27] The tenting season of 1899 was similarly ambitious.[28] With 74 cars full of animals, artists, scenery and costumes, as well as staff to support the operation, moving the show was akin to mounting a military operation.[29] Observing the intricacies involved in the task, one observer in Edinburgh, alluding to the war in the Sudan, remarked that "the War Office might take a tip, if they have not done so, of the general arrangement."[30] The potential affinity between large-scale military operations and Barnum's provincial tours was noted by other contemporaries. A season later, when the troupe performed in Berlin, Barnum's superintendent of animals observed that "the members of the [Kaiser's] Commanding Officers Staff took a great deal of interest in what they termed the 'wonderful organization of the show' which to them was far more interesting than the performances."[31]

If contemporaries had not already noticed the ubiquitous posters advertising Barnum's circus, then the arrival of the vast fleet at the railway station helped drum up interest. Many waited literally at

Fig. 3.6. "P. T. Barnum Appearing at Olympia London before His Royal Highness the Prince of Wales and Other Members of the Royal Family," 1889. Poster, printed by the Strobridge Lithographing Company, Cincinnati. Collection of the John and Mable Ringling Museum of Art, Tibbals Collection, ht2004443

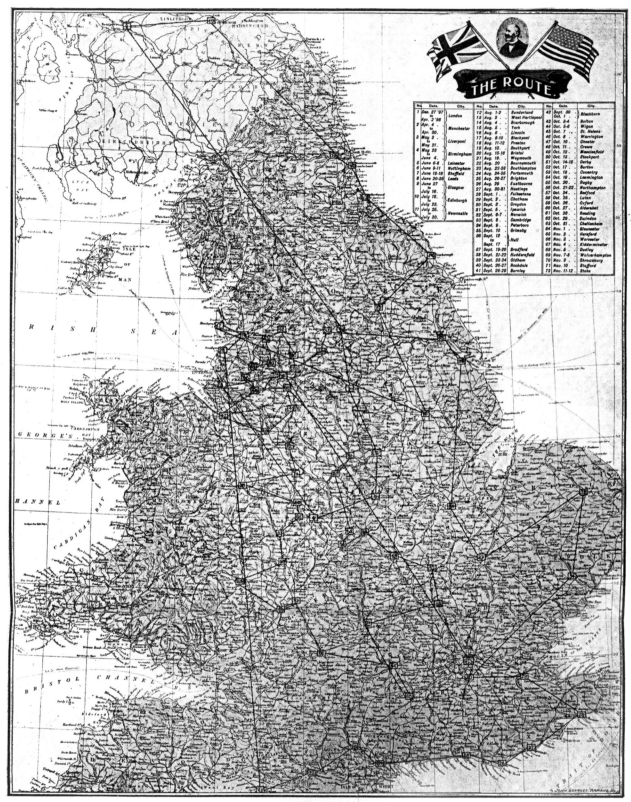

THE ROUTE

No.	Date.	City.	No.	Date.	City.	No.	Date.	City.
1	Dec. 27 '97	London	12	Aug. 1-2	Sunderland	42	Sept. 30	Blackburn
	Apr. 2 '98		13	Aug. 3	West Hartlepool		Oct. 1	
2	Apr. 4	Manchester	14	Aug. 4	Scarborough	43	Oct. 3-4	Bolton
	Apr. 30.		15	Aug. 5	York	44	Oct. 5-6	Wigan
3	May 2	Liverpool	16	Aug. 6	Lincoln	45	Oct. 7	St. Helens
	May 21		17	Aug. 8-10	Blackpool	46	Oct. 8	Warrington
4	May 23	Birmingham	18	Aug. 11-12	Preston	47	Oct. 10	Chester
	June 4.		19	Aug. 13.	Southport	48	Oct. 11	Crewe
5	June 6-8	Leicester	20	Aug. 15-16	Bristol	49	Oct. 12	Macclesfield
6	June 9-11	Nottingham	21	Aug. 19	Weymouth	50	Oct. 13	Stockport
7	June 13-16	Sheffield	22	Aug. 20	Bournemouth	51	Oct. 14-15	Derby
8	June 20-25	Leeds	23	Aug. 22-23	Southampton	52	Oct. 17	Burton
9	June 27	Glasgow	24	Aug. 24-25	Portsmouth	53	Oct. 18	Coventry
	July 16.		25	Aug. 26-27	Brighton	54	Oct. 19	Leamington
10	July 18.	Edinburgh	26	Aug. 29	Eastbourne	55	Oct. 20	Rugby
	July 23.		27	Aug. 30-31	Hastings	56	Oct. 21-22	Northampton
11	July 25.	Newcastle	28	Sept. 1.	Folkestone	57	Oct. 24	Bedford
	July 30.		29	Sept. 2.	Chatham	58	Oct. 25	Luton
			30	Sept. 3.	Croydon	59	Oct. 26	Oxford
			31	Sept. 5.	Ipswich	60	Oct. 27	Aldershot
			32	Sept. 6-7	Norwich	61	Oct. 28	Reading
			33	Sept. 8.	Cambridge	62	Oct. 29	Swindon
			34	Sept. 9.	Peterboro	63	Oct. 31	Cheltenham
			35	Sept. 10	Grimsby	64	Nov. 1	Gloucester
36	Sept. 12 to Sept. 17	Hull				65	Nov. 2	Hereford
						66	Nov. 3	Worcester
						67	Nov. 4	Kidderminster
37	Sept. 19-20	Bradford				68	Nov. 5	Dudley
38	Sept. 21-22	Huddersfield				69	Nov. 7-8	Wolverhampton
39	Sept. 23-24	Oldham				70	Nov. 9	Shrewsbury
40	Sept. 26-27	Rochdale				71	Nov. 10	Stafford
41	Sept. 28-29	Burnley				72	Nov. 11-12	Stoke

3* — Pages 18-19

Fig. 3.7. "The Route," 1898 map from Harvey L. Watkins, *Four Years
in Europe: The Barnum & Bailey Greatest Show on Earth in the Old World*
(Paris: P. DuPont, 1901), after p. 18. CircusWorld Museum, CWi-2322

the gates, as at Leeds, where "arrangements had been made to deal with the remarkable traffic."[32] After the circus was unloaded, a music band driven by a team of horses led the procession, which was composed of vans containing lions, tigers, panthers, a hyena, bears, zebras, wolves, and a "splendid drove of camels and dromedaries," their trainers and hundreds of other artists, "allegorical cars," a steam organ and 279 "fine horses."[33] So popular was it that in Nottingham, for example, "all the schools in the city were closed for the morning, and factories, warehouses and shops appeared to have suspended operations to give employees an opportunity of witnessing the procession.... Children of all ages were there in their tens of thousands, sandwiched between everybody else's legs."[34] Contemporary press reports, far from condemning the circus as a mindless distraction, asserted that school age children might actually benefit from exposure to Barnum's spectacles. A reporter in Birmingham asserted that "the school boy or school girl may have in a single tour of the collection [of Barnum's menagerie] a lesson in zoology, surpassing in interest and practical effect any that could be imparted by learned dominies in a whole month."[35]

In Nottingham, on the opening day (a Thursday which was traditionally a half-day holiday) 21,000 people attended the show and the next day, 24,000 went.[36] Given that the whole population of Nottingham, including the borough, was approximately 212,000, these attendance figures—not just the gathering at the procession which was likely more—amounted to over ten percent of the population. Among the animal acts, audiences saw seals, elephants, pigs, monkeys, dogs, and goats perform anthropomorphic stunts. Human acts included balancing, both in the air and on the ground, feats of strength, clowning, tumbling, contortionism, and

juggling. There were also freak exhibitions (absent in the British circus) featuring both humans and animals—that could be viewed in a sideshow before the performance began (fig. 3.8). Capitalizing on their novelty, Jo-Jo, "the human Skye terrier, with a face absolutely covered with hair like an animal's,"[37] the Legless Man, and others sold cartes-de-visite of themselves that later circulated throughout provincial households and served as a reminder that the Barnum circus was more than just a passing show.[38] The company's wide popularity during the two tours was experienced throughout the kingdom, with a scale of participation equivalent to the major national celebrations accompanying the sixtieth anniversary of Queen Victoria's accession to the throne, which had taken place in 1897. After seeing Barnum's in St. Helen's in 1898, one local reporter noted that "by the excitement one could easily imagine that it was the occasion of a Royal visit, or a repetition of the Diamond Jubilee proceedings."[39]

In spite of an elaborate and sophisticated public relations machinery, not all the publicity attending to Barnum's tours was favorable. In 1889 the company was entangled in a number of labor disputes. Fleeting references in the Era reveal at least four separate cases in which Barnum's employees in Britain took their grievances to local police courts. One case involved the unfair dismissal of a group of wrestlers who received no compensation.[40] It was claimed that Barnum took advantage of the fact that they were illiterate by forcing them to sign a document that led to their willing "resignation." In another case of unfair dismissal, a group of female dressers complained that their engagement was cut short though they were promised sixteen weeks of work.[41] A third case involved the dubious employment of two child apprentices without the written permission of their dance master, which was required according to the deed of their apprenticeship.[42] More seriously—from a public relations point of view—a group of eighty-three casual laborers called a strike and boycotted the show, after Barnum had reduced their pay while expecting them to perform the same work.[43] Their campaign gained traction through its association with a local trade union chapter in Hammersmith, which added to the pressure. Barnum offered these employees a higher wage, albeit not as high as their original one, an offer that was roundly rejected.[44] Barnum's was a cynical move, given that he allowed no concessions to the other workers who were less organized and attracted less publicity. In all cases, Barnum relied on the vulnerability of these individuals in order to get them to work on terms that suited him. Barnum's high-handed response to issues of condition and pay brought him into conflict with the rising power of organized labor in Britain, which was demonstrated by the successful strike by the London matchgirls (1888), the London Dock Strike (1889), and the emergence of so-called New Unionism, that attempted to reach beyond the traditional union constituency of skilled workers and sought to organize casual and unskilled labor. Barnum's management ethos aligned him with other forms of big business rather than traditional family-run circuses, which were usually able to resolve their problems with employees through a less coercive, more paternalistic, approach.

Fig. 3.8. "The Olympian Freaks, London." The Barnum & Bailey Circus, ca. 1897–98. Photograph. McCaddon Collection of the Barnum & Bailey Circus, box 27; Department of Rare Books and Special Collections, Princeton University Library

A decade later, Barnum's show returned as both a resident show at Olympia during the winter seasons of 1897–98 and 1898–99 and a touring show that went into the provinces during the tenting seasons of 1898 and 1899, as stated earlier. As a tenting operation, the company ran foul of at least one community it visited. The behavior of its laborers in setting up and tearing down the show in Newcastle in 1898 led to the Town Council's attempt to block its entry the following year. Minutes from the Newcastle Town Council meetings in this period provide a glimpse of local opinion about Barnum's show, and throw into sharp relief the problems associated with this big tenting operation whose management was sometimes lackadaisical. These minutes also offer a markedly different account of the circus from that usually found in local newspapers. The reason for the Newcastle Town Council's involvement in the discussion about the proposed visit of Barnum's circus stemmed from the fact that circuses normally paid a ground rent to local councils for the use of town squares or other public areas. In 1898 Barnum's paid 150 pounds to rent the Town Moor for six days, but after it left it was found that the company "did very serious damage to the ground and workmen were actually seen hacking it up with a joiners' ordinary axe." The consequence was that "the ground cost an enormous sum for reinstating [it]," amounting to roughly 55 pounds. When, a year later, Bailey made an application for use of the same site, he found that the councilors were seriously divided. Council discussions lasted for several months, before Bailey was finally granted permission to occupy the grounds. There was some feeling among the councilors that because the Barnum circus brought so many thousands of visitors to the city, the benefits of the visit outweighed the negatives. What eventually brought the councilors on side,

however, was Bailey's agreement to pay the increased fee of 400 pounds.[45]

Implicit in these disputes over working conditions and ground rents was a sense that the sheer scale of Barnum's operation, while it dazzled many, might also have negative connotations. The high-handed attitude toward employees and local communities revealed, some suggested, a behemoth that was alien to British culture and an affront to domestic traditions and values. Some contemporaries criticized the show for being too big, but also insisted that bigness was essentially a product of being "American." After seeing Barnum's circus perform in 1889 at Olympia, one journalist for the *Saturday Review* wrote: "it is clear that to the American mind 'greatest' and 'largest' convey precisely the same meaning." For this reviewer, quantity by no means equaled quality because if it did, the showman "would no doubt have hesitated before he adopted the grandiloquent title for his wonderful show of good, bad and indifferent materials now being exhibited at Olympia."[46]

If some contemporaries in 1889 were concerned that the sheer scale of Barnum's enterprise masked its uneven quality, and even potential mediocrity, a decade later some commentators appeared to be weary of the company's ubiquity on the ground and overexposure in print. When the company visited Norwich during the 1898 season, a local reporter in the paper *Daylight* noted: "all the week long, it's been Barnum for breakfast, Barnum for dinner and for tea, and I guess we're all getting mighty tired of it."[47] *Daylight* strove to remind its readers of the attractions of the home-grown circus. It drew attention to a show by the small British troupe Gilbert's Circus that was taking place in nearby Great Yarmouth. Its acts included "Watson's cinematographe" and "special engagement of Animata, the Great Illuminated Globe Performer, the only one in the world outside of Barnum and Bailey's."[48] However, this journalistic effort at commercial and cultural protectionism proved difficult to sustain. For all their qualms the writers at *Daylight* were obliged, albeit grudgingly, to acknowledge the popular appeal of Barnum's circus, while the paper's proprietors could hardly turn away the extensive revenue benefits of carrying the compellingly large advertisements which routinely promoted the Greatest Show on Earth in the British press.[49]

Significantly, acerbic asides, like those which surfaced from time to time in both national (*Saturday Review*) and local (*Daylight*) newspapers, rarely developed into a full-blown repudiation of Barnum's circus. One might have expected more discursive attempts to contrast the virtues of home-grown circuses, with their established, almost organic, ties to British performers, communities, and audiences, with the vices of the alien, arriviste, American circus. In fact, such starkly explicit anti-Americanism in regard to Barnum's show was rare in the British press at this time. The reason for this may simply be a consequence of the undoubted popularity of Barnum's show with the British public, or (more cynically) it may suggest the American circus's success in courting newspaper owners and editors. However, it also speaks to the myriad and complex ways in which Barnum's British venture was entwined with a wider circus culture in Britain. Far from being a static, not to say moribund, form of entertainment, the British circus was characterized by expansion and transformation throughout the nineteenth century. Barnum's tours worked in combination with, and even within, this home-grown development.

Barnum entered a circus market in Britain that had already been flourishing for several decades. Whereas, in the 1840s, there were roughly ten companies in Britain, by the 1860s, the figure was twenty-one, and by the 1890s there were approximately seventy-four.[50] Much of this growth can be accounted for by a new, commercially aggressive circus trade led by a new generation of managers and entrepreneurs. In the 1840s most of the troupes were descended from old fairground families, but by the 1860s approximately half of the companies belonged to a new breed of impresarios. By the end of the century, most managers were first generation and had companies in industrial towns where demand was high.[51] Their companies were also larger than the traditional companies in the earlier part of the century. Circus proprietors increasingly sought personnel from beyond the traditional ties of family and acquaintances by advertising in the *Era* and other papers. Far from Barnum arriving and transforming a passive British circus culture, it was Britain's existing dynamic circus market that brought Barnum into play.

The growth of the British circus was not just about numbers, however. The scale and content of the performances themselves were similarly characterized by expansion and innovation. Increased capital led to a diversification of circus programs in the 1880s and 1890s. In particular, wild animals became a star feature of some circuses, notably George Sanger's, which invested in procuring lions, tigers, and elephants from far corners of the globe. Legal influences like the introduction of protective legislation for child performers in 1879 and the lack of such protection for wild animals contributed to this development.[52] So while Barnum clearly had a considerable impact on the British circus, it is highly likely that these changes would have occurred anyway. Even the scale of Barnum's was not entirely unprecedented. George Sanger, for instance, insisted his three-ring circus predated Barnum's by several decades.[53] Even when managers appeared to be adopting the rubric of Barnum's shows, they were keen (inevitably given the boosterism that was endemic in the culture of circus managers) to emphasize their own authorship and independent development.

Moreover, the boundary between Barnum's circus and home-grown circuses was distinctly porous. At a commercial level, Barnum employed rank and file British workers, as discussed earlier with reference to the court cases brought against him in 1889. (Based on the facts established in court, neither the child apprentices, female dressers, casual male workers, nor the wrestlers were brought over from America, but were instead employed in Britain, which is why their grievances stood up in a British court.) Barnum also employed star British artists like Alfred Clarke Jr., who performed in a solo somersault and bareback jockey act for eleven months during the 1897–98 season. The ubiquitous contract defining terms and conditions of labor changed the dynamics between employer and artist in this period, making their dealings more formal and legally binding. In this case, Barnum's circus demanded Clarke's "faithful fulfillment" of his engagement by insisting that he sign an employment contract. The agreement, which granted him a salary of 20 pounds weekly, allowed the management to retain a portion of this sum as insurance of his good conduct until he had completed the engagement.[54] After his stint at Barnum's, Clarke went to work for other British troupes that demanded the same degree of loyalty and made similar arrangements to ensure it, signifying the extent to which employment practices in the circus—at least among stars—were becoming standardized in this period.[55]

Barnum's circus hired other established British stars, but not all of them were human or even alive. The most famous was Jumbo the ele-

JUMBO, THE PRIDE AND GLORY OF ENGLAND.

JUMBO, ENGLAND'S LOSS and AMERICA'S GAIN

Editorial from the London Telegraph, February 22d, 1882.

phant, who had been the darling of the British public—from the queen to the most humble servant—since the London Zoological Society acquired him in 1865 and put him on display in the London Zoo in Regent's Park. Barnum had long been interested in buying the elephant who was said to be the largest of his kind in captivity. Despite popular resistance in Britain, Barnum's offer proved more than Jumbo's trustees could refuse, and his life began anew once the showman purchased him and sent him to New York to be exhibited in his show at Madison Square Garden in the spring of 1882 (*fig. 3.9*). He performed for four seasons as the undisputed star of the Greatest Show on Earth. In 1885, after performing in St. Thomas, Ontario, Jumbo was hit from behind by an unscheduled train while he was walking, along with the other elephants in the show, down a railway track. Turning disaster to profit, Barnum arranged to salvage Jumbo's hide and skeleton, which were both exhibited in the 1886 season, and again in the 1889–90 winter season

Fig. 3.9. "Jumbo, England's Loss and America's Gain," February 22, 1882. Unknown newspaper clipping originally published in the *London Telegraph*. Bridgeport Public Library History Center

when the (now) "double Jumbo" went to London. Exploiting the elephant's popularity with the British public and their fascination with curious exhibitions, Barnum invited all to see "each ponderous bone" in Jumbo's skeleton "set up in proper place."[56] The skeleton and hide were then sent back to the United States after the show at Olympia ended, the former to be housed in the American Museum of Natural History while the latter was sent to Barnum's "pet" museum in Tufts College, where it was incinerated in an accidental fire almost one hundred years later.[57] Jumbo's sad story has more than mere sentimental purchase. The appeal of Jumbo on both sides of the Atlantic suggests that Barnum operated in a transnational world of popular entertainment, in which local cultures were rendered portable and comprehensible to audiences in more than one country.

That said, Barnum's internationalism was not indiscriminate. He took care to sequester aspects of national culture that resonated with Britons, particularly those associated with empire. Popular culture in late-nineteenth-century Britain was, as extensive scholarship has demonstrated, deeply

▲ *Fig. 3.10.* "The Barnum & Bailey Greatest Show on Earth, *The Mahdi; or for the Victoria Cross,*" ca. 1897–98. Poster, printed by the Strobridge Lithographing Company, Cincinnati. Cincinnati Art Museum, Gift of the Strobridge Lithographing Company, 1965.817

▶ *Fig. 3.11.* Principal characters in Barnum & Bailey's spectacular drama, *The Mahdi*, performed at Olympia, London, March 22, 1898. Photograph. Circus World Museum, CWi-2292

inscribed with imperial referents. Music hall acts, popular song, zoos, imperial expositions, and juvenile fiction, in myriad ways, celebrated Britain's place at the center of a worldwide empire.[58] Barnum and Bailey were clearly conscious of the appeal of popular imperialism, not to say jingoism, in Britain, and incorporated into their shows acts that dealt with race and empire. These displays revealed a confident familiarity with often highly specific and topical narratives of imperial adventure and spectacle. The most notable example of this was *The Mahdi; or for the Victoria Cross* performed at Olympia during the winter of 1897–98 (*fig. 3.10*). This show combined the tradition of the romance-adventure with a large-scale reenactment of a military encounter between British soldiers and Sudanese rebels during the ill-fated Sudan campaign of 1884–85, during which British-led forces had been defeated by the Mahdi, a self-proclaimed Islamic messianic redeem-

er, and the British Commander General Gordon had been killed. "The Mahdi" was authored by Bennet Gordon Burleigh, who had observed the 1884–85 campaign firsthand as war correspondent for the *Daily Telegraph*, but, as a Scot who had served as a mercenary in the American Civil War, also bore testimony to the complex interrelationship between Britain and the United States in this period.

"Faithfully and truthfully depicting actual scenes" from the war, the spectacle featured at least sixteen Sudanese, one of whom was said to have acted as messenger between General Gordon and the Mahdi during the siege of Khartoum, while another "native" claimed to have been rescued from a slave merchant by the imperial martyr-hero himself.[59] To add to the verisimilitude of the scene "actual officers and men of Her Majesty's force at present in England" played the members of the British cavalry and "are mounted, equipped and accoutred exactly

Atkins' has lately been 'drubbing' the fellow tribesmen of the former, and is preparing to do so again."[62]

However, the American circus's incorporation of British imperial motifs and topics was not merely a commercial response to a particular national constituency. The celebration of Anglo-Saxon dominion over peoples deemed insufficiently civilized to warrant self-determination was hardly unique to Britain in the decades in which Barnum's circus toured. Indeed, Barnum's British tours coincided with a sharpening of imperial–racial discourse in the United States. *The Mahdi* appeared, not merely in the same year that British forces returned to the Sudan to avenge Gordon's death, but also immediately prior to the United States' military campaigns in Cuba and the Philippines. Significantly, Barnum's circus's next offering at Olympia, staged in the winter of 1898–99, was a reenactment of *America's Great Naval Victory at Santiago, and the Destruction of the Spanish Fleet*, which had taken place the previous July. While one reviewer was a little underwhelmed by the technical aspects of this "grand historically correct water entertainment," he conceded that it appealed "very strongly to popular tastes and prevailing sentiment."[63] Taken together, *The Mahdi* and the *Great Naval Victory at Santiago* reveal a common transatlantic rubric of imperialism. During the Spanish-American War, many advocates of American expansionism cited the British as a model of imperial and racial hegemony worthy of emulation. Conversely, many British imperialists encouraged America to take up the "white man's burden," a phrase first coined by Rudyard Kipling in 1899 in a poem specifically intended to urge the United States to formalize its control over the Philippines.[64] British imperial boosters sought to repair, and in some cases even reverse, the schism between what were regarded as the two main branches of the

as if they were in active service in the Soudan" (*fig. 3.11*).[60] According to the program, every single accessory, from the bridle of the horses to the jewels in the warriors' swords, was said to have been transferred from East Africa to Olympia for the exhibition. The narrative was punctuated by several interludes in which "natives" performed on musical instruments and danced against a backcloth of idealized reconstructions of the desert villages from which they purportedly originated (*fig. 3.12*). By playing themselves, these actors thereby "authenticated" this representation of recent history.[61] When the circus went on tour in the provinces in the spring of 1898, several of the "native" performers in *The Mahdi* reappeared, as part of the procession prior to, and in the sideshow that accompanied, the performance. A reviewer in Leeds lauded the "truly unique sight" of fifteen camels on which "rode real Dervishes and Soudanese." He added, in what was presumably a reference to the punitive campaign to restore British authority that was currently being mounted in the Sudan, that it "would doubtless cross the minds of many of the spectators that the British 'Tommy

Fig. 3.12. "Mahdists" who performed in Barnum & Bailey's Circus at Olympia, London, 1897. Photograph. McCaddon Collection of the Barnum & Bailey Circus, box 27; Department of Rare Books and Special Collections, Princeton University Library

Anglo-Saxon world that had taken place at the end of the eighteenth century.[65] If such political ambitions were ultimately not fulfilled (not least because America, as a republic, remained uncomfortable with imperialism, at least in its formal sense), circus performance in this period dramatized a shared commitment to an imperial reading of the world.

The presence of imperial motifs in the American circus in Britain points to the circus's broader value in suggesting the complex and messy ways in which commerce and culture operated in the nineteenth century. Barnum's tours cannot be viewed in the one-dimensional terms of a foreshadowing of American economic and cultural imperialism in the twentieth century. Far from being an alien juggernaut that rode roughshod over its British competitors, the American circus worked in tandem, and often in cooperation, with the domestic circus, and British popular culture more generally. In fact, the success of Barnum's tours was predicated on an already expanding circus industry, British talent and labor, and an imperial-racial rubric (displayed in both topical referencing of recent events in British and American overseas expansion and in acts of racial caricature that encompassed both Britain's African colonies and the American South) common to the two English-speaking nations. Barnum's British tours demonstrate that the relationship between the British and American circus was characterized not by cultural colonization but by affinity and synergy, an assertion that concurs with recent research that has taken a more nuanced approach to the notion of "Americanization" in modern Europe.[66] The circus revealed the extraordinary extent of cultural hybridity in the Victorian era, and the limitations of the nation in regard to the creation and reproduction of cultural identity. These complex and fluid patterns of cultural exchange existed not merely at the level of discourse.

They were rooted in the material reality of a circus trade that operated within an international market. The circus provides further indication that, in the domains of both business and culture, globalization was a phenomenon that did not have to await the closing of the twentieth century.

Assael

1 Thomas Frost, *Circus Life and Circus Celebrities* (1875, rept. London: Chatto and Windus, 1881), 224–25. Anticipating this remark almost three decades earlier, the actor-manager Francis Courtney Wemyss cited the success of the British troupe Cook's New Circus, which performed at the Chestnut Street Theatre in Philadelphia in 1837. Francis Courtney Wemyss, *Twenty-Six Years of the Life of an Actor and Manager* (Glasgow: R. Griffin and Co., 1847), 288.

2 Poster, Circus Royal, Dock Green Hull, Aug. 29, 30, 1843, MWEZ+ n.c. 7842, Scrapbook, New York Public Library. Quoted from Brenda Assael, *The Circus and Victorian Society* (Charlottesville: University of Virginia Press, 2005), 96.

3 Poster, Astley's, Dec. 30, 1844, Astley's Files, Theatre Museum, London. Quoted from Assael, *Circus*, 96.

4 Poster, ca. Dec. 24, 1866, Printed Ephemera, Minet Library, Lambeth Archives Department, London. Quoted from Assael, *Circus*, 96.

5 Ibid.

6 For scholarship on this subject, see Michael Pickering, "John Bull in Blackface," *Popular Music* 16, no. 2 (May 1997), 181–201; Michael Pickering, "Mock Blacks and Racial Mockery: The Nigger Minstrel and English Imperialism," in *Acts of Supremacy: The British Empire and Stage, 1790–1930*, ed. J. M. MacKenzie, R. Cave and Michael Pickering (Manchester: Manchester University Press, 1991); Simon Featherstone, "The Blackface Atlantic: Interpreting British Minstrelsy," *Journal of Victorian Culture* 3, no. 2 (1998), 234–51.

7 Assael, *Circus*, 95.

8 Munby Diaries, Jan. 13, 1862, vol. 12, Trinity College, Cambridge. Quoted from Assael, *Circus*, 96.

9 Rev. H. R. Haweis, *Music and Morals* (London: Strahan, 1871), 473. Quoted from Assael, *Circus*, 96–98.

10 Munby Diaries, Dec. 28, 1861, vol. 11. Trinity College Cambridge. Quoted from Assael, *Circus*, 98.

11 *Census Return for England and Wales*, 1871, Crewkerne, RG 10/2407, 26, 29, 31, 36, Family Records Centre, London. Quoted from Assael, *Circus*, 42.

12 Entry dated March 19, 1878, Receipt Book for Messrs. Powell and Clarke's Paragon Circus, Winter Season 1877–78, Cork, Ireland. A. H. Coxe Collection, Blythe House, Olympia, Theatre Museum, London.

13 "A London Correspondent," *The Era*, Aug. 4, 1878, 4; Assael, *Circus*, 26.

14 "The Great United States Circus," *Illustrated London News*, Sept. 12, 1857, 260.

15 Assael, *Circus*, 18. Though not a circus, Buffalo Bill's Wild West Show, which arrived in London in 1887, revisited some of these themes dealing with the customs and manners of "tribal Red Indians." For a fuller discussion, see Jonathan D. Martin, "'The Grandest and Most Cosmopolitan Object Teacher: Buffalo Bill's Wild West and the Politics of American Identity, 1833–1899,'" *Radical History Review* 66 (1996), 92–123.

16 1889 poster, "P. T. Barnum's Greatest Show on Earth at Olympia," P. T. Barnum's Circus box, Mander and Mitchenson Collection, Bristol; *The Era*, Oct. 5, 1889, 15. The pound/dollar rate of exchange in this period was roughly 1:4.8. See *Economist*, Oct. 18, 1889, 1341.

17 *Saturday Review* reported there were two platforms, but the *Era* said there were three. See "Barnum's Show," *Saturday Review*, Nov. 16, 1889, 558; "Barnum at Olympia," *The Era*, Nov. 9, 1889, 9.

18 Assael, *Circus*, chap. 2; Marius Kwint, "The Legitimization of the Circus in Late Georgian England," *Past and Present* 174 (2002), 72–115; J. S. Bratton, "British Heroism and the Structure of Melodrama," in J. M. MacKensie, et. al., eds., *Acts of Supremacy*.

19 "Barnum's Show is Here: The Greatest Show on Earth Opens in a Blaze of Glory at Olympia," unknown source, Nov. 1889, Scrapbook 604, 117, Circus Friends Association, Liverpool.

20 "Barnum's Show at Olympia," *The Era*, Nov. 16, 1889, 14.

21 P. T. Barnum to Isaac T. Rogers[?], Jan. 10, 1890. Quoted from A. H. Saxon, *Selected Letters of P. T. Barnum* (New York: Columbia University Press, 1983), 316.

22 Ibid.

23 Clipping, Scrapbook #604, ca. Nov. 1889, p. 117, Circus Friends Association; A. H. Saxon, *P. T. Barnum: The Legend and the Man* (New York: Columbia University Press, 1989), 320–21.

24 "Banquet to Mr. Barnum," (London) *Times*, Nov. 9, 1889, 6.

25 "The Barnum Banquet," *The Era*, Nov. 16, 1889, 14.

26 "Barnum and Bailey's Show," *The Era*, May 7, 1898, 20.

27 Harvey L. Watkins, "Barnum and Bailey and the World," 1897–99 (n.p., n.d.), 19.

28 Ibid., 39. It visited 112 cities and towns, gave 349 performances and traveled 4,073 miles, the longest distance from one town to the next was 113 miles while the shortest was only 6.

29 This figure was given by Clarence Dean, the advance press agent, to a reporter from the *Evening Dispatch* (Edinburgh), July 20, 1898, 4.

30 "Behind the Scenes at Barnum and Bailey's," *Evening Dispatch*, July 20, 1898, 4.

31 Harvey L. Watkins, "Barnum and Bailey and the World," 41; A similar account is given in George Conklin, *The Ways of the Circus* (New York: Harper Brothers, 1921), 277.

32 "Barnum and Bailey's," *Leeds Evening Express*, June 20, 1898, 2.

33 For one local account see "Barnum and Bailey's," *Sheffield Weekly Independent*, June 18, 1898, 14.

34 "Barnum and Bailey in Nottingham," *Nottingham Daily Express*, June 10, 1898, 8.

35 "Barnum and Bailey's Show," *Birmingham Daily Mail*, May 31, 1898, 2.

36 "The Greatest Show," *Nottingham Daily Express*, June 9, 1898, 3.

37 "Barnum and Bailey," *Newcastle Daily Journal*, July 25, 1898, 6.

38 By selling these photographs, the freaks were said to supplement their wages. See Conklin, *The Ways of the Circus*, 273.

39 "The Great Show at St. Helen's," *St. Helen's Reporter*, Oct. 11, 1898, 3; a similar view was expressed when the show visited Burton. See "Barnum in Burton," *Burton Evening Gazette*, Oct. 17, 1898, 3.

40 "Action by Nero's Wrestlers," unknown source, ca. Jan. 1890. Scrapbook 604, 117, Circus Friends Association, Liverpool.

41 "Barnum's Female Dressers," *The Era*, Dec. 7, 1889, 8.

42 "Katti Lanner's Pupils," *The Era*, Nov. 30, 1889, 8. Despite the article's title, the children were apprenticed to Mr. De Francesco. See also "Letter to the Editor: De Francesco v. Barnum," *The Era*, Dec. 7, 1889, 12.

43 "On Strike at Olympia," *The Era*, Nov. 30, 1889, 7.

44 Ibid.

45 Town Council Minutes, March 15, 1899, 409–10 and June 7, 1899, 558, Newcastle Town Council Minutes, 1898–99, Tyne and Wear Archive, Newcastle.

46 "Barnum's Show," *Saturday Review*, Nov. 16, 1889, 558.

47 "The Event of the Week," *Daylight*, Sept. 10, 1898, 1.

48 Advertisement, *Daylight*, Sept. 10, 1898, 12.

49 Advertisement, *Daylight*, Aug. 27, 1898, 16.

50 Assael, *Circus*, 26. These figures are taken from a sample compiled by the author from *The Era*.

51 Ibid.

52 Ibid., 5–6.

53 "The Three Ring Business," *The Era*, Jan. 13, 1894, 13. Quoted from Assael, *Circus*, 6.

54 Barnum and Bailey Circus, employment contract for Alfred Clarke Jr., bareback rider, Sept. 8, 1897, box RP 76/1549, A. H. Coxe Collection, Blythe House, Olympia, Theatre Museum, London. Quoted from Assael, *Circus*, 37.

55 For example, Tower of Varieties and Circus, Birmingham, employment contract, n.d., to commence on Oct. 9, 1899, box RP 76/1549, ibid.; Alhambra Blackpool, Ltd., employment contract, Jan. 24, 1899, ibid.

56 1889 poster, "P. T. Barnum's Greatest Show on Earth at Olympia," P. T. Barnum's Circus box, Mander and Mitchenson Collection, Bristol.

57 Saxon, *P. T. Barnum*, 291–92, 297–300.

58 For a pioneering study see John M. MacKenzie, ed., *Imperialism and Popular Culture* (Manchester: Manchester University Press, 1986).

59 "The Barnum and Bailey Show," (London) *Times*, Dec. 24, 1897, 4.

60 R. F. Hamilton, "The Mahdi; or for the Victoria Cross," program 1897–98 season. A. H. Coxe Collection,

Blythe House, Olympia, Theatre Museum, London.

61 Ibid.; see also Annie E. Coombes, *Reinventing Africa: Museums, Material Culture and Popular Imagination in Late Victorian and Edwardian England* (New Haven: Yale University Press, 1997), 103, 105.

62 "Barnum and Bailey's," *Leeds Evening Express*, June 20, 1898, 3.

63 "Barnum at Olympia," MWEZ +n.c. 7842, n.d., u.s., Scrapbook, New York Public Library.

64 Rudyard Kipling, "The White Man's Burden," *McClure's Magazine* 5.7, no. 4 (Feb. 1899), 363.

65 Stuart Anderson, *Race and Rapprochement: Anglo-Saxonism and Anglo-American Relations, 1895–1904* (Rutherford, NJ: Fairleigh Dickinson University Press, 1981); Duncan Bell, *The Idea of Greater Britain: Empire and the Future of World Order, 1860–1900* (Princeton: Princeton University Press, 2007), 231–59.

66 For example, see Victoria De Grazia, *Irresistible Empire: America's Advance Through Twentieth-Century Europe* (Cambridge, MA: Harvard University Press, 2005).

4

AMERICAN CIRCUS POSTERS

PAUL STIRTON

According to the tagline, the poster for *Sells Brothers' Enormous United Shows* offers us "an exact representation of the many acts in two rings, mid-air, elevated stage and hippodrome." In a dazzling display, bareback riders in Roman costumes are closely followed by teams of chariots racing past in the foreground, while clowns, acrobats, and equestrian acts perform in the first of two rings (*fig. 4.1*). In the middle distance, roller skaters and trick cyclists occupy the elevated stage, above which are trapeze artists and a high-wire act. Farther in the background we can discern another bareback rider and, beyond that, horses, camels, and elephants engaged in yet another race. If this were not sufficient, the text goes on to promise, "[e]very act herein pictured, most positively seen at each exhibition—together with fifty more." These superlatives and the various figures depicted here are a staple of circus advertising. But this scene is remarkable for the quality of its printing and the sheer dynamism with which the performers in the foreground are represented.

Even allowing for exaggeration, this is a piece of dramatic description that retains its sense of overall coherence. It is easy to recognize many of the sources—sporting prints for the horses, salon paintings for the chariot race, and earlier stylized woodcuts for many of the figures in the background. But the whole scene is rendered with a degree of subtlety and skill that was only achieved in American circus posters during the decades on either side of 1900. By the early years of the twentieth century, such sophistication was becoming unnecessary in the field of mass publicity. The finest effects are achieved in composition by establishing a unified space within the massive tent, and in technique by close attention to the tone and texture in the lithographic printing. These are not particularly sophisticated printmaking devices in themselves. Yet this poster differs from most circus advertisements of the period after 1910, which rarely displayed such vigor in the representa-

Detail of fig. 4.25. Norman Bel Geddes Studio. "Ringling Bros. and Barnum & Bailey Circus," ca. 1940s. Poster. Collection of the John and Mable Ringling Museum of Art, Tibbals Collection, ht2001793

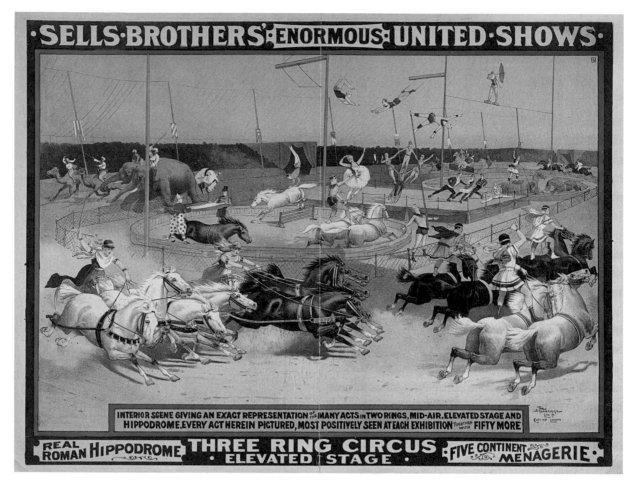

tion of the performers or such subtlety of space and tonality. Even in the early stages, many circus posters relied on emblematic representations of the figures and animals, close-up depictions of individual acts, or overlapping assemblages of different scenes in the manner of a collage. These approaches allowed for simpler description of the main figures and bolder color combinations to catch the eye of the passing spectator. The 1906 Barnum & Bailey poster for Les Rowlandes ("A Dozen Fearless French Riders in a Wild Equestro Coaching Saturnalia") shows off the advantages of the emblematic style (*fig. 4.2*). Not only can the artist fix the image of the central group in an arresting, if rather static, composition, the subsidiary scenes in ovals on either side allow for advertising Bradna and Derrick and The Riding Rooneys. What is lost in space and spectacle is more than compensated in pictorial diversity and the range of recogniz-

able elements: the poster for Les Rowlandes would probably have been easier to identify and read with just a glance.

The treatment of the panoramic interior and the rendering of light and shade, as found in the Sells Brothers' poster, was very much a nineteenth-century conception. It looks back to the high romantic treatment of equestrian and historical scenes that were the ideal of printmakers and artists of the 1820s and 1830s and it was still common in circus advertising of the 1890s before many of the basic features became conventionalized. Full-color lithography had been used widely in circus posters for a decade or two, and the Sells Brothers' image exploited many of the medium's visual effects. Note in particular the soft tonal transitions and the rendering of shadows to suggest space and movement across the foreground groups. The fact that this approach declined

Fig. 4.1. "Sells Brothers' Enormous United Shows, Interior Scene Giving an Exact Representation of the Many Acts in Two Rings, Mid-Air, Elevated Stage and Hippodrome," ca. 1890. Poster, printed by the Strobridge Lithographing Company, Cincinnati. Collection of the John and Mable Ringling Museum of Art, Tibbals Collection, ht2000443

in favor of the bolder emblematic manner of the Les Rowlandes poster may represent a move into a more modern sensibility, a simpler and more elemental mode of mass communication. But it essentially reflects the economic imperatives of advertising, revealing more about the role of the poster as a popular commercial medium than the potential of the artistic and technical means used to design and print it.

A circus poster had to inform and attract as many people as possible—young and old, town dwellers and country folk, illiterate and educated—to the few shows that the circus would hold in any single town. For some, the poster was just glimpsed from a bus or carriage. By 1900 the circus poster's priorities were established: it included striking imagery of the acts or animals, bold text advertising the name of the circus and the act, and a statement or tagline emphasizing how extraordinary the performance would be. These elements could be regarded as a basic primer for advertising in general and it is certainly true that the circus was key in the emerging American advertising industry. But the economic structure of the circus—or the business model, in modern terminology—had a number of unique features, and posters most fully satisfied these needs.

Advertising the Circus

In 1901 an editorial in the advertisers' trade magazine, *Billboard*, reported the publicist M. W. E. Franklin summing up the essence of the circus business in three words: "Printing, Parade and Performance."[1] This alliterative phrase, with its advertising ring, encapsulates the curious structure of the American circus that by this time had grown into a considerable industry. In 1900 there were over seventy circuses on the road in the United States. Many

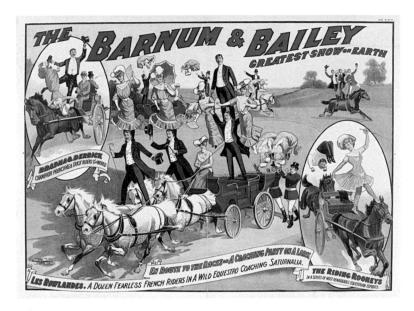

employed huge teams of men, women, and beasts; a complex network of agents, bookers, and scouts; and an advance party to prepare and check the various stops on their long routes by rail and road across the country.[2] During a typical one-day stand, the circus would arrive in the morning, set up by early afternoon, mount a parade through the town, and then give two performances, afternoon and evening, before dismantling and moving on to the next venue. There was no time to build up a local reputation based on word of mouth or newspaper reports, yet there was a pressing need to fill as many seats as possible not only to ensure profits, but to recoup the high cost of maintaining and moving such a large operation across the country. This was why Franklin emphasized "print" first in his description of the circus. Advertising by poster, herald, courier, newspaper, and other means was the main source of communicating the excitement and the specific place and date of the circus in the surrounding area. As a result, circus advertising had to achieve what later market researchers would describe as blanket or saturation

Fig. 4.2. "The Barnum & Bailey Greatest Show on Earth, En Route to the Races or a Coaching Party on a Lark," 1906. Poster, printed by the Strobridge Lithographing Company, Cincinnati. Cincinnati Art Museum, Gift of the Strobridge Lithographing Company, 1965.843

coverage in a very concentrated period of time. Every potential advertising outlet would be tapped, from stories placed in the local newspapers to radio interviews and aerial banners towed by airplanes.[3] However, the key element in every campaign was the poster, which continued to be the principal form of circus advertising from the mid-nineteenth century until it was gradually supplanted by radio and television in the 1950s and 1960s. For over a century, then, the pictorial poster was the medium that shaped the public image of the circus, while also serving as an essential element in the organization's business operation.

It has been estimated that publicity could require about one-third of the entire operating budget of a traveling circus—a considerable portion considering the staggering numbers of performers, construction and transport staff, animal handlers, provisions, and overall administration that was required to keep a circus on the road for several months at a time.[4] The publicity departments mounted massive campaigns, printing huge amounts of material and implementing a network of distribution services to rent billboards and organize billposters according to a very strict schedule. It is within this larger organizational context, rather than by conventional aesthetic standards, that one should consider the development of the circus poster, a genre that generally has been absent from mainstream histories of the poster. Its history is important, considering the number of circus posters that were printed and the role that they played in the development of the specialist show printing industry in America.

Circus publicists largely pioneered the importance of scale, coordination, and diversity in outdoor advertising. By 1884 Barnum & Bailey were in the practice of ordering several huge posters for each venue, often running to 60 or 80 sheets. The record

for the largest outdoor posters was probably the "100 sheeters" ordered by Louis E. Cooke for the W. W. Cole show in 1883; these massive advertisements stretched over 80 feet across.[5] Such colossal single posters, however, were unusual because by the 1880s most of the leading circuses had settled on an elaborate combination of poster sizes in order to take advantage of all types of surfaces. It is in this coordination of a diverse range of sizes and image types for each venue that the achievement of circus poster advertising comes into focus.

The publicity manager's role, therefore, was essential for the success of the circus's season. His first task was to prepare the orders for the printer well in advance of the tour. The order could consist of several designs in many sizes, allowing for numerous combinations of named acts, colors, and imagery. In 1916, for example, the Ringling Brothers' print order called for nine copies each of two separate designs at 24-sheet size; eight copies of four designs at each of 20-sheet, 16-sheet, 12-sheet and 8-sheet sizes; and various combinations at 15-sheet, 6-sheet, 3-sheet, and 2-sheet sizes; as well as a large number of single- and half-sheet window posters. That order added up to 2,688 printed sheets to be posted in one town. In fact, this was quite a modest load. Ringling Brothers' tour of 1911, reaching 143 towns, required almost one million printed sheets in a combination of different posters, heralds (long, narrow handbills) and couriers (booklets).[6] Delivering this bewildering range of printed paper was part of the ongoing logistics preceding the circus's move across the country.

The publicity section, or "advance," traveled ahead in up to three or four railway cars, each one scheduled to arrive at a town in a staggered sequence six, four, and two weeks ahead of the main circus.[7] With deliveries of printed paper waiting at the telegraph offices along the route, the manager of each

Fig. 4.3. Barnum & Bailey advance car and staff at the Eiffel Tower, Paris, 1901. Photograph. McCaddon Collection of the Barnum & Bailey Circus, box 26; Department of Rare Books and Special Collections, Princeton University Library

Fig. 4.4. "Map of Barnum & Bailey's Paris Bill Boards," 1901. McCaddon Collection of the Barnum & Bailey Circus, box 26; Department of Rare Books and Special Collections, Princeton University Library

Fig. 4.5. Bill Stand on the Rue de Louvre, Paris, 1901–2. Photograph. McCaddon Collection of the Barnum & Bailey Circus, box 26; Department of Rare Books and Special Collections, Princeton University Library

advance car then had to dispatch teams of bill-posters, "lithographers" (who found the smaller shop-window locations), carpenters, and banner-men (who placed cloth banners on buildings) to cover the town and surrounding area with advertising.[8] While all available billboards would have been booked by the circus already, the main task of the billposters was to seek out vacant space on buildings, gables, barns, fences, and any other unused surface in the public eye that could support a poster. This was a major spectacle in the small towns across America; there are numerous photographs of the billposters' work showing how they wallpapered their spots, or "stands," with combinations of posters of different sizes and formats. In general, the bill-poster sought to give variety to each stand, making sure that the main pictorial posters were broken up by huge "date sheets" and "streamers" carrying the key information of where and when the circus would open. The date sheets gave just that—the times and place for each venue, often simply the town's name and the date of the performance. This allowed the main lithographic posters to carry the pictorial advertisements that are now best known, and which would remain relevant over the length of the tour.

In the bigger cities the advance campaign was organized along different lines. Restrictions on the free use of vacant walls and the types of advertising material that could be posted called for a different strategy. Cloth banners were more common in built-up areas since they could be hung without marking important buildings. They could also be made in a colossal size, much larger than even the multi-sheet posters that were pasted on barns and fences in rural areas, and were particularly effective on tall buildings, where they were able to dominate the cityscape and be seen by thousands. Even in Paris, Barnum & Bailey's advertising campaign maintained its usual

diversity of scale and type, and the billposters requisitioned every available surface (*figs. 4.3–4.5*). If a city restricted billposting, there were no such restraints in the countryside, where poster advertising was at its most comprehensive and competition at its most fierce.

Out on the road, each advance car was something like a command center. This military analogy was recognized at the time, since the wide-ranging team of billposters, who often had to mount a spoiling operation against the poster campaign of a rival circus, was known as the "brigade"; one of the railway cars in the advance was called the "skirmish" car. Given the scale and complexity of these publicity operations, it becomes apparent why the circus is often seen as a training ground for the developing advertising industry in America. It certainly guided successive generations of promoters and publicity managers who were adept at planning and commissioning advertising material for posters, newspapers, and eventually radio and television.

The Status of the Circus Poster

Of all areas in popular graphics and printmaking, circus posters have received little attention from those outside of the narrow field of circus history and memorabilia. Even in the expanding study of printed ephemera and graphic collectibles, only rarely do circus graphics receive much attention, and nothing comparable to the proportion of their output by nineteenth and early twentieth-century American printers. To this day, poster auctions rarely feature circus themes, and one is more likely to encounter Polish Cyrk posters of the 1950s and 1960s than the mainstream American circus posters that were produced by the millions every year for over a century. The

problem may be their very ubiquity; the sheer number that were printed and posted throughout the United States has tended to make them seem over-familiar and conventional. But this would not explain why they rarely appear in poster exhibitions or in the collections of museums and galleries.

Instead, the reason for the neglect of the circus poster may lie in the critical history of posters in general which, in the United States at least, has tended to exclude this type from serious discussion or analysis. It is not simply a modern problem. In 1903 a test case was brought to the Supreme Court by the Courier Printing Company under the name of George Bleistein in an attempt to copyright their designs for circus posters. One of their clients, Benjamin Wallace of the Great Wallace Show, having run out of the original posters produced by Courier (*fig. 4.6*), had commissioned the rival Donaldson Lithographing Company to produce copies. Courier's attempts to protect the copyright of their designs was initially turned down on the grounds that the design had "no intrinsic value other than its function as an advertisement," and therefore could not be regarded as sufficiently artistic or original to merit copyright.[9] Although this ruling was later overturned, it is clear from the first judgment that circus posters, unlike other categories such as the art poster, and even the product poster, had little or no status in the eyes of the law. If only for the great number of posters produced, outnumbering any other field in outdoor advertising, and considering the elaborate infrastructure that supported the whole industry, the circus poster deserves the serious attention of historians. Even at the time, the scale of the circus advertising industry was frequently marginalized from other fields of mass consumption and the market. Very few early texts on advertising even mention the circus, despite the huge influence this sector had on the development of advertising as an industry.[10]

in 1892, Brander Matthews referred to the "rough effect" of the American circus poster, going on to state that it was "hopelessly unattractive when considered seriously."[11] In this, the author's sense of a hierarchy in taste is most evident since he was comparing it unfavorably with the French (and American) art poster. Even in more practical business and advertising manuals, the story was much the same. H. C. Duce's pioneering book *Poster Advertising* (1912), which claimed to be unconcerned with "the artistic possibilities of the poster, but rather to demonstrate the efficacy of poster advertising," does not illustrate a single circus poster.[12] It was not until the 1950s, with a revival of interest among graphic designers in various forms of popular culture and printed ephemera, that the circus poster began to attract an audience more drawn to the lively aspects of the design and printing than the nostalgia associated with the event it advertised. The founders of the New York studio Push Pin, Seymour Chwast and Milton Glaser, collected early circus posters and would occasionally mine these sources for inspiration and sampling.[13] There was also a broader revival of interest in wood type and display faces during the 1960s, marking a relaxation from the austere Swiss-style modernism that dominated progressive graphics in the postwar period. In this context we might observe the rediscovery of the circus poster as part of the enlargement of popular taste beyond the confines of traditional modernist criteria.[14]

The Design and Printing of the Circus Poster

The fact that circus posters were only one part of an elaborate system overseen by publicity managers may explain why they are somewhat repetitive in

The role and development of the circus poster has been equally ignored by most poster enthusiasts, although collecting circles and critical journals on posters proliferated in the 1890s and early years of the twentieth century. Writing in *Century Magazine*

Fig. 4.7. "Ringling Bros. Magnificent 1200 Character Spectacle *Joan of Arc*," 1912. Poster, printed by the Strobridge Lithographing Company, Cincinnati. Cincinnati Art Museum, Gift of the Strobridge Lithographing Company, 1965.971

Fig. 4.8. "Ringling Bros. Magnificent 1200 Character Spectacle *Joan of Arc*," 1913. Poster, printed by the Strobridge Lithographing Company, Cincinnati. Cincinnati Art Museum, Gift of the Strobridge Lithographing Company, 1965.975

terms of their style, iconography, color schemes, and layout. But this should not imply that they were unimportant, or that little attention was paid to them by the designers, printers, or clients. In fact, the reverse is true. Poster design and the overall advertising program had to be coordinated with the circus's larger touring schedule, which meant that all aspects of the campaign had to be planned precisely and in great detail. There are numerous reports of the detailed briefs given to printers by circus proprietors and publicity departments, and of close monitoring of the finished product both when delivered to the circus and when displayed to the public along the circus route. In 1912, for example, Charles Ringling's agent wrote to his printers, the Strobridge Lithographing Company, complaining about the general design and quality of their posters for the Joan of Arc spectacle, going on to explain his specific areas of concern:

> This bill has a broken title line, as you know, part of the line in the usual colors and the remainder in white. This will have to be changed on all of the bills that you have not already pasted.... You will remember Mr. Ringling often has mentioned the fact that he did not want any of the paper at any time with the title broken in colors, as this always gives the appearance of two bills and detracts greatly from the strength of the paper.

In the same letter he also reported Charles Ringling's dislike of the tonality of the costumes in some figures and "the small number of people represented in the spectacle bills, as the numbers are not at all in keeping with the title and caption lines" (*fig. 4.7*). After a profuse apology from the Strobridge Company, the following year saw a revised design more in line with Ringling's expectations (*fig. 4.8*).[15] This makes clear that the publicity managers and owners were acutely aware of the various elements in the circus poster and their impact on the audience.

The essential features of the circus poster were established relatively early. Deriving in part from theater and spectacle posters of the late eighteenth and early nineteenth centuries, the first circus posters relied on the conventionalized text or typographic lists using various bold display types and the repertoire of cuts, or standard wood engravings, found in the jobbing printer's shop. Combining as many as fifteen different display faces on a single poster—slab faces, Egyptians, italics, rustics, grotesques, relief faces, shadowed faces, and ornamented letters—the juxtaposition allowed for different types of emphasis as well as bringing variety and animation to the printed sheet (*fig. 4.9*). The design and production of wood display type is one of the success stories of the American printing industry. In the early years of the nineteenth century these items were imported from Europe but in 1828, when the New York printer Darius Wells issued his type specimen book, the American wood type industry took off.[16] Applying practical techniques for mass production of the blocks, Wells introduced such quality and efficiency to the industry that by the 1860s the tide had turned and European printers were beginning to acquire American manufactured wood type. American playbill printers were also the equal of their European counterparts in ornamental layouts, forming interesting patterns with blocks of type to further animate the sheet. Hourglass shapes, diagonals, and sinuous lines of text snaking down the sheet or newspaper column were not unknown and the eventual introduction of color allowed for impressive circus heralds (*fig. 4.10*).

The main illustrative feature of early circus posters was printed from the wood engraved blocks,

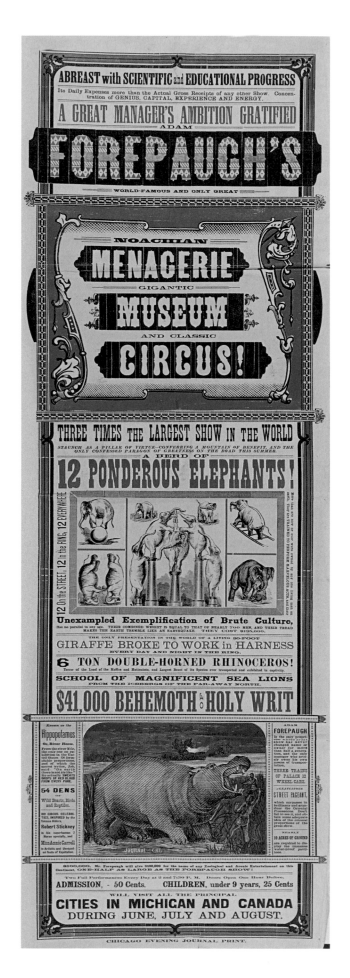

Fig. 4.9. "Welch & Delavan's Circus, Great & Grand Equestrian Fete!," August 14, 1843. Broadside, printed by Eastburn's Press, Boston. Collection of the John and Mable Ringling Museum of Art, Tibbals Collection, ht4000991

or cuts, that circulated throughout the printing industry.[17] Engraving blocks are extremely hard, made from the end grain of fruitwoods such as cherry, holly, or boxwood. When buffed and polished, the end-grain surface is very durable, requiring specialist engraving tools to incise the design. Every jobbing print shop in the country carried a stock of these cuts, generally with only a few examples of each subject area. Printers who undertook a lot of theater and circus work may have had a wider range of specialist cuts but most were likely to have just one elephant, one tiger, one horseback rider, and one acrobat to serve any number of different circuses or shows.[18] In the 1830s and 40s several innovations allowed for greater diversity and, perhaps more significantly, there were larger sizes of cuts that helped to enliven the circus poster or bill. Once Richard Hoe developed the rotary press for relief printing, larger bills of up to six by eight feet could be printed.[19] In addition, the development of softer blocks, mainly using pine instead of the close-grained fruitwoods, allowed for a larger printing surface and easier block cutting for specific designs. No longer dependent on the stock cuts, the printer could now more easily acquire new wood blocks for specific jobs or clients. This enlargement of the jobbing printer's range also came with developments in color printing because softer blocks meant that two or three separate color blocks could be cut easily for a single image, allowing for more complex multicolor illustrations.[20]

Even at this time, however, circus posters were straining at the limits of what could be achieved with woodcuts and wood engraving. The desire for more and larger pictures, especially once color could be added, indicates the extent to which circus posters required dramatic and eye-catching effects to impress their audience. The famous posters for the Raymond & Company's Menagerie for 1847, and A.

Turner and Co.'s "Extensive and Unequalled Circus" of four years later show the lengths to which the woodcut printers could go to achieve scale and diversity in their work (*figs. 4.11, 4.12*). The Raymond & Company poster incorporates some thirty-seven separate cuts, many from Thomas Bewick's *General History of Quadrupeds* of 1790, but it must have been a laborious process to set up the forme (frame) with such a range of cuts and type, and then to print the sheet. The answer to these limitations lay in the gradual improvement of chromolithography, a printing process ideally suited to producing the sort of posters that circuses, menageries, and theaters required. In effect, it was lithography that allowed for the transition from advertising based primarily on text with subsidiary illustrations to one based on images with complementary text.

Developed in the 1790s, lithography offered great freedom in pictorial description since the artist-printer could draw the image with a grease crayon directly on to a prepared limestone slab, working in sizes up to 28 by 42 inches.[21] The principle of the process is that grease and water repel one another, so when the stone is covered in water then inked, the grease-based ink will adhere only to the marked greasy areas on the stone surface. If paper is applied to the surface of the stone in a light press, the image will be transferred to the paper, giving an exact reproduction of the design in reverse. The technique was established by 1800 but it was not until the middle years of the nineteenth century that the full benefits of color lithography became available to commercial printers.[22] By then, its potential for large-scale color images was just beginning to be applied to posters.

The French lithographer Jules Chéret was instrumental in translating the techniques of chromolithography into a richly adaptable technique for posters. Many of the processes of commercial lithography had been pioneered in Britain but, for the top end of the market at least, they were employed for collectors in two related fields; the reproduction of topographical watercolors, as in the work of artist-travelers such as David Roberts and Edward Lear, and for illustrated gift books aimed at the antiquarian market. Fine reproductions of Gothic artifacts were popular, but the most famous of the early chromolithographic folios were Owen Jones's *Plans, Elevations, Sections and Details of the Alhambra* (1836–45), and *Grammar of Ornament* (1856). These set a standard for high-quality color printing in Britain, which emphasized patterns picked out with separate areas of solid, unmodulated color, as advocated by the Eng-

lish design reformers. A different tradition of color printing developed in France, free of the moralizing concern for the correct modes of ornament in design. After 1866, when he set up his workshop on Rue Borel in Paris, Chéret experimented with more diverse and variegated effects, spattering mixtures of pastel colors across the sheet. This technique, known as *crachis*, allowed for a livelier texture and lighter, more atmospheric effects that were ideally suited to his posters of lightly clad women advertising cabarets, magazines, and household goods.

These new techniques changed the basis of popular street advertising and product labeling in France, and they were gradually taken up in other countries. For a short period at the turn of the century, American circus posters seemed to embrace some of these finer effects in printing, as seen in the 1906 poster "The Barnum & Bailey Latest and Greatest Thriller: The Balloon Horse Jupiter" (*fig. 4.13*). Not only are the color transitions remarkably sensitive, the nocturnal blue light with fireworks is made more ethereal by the delicate limestone texture. Other posters of this period, such as the exceptional Barnum & Bailey poster of 1897 depicting a girl on a horse addressing a female clown, make explicit references to the French poster tradition in the iconography and asymmetrical composition (*fig. 4.14*). But this tendency did not last. The imperatives of mass advertising, economies of scale, and lithographic workshop practice led to a simplification in the color balances, less emphasis on the finer effects of the printing process, and the adoption of stock figures and compositional devices. This was only to be expected in an industry that was becoming increasingly specialized and competitive. In fact, circus advertising had matured to such an extent that by the later nineteenth century it was one of the shaping influences on the entire lithographic print-

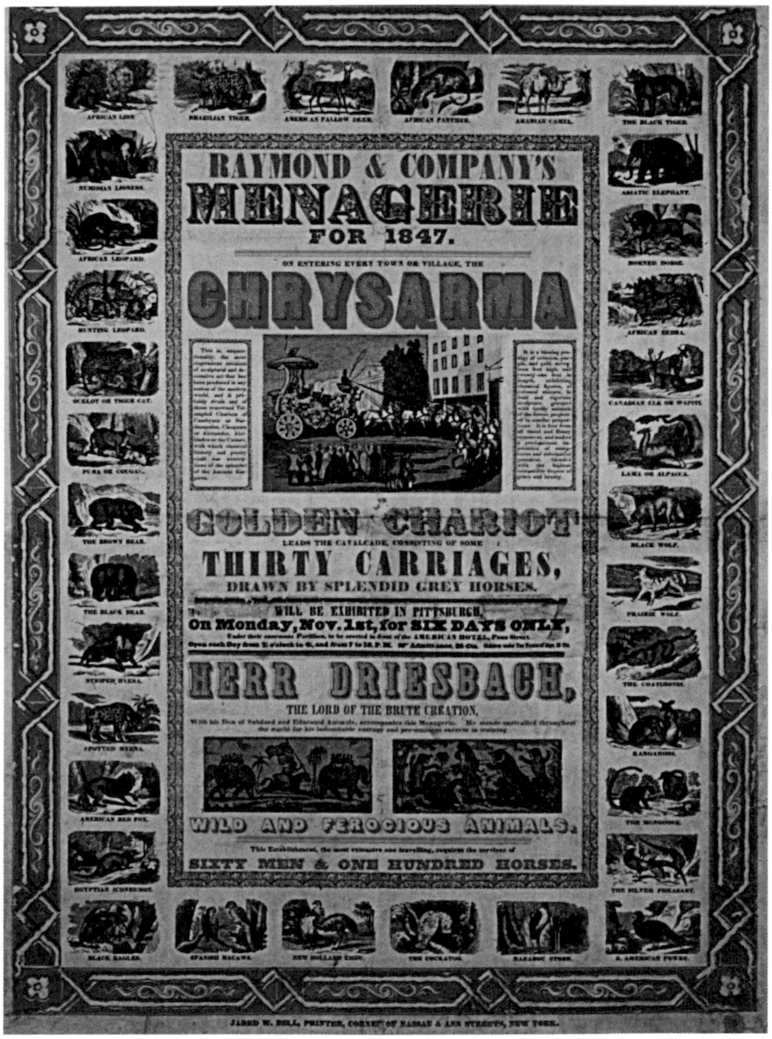

Fig. 4.11. "Raymond & Company's Menagerie for 1847." Poster, printed by Jared W. Bell, New York. Circus World Museum, CWi-2314

Fig. 4.12. "Extensive and Unequalled Circus, Enlarged and Improved for 1851, A. Turner and Co. Proprietors," May 15, 1851. Poster, printed by S. Booth, New York. Circus World Museum, CWi-2311

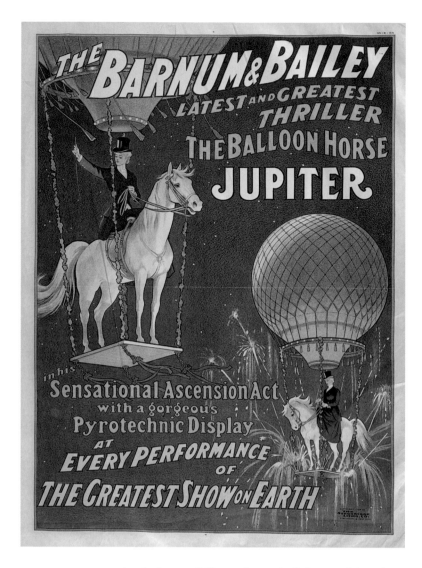

cities, largely because of the concentration of skilled printers (many from Germany) and the network of suppliers and distribution that grew up around them.[24] Cincinnati was perhaps the most famous, largely because of the Strobridge Lithographing Company, the leading printer of circus posters in the period from about 1870 to the 1920s. There were others: Buffalo was home to the Courier Printing Company, Chicago to Journal Job Print and the National Printing Company, Milwaukee to the Riverside Print Company, and Newport, Kentucky, to the Donaldson Lithographing Company. Several specialist lithographic printers, such as Cleary & Reilly, Samuel Booth and Sons, and the Richard K. Fox Printing Company, were based in lower Manhattan. Erie, Pennsylvania, home of the Erie Printing Works, was another important firm that specialized in circus and theater posters.[25]

Chromolithography was a highly skilled trade and it required expensive specialized presses but the technique allowed for massive print runs with little or no deterioration in the image quality. This marked out lithography from the earlier relief processes, notably woodcut, which was limited not only in the speed of the press work, but in wear and tear on the blocks from large print runs. Lithographs could be printed speedily and efficiently, and to a consistency unmatched by earlier processes. The only restriction was the speed of the presses, but with the addition of steam power in the 1860s and 70s, they were soon able to produce up to five thousand sheets per day.

The names of several poster designers have survived, but the bulk of those were either aspiring painters, like Edward Potthast, who transitioned to the art academy at the first opportunity, or freelance artist-illustrators who operated across the full spectrum of popular illustration for magazines, newspa-

ing industry. Where the early lithographic printers in America had quickly moved into the production of high-quality cards, scraps, and music sheets, the expansion of product labeling and advertising began to take up a large part of the industry. By the 1870s, the industry was dividing into printers specializing in smaller, labor-intensive printing jobs, often using up to fifteen stones for the extensive color range, and those who worked on a larger scale for posters and outdoor advertising.[23] Print and advertising material for the circus comprised a large part of the material in that market.

In America, the development of chromolithography became associated with certain towns and

Fig. 4.13. "The Barnum & Bailey Latest and Greatest Thriller: The Balloon Horse Jupiter," 1909. Poster, printed by the Strobridge Lithographing Company, Cincinnati. Collection of the John and Mable Ringling Museum of Art, Tibbals Collection, ht2000301

pers, and advertising. Emil Rothengatter is typical of this latter group, having worked for Strobridge in the early 1880s before turning to advertising illustration for a range of printers and products. Two figures stand out for their commitment to lithographic show posters and their association with the Strobridge Lithographing Company. Matthew "Matt" Somerville Morgan was brought over from London in the 1870s to produce cartoons for *Frank Leslie's Illustrated Newspaper*. In 1878 he was hired by Strobridge to head the printer's art department, which he did for eight years before turning his attention to painting dioramas. Although few designs can be linked to Morgan, he was responsible for establishing an efficient system for training apprentices and for the preparation of designs for printing. Henry "Harry" Ogden also began his career as an illustrator and cartoonist at *Frank Leslie's Illustrated Newspaper* before moving to Strobridge's New York office in 1881. For the next fifty years, until his retirement in 1932, he was the principal designer of circus posters in the United States. During this period he attended countless circus and theater performances, always carrying a small sketchbook in which he drew out the initial ideas for each design, which was then scaled up and refined for transfer to lithographic stones. Ogden had a particular interest in uniforms and regalia, which served him well in the description of various theater and circus costumes and paraphernalia. Later in life he was called upon to design the elaborate neo-baroque parade wagons for Barnum & Bailey, a task for which he seems to have been particularly well suited. It is uncertain how many designs Ogden saw through the press but, according to Nelson Strobridge, Ogden was responsible for most of the posters for the Barnum & Bailey Circus and for "about 98% of the circus posters we produced."[26] If this is even partly true, the number

Fig. 4.14. "The Barnum and Bailey Greatest Show on Earth," 1897. Poster, printed by the Strobridge Lithographing Company, Cincinnati. Collection of the New-York Historical Society

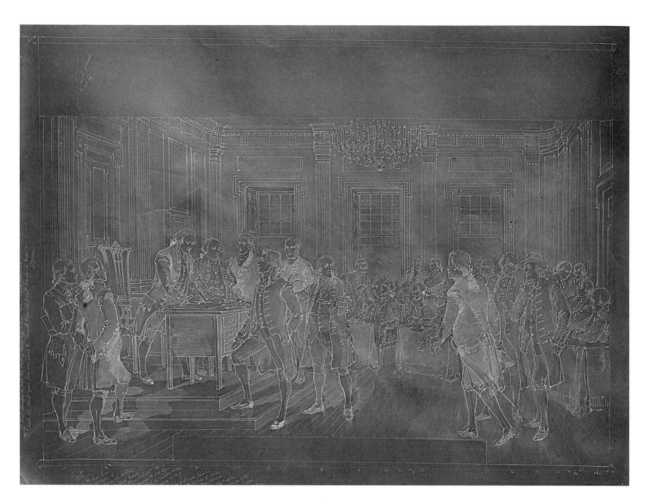

of designs must have been extraordinarily high.

Ogden did not sign his designs in the stone. Some American artists did sign their printed work, notably Rothengatter, who used the signature "E. Roe," but they are in the minority. The designers of circus and other entertainment posters in the U.S. were not independent artist-designers, as was often the case in Europe, but employees of the printing firm. Artists in France were attracted to poster design because lithography offered the freedom to draw directly on the stone, and the long-standing tradition of specialist ateliers, where master printers were ready to work alongside artists untrained in the complexities of the process. It was this tradition that gave rise to the posters of Eugène Grasset, Henri de Toulouse-Lautrec, and many other artist-designers. As familiar as these artists are to anyone with an interest in the history of graphics, they cre-ated only a small percentage of the overall output of printed posters.

Most commercial workshops in Europe and America did little specialist short-run printing and relied on a team of skilled print workers who had served apprenticeships in the trade. The designer in a large commercial printer fulfilled merely one stage in a highly organized business involving nego-tiations with clients, acceptance of the design, prep-aration and transfer to the lithographic stones, press work, paper feeders, stackers, packers, mailers, and other related jobs. Furthermore, the design and ex-ecution of the poster itself was generally the result of a series of tasks in which each stage was broken down into specialized operations in a production line. While a small pencil or ink drawing was the initial stage, it was worked up and transferred to the stone by a series of lithographers who specialized

Fig. 4.15. Harry Ogden. "Adam Forepaugh Shows: Historical Scenes and Battles of the American Revolution 4th of July 1776 Signing the Declaration of Independence for American Liberty," 1893. Glass plate negative of master advertisement design. McCaddon Collection of the Barnum & Bailey Circus, box 61; Department of Rare Books and Special Collections, Princeton University Library

in different aspects of the finished design. The most experienced hand would draw the black outlines on the stone, while others concentrated on animals, figures, landscape, or lettering.

A glass-plate negative drawn by Harry Ogden for an 1893 poster for the Adam Forepaugh spec *The American Revolution* records a first step in this process (*fig. 4.15, see fig. 13.9*). The plate, with some comments by Ogden, was presumably made before it was forwarded to the Cincinnati plant for production after consultation with the circus's management. The negative also allowed the publicity manager to make copies of the drawing for the other printing companies that the circus used for that season's advertising. In this case, Ogden's line drawing appeared in both the courier, by Empire Show Printing in Chicago, and the program for the show, which was printed by the Courier Printing Company in Buffalo. Even if a poster was designed by a known individual, the end result of circus advertising was such a cooperative effort that it could take a variety of forms. This may also explain why circus posters tended to follow design conventions that were fairly well established by the 1880s.

According to Louis E. Cooke, circus publicist and promoter, the W. W. Cole show was the first to employ lithographic posters in the early 1870s.[27] This claim can be discounted, since there are records of lithographic posters ordered from printers in the later 1840s, and several posters from the 1850s and 60s, including one for G. F. Bailey and Co. printed by the distinguished art printer and photographer Sarony, Major & Knapp of New York, in 1866 (*fig. 4.16*).[28] With somewhat more authority, however, Cooke states that W. C. Coup in 1873 was the first to commission three-sheet posters from the Strobridge Lithographing Company. Whoever did initiate this tendency, it marks the leap toward scale and spec-

tacle in advertising, which must have had a considerable impact in the locations visited by the circus.[29] It also alerted other circuses to the advantages of large-scale color posters because within a few years most had adopted this medium for their main outdoor advertising campaigns. The posters Strobridge produced for Coup in the 1870s are remarkable in

Fig. 4.16. "With G. F. Bailey & Co's Circus & Menagerie: Hippopotamus," ca. 1866. Lithograph, printed by Sarony, Major & Knapp, New York. © Shelburne Museum, Shelburne, Vermont. Gift of Harry T. Peters Sr. Family, 1959, 1959-67

Fig. 4.17. "The W. C. Coup New United Monster Shows," 1879. Poster, printed by the Strobridge Lithographing Company, Cincinnati. Collection of the John and Mable Ringling Museum of Art, Tibbals Collection, ht2004554

conception, indicating the potential of the large-scale panoramic view that lithography was well disposed to represent. For a short while, these more expansive views were a distinct category in circus posters, in contrast to the assemblage of vignette and framed items that generally characterized early circus posters. The vignette or emblematic tradition derives in part from the larger-scale theater bills that, since the individual wood blocks were small, had to incorporate several separate figures or scenes to fill the larger sheet.

Many of Strobridge's early posters already show a broad panorama and a unified pictorial field that effectively utilizes the potential of the lithograph. The W. C. Coup New United Monster Shows poster of 1879 not only incorporates the spectacle of the big top and circus site stretching back into the distance, the sweeping curve of painted and decorated railway wagons leading out of the picture in the foreground also advertises the modernity and ambition of the whole operation (*fig. 4.17*).[30] Such panoramic or bird's-eye views over the circus site are among the most striking and successful of the lithographic posters, but they are in the minority. That this approach was not taken up more widely may be due to the requirements of many circus proprietors anxious to include as many of their acts as possible in each poster. James A. Bailey was particularly concerned to advertise the full range of acts in his circus; this tended to encourage the assemblage style of different separate views and figure groups. Even here, however, many of the printers and designers showed considerable imagination arranging the various self-contained scenes in attractive compositions reminiscent of the scrapbooks and scrap screens that were popular assemblages of pictures drawn from various sources in the home.

Fig. 4.18. "Ringling Bros.: Kings of the Show World," 1905. Poster, printed by the Strobridge Lithographing Company, Cincinnati. Cincinnati Art Museum, Gift of the Strobridge Lithographing Company, 1965.1149

Another feature of this tendency is the oval medallion portraits of the circus proprietors, a staple component of the posters' designs for many decades. It was not simply vanity that prompted this display of portraiture, but the need for a reassuring image of mature and prosperous businessmen at the head of organizations that, in actuality, were often on the verge of bankruptcy. Ringling Brothers produced several posters of just their five photographic portraits, but Barnum & Bailey, Adam Forepaugh, and the Sells Brothers were each fond of presenting themselves at the top or side of their posters (*fig. 4.18*). This tendency breaks up any sense of pictorial illusion and adds a surface detail to oppose the open views of landscapes and circus interiors that could as easily be achieved with chromolithography. In fact, the various decorative borders, the cuts between separate scenes, the inconsistent scale of figures and animals, and the different levels of representation between the owners' portraits and the main scene are reminders of how complex and anti-illusionistic these graphic representations are. The arrival of the Wild West shows, above all Buffalo Bill's Wild West in 1883, helped open up the conventions of poster design into larger landscape settings with more animation and action in the figure composition but there is no consistency or clear pattern to the poster design. Buffalo Bill could as easily appear in a framed studio portrait as fighting the Indians on the wide open plains of the West (*fig. 4.19*). If anything, the variety of visual conventions is an indication of the myriad ways in which these popular images were viewed and read by their contemporary audience.

W. C. Coup partnered with Dan Castello and P. T. Barnum to form what would become the Greatest Show on Earth in 1871; during the 1870s Barnum's shows became an innovator and leader in

▶ *Fig. 4.19.* "Buffalo Bill's Wild West & Congress of Rough Riders of the World," ca. 1890s. Poster, printed by A. Hoen & Co., Baltimore. Collection of the John and Mable Ringling Museum of Art, Tibbals Collection, ht2003877

▶ *Fig. 4.20.* "Jumbo the Children's Giant Pet," 1882. Poster, printed by the Hatch Lithographic Company, New York. Collection of the John and Mable Ringling Museum of Art, Tibbals Collection, ht2004500

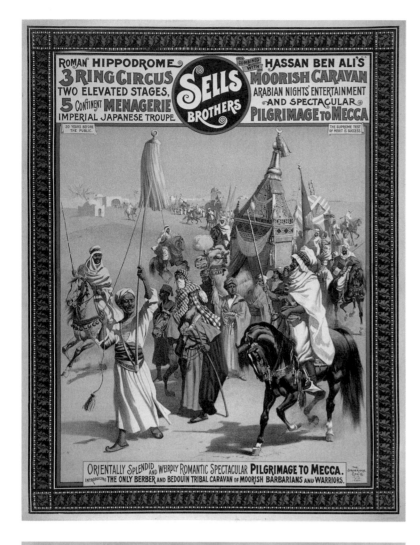

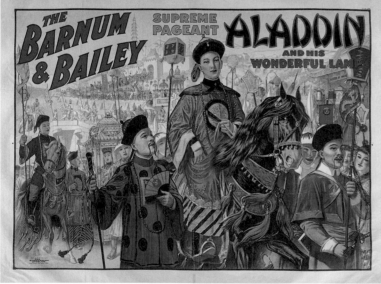

poster advertising campaigns.[31] Barnum had proven himself to be a master of publicity over the years with attractions like General Tom Thumb and Jenny Lind, and the circus offered another field in which he was able to prove his promotional skill.[32] In 1882, two years after entering into a partnership with James Bailey, Barnum introduced Jumbo to America, "the largest and heaviest elephant ever seen by mortal man either wild or in captivity." Such was the success and fame of this beast that Barnum & Bailey often advertised the elephant as a single image occupying the entire field of the poster (*fig. 4.20*). This reduction to a single motif was unusual in the 1880s but it would come to dominate the circus poster in later decades.

The subject matter or iconography of circus posters has considerable range but it can be organized into a few key types or classes, reflecting the acts that most circuses were sure to present: wild animals, especially lions and tigers, depicted either in the wild or in the ring with their trainers; equestrian acts with rearing or bareback horses; and acrobats and trapeze artists in their feats of balance and flight. Clowns were less common as the main feature in the later nineteenth century, but they became increasingly more prominent in the twentieth century, even coming to symbolize the spirit of the entire circus in posters of the modern period. It was in depictions of the circus parade and the various pageants or displays in the ring that allowed for grander designs than normal. In this last category, Sells Brothers' "Arabian Nights' Entertainment and Spectacular Pilgrimage to Mecca" of 1893 ("Orientally Splendid and Weirdly Romantic") is an unusual design revealing a firm grasp of the Salon traditions of French Orientalist painting (*fig. 4.21*). The equally sophisticated "Aladdin and His Wonderful Lamp" (1917) for Barnum & Bailey may also suggest a new set of sources beyond the normal

Fig. 4.21. "Sells Brothers: Hassan Ben Ali's Moorish Caravan, Arabian Nights' Entertainment and Spectacular Pilgrimage to Mecca," 1893. Poster, printed by the Strobridge Lithographing Company, Cincinnati. Collection of the John and Mable Ringling Museum of Art, Tibbals Collection, ht2000458

Fig. 4.22. "The Barnum & Bailey Supreme Pageant: Aladdin and His Wonderful Lamp," 1917. Poster, printed by the Strobridge Lithographing Company, Cincinnati. Collection of the John and Mable Ringling Museum of Art, Tibbals Collection, ht2000371

repertoire of standard types, in this case possibly cinematic visual conventions, since the movies were making inroads on the circus's traditional audience (*fig. 4.22*).

A striking feature of early lithographic posters for the circus is the remarkably high quality of the printing, despite the fact that many of them were displayed in random outdoor locations often for only two weeks at a time. This is almost certainly due to the exacting standards of presswork and regulated systems of preparation and printing in the specialist establishments, which ensured such a uniform quality in the finished poster. Close study of lithographs such as those illustrating Sells' Brothers Enormous United Shows (*see fig. 4.1*) and "Living Statues on Horseback" for Adam Forepaugh (*fig. 4.23*), both printed by Strobridge in the 1890s, reveal not only fine color balance, but subtle handling of tone and granulation in the surface texture, a feature of true lithography from limestone but a technique that had to be handled sensitively if it was to play a decorative role in the finished image. It remained a characteristic feature of Strobridge printing into the twentieth century, when zinc plates began to replace the traditional stones. The poster of 1909, "The Barnum & Bailey Latest and Greatest Thriller: The Balloon Horse Jupiter" attests to the continuing quality in this aspect of printing but by this time it was becoming rare, and mostly used for the smaller indoor window posters (*see fig. 4.13*).

This shift in printing quality and advertising priorities was already apparent in the years before the First World War and it would go on to become more pronounced in the 1920s and later. The most notable of these is a marked simplification in the figural elements of the poster, often reduced to a single figure or animal head, which had the added impact of greater drama and expressiveness. The

most familiar indication of this tendency is the advancing tiger leaping out of the picture toward the viewer, a design that caused considerable excitement. In February 1915 the trade magazine *The Poster* carried the notice "Applying Art to the Circus Poster" announcing that Charles Livingston Bull, "a Celebrated Artist" had been engaged "to Design a Poster of a Tiger for the Ringling Brothers." The fact that a "celebrated" animal artist and taxidermist had been commissioned was newsworthy, but his fee of one thousand dollars was a landmark in commercial art. The illustration proved to be a good investment, apart from the headlines it generated, because this design stayed in use for Ringling Brothers and Barnum & Bailey into the 1930s (*fig. 4.24*).[33] In any case, it is notable not for the identification of an individual artist but for a general tendency toward simpler and bolder designs in the character of circus posters in the period.

Such dramatic effects in the poster motifs of the 1920s were heightened by the attendant color combinations in the backgrounds. Unlike the di-

Fig. 4.23. "The Original Adam Forepaugh Shows. Living Statues on Horseback," 1894. Poster, printed by the Strobridge Lithographing Company, Cincinnati. Collection of the John and Mable Ringling Museum of Art, Tibbals Collection, ht2000425

verse settings for earlier posters, which often included the ring, members of the audience, or even a jungle landscape, the new poster style favored more general washes of a single color, eliminating any contextual information entirely.[34] This striking graphic device probably reaches its apex in the snarling leopard on a textured green ground designed by the Norman Bel Geddes Studio for Ringling Bros. and Barnum & Bailey in the early 1940s (*fig. 4.25*). This poster, which remained in use for over thirty years, demonstrates sensitive draftsmanship and stone texture with its bold color scheme. But in most similar posters, stylized animal types and strident color schemes heighten the impact of the figures and emphasize the vividness of the spectacle. Striking

and emotive as they are, very few of these later posters exploit the subtle textured effects or the modulated tonality of their predecessors.

Although lithographic printing from stones could achieve consistently high quality, especially in single-sheet window posters, the conventions of design and composition of circus posters were uneven and repetitive. The public for even the early posters before 1900 may have responded to color images and scale, but there was no premium placed on sophistication of design and layout. As a result, circus posters tended to rely on the identification of a few familiar types in which the representation need only be emblematic rather than naturalistic or formally innovative. As mentioned above, these con-

Fig. 24. Charles Livingston Bull. "Ringling Bros. and Barnum & Bailey Combined Shows," ca. 1920. Poster, printed by the Strobridge Lithographing Company, Cincinnati. Collection of the John and Mable Ringling Museum of Art, Tibbals Collection, ht2001435

ventions may have arisen through the the highly structured division of labor in lithographic printing workshops. But there was little incentive for stock posters to be individualistic. Indeed, this may have been discouraged. Many of the smaller circuses depended on generic images of standard circus fare—lions, tigers, elephants, equestrian acts, and clowns—since they could not be sure of their program in advance. With considerable mobility of performers between circuses it was impractical to advertise any single named act for a whole season unless they were a real draw, secured by an expensive contract for the whole tour. Furthermore, the printers often preferred generic designs for their paper stock that could be printed en masse during slow periods at the press and stored to be used over several years with the name of the circus and location overprinted when needed.[35] It was only the big circuses who had secured famous named acts like Jumbo, the Astounding Clarkonians, or May Wirth ("The Greatest Bare Back Rider of all Time"), who sought to raise their profile and simultaneously exploit their investment to the full with specialty posters. In this case, the mutual advantage of boosting the performer's reputation and associating the act with the circus was fully emphasized in some of the more extravagant claims of the posters. The tendency toward superlatives in advertising could almost be regarded as simply good management of the organization's investment.[36]

It also tested the designers' ability to represent the extraordinary nature of some acts. Faced with the need to demonstrate just how astounding the Clarkonians could be on the trapeze, the designer had recourse to a combination of different pictorial devices (*fig. 4.26*). Barnum & Bailey's leading act of the 1904 season was noted for performing a double somersault with a double full twist (the

so-called double double). As we are told in the text, this was "A feat never before attempted" even by these, "the most intrepid aerialists," who we can see standing proudly in their leotards in the panel on the left. For the main scene, however, the artist has placed our viewpoint high up in the air beside the acrobats near the roof of the tent so we are able to look down on the two rings far below. The other circus acts seem to have stopped mid-performance to look up and marvel at this achievement. Even in the depiction of the mid-air Clarkonians, the design struggles to describe the complex movement of the

Fig. 4.25. Norman Bel Geddes Studio. "Ringling Bros. and Barnum & Bailey Circus," ca. 1940s. Poster. Collection of the John and Mable Ringling Museum of Art, Tibbals Collection, ht2001793

Stirton

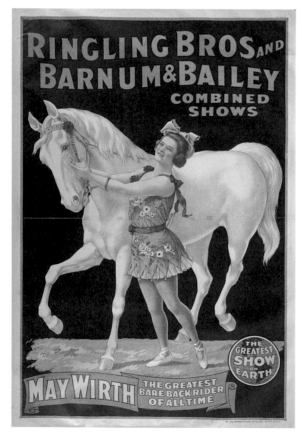

twist because the upper half of his body is facing skyward while the lower half faces the ground. It is a clumsy device but one can recognize what is going on. However, even with this distortion, it cannot have been clear enough. While wanting to keep the effect of height, which gives us a sense of danger, and also maintaining the unified open view over the interior of the circus tent, the full complexity and drama of the act was not obvious. The final strategy was to mark out the flight path of the trapeze artist with a double loop, adding numbers to explain further just what was happening.

The appeal of this poster to modern eyes lies mostly in the naive use of different visual forms while remaining clear and accessible. In this case, the results have a certain interest and even charm. However, the tendency to feature one or two famous acts in circus posters does not appear to have encouraged innovation. When certain motifs or poses had become associated with a famous act, they were often repeated in posters over many years. The poster for May Wirth, for example, produced for the Ringling Bros. and Barnum & Bailey Combined Shows in 1919 (*fig. 4.27*), suggests a type of popular printing of thirty or forty years earlier. May Wirth stands with her white horse on a green sward floating against a deep blue ground in a manner that was associated with the popular collectible lithographic handbills. And yet, this poster raises different questions regarding the status and representation of women in circus advertising at a time when women's position in American popular culture was undergoing some profound changes. The turn of the century saw the emergence of the New Woman in novels, magazines, paintings, and illustrations. Athletic, confident, educated, and independent, for the middle classes at least, this popular type was becoming a common feature in newspapers and advertising,

Fig. 4.26. "The Barnum & Bailey Greatest Show on Earth: The Astounding Clarkonians," 1904. Poster, printed by the Strobridge Lithographing Company, Cincinnati, Cincinnati. Collection of the John and Mable Ringling Museum of Art, Tibbals Collection, ht2000265

Fig. 4.27. "Ringling Bros. and Barnum & Bailey Combined Shows: May Wirth, the Greatest Horseback Rider of All Time," ca. 1925. Poster, printed by the Strobridge Lithographing Company, Cincinnati. Collection of the John and Mable Ringling Museum of Art, Tibbals Collection, ht2001475

perhaps best seen in the characteristic type of the Gibson Girl. Larger changes in society were clearly at work in the circus as well, but it would be too simplistic to see the circus as a mirror to the outside world. The circus was, by its nature and its self-promoted mystique, a different world. On the one hand, women were already a prominent feature of the performance and the publicity. This was not, however, an expression of their improved status in the larger professional hierarchy. Nevertheless, just as actresses and women writers began to gain positions of wealth and status in a male-dominated society, so many of the more successful female performers began to achieve a degree of prominence and independence in the twentieth century. May Wirth is only one of these, and the representations of her indicate her importance and celebrity within the larger organization of the Ringling Bros. and

Barnum & Bailey Combined Shows of 1919. In fact, she went on to achieve considerable success throughout the 1920s and 1930s, moving between her own troupe and solo performance with many of the leading circuses in America and Europe.

Circus posters also indicate the changing modes of dress and respectability associated with women performers. While many posters depict women acrobats and bareback riders in a prim, respectable manner that seems to deny the nature of their athletic achievements, others begin to allow more direct depiction of their less-encumbering performance costumes, which are also generally more revealing. The 1909 poster for The Könyöt Family (*fig. 4.28*), for example, seems to offer us a range of feats on horseback performed by men and women dressed as if going to a ball or presentation at court. The men wear tails and the women, formal

dresses and jewelry, just as they do in the posed formal portrait grouped round a pedestal in the center. The formal portrait is clearly derived from a studio photograph whereas the equestrian scenes appear almost absurdly stiff and artificial. How are we to interpret this? Perhaps this has nothing to do with traditional propriety but was, instead, the distinctive feature of their act—six Hungarians who dress as if going to dinner with the royal family but who throw themselves around the ring on the backs of horses. The woman up on Jupiter as he ascends beneath the balloon in 1909 is dressed in the most

formal and concealing of nineteenth-century riding clothes, but ten years later May Wirth was obviously content to be depicted in her light costume and tights (*see figs. 4.13, 4.27*).

This more revealing but also more vigorous representation of women performers would become the norm from the 1920s onward. It made for a more spectacular as well as a more accurate depiction of the performance to come. It is true that many opportunities were taken to reveal groups of scantily clad women, especially in the Oriental displays and in the popular revivals of classical scenes such as

Fig. 4.29. "The Barnum & Bailey Greatest Show on Earth: *The Spectacle of Balkis—A Veritable Vision of Ancient Glories*," 1903. Poster, printed by the Strobridge Lithographing Company, Cincinnati. Collection of the John and Mable Ringling Museum of Art, Tibbals Collection, ht2000257

the chariot race. The Barnum & Bailey poster for the *Spectacle of Balkis* (the Queen of Sheba) of 1903 (*fig. 4.29*) is one of the more explicit of these and quite early for this degree of exposure. Circuses were hardly alone in revealing more of a woman's body than would normally be acceptable. If anything, it reflects a parallel development in early films in which the Bible and the ancient world offered any number of stories to explore the exotic and the sensational while maintaining a degree of respectability, even morality in the whole affair. In fact, it is striking how few, if any, depictions of women in circus posters have recourse to the outright salacious. This may be due to a distinct separation between the different categories of popular entertainment in the United States. The various acts often moved between the circus and vaudeville, implying a certain overlap or kinship between these two forms. But a move into burlesque would have been unacceptable for an industry that relied on a traditional small-town family audience.

While respectability in the content of circus posters was certainly maintained throughout the twentieth century, the same could not be said for printing and design standards. Even as the conventions of composition and iconography have remained fairly consistent, the standard of color printing and the reliance on photographs has greatly diminished the graphic impact. Even here, however, we should beware of adopting a critical tone based on some supposed standard of previous excellence. The more recent posters of the late twentieth and even twenty-first centuries are competing for the attention of children and adults whose visual experience is undergoing dramatic changes in both imagery and modes of reading and using pictures. As discussed at the outset, circus posters have always wanted serious attention as documents of a particular way of looking and of engaging with the performative nature of the circus. Current circus posters may still tell us as much about the pattern of production and consumption of visual information as the social and economic structure of a traditional but changing industry. Given the inroads that new media have made on established forms of popular entertainment in the last twenty years, it is surprising how long the traditional poster has continued to be a major form of public advertising for the circus. In the second decade of the twenty-first century, circus posters are still appearing on the traditional routes followed by modern, if much reduced, circuses. These contemporary images still have a strong resemblance to circus posters of a hundred years ago. Why this should have remained so is a complex question, but a large part of the answer surely has to do with nostalgia. In an age of multifarious social media, performance on demand, and access to a bewildering range of images and performances online, the circus is something of an anachronism. But it still attracts an audience. And since posters are part of the total experience of the circus, they have retained something of their original character and form.

1 "One of the great general agents in the show business in this country, M. W. E. Franklin, has coined an aphorism which will be endorsed by every circus man. He says there are three P's essential to the success of showmen. They are: Printing, Parade and Performance. These three requisites are intimately associated, and without the trinity being closely kept together and considered, the show, no matter how great in any one particular, must fail. Good printing first attracts the attention of the public; the parade arouses the interest of the multitude and draws them to the show; the good performance creates talk and favorable comment, which follow the show, throughout the season." Quoted in Jack Rennert, *American Circus Posters* (Baraboo, WI: Circus World Museum, 1984), introduction, n.p.

2 The number of circuses on the road in any year is uncertain due to incomplete records. C. G. Sturtevant counted 78 different circuses in his listings for 1900. See C. G. Sturtevant, "Who's Who in the American Circus," *Circus Historical Society,* http://www. circushistory.org/History/Sturtevant1900.htm (accessed April 6, 2012). For more on this, see Robert L. Parkinson, *Directory of American Circuses, 1793–2000* (Baraboo, WI: Circus World Museum, 2002).

3 Reports of these can be found repeatedly in the circus pages of *Billboard* magazine. See for example *Billboard*, March 19, 1955, 63, which reports the Hunt Bros. circus employing an airplane in 1943, but proposing to acquire a helicopter for future aerial advertising.

4 This rough proportion is repeated in many books, although generally without figures to support it. In the course of reviewing his career in the 1880s and 1890s, W. C. Coup wrote, "It may not be generally known to the public, but it is a fact, that nearly one-half of the entire expenditure of a circus is incurred in the work of the advance brigades. The advertising material, its distribution, express, freight and cartage, together with the salaries, transportation and living expenses of seventy-five to one hundred men, amount to vast sums of money." W. C. Coup, *Sawdust & Spangles: Stories and Secrets of the Circus* (Chicago: Hubert S. Stone, 1901), 104.

5 Louis E. Cooke, "Charles H. McConnell," *Newark Evening Star*, Dec. 2, 1915, n.p. This was one of a series of articles written by Cooke in the newspaper between 1915 and 1916 under the general title "Reminiscences of a Showman."

6 Charles P. Fox and Tom Parkinson, *Billers, Banners and Bombast: The Story of Circus Advertising* (Boulder, CO Pruett Publishing Company, 1985), 55–56.

7 For the most detailed account of the "advance," see ibid., chap. 3.

8 As reported: "The roster of advertising car No. 3,

Forepaugh–Sells Bros. Show: H. A. Mann, manager; Harry Thorp, boss bill poster; assistant bill posters, Alf. Belfrey, George Mulvey, Ed Guyon, Charles Morelles, Ed Baker, W. H. Cohn, W. H. Bryson, Matt. Smith, H. V. Lewis; lithographers, H. V. Pennypacker, Louis Bowers, Frank Baker; banners, Walter Gilmore, William Curtis." *Billboard*, June 1, 1901, 6.

9 See Bleistein v. Donaldson Lithographing Company, 188 U.S. 239 (1903).

10 See for example, Harry Tipper and George Burton Hotchkiss, *Advertising*, Modern Business, vol. 4 (New York: Alexander Hamilton Institute, 1914). There is no mention of the circus in this standard manual tracing the history and modern practice of advertising.

11 Brander Matthews, "The Pictorial Poster," *Century Magazine* 44 (Sept. 1892), 748–56.

12 Herbert Cecil Duce, *Poster Advertising* (Chicago: Blakely Printing Co., 1912), 6.

13 Seymour Chwast and Steven Heller, *The Push Pin Graphic: A Quarter Century of Innovative Design and Illustration* (San Francisco: Chronicle Books, 2004), 248.

14 The song "Being for the Benefit of Mr. Kite" on the Beatles' 1967 album *Sgt. Pepper's Lonely Hearts Club Band* was inspired by a circus poster of 1843; this tendency to find humor and a new sensibility in Victorian popular printing is perhaps best seen in both the title and the graphics of Monty Python's Flying Circus, launched in 1969. Recently, the 2010 exhibition *The Amazing American Circus Poster: The Strobridge Lithographing Company*, organized by the Cincinnati Art Museum and the John and Mable Ringling Museum of Art, was something of a landmark for its presentation of circus posters.

15 Quoted in Fred D. Pfening III, "The Strobridge Lithographing Company, the Ringling Brothers, and Their Circuses," in *The Amazing American Circus Poster: The Strobridge Lithographing Company*, ed. Kristin L. Spangenberg and Deborah W. Walk (Cincinnati: Cincinnati Art Museum, 2011), 37.

16 For an account of the American wood type industry see David Consuegra, *American Type Design and Designers* (New York: Allworth Press, 2004), 9–11.

17 Charles Philip Fox, ed., *Old-Time Circus Cuts* (New York: Dover, 1979).

18 Workshop practice in the show printing trade is discussed in Derek Forbes, *Illustrated Playbills* (London: Society for Theatre Research, 2002).

19 Matthew Wittmann, "Menageries and Markets: The Zoological Institute Tours Jacksonian America," *Common-Place* 12, no. 1 (Oct. 2011), n.p.

20 Richard Flint, "A Great Industrial Art: Circus Posters, Business Risks, and the Origins of Color Letterpress Printing in America," *Printing History* 25, no. 2 (2009), 18–43.

21 Printing industry standards for the size of lithograph

sheets were fixed at 28 x 42 inches in the 1890s. Two decades later, in 1912, the standard size of billboards was fixed to support twenty-four separate sheets. Kristin L. Spangenberg, "The Strobridge Lithographing Company: The Tiffany of Printers," in *The Amazing American Circus Poster*, 25.

22 For a history of early lithographic printing, see Michael Twyman, *Breaking the Mould: The First Hundred Years of Lithography* (London: British Library, 2001).

23 Of the former group, the best-known early lithographers in the U.S. were John H. Bufford (1810–1870) and Louis Prang (1824–1909), both based in Boston. See Philip B. Meggs, *A History of Graphic Design* (New York: Van Nostrand Reinhold, 1992), 156–63.

24 See Georgia B. Barnhill, "Commercial Nineteenth-Century American Lithography: An Economic History," paper presented at "Representations of Economy: Lithography in America from 1820 to 1860," Ninth Annual Conference of the Program in Early American Economy and Society, Library Company of Philadelphia, Oct. 15, 2010.

25 Fox and Parkinson, *Billers, Banners and Bombast*, 26–33.

26 Manuel Rosenberg, "Billing the Greatest Show on Earth," interview with Nelson Strobridge in *The Artist and Advertiser* 2, no. 2 (Feb. 1931), 5. Quoted in Spangenberg, 23.

27 Louis E. Cooke, "Reminiscences of a Showman," *Newark Evening Star*, Dec. 2, 1915, n.p.

28 Fox and Parkinson, *Billers, Banners and Bombast*, 14, 15, 26.

29 Cooke, "Reminiscences of a Showman." (New Jersey), Dec. 2, 1915.

30 The Harold Dunn Collection, Sarasota, Florida. Illustrated in Jack Rennert, *100 Years of Circus Posters* (New York: Darien House, 1974).

31 Stuart Thayer and William L. Slout, *Grand Entrée: The Birth of the Greatest Show on Earth, 1870–1875* (San Bernardino, CA: Borgo Press, 1998).

32 A. H. Saxon, *P. T. Barnum: The Legend and the Man* (New York: Columbia University Press, 1989).

33 Harriet S. Flagg, "Applying Art to the Circus Poster," *The Poster* 6 (Feb. 1915), 37.

34 See, for example, the 1918–19 poster for the Ringling Bros. and Barnum & Bailey Circus, celebrating the union of the two circuses. It employs just three pictorial elements—the heads of a clown, a girl, and a polar bear—against a solid blue ground. Collection of the John and Mable Ringling Museum of Art, Tibbals Collection, ht2001440.

35 Fox and Parkinson, *Billers, Banners and Bombast*, 38–41.

36 In an article in *The American Magazine* of September 1919, John Ringling claimed that it was his brother Charles who had created the new language of the circus poster. "The language of the circus poster

is unique. Originally it was the result of opposition shows striving to outdo one another in startling announcements. Charles, who is the greatest scholar in the family, and an authority on words, created a new vocabulary and the style caught public fancy. We understand now, although we did not at the time, that we had struck upon the child-appeal in another form. All children and all primitive minds, love big words, and love exaggeration." Quoted in Charles Philip Fox, *A Ticket to the Circus* (Seattle: Superior Publishing Co., 1959), 45.

5

SHELBURNE MUSEUM'S COLCHESTER POSTERS AND CIRCUS ADVERTISING

KORY W. ROGERS

In 1991 workers replacing the external siding on Harold and Gladys Degree's home in Colchester, Vermont, discovered a cache of late-nineteenth-century circus posters hidden under the rotten clapboards (*fig. 5.1*).[1] Featuring exotic animals and daring performers, the posters advertised the July 26, 1883 show of The Great Forepaugh Museum, Menagerie, Triple Circus, and Roman Hippodrome in the neighboring city of Burlington. After being hidden for over a century, the bright colors and eye-catching imagery of the posters brought traffic on Colchester's Main Street to a screeching halt, just as they had many years before. As word spread about the uncovered posters, a local media storm developed. Responding to the overwhelming public interest in viewing the posters, the homeowners donated them to Shelburne Museum, one of the country's unique repositories of art, architecture, design, and Americana. The gift was proffered with the stipulation that the museum remove the fragile advertisements as quickly as possible to allow the renovation project to continue unimpeded.

Immediately a team of curators, conservators, and carpenters was dispatched to the scene to assess the situation and determine the safest and most expedient way to detach the posters from the walls. It was during their initial inspection that the conservators detected the presence of a second layer of posters underneath the Forepaugh ads, which complicated matters. After spending hours under plastic sheeting in inclement weather attempting to remove the gorilla poster using small metal spatulas to dislodge the two layers of paper from their board backing, conservators determined that the most expeditious way to extract the posters was to cut out sections of the walls with the posters still attached (*fig. 5.2*). Conservators exploited the natural tears in the paper where the wall slats had contracted and expanded over a century, noting that it was easier to mend a straight, clean cut than a jagged, torn edge. The

Detail of fig. 5.11. "Nala Damajante," 1883. Poster. © Shelburne Museum, Shelburne, Vermont, Gift of Harold and Gladys Degree, 1991-18.1

the five so-called Colchester posters that exposed the underlayer of ads, revealing evidence of a forgotten advertising war fought between the Forepaugh show and a smaller rival, the John B. Doris Great Inter-Ocean Museum, Menagerie, & Circus.[2]

Three of the five large Forepaugh posters, measuring seven by three feet, including the giraffes, the Japanese wirewalker, and the bicycle thrill act, were sent to the Northeast Document Conservation Center (NEDCC) in Andover, Massachusetts, for treatment. There conservator Bucky Weaver separated the top posters from their substrates, unveiling the hidden layer of advertisements from John B. Doris's Great Inter-Ocean Circus. Printed by James A. Reilly of New York, the first poster to be removed from its boards was "Little All Right, The Japanese Marvel depicted in His Perilous 'Slide for Life,'" which revealed two smaller, one-sheet (28-x-42-in.) posters (*fig. 5.3*). Positioned under Little All Right's torso, the top poster featured a three-quarter profile bust of the Great Inter-Ocean's proprietor, John B. Doris (*fig. 5.4*). Directly under the portrait of Doris, the lower poster portrayed the acrobatic feats of Ella Stokes, the star equestrienne who "shines with a bright effulgence which completely shadows all the lesser luminaries of the arenic firmament" (*fig. 5.5*).[3]

The second large poster conserved at NEDCC depicted a tower of five giraffes, which was actually false advertising, because at the time Forepaugh's menagerie contained only two of the long-necked ruminants (*fig. 5.6*).[4] Below the giraffes, another set of two smaller Great Inter-Ocean posters was uncovered. The top poster portrayed a male bareback rider believed to be Signor Don José Ramirez, the Human Whirligig, standing astride the back of his Andalusian

remaining four posters were extracted from the house's exterior board by board and were stored disassembled at the museum for almost twenty years. Thanks to the support of generous donors, the Shelburne Museum recently conserved four out of

horse (*fig. 5.7*).[5] Advertised as a former performer in the Circus of His Majesty King Alfonso in Madrid, Signor Ramirez was billed as "the only artist in the world who has succeeded in turning a somersault while riding sideways."[6] The lower poster depicted Clarke's Slave Cabin Jubilee Singers, Shouters and Juba-Patters performing their "plaintive pathetic renditions of plantation melodies," while riding a "crystal chariot" in Doris's free street parade, described as a "world of wonders on wheels" (*fig. 5.8*).[7] In keeping with the minstrel tradition in American circuses, Forepaugh's street parade also had a "canvas tableau, with slave troupe of minstrels."[8]

Captioned "Look at Leonati, the Gymnastic Autocrat of Aerial Art," the third poster conserved at NEDCC prominently featured the fifty-foot-tall spiraling roadway on which the performer rode a "slender" bicycle (*fig. 5.9*). Thrill acts incorporating tall spiral ramps such as Leonati's were popular around the turn of the century; these included Leon Laroche's Mysterious Ball routine, in which the artist encapsulated himself in a metal ball and rolled up the winding roadway.[9] Beneath Leonati, conservators discovered a large poster of a Hyæna Striata Giganteum, or a giant striped hyena (*fig. 5.10*). Viewers were titillated by the African canine shown gnawing on human skeletal remains. Both posters had been punctured with a circular hole years back when the house was wired for electricity.

The sole ad attached to the southeast façade of the Degrees' home was the poster of Nala Damajante, The Hindu Snake Charmer and it was treated by independent conservator Mary Jo (M. J.) Davis at her laboratory in Vermont's Northeast Kingdom (*fig. 5.11*). Originally the same size as the four other large Forepaugh posters, the image of Damajante was accidentally damaged during the removal of the siding and only the upper half of the poster has sur-

vived. Shown coiled by constrictors, the exotic Damajante was described as "the most wonderful manipulator of venomous reptiles ever seen in the world."[10] Her most distinguishing physical feature, her exotic, voluminous, afro-textured hair, was a vestigial characteristic of the fictitious circassian lady whose identity became inextricably conflated with female snake charmers.[11] Underneath Nala

Fig. 5.2. Gorilla, 1883. Poster, printed by Russell, Morgan & Co., Cincinnati. © Shelburne Museum, Shelburne, Vermont, Gift of Harold and Gladys Degree, 1991-18.3

Damajante, Davis discovered an extremely rare portrayal of John B. Doris's star attraction: Millie-Christine, the Two-Headed Nightingale, conjoined sisters who were treated as one individual (*fig. 5.12*).

They were portrayed in elegant red dresses, carrying attributes that reflected their different personalities within a domestic setting, all allusions to beauty and femininity. Millie-Christine's "peculiar and strange form" was so extraordinary that she became collateral damage in Adam Forepaugh's circus war with John B. Doris (*see figs. 5.12, 5.13*).

Circus wars broke out when the touring routes of two rival shows competed in a geographical region. Competition for limited audiences resulted in vicious advertising campaigns; subterfuge and sabotage undermined the perceived interlopers' credibility and suppressed audience turnout. What ensued was a war of words between the two circuses' "advance departments."[12] Traveling in private railroad cars weeks ahead of the circus, the advance team was responsible for publicizing the coming attraction by bombarding communities and the surrounding region with print media. Comprising press agents, billers, banner-men, and programmers, the advance team carried out their orders with militaristic precision, papering buildings with posters, placing ads in local newspapers, handing out two-sided showbills called "heralds," on street corners, and distributing couriers (multipage pamphlets comparable to modern-day store circulars) through the mail. (See chapter 4, "American Circus Posters.")

Within the advance department, smaller special operations called "brigades" conducted oppositional maneuvers when the routes of two circuses collided.[13] Their arsenal included stacks of posters and defamatory broadsides known as rat sheets, deployed in guerrilla-style warfare. As evidenced on the Degrees' home, current posters were covered over by the competing circus. The sheer volume of

Fig. 5.3. "Little All Right, The Japanese Marvel in His Perilous 'Slide for Life,'" 1883. Poster, printed by James Reilly, New York. © Shelburne Museum, Shelburne, Vermont, Gift of Harold and Gladys Degree, 1991-18.2

posters plastered about was staggering, as it was not unusual for a single show to blanket a community in five to eight thousand posters, resulting in "circus advertising at its most, not its best."[14]

Rat sheets were scurrilous broadsides containing outrageous and libelous statements fabricated to assassinate the character of the opposition, including proprietors, performers, and press agents (*see fig. 1.16*). Forepaugh's rat sheets were notoriously vicious, like the one his show issued after the death of President James A. Garfield, asserting that Doris's press agent, J. V. Strebic, "openly proclaimed the assassination of our late honerable president a

just retribution and upholds his murderer, Guiteau, as a saint and wants to see him honored with a monument of gold!"[15]

It was common for circuses like the Great Forepaugh Show and the Great Inter-Ocean Circus to become embroiled in long-standing feuds, carrying the animosity over from encounters during previous seasons. These conflicts had a tendency to amplify and take on a life of their own. In his book *Sawdust & Spangles: Stories and Secrets of the Circus*, the showman W. C. Coup described how these clashes sometimes spun out of control, stating "the rivalry between two shows often costs thousands of dollars

Fig. 5.4. "John B. Doris' Great Inter-Ocean Museum, Menagerie, & Circus," 1883. Poster, printed by the Strobridge Lithographing Company, Cincinnati. © Shelburne Museum, Shelburne, Vermont, Gift of Harold and Gladys Degree, 1991-18.7

and is sometimes kept up by the agents long after the proprietors have become reconciled."[16]

In the summer of 1883 John B. Doris and Adam Forepaugh's circuses crossed paths in Vermont, igniting such a war. Both shows were scheduled to play similar routes through the Green Mountain State that included a performance in the city of Burlington, located on the shores of Lake Champlain. Doris arrived in the Queen City first on June 22, followed a month later by Forepaugh on July 26. Doris and Forepaugh were both contending for the patronage of Burlington's 11,374 residents and the 21,418 people who lived in the Lake Champlain Valley.[17] In order to make a profit, each showman had to neutralize his competition. The stakes were particularly high

for Forepaugh, which was the larger operation and performed in a big top that measured 214 by 364 feet and was capable of accommodating up to 12,000 spectators for each performance.[18]

In an attempt to preempt Doris, Forepaugh launched the first volley in the battle when he dispatched his aptly named "skirmish brigade" to Vermont more than a month in advance of his scheduled performance to flood the Burlington area with ads.[19] As it was unusual for circuses to promote so far in advance, Forepaugh felt the need to explain his actions in a lengthy article published in the region's largest newspaper, *Burlington Daily Free Press & Times,* on June 14.[20] In the article titled "Why? Mr. Forepaugh," the showman answered the question,

Fig. 5.5. "John B. Doris' Great Inter-Ocean Museum, Menagerie & Circus: Ella Stokes," 1883. Poster, printed by the Strobridge Lithographing Company, Cincinnati. © Shelburne Museum, Shelburne, Vermont, Gift of Harold and Gladys Degree, 1991-18.8

"Why do you announce and advertise your coming so far ahead of your appearance?" To which he paternalistically replied, "To let the people know that Adam Forepaugh is coming with the largest show in the world." He went on to warn, "If I did not let the people know that I was coming, some would be led into throwing their money away on the small affairs that go about deceiving the people. For I am sorry to say that some showmen, who are not an honor to the fraternity, borrow the best lines of their advertisement from my announcements, or give free rein to their imaginations."

Undoubtedly the "small affair" mentioned in the article was intended to slight John B. Doris's Great Inter-Ocean Circus, which was indeed a smaller two-ring show. The clash between Doris and Forepaugh was a David and Goliath story where the former was outmatched by the latter. Whereas Forepaugh could afford to flood the Burlington media market with newspaper ads more than a month in advance of his show, the first newspaper ad for the Doris show appeared two days before their scheduled performance, suggesting its much more limited resources and the corresponding importance that posters played in its overall advertising strategy.

It was obviously the location that attracted Doris's billers to the Degrees' home, which was prime real estate for circus advertising. Built next to Colchester's general store near a busy intersection on Main Street, the house was clearly visible to both east- and westbound traffic. In the summer of 1883 the house lacked its exterior siding, a fact that probably made the prospect of pasting posters to it more palatable to the original homeowners. As was customary at the time, the residents would have received free tickets for permitting the circus to turn the outside of their home into a billboard.

In 1883 Adam Forepaugh celebrated his nineteenth season as the owner and proprietor of his circus by adding a Roman hippodrome to the lineup of his attractions. Patterned after the elliptical racetracks of ancient Rome, the half-mile course ran around the show's three performance rings directly in front of the audience. From the grandstands, spectators watched chariots, bicycles, and various species of animals, including 150 horses, 25 elephants, camels, and monkeys riding on donkeys, race around the tent.[21] Forepaugh's decision to include the hippodrome may have been influenced by the increased public interest in chariot racing after the publication of Lew Wallace's best-selling novel *Ben Hur: A Tale of the Christ* in 1880.[22]

Inside the show rings Forepaugh added fifty new performers of "different grades," for the 1883 tour.[23] Among the new recruits, Leonati, the Spiral Ascentionist (*see fig. 5.9*) performed a thrill act in which he rode a bicycle "upward, onward, around

Fig. 5.6. "Great Forepaugh Show, Museum, Menagerie, Triple Circus and Roman Hippodrome," 1883. Poster, printed by Russell Morgan & Co., Cincinnati. © Shelburne Museum, Shelburne, Vermont, Gift of Harold and Gladys Degree, 1991-18.4

and down the dizzy curving course," of a fifty-foot-tall spiral ramp.[24] Audiences were also treated to the aerial acrobatics of Little All Right, the Japanese Wirewalker, who performed his "marvelous slide for life" down a tightrope, using a paper para-

sol and fan to balance himself as he glided down the wire (*see fig. 5.3*). The inclusion of Little All Right in the Forepaugh show was a tribute to the abiding public interest in all things Japanese and John B. Doris also presented a similar act with his "original and only Royal Japanese Circus in America."[25] In the act, one of the Japanese equilibrists performed on a slide identical to that of Little All Right's. In the circus business, imitation was not always perceived as the highest form of flattery, but it was standard practice for showmen, especially Forepaugh, to plagiarize innovative or popular acts and promote them as unique and original.

Born Adam Forebaugh in Philadelphia in 1831, the showman changed the spelling of his surname to allude to the exotic quadrupeds in his circus menagerie.[26] A meat dealer and livestock trader, Forepaugh threw his hat into the circus ring in 1864 when he took possession of the Tom King Circus to recoup a bad debt for horses he sold to the show.[27] For the next twenty-seven years Forepaugh expanded his circus and challenged Barnum & Bailey for the title of the largest and best show in the United States in the late nineteenth century.

A savvy businessman and fierce competitor, Forepaugh earned a reputation for his aggressive and antagonistic behavior. He was perhaps best known for his ongoing public disputes with P. T. Barnum. During the so-called Elephant War Forepaugh provoked Barnum's ire by publicly demeaning the less-than-ivory complexion of Toung Taloung, the sacred white Siamese elephant Barnum had imported at great expense in 1884.[28] A master at publicity, Forepaugh devised his own white elephant using whitewash, a ruse that was quickly foiled by the press and secured his reputation as a trickster.[29] This was a reputation that was hard for Forepaugh to shake and was exploited by

Fig. 5.7. "Signor Don José Ramirez," 1883. Poster, printed by James Reilly, New York. © Shelburne Museum, Shelburne, Vermont, Gift of Harold and Gladys Degree, 1991-18.10

Fig. 5.8. "John B. Doris' Great Inter-Ocean Museum, Menagerie & Circus: Clarke's Slave Cabin Jubilee Singers," 1883. Poster, printed by the Strobridge Lithographing Company, Cincinnati. © Shelburne Museum, Shelburne, Vermont, Gift of Harold and Gladys Degree, 1991-18.9

his detractors, who claimed the showman allowed con artists on his show grounds.

John B. Doris (1847–1912) initiated his first season as the sole owner and proprietor of The Great Inter-Ocean Museum, Menagerie, & Circus in 1883, a year after his longtime business partner George H. Batcheller had retired and sold his stake to Doris.[30] The two men had begun collaborating several years earlier, managing concessions for various circuses, before starting their own show based out of Providence, Rhode Island in 1879.[31] According to Doris, their spectacular financial success was behind Batcheller's decision to quit showbiz: "being satisfied with the handsome competency his share in our profits had secured for him, desired to retire, and sold his interest to me, for a sum that I once regarded as being beyond my wildest ambition to possess, but which I am happy to say, I was abundantly able to spare."[32]

The publicity for Doris's show bragged that he spared no expense in acquiring new sensational acts for his show and this undoubtedly affected his profit margin. The highest wage earner by far was the show's leading act, Millie-Christine, the Two-Headed Nightingale; Doris had coaxed the siamese twins out of early retirement for the astronomical sum of 25,000 dollars per annum—more than half a million dollars today (*see fig. 5.12*).[33] Millie-Christine's position in the spotlight made her the primary target for Forepaugh, who could not find a comparable performer and relied on racist and derogatory advertisements to defame her reputation.

The 1883 Doris circus tour featured other impressive acts, including the British sensation Zazel, "the only human projectile ever shot from a cannon loaded and exploded by real gunpowder."[34] Other notable performers included the bareback riders William Showles, Don José Ramirez (*see fig. 5.7*), and

▲ *Fig. 5.9*. "Look at Leonati, the Gymnastic Autocrat of Aerial Art, Forepaugh Shows, Museum, Menagerie, Triple Circus & Roman Hippodrome," 1883. Poster, printed by James Reilly, New York. © Shelburne Museum, Shelburne, Vermont, Gift of Harold and Gladys Degree, 1991-18.5

HYÆNA STRIATA GIGANTEUM. THE ONLY LIVING SPECIMEN IN AMERICA

For the billers in Forepaugh's skirmish brigade it must have felt like sweet revenge when they covered over Doris's poster of Millie-Christine, the Two-Headed Nightingale with their own image of Nala Damajante, the Hindu Snake Charmer (*see fig. 5.11*). At the time, the conjoined siblings were suing Adam Forepaugh for libel in United States Circuit Court in the District of Indiana.[35] *Millie Christine v. Adam Forepaugh* alleged that the showman "composed and published show bills," that were libelous and circulated them throughout the city of Fort Wayne and the surrounding countryside.[36] The incident occurred when the touring routes of The Great Inter-Ocean and The Great Forepaugh circuses collided in northeastern Indiana in May of 1882. According to the complaint, Forepaugh knowingly and willingly distributed scurrilous rat sheets with the "malicious intent to injure the plaintiff in her said business of exhibiting herself for gain, and with the malicious intent to deprive this plaintiff of the patronage of the public."[37] In so doing, Forepaugh was accused of damaging the twins' livelihood and their ability to "amass some means by which she hopes to become independent, and beyond the danger of want."[38] For defamation, Millie-Christine sued Forepaugh for compensatory damages in the amount of 25,000 dollars, or one year of her salary.[39]

In the complaint, Millie-Christine's attorney quoted one showbill, or rat sheet, allegedly issued by Forepaugh attacking Batcheller and Doris's Inter-Ocean Circus, that read:

> The one great feature this concern extensively advertises is a horribly repulsive negro monstrosity. No lady would knowingly ever look upon it. Little children cover their faces with

Ella Stokes (*see fig. 5.5*), as well as the three acrobat Seigrist Brothers, six Siberian skaters, and Prof. Wingfield's dog circus. Doris's menagerie exhibited a wide variety of exotic animals, including two striped hyenas (*see fig. 5.10*), the great Egyptian Bovalapus, a "rare amphibious animal (water buffalo), vampire bats, and a baboon-like creature advertised as the 'lion slayer.'" Although not as large as Forepaugh's show, the John B. Doris Inter-Ocean Circus seemed to offer patrons an impressive array of attractions.

Fig. 5.10. "Hyæna Striata Giganteum, The Only Living Specimen in America," 1883. Poster. © Shelburne Museum, Shelburne, Vermont, Gift of Harold and Gladys Degree, 1991.18-11

their hands when encountering this frightful malformation and the sooner this hideous human deformity is hid from public view the better it will be for the community. All good Christian people can but regret that this afflicted object should be hawked over the country to satisfy the greed of a couple of sideshow exhibitors.[40]

The rat sheet's cruel claim that the conjoined but attractive twins Millie-Christine were a "horribly repulsive negro monstrosity," is demonstrably untrue (*fig. 5.13*). The nature of her "indissoluble union" was well documented and publicized. In a precedent set by P. T. Barnum's handling of his assorted human curiosities, Millie-Christine, like others with extraordinary physical configurations,

Fig. 5.11. "Nala Damajante," 1883. Poster. © Shelburne Museum, Shelburne, Vermont, Gift of Harold and Gladys Degree, 1991-18.1

was subjected to frequent invasive medical examinations, which were published for promotional purposes.[41] Medically described as a symmetrical pygopagus, the sisters were two fully developed individuals joined at the sacrum so that they "stand not quite back to back, rather sideways."[42] In addition to highly detailed anatomical descriptions, the medical reports contained statements attesting to the girls' attractive appearance. One observer testified that the girls were "well formed," another proclaimed them to be "pleasing to the eye," with "splendid Caucasian heads."[43] A courier published by Doris a year later, for the 1883 touring season, refuted the vituperative accusations of Forepaugh's rat sheet by describing Millie-Christine as possessing "two perfect, beautifully shaped heads, two gracefully formed necks and four arms and four lower limbs. A single perfect body," adding "Not the least deformity of limb, body or feature will be found."[44]

The assertions that "no lady would knowingly ever look upon it" and that "children cover their faces with their hands" in her presence were also greatly exaggerated. Before signing on with the Great Inter-Ocean in 1882, Millie-Christine had a long and prolific career in Europe and the United States, where the act was viewed by potentates and respectable audiences. In England, Millie-Christine was granted an audience with Queen Victoria and Prince Albert, who, "went down with the children to see an extraordinary object, far more extraordinary than the Siamese Twins."[45] Instead of being repulsed by a "monstrosity," the Queen recorded her impressions of the twins' appearance as being "very dark coloured, if not exactly negros & [they] look very merry & happy."[46]

After multiple continuances, settlement negotiations, a withdrawal of the complaint, and then

Fig. 5.12. "Millie Christine, The Two-Headed Lady," 1883. Poster. © Shelburne Museum, Shelburne, Vermont, Gift of Harold and Gladys Degree, 1991-18.6

Fig. 5.13. Ollivier & Co., New York. "Millie Christine, the Two-Headed Nightingale," ca. 1875. Carte-de-visite. © Shelburne Museum, Shelburne, Vermont, 2010-1.1

refiling in 1883, the lawsuit, in the end, was never adjudicated. As biographer Joanne Martell explained in her book *Millie-Christine: Fearfully and Wonderfully Made*, "trying to pin down roving circus people to trial appearance dates could strain the patience of any administrator."[47] Although Millie-Christine's lawsuit was a legitimate cause of action, it was common practice for circuses to use the legal system of Indiana as a means of retaliation against their rivals.[48] According to the inveterate showman W. C. Coup, "[o]nce we became involved in one of these contests and the opposition, in order to harass us, actually had four of our men arrested in different states on charge of libel. The Indiana libel laws were very severe and in each instance we were compelled to give a heavy bond for the release of our man."[49]

The 1883 skirmish in Colchester was thus just one facet of an abiding and acrimonious rivalry between the two shows.

◆◆

Perhaps it was a testament to the efficacy of Forepaugh's skirmish brigade and their tactics to marginalize their competition, or perhaps it was an indictment against the size and quality of Doris's show, but the local Burlington press took little note of the Great Inter-Ocean Circus's performance in the Queen City. Sandwiched between announcements for the local high-school graduation ceremony and the university glee club's performance, a short review under the "City Notes" section of *Burlington*

Fig. 5.14. Forepaugh Circus Parade in Montpelier, Vermont, July 19, 1892. Photograph. Vermont Historical Society

Daily Free Press & Times declared, "Doris' circus has come and gone." In six short sentences the critique praised the Great Inter-Oceans' street parade as "good and long," the menagerie as, "not large, but interesting and good," and the ring performance as "excellent." The writer went on to qualify his enthusiasm in the last sentence, stating, "On the whole the circus, though it can not rival Barnum's or Forepaugh's in size, is very good as far as it goes."

On the other hand, Forepaugh's show was well documented in a lengthier and laudatory critique published in the paper.[50] According to the article, ten thousand people "from the surrounding country and from across the lake took advantage of the cheap excursion rates," offered by both the ferries and railroad to attend the afternoon performance.[51] The review called the street parade an "attractive pageant," and declared the menagerie was "first-class" based on the quantity of elephants it contained. As far as circusgoers were concerned, the quality of a show was judged by the number of its pachyderms and Forepaugh's "quarter of a hundred" made his show "without [a] doubt the finest circus on the road to-day."[52] An 1892 photograph of the Forepaugh parade in Montpelier, Vermont, shows how an impressive elephant display drew in the crowds (*fig. 5.14*).

The newspaper went on to describe the scene under the big top as "remarkably novel and elaborate," mentioning by name the "Hindoo" snake charmer Nala Damajante and Leonati's thrilling ascent and decent. Those in attendance during the afternoon show were treated to an unexpected performance when a pickpocket named Oyster Jim was apprehended by a Pinkerton agent hired by Forepaugh.[53] The thief was "introduced to the audience" and "marched around the hippodrome track while the band played the 'Rogue's March.'"[54] It has been suggested that the arrest of Oyster Jim was a publicity stunt coordinated by Forepaugh to contradict his reputation for allowing grift in his show, lulling the audience into a false sense of security.[55] After a "good night's business," Forepaugh's circus experienced a series of mishaps that temporarily delayed their exodus from Burlington until 7:00 a.m. the following day.[56] One of the show's trains derailed in a tunnel on the outskirts of town, "smashing two flat and two stock cars."[57] During the commotion, one of the big center poles fell on top of a canvas man, severely injuring him.[58]

Competition between rival showmen like Adam Forepaugh and John B. Doris had a profound and positive impact on the development of America's itinerant circuses, inspiring both artistic creativity and technological innovation. But these same rivalries were also responsible for the development and implementation of disreputable and unethical business practices that skirted and often broke the law with few consequences. The recent conservation of Shelburne Museum's Colchester Posters brought attention to this circus advertising war.

1 Gail S. Rosenberg and Angela Patten, "1883 Forepaugh Posters Discovered in Vermont," *Bandwagon* 35, no. 4 (July–Aug. 1991), 34.

2 Kory Rogers, *Shelburne Museum's Circus Collection* (Shelburne, VT: Shelburne Museum, 2010), 10–11.

3 John B. Doris Great Inter-Ocean Museum, Menagerie, & Circus, courier, Shelburne Museum Library/Archives ms 398, 10.

4 "Route Book of the Great Forepaugh Show, Circus, Hippodrome, and Menagerie," season of 1883, www.circushistory.org/History/Forepaugh1883.htm (accessed Jan. 30, 2011).

5 The attribution of the identity of the equestrian portrayed in fig. 5.7 as Signor Don José Ramirez by the author was made after comparing the poster with an image of the rider published on page 12 in the John B. Doris Great Inter-Ocean Museum, Menagerie, & Circus courier in the collection of Shelburne Museum's Library and Archives.

6 John B. Doris Great Inter-Ocean Museum, Menagerie, & Circus, courier, Shelburne Museum Library/Archives ms 398, 12.

7 Ibid., 15.

8 "Route Book of the Great Forepaugh Show, Circus, Hippodrome, and Menagerie," season of 1883.

9 Ricky Jay, *Learned Pigs & Fireproof Women: Unique, Eccentric and Amazing Entertainers* (New York: Villard Books, 1986), 201–12.

10 Anne Geggis, "Amazing Human Feat," *Burlington Daily Free Press & Times,* June 5, 1991, B1.

11 Robert Bogdan, *Freak Show: Presenting Human Oddities for Amusement and Profit* (Chicago and London: University of Chicago Press, 1990), 235.

12 Charles Philip Fox and Tom Parkinson, *Billers, Banners, and Bombast: The Story of Circus Advertising* (Boulder, CO: Pruett Publishing, 1985), 51.

13 Ibid., 63.

14 Ibid., 1, 203.

15 Joanne Martell, *Millie-Christine: Fearfully and Wonderfully Made* (Winston-Salem, NC: John F. Blair, 1999), 222.

16 W. C. Coup, *Sawdust & Spangles: Stories & Secrets of the Circus* (Chicago: Herbert S. Stone, 1901), 113.

17 *Walton's Vermont Register and Farmer's Almanac for 1883* (White River Junction, VT: White River Paper Company, 1883), 56.

18 "Route Book of the Great Forepaugh Show, Circus, Hippodrome, and Menagerie," season of 1883.

19 "Forepaugh in Vermont," *Burlington Daily Free Press & Times,* June 21, 1883, 3.

20 "Why! Mr. Forepaugh Answers," *Burlington Daily Free Press & Times,* June 14, 1883, 1.

21 Herald, "Forepaugh Show," 1883, Show Bill Printing House Avil and Co., Collection of Shelburne Museum 27.4-132.

22 John Culhane, *The American Circus: An Illustrated History* (New York: Henry Holt, 1991), 104.

23 "Route Book of the Great Forepaugh Show, Circus, Hippodrome, and Menagerie," season of 1883.

24 Quote taken from advertisement posted at http://yesterdaystowns.blogspot.com/2007_04_01_archive.html (accessed Jan. 28, 2011).

25 John B. Doris Great Inter-Ocean Museum, Menagerie, & Circus, courier, Shelburne Museum Library/Archives ms 398, 9.

26 "Old Adam and New Noah," *New York Times* (June 19, 1887), www.nytimes.com (accessed Jan. 26, 2011).

27 Culhane, *American Circus,* 136.

28 Ibid., 135–36.

29 Ibid., 136.

30 John B. Doris Great Inter-Ocean Museum, Menagerie, & Circus, courier, Shelburne Museum Library/Archives ms 398, 2.

31 Tom Ogden, *Two Hundred Years of the American Circus: From Aba-Daba to the Zoppe-Zavatta Troupe* (New York: Facts on File, Inc., 1993), 39.

32 John B. Doris Great Inter-Ocean Museum, Menagerie, & Circus, courier, Shelburne Museum Library/Archives ms 398, 2.

33 Ibid., 8.

34 Ibid., 16.

35 Martell, *Millie-Christine,* 221–26.

36 Millie Christine v. Adam Forepaugh, United States Circuit Court (District of Indiana, 1882).

37 Ibid., 2.

38 Ibid., 1.

39 Ibid., 5.

40 Ibid., 3.

41 Ibid.

42 Ibid.

43 Millie Christine McCoy, *History and Medical Description of the Two-Headed Girl* (Buffalo, NY: Warren Johnson, 1869), 23, 28.

44 John B. Doris Great Inter-Ocean Museum, Menagerie, & Circus, courier, Shelburne Museum Library/Archives ms 398, 8.

45 Martell, *Millie-Christine,* 164.

46 Ibid. 165.

47 Ibid., 228.

48 Neil Harris, *Humbug: The Art of P. T. Barnum* (Chicago and London: University of Chicago Press, 1973), 249.

49 Coup, *Sawdust & Spangles,* 113–14.

50 "The Circus," *Burlington Daily Free Press & Times,* July 26, 1883, 3.

51 Ibid.

52 Ibid.

53 "A Pickpocket Comes to Grief," *Burlington Daily Free Press & Times,* July 26, 1883, 3.

54 Ibid.

55 *Shelburne Museum Newsletter,* Summer 1991, 3.

56 "Route Book of the Great Forepaugh Show, Circus, Hippodrome, and Menagerie," season of 1883.

57 Ibid.

58 Ibid.

6

ᵀᴴᴱ CIRCUS PARADE

GREGORY J. RENOFF

In the late winter of 1995 circus aficionados in Richmond, Virginia, eager to catch a glimpse of the animals from the Ringling Bros. and Barnum & Bailey Circus on their city's streets, needed to conduct an urban safari. With the show remaining quiet about the time and route that it would use to move its animals from their railroad cars to the Richmond Coliseum, locals resorted to calling the police to find out when and where the procession would take place. Those Virginians who succeeded in their search witnessed a largely silent line of elephants, horses, camels, ponies, zebras, and llamas moving without fanfare through the darkened streets of the city. In response to these efforts, the show issued a news release reminding its fans that its "animal walk" was "not a parade." Instead, was a "logistical necessity" needed "to move our animals from the circus train" to the performance site.[1]

At one time, industry impresarios would have considered such talk as akin to suicide for the circus industry. As the entertainment trade journal *Billboard* argued in 1926, "Cutting out the circus parade is equivalent to cutting off the supply of circus fans."[2] Between the 1830s and the 1920s, these processions had signaled the start of the unofficial holiday known as Circus Day, the date on the calendar that a troupe performed in a specific community (*fig. 6.1*). Because Americans gauged the quality of a concern by its parade, circuses deployed elaborate wagons, secured hundreds of gorgeous horses and exotic animals, outfitted show members with fantastic costumes, and employed dozens of talented musicians to provide their pageants with a spirited soundtrack, all in an effort to make their shows as alluring as possible. When it moved through the main streets of a community, a circus procession served as a living, moving advertisement for a concern, expressly designed to turn parade watchers into circus attendees.[3]

At the industry's Gilded Age peak, circus parades competed with ethnic, military, and holiday processions for the attentions of Americans.[4]

◄ *Detail of fig. 6.9.* Michael Maslan. "A Forty-Horse Team in the Barnum & Bailey's Circus Parade, Chicago, Illinois," 1904. Photograph. © Michael Maslan Historic Photographs/Corbis

Despite the ubiquity of these other parades, circus caravans invariably attracted thousands of spectators who packed streets, craned their necks out of windows, and peered down from rooftops, all in an effort to witness the public displays put on by the era's biggest and most sensational popular entertainment concerns. These crowds of people, along with the pageants they turned out to see, possessed the power to disrupt the normal course of activity in a community by shutting down schools, civic institutions, and businesses. When the circus came to town, the parade set the celebratory tone for the duration of Circus Day.

Still, the power of a circus parade went beyond stopping traffic and closing businesses. By their very nature these pageants turned a community's streets into an open-air theater and produced a sense of democratic spectatorship that allowed anyone, regardless of color or class, to take in the parade without spending a cent. This sense of rough equality and shared experience among those that feasted their eyes on circus parades helped make them what scholar David Rockwell has described as awe-inspiring "live experiences that require communal participation," or spectacles.[5]

Here it is important to underscore and expand upon Rockwell's point. As literary theorist Mikhail Bakhtin wrote about carnival, "it is not a spectacle seen by the people; they live in it, and everyone participates because its very idea embraces all the people."[6] This same sense of active participation—as opposed to passive spectatorship—held true for circus parades. When they turned out for these public displays, Americans did more than just watch the delights that rolled past them. They stared, laughed, cheered, yelled, and sometimes even participated in the parades themselves in official and unofficial capacities. In doing so, they played an essential role in

Fig. 6.1. "Sells-Floto Super Combined Circus," 1919. Poster, printed by the Strobridge Lithographing Company, Cincinnati. Collection of the John and Mable Ringling Museum of Art, Tibbals Collection, ht2000696

making the circus parade, and Circus Day by extension, into a true communal celebration. Without joyous crowds to experience it, a circus parade was nothing more than a slow-moving caravan of horse-drawn wagons and exotic animals.

Despite their centrality in American life, circus parades began to recede from the national scene by the early twentieth century. While some smaller shows continued to offer parades into the 1930s, the industry's leading owners, faced with the challenges of trying to process through an urban landscape festooned with low-hanging wires, regulated by stoplights, and dominated by automobiles, began to curtail or end their free street displays. Commenting on the elimination of its parade, a Barnum & Bailey Circus official told the *New York Times* in 1903 that Manhattan's streets had become "impassable" for the troupe's animals, not to mention challenging for the "multi-thousand-dollar cars, 'open dens of wild beasts, and mounted cavaliers and ladies in picturesque costumes.'"[7] Although this process moved unevenly across the country, by the 1920s almost all sizable circuses had eliminated their free daily pageants.

Despite their decline, the content of these processions and the celebratory impulses they inspired have found outlets in different guises and have experienced rebirths throughout the twentieth and into the twenty-first centuries. The same spirit of release and commercialism that animated circus parades thrives today within the Macy's Thanksgiving Day Parade, an outgrowth of and successor to circus parades in New York City. Since the 1960s, Milwaukee's annual Great Circus Parade has provided a nostalgic reenactment of the great pageants of the past. The evolution of these events from novelties to civic institutions, thanks in no small measure to the participation of ordinary Americans in them, demonstrates the cultural power that these spectacles rooted in the circus continue to have in American life.[8] And despite Ringling Bros. and Barnum & Bailey's occasional efforts to limit the attention given to its animal walks, circus fans flock to these unofficial parades. Circus showmen neither invented the parade nor stage them today but their innovations expanded and prefigured almost all of the elements that make some of the greatest American parades not just spectacles, but truly spectacular.

The first organized circus parades in America reflected the realities of itinerancy as much as advertising. After the 1825 development of a portable canvas tent gave showmen the ability to dispense with the need for wooden buildings to host their performances, they set out to tour the American backcountry. While some shows moved from place to place by way of steamboat, by the late 1820s increasing numbers of traveling concerns ambulated via wagon, performing in one location and then traveling in the darkness along America's primitive road network to the next performance site.[9]

In short order, showmen recognized that their caravans, with their lines of wagons, men on horseback, and occasionally an elephant, invariably captured the attention of locals as they trundled their way to the next tour stop. In fact, the movement of a show's wagon train from the outskirts of town to the show lot represented the most effective means of announcing that a performance would soon commence. In his discussion of this first generation of shows, veteran circus man Gil Robinson observed that since these early troupes had no mechanisms in place for advertising, they wholly "depended on the caravan to stir up public interest." Once a show approached a community, a rider loped ahead of the wagon train and headed to the center of town to herald the circus's arrival with a trumpet blast. The

LITH. AND PRINTED IN COLORS BY G. & W. ENDICOTT N. YORK.

THE GREAT EGYPTIA

Drawn by Camels imported from the Deserts of Arabia for Crane & Co's great Oriental Circus, the largest Equestrian and Zoological Establishment in the

convoy that followed the trumpeter then served to publicize that day's performances.[10]

Billposting, or the use of pictorial advertising, soon provided a new reason for parading. While eye-catching posters tacked up at every country cross-roads, barn, and mill within a twenty-mile radius of town might promise an amazing display of rare animals, daring equestrians, and hilarious clowns, not every circus delivered what it promised on its posters. "Notwithstanding so much tall bragging in bills and advertisements," one Ohio newspaper editor wrote in 1847, the circus he saw "was a miserable affair in general. Some two or three thousand persons were humbugged out of their half and quarter dollars."[11]

In order to lessen public suspicion, circus owners began using their parades as a means to demon-strate convincingly that their shows deserved patronage. After the long overnight ride, showmen dismounted their wagons and horses on the outskirts of town and set out to make themselves, the show's stock, and their wagons presentable. They curried dirty horses and scraped mud from the sideboards and wheels of wagons. They washed the dirt from their faces, slicked down their windswept hair, and donned their costumes before proceeding down the community's main street.[12] During the nineteenth and early twentieth centuries, Americans learned to judge the quality of a show by the parades that show-men staged, rather than by the vainglorious claims that they made on their advertising materials.[13]

In order to further impress locals—and to en-courage them to buy show tickets—impresarios had

Fig. 6.2. "The Great Egyptian Dragon Chariot," 1849. Lithograph, printed by G. & W. Endicott, New York. Courtesy, American Antiquarian Society

DRAGON CHARIOT,

Caravan consists of Real Syrian Camels much larger than any ever before imported. Two of the number are Sacred White Camels or Albinos.

The whole of this Immense Establishment will exhibit at

1849

begun to deploy elaborately crafted and richly hued wagons by the 1840s. Taking inspiration from the conveyances of European royalty, this new generation of circus wagon featured meticulously crafted wood and skillfully painted tableaux (*fig. 6.2*).[14] Most typically, the first conveyance that a showman procured with the parade particularly in mind was a bandwagon. Showmen invested in opulent bandwagons in order to provide a spectacular rolling stage for their musicians to perform on as the show moved through town. For example, the Robinson & Elred Circus announced that its "celebrated Brass Band" would be carried in its "Chariot of the Sun, a magnificent work of art, constructed at an enormous expense [and] ... drawn by 20 beautiful Cream Horses, caparisoned in the most superb style."[15] Behind a show's ornate band-wagon came costumed performers on horseback, wheeled animal cages, and an elephant or two.

By mid-nineteenth century, circus men sought to stand out from their competitors by sparing no expense in outfitting their bandwagons. The Raymond & Waring Circus featured a five-thousand-dollar gilded bandwagon that measured thirty feet in length and required a clearance of twenty feet.[16] Not to be outdone, the Bailey & Co.'s Circus kicked off its daily Grand Cavalcade with a regal bandwagon pulled by an elephant in harness.[17] By the end of the wagon-show era, showmen deployed extraordinarily extravagant conveyances and teams:

At the head of the line came Dan Castello's herd of camels, eight in number .... The camels were

Renoff

in harness, and following them came four beautiful horses, the twelve animals drawing the "Car of Theodorus," a chariot constructed at immense expense.... It was a splendid car, being handsomely ornamented with gilt figures upon the sides and shone resplendent in the sun. In the centre of the establishment was a huge gilt figure of a dragon, in front and back of which sat the members of the fine band which accompanies the show, and whose excellent music was delightful to hear.... The car is the most superb thing of the kind that has ever been brought out, and is, of itself, a big show.[18]

The *Savannah Morning News* reporter's observation that this wagon itself was "a big show" underscores the success that showmen like Castello had in transforming their once-modest processions into spectacular attractions in and of themselves.

With these extravagant carriages at their head, wagon-show-era circus parades served up a sensory feast to Americans. Consider, for example, the soundscape of nineteenth-century towns and cities. In these places possessed of what historian Mark M. Smith has dubbed "rural quietude," the calls of

animals, voices of men, and church bells dominated the auditory environment, and the rumble of an approaching railroad or the roar of a steam-powered mill represented a significant departure from the workaday norm.[19] Likewise, picture a visual landscape where buildings stood painted in largely muted hues, horse teams came matched by ability rather than color and conformation, and conveyances were designed for practicality more than ornament.[20]

When they entered this subdued environment, circus parades attracted attention and stirred emotions by producing an explosion of tumult and riot of color. For instance, in September 1858, the Sand's, Nathan's & Co. circus shattered the tranquility of morning in the Pennsylvania hamlets of Tioga and Troy, population 1,157 and 1,418, respectively, by processing through the streets with a line of "Artists, Horses, Ponies ... Carriages, Wagons," and a glittering brass band.[21] Yet the *pièce de résistance* of this show's street display was a brand-new innovation in the circus business, a steam-powered organ, or calliope (*fig. 6.3*). Drawn by six elephants, the show's rig featured one wagon for its player, keyboard, and whistles, and a trailing vehicle that transported the rolling instrument's steam engine. When the show's advertising promised it could be "distinctly heard for ten or twelve miles," locals who witnessed this steam-belching, half-animal, half-machine rig and experienced the ear-piercing din that it unleashed in their communities, likely took the ad at its word.[22]

Small towns aside, circus men made sure to outfit their shows with trappings sufficient to draw attention even in larger communities. When a circus rolled through the bustling mill town of Pittsfield, Massachusetts, in 1846, the local paper reported, "The Mammoth National Circus of Messrs. Welch & Mann made a splendid entrée into our village this (Wednesday) morning, and attracted much notice.

Fig. 6.3. Parade scene of the Ringling Bros. Circus in Decatur, Illinois, showing a rear side view of a steam calliope, 1908. Photograph. Circus World Museum, CWi-1363

Their 'Magnificent Band Chariot (drawn by 10 cream colored horses), with 14 talented musicians, playing some of the most popular airs,' is a great affair."[23] Behind gilded bandwagons pulled by perfectly matched teams came mounted performers holding vibrant flags that fluttered in the breeze, with men clad in suits of armor that clanked, squeaked, and glinted in the sun as the riders processed past the assembled masses. Bringing up the rear, colorful banners bedecked gaily painted animal cages, from which emanated the roars and growls of wild animals.

Over the cacophony of street life in the busy port city of Salem, Massachusetts, a circus company turned the head of a local newsman in 1835:

> There never was a place so filled with strange sights and sounds as was ... Salem, during the latter part of last week. One pair of eyes seemed to be hardly sufficient ... to take in all of the wonderful, the beautiful, the comical, the ridiculous, which solicited attention ... on every side. *Here* are two huge elephants, a band of music, and a train of wagons, lumbering through the streets.... *There* is a procession of Circus mummers in the most fantastic garb, mounted upon piebald horses, with trumpets sounding, and clowns ... chattering on the necks of their steeds.[24]

Showmen outfitted and organized circus parades in order to create a noisy, vibrant moving spectacle replete with enough color, sound, and motion to enthrall onlookers, regardless of whether they dwelled in small villages or large cities.

Americans reacted to these pageants in a variety of ways. First and foremost, they watched them with rapt attention. For example, a New Hampshire newspaper applauded the 1835 arrival of a show by writing that its "approach was announced by well-executed national airs from a large and distinguished band of music, drawn by four elegant bays, in a splendid music carriage. The train of wagons and cages was much more numerous than we have ever seen before, and both equestrians and pedestrians gathered in the streets to watch the passing parade."[25] In Columbus, Georgia, the citizenry "turned out en masse" in 1867 to see the Castello Circus's "grand cavalcade, headed by a brass band" with its "wagon drawn by six white horses, with nodding plumes" make its way through the streets, followed by "knights in full armor ... ladies gaily caparisoned, a baby elephant, a phaeton with four tiny ponies attached ... [and] a lion loose upon the top of a wagon."[26]

Parades of this caliber inspired some people to do more than watch. As the Bailey and Co.'s wagons made their way through the streets of Columbus, locals expressed their approval by first welcoming them "by loud and vociferous yelling." As the trailing caissons passed by, the uproarious throng of Georgians then "escorted them to their quarters in large crowds."[27] In the same city, an "immense crowd of darkies and little people white and black" escorted Stone & Murray's Grand Circus's bandwagon to the show grounds.[28] In the Empire State, Brooklynites rapturously "followed" the lion cage wagon from Howe's Great Circus as it clattered along the city's cobblestone streets, even though the show's big cat menacingly "glared" at them as they walked alongside its wheeled enclosure.[29] When Americans experienced circus parades, they did more than watch them. They joyously participated in them as they transpired. In doing so, they transformed commercial processions into communal celebrations.

As the 1870s dawned, the industry's leading showmen took advantage of advances in transportation technology and the concomitant development of a national railroad system to shift their main mode of itinerancy from wagon to rail. In practice this meant that circus owners could significantly increase the mileage their outfits could cover in a single season, but it also limited their tour stops to sizable communities along railroad lines.[30]

Along with easing their ability to ambulate, this transition from road to rail allowed showmen to exploit the demographic changes resulting from the movement of Americans from rural to urban areas. Between 1860 and 1900, American cities experienced a rate of population growth that outstripped that of rural areas, with urban communities growing rapidly.[31] For instance, Philadelphia's popu-

lation increased from 565,529 in 1860 to over a million in 1900, joining New York and Chicago as the third American city with a populations of over one million inhabitants.[32] Baltimore, Boston, and St. Louis likewise could all count more than a half million residents in 1900.[33] This marriage between a relatively efficient transportation network and explosive population growth provided circuses with the conditions that allowed them to draw larger audiences than ever before and to become America's preeminent mass entertainment.[34]

With leading circuses now bypassing small towns, their performance locations became magnets for rural people, who headed to town on Circus Day

THE GRAND LAY-OUT.

in order to take their places in the streets alongside town and city dwellers during the morning parade (*fig. 6.4*). For example, as dawn broke on an October 1899 morning in Fayetteville, Arkansas, "every road leading to this city bore a steady stream of happy and expectant country people from as early as five o'clock."[35] In Columbus, Georgia in 1877, "country people from all directions were flocking to the city to see the circus...large forces may be expected from the surrounding country 'for many miles around.'"[36]

The resulting crowds of city and country people comprised individuals drawn from a wide range of groups. In Boston, people "flocked in from all the suburban districts and lined the sidewalks the entire length of the route. At central points...there were immense crowds of people, men, women and children. All classes of society were represented."[37] The railroad town of Bainbridge, Georgia, hosted "people, old and young, white and black" who moved "shuffling and scuffling to get eligible positions from which to 'see the bandwagon.'"[38] As a *New York Times* reporter summarized, "hastily compiled statistics indicate that the entire census of the city, young and old, male and female, 999 [*sic*] percent, was in the streets, on the steps, or located at the different vantage windows of the hotels where the great procession was to pass."[39] On Circus Day, parades drew thousands of people of all classes and colors into the streets.

As a procession's advent approached, people moved to seize vantage points from which to see it move through the streets. The sight of Forepaugh's Circus forming its line of march sent "thousands of people" in St. Louis "running to see the grand procession" in 1877 (*fig. 6.5*).[40] As a pageant prepared to move through Denver, the city's circus fans "perched themselves on railings, like so many buzzards on a roost, and craned their necks out of win-

dows looking for the elephants, the ponies and the bespangled women."[41]

Part of the eagerness of locals to witness these processions stemmed from their spectacular scale. By making use of the increased freight capacity offered by rail cars, showmen vastly expanded the number of wagons and performers, both animal and human, in their parades (*fig. 6.6*). The largest traveling shows of the 1850s displayed twenty or so wagons—along with a few dozen horses, ponies, and elephants—in their parades (*fig. 6.7*). However, a representative railroad-era parade staged by the Barnum & Bailey Circus in 1895 included

four hundred horses, 300 performers, all splendidly mounted; 7 open dens of wild beasts, with a male or female trainer in each; 2 droves of camels and 400 ponies.... All of the crowned heads of the world—the reigning sovereigns—in coaches of state, in royal robes, on horseback, surrounded with escorts; the military uniforms of all nations, in groups and in picturesque Oriental style...with golden chariots, containing the zoological collection and the allegorical chariots, illustrating nursery rhymes and children's fairy stories.

These were all trailed by twenty-four elephants and a steam calliope.[42] Parades by well-capitalized circuses of the late nineteenth century routinely measured over a mile in length and took more than an hour to run their course.[43]

As the twentieth century approached, showmen found a new way to draw attention to their cavalcades when they opened their stands in America's largest cities. While almost all prior circus parades had occurred in the daylight hours, by the 1880s some circus entrepreneurs began staging parades in the evening and illuminating them with a variety of sources. As a Chicago scribe informed his readers after taking in one of these nighttime pageants, "the illuminations were the feature. There were two or three or four, sometimes even five, colored lights upon each wagon, while there were reflectors upon wagons at various points in the parade flashing light to both front and rear. Viewed from a distance it was a long row of colored lights with occasional punctuation, in the form of pyrotechnic wagons," producing "without a doubt the most noticeable procession

... ever seen in Chicago."[44] The Great London Circus added further incandescence to its twilight spectacle in the same city by heading it up with fifty armored knights carrying torches ablaze with red and green colored flame. Behind the marchers came a parade illuminated by Chinese lanterns, torches, and calcium lights, with the show's bandwagons dispensing "calcium lights as well as music. On the highest seats torch bearers manipulated red, blue and green fire, or occasionally sent up Roman candles. The last was the certain signal for renewed cheers from the juveniles."[45] By utilizing everything from flambeaux to fireworks, circus men set the streets—and their processions—aglow when they processed through America's largest cities.

While people hallooed, whistled, and walked alongside these processions as they wended their way to their exhibition sites, late-nineteenth-century circus men gave locals the chance to further participate in these public events. In order to intensify the visual impact of their open-air spectacles, circus owners recruited upwards of a thousand volunteers to parade with their shows while carrying torches, and sought to guarantee the return of their property by compensating each torch-bearer with a dollar, or a ticket to the show, when he or she turned it in at the end of the parade.[46] In Manhattan, a Barnum & Bailey parade featured "red fire ... burning on all the wagons and chariots, and torch-bearers, walking in line on each side, increased the glare and made the profuse display of gilt and silver, spangles, mirrors, and brilliant colors more brilliant than would be possible in daylight."[47] While circus fans of all ages queued up for their chance to become

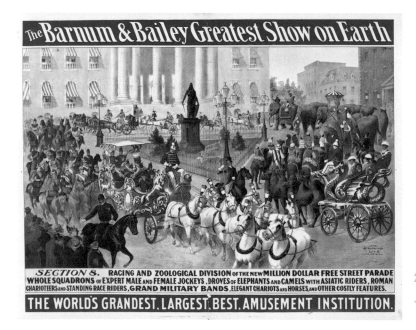

Fig. 6.6. "Gorgeous Street Parade by W. W. Cole's Grand Concorporation!" 1878. Fold-out advertisement. Circus World Museum, CWi-2320

Fig. 6.7. "The Barnum & Bailey Greatest Show on Earth, Section 8. Racing and Zoological Division of the New Million Dollar Free Street Parade," ca. 1902. Poster, printed by the Strobridge Lithographing Company, Cincinnati. Cincinnati Art Museum, Gift of the Strobridge Lithographing Company, 1965.784

a torchbearer, children, in particular, took to this task with great zeal. The *New York Times* reported in 1890 that scores of young torchbearers "trudged with the parade right alongside of the steam organ, the den of lions, the team of streaked zebras, and other startling components of the procession."[48]

Whether day or the night, crowds took command of streets and sidewalks as these cavalcades moved through American communities (*fig. 6.8*). "The sidewalks were literally packed," Philadelphia's *North American* reported, "and no little amount of work fell to the police, who were kept busy keeping the mob under control."[49] In Milwaukee, "All the principal down-town streets were crowded . . . . Third Street and several other thoroughfares were so crowded that pedestrians were obliged to walk in the roadway."[50] Thoroughfares in Pittsburgh "over which the parade passed were crowded and street traffic for a time was practically suspended."[51] Highlighting the tumultuous scene on Chicago's streets during a circus parade, an *Inter-Ocean* scribe questioned whether "there has been such another popular outpouring since the time of the riots."[52]

By the last decade of the nineteenth century, the success of circuses in attracting huge throngs to their parades began to run headlong into the desire of municipalities to maintain a free flow of traffic in their increasingly crowded streets. While growing urban population densities maximized the potential customer base for circuses, congested thoroughfares presented serious challenges for urbanites. In the decades before traffic signals became urban fixtures, helter-skelter traffic movements saw horse- and mule-drawn conveyances attempting to move in the face of oncoming electric streetcars, and mounted riders and pedestrians seeking to avoid being hit by both.[53] "So far as legitimate locomotion is concerned," a reporter visiting Manhattan in 1905 explained to his readers, "conditions are pretty near unbearable," with vehicles often moving "at a snail's pace" through Gotham's teeming streets.[54] Considering the same issue, in 1897 a Boston editor decried the interrelated urban "evils" of the "congestion of street traffic" and "delays in traveling through the central part" of his city, which he argued would only worsen in the coming years.[55]

Unsurprisingly, by the last decade of the nineteenth century, showmen began to face complaints about deleterious effects that their parades had on urban traffic flows (*fig. 6.9*). In 1894 the *Milwaukee Journal* reported that a local street railway company official "was extremely indignant" about even "the thought of stopping the [street] cars for a circus

▲ *Fig. 6.8.* Robert L. Bracklow. Barnum & Bailey's circus parade, New York, ca. 1900. Photograph. © Photo Collection Alexander Alland, Sr./Corbis

parade." Since these events halted "all the traffic of the city," he argued, they produced "no end of inconvenience to thousands of citizens, besides causing a great financial loss to the street railway company."[56] Despite this official's denunciation, circus companies tried to reconcile their cavalcades with urban traffic conditions by periodically halting their line of march to allow idling streetcars to travel athwart parade routes.[57]

Still, in practice such accommodations often proved less than satisfying. An 1887 Barnum Circus procession "kept the streets thronged and car drivers swearing" as they struggled to transport their passengers through Brooklyn and to keep their teams of horses from bolting as the show's elephants passed.[58] In Pittsburgh, "the thoroughfares over which the parade passed were crowded and street traffic for a time was practically suspended, as all the street car lines were tied up until the procession

had gone by."[59] Of course, any serious traffic complications that arose during a cavalcade had the potential to paralyze an entire city. When a cable car wreck coincided with a circus procession in midtown Manhattan in 1896, ten thousand parade watchers mobbed the accident scene, and as a result, "Broadway was almost entirely blocked for three hours. During that time not a car moved from Houston Street to Union Square."[60]

Circus animal handlers likewise struggled to maintain control over their charges in the face of the sensory overload produced by modern environments. In New York City, a group of elephants passing under an elevated train platform bolted when a train suddenly rumbled across it.[61] Even smaller communities did not offer a complete respite from these challenges, as those in the vicinity of a Beloit, Wisconsin circus parade discovered in 1900 after a steam pile driver spooked a hitch of ponies, sending onlookers scrambling to avoid the runway wagon.[62]

As a result of these factors, some circus companies began eliminating their parades as early as 1902.[63] While industry insiders and observers remained split about the wisdom of this move, those in favor of omitting the feature saw their position bolstered by the Barnum & Bailey Circus's 1905 announcement that it would no longer parade. In an attempt to mitigate public disappointment with this decision, J. A. Bailey, the show's manager, suggested that the results of "a careful investigation" by the show had found that "the circus parade is no longer popular" with Americans. He also claimed that regardless of the feature's purported appeal, the show's scale had simply grown "too big" for it to caravan before performing.[64]

At the same time, however, the show's statements to the press hinted at the real reasons behind the move. J. A. Bailey reminded the *New York Times*

Fig. 6.9. Michael Maslan. "A Forty-Horse Team in the Barnum & Bailey's Circus Parade, Chicago, Illinois," 1904. Photograph. © Michael Maslan Historic Photographs/Corbis

that by cutting out the parade, the show would now uniformly apply a policy that it already followed when it appeared in America's biggest cities. "We have not given a parade in New York, Chicago, or other large cities for years," he said.[65] Two years later, a Barnum representative offered a further explanation by admitting that the "interference with public traffic" caused by parades had played a significant role in the show's decision.[66]

As the automobile became an increasingly common sight in American cities, the anti-parade movement picked up steam. In 1914, the Atlanta city council barred circus parades from the city's downtown shopping district on the behest of merchants who successfully argued that these displays "demoralized" their business operations when their automobile-driving customers faced "congested traffic" as they tried to patronize their stores on Circus Days.[67] A decade later, a press agent explained to a Chicago daily that since the city was "so large, with so many automobiles and street cars and subway entrances cluttering up the downtown streets," parading had become impractical.[68] This opinion certainly reflected the impact that parades like those staged by Ringling Bros. and Barnum & Bailey in 1920 had on life in Chicago. The massive display "jammed" the surrounding streets with idling automobiles, halted streetcar traffic, and even forced the city's fire department to find alternate routes for its equipment.[69] In the end, even Charles Ringling, who had stood fast in face of industry pressure to cease parading, decided to cut out the feature in the early 1920s. With regret, he conceded in the pages of *Billboard* that "traffic conditions in the modern city" simply made it "impossible" to "haul the massive bandwagons...through the down-town streets." By the mid-1920s the circus parade had largely become a thing of the past.[70]

Here it is important to underscore that it was the changing nature of America's biggest cities, and not the effectiveness of the circus parade as an advertising tool or popular draw, that had led to its decline. Indeed, in smaller cities, some second-tier circuses still paraded, their processions arousing keen interest. Two decades after J. A. Barnum had claimed that the feature had become unpopular, "thousands of spectators" swarmed the streets of Lewiston, Maine during a parade, with women and children literally climbing on a hippo cage wagon during a pause in the procession.[71] In Reading, Pennsylvania, the superintendent of public schools dismissed the city's students early so they could take in a 1917 parade, allowing them to join a crowd that numbered in the thousands.[72] Even as late as 1925, a procession "thrilled" throngs of citizens in St. Petersburg, Florida, who watched the show pass through the city's downtown.[73]

The tremendous enthusiasm that Americans exhibited for circus parades—and their effectiveness as an advertising tool—encouraged their appropriation by another commercial enterprise: Macy's department store. To be sure, the New York–based retailer did not invent the holiday parade; in 1920, Philadelphia's Gimbel Brothers Department Store presented a small Thanksgiving Day parade with a finale that saw Santa Claus ascend a ladder into the store's toy department.[74] But Macy's 1924 Big Christmas Parade (Macy's did not call it a Thanksgiving Day Parade until 1935), did set a new standard for such holiday spectacles, and in doing so, drew on circus parades for its form and content.[75]

In its publicity material, Macy's proclaimed that its procession would allow for the "welcoming" of Santa Claus to New York.[76] Yet little else in its inaugural parade, other than the jolly figure in his red suit, reflected the traditional content of

Christmas. Instead of the trappings of Christmas, the store's advertising (*fig. 6.10*) promised spectators that they would see a "tremendous pageant of … elephants, bears, camels, monkeys, clowns, brass bands . . . and everything that makes a real Circus Parade so dear to everyone." In sum, it was an advertising campaign that the leading circus entrepreneurs of the Gilded Age would have been happy to endorse for their own shows.[77]

Along with Santa Claus and its circus features, Macy's also sought to appeal to children by displaying floats themed on traditional nursery rhymes and folk tales. Yet in this case as well, circus men had offered up this content in their processions in decades past by deploying parade wagons with motifs such as the Old Lady Who Lived in a Shoe and Little Red Riding Hood.[78] In fact, circus impresarios had even anticipated Macy's use of Santa Claus. In 1883 the Barnum & London Circus parade offered up a representation of "Santa Claus, drawn by reindeer" for "the amusement of the little folks" who turned out for its parades.[79]

In light of the tremendous success that circus men had achieved in creating a sense of spectacle—

and a desire to spend—through their public displays, it is unsurprising that Macy's first parade drew so heavily from circus processions.[80] As historian William Leach has shown, Macy's owners intended to use the parade to publicize their store, appeal to children, and to drive consumer spending.[81] Circus men, if nothing else, had demonstrated that their spectacles, with their clowns, elephants, and brass bands, could capture the attention of a city's residents, particularly its children, and encourage people of all ages and classes to eagerly hand over their money for tickets. While Macy's was in the business of selling consumer goods instead of an entertainment experience, ultimately its goal with its parade was the same that circuses had pursued a generation before. This intersection between the two seemingly disparate spectacles was not lost on the *New York Times*, which wrote, "To children [the Macy's parade] has the same appeal as the old time circus parade."[82] Whether they sought to sell tickets or toys, parades with circus content drew crowds and drove spending.

Macy's pursued those ends with its inaugural parade. Macy's 1924 parade began uptown on 145th Street and wended its way down Broadway to the store's Herald Square location. With store employees and some professional entertainers comprising the marchers, the parade passed "men, women, and more especially children" lining the sidewalks "sometimes four and five deep." In a dynamic similar to that of circus parades drawing people to the circus lot, the attention the parade garnered along the way helped swell the crowd around the store to upwards of ten thousand New Yorkers, with children, according to the *New York Times*, "in the majority" (*fig. 6.11*). When the parade arrived at Macy's, Santa Claus ascended to the portico above the store's entrance and then unveiled the store's

Fig. 6.10. "Big Christmas Parade!" 1924. Poster. Macy's

Christmas window display. Almost immediately, "the police lines gave way and with a rush the enormous crowd flocked to the windows."[83]

At first glance, it is surprising that Macy's succeeded in organizing and staging a procession in the streets of America's biggest city at a time when large urban areas had become inhospitable for circus parades. Macy's, however, labored to make sure that its parade would not encounter the same pitfalls as circuses had had with their big city processions in the early twentieth century. Macy's, unlike circus companies that sought to parade on whichever days their tours arrived in New York, held its parade on a New York State holiday, when the traffic on the city's streets would be light and could be rerouted without significant difficulty.[84] Macy's also requested and was granted "special permission" from New York City officials to hold the parade. Indeed, the political connections of Macy's owners played a significant role in making certain that the parade became an annual event; when the store faced charges

from religious and patriotic groups that its 1924 cavalcade served to desecrate a religious holiday, Macy's reached out to the city's police commissioner, who supported the store in its effort to continue its feature in future years.[85]

Since 1924, the Macy's Thanksgiving Day Parade has become a New York institution, and perhaps saw its biggest and most lasting change in 1927, when it added its trademark character balloons to the event. While the introduction of these balloons helped signal Macy's movement away from an overt circus theme, Macy's has occasionally revisited it. In 1948 Macy's hired professional circus performers, including clowns, to march in its parade.[86] Along with Hollywood luminaries, the store featured "a full fledged live circus" as part of its 1955 procession.[87] Six years later it presented its "Thanksgiving Day Parade and Circus," which featured elephants, equestrians, and a trapeze act in front of its Herald Square store.[88] The store's continued reliance on circus themes, along with the parade's general simi-

Fig. 6.11. Santa Claus rides a parade float down Broadway during the annual Macy's Thanksgiving Day Parade, November 26, 1925. Photograph. © Bettmann/Corbis

larity to those staged by circuses in decades past, led the *New York Times* to editorialize in 1954 that "there is a distinct circus flavor to the spectacle."[89]

Macy's found a further way to turn its parade into a spectacle by giving ordinary Americans a chance to join Macy's employees in the line of march. As early as the late 1920s, Macy's had invited bands from the New York National Guard to provide a soundtrack for its spectacle.[90] In the late 1940s, however, Macy's reached out to other bands and color guards from the New York area, including those comprising young people.[91] By the 1950s, musical groups from across the country marched in the parade alongside store employees, which today includes everything from cheerleading squads and jump rope teams to color guards to marching bands.[92] Today Macy's takes a similar approach to the staffing of its balloon handlers. Although Macy's employees comprise the vast majority of the individuals who guide the store's airborne characters along the parade route, in recent years Macy's has allowed its employees to "sponsor" friends and family members who

have an interest in becoming one of the hundreds of balloon handlers needed for the parade.[93]

By allowing groups and individuals from around the country to participate in its parade, Macy's, much like circuses had done when they allowed urbanites to serve as torchbearers, helped make its spectacle an inclusive event that celebrated community as well the institution sponsoring the parade. This is reflected in the excitement and sense of accomplishment that participants feel when their organizations take their place in the line of march (*fig. 6.12*). "This is a dream come true for these guys," Miami University's marching band director said as the band prepared to march in the 2003 parade. "It's a dream come true for me. This is a very big stage we are going to be performing on."[94] After participating in the 1999 parade, a Wisconsin high school musician agreed, describing the "thrill and excitement" of marching down Fifth Avenue with his school's band as "intoxicating."[95] A sixteen-year-old Arizona marching band member reaffirmed the electrifying nature of the experience, exclaiming with tears in his eyes as he stood in the line of march: "Amazing. So amazing. It's surreal. It's completely mind-boggling."[96] Finally, a volunteer balloon handler explained the positive effect this experience had on her and her "teammates" who were charged with keeping a fish balloon on course: "[We] sport idiotic grins as we cart the fish down the first few blocks. We don't notice the cold anymore, as we focus on our mission of making 2 million people—in crowds 50-people deep on some blocks—feel as happy as we do."[97]

While the Macy's parade has evolved from its circus beginnings, it does offer the same democratic appeal that was one of the hallmarks of American circus parades. Today, well over three million people regularly fill the streets of the Big Apple to take part in the event.[98] As Jean McFaddin, Macy's parade

Fig. 6.12. Brendan McDermid. Balloons make their way down Seventh Avenue during the 83rd Macy's Thanksgiving Day Parade, November 26, 2009. Photograph. Brendan McDermid/Reuters/Corbis

director, said in 1988, "It is a celebration. The rich, poor, old, young, healthy, sick love it" (*fig. 6.13*).[99] Indeed, anyone can crowd along the police lines that demarcate the line of march, including the homeless man who in 2004 stood with the masses and watched, drinking a Starbucks beverage, as the parade's oversized balloons floated by him.[100] Still, the privileged individuals who wanted to avoid the press of the crowd could secure luxurious perches for parade viewing, such as the tony Trump International Hotel and Tower, which in 2009 offered rooms overlooking the route for $595 per night.[101]

Even as Macy's Thanksgiving Day Parade became an integral part of New York City's cultural fabric, circus parades proper were a waning phenomenon in American life. In fact, by the late 1920s discussions of circus processions began to take on a nostalgic tone as observers began using terms such as "old time" when writing or speaking about them.[102] For instance, one circus that continued the tradition did so in 1936, according to the *Los Angeles Times*, because it "prides itself on being old fashioned."[103]

Nostalgia aside, almost all post-1930s parades were a far cry from those of the Gilded Age. Since the largest and most heavily capitalized circuses no longer paraded, the processions offered up by smaller outfits often proved less than satisfying in practice. In a dynamic that dated back to the antebellum era, residents of Lewiston, Maine expressed their "bitter disappointment" in 1948 that after turning out for a "much publicized" street parade, the King Brothers Circus offered up nothing more than "four elephants, a lone lion, four horses, a band and score of performers." In the wake of its poor showing, the concern's management explained to the local paper that it was "not equipped to stage the type of processions which thrilled and awed the young and old alike a score of years ago."[104]

Ultimately, however, this sense of nostalgia and desire to see a real "old-time" circus parade spurred the drive for a re-creation of a nineteenth-century circus parade by a Baraboo, Wisconsin–based institution dedicated to preserving the history of the traveling circus. In 1962 the Circus World Museum's director, C. P. "Chappie" Fox, set plans into motion to present a parade featuring the museum's large collection of restored vintage circus wagons. With the coffers of the museum not full enough to fund such a spectacle, Fox approached a number of Wisconsin businessmen in the hopes of finding sponsors for the parade. After a number of rejections, Fox sat down with a Milwaukee–based investment executive, and showed him vintage photographs of circuses parading past huge throngs of onlookers. "Do you mean," the executive incredulously said to Fox, "these crowds jammed the streets to see a circus parade?" Sensing the marketing potential inherent in such an event, the executive quickly recruited Milwaukee's Schlitz Brewing Company as a corporate supporter, and plans for presenting what has come to be known as the Great Circus Parade in the streets of Milwaukee were underway.[105]

In the run up to the inaugural parade, Fox and the other organizers invited individuals from around

▶ *Fig. 6.13*. Philip Gendreau. Crowds watching the Macy's Thanksgiving Day Parade, 1956. Photograph. © Bettmann/Corbis

the country to contribute to their effort. Along with dozens of volunteers who leapt at the chance to do everything from help prepare circus wagons to pick up elephant dung, they received pledges of assistance from horsemen, who volunteered their time and the requisite number of draft horse teams so the museum's circus wagons could roll once again.[106] And much like the Macy's Thanksgiving Day Parade, organizers would provide a musical soundtrack for their cavalcade through the participation of marching bands, in this case thirty-five municipal, fraternal, and church bands hailing from around Wisconsin.[107] Finally, the Ringling Bros. and Barnum & Bailey Circus offered up some performers to fill out the procession and some of its exotic animals so the museum's antique cage wagons could be filled with wild beasts and locals could be awed by the presence of the show's elephant herd.[108]

As the sun rose in the Milwaukee sky on the Fourth of July 1963, the five-mile-long parade got underway. In front of an estimated 400,000 people, approximately 3,000 participants, and hundreds of horses, some pulling antique wagons, took part in

the first circus parade in Milwaukee since the 1920s (*fig. 6.14*). Spectators filled the sidewalks, peered out of windows, and looked down from rooftops as the parade made its way through downtown Milwaukee. Other more ambitious souls sat atop stepladders they had brought downtown, stood on mailboxes, or literally hung from light poles.[109] As the cavalcade moved, onlookers followed the best traditions of circus parade attendance by cheering, whistling, and waving at the "most wondrous" spectacle.[110]

Much like the Macy's Thanksgiving Day Parade, the Great Circus Parade put down roots and grew from its first iteration, and in doing so, became a point of civic pride for Milwaukee and its residents. By 1967, the parade attracted crowds of 600,000 people and featured over fifty wagons, and marching units drawn from around the country.[111] While the parade has been staged in Chicago and Baraboo, Wisconsin, it was cancelled in 1968 due to fear of civil unrest, and now will probably be held in Milwaukee every few years rather than annually in order to provide time for fundraising. It still remains a key institution in the eyes of many in Milwaukee.[112] Recently, Milwaukee Mayor Tom Barrett led efforts to restore funding and to return the parade to his city in 2009, saying it would attract "hundreds of thousands of people" who would "travel to our city or be in our city to celebrate what I consider to be one of the great family traditions that we have had here in our community."[113]

While the event has brought joy to the people who traveled from all over the world to see what one parade coordinator called the "people's parade," the experience also has made lasting impressions on the event's volunteer participants.[114] Marching band musician Dick Farvour said in 1995 that despite the challenge of performing in blazing summer heat, it is "the greatest experience in the world, exhausting

▲ *Fig. 6.14*. John Leongard. The Sauk County circus band performs from the top of the Lion and Mirror Bandwagon during the Schlitz Circus Parade, July 4, 1964. Photograph. Time & Life Pictures/Getty Images

171

and exhilarating."[115] Horseman Paul Sparrow, who drove a circus wagon pulled by a forty-horse hitch in parades during the 1980s, explained that driving such a long line of equines was personally "exciting" for him, but ultimately he participated because of the crowd's reaction when he rolled down the street. When "people stood and applauded," as he drove his team through the city, he could only think to himself, "wow, what a feeling."[116] Jim Cheski, a parade volunteer, concurred with Sparrow in 1991 in describing the impact that the Great Circus Parade had on spectators, saying that along the route there "were kids with eyes bright and big as saucers and tears in people's eyes. Once a young woman came up to me with tears in her eyes and she hugged me, and I am just a small part of it. That is the big reward."[117] As in the case of the Macy's parade, the Great Circus Parade's "big tent" approach to its staging allowed for the inclusion of a broad range of participants, making it a true community celebration.

Despite the influence and impact that circus parades have had on American public culture, America's leading circus, the Ringling Bros. and Barnum & Bailey Circus (RBBBC) maintains that it does not present parades. Even so, the show does stage an "animal walk," necessitated by its need to move its animals from its train to its performance sites. "In every city," RBBBC spokeswoman Barbara Pflughaupt noted in 2004, "we have to walk our hoofed stock from train to the arena."[118] While the RBBBC has at times, as it did in Richmond in 1995, sought to downplay the event, the show does issue press releases detailing the date and time of these unofficial parades, and even maintains a toll-free "Animal Walk Hotline."[119]

While the animal walk may appear to be a contemporary successor to the circus parade, in fact, these marches date back to the late nineteenth cen-

tury. In 1887 the Barnum show moved its animals from Mott Haven, New York, across the Harlem River, and through the darkened streets of Manhattan to Madison Square Garden with little fanfare. The *New York Times* reported: "The reception in New York was very informal. No bands played and there were no speeches of welcome. A dozen spectators climbed upon a pile of ties to see what was going on and be out of the animals' way."[120]

Yet in other years, these unadvertised processions drew large crowds. A daytime movement of animals in 1935 brought "thousands" of New Yorkers into the streets to see fifty elephants and dozens of circus wagons move into Madison Square Garden.[121] Similarly, "all the policemen in New York," a scribe informed his readers in 1939, "couldn't have kept the youngsters from trailing along in the street, whooping with joy at the zebras and pointing at the dromedary . . . the din was terrific as the impromptu parade passed through the Italian section [o]n First Avenue" on its way to the Garden.[122] Nonetheless, even the cover of darkness did little to lessen the enthusiasm shown by New Yorkers, particularly the youngest among them. A *New York Times* reporter, watching a 4 a.m. procession transpire, marveled at the "many small boys" who moved "running and shouting" alongside wagons and elephants. "How they knew it was coming no one knew," he wrote in 1909. "But there always seems to be an underground wire which tells the boys when the circus is to arrive, and they are always ready for it."[123]

In an example of the old becoming new again, RBBBC officials, like their antebellum predecessors, by the second half of the twentieth century had come to appreciate that moving their animals through town could serve not only as a "logistical necessity," but also as a promotional device. One way the show accomplished this was by inviting journalists and

other officials to play starring roles in their animal walks. In Milwaukee, for instance, local news personalities got to hitch a ride on top of the show's pachyderms in 1969 as they lumbered from their train cars to the Milwaukee Arena.[124] Five years later, the show expanded the professions of its elephant passengers to include a local preacher and a politician as the show opened its stand in Palm Beach.[125]

While these marches occur all over the country, perhaps the nation's most dramatic animal walk takes place in New York City. When the show moves its animals from Queens to Manhattan, it takes its animals through the Queens-Midtown Tunnel. In order to not create a traffic jam of monstrous proportions, the tunnel authority grants the show the full use of one tube during the middle of the night. In this way, RBBBC can move, as it did in 1993, "18 elephants, 34 horses, 4 zebras, 2 camels and 2 llamas" in a journey under the East River that takes about twenty-five minutes to complete.[126]

The surreal sight of elephants emerging from a tunnel and passing through tollbooths is enough to encourage hundreds of New Yorkers to stay up all night to wait for the show to arrive.[127] When the elephants make their way up the ramp and into the city, cheers ring out from the assembled masses, peppered by boos and jeers from protestors from People for the Ethical Treatment of Animals (*fig. 6.15*).[128] Along with the show's supporters and detractors, distinguished public officials sometimes greet the RBBBC's animals, as in 1995, when they received a special welcome from the city's mayor, Rudolph W. Giuliani, who brought his son Andrew out to greet the show's elephants after they exited the tunnel.

After bidding the mayor and his family farewell in 1995, the animals and their handlers headed for the Garden. But their reception was far from complete. A *New York Times* reporter noted that during this less than two-mile journey, the show's elephants strolled past "hundreds of female students" from Stern College, who "jumped up and down and danced to welcome the huge beasts." Further along the way, the animals passed two brothers, who, along with a dozen friends, engaged in their annual ritual of donning elephant trunk noses in order to welcome the pachyderms. "I wasn't born an elephant fan," one of the brothers told the journalist while sporting a Babar shirt. But after witnessing a late 1980s animal walk, he realized, "what a great reason to party. Somebody had to welcome elephants. I saw my opening and I seized it."[129]

The enthusiastic response of New Yorkers to RBBBC's animal walks reaffirms the fact that the enthusiasm of ordinary people is what transforms a simple movement of exotic animals into a circus parade. In fact, the first circus parades were not organized events; locals who saw circus wagons and animals move through their towns during the ante-

Fig. 6.15. Ray Stubblebine. Ringmaster Chuck Wagner rides the elephant Karen along Seventh Avenue as the midnight parade of pachyderms heralds the annual arrival of the Ringling Bros. and Barnum & Bailey Circus at Madison Square Garden in New York, March 18, 2008. Photograph. © Ray Stubblebine/Reuters/Corbis

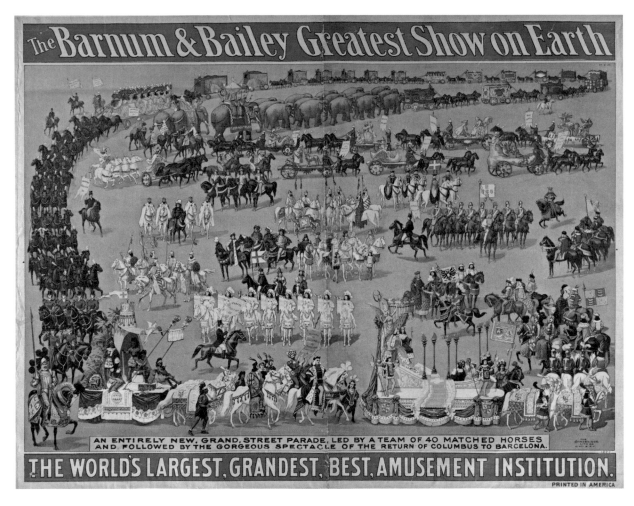

Fig. 6.16. "The Barnum & Bailey Greatest Show on Earth. An Entirely
New, Grand Street Parade," 1897. Poster, printed by the Strobridge
Lithographing Company, Cincinnati. Collection of the John and Mable
Ringling Museum of Art, Tibbals Collection, ht2000175

bellum period simply could not help but take notice. As that century progressed, circus parades reached their pinnacle, with showmen deploying dozens of extravagant wagons, hundreds of exotic animals and talented performers, and scores of spirited musicians in an effort to make their grand entrée into town an event that was worth traveling many miles to see (*fig. 6.16*). As with the animal walks of today, circus parades drew people of all walks of life into the streets as to not miss these spectacles.

Likewise, the circus's cultural flexibility has allowed for its continuing relevance in American life. Even though parading by traveling shows had become wholly impractical by the early twentieth century, the successful resurrection of the event in the form of the Great Circus Parade has demonstrated the form's continuing power. Similarly, Macy's use of circus content for its early parades and its regular return to circus motifs reaffirms the fact that the circus remains relevant in American public life and has a role to play in a range of spectacles.

Ultimately, however, the circus has maintained its place in American spectacles because parade organizers ranging from late-nineteenth-century showmen to those of the Great Circus Parade comprehend that public inclusion generates public enthusiasm. That is, by allowing ordinary people to carry torches or serve as parade volunteers, circus parades become celebrations of the community as much as of the event itself. In the final analysis, parades draw their energy from the presence and participation of ordinary people; without them, a line of elephants moving through a city would just lumber silently through the streets.

Renoff

1 "Circus Comes to Town on Tiptoe," *Richmond Times-Dispatch*, Feb. 14, 1995.

2 "Circus Parades," *Billboard* 38 (April 10, 1926), 48.

3 "Abandonment of the Parade," *Billboard* 18 (June 23, 1906), 18.

4 On the history of nineteenth-century parades, see Susan G. Davis, *Parades and Power: Street Theater in Nineteenth-Century Philadelphia* (Philadelphia: Temple University Press, 1986); Simon P. Newman, *Parades and the Politics of the Street: Festive Culture in the Early American Republic* (Philadelphia: University of Pennsylvania Press, 1997); Mary P. Ryan, "The American Parade: Representations of the Nineteenth-Century Social Order," in Lynn Hunt, ed., *The New Cultural History* (Berkeley: University of California Press, 1989), 131–53.

5 David Rockwell and Bruce Mau, *Spectacle* (New York: Phaidon, 2006), 19.

6 Mikhail Bakhtin, *Rabelais and His World* (Bloomington: Indiana University Press, 1984), 7.

7 "No Circus Parade This Year," *New York Times*, March 8, 1903, 7, http://query.nytimes.com/mem/archive-free/pdf?res=F40814F73A5412738DDDA108 94DB405B838CF1D3 (accessed Feb. 24, 2012).

8 Matthew Roy, "A Change in Tradition," *Virginian-Pilot*, Feb. 22, 2006, B1.

9 Stuart Thayer, *Traveling Showmen: The American Circus before the Civil War* (Detroit: Astley and Ricketts, 1997), 45–56.

10 Gil Robinson, *Old Wagon Show Days* (Cincinnati: Brockwell, 1925), 28.

11 *Eaton* (Ohio) *Register*, Aug. 26, 1847, quoted in Stuart Thayer, *The Annals of the American Circus, 1793–1860* (Seattle: Dauven and Thayer, 2000), 207.

12 Charles Philip Fox and F. Beverly Kelley, *The Great Circus Street Parade in Pictures* (1978; rpt. Mineola, NY: Dover, 1990), 1.

13 Thayer, *Traveling Showmen*, 35–44.

14 Helen Stoddart, *Rings of Desire: Circus History and Representation* (Manchester: Manchester University Press, 2000), 22.

15 "Robinson & Elred's Great Southern Circus," *Columbus* (Georgia) *Enquirer*, Dec. 24, 1850.

16 Fox and Kelley, *Great Circus Street Parade*, 2–3.

17 "Bailey and Co.," *Columbus* (Georgia) *Times*, Dec. 28, 1858.

18 "The Great Circus," *Savannah Morning News*, Nov. 24, 1868.

19 Mark M. Smith, *Listening to Nineteenth-Century America* (Chapel Hill: University of North Carolina Press, 2001), 120.

20 Roger W. Moss, *Century of Color: Exterior Decoration for American Buildings, 1820–1920* (Watkins Glen, NY: American Life Foundation, 1981), 10–12.

21 For the populations, see Thomas Baldwin and J. Thomas, *A New and Complete Gazetteer of the United States: Giving a Full and Comprehensive Review of the Present Condition, Industry, and Resources of the American Confederacy* (Philadelphia: Lippincott, Grambo & Co., 1854), 1152, 1162; "Sand's, Nathan's, & Co's," *Tioga County Agitator*, Sept. 2, 1858.

22 Ibid.

23 "Mammoth National Circus," *Pittsfield Sun*, May 7, 1846.

24 *Salem Gazette*, May 12, 1835.

25 (Portsmouth) *New Hampshire Gazette*, May 18, 1835, quoted in Thayer, *Annals of the American Circus*, 149.

26 "The Circus is Here," *Columbus* (Georgia) *Daily Sun*, Nov. 19, 1867.

27 "Bailey's Circus," (Columbus) *Daily Sun*, Dec. 29, 1858.

28 "The Circus," (Columbus) *Daily Sun*, Nov. 17, 1868.

29 "Howe's Great Circus in Brooklyn," *New York Times*, Nov. 7, 1865, www.nytimes.com/1865/11/07/news/amusements-union-mass-meeting-at-elizabeth-nj.html (accessed April 16, 2012).

30 Janet M. Davis, *The Circus Age: Culture and Society under the American Big Top* (Chapel Hill: University of North Carolina Press, 2002), 15–25.

31 Joel Shrock, *The Gilded Age* (Westport, CT: Greenwood Press, 2004), 2.

32 Russell F. Weigley, "The Border City in Civil War, 1854–1865," in Russell F. Weigley, ed. *Philadelphia: A 300 Year History* (New York: W. W. Norton, 1982), 366.

33 "Urban Population of the United States," *National Geographic* 12 (Jan. 1901), 345.

34 Davis, *Circus Age*, 1–14.

35 "The Circus is Here," *Fayetteville* (Arkansas) *Observer*, Oct. 5, 1899.

36 "Come to the Circus," (Columbus) *Enquirer-Sun*, Nov. 29, 1877.

37 "The Great Circus," *Boston Daily Advertiser*, June 7, 1880.

38 "The Circus," *Bainbridge* (Georgia) *Democrat*, Oct. 23, 1890.

39 "Barnum's Great Parade," *New York Times*, March 11, 1884, 2.

40 "The Big Show," *St. Louis Daily Globe-Democrat*, May 29, 1877.

41 "Old John's Circus," *Rocky Mountain News*, Aug. 12, 1873.

42 "Moving the Circus Animals," *New York Times*, March 24, 1895, 5; "The Street Pageant To-Night," *New York Times*, March 27, 1895, 3; "The Niagara Suspension Bridge," *Pittsfield Sun*, July 19, 1849.

43 Gregory J. Renoff, *The Big Tent: The Traveling Circus in Georgia, 1820–1930* (Athens: University of Georgia Press, 2008), 85; Jerry Apps, *Ringlingville USA: The Stupendous Story of Seven Siblings and Their Stunning Circus Success* (Madison: Wisconsin Historical Society Press, 2005), 143–45; "Ten Thousand Saw It," *Savannah Morning News*, Nov. 9, 1895; "The Ringling's Big Show," *Savannah Morning News*, Nov. 7, 1896.

44 "Seen in a New Light," (Chicago) *Daily Inter-Ocean*, April 9, 1896.

45 "The Twilight Parade," (Chicago) *Daily Inter-Ocean*, June 17, 1879.

46 "The Greatest Show," *New York Times*, March 11, 1888, 2; "The Circus is Coming to Town," *New York Times*, March 29, 1896, 8.

47 "Many Sightseers," *New York Times*, April 1, 1897.

48 "Barnum's Annual Debut," *New York Times*, April 12, 1890, 5.

49 "The Circus Parade," (Philadelphia) *North American*, April 18, 1891.

50 "A 'Bran[d] New Circus in Town,'" *Milwaukee Journal*, July 18, 1892.

51 "Ringling Bros' Circus Parade," *Pittsburgh Press*, July 3, 1901.

52 "The Twilight Parade," (Chicago) *Daily Inter-Ocean*, June 17, 1879.

53 M. G. Lay, *Ways of the World: A History of the World's Roads and of the Vehicles that Used Them* (New Brunswick, NJ: Rutgers University Press, 1999), 186–87.

54 "Travel in New York," *Baltimore Sun*, July 9, 1905.

55 "Rapid Transit," *Boston Daily Advertiser*, May 15, 1897.

56 "Orders to Run Cars," *Milwaukee Journal*, June 11, 1894.

57 "The Circus Does Not Seem the Same, Somehow," *Hartford Courant*, June 10, 1917.

58 "Barnum Opens in Brooklyn," *New York Times*, April 26, 1887, 2.

59 "Ringling Bros' Circus Parade," *Pittsburgh Press*, July 3, 1901.

60 "Broadway Cable Cars in Tangle," *Chicago Daily Tribune*, April 2, 1896.

61 "The Greatest Show," *New York Times*, March 11, 1888, 2.

62 "Circus Ponies Run Away with a Cage Filled with Monkeys," *Chicago Daily Tribune*, June 23, 1900.

63 "Circus Parade Is Cut Out," *New York Times*, Oct. 12, 1902, 26.

64 "No More Circus Parades," *New York Times*, April 15, 1905.

65 Ibid.

66 "Too Big to Parade," *Reading Eagle*, April 13, 1907.

67 "Circuses Barred from Peachtree and Whitehall," *Atlanta Constitution*, Nov. 17, 1914; Circus Solly, "Under the Marquee," *Billboard* 26 (Dec. 12, 1914), 23.

68 "Chicago Too Crowded for Circus Parade," *Chicago Daily Tribune*, Aug. 15, 1924.

69 "In Our Busiest Streets at the Busiest Hour," *Chicago Tribune*, April 14, 1920.

70 Charles E. Ringling, "Minus the Circus Parade," *Billboard* 36 (Dec. 13, 1924), 6.

71 "Huge Circus Encamps on Lewiston Soil," *Lewiston*

Evening Journal, June 27, 1918.

72 "Lessons Make Way for the Parade," *Reading Eagle*, May 9, 1917.

73 "Circus Parade Thrills Crowds," (*St. Petersburg, Florida*) *Evening Independent*, Sept. 25, 1926.

74 Library of Congress, "Thanksgiving Timeline, 1541–2001," *Thanksgiving—For Teachers (Library of Congress)*, http://www.loc.gov/teachers/classroom-materials/presentationsandactivities/presentations/thanksgiving/timeline/1541.html (accessed July 24, 2010); Hennig Cohen and Tristram Potter Coffin, *America Celebrates!: A Patchwork of Weird & Wonderful Holiday Lore* (Detroit: Visible Ink Press, 1991), 326.

75 Robert Grippo and Christopher Hoskins, *Macy's Thanksgiving Day Parade* (Charleston, SC: Arcadia, 2004), 39.

76 Ibid., 10.

77 Ibid., 10.

78 "The Circus is Coming to Town," *New York Times*, March 29, 1896, 8.

79 "Barnum's Parade," *New York Times*, March 24, 1883, 8.

80 Renoff, *The Big Tent*, 67–84.

81 William Leach, *Land of Desire: Merchants, Power, and the Rise of a New American Culture* (New York: Vintage Books, 1993), 334.

82 "Pushing Holiday Trade," *New York Times*, Nov. 14, 1926, E18.

83 "Greet Santa Claus as 'King of Kiddies,'" *New York Times*, Nov. 28, 1924, 5.

84 "Legal Holidays," *The Tribune Almanac and Political Register* 17 (Jan 1905), 233; "Helium Monsters Invade Broadway," *New York Times*, Dec. 1, 1933, 21.

85 Leach, *Land of Desire*, 334.

86 "Thanksgiving Parades Draw Large Throngs," *Billboard* 60 (Dec. 4, 1948), 49.

87 "Thanksgiving TV Spotlight," (Bridgeport, CT) *Sunday Herald*, Nov. 20, 1955.

88 "Thanksgiving Day Parade in Color," (Cape Girardeau) *Southeast Missourian*, Nov. 17, 1961.

89 "Macy Parade," *New York Times*, Nov. 25, 1954, 28.

90 "100,000 Children See Store Pageant," *New York Times*, Nov. 30, 1928, 25; "Helium Monsters Invade Broadway," *New York Times*, Dec. 1, 1933, 21.

91 "Six Giant Balloons in Store's Pageant," *New York Times*, Nov. 21, 1948, 42.

92 Meyer Berger, *Meyer Berger's New York: A Great Reporter's Love Affair with a City* (New York: Fordham University Press, 2004), 112; Howard Wilkinson, "Local Kids Ready to Step Out," *Cincinnati Enquirer*, Nov. 26, 2003.

93 Tamara Simpson Girardi, "2 Teachers to be Balloon Handlers in Macy's Parade," (Pennsylvania) *Valley News Dispatch*, Nov. 23, 2008.

94 Wilkinson, "Local Kids Ready to Step Out."

95 Tom Ribbens, "March in the Rain," *Milwaukee Journal Sentinel*, Jan. 3, 2000.

96 Michelle Woo, "Gilbert Band Heats up NYC," *Arizona Republic*, Nov. 26, 2004.

97 Kathy Jones, "I Love A Parade: A Diary Of The Macy's Thanksgiving Day Parade, Ground-Zero," *Newsweek*, Nov. 24, 2000, http://www.thedailybeast.com newsweek/2000/11/24/i-love-a-parade.html (accessed Feb. 4, 2012).

98 Beth Whitehouse, "Macy's Parade: Where to Watch on Thanksgiving," (New York) *Newsday*, Nov. 23, 2008, www.newsday.com/search/macy-s-parade-where-to-watch-on-thanksgiving-1.754 247 (accessed April 2, 2012).

99 "The Best Parade on Television," *Lodi* (California) *News-Sentinel*, Nov. 24, 1988.

100 Patrick Healy, "At 64 Degrees, with 59 Balloons, One Perfect Thanksgiving Day Parade," *New York Times*, Nov. 26, 2004, A1.

101 Clyde Haberman, "A Public Street Turned Private on Macy Day," *New York Times*, Dec. 1, 2009, 27.

102 "Sparks Circus to Give Parade," (St. Petersburg) *Evening Independent*, Oct. 24, 1929; "Revival of Circus Parade to Feature Pageant Program," *Sarasota Herald*, Feb. 20, 1937.

103 Timothy G. Turner, "Old Time Circus Parade Thrills Los Angeles," *Los Angeles Times*, Sept. 22, 1936.

104 "Circus Parade Dismal Failure," *Lewiston Daily Sun*, July 1, 1948.

105 C. P. "Chappie" Fox, *America's Great Circus Parade: Its Roots . . . Its Revival . . . Its Revelry* (Greendale, WI: Country Books, 1993), 16–17.

106 Bruce B. Brugmann, "Circus Parade Stirs Baraboo with Activities of Yesteryear," *Milwaukee Journal*, March 25, 1963; Bruce B. Brugmann, "Horses Will Power Circus Parade Units," *Milwaukee Journal*, April 24, 1963.

107 "Forty Old Cars to Pace July 4th Circus Parade," *Milwaukee Journal*, June 22, 1963; "400,000 See Circus Parade in Milwaukee," *Chicago Tribune*, July 5, 1964; Karin Winegar, "The Circus is Coming on Wheels," *New York Times*, June 30, 2002, D19.

108 Fox, *America's Great Circus Parade*, 21; "I Love a Parade," *St. Petersburg Times*, June 23, 1963.

109 Robert N. Leipzig, "425,000 Cheer Parade," *Milwaukee Sentinel*, July 5, 1963.

110 "Milwaukee Salutes 4th with a Parade," *New York Times*, July 5, 1963, 32; Robert N. Leipzig, "425,000 Cheer Parade," *Milwaukee Sentinel*, July 5, 1963.

111 George Bushnell, Jr., "Milwaukee Recreates Old-Time Circus Parade," *Chicago Tribune*, June 18, 1967.

112 "Schlitz Cancels Parade in Milw.," *New Pittsburgh Courier*, May 4, 1968; "Great Circus Parade Returns to Milwaukee after Six Years," *USA Today*, June 29, 2009, www.usatoday.com/travel/destinations/2009-06-29-milwaukee-circus-parade_N.htm (accessed April 2, 2012).

113 Associated Press, "Circus Parade Returning, but Funds Still Needed," *WISN—Milwaukee*, March 13, 2008, http://www.wisn.com/entertainment/15589403/detail.html (accessed July 25, 2010).

114 Ben Barkin, "Size of Crowd at Circus Parade Not as Important as Response," *Milwaukee Sentinel*, Aug. 30, 1989.

115 Ernst-Ulrich Franzen, "Drums, Sweat, and Cheers Endure," *Milwaukee Journal-Sentinel*, July 17, 1995.

116 Paula A. Poda, "Crowd's Glee Spurs Forty Horse Hitch, 10 Ton Wagon," *Milwaukee Sentinel*, July 17, 1989; Rachel N. Anastasi, "Forty Horse Hitch a Kinetic Sculpture," *Milwaukee Sentinel*, July 10, 1989.

117 Kathleen Waterbury, "Parade Stirs Volunteer Spirit," *Milwaukee Sentinel*, July 12, 1991.

118 Michael Pollak, "Hoofing it to Midtown," *New York Times*, Feb. 29, 2004, C42.

119 Staff Reports, "Circus Animal Walk Planned for Tuesday," *News-Record.com*, Feb. 8, 2010, http://www.news-record.com/content/2010/02/08/article/circus_animal_walk_planned_for_tuesday (accessed July 26, 2010); Ringling Bros. and Barnum & Bailey Circus, "Pachyderm Parade on Capitol Hill Celebrates St. Patrick's Day and Marks the Arrival of Ringling Bros. and Barnum & Bailey Circus to Washington, D.C.," *marketwire.com*, March 12, 2009, www.marketwire.com/press-release/Pachyderm-Parade-on-Capitol-Hill-Celebrates-St-Patricks-Day-Marks-Arrival-Ringling-Bros-960493.htm (accessed July 27, 2010).

120 "Eight Elephants Arrive," *New York Times*, March 11, 1887, 2.

121 "Circus Elephants Parade into Town," *New York Times*, April 8, 1935, 21.

122 "Young Circus Fans Overwhelm Police," *New York Times*, April 2, 1939, 22.

123 "Weary Circus Here after a Long Trip," *New York Times*, March 18, 1909, 18.

124 "Big Show on Parade Today," *Milwaukee Sentinel*, Oct. 21, 1969.

125 "Circus Parade Today," *Palm Beach Post*, Jan. 17, 1974.

126 Diane Ketcham, "Herd in the Tunnel," *New York Times*, April 4, 1993, L.I. 3.

127 "Mike Allen, "These Days, the Circus Animals Sneak into Town," *New York Times*, Feb. 19, 1995, 28.

128 Jacob E. Osterhout, "Ringling Bros. Circus Elephants Prepare for a Safari through NYC," (New York) *Daily News*, March 22, 2009; Stephanie Feuer, "Tunnel Visions," *New York Times*, March 16, 2008, CY 3.

129 Michael T. Kaufman, "Heavy Tread of Elephants Makes Hearts Lighter," *New York Times*, March 24, 1995, 33.

7

CIRCUS MUSIC
IN AMERICA

LEON BOTSTEIN

In the evening of January 12, 1942, the legendary choreographer George Balanchine telephoned his old friend Igor Stravinsky, who was in the midst of a card game with his wife. Balanchine asked whether Stravinsky would be interested in writing a short ballet for elephants for the Ringling Bros. and Barnum & Bailey Circus, which was to open their touring season at Madison Square Garden in early April. After asking how long the piece had to be, Stravinsky agreed. He was eager to gain a firmer foothold in what was still for him a new country and he was relieved that the piece had to be short. He completed the score of *Circus Polka*, as his piece ultimately came to be known, in February of 1942.[1]

The choreography by Balanchine included fifty elephants and fifty dancers in fluffy pink outfits (*fig. 7.1*). The star was a small veteran elephant, Miss Modoc, who carried Balanchine's wife, Vera Zorina. Balanchine paid homage to the traditions of the American circus. With a considerable dose of humor, he respected the power of the circus to invert expectations on a spectacular and grand scale. He made elephants look graceful, as the circus had for generations, and he humanized them, crowning the star elephant with his wife and surrounding the rest with ballet dancers. The work premiered on April 9, 1942, with the title "The Ballet of the Elephants" (*fig. 7.2*). It was about four minutes long.

The event was a great success. It ran for 425 performances. The piece is scored for a typical circus band of the period, an era that actually marks a high point in the development of American circus music. Stravinsky called for a flute, four clarinets (two solo parts), alto and baritone saxophone, seven cornets (including two solo cornets and two baritone cornets), two horns, four trombones, two tubas, and percussion (big drum, side drum, cymbals, and xylophone). *Circus Polka* opens with a loud flourish and then segues into a lively, sharply punctuated, gracious but discontinuous and asymmetrical

◄ *Detail of fig. 7.14.* Frederick Whitman Glasier. "Victor Robbins and the Sells-Floto Circus Band," 1924. Photograph. Collection of the John and Mable Ringling Museum of Art, Glasier Glass Plate Negative Collection, 1359

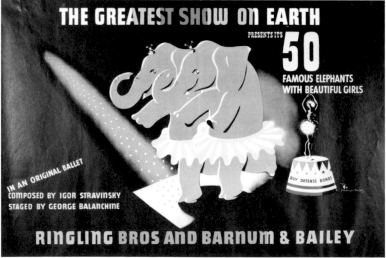

polka. Toward the end, as the sound gathers steam, a brassy quote from Schubert's famous *Marche Militaire* is introduced and brings this adorable miniature to a dramatic close. The work is unmistakably Stravinsky: humorous, angular, mischievous, and lyrical.

But the anticipated continuity of a polka is distorted by abrupt pauses and shifts in sonority. Despite the unmistakable surface homage to circus music, which had long included polkas (*fig. 7.3*), the piece was distinctly modern and often not entirely considerate of the elephants. But Stravinsky liked the piece enough to arrange it subsequently for piano and also for full orchestra, in which forms it survives

▲ *Fig. 7.1.* George Balanchine, director of the "Ballet of the Elephants," instructs Modoc, the elephant ballerina, on new steps, 1942. Photograph. © Bettmann/Corbis

▲ *Fig. 7.2.* E. McKnight Kauffer. "The Greatest Show on Earth Presents Its 50 Famous Elephants with Beautiful Girls," 1942. Poster. Circus World Museum, CWi-2302

in the concert repertory. *Circus Polka* seems never to have made it back to the circus.

In 1942 the leader of the circus band at Ringling was none other than Merle Evans, the undisputed Maestro of the Circus, or Toscanini of the Big Top (*fig. 7.4*).[2] Elephant music had never been the favorite part of the show for Evans, probably the last great circus band director. By the 1930s Evans had become the most visible and successful musician in the history of the American circus. He was band director for the Ringling Bros. and Barnum & Bailey Circus from 1919 to 1969, well after the heyday of the American circus had passed. He is reputed to have missed only one day of work in fifty years and in more than 30,000 performances (some sources are more modest and cite only 18,200 performances). Having started at 60 dollars a week and closing his career earning 800 dollars, Evans was grateful. Being a circus musician was hard work but he felt it was decently enough paid, which is why in the 1940s he crossed swords with the musicians' union, considering his peers in the classical and popular fields as not nearly as hard working, disciplined, or admirable as the best circus musician.

Evans's chip on his shoulder with regard to classical music was not too great; like his predecessors he saw no need to rank music into an invidious hierarchy. Evans was dismayed, however, at having to witness the death of the art form he had perfected (he died in 1987 at the age of ninety-six). He observed the gradual replacement of live band musicians playing on acoustic instruments—his largest circus band, after World War II, consisted of thirty-six wind, brass, and percussion players—by not only standard rock and roll music, but also recorded sound and ultimately digitally synthesized music.[3]

The 1942 spectacle of fifty young elephants and fifty ballerinas (Stravinsky is reputed to have agreed

Fig. 7.3. P. H. van der Weide, *Hippodrome Polka*, sheet music (New York: T. S. Berry, 1853). Lithograph, printed by Sarony & Major, New York. Rare Book, Manuscript, and Special Collections Library, Duke University, Durham, North Carolina

Fig. 7.4. Merle Evans conducts the Ringling Bros. and Barnum & Bailey band, 1946. Photograph. Circus World Museum, CWi-2287

to write the piece only if the elephants were young) dancing to music by Stravinsky in Madison Square Garden during The Greatest Show on Earth, under the big top, did not amuse Evans (*figs. 7.5, 7.6*). He was skeptical. "Now good elephant music is something with a solid beat—a march, one step, schottische, fox-trot, waltz or cake-walk," he commented. Evans could not find "any beat" at all in Stravinsky's music. It "was all chopped up…it wasn't what the elephants needed, or deserved." Evans and his men, who found the piece exceedingly hard, were glad when the run was over.[4]

Circus Polka had required too much rehearsal for Evans and its structure and profile were too un-derstated for elephants. Evans tried to minimize the problem in classic circus fashion. In order to set the Stravinsky elephant number up properly and cue the elephants effectively, *Circus Polka* was "sandwiched" (as Evans put it) between Weber's "Invitation to the Waltz" (the title Evans gave Weber's *Invitation to the Dance*) and Ponchielli's *Dance of the Hours*. Evans recalled, "We had to run those elephants in with mu-sic they knew or they'd never get started. And we had to get them out when their turn was over." But the crowd seemed delighted, as were Balanchine and his wife. True to circus tradition, the improbable, unex-pected, and bizarre had occurred, creating for the audience a welcome contrast to daily life.[5]

Good fun may have been had by all, but Evans still dismissed *Circus Polka* as "Harvard" music. The music highlighted a sharper divide between the cul-ture of the circus and so-called classical highbrow music than Evans realized existed. But as he knew, that was not really the whole issue. The culprits, as they would come to be seen by many in Evans's gen-eration, were precisely the signatures of modernism Stravinsky employed that threatened to dominate musical practice. The unnatural-sounding moder-nity, surface irregularity, and unpredictable discon-

tinuity in *Circus Polka* bothered Evans. His angry quip about Harvard hinted at one of the consequenc-es of the rise in the prestige and use of formal school-ing in America during the 1930s. Evans held book learning responsible for the collapse of a historic alliance between the classical and concert traditions of music and American circus music that brought all social classes together. After the war ended Evans sensed, with dismay, an ever-widening gulf between the culture of popular entertainment and the seem-ingly arcane and exclusive concert world, ever more dominated by a snobbery among critics and the high-brow public, a snobbery quite foreign to the profes-sional credo shared by most musicians in both the circus and on the concert stage.

Stravinsky seemed to be poking fun at Ameri-can circus music even though, as Evans knew best, the circus had for generations been the venue in which most Americans heard their first live classical music performances given by a large, sonorous en-semble (*fig. 7.7*). The circus was a highly visible means of access to legendary moments from the opera and concert world for the general public, regardless of class and region. That bridge to the classical music repertoire survived intact, despite competition first from the radio, and subsequently from the advent of the sound film. The list of compositions Evans per-formed at Madison Square Garden as Bandmaster of the Ringling Bros. and Barnum & Bailey Combined Shows in 1927 included selections by, among others, Rossini, Liszt, Goldmark, Wagner, Boito, Meyerbeer, Mendelssohn, Tchaikovsky, Beethoven, Verdi, Puc-cini, Saint-Saëns (from *Samson and Delilah*, not the *Carnival of the Animals*), Massenet, Svendsen, and Schubert.[6] Although a distinct circus repertoire of marches, tunes, and dances came into being, the de-mand for music in the circus—the need for longer selections, music appropriate to specific acts, and

Fig. 7.5. "Ballet of the Elephants" at Madison Square Garden, 1942. Photograph. Circus World Museum, CWi-2300

Fig. 7.6. Allen Lester. "Ballet of the Elephants" at Madison Square Garden, 1942. Photograph. Circus World Museum, CWi-2301

more variety at parades and concerts before and during pauses between shows—was so great that selections from the standard concert and opera repertoire regularly were put to good use.[7] This use of fragments from the classical and operatic repertoire to accompany visual effects and stunts, first pioneered in the American circus in the nineteenth century, was appropriated with a vengeance in the twentieth by animated Hollywood cartoons with sound.[8]

A fluidity in European and North American culture among and between several types of music—rural folk genres, urban street music and dance hall music for casual entertainment, popular song, secular instrumental music, light theater music, and the musical theater with pretentions to art—was pronounced from the late eighteenth century (consider the German Singspiel, Mozart's *Die Zauberflöte*, Beethoven's *Wellington's Victory*, and operetta music) through

the end of the nineteenth century. For most of the nineteenth century in the United States, circus and opera experienced parallel lives. Indeed, the expansion of classical music in America occurred during the great age of the traveling circus, between the 1870s and the mid-twentieth century, when smaller towns and cities had little or no access to what was essentially still an exclusively European art.[9] For immigrants who had come from Europe, particularly Germany and Central Europe, the traveling circus brought nostalgic fragments of a familiar musical culture to the New World. It was P. T. Barnum, after all, who, in an effort to recover from failure successfully restored his reputation as a showman by bringing the Swedish Nightingale, Jenny Lind, to America in a legendary and historic concert tour in 1850.[10]

The Lind tour was a landmark event for music in America. Similar in scope to later circus tours, it

Fig. 7.7. Edward J. Kelty. Ringling Bros. and Barnum & Bailey Combined Circus & Side Show, Madison Square Garden, New York City, 1940. Photograph. Collection of the John and Mable Ringling Museum of Art, Tibbals Collection, ht0004854

generated interest in European concert music and opera. Barnum therefore followed up quickly with the closest equivalent to a circus: a touring orchestra with a few outsized instruments (oversized drums and brass) playing, with startling precision and verve, everything from classics to recent dance music—quadrilles. In the 1853–54 season Barnum brought a Frenchman who worked in England, Louis-Antoine Jullien (1812–1869), a flamboyant and sartorially unsurpassed conductor and his orchestra for over two hundred concerts in America. Jullien, like that protean figure, the legendary pianist and composer Louis Moreau Gottschalk (1829–1869), whom Jullien influenced and was truly an American original, believed in the happy and beneficial interplay between popular music and concert music. Jullien and Gottschalk were both consummate showmen who grasped the idea that a concert, especially on a tour, was a visual spectacle that demanded antics and surprises, much like the circus. Using rail transportation, Gottschalk, between 1862 and 1865, gave over a thousand concerts coast to coast, filled with the full range of repertoire, from popular song and dance to pure classical works.[11]

Barnum, Jullien, and Gottschalk were trailblazers for what would emerge as a popular late-nineteenth- and early-twentieth-century practice: booking strenuous tours by European musical celebrities, singers, and instrumentalists, coast to coast, from town to town (Hans von Bülow, Anton Rubinstein, Pablo Casals, and Sergey Prokofiev all experienced this, for example), performing as legendary or upcoming stars. The promotional habits and audience expectations in American concert and operatic life, particularly involving visitors and acts from afar (e.g., traveling opera companies and later orchestras and ensembles) owe, for better or worse, a great debt to the habits and patterns pioneered by the American traveling circus after 1870.

Circus and concert promoters capitalized on the public's anticipation of a striking spectacle and their delight in improbable feats of virtuosity. The circus, concert life, and opera all exploited the public's weakness for stars and its eagerness for the exotic. They traded shamelessly on the unique reputation of personalities. Since circus and concert life offered only seasonal and periodic entertainment, the entrepreneurs in charge cultivated the momentum of anticipation that only rarity and scarcity, sustained merely through memory, can create. P. T. Barnum's ambitions to bring lucrative and imposing spectacles befitting a young and expanding America can therefore be compared to the frustrations and aspirations of early-nineteenth-century opera promoters, particularly in New York City, from Lorenzo da Ponte (Mozart's librettist for *Figaro*, *Don Giovanni*, and *Cosi fan tutte*) to the founders of the Metropolitan Opera in the early 1880s.[12]

Given this context, it was sad and ironic that Evans was annoyed. After all, Stravinsky (who had little respect for performers in general) quoted from a legendary and familiar Schubert tune already used in circuses and thereby acknowledged the debt concert and opera music in America owed to the popularizing traditions of circus musicians. Furthermore, precedents—connections between the circus and classical music in America in the twentieth century—were not hard to find. William Schuman (*A Circus Overture*), Ernst Toch (*Circus Overture*), and Walter Piston (*The Incredible Flutist*) all would write music inspired by the circus. The circus played a particularly important part in the early life of America's most respected and well-known (and homegrown) twentieth-century modernist, Charles Ives, the master borrower of familiar tunes and sounds from the everyday world around him. Ives wrote a tribute to the circus and its music entitled

Circus Band, a march, shortly after completing his undergraduate years at Yale.

For Ives, writing music was an adventure in autobiography. His scores are filled with nostalgic references to his childhood in Danbury, Connecticut, where his father was a bandmaster. Ives's father never performed in a circus, although in the 1870s, traveling troupes often had to hire local musicians to flesh out the band for circus-day performances. Ives's boyhood memories of the circus coming to town, with its lavish-looking parade on the main street led by a circus band, left a lasting impression and inspired him.[13] Ives later wrote a song to the tune of the march. The song, also known as "The Circus Band," exclaims: "Ain't it a grand and glorious noise?" Written in 1902, the song was published in 1922 privately by Ives himself in his landmark *114 Songs* (the march itself was composed in 1899).[14]

Ives grouped "The Circus Band" with five other "street songs and pieces" whose texts he deemed "traditional." The song opens with a brief, loud introductory fanfare followed by a fast "quickstep" with two verses in duple meter that end quietly. Then comes a slower, softer middle section in 6/8 meter (that alternates between and combines triple and duple time), with one verse that is repeated, and in a fashion that ends the song with a loud, raucous, and abrupt closing flourish. Ives's text, clearly his own adaptation of something he may have remembered, reveals the essence of his generation's lifelong fascination with the culture of the circus:

> All summer long, we boys dreamed
> 'bout big circus joys!
> Down Main Street, comes the band,
> Oh! Ain't it a grand and glorious noise!
> Horses are prancing, Knights advancing;
> Helmets gleaming, pennants streaming,

> Cleopatra's on her throne!
> That golden hair is all her own.
> Where is the lady all in pink?
> Last year she waved to me, I think,
> Can she have died? Can! That! Rot!
> She is passing but sees me not.

Ives captured the traveling American circus succinctly: the bustling parade, the crowds, the anticipation each year, the historical costumes and spectacles, the exotic acts, and the expectation of freaks and wonders.

Ives particularly liked this work, which is why there are so many versions. They all evoke the experience of a totally enthralled young spectator watching a circus come to town. The final version of this charmingly dissonant and arresting but still jaunty, lively two-minute number is for chorus and orchestra. It was produced in the 1930s under Ives's supervision. Ives had stopped composing by then, but his memory did not fail him. When he helped George F. Roberts complete this last version, the "orchestra" he insisted on was little more than the small-size circus band characteristic of the midcentury, the type Ives might have remembered hearing and seeing when he was five or six, with piccolo, flute, two clarinets, one horn, one trumpet, percussion, and one or two violins—no lower strings—the kind of band that either could march or fit easily on a bandwagon and still play.[15]

"The cornerstone of circuses in America has always been music," a leading circus historian and devotee observed. Indeed, "without music we should never have had a circus parade, sideshow, big top performance, concert or after-show."[16] This catalogue of events makes the point that in the circus, music was continuous. The expectation for the public was, from start to finish, within the circus, to encounter spectacular visual entertainment extending over a wider scale of experience, reality, and geography than found in the daily life of the circusgoer. The anticipation at the circus was that it would invite extremes of delight, fear, awe, terror, incredulity, and amazement. From astonishment at the presentation of exotic cultures, the reenactments of heroic and patriotic history, to laughter at parody and satire in the work of clowns, to wonderment at tricks, midgets, fat people, giants, and other unbelievable spectacles (such as elephants dancing with pretty girls), a welcome artificiality and unreality dominated at the circus.

In New York City, which was until the mid-1920s an immigrant city made up of people from distant countries, and from the 1930s, a destination point for migration internal to the nation, the circus offered that rare public spectacle at which no one was quite "at home," privileged, or given priority by the spectacle. There were no "normal" people in the ring, only exceptional artists and animals. All spectators were rendered equal by the contrast between the inside of the ring and the public, and by the grandeur, ambition, and excess of circus entertainment. The circus privileged no particular language or religion. The language of the circus was primarily gestural and visual. And this language in turn was framed, circumscribed, controlled, and defined by the constant presence of music. To enjoy the American circus of the late nineteenth century, fluency in English was not required—except perhaps when the singing clowns performed.

One of the roots of the decline of the American circus during the mid- and late-twentieth century lies in the success it had in establishing norms with respect to the role of music in the urban culture of modernity. The circus's demise coincided with the development and spread of competitive forms of visual public entertainment framed by a continuous narrative but reminiscent of the circus experience in their need for and exploitation of the constant collaborative presence of music. Movies and later television amalgamated the illusion of realism from the naturalist theater with the realm of fantasy characteristic of the circus, particularly the circus's capacity to evoke the extremes of human emotion and response in the audience. Music enhanced the element of fantasy.

The moving picture, albeit a novel twentieth-century form of public entertainment, resembled the circus. It required a public arena and was framed by music. There was never, actually, a silent film (as producer Irving Thalberg famously remarked), just as there seems never to have been a circus without music.[17] The first films, those without a soundtrack, were produced in the expectation that music would accompany the visuals and introduce the film. The music was either entirely composed to fit the film, or improvised anew at each showing, using forces ranging from a solo piano to a whole symphony orchestra, particularly during the 1920s in Europe and North America, when the first experiments using recorded sound (not on the film itself) were heard.

The legacy of the circus as a model of modernity's craving for complex visual temporal entertainment requiring music may be the American circus's most audible legacy. However, what has become the norm for films and television, including the music video—the circuslike omnipresence of music in an indispensable supporting role—has left its mark on everyday life. What was expected at a circus—that no event in time would take place in silence (without musical sounds)—was transferred in the 1950s beyond the motion picture to daily life itself. Muzak, ambient music in malls, shops, and restaurants, transformed the quotidian so that it more closely resembled a circus. This is not entirely surprising, since the circus's popularity in the rapidly growing urban centers of America rested on its capacity to break the monotony, peculiar silences, and mechanical sounds of the urban environment by reframing time using the artificial sensibilities of the temporal experience uniquely generated by music. The difference, in the end, was that in the circus, music was center stage and eagerly awaited and remembered, whereas in movies and in daily life, by the end of the twentieth century music became a banal assumption and subsumed into a background, indistinct and hard to remember. There is now so much canned ambient sound at all times that it is hard to imagine the thrill of the music of the circus as demarking the boundary between dream and reality.

Nonetheless, it was the circus, through music written specifically for it and through its adaptations of popular and concert classical music, that developed the gestures of musical continuity we have come to understand and respond to thoughtlessly as we pursue our daily lives. These musical gestures are designed to heighten, minimize, or delay expectations of that which we might see and encounter. They derive from circus routines, including the snare drum roll, slow lugubrious music in minor keys; quick dance rhythms; repetitions designed to elongate tension; the perception of time; sonorities planned to denote distance, scale, and size; as well as commonplace examples of tone painting—trills for birds, for example. The use of musical rhetoric in the circus, notably sonority and repetition, popularized a musical rhetoric of cues that advanced and deepened narration and illustration.

However, circus music was certainly continuous, but although it was subordinate, it was never irrelevant. The heritage of continuity, precise coordination, and discrete subordination permitted circus habits to become the bedrock of the narrative uses of music in film and television. Music, both in the circus and on the screen (so to speak) is indispensable because it invites the individual and the group to adjust to and accept an artificial distortion of an internalized adjustment to external clock time—the rational standard division of work and daily experience in a manner compatible with measurable units of seconds, minutes, and hours. Circus music interrupted that expectation through a distortion by music, one that had the effect of heightening our experience of the visible spectacle.

The allure of the circus during its heyday was that as an archaic fragment of pre-industrial culture (although adapted to industrial modernity by the railroad), it returned its public to an attachment to a time sensibility distinctly not dependent on the industrial and agricultural practices of modernity and urban life. The circus represented effectively the power of music to control the subjective experience of time. That is why music was indispensable: it defines and frames the circus. Music invites the spectator to park the uniform sense of time at the door of the big tent. By offering a different experience of elapsed time and the intensification of time as it moves in tandem with a visual experience, the circus and then the screen constructed a distinct alternative framework for emotional response. Music, not the clock, defined the sense of time and duration.

Music in the circus and on the screen functioned as means by which strong emotional experiences were rendered more intense, compact, and refined. The dreamlike expansion of memory and speculation inspired by the circus seemed also persuasively enlarged through music in the imagination to encompass years and centuries forward and back. Music enabled the artificiality and unreality of the circus spectacle to have a great emotional impact.

It was the circus that therefore shaped the amorphous quasilinguistic manner in which music has come to support and illustrate mental pictures for modern spectators, to conjure them in real time and in memory so that the reception of ideas and story lines imbedded not only in circus acts and movies, but in life, is deepened, for better or for worse.

There were always different types of music at the American circus, not one form of circus music, but many circus musics (*fig. 7.8*).[18] The circus musician came to be called a "windjammer" (owing to the extent and frequency of blowing into an instrument that working a circus required). The wind and brass band was the leading part of the music at the circus

from the 1870s to the 1960s and was often prominently featured on circus heralds (*fig. 7.9*).[19] Band directors or leaders were crucial to the circus and to the successful integration of spectacle and music.[20] But circuses also featured a wide variety of other kinds of music, including calliopes, minstrel and sideshow bands, and novelty acts like the Ringling Bros.' Elephant Brass Band (*fig. 7.10*). Larger circuses sometimes required two bands, because the working day was incredibly long and hard. After all, nothing went on at the circus without mu-

sic. By the 1890s, in huge one-ring tents and in the three-ring circus configuration, a concert was introduced, often at the top of the show. Circus sideshow bands worked to attract attention and ultimately customers for the main show. These smaller groups, during the twentieth century in the Northeast, became almost exclusively African American in composition. Dixieland music was a feature of the sideshow.[21]

Music became so important to the American circus and its reputation that the circus by the mid-nineteenth century produced its own musical personalities and stars. Although some late-eighteenth-century accounts describe a single tambourine being used to accompany equestrian feats, John Bill Ricketts's seminal American circus featured "an excellent band of music playing all the time," likely consisting of drums, trumpet, and fifes.[22] By the 1830s, the size of the band had expanded and the dozen musicians in a broadside for a J. R. Howe's New York Menagerie were portrayed playing a mix of woodwind and brass instruments in addition to a drummer (*fig. 7.11*). America's first circus musician star was Edward "Ned" Kendall (1808–1861), who played the keyed bugle and was by all accounts so famous that crowds flocked to circuses where he was playing just to hear him (*fig. 7.12*). The Kendall family came from Rhode Island and Boston. Ned's brother James worked the other side of the proverbial nineteenth-century band-music street, playing in the Boston Brigade Band, a legendary non-circus ensemble that Ned himself would ultimately lead. Kendall made his circus debut in 1837 in Albany, New York, and worked for one of the first railroad circuses, the Spaulding and Rogers show in the 1850s. He worked for a variety of circuses over his career and his skill and fame were so legendary that (for perhaps the first time) a public "battle," a contest, on the

▲ *Fig. 7.10.* "Ringling Bros. World's Greatest Shows: The Funny, Wonderful Elephant Brass Band," ca. 1899. Poster, printed by the Courier Company, Buffalo. Courtesy of the Library of Congress Prints and Photographs Division

keyed bugle was held in 1856. Kendall soft-pedaled his circus career as the antebellum circus was the object of considerable derision from many clergy and ostensibly respectable critics. Its reputation for relative respectability was achieved only decades after Kendall's death.[23]

Carl G. Clair (1868–1911) was an Iowan (as was his slightly older contemporary, George Gauweiler, leader of Adam Forepaugh's circus band and a former military band musician who died in 1901) who worked for Barnum & Bailey at the turn of the century and rose to stardom as a bandleader and composer of circus music. He led the band for Barnum & Bailey during its European tour from 1897 to 1902. Also on the

▲ *Fig. 7.11.* Detail of "J. R. & W. Howe & Co's New York Menagerie," 1834. Poster. Somers Historical Society

▲ *Fig. 7.12.* Dominque C. Fabronius, *Edward Kendall*, ca. 1855. Lithograph. From the collections of the Henry Ford, 00.19.343

tour was Walter P. English (1867–1916), a tuba player and famous as a composer of circus tunes who took over when Clair fell ill. Even during the heyday of the traveling circus, after the expansion of the railroads, circus musicians often had to work elsewhere. Circus jobs were mostly seasonal. Like Kendall before him, English played in non-circus concert bands. Other circus players worked in bands on river showboats. Another circus legend, Henry Fillmore (1881–1956), was an Ohio conservatory-trained musician, a slide trombone player famed for his circus marches.

Many early American circus musicians came from Europe, from Germany, the Czech lands, and Italy. In some instances they brought European circus repertoire to America, including marches by Julius Fucik (1872–1916), the noted Czech band composer. Among these distinguished immigrants was an Italian, Allesandro Liberati (1847–1927), a

virtuoso cornet player (who once played in the Boston Brigade Band) known for the circus concerts he gave before the show began.

Liberati, along with Karl L. King (1891–1971) a euphonium player, bandleader, and composer who wrote a host of perennial favorites (including "Barnum and Bailey's Favorite" and "Eclipse Galop,") became noted for the precision and virtuosity of their bands (*fig. 7.13*). Longtime bandleader Vic Robbins (1896–1970) and Fred Jewell (1875–1936), composer of "The Denver Post" and "The Screamer" and also a calliope player,[24] were among the most assiduous in bringing to American audiences in small towns and cities not only their own original music tailored for circus use, but highlights of the classical and romantic concert and opera literature arranged for woodwind and brass band (*fig. 7.14*).[25] And then there were the great black minstrel and circus leaders, the most famous of whom was P. G. Lowery (1870–1942), a brilliant cornet virtuoso who worked the sideshows for the Ringling, the Cole, and the Robbins Brothers circuses and toured as a leader of several minstrel bands (*fig. 7.15*).[26]

But apart from parade music and preshow concerts, there was the very heart of the music for the circus, music written and adapted to accompany particular acts. A large portion of circus music sounds essentially similar to non-circus marches and dances, if somewhat more cheerful and exuberant. But unlike the imperial-sounding grand marches associated with bandstands in parks and military parades (e.g., those by John Philip Sousa), much of the circus repertoire needed to give spectators quite specific acoustic markers for distinct types of events. When required, circus melodies often had wide intervallic leaps, sound effects (a trombone "smear"), and highly marked transitions (Henry Fillmore's "Shoutin' Liza Trombone"). The emphasis

▲ *Fig. 7.13*. Karl L. King, ca. late 1930s–early 1940s. Photograph.
Circus World Museum, CWi-2362

Fig. 7.14. Frederick Whitman Glasier. "Victor Robbins and the
Sells-Floto Circus Band," 1924. Photograph. Collection of
the John and Mable Ringling Museum of Art, Glasier Glass Plate
Negative Collection, 1359

Fig. 7.15. "P. G. Lowery's Band & Minstrels, Ringling Bros. and Barnum
& Bailey Circus," ca. 1919. Photograph. Photographs and Prints
Division, Schomburg Center for Research in Black Culture, The New York
Public Library, Astor, Lenox and Tilden Foundations

▲ *Fig. 7.16.* Frederick Whitman Glasier. Ringling Bros. Circus, Swan Bandwagon lining up for the street parade, ca. 1905. Photograph. Collection of the John and Mable Ringling Museum of Art, Glasier Glass Plate Negative Collection, 1376

▲ *Fig. 7.17.* Bill Bailey. "Ringling Bros. and Barnum & Bailey: Liberty Bandwagon," 1943. Poster. Collection of the John and Mable Ringling Museum of Art, Tibbals Collection, ht2001727

in rhythm was not limited to mere pavement-pounding regularity and predictability, but frequently featured tantalizing syncopation designed to suggest extreme difficulty (King's "Wyoming Days"). Punctuation by sharp accents and dramatic, exaggerated flourishes were commonplace, befitting a grand and dramatic visual tableau (Jewell's "Floto's Triumph").

The so-called trios, the lighter and often less bombastic inside sections of a march, could be more contrasting in mood and more varied than in a concert march. And true to their function, circus marches gave room and reign to virtuosity—particularly fast solos for single instruments (Jewell's "High and Mighty").[27] By the early 1900s the circus was successful enough to spawn players who understood the distinct vocabulary and were able to improvise, add repeats, and cut and paste as they went, using the same material, varying it only slightly, adding solos and modulating when necessary. A circus performance was different each time. Precision in coordination between the acts and the music made both seem persuasively spectacular.

Circus songs and marches also had to keep the audience from flagging and generate excitement, particularly just before acts began. Fillmore was especially adept at so-called "screamers," upbeat fast marches (faster than any military march) designed to whip up audience frenzy. Music also was needed to "run off" the show and bring it to a close, often with over-the-top closing numbers.

Last but not least, the circus march had to be flexible and be able to adjust quickly and seamlessly to what was happening in the ring. Part of the excitement of the circus experience was the tension of eye and ear coordination, watching how the bandleader and his players anticipated, caught, and amplified the amazing acts using music. Time had to be elongated or cut. Gaps were filled and silences broken with improvised connective material, including the suspense-filled drum roll, backed up by interventions by percussion—cymbals, big drum, triangle—and fanfares to illustrate a memorable moment, particularly in the high-wire acts. But at the core, all circus music sounded familiar to the audience, connected to musical sensibilities outside of the perimeter of the circus.

The exception to this came when the circus brought exotic acts from abroad—from Africa and Asia—and when it illustrated the Native American presence (King's "Passing of the Red Man"), in war and peace, and when freak acts happened. The music had to show "Oriental" exoticism and palpable distinctiveness or strangeness, using even ragtime elements (Lowery's "Prince of Decorah"). Some pseudo-exotic tunes carried generic titles, such as "Bravura," written by the circus composer Charles Edward Duble (1884–1960); others advertised the specific character of the foreignness: "March to Mecca" and "Fan-Tan."[28] But they still sounded unmistakably like circus music despite their evident markers of exotic difference. All circus music, by playing off recognizable musical elements, supported the inverted reality of the circus. The music defied the everyday by its twists (often improvised in performance) on ordinary march, dance, and song music, just as the acrobatic acts witnessed in the ring were mind-boggling extensions of normal movements.

And there was considerable explicit musical patriotism on display at the circus. Circus parades, in which the bandwagon was a star attraction, were entirely celebratory and inherently patriotic (*figs. 7.16, 7.17*).[29] "The Star-Spangled Banner" had its most persuasive advocate in its use in the circus under the leadership of William Sweeny (1856–1917), who was the bandmaster for Buffalo Bill's Wild West Circus and author of innumerable Buffalo Bill circus marches. At the turn of the century, American imperialist fervor at the circus did not lag far behind, as the popularity of Russell Alexander's "The Storming of El Caney," a gallop from 1903 inspired by a battle in the Spanish-American War reveals.[30]

Animal acts demanded their own repertoire, particularly horses (Jewell's "They're Off"), seals (King's "The Walking Frog") and elephants (Jewell's "Galop-Go!"). But acrobats too required special numbers, many of them adapted imports (J. Strauss Jr.'s "Thunder and Lighting," the "The Flying Trapeze" from England, and Alfred Margis's "Valse Bleu" from France). Clowns, especially if silent, were quite dependent on music specially designed for their use (Jewell's "Trombone Blues"). One favorite, King's "Broadway One-Step," although written for clowns, ended up in trampoline stunts, bareback feats, and bicycle acts, as did "Stop It!" a delightful circus piece written by a silent film industry composer, Mel B. Kaufmann (1879–1932). Among the most popular clown tunes was "Shoutin' Liza Trombone," which featured a quote from the "Hallelujah" chorus of Handel's *Messiah*.

Singing clowns needed to improvise lyrics on songs written explicitly for them. In the 1880s, circuses, particularly those of Adam Forepaugh, highlighted singing comic clowns. When circuses were smaller and had only one ring, the singing clown was featured as an elite performer who engaged the audience by getting it to sing along, a practice that led to particular type of publication, the songster, published with lyrics only (*fig. 7.18*). The circus songster was a genre sold well beyond circuses themselves that flourished before the turn of the century.[31]

Fig. 7.18. Johnny Patterson's "Great London Circus Songster" (New York: Clinton T. DeWitt, 1878). Somers Historical Society

Dan Rice (1823–1900) was certainly the most famous of all American singing clowns, and at the height of his career in the 1860s he was the best-paid circus performer in America. But Rice was more than a circus performer. His claim to fame and notoriety (a 2001 biography was entitled *Dan Rice: The Most Famous Man You've Never Heard Of*) includes his use of a circus bandwagon to campaign for Zachary Taylor.[32] Rice is credited with inventing the mixed entertainment show that became central to the circus and helped define vaudeville. His circus acts apparently inspired an Arkansas newspaper to dub it "the greatest show on earth," a term that stuck. Rice was immortalized by Mark Twain (who saw him work) in *The Adventures of Huckleberry Finn*. P. T. Barnum envied him and many spectators idolized him, making him the best suspect for what became the visual image of Uncle Sam.

Rice was noted for his capacity to improvise. But what links Rice, an early star who died amid the heyday of the modern circus, to the musical elements of the circus experience was more than his singing in comic routines. Rice embodied the idea that the circus was at one and the same time a democratic spectacle and a sophisticated art. He was convinced that popular and high art could be integrated. Just as the circus bands brought concert classical music to the larger public, Rice did more than any other American to popularize Shakespeare through parodies he staged involving acting and singing. Humor and high literature were conveyed through satire that invited, through laughter, respect and curiosity for literature. The popularity of Rice also suggests that from the start, the circus in America, particularly in large cities like New York, attracted spectators from all social classes, ranging from the highly educated and literate to the illiterate, poor laboring classes.

As the circus expanded, star singing clowns were replaced by larger groups of clowns and one standard act that developed was the burlesque clown band (*fig. 7.19*). The clowns often also appeared alongside black minstrel groups in the circus after-show concerts and sideshows. By 1900 these were not only concerts of sorts, but also often featured comedy routines with performers not seen in the main rings; it was essentially a variety show, with music ranging from banjo playing to juggling, a predecessor to vaudeville and the television variety show of the 1950s and 1960s—a comic predecessor of Ed Sullivan.

But whether it was a song or a march, each piece of circus music, lasting from one minute to ten, was marked by simplicity, clarity, and repetition, employing only slight variation and carrying a descriptive title (*fig. 7.20*).[33] The music always implied

 *Fig. 7.19. Clown band, ca. 1920. Photograph. Circus World Museum, CWi-2293*

Fig. 7.20. W. W. Cole's Grand Zoological March, sheet music (Cincinnati: John Church & Co. Music Publishers, 1877). Lester S. Levy Collection of Sheet Music, box 103, item 103.120; Department of Rare Books and Manuscripts, Sheridan Libraries, The Johns Hopkins University

a story. Those stories, tied to pageants, grand entrances and exits, and equestrian displays, often carried an educational function and were even drawn from the legends of ancient history. G. F. Mitchell's popular "Caesar's Triumphal March" from 1898, the "Ramses" march from 1911 written by J. J. Richards (leader of the Ringling Bros. band 1911–19), King's "Cyrus the Great," and Fucik's famed 1900 "Entry of the Gladiators" (a real hit) were all written with specific images in mind. All these works were used in parades. In this context, circus music functioned as an instrument of memory, enabling hearers, after the fact, to conjure up, through sound images of unique tableaux and reenactments of history and life in distant lands that lingered long after the circus had left town.[34]

The exotic and unique sound of circus music was not entirely dependent on what composers wrote. Circus music sounded distinct because the circus featured its own idiosyncratic instruments. Early on, the American circus featured bizarre and unique instruments, the most important of which

was the calliope (*fig. 7.21*). The calliope, a singularly American invention designed for outdoor use, made its appearance in the 1850s. The first calliope was seen and heard (apparently as far as five miles away) in 1855, replete with fifteen whistles through which steam from a boiler was pushed. It was so incredibly loud that Worcester, Massachusetts, where its inventor Joshua C. Stoddard was from, banned its use.[35]

Ultimately Stoddard lost control of production and successor companies developed a keyboard version. The first "practical" calliopes were designed for steamboats, notably on the Mississippi. Steam was ultimately replaced by compressed air and the calliope went onshore to become a signature instrument of the American circus. They were placed on elaborate wagons and played a large role in the opening parades, but were also on occasion used inside the tent (*fig. 7.22*). The calliope's projection over large distances was a virtue in the era before amplification. Indeed, as the scale of the circuses grew, and with it the size of the crowds, weaker sounds (e.g., strings) disappeared, in favor of instruments that could be heard without difficulty from a distance, particularly those sounding at very high ranges or very low ones—piccolos and bass tubas. Wind and brass instruments paraded not only on foot but seated on the very same kind of ornate bandwagon later built for calliopes. Windjammers and calliopes made not only a flashy sight but unmistakable sounds as bandwagons paraded through the streets.[36]

In addition to the calliope and the circus band's easily discernable percussion, American circuses employed bagpipes, metal chimes, and briefly in the twentieth century, a contraption called the Una-Fon, a short-lived monstrosity invented in Chicago in the 1930s. The Una-Fon anticipated the economic efficiency of synthesized sound. Too ahead of its time, it

Fig. 7.21. Mabel Chipman. Great Pan-American Shows, steam calliope wagon, 1902. Photograph. Circus World Museum, CWi-182

vanished quickly. But it was a harbinger of bad news for the circus musician. A type of electronic organ, the Una-Fon could, using only one player, emulate the sound of a large brass band through the placement of oscillators on each and every note.[37]

By the end of the twentieth century, as the Una-Fon's brief if premature career suggests, the circus in America would change its character and cede its place of pride in the imagination of the wider public. As a form of mass public entertainment, the spectacular grand American circus would give way to new forms, including the motion picture and the rock concert. The music traditional of the circus would become an object of nostalgia, along with its sonorities, rhythms, and texts. Even the "pops" concert tradition, pioneered in Boston and Cincinnati using symphony orchestras in potpourri programs reminiscent of circus concerts, slowly began to lose its audience as the century came to a close.[38]

A sharp dip in the fortunes of the American circus in the 1960s paved the way for a revival of the more intimate one-ring circus in the early twenty-first century. The public began to seek out small circuses that used wind band players and sought to restore a rapport with the audience nearly impossible in the context of venues like Madison Square Garden. The modest renaissance of the small one-ring circus and the emphasis on live music in the popular Cirque du Soleil reveal just how integral music was to the circus in its prime; they and their playing had been main attractions and indispensable to the effectiveness of the circus. Together music and spectacle transformed the quotidian and challenged the boundaries of normal experience and expectations.

The primary musical residue of the American circus is not to be found in its repertoire or traditions of entertainment. The circus helped render permanent, as features of modern urban life, the demand

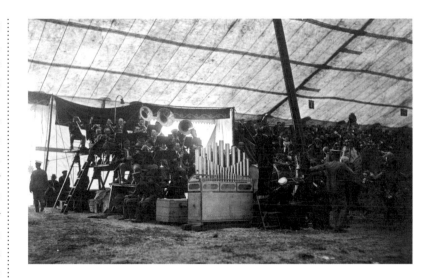

for ubiquitous musical accompaniment to the passage of time and a dependence on music as communicative of events we see because we understand music as descriptive of events and our reactions. It paved the way for the introduction of music as a necessary continuous dimension of our noisy industrial urban environment. The circus helped educate a democratic public about the varieties of repertoire and styles. It created, for a democratic culture, a shared vocabulary for masses of citizens, a vocabulary of nonlinguistic signs and sound effects, a music by which a diverse populace can recognize the world around it, dream about the unknown and the mysterious, and revel in mere spectacle and synthetic grandeur while experiencing sorrows and joys, all without speaking.

Fig. 7.22. Interior tent view of Barnum & Bailey band with calliope, 1924. Photograph. Circus World Museum, CWi-2294

1 The best account of the Stravinsky-Balanchine commission can be found in Charles M. Joseph, *Stravinsky and Balanchine: A Journey of Invention* (New Haven: Yale University Press, 2002), 167–74. See also Eric Walter White, *Stravinsky: The Composer and His Work*, 2nd ed. (Berkeley: University of California Press, 1984), 412–14.

2 See Francis Beverly Kelley, "Toscanini of the Big Top," *Saturday Evening Post*, Aug. 21, 1943, 21–22, 37–38; also Robert L. Parkinson, "Merle Evans," from the booklet included in the five-LP boxed set, *A Tribute to Merle Evans: An Anthology of Circus Music,* featuring the New England Conservatory Circus Band conducted by Merle Evans, Crest Records, 1970, 33⅓ rpm. The anthology, including Parkinson's essay, was reissued by Windjammers Unlimited on compact disc in 1997.

3 See Gene Plowden, *Merle Evans: Maestro of the Circus* (Miami: Seeman, 1971). For a recording of the Evans band, see *Circus Music from the Big Top: The Merle Evans Circus Band Legacy* (International CD 356).

4 Plowden, *Merle Evans*, 132–38.

5 Ibid., 136–38.

6 Evans's complete repertoire list for 1927 is found in *White Tops*, Nov.–Dec. 2003, 36. It includes also selections by Fritz Kreisler, Johann Strauss, Jr., and Arthur Sullivan.

7 For a representative list of specific circus repertoire, see Sverre O. Braathen, "Recorded Circus Music," *White Tops*, March–April 1966, 27–28, and Joseph T. Bradbury, "The Historian's Column," *White Tops*, May–June 1968, 28–29.

8 See Daniel Goldmark, *Tunes for 'Toons: Music and the Hollywood Cartoon* (Berkeley: University of California Press, 2005).

9 The finest general social history of the circus in America is Janet M. Davis, *The Circus Age: Culture and Society under the American Big Top* (Chapel Hill: University of North Carolina Press, 2002).

10 On the Jenny Lind tour, its reception, and impact, see Katherine K. Preston, "Art Music from 1800-1860," in *The Cambridge History of American Music*, ed. David Nicholls (Cambridge: Cambridge University Press, 1998), 203–4; Charles Hamm, *Music in the New World* (New York: W. W. Norton, 1983), 217–19; and Richard Crawford, *America's Musical Life: A History* (New York: W. W. Norton, 2001), 186–90.

11 S. Frederick Starr, *Bamboula! The Life and Times of Louis Moreau Gottschalk* (Oxford: Oxford University Press, 2000), esp. 149–50.

12 See Irving Kolodin, *The Metropolitan Opera, 1883-1935* (Oxford: Oxford University Press, 1936), 1–7. See, in addition to the standard works cited in the previous note, Max Maretzek's two-volume memoir *Revelations of an Opera Manager in 19th-Century*

America. The first volume was published in 1855, the second in 1890, and the whole edited by Charles Haywood and reprinted by Dover: *Revelations of an Opera Manager in 19th-Century America: Crotchets and Quavers & Sharps and Flats* (New York: Dover, 1968). Maretzek came to New York in 1848 and ran opera in New York in a manner that rivaled Barnum.

13 See Stuart Feder, *The Life of Charles Ives* (Cambridge: Cambridge University Press, 1999), 1–45 and *Charles Ives: "My Father's Song." A Psychoanalytic Biography* (New Haven: Yale University Press, 1992), 312.

14 Charles Ives, *114 Songs*, no. 56, 128–30. Ives's date in this publication is 1894. There is no need to go into the intricacies of Ives's catalogue and the issue of dates. For more on the origins of the piece, see John Kirkpatrick, ed., *Charles E. Ives: Memos* (New York: W. W. Norton, 1972), 36, 148, 171.

15 For more on "The Circus Band," see Crawford, *America's Musical Life*, 506–8, and J. Peter Burkholder, *All Made of Tunes: Charles Ives and the Uses of Musical Borrowing* (New Haven: Yale University Press, 1995), 27, 372.

16 Sverre O. Braathen and Faye O. Braathen, "The Parallel Development of Circuses and Bands in America," *Bandwagon*, Nov.–Dec. 1972, 4.

17 Rick Altman, "The Silence of the Silents," *Musical Quarterly* 80, no. 4 (1998), 648–718.

18 Jean M. Bonin, "Music from the 'Splendidest Sight': The American Circus Songster," *Notes* 45, no. 4 (June 1989), 700.

19 C. H. Amidon, "From Where Came Our Circus Music," *White Tops*, March–April 1975, 25–29.

20 See the list of band directors in *White Tops*, April–May 1944, 16.

21 Sverre O. Braathen and Faye O. Braathen, "Parallel Development of Circuses and Bands," 4–8; and "How Do You Like Your Circus Music?" *Bandwagon*, Aug. 1957, 5.

22 James S. Moy, "Entertainments at John B. Ricketts's Circus, 1793–1800," *Educational Theatre Journal* 30, no. 2 (May 1978), 187–202.

23 Robert Kitchen, "19th-Century Circus Bands and Music," *Bandwagon*, Sept.–Oct. 1985, 14–17, and "Edward Kendall: America's First Circus Bandmaster," *Bandwagon*, July–Aug. 1977, 25–27.

24 For a good collection of circus music, with short historical notes for the music of each number, see William E. Studwell, Charles P. Conrad, and Bruce R. Schuenemann, eds., *Circus Songs: An Annotated Anthology* (New York: Haworth, 1999), 1, 10, 11, 28, 39–40, 89–90, 87–88. The basic sheet music for all the specific numbers cited can be found in this volume.

25 The information in this, the previous, and following paragraphs on the careers of a select few band leaders is drawn primarily from the work of Sverre O. Braathen, the leading authority on American circus

bands. See Sverre O. Braathen, "Circus Bands: Their Rise and Fall..." (self-published pamphlet, n.d.); "Circus Windjammers," *Bandwagon* 15, no. 3 (May–June 1971), 12–23; "Chords and Cues," *Bandwagon* 15, no. 5 (Sept.–Oct. 1971), 4–15. See also Richard E. Prince, "Victor H. Robbins, American Bandmaster," *Circus Fanfare* 18, no. 5 (1988). Stuart Thayer, "Carl Robinson, Bandleader," *Bandwagon* 35, no. 4 (July–Aug. 1991), 16–19; and Carl Landrum, "George Gauweiler, Band Master," *Bandwagon* 25, no. 1 (Jan.–Feb. 1981), 17–20.

26 Clifford Edward Watkins, *Showman: The Life and Music of Perry George Lowery* (Jackson: University of Mississippi Press, 2003), 81–89, and "The Travels of the Showman Perry G. Lowery," *Bandwagon*, March–April 2004, 22–26.

27 Studwell et al., *Circus Songs*, xiv–xv.

28 Ibid., 12 and 19, 141–42, 95–96.

29 The design and scale of these wagons could be intricate and grand. See Charles Avidon and Stuart Thayer, "Early Parades, Early Bandwagons," *Bandwagon*, Nov.–Dec. 1977, 32–34, and Richard E. Conover, *The Fielding Bandchariots* (Xenia, OH: Richard E. Conover, 1969), a history of the Fielding Company in New York that manufactured the most famous of all circus bandwagons.

30 Studwell et al., *Circus Songs*, 30, 212–16.

31 Fred D. Pfening, "Circus Songsters," *Bandwagon* 1, no. 6 (Nov.–Dec. 1963), 10–12, and Bonin, "Music from 'The Splendidest Sight,'" passim.

32 David Carlyon, *Dan Rice: The Most Famous Man You've Never Heard Of* (New York: Public Affairs, 2001).

33 A reasonable selection of circus music can be heard on *Under the Big Top* (Angel Records CD 54728), 1993, performed by The Great American Main Street Band, a group made up of 17 players, some distinguished classical orchestra musicians from New York City.

34 Studwell et al., *Circus Songs*, 5, 24, 10, 11, 60–61, 179–80, 85–86, 91–92.

35 See Clarence Wilson, "First Steam Calliope Worcester Invention," *White Tops*, June–July 1944, 17; Fred Dahlinger, "Steam Calliopes in the Billboard," *Bandwagon* 13, no. 4 (Sept.–Oct. 1969), 24–27; Fred Dahlinger, "The Origin of Early Circus Calliope Instruments," *Bandwagon* 25, no. 4 (July–Aug. 1981), 18–19; Richard E. Conover, "The Early Stoddard (American Steam Music Company) and other pre-1900," *Bandwagon* 13, no. 6 (Nov.–Dec. 1969), 14–25; Barbara Owen, "Calliope," in *New Grove Dictionary of Musical Instruments*, ed. Stanley Sadie (London: Macmillan, 1984), 1: 301–2.

36 Fred H. Phillips, "Centennial of the Calliope," *White Tops* 28, no. 2 (Jan.–Feb. 1955), 2, and Robert J. Loeffler, "A Critical Re-Examination of the History of the Steam Calliope," *White Tops*, part 1: Nov.–Dec. 1955, 17–21, part 2: Jan.–Feb. 1956, 17–21.

37 See Hugh Davies, "Una-Fon," in *New Grove Dictionary of Musical Instruments*, 3: 700.

38 It is interesting to consider the impact of the use of music in the circus on the Broadway musical, another uniquely American adaptation of a European model, where music interrupts action. An exception was Billy Rose's *Jumbo*, a circus musical from 1935. See Geoffrey Block, "Bigger than a Show—Better than a Circus: The Broadway Musical, Radio, and Billy Rose's *Jumbo*," *Musical Quarterly* 89, nos. 2–3 (2007), 164–98. In the show, bandleader Paul Whiteman entered on a great white stallion.

FRED DAHLINGER, JR.

^{THE} AMERICAN CIRCUS TENT

The public knows the circus as the unique combination of human athletes and trained animals collaboratively performing together in a circular ring. Yet, the iconic image that is most frequently associated with the traveling circus is the venue architecture that imbued the enterprise with mobility and identity: the tent.

The tent city was the portable architecture of the traveling circus—usually coming once a year, disrupting the daily work and school rituals by providing a day of diversionary entertainment. It was enjoyed by children of all ages, whether boys and girls accompanied by relatives or nostalgic adults seeking to recapture the innocence of their youth. Customers approaching the circus experienced a diverse arrangement of concession offerings and ticket wagons, flanked by the sideshow, with its silver-throated talkers and beckoning bannerline of attractions (*fig. 8.1*). Great anticipation accompanied the entry into the

marquee, the circus main entrance, which led to the menagerie, filled with an array of wild and exotic animals. The culminating goal of the day's visit was the iconic big top, filled with multiple rings, elevated stages, and aerial apparatus, all surrounded by a hippodrome track and seating.

The big top is embedded in the American mind; many in the general public had lesser opinions of building venues. The anonymous author of the 1897 Ringling Bros. *Circus Annual* observed: "There are a great many people who believe that a circus cannot be a real circus unless it be seen under canvas, with dirt rings and the sawdust smells that go with it." Beyond the big top, in the area known to show folks as the "backyard," were the numerous other tents, sometimes twenty or more, which were required to conduct the daily rituals of circus life.

The winner of the Fédération Mondiale du Cirque's 2010 photography contest was a photograph of a Russian circus chapiteau, or tent. The media announcement from August 31, 2010 characterized its

significance: "This year's 'best of show' is perfect because it is not only great photography but also highlights the importance of the travelling tent in the popular conception of 'Circus.' . . . [L]ike the chapiteau, one must look inside to discover the mystery and delights of Circus."

The Pavilion

Introduced in 1825 as the "pavilion," the portable big top was improved and expanded for a century, ultimately housing over 16,000 people at a single performance in 1924. Significantly, the portable enclosure initiated the pervasive Americanization of the British-originated modern circus. Constant daily moving to a different community from late spring to early fall brought about the development of management and logistical practices, advertising meth-ods, transportation technologies, performance features, and other innovations that gave the circus a unique identity and role in North American life and culture. Shaped by domestic geography, weather, and population demographics, it evolved along entirely different lines than period European shows, other than in the content of the ring performance.

The performance art known as the circus was initiated in the United States in Philadelphia on April 3, 1793, a derivative of predecessor activity that took place in England starting in 1770. Until 1825, the equestrian exercises and associated acrobatics, clowning, and other feats of physical agility were staged inside temporary wooden amphitheaters with conical canvas tops erected only in larger cities.[1] The term *circus*, originally the name for the structure housing the activities, was not applied to the performing troupe identity nor did it serve as a title brand until 1824.

Fig. 8.1. Harry A. Atwell. Ringling Bros. and Barnum & Bailey midway to big top, Chicago, 1925. Photograph. Circus World Museum, CWi-2338

Having satisfied the audiences available in the population centers for three decades with weeks-long appearances, circus proprietors recognized opportunity to seek new territory as the population moved westward. That ambition was realized in November 1825, when J. Purdy Brown and his partner Lewis Bailey instituted the use of a round tent, an elevated top enclosed with a sidewall reaching to the ground, to house their enterprise. It was such a revolutionary transformation that advertisements for the troupe were headed by "Pavilion Circus," so as to differentiate it from the building presentations of the previous thirty-two years. Advertisements informed: "The Pavilion secures Ladies and Gentlemen from the weather, and covered seats offer comfort and convenience."[2]

No comment has been found as to the inspiration for the new style enclosure, but it was surely suggested by prior use of traveling theater companies (1823) and especially itinerant menageries (1824).[3] An 1847 engraving of a small menagerie tent, labeled as such on the sidewall, portrays a canvas that may have been one assembly. The top and side appear to be one integrally sewn piece, with no external rope guys or stakes, suggesting that either the poles were embedded into the earth or there was an internal support skeleton.[4]

Circus historian Stuart Thayer ascertained that 1825 was Brown's first season as a proprietor. With a career that speaks to major innovations, as an insightful novice he may have sensed that the established shows already fulfilled the prime eastern city dates and thereby decided that by becoming more mobile he could visit the hinterlands, which were not reachable by those showmen utilizing the temporary amphitheater methodology. The exploitation of new territory by road, river, and ultimately railroad was often the hallmark of the most success-

ful North American circus proprietors. Brown's action eventually made the circus the most favored and common entertainment in the countryside.

Without reservation, the decision to use a tent and the subsequent successful implementation of the apparatus was the single most important action taken in the history of the American circus. The choice impacted the ring performing arts, lifestyles, logistics, capital and expense, technology, and every other conceivable aspect of the industry.[5] The canvas-enclosed rituals and traditions that were established set the ring shows, which were sometimes called the "horse opera," decidedly apart from traveling theater heritage.[6]

The tent provided a readily movable housing for ring performances and the audience. It was one that was erected, performed in, then taken down and transported between communities every day of the week except Sunday, the single-day stand ritual starting as early as May 1826.[7] Principal features of the interior space were a nominal forty-two-foot ring and a surrounding space for the audience, with an entry slit for the audience and a back door for performer access and egress.

Nathan Howes and his partners were the first to follow the Brown and Bailey lead. Their sixty-foot-diameter top provided an audience pit space about ten feet deep, surrounding the ring.[8] Seating, illumination, and other appurtenances would be added to the simple canvas outfit during the coming years, providing a more complete venue for the operation. By 1836 all other American circus proprietors had done likewise, there being no temporary wooden and canvas structures erected in that season or thereafter.[9]

In little more than a decade vernacular existed to describe a portable enclosure. In 1837 it was a "complete set of Canvass with top, sides, poles, chains, guy stakes and all fixtures." This one measured 75 by 100 feet, meaning that it was a round top with a 25-by-75-foot rectangle between the half-circles, there being two center poles. In the shorthand that developed later it would have been designated a "75 x 100."[10]

Circus Fence

The circus business moved from amphitheater to pavilion operations during a single decade, but within that time the transition was not totally consistent. Four sources from the second half of the nineteenth century commented on the absence of a top piece. Their collective observations, though secondary, cause us to conclude that some early shows were intentionally presented in the open air, concealed only from ground-level prying eyes by the use of "side canvas," what came to be known as the "sidewall."

The innovator in the use of hanging canvas pieces for concealment was the traveling menagerie. Benjamin Brown was of the opinion that his brother, Christopher Columbus Brown, had introduced the use of canvas strips on Edward Finch's itinerant beast outfit in 1823. The ten-foot-tall, fifty-foot-long pieces created a view-blocking entryway to the door of the barn where the mammals were stabled and exhibited.[11]

Chess L. Briarmead, a circus history chronicler, wrote in 1875: "I might instance a circus which gave some exhibitions between Baltimore and some important objective point. There was no top to the canvas, and in one place a number of students undertaking to obtain a gratuitous view of the performance from the roof of the Academy, which stood by, the clown brought the house down by an allusion to the crows that were going to roost. So, too, of a

circus about 1827, which my informant thought was Brown's."[12] A noted clown and pantomime performer, Tony Denier, who was in the business as early as 1862, wrote in his 1877 training volume: "Few people have any idea how very crude a thing the American circus was as late as 1828.... [T]here was no roof to the ring enclosure ... oft-times startling early-arisen villagers into joyous expectation by their white canvas fence at break of day.... A tent was substituted for the old-fashioned circus fence, that showers might no longer be actual calamities."[13]

An unpublished manuscript from about 1891, written by longtime circus agent John Dingess, informed that traveling shows predating Howes intentionally had no top. "Previous to this, the circuses used to show with a sidewall only, which was made of very heavy drilling called Methnen [sic] Duck."[14] Finally, the generally reliable memoir of circus rider John H. Glenroy tells of a period in the 1850s that causes some confusion about the meaning of tent. "Our circus tent also was peculiarly fitted up, it having no top."[15] He and the remainder of the cast performed in a sidewall enclosure in the tropics. In the early days of the traveling circus, typically a single performance was staged in the afternoon, when no artificial lighting was necessary.

The inability to readily secure a center pole each day locally provided a rationale for the circus fence or sidewall construction. The tent had been embraced, but on days with pleasant weather the architecture was reduced to the minimum to prevent casual viewing of the ring action. It also reduced the labor by the performers and others to erect the enclosure.

A cloth ribbon placed around a series of poles a few feet high was the first definition of the circular circus ring, the wooden ring curb and earthen or tanbark ring bank coming later. Showman Aron (also

Aaron) Turner, a Howes partner in 1826, had no tent of his own when he went out in 1830. In the fashion of the ring barrier, he used a length of canvas placed around a set of six-foot-tall poles that were positioned in a circle to define his enclosure. It was a means to enter the trade with less capital investment than a complete tent with top.[16] In the future, when the top was not available due to damage or loss, the operation was said to be "sidewalled" or "corralled."[17] Clearly having a side to obstruct ground viewing carried a different meaning than a top, which prevented aerial viewing, but the latter also protected the operation from weather. For that reason, the subsequent use of "top" instead of pavilion, is thought to be derived from the physical position of the material, as with "side" canvas, as opposed to being compared to the child's toy, a spinning top.

Over time, "top" came to mean the entire tent assembly, as in the "white tops," a romanticized phrase referring to the newly fabricated canvas equipage before it became soiled and stained through contact with earth and grass. The portable architecture denoted the choice of itinerant employment and lifestyle. "White tents" and "white tops" became a favored phrase in the trade, as clear from circus news column headings in journals: "News of the White Tents," 1890 *New York Clipper*; "Tent Shows," 1900 *Billboard*; "With the White Tops," 1907 *Show World*; and *Chatter from around the White Tops*, the 1927 title of the Circus Fans Association's journal.

The Circus Day Ritual

Initial overland circus travel required the use of saddle horses and a couple of carriages, an omnibus or two, and a few wagons pulled by work animals to convey the personnel, the tent, and the performance properties. The show was typically presented on level, cleared land, often adjacent to a hotel, where the cast and crew lodged overnight and were fed, with the animals bedded and cared for in the associated stable. Following the public arrival of the caravan, the next priority was the erection of the circus enclosure.

The wagons drew up around the square in front of the Court House and a multitude of long poles and bales of grimy canvas were unpacked and thrown down. In the center of the green . . . a stake was driven by one of the odd men, the forerunners of the present "tent men," one end of a long tape was held to this stake by him and one of his comrades took the other and ran round with it in a circle, dropping here and there at regular intervals other stakes destined to hold the ropes. A smaller circle was marked off and along its circumference a row of pillars erected, while in the center was raised the great center pole of the tent. Then the canvas was raised and made secure, the ropes drawn taught, a booth erected to serve as a dressing room, and all was ready when the ring had been hastily turned up in the green turf and rows of wooden benches arranged in circles.[18]

The temporary architecture drastically altered the local landscape as well as the temperament of the community that anxiously anticipated the presentation by visitors from some distant place: "It stands out on the green, in beautiful proportions, erected suddenly, as if by magic. A flag floats over its summit, on whose ample folds is inscribed 'Circus.' All things are ready for the evening's sport, and a death-like silence reigns over the village."[19] Initially it took about an hour to erect the pavilion. The duration and scope of the undertaking expanded greatly in the years to come, in size, complexity, and expense, but the basic tent erection spectacle quickly became an expected ritual that came to be known as Circus Day in communities across America during the summer.[20]

To encourage the public to arrive at the circus lot early, by the 1840s a free act was offered, providing opportunity to sell refreshments and snacks, or tickets to the accompanying "outside shows." Among the earliest of such presentations was the ascension of an inclined rope, from the ground to the top of the center pole. It accentuated the height of the canvas structure, which was exaggerated in the advertising by as much as 50 percent. Still, in many communities, the center pole may have been second only to the church steeple in height—the two peaks representing moral views that were sometimes in conflict.

Basic Construction

The circus tent was an engineered combination of specially woven and sewn lightweight fabrics (tight-weave canvas duck for the top and drill with diagonal ribs for sides) and drawknife-shaped tree trunks and limbs. Long, spindly poles and stakes were visually juxtaposed against the broad expanse of the canvas membrane that they supported effortlessly in the air. The symbiotic assembly of parts was secured to the earth by rope or chain guys stretching from the peaks of poles to the stakes, which were termed "guy pins" in 1837. Similar tents were used for revival meetings and university assemblies, at agricultural fairs, and for political campaigns, but nothing quite equaled the circus pavilion in appearance and appeal. The plain and simple exterior appearance was quite dif-

ferent from the colorful, much-anticipated entertainment that magically transformed it at show time.

Circus pavilion fabrication expertise originated in the sail-making and military tent trades. A noted American novelist made the first connection, witnessing a performance "under a pavillion of sail-cloth."[21] The sewing of reinforcing ropes to sail material was reported as one reason why sail makers went into the circus top trade, where the same technique was employed.

The paucity of early patents issued for fundamental tent construction suggests that they were a pre-existing art. The subsequent absence of protective documents indicates that few details, extremely simple as necessary for over-the-road utilization, were ever devised, or judged worthy of the expense of patent protection and the added income it might generate. As a result, it is not the development of technology that delineates the story of American circus tents; it is focused largely on their utilization and proliferation.

Tent designers and makers had knowledge of drafting or geometry to establish the difference in lengths and areas between when the top material was sewn on a flat surface and how it would hang when it was erected in the air, the latter governing the dimensioning process. The sail loft or tent maker purchased bolts of suitable goods from a mill or merchant. Unrolled and laid flat, pieces were cut to the requisite shape, and then edged or sewn together, side by side, to make the specified top shape: an entire circle, a half-circle, a wedge-shaped piece, or a rectangle. The subassemblies were brought together in the field, with lacing connecting them together to create the circular or oval shape of the top piece.

The sidewall comprised one or more lengths of rectangular sewn pieces, erected end to end, and hung between side poles. It was suspended in part by attachments encircling the outer circumference of the top piece. At a chosen location, the sidewall ends were simply folded back to provide an entrance slit for customers. There were no ports to establish natural ventilation, other than the central penetration for the center pole. Lowering of the sidewall to promote a crosswind was the means typically employed to flush stagnant or heated air from inside the tent. By 1856 a "sun skirt" or "rain curtain," a longitudinal flap typically with a scalloped lower edge surrounding the periphery of the top piece, covered the joint line and provided a limited seal against weather entry. Such a detail is seen on a British non-circus tent erected in 1844, though it lacked a sidewall.[22]

The Sands, Nathans & Co. pavilion depicted in a lithograph dated September 16, 1856 for an engagement at Massillon, Ohio, may represent one style in common use before and after the invention of the quarter pole in 1847 (*fig. 8.2*). The top piece appears to have a reinforced grommet around the center pole, suggesting a "push-pole" style arrangement. In that system, the center pole was laid on the ground and the top pieces were placed over it. A spike at the top end of the pole went through the reinforced hole and the pole was then manually pushed upward to raise the peak of the tent. The grommet bore the weight of the top canvas.

Top pieces made from more than one piece of canvas were fastened together by a lacing line, called a "key," which was woven through a series of holes. It was a weak system, prone to leakage. On May 7, 1878, New York tent maker Max R. Kunkely was granted U. S. Patent 203,279 for an improved method of lacing that was more resistant to weather entry (*fig. 8.3*). His "lap lacing" advance consisted of a series of interlocking loops and an overlapping flap to cover and seal the joint. Kunkely's invention made the top assembly

Fig. 8.2. "Mme Isabel in Her Grand Ascension Outside of Sands, Nathans, & Co.'s Circus," 1856. Poster, printed by Sarony & Co, New York. Courtesy American Antiquarian Society

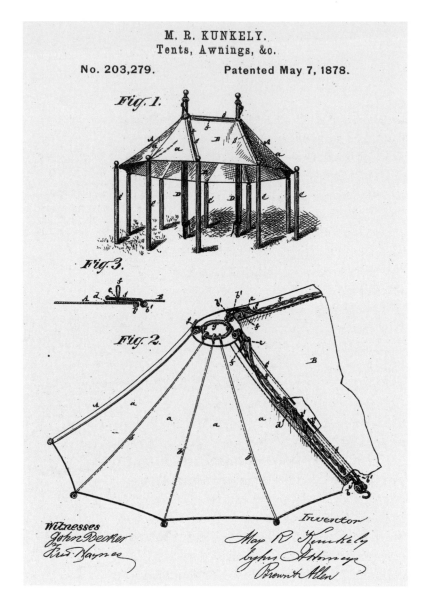

The Tent City

Development of the overland and the railroad circus between the first pavilion in 1825 and the initial three-ring circuses of 1881 precipitated the proliferation of purpose-specific tents. The aggregation of tents on the circus lot is an example of form following function, each addition representing an advance in circus technique, operating efficiency, revenue increase, expense reduction, or splendor. It was a unique configuration that readily came to mind when viewing other postwar landscapes. A decade after the United States had been mobilized for the Civil War, the circus was portrayed as a moving army encampment, a concept readily understood by the public. "But the city [Washington, DC] is somewhat on the circus principle of big tent and side shows, and as we had too little time for the latter, we bent our steps to the Capitol."[25] There was also an observed, deliberate hierarchy to the one-day-long, temporary architecture, as an editor noted in 1870. The performance pavilion was the acknowledged center of the circus cosmos. "The tent is stretched in a large field, and there are other tents adjacent—moons, as it were, to the great planet. Flags wave gayly from the tops of poles. There is a long line of vans and a tent of horses. What a peaceful encampment!"[26]

Circus men portrayed the community of tents as a movable city that arrived in the glimmer of the dawn and removed itself in the darkness of night, the business of entertainment conducted during the brief one-day interlude from everyday life. The aggregation of circus tops on the show lot was dubbed the "Magic City" in 1872 Barnum circus newspaper advertisements.[27] The development of the tent city reveals where owners focused their attention and invested their capital. Charles H. Day said of the late 1870s: "managers were swelling to

stronger and more durable, especially in high winds, and improved the comfort level inside the top. The simple system won out over competing methods and became the accepted standard in the trade.[23]

By the mid-nineteenth century limited knowledge of small tent construction and pricing was being disseminated via agricultural journals, but no details were shared in the circus trade journals that were initiated a few years later. The Industrial Fabrics Association International can trace an origin to 1912. A comprehensive treatise on tents was finally published in 1914.[24]

Fig. 8.3. Max R. Kunkely. Patent US 203279, May 7, 1878. U.S. Patent and Trademark Office

burst to increase their dimensions, both on the bill-boards and on the lot."[28] Circus pavilions were often the largest structures seen in nineteenth-century American communities.

The circus lot became an increasingly curious temporary commune. It was a mixture of the circus, menagerie, outside shows, itinerant and local vendors, and others seeking to earn some money from the assembly of city and hinterland folks.

The difficulty of donning circus costumes in the hotel, making one's way to and from the pavilion whatever the weather, and having a place to relax between the grand entrée and the ring appearances, was resolved with the addition of a second canvas. Likely introduced in the 1820s, but known from 1834 and by inclusion in an 1837 inventory, the first tent addition was the dressing room. Vertical canvas barriers divided it into two separate spaces, half to house ring properties, or props, and the other half divided again in two, for men and women. Horses were picketed immediately outside and conveniently led into the ring.[29]

The next addition was an outgrowth of the traveling menagerie, a collection of three or more animals conveyed on wagons or walking between communities. They commenced operations independent of the circus in 1813. Ring attractions were added to augment their educational animal presentations, thereby generating a confusing array of field shows. There were infrequent and various combinations with circuses starting in 1828. J. Purdy Brown, innovator of the circus pavilion, was also the first proprietor to place a combination circus and menagerie on tour, doing so in 1832. Thereafter the two entities were frequently consolidated, one-time menagerie proprietors increasingly becoming circus men as the independent animal shows went into decline.[30] Some circus proprietors ardently em-braced the menagerie as an added attraction on their lot, since it attracted additional Christian clientele that would not otherwise visit the circus. Other showmen decided that exotic beasts provided no pecuniary benefit, or required too much investment and maintenance and excluded them altogether.

Some confusion was created by combined circus-menagerie operations, involving their marketing identity, so as to play games with municipal licensing practices as well as pulpit preachers who decried the circus but visited the menagerie. When local laws and license practices were discriminatory against one or the other, a show might favor or drop one name—circus, or menagerie—in favor of the other, or employ a euphemism. The Van Amburgh & Co.'s Mammoth Menagerie and Great Moral Exhibition of 1862 featured not only a splendid and diverse exhibition of animals, it also presented a performance in a ring. The elements included the elephant Tippo Saib in conjunction with a perch act by acrobat Professor Nash; a performing Shetland pony named Black Diamond; a monkey, Jocko, riding another pony, Prince; and a bucking mule, the Maltese Jack. Lacking an equestrian act and a clown, the Great Moral Exhibition was not a circus by the typical and sometimes legally enforced definition, but most citizens would have judged it to be one. A male or, especially, a female performer in a figure-exposing costume typically fueled contemporary moral objections to the true circus.[31]

By the 1870s, circuses were identified either as solo establishments—a ring show only—or as a combination of a circus and a menagerie, each possibly having outside shows unless the proprietor was against them.[32] Lewis B. Lent typified the owners who were against "cat caravans," as circus scribe Charles H. Day termed the menageries. He and his kindred spirits focused on perfection in a single ring, hiring premiere artists, featuring a great band of skilled musicians, and thereby created a brand aligned with New York.[33] Adam Forepaugh, who added the large and diverse Mabie menagerie to his big circus in the spring of 1865, exemplified the finest of the circus and menagerie combinations. Animals were housed inside the circus pavilion, to one end of an oval tent layout, or lined the interior of the sidewall in a large round top, with a walkway between them and the back of the tiered seats.

Increasing daily revenue was a paramount interest for circus entrepreneurs and the next tops to be found on the show lot reflected that priority. "Outside show" described the catch-penny concerns

that sought ticket buyers outside the pavilion. In time, the phrase was truncated and conjoined to "sideshow," with "museum" used interchangeably for many years, as well as "annex."[34] Their appearance was noted as early as the mid-1830s. An 1860s observer declared: "The side show . . . is an institution of itself—one in which considerable money is invested with some concerns, while with others not so much capital is required."[35]

Early sideshows were usually conducted under a "privilege" sold by the circus owner, a practice discontinued in later years, when proprietors directly hired their own attractions or retained a sideshow manager to do so. Other privileges included refresh-

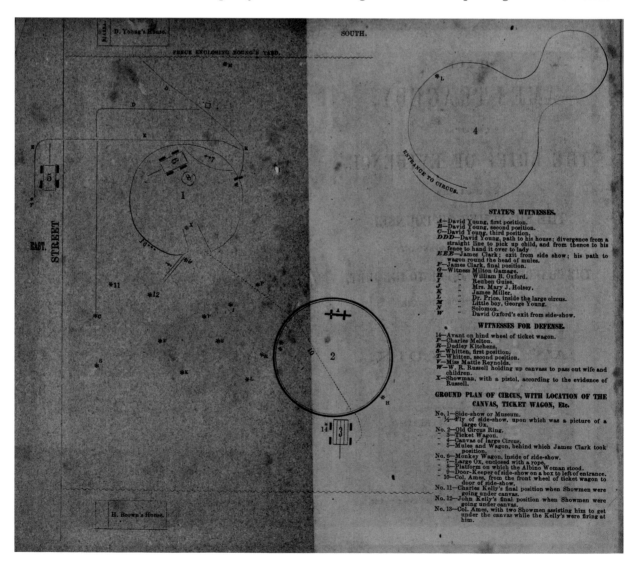

STATE'S WITNESSES.

A—David Young, first position.
B—David Young, second position.
C—David Young, third position.
DDD—David Young, path to his house; divergence from a straight line to pick up child, and from thence to his fence to hand it over to lady.
EEE—James Clark; exit from side show; his path to wagon round the head of mules.
F—James Clark, final position.
G—Witness Milton Gamage.
H—"   William B. Oxford.
I—"   Reuben Guise.
J—"   Mrs. Mary J. Holsey.
K—"   James Miller.
L—"   Dr. Price, inside the large circus.
M—"   Little boy, George Young.
N—"   Solomon.
W—"   David Oxford's exit from side-show.

WITNESSES FOR DEFENSE.

14—Avant on hind wheel of ticket wagon.
P—Charles Melton.
R—Dudley Kitchens.
S—Whitten, first position.
T—Whitten, second position.
V—Miss Mattie Reynolds.
W—W. R. Russell holding up canvas to pass out wife and children.
X—Showman, with a pistol, according to the evidence of Russell.

GROUND PLAN OF CIRCUS, WITH LOCATION OF THE CANVAS, TICKET WAGON, Etc.

No. 1—Side-show or Museum.
"   1½—Fly of side-show, upon which was a picture of a large Ox.
No. 2—Old Circus Ring.
"   3—Ticket Wagon.
"   4—Canvas of large Circus.
"   5—Mules and Wagon, behind which James Clark took position.
No. 6—Monkey Wagon, inside of side-show.
"   7—Large Ox, enclosed with a rope.
"   8—Platform on which the Albino Woman stood.
"   9—Door-Keeper of side-show on a box to left of entrance.
" 10—Col. Ames, from the front wheel of ticket wagon to door of side-show.
No. 11—Charles Kelly's final position when Showmen were going under canvas.
No. 12—John Kelly's final position when Showmen were going under canvas.
No. 13—Col. Ames, with two Showmen assisting him to get under the canvas while the Kelly's were firing at him.

ment and snack stands, gambling, clothesline (theft of locally drying wash), and the "concert," the minstrel or variety show staged after the ring performance and for which was paid an additional fee. The ranks of circus proprietors are populated with numerous men who accumulated their capital handling privileges. The sideshow operator typically furnished his own tent and other apparatus, such as platforms, having an outside "talker" or "blower" to verbally attract patrons with their auctioneer-like banter to what was known as the "kid show" by 1870.[36]

Circus proprietor Col. C. T. Ames was murdered on his circus lot in 1870. An account of the trial of the accused assailant included the earliest known sketch documenting the plan of a circus lot, one that delineated the sideshows (fig. 8.4). It depicts the following elements: the round-top pavilion with a peculiar entrance; a smaller circular dressing-room top connected by sidewall to the circus; a banner of

a large ox and the doorkeeper out front of the sideshow or museum tent that housed a "happy family"–style monkey cage, an ox in a pen, and a platform for the albino lady inside; and a ticket wagon near a previously used circus ring. Not included were the horses, carriages, and baggage wagons used for show transportation. The arrangement was typical of circuses that utilized a local hotel and stable, and had no attached menagerie.

It was not uncommon for a circus to have several sideshows. The Champion Circus fielded by Frank J. Howes in 1865 had three, one of which was a full wild-animal presentation.[37] The Howes show exemplified the development of the tent city up to the end of the decade (fig. 8.5). The pavilion, a round top approximately one hundred feet in diameter with one row of quarter poles, dominated this lot by the river. The dressing-room top is nearly hidden behind it (back, left), while the profitable concession

Fig. 8.4. Col. C. T. Ames, circus plan, 1870. From Weston & Combs, *The Ames Circus Tragedy at Dawson, Terrell County, Georgia, November 2d, 1870* (Macon, GA: J. W. Burke & Co., 1871), Circus World Museum, CWi-2304

Fig. 8.5. Frank J. Howes's Champion Circus lot, 1865. Tintype. Fred D. Pfening III Collection

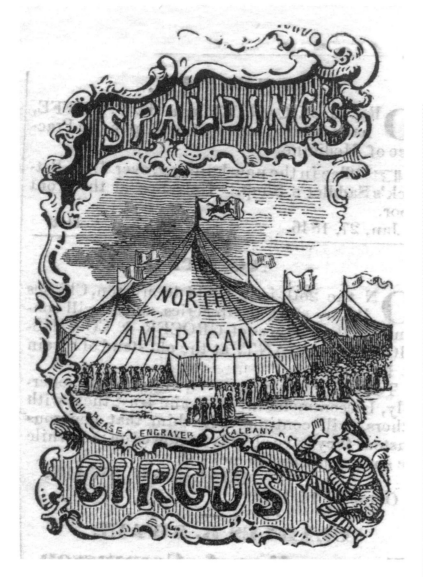

stands, three sideshows, and ticket wagon are all readily accessible in front. A combination circus and menagerie would have had another large round top, but Howes was satisfied with George W. "Popcorn" Hall presenting a smaller animal presentation as a sideshow. This overland show was dismantled and then loaded onto baggage wagons on the right side of the lot.

Reducing daily expenses was another important goal for the circus owner, the highest of them being the room and board costs for the troupe and horses. To that end, the dressing top sometimes doubled as a stable at night. The constant bills for

hotel lodging, meals, and horse stabling and bedding rose as circuses expanded, causing more than one circus proprietor to seek relief from the increasing expense. It came in the form of a camp outfit, an assembly of at least two tents, a cookhouse, and stables, which provided sleeping and bedding accommodations for the working men and horses on the lot. The proprietor, treasurer, and performers stayed in hotels. The first circus to implement the practice was the Mabie show, which did so in 1858.[38] This change truly fostered the general concept of the circus as a self-sustaining encampment, providing another allusion to the military precision of the undertaking.

The traditional gypsy caravan was never part of the American circus vehicle fleet, but some overland shows did utilize dormitories on wheels to house the personnel on the lots. The practice seems to have become more prevalent after the rise of the railroad circus, which relegated the smaller overland outfits to the more sparsely settled hinterlands where lodging space was not available.[39]

The end result of the expansion of the tented city was that by the 1860s a circus proprietor generally owned a number of tops of varying sizes. The 1856 Pentland show had a 105-foot-diameter round top and a 32-foot-diameter dressing room, three other tents of unspecified purpose measuring 50 and 30 feet in diameter, and one 34-by-20-foot tent, presumably rectangular.[40] The circus operated by L. B. Lent in 1865 possessed six tents: five round tops with diameters of 120, 118, 50, 45 and 44 feet, and one "oblong" measuring 28 by 44 feet, with no purposes stated for any.[41] Tents could be applied to different purposes by showmen, thus only the dimensions and specific shape were of importance in sale listings. A dressing room from a large circus could serve as a small sideshow for another. The antebellum proliferation of tops was a harbinger of postwar developments.

Fig. 8.6. "Spalding's North American Circus," Urbana, New York, Sept. 16, 1847, newspaper advertisement for New York engagement. Richard H. Pease, engraver and lithographer, Albany. Circus World Museum, CWi-2309

The Expanding Pavilion

◆◆

The pavilion dominated the architecture of the circus encampment and continued to grow and develop as field shows evolved toward their peak years of influence and appreciation in North America.[42] Audience capacity and associated revenue generation, working hand-in-hand with performance features, ultimately led to the three-ring circus of 1881, and in 1914 to the ultimate layout of three rings and four stages, all surrounded by a broad hippodrome track. Dimensionally, the pavilion width, length, and height were modified to satisfy the requirements of the business plan.

The two decades after 1825 were a period of experimentation with the shape and size of pavilions. Stuart Thayer's research revealed that there was no fixed standard, in part because the circus and the allied traveling menagerie were themselves evolving, independently and in conjunction with one another. Round tops were the prevalent shape, usually not more than 110 feet in diameter, with some claimed to be as large as 140 and 160 feet. Oval tents—rounds with one or more middle pieces and multiple center poles—were also employed.

The first physical limit to be reached was the diameter of the round top. About 1844, the pavilion with the North American Circus owned by Gilbert R. Spalding was "80 by 90 feet in diameter."[43] The substantial increase in tent diameter caused the canvas to sag between the center and the side poles, interfering with the line of sight from upper seats to aerial acts. Spalding eliminated the problem in 1847 by erecting four intermediate support poles just outside the ring.[44] They divided the round top into quarters, thus the apparently derived terminology "quarter poles." Spalding started with four quarter poles and then increased to eight, but whether they were positioned in one or two circles is unknown.

As pavilion dimensions grew, the top material alone could not endure the stresses imposed upon it by its own weight, plus absorbed water and soil. At some unknown date a network of ropes was sewn on the underside of the canvas, to reduce the deadweight stress in the membrane. These were termed "section-ropes" in Kunkely's 1878 patent. They served as support ribs, also eliminating any increased stress caused by the intermediate presence of the quarter poles.

The 1847 engraving depicting Gilbert R. Spalding's North American Circus provides the earliest iconography of American show tops (*fig. 8.6*). It reveals the presence of four external ropes securing the center pole in a vertical position. They strongly suggest that the center pole was of the "bail-ring" type; a tent in that style was in use for non-circus purposes in Great Britain by 1844.[45] The inner circle of the canvas top was secured to this metallic ring, which was then lifted aloft by means of pulleys or block and tackle. Spalding's quarter poles were also of the bail-ring style.[46] The use of the circular metal ring might signal two important features of later circus tops: the initial division of the round-top canvas into four or more pie-shaped sections, which were laced together along radial lines, and the application of section ropes, spanning from the bail ring to the sidewall, to support the canvas and develop the support of the quarter pole over a larger area, thereby preventing localized tearing.

The quarter pole innovation may have been inspired by Spalding's desire to increase audience capacity through the use of seats with a larger number of tiers, or rows, placing the outermost seats at a higher elevation. In conjunction with the poles added in 1847, Spalding reportedly had a 17-foot-wide canvas ring added around the periphery of the top, the addition of which required the use of a second set of

side poles. Two years later a lithograph described his pavilion as being 15,000 square feet, nominally 138 feet in diameter, with a capacity of a thousand people.[47]

In effect, Spalding's invention allowed for a multiple-piece, round, bail-ring top with a center pole, side poles, and two rows of quarter poles. It was readily erected and dismantled; withstood typical storms and winds; and provided an expanded seating area with improved viewing. It was the basis of later, larger tents. Other than lacking a middle piece, which others had already accomplished, Spalding's tent embodied the essential elements necessary for tremendous expansion of the pavilion. His top was

at the cutting edge in its day, a substantial advance over others and for that reason was illustrated at the head of his newspaper advertisements.

The interior of the Spalding & Rogers pavilion was the central focus of an 1849 poster (*fig. 8.7*). The street parade—depicted in vignettes around the periphery of the print—wound through the principal streets, displaying the show's fine artists, horses, vehicles, wardrobe, and music. The procession led everyone to the lot, represented by the two tents in the upper left, where the townspeople gathered outside, then proceeded inside for the performance. The pavilion had the characteristic center pole, with a "mud block" at the base to prevent sinking into the

▲ *Fig. 8.7.* "Spalding & Rogers North American Circus," 1849. Poster, Richard H. Pease, engraver and lithographer, Albany. Courtesy American Antiquarian Society

soft earth. A chandelier provided illumination for evening shows, while the four quarter poles eliminated sag from the top. The staked ring curb, tiered seating, front and back doors (for guests' and artists' entry and exit), and bandstand defined the state-of-the-art circus pavilion architecture of the period. It had taken twenty-five years from Brown's initial innovation to reach a plateau that would serve as the platform for further expansion.

Joe Pentland's 1856 top incorporated quarter poles, the name found in an 1857 sale document for the circus.[48] An advertising cut from L. B. Lent's National Circus of 1857 is the earliest to portray a circus pavilion with two rows of quarter poles.[49] On the 1875 Barnum Hippodrome they were identified as long and short quarter poles, according to the height of the canvas they supported. On the 1905 Barnum & Bailey show the longer, inside row quarter poles were called "half poles," a characterization that has not been found elsewhere. With two rows of quarters to prevent sagging, tent makers were able to furnish a top that reached 200 feet in diameter by the mid-1870s.[50]

An alternative to enlarging the diameter of the tent was to divide the round top into halves and place what became known as the center piece or middle between them.[51] This required a second center pole, the single performance ring situated between the pair. It essentially split the impact of a single diameter, creating different width and length dimensions for the pavilion. The available accounts are not always definitive in their language, but it seems that an oval-shaped tent was placed into use as early as 1834 (an 80-foot round with a 40-foot middle), with an equally wide tent and perhaps as many as three or four middles employed in 1844 (80 × 200).[52]

Oval-shaped pavilions and larger diameter round tops were used by showmen with combination circus and menagerie operations, enabling them to house everything under one top. In 1868 Fayette Lodawick "Yankee" Robinson employed a "zoological panorama," presumably a longitudinal canvas panel painted with lifelike animal scenes to physically separate the circus and the menagerie within his single large top.[53]

The large, oval-shaped performance pavilion dominated the lot in a photograph documenting the engagement of an unidentified circus on the west side of St. Paul, Minnesota about 1874 (fig. 8.8). With two middle pieces, it was larger than the entire balance of the show. The cookhouse and stable tents are seen at the far left. The right area is filled with the sideshow and bannerline, two concession stands, the ticket wagon, and an unusual menagerie, wherein several top pieces are surrounded by a single sidewall. People have started to arrive by horse and buggy, while the wind has the center pole flags snapping in its clutches. It is a warm day, as determined by the fact that some of the sidewall has been lifted to help ventilate the top.

The height of the pavilion, established by the length of the center pole, was generally proportioned to the diameter of the round top, and later to the width of the oval tent. Fashioned from a single tree trunk, they were always a single, solid piece,

▶ *Fig. 8.8.* Circus on the west side of St. Paul, Minnesota, ca. 1874. Photograph. Minnesota Historical Society, negative 37515

necessary to sustain the load of the canvas and weather. Initially the diameter and length of the pole were limited by the ability of a crew to raise them with no more assistance than a team of horses and possibly block and tackle. Transport by wagon probably imposed a weight limitation that was influenced by the locale and road conditions. The conversion to rail operations meant that the pole and the wagon upon which it was placed could not exceed the length of a flatcar. In the 1870s this was between thirty and forty feet, reaching sixty feet in the early 1880s and seventy feet after 1919.

More Tents, More Rings

Yankee Robinson jumped to the forefront of showmen in 1856 with his Quadruple Show, the name originating with his four tops. They housed a menagerie, big show, museum, and black minstrels, all seen for one admission price. It anticipated the three-tent configuration that became the standard several decades later, but few if any showmen followed his lead, presumably because of the expense, labor, and logistics associated with four separate tops.[54]

Gaining momentum and expanding with other American enterprises in the post–Civil War years, the American circus stepped forward with greater plans than ever before. Forepaugh reportedly had the biggest tent of any showman in 1867, a 120-foot round with two 40-foot center pieces, held aloft by three center poles and sixteen quarter poles.[55] He initiated a new era by dividing this combination circus and menagerie into two big tents for 1869.[56] Forepaugh's newspaper advertisements advised readers to see the diagram of the interior—a drawing that must have been illustrated in other materials. Shows having two large tents, for a menagerie and

Fig. 8.9. "J. E. Warner & Co.'s Museum, Menagerie and Circus," 1871. Herald. Courtesy of Michigan State University Museum, 1413.7

a circus, were not a great novelty, having been done previously, but Forepaugh took his dividing action at a fortuitous time. The argument has been advanced that the pillars of the circus, the performance, the menagerie, and the sideshow (or museum) had grown so large that each required individual housing.[57]

Joseph E. "Joel" Warner used the divisional concept when inaugurating his much-publicized three-tent configuration of circus, menagerie, and sideshow (museum) for 1871. Other showmen, such as John Robinson, followed Warner's lead that year, promoting the three-top configuration. Warner's advertising portrayed his novel three-tent circus scheme to the public, a step somehow beyond Yankee Robinson's 1856 four tops and Forepaugh's 1869 two-tent concept. Notably, unlike other circuses, the museum or sideshow was included in Warner's single 25-cent admission price, which may have been the true novelty of his innovation. His action was perhaps more a marketing ploy than a meaningful inflection in the history of circus tents. Warner explained his action in a pronouncement in one of his heralds: "Thus arranged [in three separate tents], the 'entire community' and particularly that portion opposed to circuses may with the utmost propriety visit our entertainments accompanied by their families" (*fig. 8.9*).[58]

It was thus a separation to satisfy moral objections, which actually ended up increasing the daily take by catering to the objectors. Those who disapproved of the ring entertainments could safely visit Warner's first two tents and never lay eyes upon the offending performers. In reality, many simply followed the crowd, hoping that it would provide them with anonymity. Such covert visitations often drew mention in local newspapers, who chided the hypocrites for their deceitful actions. A favored excuse

was that their children wanted to see the circus and could not go unaccompanied.[59]

P. T. Barnum and his agents, seldom shying away from challenge or opportunity, took anti-entertainment attitudes on in several ways. Although the performance pavilion and all that it housed was the primary goal, the word *circus* and descriptions of its attractions were downgraded in show advertising. The word *circus* was absent in the fully developed title: P. T. Barnum's Great Traveling World's Fair, Museum, Menagerie, Polytechnic Institute and International Zoological Garden. Under the heading "Public Amusement" in the 1872 advance courier, an anonymous writer declared: "America is on the amend in regard to public amusement." In a verbose way, an argument was made that the attractions of the Barnum show had been elevated so as to avoid previously disparaged elements and qualities. Ratcheting up a notch, the 1873 advance courier reprinted the same article under the heading "Popular Amusements a Necessity" and added a practice of "Free Admission to the Clergy," to inveigle their attendance by the use of free advance tickets. If they did not arrive in advance by mail, they would be issued directly upon application at the ticket wagon.

Three tents ultimately became the standard configuration for the American circus, but not until later. Abandoning rationality after just one year, circus publicity in the 1870s aggrandized four, six, or more tent configurations. More was always better. There were also multiple round-top pieces surrounded by a single sidewall, with disorienting interior labyrinths, and other unusual and novel configurations of canvas and poles. The emphasis on multiple tops became so important that the Barnum show's 1873 advance courier carried an article about "canvas shows," outfits with ten to twelve largely empty tents,

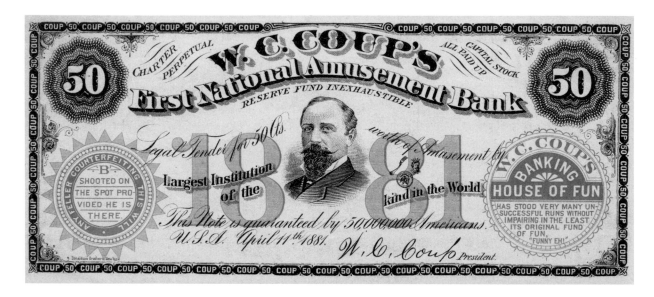

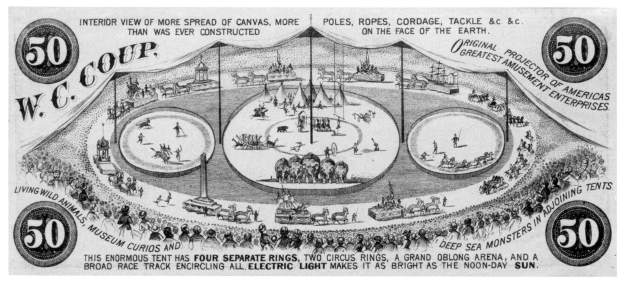

wherein the visitor had to imagine each filled with something, so limited were their contents.

The circus action reflected the 1870s and 1880s industrial-era philosophy of giant undertakings. Shows played the numbers game with everything that could be counted, including railroad cars, horses, cages, elephants, and tents, which were among the most readily ascertained. There were novelty installations, innovations that lasted a couple of seasons until familiarity or reality abated their significance. These included multiple menagerie tents, from two to as many as seven; additional sideshow and museum tops; a public rest tent; aquarium tents; the horse fair; and "black tops," made with dyed canvas, for the presentation of magic illusions and early films.

The growing appeal of the invigorated circus increased daily attendance. Dan Castello recounted that it was he who suggested to P. T. Barnum that a

Fig. 8.10. "W. C. Coup, Original Projector of America's Greatest Amusement Enterprises, Interior View of More Spread of Canvas, More Poles, Ropes, Cordage, Tackle, &c &c than Was Ever Constructed on the Face of the Earth," 1881. Handbill. Circus World Museum, CWi-2335A, 2335B

second ring was necessary to accommodate the enormous crowds that jammed their huge overland circus in 1871 and the version placed onto a special train of specially built railroad cars in 1872.[60] For 1873 the firm added a second ring, which was also surrounded by a hippodrome track where processions and races could be staged.[61] The Barnum pavilion was remembered as a 150-foot-diameter round with three 50-foot middles, but a photograph of the 1873 lot shows only a three-pole arrangement, perhaps a 150-by-250-foot configuration.[62] Before merging with the Barnum show for 1881, the two-ring Great London, owned by James A. Bailey and James E. Cooper, toured with a top that measured 186 by 270 feet, indicating some modest growth.[63]

The disparity between smaller and larger outfits increased further in 1881, when two circuses, the new Barnum & Great London combination and that of W. C. Coup, both brought out the first American three-ring circus in a tent. It's generally believed that the Barnum outfit backed into the concept after plans for a conventional two-ring circus for domestic presentation and a single-ring show for touring Europe collapsed.[64] With three rings' worth of artists signed, the decision was made to put forth the world's first three-ring circus.[65]

Coup, who had been Barnum's partner between 1871 and 1875, had a circus about half the size in 1881 and the ambition to go toe to toe with the bigger outfit. Both had a three-ring and hippodrome track configuration, mandating an oval pavilion with three middle pieces and four center poles. Coup illustrated his peculiar arrangement on the back of a handbill (*fig. 8.10*). It was issued in the form of faux legal tender, assigned a value of "50 Coup," ensuring that it would grab more attention than the simpler trade cards in use. His agent exaggerated the hippodrome track into a fourth ring and de-

scribed the center ring as a "grand oblong arena." Circus illustrators were masters at romanticizing features and stirring the imagination. When shows inserted middle pieces between the half-round ends, they usually removed the center poles from the middle of the ring, but that was not the case in this portrayal of Coup's unique layout.

Dimensions are not available for Coup's 1881 three-ringer and conflicting data survives for that of Barnum & Great London. The Sells Brothers also reportedly went with three rings, under a 120-foot round with three 50-foot middles.[66] Prime competitor Adam Forepaugh, equal in all parameters and sometimes greater than the Barnum operation, fielded a 214 by 379 in 1883 and in the next season the Barnum show had a 212 by 432.[67] Each show could honestly brag that they had the largest pavilion by selectively citing just one dimension. People continued to witness the time-honored ritual of the erection of the circus city, but it had extended into a several-hour process by 1888 (*fig. 8.11*).

The three-ring configuration became an icon of the American circus. In an era when giant sizing was becoming commonplace in society and industry, the circus simply followed suit. As with all things circus, the linear arrangement of the rings was subject to variation and experimentation. The availability of certain acts from variety and vaudeville houses, such as trick bicycling, roller-skating, and

Fig. 8.11. Barnum & Bailey Circus center poles, South Bend, Indiana, July 21, 1888. Photograph. Collection of Howard Tibbals

dancing, all of which required a secure flat surface, was one reason why some shows substituted a slightly elevated wooden stage for one of the rings.

A standard was reached in 1890, when the first arrangement of three rings with two stages between them was implemented by Barnum & Bailey. That season also marked the debut under canvas of Imre Kiralfy's production *Nero, or the Destruction of Rome*, the first of nearly three decades of extravagant spectacles presented on a theaterlike stage with special backdrops and props that displaced considerable seating space. James A. Bailey presumably added the two square stages between the three rings to lengthen the tent and recover lost seating space and revenue. He also reduced the number of performance displays, or act changes, from a near-typical seventeen in 1889 to just eight in 1890 and twelve in 1891. Further, not all five activity locations were occupied by performers at all times throughout the program. Every performance comprised a band concert, top-quality ring, stage talent, multiple hippodrome track races, and the grand operalike spectacle, plus admission to the menagerie. For the price of one ticket, Bailey's customers were given full sensory overload.[68]

The circuses that comprised three or more rings often drew negative comment, whether a cartoon that portrayed a man cross-eyed from seeing the three-ring show or a more insightful complaint from an 1884 observer.[69] "This three-ring idea has produced a change that is decidedly detrimental to the merit of any good performance or act. Performers of merit will always exert themselves when their efforts receive applause; but where two or three acts are going on at once, if any applause is given the question is: *Who* is being applauded? These acts must all finish at one time, no matter if one of the artists can do much more and better than anyone else."[70] The simultaneous acts diluted the apprecia-

tion for the best ring stars and had the ultimate effect of lessening the overall quality of the circus.

Al G. Field recalled in his 1912 memoir that "the old clown was best man with a circus. He was the entertainer, the leading man."[71] Despite their once fundamental and primary role, the talking and singing clowns, who had gained prominence via the ringmaster (straight man)—rider (artiste)—clown (buffoon) trio that defined the quintessential one-ring circus activity, were the first casualties of the expanded arena. Their engaging verbal discourses, which once inspired belly laughs, and their knowing political jabs that used to be met with assenting nods, could no longer be heard throughout the immense pavilion. The solo star clown was replaced by a cadre of nameless sight-gag presenters that ultimately reached fifty in number.[72] The name-brand clown was out of a job, but expansion of the performance top gave many more artists with different skills employment during the heyday of the multiple-ring circus.

From Pavilion to Big Top

The Barnum show performance tent of the 1870s was described by a variety of terms, including pavilion, but a simplification of their 1877 description, "big top canvas," is the one that gained the widest and most permanent acceptance of all.[73] Charles McLean was the Master of Pavilions from 1873 to 1907 (except 1893) and the phrase likely came out of daily use during his tenure. By 1883, "big top" was the name being used consistently in show documents.[74] The Ringling Bros. World's Greatest Shows started to regularly use "big top" by 1891.[75]

Though used internally by circus personnel as early as 1877, it was almost two decades before "big top" came into popular usage. A recent search of digitized newspapers revealed the first publication of "big top" in 1887, with other singular examples in 1889, 1893, 1895, and 1897.[76] With the exception of 1893, with a Ringling connection, all of the other examples were in association with circuses owned and operated by James A. Bailey. That takes on more significance when one realizes that major publications using the term in the late 1890s were all based on visits to his Barnum & Bailey troupe. The popularization of the term may also be attributed in part to Bailey's legendary longtime press agent Richard F. "Tody" Hamilton, who served the show from 1881 to 1907. Thus, to some degree, the Greatest Show on Earth can be accorded recognition for having supported the proliferation of the expression "big top."[77]

The Biggest Big Top

That typically American characteristic, the desire to know who had the biggest, is a rather difficult task when it comes to ranking big tops. The limited survival of business records and technical or contract documentation forces reliance upon a patchwork of alternative sources that must be judged separately for their accuracy and reliability. Further complicating the task are the individual dimensions, which could be cited in any number of ways to make the whole seem larger. The data below represent the leading candidates for the largest big tops, as ranked by square footage as encircled by the sidewall, once it was erected and guyed out (*table 8.1*).

BIG TOP SIZES

Year	Show	Width ft.	Length ft.	Middles qty–ft.	Center Poles qty	Area sq. ft.
1905	Barnum & Bailey[78]	278.87	523.37	5–48.9	6	129,232
1898	Barnum & Bailey[79]	240	525	5–57	6	113,616
1875	America's Racing Association[80]	214	574	6–60	7	112,989
1875	America's Racing Association[81]	250	400			85,563
1892	Barnum & Bailey[82]	220	500	5–56	6	99,594
1883	Barnum & London[86]	250	450			99,063
1905	Coney Island Hippodrome[83]	210	490	5–56	6	93,419
1916	Barnum & Bailey[84]	200	510	5–50, 2–30	8	93,400
1919	RBBB[85]	200	500	5–60	6	91,400
1853	Franconi's Hippodrome[88]			4	5	87,120
1853	Welch's Hippodrome[89]			2	3	87,120
1883	W. W. Cole[87]	250	400	3–50?	4	86,563
1884	Barnum & London[90]	212	432	4–55	5	81,921
1913	Ringling Bros.[91]	190	450	4–50, 1–60	6	77,739
1894	Barnum & Bailey[92]	180	440	5–52	6	72,234
1875	Barnum Hippodrome[93]	200	400	5–40	6	71,400

Table 8.1. Big top sizes of major circuses.
RBBB—Ringling Bros. and Barnum & Bailey

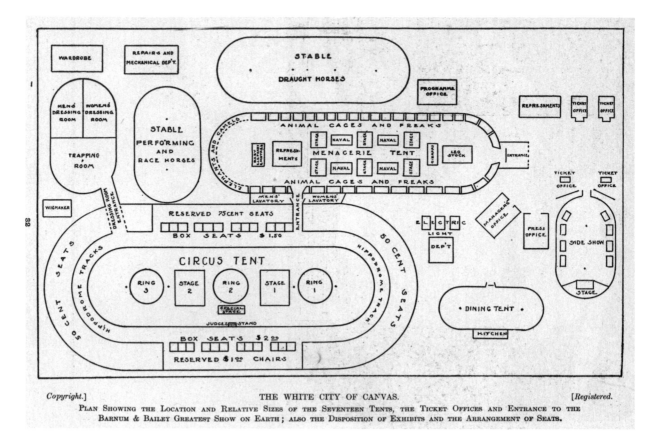

THE WHITE CITY OF CANVAS.

PLAN SHOWING THE LOCATION AND RELATIVE SIZES OF THE SEVENTEEN TENTS, THE TICKET OFFICES AND ENTRANCE TO THE
BARNUM & BAILEY GREATEST SHOW ON EARTH; ALSO THE DISPOSITION OF EXHIBITS AND THE ARRANGEMENT OF SEATS.

After the deaths of Forepaugh in 1890 and Barnum in 1891, James A. Bailey occupied the pinnacle of the American circus. His Barnum & Bailey outfit was truly the Greatest Show on Earth. It is thus unknown why, when his tent was already the largest, that spurious data exaggerating its size was released in England in 1898, only to be unrealistically increased in 1905, the third year of his less-than-triumphant return to the United States. We can only hypothesize that Bailey felt pressured by the increasingly competitive Ringling brothers, who by the time Barnum & Bailey returned to the U.S. for 1903 had equaled his market. The Bailey data, the two top entries, must be disqualified by their unrealistic widths and data on the poles supporting the canvas. The center pole lengths were given as 65 feet, which was impossible when the show flatcars were only 60 feet long. Authoritative evidence for the European big top set the center pole length at just 58 feet, within the 60-foot flatcar length.[94]

Upon the return to the United States for 1903, a contract was given to tent maker William Lushbaugh for the Barnum & Bailey tops. With center poles measuring 60 feet tall, and quarters of 45 and 35 feet, it was indeed a very tall top, perhaps reflecting European influence or additional space for aerial and thrill act presentation. An advertisement taken by Lushbaugh in the 1903–4 Barnum & Bailey route book illustrated the behemoth interior space and declared it "The Largest Tent Ever Made."[95]

Circuses never passed by an opportunity to boast about the immensity of their operation, some going to the extent of publishing a layout of the tents in the show's advertising courier (*fig. 8.12*). While the plan shows the tops used during the European tour from late 1897 to 1902, a similar configuration applied to the return tour in 1903. In that year Bailey staged what was likely the most massive and magnificent circus seen anywhere until that time. In fact, it was so elaborate that the staff and crew were un-

Fig. 8.12. Barnum & Bailey Circus tent layout, 1903. Plan from *The Official Programme and Book of Wonders Combined of the Barnum & Bailey Greatest Show on Earth* (New York: George Arlington, 1903), 32. Circus World Museum, CWi-2343

able to maintain the normal daily rituals. The incredibly heavy apparatus caused frequent logistical problems, late or canceled performances, and forced abandonment of the parade from 1905 to 1907. Bailey was compelled to have his experienced boss canvasman, Charles McLean, return from Europe to get it back under control in mid-season. Whether the big top was astounding in size is unknown, since no one recorded its dimensions.

Seven hippodrome shows with circus acts toured the U.S., two in 1853 and five between 1874 and 1877. One circus veteran claimed that the America's Racing Association had the largest spread of canvas that was ever put up in the United States at that time, but the top-ranked entry from 1875 has no documentation other than a "remember when" squib from nearly fifty years later.[96] The dimensions of the Barnum Hippodrome are from an auction sale catalogue and were confirmed by W. C. Coup. The Franconi and Welch 1853 hippodrome tent entries have no documentation other than published claims of "two acres" (87,120 sq. ft.).

From 1884 to 1889 the Barnum & London show issued numbers declaring that their big top had a 252-foot round with a 488-foot length. It was not uncommon for the dimensions of the stake lines to be added to those of the canvas, adding another fifteen to twenty feet around the entire periphery of the actual top. Those numbers may have defined the entire tent apparatus, but not the actual sidewall-defined area. The fabricator of the Barnum show felt compelled to inform the trade that it was actually a 212-foot round with a 432-foot length.[97] The correction is of interest because Bailey probably continued to inflate the published numbers into the 1890s, suggesting that the 1892 numbers were more akin to those of 1894. The Barnum and Cole shows both claimed 250-foot rounds in 1883, a dimension that

simply is not realistic. Cole's final hippodrome tent of 1886 was a mere 170 by 320.[98]

The 1908 Coney Island Hippodrome top was a true monster, "said to be the largest in the world," a description that brought no objectors. The dimensions were printed in a contemporary news report and have a ring of authenticity.[99] It briefly housed a four-ring circus in Coney Island. The static placement may explain the extraordinary width, which was hardly typical of a road show big top. Depending upon the stretch of the canvas, the Coney Island top would have been equaled by the 1916 Barnum & Bailey big top.

Big tops exceeding 200 feet in width were rare. Ernest Chandler's authoritative 1914 volume *Awnings and Tents, Construction and Design* stated: "The dimensions of the largest tops manufactured, such as those furnished to the three-ring shows, measure 450 by 200 feet."[100] This would be a 200-foot round with five 50-foot middles, covering three rings and two stages. It turns out that Chandler's design matches that for the 1916–17 Barnum & Bailey show, supporting Chandler's dimensions. This top was reportedly specified by John H. "Happy Jack" Snellen, the long-time boss canvasman.[101]

The final candidate was the big top put into service by Ringling Bros. and Barnum & Bailey Combined Shows in 1919. This biggest circus of all time was only incrementally larger than the two shows that were merged to form it. Strictly by the numbers, the Ringling Bros. and Barnum & Bailey big top covered less area than the two valid top entries. However, two additional 30-foot middles, visible in 1919–20 photography, were added for major city engagements. They yielded a 200-by-560, 8-pole big top covering 103,400 square feet, 10 percent larger than the Coney Island Hippodrome and Barnum & Bailey big tops. Ringling Bros. and

Barnum & Bailey boss canvasman James A. "The Whale" Whalen told people that the basic 200 by 500 was sometimes stretched out to a 210 by 510, which encompassed an area of 110,219 square feet, making it about 18 percent larger.

For these reasons, the 1919–20 Ringling Bros. and Barnum & Bailey tent is recognized as the largest circus big top. By comparison, a regulation National Football League playing field is 160 feet wide by 360 feet long, covering 57,600 square feet. America's largest big top, stretched to its maximum, covered an area nearly equivalent to two NFL fields. The basic 1919 Ringling–Barnum configuration remained in effect through 1938 and was reintroduced for 1946 and 1947. A 1923 trade report described it as "the largest tent built for circus purposes." Fittingly, on September 13, 1924, a crowd formally tallied in circus accounting records at 16,702 filled it during the matinee in Concordia, Kansas, setting the all-time circus big top single audience record.[102]

The immensity of a 200-foot-wide by 500-foot-long space is brought into focus by a photograph of the interior of the big top with the 1925 Ringling Bros. and Barnum & Bailey Combined Shows (*fig. 8.13*). Ten to fifteen thousand customers often watched the performance as it was staged in three rings and on four stages, as well as around the broad hippodrome track and at multiple locations high in the air. Stirring music from a fifty-piece band filled the top, interspersed with periodic introductions by the announcer and the blasts from the equestrian director's whistle that signaled the change of acts. An endless mixture of aromas and noxious odors, from popcorn, perfumed ladies, the animals, and occasional wafts of fresh air, all mixed under the canvas as it leisurely waved in the balmy summer breezes. With so much activity filling all the senses, it was easy for children of all ages to forget the present and step back into the past, inside the big top.

American Circus Tent Influence in Europe

The British originated the circus that John Bill Ricketts introduced to Americans in 1793 and the favor was returned in the 1840s, when the tent was promoted by showmen arriving in England from the United States. British equestrian Thomas Cooke returned home from the U.S. in 1840. He erected a wooden structure on the Dock Green in Hull and then went to Nottingham and Gainsborough, reportedly touring the northern and midland counties with a circus under a pavilion. Though Cooke is commonly credited with introducing the tented circus to Britain, primary documentation has not been found.[103]

Though he was possibly the first, whatever the nature of Cooke's effort was substantially eclipsed by the broader actions of bareback rider Richard

Fig. 8.13. Harry A. Atwell. Ringling Bros. and Barnum & Bailey Combined Shows big top interior, Chicago, 1925. Photograph. Circus World Museum, CWi-2337

Sands, who took his American Circus troupe to England in 1842. He exhibited under "a splendid and novel Pavilion, made after an entirely new style." It was advertised to be 260 feet in circumference, or just under 83 feet in diameter, with carpeted portable seats that could sit 1,000 and space for 1,500 more.[104] British showmen immediately followed suit. William Batty's 1843 canvas measured 65 feet tall and 300 feet in circumference (95 ft. 6 in. in diameter) and seated 1,400. Batty's tent was an interesting second-hand apparatus. It had previously served to house the January 17, 1842 ceremony when Prince Albert laid the first stone of the new Royal Exchange in London. Thomas Hosmer Shepherd portrayed it in an engraving published in 1842, possibly the earliest view of any British circus pavilion. Shown as a round top with striped canvas, a large circular chandelier was suspended from the single center pole.[105]

Numerous engravings in 1840s British illustrated journals confirm that the British were accomplished tent makers. They housed fairground shows starting in the early nineteenth century. The circumstances suggest that the decision to shift from circus building to pavilion had little to do with tent fabrication capability, or specific design, being based upon itinerancy and the economics of constructing a wooden circus structure.[106] Another important factor was the proliferation of circus amphitheaters in communities throughout England, the primary need for tents being when smaller cities and towns were on the route.

In time, British circus men introduced the portable top to continental Europe, known in France as the *tente américaine*.[107] Despite starting from the

Fig. 8.14. James Geraty after Frederic Arthur Bridgman. *The American Circus in France*, 1876. Engraving from *Appletons' Art Journal*, Feb. 12, 1876, 219. Print Collection, Miriam and Ira D. Wallach Division of Art, Prints and Photographs, New York Public Library, Astor, Lenox and Tilden Foundations

same 1840s traveling format, American and European circuses developed along different lines, establishing individual big top identities that largely remain in place today.[108]

Artist Frederic Arthur Bridgman captured the essence of the Grand Amphithéatre Portatif d'Été housing the Grand Cirque Américain toured by American equestrian James Washington Myers and his partner Richard Bell through France from 1867 into 1870 (*fig. 8.14*). The artist's collage captured all of the essential elements of the mid-nineteenth-century circus: the top and sidewall, center and quarter poles, chandelier and trapeze suspended off the center pole, the elevated guest seating and bandstand, the audience transfixed on the ring artists or eyeing one another, the ring trio of riders—clowns—ringmaster (and apprentice), and a Native American capturing the attention of a small boy, all under a sunlit

matinee performance. Bridgman's work, "painted with rare skill," was originally called "Breton Circus." Laying the foundation for his career, it was first exhibited at the Paris Salon of 1870, repurchased by Bridgman in 1889, and has not been documented since he exhibited it in Paris in 1907. This engraving is the only known illustration of the painting.

Tent Interior Conditions

Over time, the nostalgic interest in the big top experience of long ago has only grown. But in the big top, most every sense was assaulted in some manner, which no doubt wore on the audiences through the hours-long string of performances. Yet, Americans were clamoring for any diversion from everyday life. "Summer complaint," a malady afflicting more wom-

Fig. 8.15. "Ringling Bros. World's Greatest Shows," 1913. Poster, printed by the Strobridge Lithographing Company, Cincinnati. Circus World Museum, CWi-2325

en than men, resulted from inadequate ventilation of tents, the stale air aggravated by the fumes from animal excrements. It could readily become unbearable, especially on sultry days. The description of a circa 1870 "country circus" illustrated the conflict that existed between physical discomfort and the desire to be entertained. "We are all sitting gasping as well as gaping. It is three o'clock of one of the most torrid days, and we are packed upon the narrow board seats under the canvas roof. All the women and most of the men are fauning, and to the right of us and to the left of us it is one volley of 'whew!' 'whew!' The men ease their necks in their sticky collars; but we none of us take our eyes off the ring. If we had never seen a man or a horse before we could not stare more steadfastly."[109]

Death under the White Tops

Disasters that have taken lives at the circus suggest to some casual observers a careless attitude by circus people toward their clientele. An examination of period literature strongly disagrees, confirming a bona fide commitment by showmen to protecting their guests from recognized hazards. The death-defying stunts staged under the big top intentionally positioned trained performers in harm's way. That was not the case with the audience, who was there to vicariously enjoy the stomach-tightening thrills and then safely go home to discuss the experience with family and friends.

For that reason, the horrific loss of 168 lives in a Ringling Bros. and Barnum & Bailey big top fire at Hartford, Connecticut on July 6, 1944, endures as a black mark on the history of the circus. It has been memorialized by some as "The Day the Clowns Cried," the melodramatic title of a 1953 *Reader's*

Digest article.[110] But actually, rather than crying, the circus clowns, stunned in a grief-stricken state like other circus employees, tried futilely to assist in the rescue of the already doomed guests. Later, like many shocked veterans of World War II, they seldom discussed the tragedy with others, silently suffering what would today be known as post-traumatic stress disorder.

Tent fires were not unlike other structure losses in an era of wooden construction and open-flame illumination. It is forgotten today that the nineteenth century, with common practices such as lit candles on Christmas trees, was an era of conflagrations that frequently destroyed multiple homes, city blocks, and countless human lives. The lack or failure of building codes, late development of fire-fighting practices and technology, untrained volunteer firefighters, and other factors all contributed to an era of tremendous fire losses.

Half of the dozen known circus big top fires were caused by artificial illumination that either malfunctioned or was brought into contact with the canvas during a blowdown. Oil and gasoline lamps, with the fuel stored in tanks and metered into the burners, were the principal culprit. Candles, generated gas systems, and electric lights did not carry with them the hazard of the liquid fuel devices. Some fires were readily extinguished, while in others the tops were lost. In only one incident—in 1944—was there a loss of life. If the 1944 circus fire had a positive result, it was the change in applicable fire codes and unilateral implementation of fire-retardant chemicals in circus and other tents to mitigate whatever circumstances might initiate or sustain combustion. There has been no circus big top fire in the United States subsequent to the Hartford tragedy.

The Hartford tragedy stands in stark contrast to the afternoon of May 20, 1910 in Schenectady,

New York, when the Barnum & Bailey big top—filled with some twelve to fifteen thousand guests, mostly women and children—was destroyed by fire as equestrian director Edward Shipp's whistle was about to open the matinee performance. Attempts to extinguish the small blaze from spreading to the entire top proved futile, even after canvasmen went atop the canvas with water to fight the flames. The employees refocused their actions on assisting with crowd evacuation. All present, along with the city and the entire circus community, were relieved that there was no loss of life, only the destruction of the canvas and scorched seating and performance apparatus. The timing was critical, for in the quiet, undivided attention that immediately preceded the performance it was possible to command the full cooperation of the assembly. The only injury was suffered by a woman who fell from the top of the seats. A member of the audience, a careless cigar smoker who had been told to quit smoking, was quickly identified as the source of the blaze.[111]

The Big Top, Still with Us

From the 1840s to the 1930s, circus advertising frequently featured either the big top or the entire canvas-covered aggregation as an iconic image. The technology and daily logistics that made them possible had been perfected for several decades before the Ringlings caused a splendid 1913 lithograph to pay tribute to the "Magic Moving City of Tents, the Home of Many Marvels" (*fig. 8.15*). With America more mobile than ever before, the circus had good reason to aggrandize their ability to move on a daily basis. Circus tents were so much a part of the circus experience that when Ringling Bros. and Barnum & Bailey Combined Circus advertised a 1936 engage-

ment inside Chicago's Soldier Field, the posters specifically advised "under canvas."

The striking of the Ringling Bros. and Barnum & Bailey Combined Shows' big top in a Pittsburgh suburb in July 1956 marked the end of an era. Characterized by many as the end of the tent shows, it actually marked the final season of only the railroad tent circus. The Greatest Show on Earth was outlived by the Clyde Beatty Circus, another rail-based operation that worked outdoors. For the following year both circuses were converted to truck operations, with Ringling Bros. and Barnum & Bailey forsaking the tent for indoor venues, establishing a system that remains in use more than half a century later.

The Beatty show, now under different ownership and known as Cole Bros., retained the outdoor big top. Other circuses moving over the highways by truck and personal vehicle also embrace the big-top rituals in developed in the nineteenth century. Recognizing the economics involved and advanced materials technology, canvas was superseded by vinyl and American manufacturers were replaced by European vendors. They furnish physical configurations based principally on continental designs. Multiple "masts," rather than poles, now typically hold aloft membranes that hardly resemble their American ancestors in shape or color.

The tent has not died out as a home for the circus, but the great majority of Americans now see the ring spectacle indoors, where comfort has superseded the vagaries of outdoor presentation. But the air-conditioned, permanent environment has lost much of the dynamic experience of the nostalgic annual summertime show, with its flapping canvas, odors, sounds, and excitement that closely connected Americans with their land.

1 John H. Glenroy, *Ins and Outs of Circus Life* (Boston: M. M. Wing & Co., 1885), 27, described an 1839 winter circus constructed with board sides and a canvas roof. Christian Dupavillon, *La tente et le chapiteau* (Paris: Editions Norma, 2004), 106, includes an aquatint depicting the canvas top and wooden sidewall enclosure of the 1830 Cirque Bouthors, a structure probably similar to those that were in use in America before the implementation of the tent. Itinerant circuses never ceased contracting for building appearances following implementation of the pavilion. A number of structures designed exclusively for the circus were erected or converted for their use during the nineteenth century. Numerous theaters, arenas, armories, and other public assembly structures in larger communities also housed short-term circus engagements. Shortly after the beginning of the twentieth century an adequate number of suitable interior spaces existed to enable a few showmen to contract winter routes or spring openers and selected summer dates utilizing indoor venues. Yet, the image and existence of the traveling circus from the early nineteenth century through the twentieth was one that was closely associated with the use of a tent.

2 *Pavilion* was derived from the French term *pavillon*, from the Latin *papilio* or *papilionis*, meaning butterfly or tent. Quote from Brown & Bailey advertisements in unidentified newspaper for engagement on Oct. 25, 1826, Fred D. Pfening III collection, in *Bandwagon* 50 (Sept.–Oct. 2006), 12; and *National Journal*, Oct. 31, 1825.

3 William L. Slout, *Theatre in a Tent* (San Bernardino, CA: William L. Slout, 2000), 55–71, provides reference to an 1823 traveling tent theater and develops the storyline into the history of Chautauqua and tent repertoire theater tops, and to a lesser degree those used by evangelists. Col. Hugh Lindsay (1804–1860), a clown and singer with John Miller's menagerie in the fall of 1824, wrote that he was "to help raise the canvass" and also "drive the camels," duties that suggest the background of the phrase "to be generally useful." He stated that in 1825 Miller's menagerie used a "canvass tent." See Col. Hugh Lindsay, *History of the Life, Travels and Incidents of Col. Hugh Lindsay* (Philadelphia: n. p., 1859), 25. Charles Finney (1792–1875) used a tent for revival meetings as early as the mid-1830s. A representation of his top is in Geoffrey Blodgett, "Father Finney's Church," *Timeline*, Jan.–Feb. 1997, 21–33.

4 Designed by Edward Purcell and engraved by Alexander Anderson, the image was published in Renesselaer Bentley, *The Pictorial Reader: Containing a Variety of Useful and Instructive Lessons upon Familiar Subjects: With Illustrations to Render Them Interesting and Attractive* (New York: George F. Cooledge & Brother, 1847), 80. Information courtesy of Matthew Wittmann. It was reproduced in John and Alice Durant, *Pictorial History of the American Circus* (New York: A. S. Barnes and Company, 1957), 60.

5 Stuart Thayer wrote extensively about the American traveling circus of 1825 to 1860, including the origination of the tent and its subsequent development and influence upon the genre. His relevant works include: "One Sheet," *Bandwagon* 20 (May–June 1976), 3, 27; "Notes on the History of Circus Tents," *Bandwagon* 30 (Sept.–Oct. 1986), 28–30; "The Oldest of Showmen, The Career of Benjamin F. Brown of Somers, New York," *Bandwagon* 50 (Sept.–Oct. 2006), 10–16; *Traveling Showmen, The American Circus before the Civil War* (Detroit: Astley & Ricketts, 1997); *Annals of the American Circus 1793–1860* (Seattle: Dauven and Thayer, 2000); *The Performers* (Seattle: Dauven and Thayer, 2005); and "Stuart Thayer's American Circus Anthology," a compendium of his articles published in *Bandwagon*, http://www.circushistory. org/Thayer/Thayer.htm (accessed April 1, 2010).

6 "Horse opera" was initially applied to Astley's circus presentations in *The Adventures of Hajji Baba of Ispahan in England* (London: John Murray, 1828), 2: 79. This "more tasteful term," appealing to "respectable" people, was quoted in *Knickerbocker* 49 (May 1857), 526, concerning the circus in New Orleans, and applied previously on July 10, 1850 by the *Orleans Republican* (Albion, NY) to the Van Amburgh Menagerie, which included ring activity.

7 Thayer, *Annals*, 7.

8 John A. Dingess, untitled typescript, ca. 1891, 273, Hertzberg collection, Witte Museum.

9 A unique exception was the Paris Pavilion, an imported, prefabricated, modular-panel building with a canvas top that Dan Rice toured from April to November 1871. See William L. Slout, "Recycling of the Dan Rice Paris Pavilion Circus," *Bandwagon* 42 (July–Aug. 1998), 13–14, 16–21. Though there were reportedly earlier examples in the same line in England, Charles Henry Keith received British 1882 patent no. 753 for a structure assembled from ten portable vehicles outfitted with seating, enclosed by a canvas top supported with a center pole. W. C. Coup also proposed a modular and portable "opera house" in 1882. See "A Novelty, A Portable Opera House is the Last Great Scheme," *Jersey County* (Jerseyville, IL) *Democrat*, Oct. 26, 1882.

10 Auction list for eastern section of Zoological Institute, Aug. 22 and 23, 1837, Elephant Hotel, Somers, New York, Laura Howe Nelson collection, Somers Historical Society.

11 Thayer, "The Oldest of Showmen," 11.

12 Chess L. Briarmead, "The American Circus," *New York Clipper Supplement*, April 17, 1875, 2.

13 Tony Denier, *How to Join the Circus and Gymnasium* (New York: Happy Hours Company, 1877), 4, 5.

14 Dingess, untitled typescript, 273. A later circus compiler declared "canvas sided enclosures too unsatisfactory because of the constant threat of inclement weather." See R. W. G. Vail, *Random Notes on the History of the Early American Circus* (Barre, MA: Barre Gazette, 1956), 88. Methuen duck, an industry standard fabric, was produced in the Massachusetts city of the same name by the Methuen Company.

15 Glenroy, *Ins and Outs of Circus Life*, 107.

16 Isaac J. Greenwood, *The Circus, Its Origin and Growth Prior to 1835* (New York: Dunlap Society, 1898), 113. George F. Bailey's recollection of Turner's top pertained to 1848, not 1830, as Thayer interpreted the statement. See "Talk with a Showman," *Lebanon* (Ohio) *Patriot*, June 26, 1879. Dingess, untitled typescript, 273, contains an unreferenced quote confirming pre-1826 sidewall usage: "Previous to this [Howes' use of a pavilion], the circuses used to show with a side wall only."

17 The latter term is in *New York Clipper*, July 20, 1923, 3.

18 Horace Townsend, "The Old-Time Circus," unidentified clipping, scrapbook SBK17, n.p., Circus World Museum (hereafter CWM).

19 [Samuel Ward, Jr.], "Circus," *Knickerbocker* 13 (Jan. 1, 1839), 70–71.

20 Cleveland Moffett, "How the Circus Is Put Up and Taken Down," *McClure's* 5 (June 1895), 49–61, describes the erection of the 1894 Barnum & Bailey tent city.

21 Nathaniel Hawthorne, *American Notebooks* (New Haven: Yale University Press, 1932), 64–65.

22 *Illustrated London News*, Aug. 26, 1844, 260.

23 William H. Lushbaugh, a competitor, received U.S. Patent 318,382 on May 19, 1885 for a less desirable and more complex assembly concept.

24 See "Cost and Construction of Tents," *Ohio Cultivator* 8 (Feb. 1, 1852), 40. Circus tents are included in Ernest Chandler, *Awnings and Tents, Construction and Design* (New York: Ernest Chandler, 1914), the first comprehensive treatise to be published on the topic.

25 Mrs. H. A. Bingham, *The Ladies Repository, A Universalist Monthly Magazine for the Home Circle* 39 (1867), 204.

26 "Editor's Easy Chair," *Harper's New Monthly Magazine* 41 (June–Nov. 1870), 779.

27 Clipping from unidentified 1872 newspaper, CWM, cited in Philip B. Kunhardt, Jr., et al., *P. T. Barnum, America's Greatest Showman* (New York: Knopf, 1995), 224.

28 Charles H. Day, "Making Much of Music," *Billboard*, May 11, 1901, 7.

29 Thayer, *Traveling Showmen*, 60; *Catalogue of the Great Sale of the Property Belonging to the 2d Section of the Zoological Institute . . . November 13, 1837*, Howard C. Tibbals collection; John J. Jennings,

Theatrical and Circus Life (St. Louis: Dan Linahan & Co., 1882), 528.

30 Stuart Thayer also researched and wrote about early menageries. His works include: Thayer, "One Sheet," *Bandwagon* 18 (Sept.–Oct. 1974), 23; and Thayer, "A History of the Traveling Menagerie in America," *Bandwagon* 35 (Nov.–Dec. 1991), 64–71 and 36, 1, 31–36. Thayer, *Annals*, 125–26, covers Brown's circus and menagerie consolidation.

31 Data in *Biographical Sketch of I. A. Van Amburgh, and an Illustrative and Descriptive History of the Animals Contained in this Mammoth Menagerie and Great Moral Exhibition* (New York: Samuel Booth, 1862), CWM. Janet M. Davis, *The Circus Age, Culture and Society under the Big Top* (Chapel Hill: University of North Carolina Press, 2002), 82–141, discusses female nudity at the circus.

32 Thomas Frost, *Circus Life and Circus Celebrities* (London: Tinsley Bros., 1876), chap. 13, about American circuses, clearly makes this point.

33 Day, "Making Much of Music," 7.

34 Stuart Thayer, "The Outside Shows," *Bandwagon* 36 (March–April 1992), 24–36, explores the character of the temporary and artificial community spawned by the one-day presence of the circus.

35 Frost, *Circus Life*, 248. Lewis B. Lent did not believe in sideshows. His 1870 newspaper advertisements declared:

"No Catchpenny Side Shows Are Allowed with this Establishment." *Toledo Blade*, June 28, 1870.

36 Frost, *Circus Life*, 248–50 and Jennings, *Circus and Theatrical Life*, 533–35. The earliest known privilege contract dates from 1841. See Thayer, *Annals*, 179. Harvey W. Root, *The Ways of the Circus, Being the Memories and Adventures of George Conklin, Tamer of Lions* (New York: Harper & Brothers, 1921), 151, mentions the clothesline privilege.

37 "The Career of George W. Hall, Jr., an Old-Timer in the Show Business," *Billboard*, June 24, 1922, 49.

38 Stuart Thayer, "The First Cookhouse," *Bandwagon* 36 (July–Aug. 1992), 25.

39 Frost, *Circus Life*, 39, describes a fold-out hotel and wagon-mounted range on a Van Amburgh show. Coup placed bunks inside baggage wagons on the 1871 Barnum show, which was also an overland outfit. See Stuart Thayer and William L. Slout, *Grand Entrée, The Birth of the Greatest Show on Earth* (San Bernardino, CA: Borgo, 1998), 22.

40 Handbill for Jan. 6, 1857 auction of the Pentland circus, source unknown, photographic copy reproduced in *Bandwagon* 18 (Sept.–Oct. 1974), 22.

41 Sale advertisement by L. B. Lent, *New York Clipper*, Jan. 6, 1866, 311.

42 The Golden Age of Circuses, a name typically applied to the era, is described as characterizing the period 1871–1915 in Earl Chapin May, *The Circus from Rome to Ringling* (New York: Duffield & Green, 1932). His specific criteria are not only inconclusive, but in some cases in error as to date.

43 "Full of Interest, Reminiscences of a Veteran Amusement Manager. An Interview with Mr. G. R. Spalding," *St. Louis Republic*, Feb. 1, 1880.

44 Clipped Spalding advertisement for Sept. 16, 1847 engagement at Urbana, New York, CWM. Burr Robbins, who joined Spalding & Rogers in 1858, stated that the firm originated quarter poles in *Billboard*, Jan. 19, 1907, 22.

45 *Illustrated London News*, Aug. 26, 1844, 260.

46 C. G. Sturtevant, "Getting It Up and Down," *Billboard*, March 24, 1928, 187. "Bail-ring" is in Kunkely's 1878 patent. It was given as "bale-ring" in 1895 by Moffett, "How the Circus Is Put Up and Taken Down," 53; both spellings are in use today.

47 Sturtevant. Spalding & Rogers North American Circus lithograph, inscribed with date for Wooster, OH, June 14, 1849, American Antiquarian Society, no. 152471.

48 Handbill for Jan. 6, 1857 auction of the Pentland circus, photographic copy, *Bandwagon* 18 (Sept.–Oct 1974), 22.

49 Lent advertisement in (*Little Rock*) *Arkansas State Gazette & Democrat*, Sept. 8, 1857. The American Antiquarian Society holds a poster of the traveling version of the 1853 Franconi's hippodrome that portrays it with two sets of quarter poles, but no corroboration for the representation has been found (no. 408569). The area was given as two acres, the same as Welch's hippodrome tent of the same year, which had six intermediate supporting poles between the three center poles and the side poles. See Stuart Thayer, "Rufus Welch's Worst Season," *Bandwagon* 34 (Nov.–Dec. 1990), 66–68.

50 *Sale Catalogue of Show Property to be Sold by the P. T. Barnum Universal Exposition Co.*, at Public Auction (n. p., [1875]), 4; Barnum & Bailey "Wonderland" courier for Allentown, PA, May 6, 1905.

51 *Sale Catalogue... P. T. Barnum* (n. p. [1875]), 4. "Centre piece" was in *New York Clipper*, June 1, 1867, 63. "Center piece" was used in Kunkely's 1878 patent and appears as a compound word in W. C. Cole's ad in *New York Clipper*, Nov. 20, 1886, 576.

52 Thayer, "Notes on the History of Circus Tents," 29; Thayer, *Traveling Showmen*, 61.

53 Olive Logan, *Before the Footlights and Behind the Scenes* (Philadelphia: Parmelee & Co., 1870), 367.

54 Newspaper ad for Kewanee, IL, Sept. 24, 1856, CWM. Robinson's ad said the pavilion had five center poles, but the graphic shows a three-pole combination circus and menagerie.

55 *New York Clipper*, June 1, 1867, 63. One of the two Van Amburgh menageries had a four-pole top that covered less area.

56 Charles H. Day, "Barnum on the Tented Field," *New York Clipper*, July 6, 1872, transcribed in William L. Slout, *Ink from a Circus Press Agent* (San Bernardino, CA: Borgo, 1995), 51, 98, note 38. Day later assigned the innovation to Forepaugh's agent, Joel Warner, who told him it was implemented at St. Louis in Sept. 1868, whereas Forepaugh said it was 1869 at Louisville, Kentucky. *Billboard*, Dec. 19, 1906, 40. Forepaugh did not play west of Indiana in 1868, but appeared in both Louisville (May 10–13) and St. Louis (Sept. 6–11) in 1869.

57 Thayer and Slout, *Grand Entrée*, 19.

58 Stuart Thayer, "Joseph E. Warner—Pioneer of the Three-Tent Circus," *Bandwagon* 14 (Jan.–Feb. 1970), 20–23, discusses Warner's show, but not the others of 1871, which included Barnum, Older, Forepaugh, and possibly others. Warner advertised a specific "three," others just did it without public recognition. The Warner herald is at the Michigan State University Museum, no. 1413. John Robinson advertisement in *Our Home Journal* 2 (Dec. 16, 1871), 367.

59 Religious and other attitudes toward circus attendance are reviewed in Gregory J. Renoff, *The Big Tent, The Traveling Circus in Georgia, 1820–1930* (Athens: University of Georgia, 2008), 49–67.

60 "Ancestor of Clowns, Old Dan Castello Talks of His Experiences of Long Ago," *Syracuse Standard*, undated clipping, CWM.

61 Ibid. Charles Day credited William C. Coup with originating performances with two rings in *Billboard*, Jan. 5, 1907, 20. The Great Eastern also added a second ring in 1872, their first tour. William L. Slout investigated the claims and counter-claims for multiple rings in "Two Rings and a Hippodrome Track," *Bandwagon* 44 (Nov.–Dec. 2000), 18–21, and "Chicken or the Egg; A Double Ring Controversy," *Bandwagon* 51 (Jan.–Feb. 2007), 29–36. It is a common error to count the number of middle pieces and assume that the count represents the number of rings or stages inside the tent. They were sometimes placed outward from the end poles, to the side of inner poles, and rings sometimes encircled center poles.

62 F. C. Cooper, "The Oldest Showman Active," *Billboard*, June 22, 1912, 23. The photo from CWM is in Kunhardt, *P. T. Barnum*, 232–33.

63 *Brooklyn Daily Eagle*, May 5, 1880.

64 Fred D. Pfening III, "A Documentary History of the Barnum and London Circus in 1881," *Bandwagon* 52 (Nov.–Dec. 2008), 5–70. George Speaight, *A History of the Circus* (London: Tantivy Press, 1980), 108, assigns the first three-ring circus, 1860, to British showman George Sanger, but no period confirmation has been brought forth. The temporary arrangement was reportedly rejected by the

performers and public alike. Speaight also lists subsequent European attempts with the format (140).

65 The configuration is confirmed in the 1881 route book and program. Three rings did not immediately reign supreme; Barnum & Great London utilized several rings, stage arrangements, and even a water-filled diving basin in the 1880s.

66 The Sells dimensions are in Jake Posey, *Last of the 40-Horse Drivers, The Autobiography of Jake Posey* (New York: Vantage Press, 1959), 18. A 216 by 378 having three 54-foot middles was offered in the Barnum & London surplus sale ad in *New York Clipper*, Nov. 11, 1882, 557. Old tents were typically sold after they had served a year in storage as a backup. Charles McLean recalled the 1881 top as a 175 with four 50s, but the show was only three rings. His 1882 data is similarly unreliable. See Cooper, "Oldest Showman," 23.

67 C. G. Sturtevant, "My Friend, Jimmy Whalen," White Tops, Dec. 1941–Jan. 1942, 5–7; *New York Clipper*, May 31, 1884, 166, which concurred that Forepaugh's tent was wider but shorter.

68 Observations derived from Barnum & Bailey programs, CWM.

69 Sketch by F. M. Howarth in *Life*, May 30, 1889, as reproduced in Durant, *Pictorial History*, 79.

70 "Tanbark Odds—and—Ends," *New York Clipper*, Nov. 24, 1884, 582.

71 Al G. Field, *Watch Yourself Go By* (Columbus: n. p., 1912), 275.

72 "The Clown Business," *Eldora* (Iowa) *Weekly Ledger*, June 2, 1887. Coincident with the tent change, some felt that the best turners of a comical phrase were going into journalism. See *The Nation*, Aug. 3, 1882, 83. The variety and vaudeville stage also beckoned them.

73 Robert Good, "Route Book, Season of 1877, P. T. Barnum's New and Greatest Show on Earth" (Philadelphia: Spangler and Davis, 1877), typescript, 3. George Washington Harris, "A Sleep Walking Incident," *Spirit of the Times*, Sept. 12, 1846, uses "big-top" to mean a nightcap and associates petticoats with a circus tent, but the association is ambiguous and was not sustained in show or popular use.

74 It is employed in the 1883, 1884, and 1885 Barnum & London route books.

75 The phrase appears consistently in 1891 to 1895 Ringling Bros. route books.

76 *Eldora* (Iowa) *Weekly Ledger*, June 2, 1887; *Pittsburgh Dispatch*, Sept. 23, 1889; *Cedar Rapids Evening Gazette*, Aug. 2, 1893; *Fort Wayne Sentinel*, May 22, 1895; and *St. Paul Globe*, July 14, 1897.

77 Moffett, "How the Circus Is Put Up and Taken Down," which was widely quoted in newspapers; Charles Theodore Murray, *A Modern Gypsy, A Romance of Circus Life* (New York: American Technical Book, 1897) 36; Charles Henry Jones, "Transporting the Greatest Show on Earth," *Ludgate Illustrated* 6 (new series), Sept. 1898, 399–408. A summary biography of Hamilton is in William L. Slout, *Olympians of the Sawdust Circle* (San Bernardino, CA: Borgo Press, 1998), 121–22.

78 Barnum & Bailey "Wonderland" courier, 1905.

79 Jones, "Transporting the Greatest Show on Earth," 399.

80 *Billboard*, Oct. 21, 1922, 73; and transcript of 1879 W. C. Coup interview in Stuart Thayer papers.

81 (Syracuse) *Sunday Courier*, May 16, 1875.

82 Col. C. G. Sturtevant, "My Friend, Jimmy Whalen"; and Fred Warrell, "The Circus, A Mechanical Wonder Show," *Popular Science* 103, no. 1 (July 1923), 21–23, 83.

83 *Variety*, June 6, 1908, 13.

84 C. G. Sturtevant, "My Friend, Jimmy Whalen."

85 Ibid.

86 *Milwaukee Daily Journal*, June 5, 1883.

87 *Sedalia* (Missouri) *Bazoo*, Sept. 20, 1883.

88 Lithograph, "Franconi's Hippodrome," 1853, American Antiquarian Society, no. 408569.

89 *Bandwagon* 34 (Nov.–Dec. 1990), 6, 67.

90 *New York Clipper*, May 31, 1884, 166.

91 *Bandwagon* 37 (Mar.–Apr. 1993), 2, 13.

92 Moffett, "How the Circus Is Put Up and Taken Down," 50.

93 *Sale Catalogue of Show Property . . .*, 4; W. C. Coup, *Sawdust & Spangles: Stories & Secrets of the Circus* (Chicago: Herbert S. Stone, 1901; rpt. Paul Ruddell, 1961), 134, states 225 by 425/450.

94 List dated March 29, 1901, Joseph T. McCaddon Papers, Manuscripts Division, Princeton University Library, entry on Richard E. Conover collection note card.

95 Charles Andress, *Day by Day with Barnum & Bailey* (Buffalo: Courier Co., [1904]), 108; pole lengths in Joseph T. McCaddon Papers, Manuscripts Division, Princeton University Library, per Richard E. Conover collection note card abstract.

96 W. Quinett Hendricks, *Stranger Than Fiction* (n.p.: W. Quinett Hendricks, 1928), 26.

97 *New York Clipper*, May 31, 1884, 166.

98 It was advertised as being offered at auction in *New York Clipper*, Nov. 20, 1886, 576.

99 *Variety*, July 25, 1908, 15. Some references erroneously identify it as the former 1905–6 Carl Hagenbeck circus top, but that tent measured only 150 by 290 feet.

100 Chandler, *Awnings and Tents*, 306.

101 The Barnum & Bailey and Ringling Bros. big tops of 1913 housed three rings and two stages, but their dimensions are unknown. The Barnum & Bailey show went with three rings and four stages surrounded by a hippodrome track for the 1914 season. The two outer stages could have been positioned between the two outermost center poles and the hippodrome track, with the introduction of the mammoth eight-pole top first taking place in 1916. Ringling Bros. retained their three rings and two stages configuration throughout the 1910s. The layout information was compiled from show programs.

102 *Billboard*, Feb. 24, 1923, 82. The record crowd is substantiated in a daily expense ledger entry in the Ringling Bros. and Barnum & Bailey Business Records, CWM. Paid attendance was 15,686, indicating the show redeemed 1,016 complimentary tickets, about 6 percent of the total.

103 W. F. Wallett, *The Public Life of W. F. Wallett, The Queen's Jester: An Autobiography*, John Luntley, ed. (London: Bemrose and Sons, 1870), 54–62, covers Cooke's returning operation but makes no specific mention of a pavilion. *Hull Packet*, July 10, 1840 stated that Cooke's circus would require two months to erect, and on October 23, 1840 reported the Mart opening.

104 *Trewman's Flying Exeter Post*, June 15, 1843, courtesy Paul Griffiths.

105 Charles Mackie, *Norfolk Annals* (Norwich, England: Norfolk Chronicle, 1901), 1: 425, referenced without attribution in George Speaight, *A History of the Circus* (London: Tantivy Press, 1980), 43–44.

106 See *Illustrated London News*, July 2, 1842, 120; May 20, 1843, 334; and May 9, 1846, 301.

107 Dominique Jando to author, e-mail, May 27, 2010.

108 Christian Dupavillon, *Architectures du cirque, des origins à nos jours* (Paris: Éditions du Moniteur, 2001) is the best survey of European circus building and tent history, but unfortunately it does not explore the cross-continent influences and different growth patterns. The menagerie and sideshow, being considered fairground attractions, generally did not become aligned with the European circus.

109 "Editor's Easy Chair," *Harper's New Monthly Magazine* 41 (June–Nov. 1870), 780–81.

110 T. E. Murphy, "The Day the Clowns Cried," *Reader's Digest*, June 1953, 59–62.

111 "Circus Tent Burns, 15,000 March Out," *New York Times*, May 22, 1910; "Blaze at Big Circus," *Washington Post*, May 22, 1910.

9

ELEPHANTS AND THE AMERICAN CIRCUS

SUSAN NANCE

Imagine yourself in the wings at Madison Square Garden. It is March 30, 1955, and tonight the Ringling Bros. and Barnum & Bailey Circus is putting on a special performance featuring Hollywood celebrities. One of the stars of the show is preparing to enter the ring. She wears a preposterous costume and blinks against a crush of photographers. Indeed, millions clamor to see her and many believe they know who she is and that they understand her private personality and her desires.

We know today that they were wrong. Many years after her death, we know that her inner reality was not represented by the images she posed for nor by the persona her publicists and fans projected onto her. Behind the scenes, often she labored unhappily to entertain her public while many of the people around her were failing her grievously.

Of course, I speak here of the circus elephant. Did you think I was referring to Marilyn Monroe?

This is understandable, for Monroe was and still is instantly recognizable as an iconic star of the mid-twentieth century. Yet, in this case, to be distracted by Monroe is a useful confusion. Seeing an image of Marilyn Monroe perched on a circus elephant not only points out our tendency to overlook the animals central to so many human stories, it also hints that perhaps that elephant had more in common with Monroe than we might suspect (*figs. 9.1–9.3*).

Both the dumb blonde and the circus elephant were show business inventions, manufactured clichés that presumed men had the power to take and use—or at least visually consume—whatever and whomever they desired because the object of their interest wanted it that way. Riding an elephant colored pink for the event, Marilyn Monroe anchored the Valentine's Day segment of the 1955 spec, or spectacle, called *Holidays* and only worked for the circus for one night. The elephants held by circuses never had that choice. Their captivity made circus life more incredible but also more dangerous. How and why

---

The elephant as entertainment feature, promotional icon, and unpaid labor source was a profound American innovation in the global art, business, and logistics of circus. It all began with the mobile animal exhibitions of the early republic. They offered Americans any number of domestic or imported species presented in barns or empty lots, and even a moose from Maine might seem exotic in Savannah or Philadelphia. But with their gray skins, flapping ears, somber countenances, and wiggling trunks, the elephants traveling the nation were far more incredible and endearing.

Those first elephants were juvenile Asian females and males. Babies offered many advantages to the showman, initially ease of management, since they were smaller than a horse and modest in power and appetite. Because they were separated from adults who might have shown them elephant cultures, they were not wise to the need to avoid humans. Nor did they scratch and bite like other captive animals, but engaged gently with people by snuffling around with their little trunks in visitors' pockets. The curious who heard of this behavior came to the shows with food hidden there, expecting to feed and pet the elephant.

All these juveniles died within a few months or years of their arrival in America. Since early showmen operated in almost total ignorance of the species' habits and needs, elephants suffered various kinds of mismanagement, including improper feeding, falls from bridges that produced fatal injuries, drowning while being driven through swollen rivers, or exposure to the gunshots of locals made angry by the cultural and economic liberalization elephants represented.[1] Still, the public loved seeing elephants and the creatures seemed to present an opportunity that could not be missed. As the century progressed, impresarios and speculators continued importing

circus people persevered with keeping and showing these animals—especially when individual elephants made it clear they were not party to the human ethos "The Show Must Go On!"—is something we should not take for granted. A look at the origins, life cycles, and ultimate disposition of the animals that made the American circus possible actually reveals the full experience, talent, and labors of the people who created these complicated but fragile institutions. It is also a fraught and ambivalent tale that exposes the circuses at their most ingenious and glamorous, their most hidebound and unimaginative.

Fig. 9.1. Weegee (Arthur Fellig). *Beauty on the Beast*, 1955. Photograph. International Center of Photography/Getty Images

Fig. 9.2. Weegee (Arthur Fellig). *Whoa Nelly*, 1955. Photograph. International Center of Photography/Getty Images

Asian and eventually also a few African elephants. These creatures survived for longer periods than their predecessors, although they were still just teenagers in elephant years. To innovate their entertainment offerings, menagerie men trained them for a broad array of tricks that told audiences elephants had an innately theatrical, humorous nature. Often marketed with exotic names that spoke of their distant origins—Hannibal, Mogul, Tippo Saib, Siam—circus show patter and print advertising offered antebellum elephants as actors and performers. Even simple bits, like stepping over a prone trainer or raising a trunk in a salute to the crowd, showmen said, attempted to demonstrate that elephants were "sagacious" animals; namely, intelligent

and powerful beings who sought human masters.[2] Circus advertising or designer's mock-ups of elephant costuming showed imagined elephants with a skipping gait and trunks held high in joyful performance, not the solemn-looking elephants fans encountered at the circus (figs. 9.4–9.6).

A narrative emerged in those years—and is with us still today—that all circus elephant training was done by "kindness," that is, repetition of an act by an elephant rewarded by a human trainer. By this argument, all that was required to get an elephant to stand on her head was practice, praise, and a pile of carrots. Audiences loved this flattering and familiar idea, since they might train a pet dog to shake a paw just so and it helped to recast elephant captivity as a

▲ Fig. 9.3. Michael Ochs. *Marilyn Rides a Pink Elephant*, 1955. Photograph. Michael Ochs Archives/Getty Images

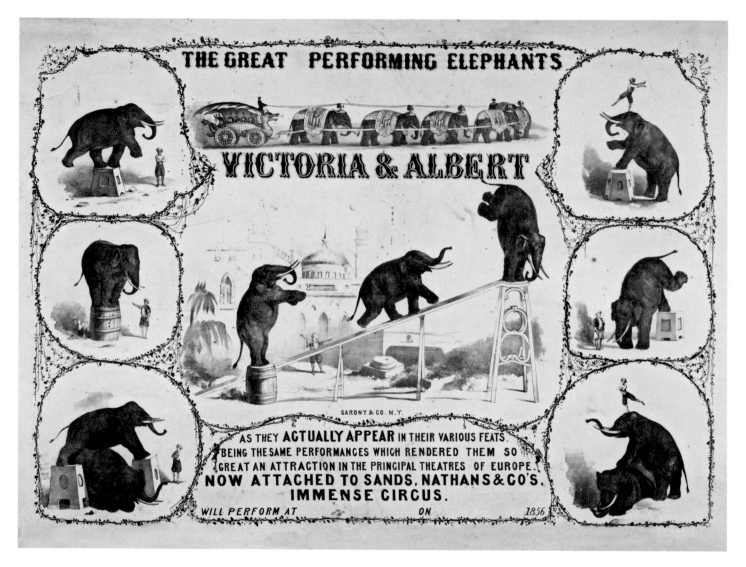

kind of animal education and improvement. From the showman's perspective, the idea of kindness training edited out the ugly logistical realities of working with animals who weighed thousands of pounds and became increasingly unpredictable or outright aggressive as they neared adulthood.

To be sure, already in the antebellum years there were detractors. Some worried the elephants were being forced to perform dangerous stunts against their wills, such that animal tricks were a crass manipulation of public sentiment for profit. Yet, by and large, nineteenth- and early-twentieth-century Americans would troop enthusiastically to the shows because they believed God had given man power over the natural world to exploit as he saw fit. Indeed, the nation's growing affluence was premised on animal use of all kinds, trained elephants being only the most glamorous example.

Fig. 9.4. "The Great Performing Elephants Victoria & Albert . . . Now Attached to Sands, Nathans & Co's Immense Circus," 1856. Poster, printed by Sarony & Co., New York. Courtesy American Antiquarian Society

Yet, why elephants? Why did the circuses not restrict themselves to trick horse riding or monkeys trained to ride dogs? The circus is not simply an unchanging series of acts but the timeless art of creating an audience experience that mixes laughter, awe, and incredulity with a little bit of fear. No one animal produced all of these in the mind of the viewer as well as an elephant, or ten. Grand, powerful, and surreal in appearance, they seemed natural symbols for ambitious and apparently wealthy circus impresarios of the post–Civil War circuses. An elephant arms race would begin in the 1850s, when the century's entertainment titan, P. T. Barnum, entered the merging circus menagerie business. He challenged his competitors and the audience with an advertised "Team of Ten Elephants" in a single production.[3]

Barnum was a famous risk taker and, in effect, posed a troubling question to the industry: Is a herd of elephants in one show good for a circus, or even the circus business as a whole? This question would seemingly go unanswered as the most prestigious rail circuses made elephant herds a competitive necessity, whatever the price. Gilded Age circus impresarios, in turn, told audiences that they were a patriotic and privileged public deserving the most extraordinary show money could buy. By then, show business wisdom had it that elephants functioned "as an advertisement" for circuses, incredible logos that distinguished their entertainment from all others.[4] The bigger the elephant herd, the more prestigious the show. By this theory of "mammoth show" marketing, circuses of means spent liberally on all visible aspects of their productions, many believing that public knowledge of that risky spending drove ticket sales because it flattered both the nerve of the impresario and the privileges of a national citizenry with aspirations to global power. In such an atmosphere, even a single

elephant could make a small circus seem a little spectacular (*fig. 9.7*).

Elephants came advertised with names, weights, heights, ages, habits, and other biographical information that lent personality to a circus company

Fig. 9.5. Jose de Zamora. Design for an elephant costume for Ringling Bros. and Barnum & Bailey Circus, likely for either the 1958 or 1963 season. Watercolor on paper. Collection of the John and Mable Ringling Museum of Art, Tibbals Collection, ht3001826

Fig. 9.6. "G. C. Quick & Co.'s Performing Elephant Bolivar," ca. 1850. Lithograph, printed by G & W Endicott, New York. Collection of the John and Mable Ringling Museum of Art, Tibbals Collection, ht2004401

brand. So did the circuses show Americans how to perceive an animal as famous by consuming such human-made stories about him or her, a phenomenon that would proliferate in the twentieth century.[5] The most prominent early example was an adult African elephant known as Jumbo. Purchased by Barnum from the London Zoo in 1882, he was purported to be the largest elephant in the world and to have a fondness for children. In both Britain and America his fame made him a kind of national pet. Barnum had obtained Jumbo from London over public protests in Britain, such that to many Americans Jumbo seemed to mark the increasing global power of the United States at the expense of an old rival.[6] Many ticket buyers took this all with a grain of salt, of course, knowing that animals like Jumbo had no cognition of the entertainment and media industries they supported. By that view, Jumbo was a satire on American bravado—that is, until he died in an industrial accident, hit by a train in St. Thomas, Ontario in 1885 (*fig. 9.8*).

By the turn of the twentieth century, the American circus as mass culture and as industry was a raging success, even if individual companies did go bankrupt with some regularity. And this is where the less glittering but more compelling backstage part of the story begins.

Circus life has always been one of constant toil and exhaustion made all the more intense by a sense of being scrutinized as an outsider by the mainstream of American society. Plenty of circus folk spoke of their love-hate relationship with the public, collectively in love with the circus but always ready to criticize. Especially irksome was that among that judgmental public were many Americans who behaved terribly at circus shows, harassing workers and animals or sabotaging equipment. That contrast—the apparent romance of working for an adored circus

Fig. 9.7. Wallace G. Levison. Three boys walking down Atlantic St. near Nevins St., Brooklyn, with an elephant from the Barnes Circus, June 1891. Photograph. Time Life Pictures/Getty Images

Fig. 9.8. "P. T. Barnum's Greatest Show on Earth & The Great London Circus … The Giant African Elephant Jumbo," 1882. Poster, printed by the Strobridge Lithographing Company, Cincinnati. Collection of the John and Mable Ringling Museum of Art, Tibbals Collection, ht2004513

coupled with frequent misery behind the scenes – was captured in 1882 by the route book for the P. T. Barnum's Greatest Show on Earth & the Great London Circus. That season the unit acquired Jumbo while already saddled with a large herd of elephants, who raced in the ring as a feature of the show:

Sunday, April 9th. New York, N.Y.

On Sunday morning, April 9th, the long expected, best advertised, new sensation, the Mastodon Elephant Jumbo, arrived from London on the steamship Assyrian Monarch. It was early in the morning when the steamer was moved to Pier 1, North River, but it took until twelve o'clock at night to get Jumbo on terra firma. Eight horses were on hand, and hitched to the cage on wheels, commence their march up Broadway. The rain was pouring in torrents and the management as well as the large delegation of employees who on foot escorted the new visitor will not soon forget the drenching they received.

Monday, April 10th. New York, N.Y.

Jumbo was first introduced to the American public and became a part of the Great Show, the talk of all New York and the sensation of the day.

Monday, April 24th. Philadelphia, Pa.

Arrived 10 o'clock Sunday morning. The special car built for Jumbo could not stand the strain of his enormous weight and the running gear gave way on arrival. This was repaired during the week.

Monday, May 22nd. Brooklyn, N.Y.

Scott, Jumbo's keeper, returned to the show cured of the injuries inflicted on him by Jumbo accidentally pressing him against the side of his car.

Saturday, June 17th. Boston, Ma.

Saturday being Bunker Hill day, . . . The herd of elephants gave a free swimming exhibition at 8 a.m. in the pond at Boston common.

Wednesday, August 2nd. Troy, N.Y.

In the evening as the small elephants were being conveyed to their cars, they were attacked and stampeded by a gang of Trojan roughs. They ran in all directions, two of them rushing into an iron foundry which they soon cleared by indiscriminately slinging around all the red hot irons they could find. Another two ran into a corn field, after upsetting half a dozen people.

Friday, August 25th. Binghamton, N.Y.

Henry Morgan's elephant ran close to the poles, throwing him in the way of the other racing elephant, who, stepping on him broke his leg. William Hicks, jockey, was thrown from his horse and broke his breast bone. Both left . . . under medical aid.[7]

How could one sufficiently prepare an elephant or one's employees for this life?

Step one was acquisition. Since elephants did not breed with any success in the United States (whether because they were too young, physiologically stressed, or continuously confined), showmen acquired them from Africa and Asia through animal dealers.[8] From 1796, when the first two-year-old Asian female came to New York from Calcutta, until the 1973 Endangered Species Act effectively banned importation into the U.S., there was little innovation in acquisition or transport of the species. Baby or juvenile elephants were collected, if African, on hunting expeditions wherein adult elephants were slaughtered and their young captured, and if Asian, purchased from the centuries-old South Asian mahout-run elephant capture and training systems. Aboard ships bound for New York, young

elephants sold tickets like nothing else, he, for one, put it plainly that elephants strained circuses as "the most expensive luxury" because they were "expensive to feed."[10] That was just the beginning. Elephants also increased labor costs, and the largest shows might typically have a team of "elephant men" consisting of a superintendent of elephants and up to ten assistants to manage twenty elephants (while a pair of men could manage ten horses or caged animals by themselves). Elephants further needed barrels of water and specially reinforced temperature-controlled stock cars. And elephants required cash, since they frequently obliged circus managers and owners to pay off townspeople and audience members for elephantine damages to property and person.

Why so? Consider this scenario: one earns a living by camping across the countryside on a tight schedule with, say, five or ten creatures each weighing around 6,000 pounds and wielding colossal strength. These creatures are driven by instinct to move and forage most of the day and seem constantly mischievous and restless. They can walk through the walls of all but the most reinforced concrete structures (unavailable until the early twentieth century, in any event). They are easily frightened and made destructive by one another or humans. In theory, no amount of manpower might be able to control them if they were to reject that control.

So, to meet and cultivate audience demand, circus people had to create a kind of continuous-containment management. First, they adapted the time-tested technique of simply tying elephants to immovable objects. Keepers chained elephants at the ankle to stakes and anchors in the ground or the floor of a railcar, box van, or stock trailer at all times when not performing in the ring or being worked by trainers.[11] Yet this did not solve all the logistical prob-

elephants, known as "punks," were far easier to contain, direct, feed, and water than adults. Still many of these babies died en route since endangered by separation from their matrilineal family groups and the suckling that was normal at that age (figs. 9.9, 9.10).[9]

Step two was containment. The daily management and transport of the world's largest and most powerful species was very hard work. Although Otto Ringling and many others believed

Fig. 9.9. H. F. Davis. Elephants from the Blackpool Whitsun Circus being unloaded at Tilbury docks, May 1928. Photograph. Topical Press Agency/Getty Images

Fig. 9.10. Fox Photos. Baby elephants from Burma in the hold of a ship, bound for London where they will join a circus, 1935. Photograph. Fox Photos/Getty Images

lems elephants introduced. Even more exasperating than the elephant's desire to roam was his trunk. While audiences found an elephant's trunk whimsical, to circus people they could be dexterous, terrifying tools. They said that bored or frustrated elephants used them to tinker with costumes and circus equipment, free themselves from chains and shipping containers, rattle chains, pester horses, and strike out with enormous force at people. Thus did animal managers develop all sorts of hobbles and harnesses in often futile attempts to calm elephants artificially. For instance, the Barnes Circus elephant Black Diamond wore a metal bar bolted across his tusks over his trunk to keep him from fully extending it. He also wore ankle chains connected to a chest harness so as to slow his movement, although he killed a number of people nonetheless.[12]

Most elephants survived these intensive restraints by stereotypic weaving. Although the behavior appeared rhythmic and romantic to many human observers, it showed elephants working hard to cope with an inability to practice species-typical behaviors, behaviors elephants could temporarily suppress but which could never be trained out of an elephant entirely (*fig. 9.11*).[13]

From the antebellum years, when two elephants might be driven on foot from town to town, to the rail and truck era, when circus elephants lived in intensively confined herds of unrelated individuals, elephants improvised ad hoc communities. Trainers said pairs of elephants often formed strong friendships and might be seen caressing trunks. Other times, the close quarters produced aggression among particular elephants (since they were unable to interact freely and determine hierarchies), especially males, who normally lived in loosely knit competitive groups in the wild. If a trainer was lucky, an older female in a herd would assert herself as dis-

ciplinarian. Since free elephant females and juvenile males live in matrilineal family groups, even in captivity a stand-in matriarch was an authoritative presence. She could calm an uncooperative elephant or persuade him or her to follow human direction, unknowingly functioning as "chief assistant" to the head elephant man, as circus vet Doc Henderson put it.[14]

Step three was training. Elephants performed in the ring and parades and all the while there were no bits, no reigns, and no cages to restrain them. They appeared before crowds accompanied only by a handler who had no obvious physical power over them. How did circuses produce the fantasy of the sagacious elephantine performer at liberty in America with actual living elephants?

Veteran elephant man George "Slim" Lewis, for one, addressed this mystery. He admitted that circus shows and advertising offered an "idealistic viewpoint," which portrayed "all elephants as big, kind and lovable." As a kid at the circus, he said, he too "saw

Fig. 9.11. Marty Lederhandler. Three of the elephants with the Ringling Bros. and Barnum & Bailey Circus are chained with their trainer Ed Healey before performing, Madison Square Garden, April 3, 1957. Photograph. AP Photo/Marty Lederhandler

them taking abuse with no apparent resentment or sign of retaliation, and they seemed a lot more amiable and pleasant to live with than people." As an adult working with elephants, he learned that in fact the fantasy was produced by a trainer and elephant sharing respectful apprehension for one another, with the trainer simply more determined to assert himself as boss. Lewis and many of his colleagues thus felt foiled by circus advertising that continued to sell elephants as pets: "People just can't seem to get it through their heads that the average elephant is quiet and docile, in spite of visiting strangers, only because its handler is there," he said. "Only the respect it pays its handler [keeps] it in check . . . and, to get down to blunt facts, this quality begins with fear: fear of punishment and discomfort."[15]

Indeed, since the early nineteenth century, both European and native-born elephant trainers in the U.S. had been using the ancient South Asian practice of breaking elephants. It required tying an elephant down and beating him or her with heavy poles or stakes until he or she ceased struggling and vocalized a sound of "resignation," a process that was exhausting for all involved and could last up to thirty minutes. Thereafter, elephant control came from enforcing a balance between reward (to communicate to an elephant, say, that finishing the commands leads to eating hay outside) and pain aversion (such as using an elephant hook to put pressure on an elephant's skin so that he or she understood that it hurts to step off the pedestal without a command to do so), with occasional re-breaking as needed. This process was on average less successful with male elephants, such that by the interwar years most circus elephants were females, although commonly known as "bulls" by then to obscure that fact. Unaware of the elephant's full experience, the audience only saw an artistic or humorous display as the psychological mechanics of the training was invisible so as not to complicate the effect of the trick (*fig. 9.12*).

The notorious goad, or elephant hook, was a fixture in circuses that revealed how intentions of kind animal management did not always match up to work-a-day practice. Tiny Kline, who worked as an elephant girl for the Al G. Barnes Circus, was typical in this. In her memoirs she insisted that it was "a general fact that elephants love their trainer. . . . Only rarely does an exasperated caretaker use that hook at the end of the stick elephant men always carry, on top of the ear, the only tender part of the elephant's body."[16] Yet, in Kline's day, as before and since, the industry was loaded with successful handlers who motivated elephants primarily by painful hooking rather than patient friendship.

Fig. 9.12. Lilo Hess. Circus elephant sitting on stand while being trained, 1947. Photograph. Time Life Pictures/Getty Images

Kline would complain of one heavy-handed trainer who hooked the elephants so harshly that "my costumes were always stained with blood from the bulls' trunks." And even Kline was not wholly innocent. Working in the ring with one uncooperative female known as Babe, she told one of the keepers "to stand in the wings and show her the hook" during their act so as to intimidate Babe into compliance without the audience's knowledge.[17]

The open secret in the business about how the head elephant man and his team of handlers controlled their elephants put people on edge. Plenty of circus workers—from acrobats to roustabouts—disliked and even feared elephants and their intimidating human handlers. "The minute I saw the elephants lined up outside the kraal I knew I'd made a mistake," wrote circus performer Connie Clausen of her first contact. "There must have been fifty of them. They all looked exactly alike—terrifying—and they all looked mad. They tossed their heads from side to side, they beat the ground with their trunks, and their great ears seemed to be stirring up a minor hurricane."[18]

Clausen's fear was not unfounded. In spite of the assertive work of trainers and handlers to dominate elephants, "for every man killed by claws and fangs [in a big cat act], a half-dozen are gored or trampled backstage by elephants, and without the attendant publicity," Slim Lewis would warn. "A bull hand often is a nobody, and if his death rates a paragraph in the newspapers, it is as 'an unfortunate accident.'... It used to be cheaper to hire another handler than it was to buy an expensive elephant, and if it was only a circus roustabout who got it, the incident was hushed up."[19] In fact, ever since the elephant Mogul assaulted a barnman in 1835 by striking him on the face with the trunk and drawing blood, there had been a debate simmering behind the scenes over circus elephant use.[20] Many circus people knew that

public relations duties and ring performances featuring unchained elephants posed a risk to public safety while endangering elephants who displayed an exaggerated startle response or were otherwise unpredictable. Yet, we hear little about these dilemmas of the business, not just because of company "hush ups" but because circus workers kept that debate largely private. By the old circus wisdom, whatever goes on behind the scenes, whether immoral, negligent, or even criminal, one does not let on to the rubes since their fantasies about the glamour of circus life sustain one's livelihood (fig. 9.13).

Step four was disposition. Despite romantic stories of circus elephants purported to be one hundred years old, optimally elephants live only sixty years or so. While a few female elephants lived and worked in circuses into their fifties, most females left by their twenties or thirties, most males by their early twenties. Circus companies sold off to zoos or animal dealers older elephants who became slow or recalcitrant in adulthood. And certainly, plenty died young due to the tent fires, train wrecks, and other accidents that haunted the circuses. Still others died from mysterious illnesses or poisonings by aggrieved employees.

More notable from the public's point of view was that until World War II, circus companies killed

Fig. 9.13. Child greeting an elephant at the Ringling Bros. and Barnum & Bailey Circus, n.d. Photograph. Collection of the John and Mable Ringling Museum of Art, Tibbals Collection, ht0000744

some of their elephants with premeditation. Heavy importation of elephants in the Gilded Age had drawn many inexperienced people into the industry as handlers, while the elephants they managed each year grew older. By the turn of the century, plenty of those elephants were adults struggling against the requirement to stay calm and obedient. When they lashed out and injured or killed a member of the public, the circuses and the press criminalized that behavior with "execution" rituals meant to assuage popular anger over the public safety hazard circus elephant herds posed. Among the famous dead: Fritz, strangled in 1902 by the Barnum & Bailey Greatest Show on Earth Company while on tour in France; Gypsy, a Harris Nickel Plate Shows elephant shot to death in 1902 at Valdosta, Georgia, where she ran from her keeper; Topsy, a discarded circus elephant electrocuted by Thomas Edison at Coney Island in 1903; the famous Columbia, first elephant born on U.S. soil but killed at Barnum & Bailey's winter quarters in 1907 because her socially deprived upbringing made her uncontrollable; Mandarin, father of Columbia, strangled then dropped off the side of a ship into the Atlantic by Barnum & Bailey in 1902; Mary, hanged by the Sparks World Famous Shows Company in 1916 at Erwin, Tennessee. In a particularly noted example, in 1929 at Kennedy, Texas staff of the Al G. Barnes Circus publicly poisoned the male known as Black Diamond after he killed for the fourth time. In that instance, the subject of his power was a parade spectator, Eva Donahoe, whom the elephant grabbed with his trunk, threw to the ground, and rammed with his

Fig. 9.14. Black Diamond in chains on the way to the firing squad, 1929. Photograph. Circus World Museum, CWi-2339

tusks, smashing one side of her skull. Circus staff had already attempted to control Diamond by bolting a steel bar across his tusks to limit the reach of his trunk, later binding it with chains. Black Diamond survived the poisoning attempt, only to be led off to a firing squad, where he was shot repeatedly by local law enforcement officials until he finally collapsed and died (*fig. 9.14*).

Thus did many twentieth-century Americans come to hate circus elephants as "vicious" "brutes" who "mangled," "crushed," or "attacked" people, as the newspapers sensationalized. Often described as "mad" or "angry," these elephants were either males in musth or abused adult elephants so traumatized that they appeared "insane" to observers.[21] The 1941 Disney film *Dumbo* spoke to public knowledge of

▲ *Fig. 9.15*. Harold M. Lambert. Two circus elephants wearing giant clown costumes, 1941. Photograph. Harold M. Lambert/Hulton Archive/ Getty Images

circus elephant dysfunction: Dumbo's mother, Mrs. Jumbo, is locked away in a wagon as a "mad elephant" when she assaults a circus visitor who ridicules Dumbo's ears. After *Dumbo*, as a rule the circuses hid from the public the disposition of elephants made psychotic by circus management, as well as those injured or accidentally killed in their care.

In doing so, the circuses lost a bit of their power since for many Americans elephants were interesting because of the contradictions they represented, a species at times gentle and obedient, at times frightening and incomprehensible. "That piercing primeval trumpet; that wrinkled, seemingly elastic trunk; and those solid squared-off legs, tiny eyes, and long, siren lashes are all strictly elephant, nothing else," explained Connie Clausen in 1961. "Certainly their intelligence, ability to respond to affection and that hint of jungle violence that lay beneath their apparently easy-going natures made them fascinating."[22] If stardom is created by the uniting of divergent elements, then truly the circus elephant was the original

American star, glamorously mysterious because beautiful, tragic and dangerous all at once (*fig. 9.15*).[23]

And this is where Marilyn Monroe rides back into the story on that pink elephant. That night in 1955 the Ringling Bros. and Barnum & Bailey Circus invited her to Madison Square Garden for their promotional spring charity show (*fig. 9.16*). Since the 1940s, each year the circus had put on a star-studded performance to promote the upcoming season. A rash of bankruptcies in the industry and a changing media context meant that no longer did circuses have the biggest stars but had to borrow them from Hollywood, a community itself reeling from the new popularity of television.[24]

Despite the serious undercapitalization of the circus business, Ringling Bros. still held fifty elephants, while most companies owned five or less.[25] A 1952 "elephant census" commissioned by the trade journal *Billboard* counted only 126 elephants held by circuses. They were losing ground to other modes of entertainment featuring the species and the same survey noted 142 more elephants in stationary animal shows, zoos, carnivals, and exotic animal dealers' stocks serving private parties, and television and film productions.[26]

The age-old riskiness of running logistically complicated circuses and the still frequent insolvency of individual shows had produced a chronic transience in human-elephant relationships in the U.S. Heightened by the postwar crisis in the circus trade, that transience threw into high relief how people still saw elephants as impermanent inventory. To be sure, stories were known of the devoted trainer who spent decades with the same beloved elephant or rescued an old elephant from cruel colleagues.[27] Yet, most spoke very frankly about owners who sold, leased, or rented elephants at will, often over the desperate objections of the elephant's trust-

Fig. 9.16. Weegee (Arthur Fellig), *What a Ride*, 1955. Photograph. International Center of Photography/Getty Images

ed trainer, with no assurance or concern for their welfare. And everyone knew about the unsentimental animal dealers who could get a person "anything, anytime," no questions asked.[28] Midcentury want ads in *Billboard* attest to the sad traffic in elephants in those years:

ELEPHANT FOR SALE One Elephant too many. Large, gentle. Good single routine. Pushes, pulls. Cheap for quick sale. C. A. Vernon Phone 3650—Bryan, Texas.

CHEAP—TRAINED ELEPHANT, FEMALE, eight tricks, actual weight, three tons; anyone can handle. Call Elma Fulbright, 4293, Saline, La.

FOR SALE 2 Elephants, trained for circus and TV acts. $4,000.00 for both. HARRY RIMBERG 408 W. 14th St. New York City Phone: Chelsea 2–8765

ELEPHANT Five feet three inches, six years old, intelligent, gentle, trained by Louis Reed. Can stand, sit on tub, lie down, stretch out, play harmonica, etc. $3,000 F.O.B. Call West Winfield 65302 before Feb. 29. MRS. KENNETH DAVIS Star Route, West Winfield, N.Y.[29]

▲ *Fig. 9.17.* Jonathan S. Blair. Circus elephant pulls a car and trailer from a muddy meadow, March 1972. Photograph. National Geographic / Getty Image

This trade continued, yet by the 1970s Asian and African elephant populations were shrinking quickly due to the ivory trade and human encroachment on elephant habitats. So had the "spectacular" circus elephant performer fallen out of favor by then. Public knowledge of the plight of free elephants inspired a resurgence of the idea that many comedic and acrobatic elephant tricks—like standing on one foot or being mounted by a tiger—were unsympathetic presentations. Since then, audiences have favored more seemingly "natural" bits like elephant rides, parade marches, and only the most basic posing in the ring (*fig. 9.17*).[30]

Just as long as there have been people counterintuitively terrified by circus clowns, there have been people made angry or sad by the sight of a circus elephant. Only recently did a critical mass of Americans have the ability to air these feelings with the help of new consumer technologies. The tide certainly shifted that day in 1994, when citizens armed with handheld video cameras taped the public killing of the chronically abused Hawthorne Corporation circus elephant Tyke in a Honolulu alleyway after she ran from the ring (she now has her own Wikipedia and YouTube pages filled with such user-generated content.[31]) These kinds of depictions of elephants were common before the 1940s but were pushed underground by circuses when the industry stumbled at midcentury. Nowadays, such difficult images leak out past their disciplined marketing programs, recorded by citizens who witness unscripted events or divulged by whistle-blowing circus employees.

Since Tyke, on-site protests and editorials denouncing animal circus acts have become as much a part of circus day in America as elephants. An explosion of competing online and television content—from National Geographic Channel to the vast website networks of reform groups like People for the Ethical Treatment of Animals—contextualizes the controversy over circus elephant use and encourages consumers to be far more worried about animal experience than they once were. Parents still take their kids to the circus, of course, and ultimately they will decide if the time-honored American art form of the traveling circus will survive better with or without elephants.[32]

1 There are many dozens of these cases, and the pattern continues today in spite of our far greater knowledge of elephant biology and welfare needs. For some early examples of accidental deaths of Betsey, Horatio, and Victoria, see "Infernal Transaction—Death of the Elephant," *Boston Gazette*, July 29, 1816, 1; "Shocking Calamity!" *New Hampshire Sentinel* (Keene), Sept. 23, 1820, 3; "From California," *New York Times*, July 31, 1860, 2.

2 Harriet Ritvo, *The Animal Estate: The English and Other Creatures in the Victorian Age* (Cambridge, MA: Harvard University Press, 1987), 25–26, 37.

3 See for instance, "Grand Entrance of the Asiatic Caravan, Museum and Menagerie of P. T. Barnum," *Farmer's Cabinet*, July 31, 1851, 4; "P. T. Barnum's Grand Colossal Museum and Menagerie," *Daily Quincy* (Illinois) *Whig*, Aug. 19, 1853.

4 Charles H. Day, "The Elephant as Advertisement," *Billboard*, March 23, 1901, 6, rpt. in Charles H. Day, *Ink from a Circus Press Agent* (San Bernadino, CA: Borgo Press, 1995), 66–67.

5 Randy Malamud, "Famous Animals in American Culture," in *A Cultural History of Animals in the Modern Age*, ed. Randy Malamud (Oxford and New York: Berg Publishers, 2007), 5.

6 Ritvo, *Animal Estate*, 232.

7 Alvaro Betancourt [Stewart], comp., "My Diary, or, Route Book of the P. T. Barnum's Greatest Show on Earth and the Great London Circus for the Season 1882," 1882; box 47, "Miscellaneous Materials: Route Books," McCaddon Collection, Special Collections and Rare Books, Princeton University Library, Princeton, NJ

8 Staff at North American zoos, at Carson & Barnes "Endangered Ark Foundation" in Hugo, OK, and Ringling Brothers' Florida "Elephant Conservation Center" breeding/winter quarters facilities have recently resorted to artificial insemination to try to produce more elephants for entertainment and show since elephants are notoriously reticent to breed naturally once removed from life at large in Asia and Africa. It is not clear if these attempts at breeding, especially by impregnating juveniles (since later in life captive females develop infections and other health problems that inhibit oestrus and impregnation), will succeed, since captive-born elephants usually die before age five from disease or maternal deprivation. Indeed, elephants will possibly go extinct in the U.S. in the next few decades, perhaps around the time Asian elephants are predicted to go extinct in the wild due to human encroachment on their habitats. Shana Alexander, *The Astonishing Elephant* (New York: Random House, 2000), 255; Raman Sukumar, *The Living Elephants: Evolutionary Ecology, Behavior and Conservation* (New York: Oxford University Press, 2003), 388–89.

9 Ros Clubb, Marcus Rowcliffe, Phyllis Lee, Khyne U. Mar, Cynthia Moss, Georgia J. Mason, "Compromised Survivorship in Zoo Elephants," *Science* 322, no. 598 (Dec. 12, 2008), 1649.

10 Otto Ringling quoted in Jerry Apps, *Ringlingville USA: The Stupendous Story of Seven Siblings and Their Stunning Circus Success* (Madison: Wisconsin Historical Society Press, 2005), 141.

11 Today chaining remains a necessity whenever an elephant is not being actively monitored by keepers with a goad, the limited use of electrified paddocks in the industry notwithstanding.

12 Jay Teel, *The Crime and Execution of Black Diamond, The Insane Elephant* (Ansted, WV: Petland Press, 1930), folder 15, vol. 8, Leonidas Westervelt Circus Collection, the New-York Historical Society, New York.

13 There is a large scientific literature on stereotypic elephant behaviors. See, for instance, Janine L. Brown, Nadja Wielebnowski, and Jacob V. Cheeran, "Pain, Stress and Suffering in Elephants," in *Elephants and Ethics: Toward a Morality of Coexistence*, ed. Christen Wemmer and Catherine A. Christen (Baltimore: Johns Hopkins University Press, 2008), 125–26; Ted H. Friend, "Behavior of Picketed Circus Elephants," *Applied Animal Behaviour Science* 62 (1999), 73–88; Ted H. Friend and Melissa L. Parker, "The Effect of Penning Versus Picketing on Stereotypic Behavior of Circus Elephants," *Applied Animal Behaviour Science* 64 (1999), 213–55.

14 J. Y. Henderson, *Circus Doctor; as Told to Richard Taplinger* (New York: Bantam Books, 1952), 55.

15 George "Slim" Lewis, *I Loved Rogues* (Seattle: Superior Publishing Company, 1978), 28–29, 57.

16 Tiny Kline, *Circus Queen and Tinker Bell: The Memoir of Tiny Kline*, ed. Janet Davis (Urbana and Chicago: University of Illinois Press, 2008), 175. To be sure, there were some elephant men who strove to achieve the ideal Kline and others described, using the hook forcefully only to interrupt dangerous elephant action or to defend themselves against a suddenly aggressive animal. On this shade of elephant training, see John Lehnhardt and Marie Galloway, "Carrots and Sticks, People and Elephants: Rank, Domination, and Training," in Wemmer and Christen, eds., *Elephants and Ethics*, 167–84.

17 Kline, *Circus Queen and Tinker Bell*, 199–200.

18 Connie Clausen, *I Love You Honey, But the Season's Over* (New York: Holt, Rinehart and Winston, 1961), 31.

19 Lewis, *I Loved Rogues*, 4–5.

20 "The Elephant," *Farmer's Cabinet*, April 24, 1835.

21 Elephant musth is a state of physical discomfort, irritability, and aggression occurring periodically beginning in puberty at around ten years of age (although there has probably been great variation in this in elephant history, as there is today, due to differences in diet and other factors among male elephants). The experience drives bull elephants to attain the necessary "sociological maturity" for reproduction, but also is suspected to make male elephants feel terrible, certainly physically and probably mentally. While in this state, a gland on either side of a bull's head drips a noxious fluid that drains into the mouth, he may dribble urine and otherwise appear unsettled and aggressive to other elephants, people, or any animal. Since they cannot be worked safely or efficiently at that time, many elephant handlers in Asian lumber camps simply tether musth elephants to trees and wait the process out, which can take weeks. Sukumar, *Living Elephants*, 100–103.

22 Clausen, *I Love You Honey*, 197.

23 Christine Geraghty, "Re-examining Stardom: Questions of Texts, Bodies and Performance," in *Stardom and Celebrity: A Reader*, ed. Sean Redmond and Su Holmes (London: Sage Publications, 2007), 98.

24 "Line up Told for Ringling N.Y. Telecast," *Billboard*, April 2, 1955, 57, 64; J. P. Shanley, "Circus on Video: Improvements Noted in Coverage of Big Show After Seven-Year Lapse," *New York Times*, April 3, 1955, X15; "Old-Time Circus Opens at Garden," *New York Times*, March 31, 1955, 30; Jim McHugh, "Word Must Be 'Greatester' on Ringling Show," *Billboard*, April 9, 1955, 1, 48, 80, 135.

25 "20 New Additions Bring R-B Elephant Herd to 50," *Billboard*, Oct. 23, 1954, 60.

26 "Elephant Census," *Billboard*, April 12, 1952, 65; "It Couldn't Be They Weren't at Home," *Billboard*, April 26, 1952, 53.

27 The tales of Ralph Helfer with Modoc and Murray Hill were noted examples. Ralph Helfer, *Modoc: The Story of the Greatest Elephant that Ever Lived* (New York: Harper, 1998); Gary Ross, *At Large: The Fugitive Odyssey of Murray Hill and His Elephants* (New York: Random House, 1992).

28 Bob Cline, *America's Elephants!* (n.p.: T'Belle LLC Publications, 2009), 23.

29 "Elephant For Sale," *Billboard*, Jan. 8, 1955, 47; "Cheap—Trained Elephant," *Billboard*, Dec. 17, 1955, 80; "For Sale," *Billboard*, April 28, 1956, 71; "Elephant," *Billboard*, Feb. 23, 1959, 61.

30 Nigel Rothfels, "Why Look at Elephants," *Worldviews: Environment, Culture, Religion* 9, no. 2 (Summer 2005), 166–72.

31 Will Hoover, "Slain Elephant Left Tenuous Legacy in Animal Rights," *Honolulu Advertiser*, Aug. 20, 2004, http://the.honoluluadvertiser.com/article/2004/Aug/20/ln/ln19a.html (accessed May 4, 2010).

32 Richard Corliss, "That Old Feeling IV: A Tale of Two Circuses," *Time*, April 20, 2001. http://www.time.com/time/arts/article/0,8599,107192,00.html (accessed Feb. 26, 2008).

10

HORSES ^{AND} CAT ACTS IN THE EARLY AMERICAN CIRCUS

BRETT MIZELLE

Animals have been an integral part of the modern circus since its formation in the late eighteenth century. For millions of people in the past two centuries, a public amusement simply was not worth being called a circus without the animals that both entertained patrons and provided the labor that made the circus possible. As an itinerant form of American popular culture, the circus brought excitement to wherever it traveled, providing many Americans with their first encounter with wild animals and displays of mastery over familiar, domesticated animals. The circus was an important site where the natural world was tamed, trained, and partially brought under human control, and where ideas about and practices toward nonhuman animals were mobilized to a wide range of purposes.

Although some wild animals, such as elephants, and domesticated species, such as horses, are immediately associated with the circus, a wide variety of animals have played parts in this important form of American popular culture. Domestic animals such as horses, dogs, and pigs were familiar to Americans but appeared in new and exciting contexts in the circus. Wild and exotic animals appeared as curiosities in menageries and were exhibited in animal acts with human trainers, demonstrating human mastery over the natural world. Of the many exotic animals associated with the circus, charismatic megafauna such as lions, tigers, bears, and elephants have had the greatest appeal. Other species, such as monkeys, have been the centerpieces of comic performances; the appeal of these and many other humorous circus acts comes from blurring the distinctions between the human and the animal, the wild and the domesticated.[1] At the circus, fierce wild animals from exotic foreign and domestic places could be seen as at least partially domesticated, forced to do the bidding of humans while retaining their wildness. Likewise, domesticated animals such as dogs and pigs were used in comic performances

◄ *Detail of fig. 10.16.* Eliphalet M. Brown. "Miss E. Calhoun, the Celebrated Lion Queen, as She Appears with Her Group of 9 Lions, Tigers & Leopards, Now Attached to Van Amburgh & Co.'s Magnificent Collection of Living Wild Animals," 1848. Lithograph, E. Brown, Jr. lithographer; printed by Sarony & Major, New York. Courtesy, American Antiquarian Society

and demonstrations of "animal sagacity" that playfully inverted categories of the human and the animal, destabilizing the category of the human. Central to all of these performances were partnerships between humans and animals in which both parties possessed substantial agency, making the outcomes of these performances, despite extensive training, always somewhat indeterminate.

Given the tremendous variety of animals, their changing modes of display and performance, and the myriad cultural meanings attached to their exhibition in the circus, a comprehensive survey of animals in the American circus is beyond the scope of any individual writer.[2] Although there are some outstanding studies of the circus and its animals, some focus on particular species, genres of performance, or individual celebrity animals. This chapter examines two major human–animal assemblages in the American circus through approximately 1860, the period before what is generally referred to as the golden age of the circus.[3] Activities and developments in the United States will be explored, but with detours to Europe, inevitable because the circus has always been a global phenomenon, with animal and human performers circulating throughout the world and with exotic animals imported from virtually everywhere Europeans and Americans were exploring and expanding their empires.

The horse, a species deeply connected to human history and development, was the original circus animal. Horses were an integral part of the working environment, crucial to human progress and mobility. Their centrality to the circus exemplifies how labor and pleasure, work and spectacle overlapped as a quotidian human–horse relationship was made marvelous. The early American equestrian circuses developed in parallel with exhibitions of exotic and performing animals, first in the form of fixed and itinerant displays of individual animals, then in the shape of traveling menageries that shared many features with the equine and human performance-centered circus. There were, of course, several contact points between the two forms, including the early addition of the elephant to the circus and the merging of equestrian performances with other animal acts. While exhibitions of individual lions began as early as the 1720s, performances in which keepers entered cages filled with multiple wild animals, especially lions and tigers, became incredibly popular beginning in the 1830s and are most associated with the American animal trainer Isaac Van Amburgh, the subject of the second part of this essay.

Both the circus, with its human and equine performers, and the menagerie, with its often brutal displays of human dominance over wild nature, were contested in the nineteenth century, just as the captivity of animals in the circus and zoo is challenged today. While concern over the treatment of animals was growing, the circus was also suspect as a form of leisure and for the supposedly disreputable character of the humans involved. Efforts to make circus and menagerie performances respectable, often by wrapping them in scientific, historical, literary, or biblical contexts, remind us that these performances were important parts of an expanding and contested American popular culture in the nineteenth century. Ultimately, the circus became an American cultural institution in part because its inclusion of exotic animals helped to legitimize its other acts by imparting lessons about the natural and social order. Combining the exotic animals of the menagerie and the equine and human performers of the circus authorized the show to promise "instructive amusement," adding a pedagogical rationale for the circus that enhanced its respectability. Today circuses featuring animals, especially wild animals such as elephants and lions, are on the wane, increasingly prohibited by law and disdained by a public that has developed different understandings and expectations of animals. That contemporary animal acts delegitimize the circus reflects profound transformations in our ideas about and practices toward animals in the past two centuries.

The Horse, the Original Circus Animal

Although, according to legend, P. T. Barnum insisted that "clowns and elephants are the pegs upon which the circus is hung," the American circus from its late-eighteenth-century origins was centered upon the human–horse relationship and featured a wide range of equestrian feats. While horses have been used in many types of entertainments throughout history, they became the cornerstone of the modern circus. The Englishman Philip Astley, a former sergeant major in the cavalry, was an excellent horseman who observed that the public was interested in trick riding. He opened a riding school in London and pioneered the use of the circus ring, which enabled riders to balance by using centrifugal force. By 1770 he was teaching riding in the mornings and performing "feats of horsemanship" in the afternoons. To entertain people between riding sequences, Astley added clowns, jugglers, tightrope walkers, and gymnasts to his performances, creating the mix of entertainments that remains a hallmark of the modern circus.[4]

Astley opened permanent amphitheaters for performances in London in 1773 and in Paris in 1782. Many of his riders eventually became his competition, including Charles Hughes, who opened the Royal Circus and Equestrian Philharmonic Academy in London in partnership with Charles Dibdin. Other riders spread exhibitions of equestrianism throughout Europe and across the Atlantic. John Sharp rode "two Horses, standing upon the Tops of the Saddles, with one foot upon each, in full Speed" in New England in 1771 while a Mr. Foulks, who claimed to have performed before royalty in England, performed in New York City in the same year. Jacob Bates did acrobatics on horseback in 1773 along with the comedy riding act "The Tailor's Ride to Brentford," based on the popular tale of an inept effort to ride a horse to vote in an election.[5]

During the revolutionary crisis with Britain, the American Continental Congress prohibited traveling shows to promote virtue among the American people and draw a contrast with British extravagance and dissipation.[6] After the revolution, Thomas Pool was advertised as "the first American that ever exhibited . . . Equestrian Feats of Horsemanship on the Continent" before his 1785 performances in Philadelphia. In addition to mounting and vaulting feats, Pool performed an Americanized variation of the comic act about poor horsemanship, retitled "The Taylor Humourously Riding to New York" and exhibited three horses that would "lay themselves down as if dead."[7] Pool moved to Boston in 1786 and opened a riding school to teach horsemanship to accompany his performances in the ring.

The key figure in the development of the circus in the United States was John Bill Ricketts, who began his career with Hughes in London. Ricketts opened a riding school and equestrian circus in Philadelphia in 1792, promising that "the citizens of this metropolis will experience considerable gratification from this new field of rational amusement." In addition to displaying his own "surprising feats of horsemanship," Ricketts "offered lessons to men and women in the handling and riding of horses," making the instructiveness of his exhibition explicit at a time when popular culture was still viewed with suspicion.[8] Initially performing solo, Ricketts executed his equestrian feats "with the utmost taste and gracefulness; all his attitudes are well chosen, & none of them of such a nature as to injure the feelings."[9] Ricketts was called "perhaps the most graceful, neat and expert public performer that ever appeared in any part of the world" by a writer in Philadelphia in 1794.[10] Broadsides and handbills for Ricketts's performances featured enticing images of vaulting and trick riding, including a feat in which

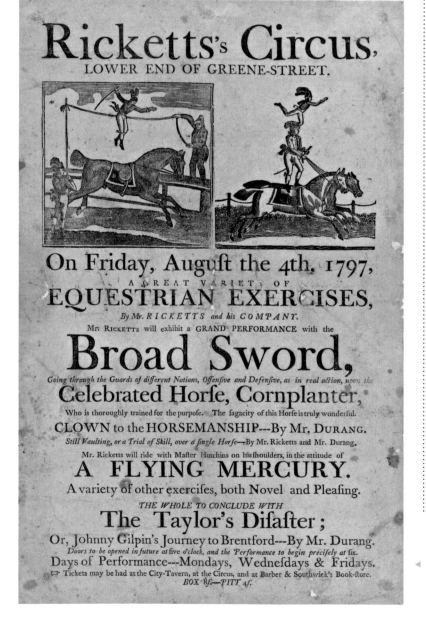

Ricketts stood on the back of two horses with a boy standing on his shoulders "in the attitude of a Flying Mercury" (*fig. 10.1*). Ricketts constantly modified and expanded his shows to keep them fresh, adding a variety of other performers and experimenting with other novelties, such as pony races (*fig. 10.2*). Over time, theatrical components and pantomimes were added, as were historical and patriotic entertainments, including one based on the suppression of the Whiskey Rebellion.

Ricketts's professionalism and patriotism helped to legitimize the circus as a form of popular entertainment, as did his cultivation of the patronage of George Washington, who attended the circus in 1793 and gave Ricketts one of his horses, Jack, in 1797. Most horses were not themselves celebrities in the early circus, although Ricketts's horse Cornplanter could supposedly leap over a horse of his own height, take off his own saddle, and perform other feats.[11] Ricketts's spectacles attracted large and diverse audiences for many years, although in 1797 he began to separate the dramatic and the equestrian, being convinced, in the recollection of the actor John Durang, "that a[n] equestrian performance blended with dramatic performance would never agree or turn out to advantage." Cultural historian James S. Moy has argued that Ricketts saw "the stage as a moral vehicle and the circus ring a medium for pure entertainment" and began to emphasize the equestrian. Although Ricketts regularly traveled from South Carolina to Canada to perform before new audiences, the destruction of his circus building in Philadelphia by fire in 1799 led him to pursue opportunities elsewhere. After a failed stint in New York, Ricketts headed to the West Indies but was lost at sea en route to England in 1800.[12]

After Ricketts's death, other performers stepped in to provide the public with mixed entertain-

Fig. 10.1. "Ricketts's Circus, Lower End of Greene-Street: On Friday, August the 4th, 1797." Broadside. Popular Entertainment Collection, Harvard Theatre Collection, Houghton Library, Harvard University

ments centered upon displays of horsemanship. In the first decade of the nineteenth century, the circus troupe of Victor Pepin (an American of Acadian descent) and Jean Breschard (a Frenchman) featured riders specializing in various tricks, including Roman standing (riding and controlling two to four horses), *voltige* (vaulting on and off a horse's back), *corde volante* (leaping over objects and then landing on the saddle), and somersaulting (*fig. 10.3*). Mme Breschard, who jumped her horse through two barrels, was promoted "for her elegance of person and astonishing feats of female activity united with all the ease of Parisian manners."[13] In addition to these spectacles, Pepin and Breschard presented The Incombustible Horse (named Tyger), who had been trained to stand patiently amid exploding fireworks.

Cayetano Mariotini, a skilled horseman, joined Pepin and Breschard, but eventually formed his own circus. This company was the first to show an elephant—the animal known as Old Bet—in New York City in 1812.[14] He exhibited extensively in New Orleans, where he died of yellow fever in 1817. James West arrived with his company from England in 1816, introducing the hippodrama to the United States through a performance of "Timor the Tartar." Hippodramas were generally staged in East Coast theaters and enabled circus equestrians to make a good deal of extra money as they performed with their horses in exciting spectacles featuring battle scenes and chases. The performer Charles Durang recalled the shouts and screams of the audience at the final scene of "Timor," in which "Zorilda, mounted on her splendid white charger, ran up the stupendous white cataract to the very height of the stage." Throughout the spectacle, "ramparts were scaled by the horses, breaches were dashed into, and a great variety of new business was introduced. The horses were taught to imitate the agonies of death and they

PONEY RACE WITH REAL PONIES AT THE PANTHEON, AND RICKETTS's AMPHITHEATRE, PHILADELPHIA. Jan.ʸ 14.ᵗʰ 1797.

did so in a manner that was astonishing."[15] Equestrian dramas remained important aspects of American popular culture for decades, with perhaps the most notable performance that of Adah Isaacs Menken as *Mazeppa* in the 1860s. In the later nineteenth century, public fascination with these spectacular battle scenes and chases would reach its apex in the Wild West show.[16]

The Wild West show, a spectacle most associated with Buffalo Bill Cody, provided the template for a new kind of horse act in the wake of the Civil War, one that dramatized recent American history to promote American progress and empire. These horses were described as untrained and "natural" in the show's publicity, which added "the horses are as they were intended to be, and the men ride as horses should be ridden. They are not trained to act before the limelight, neither are any of them subjected to tortures in order to serve the whims of their masters."[17] This emphasis on naturalness was fitting given the Wild West show's content, but also reflected an interest in the innate nature of the horse at a moment when these animals were gradually disappearing from the urban environment and Native Americans were vanishing from the Western landscape.

Fig. 10.2 "Poney Race with Real Ponies at the Pantheon and Ricketts's Amphitheatre, Philadelphia," January 14, 1797. Lithograph. Collection of the York County Heritage Trust, York, Pennsylvania

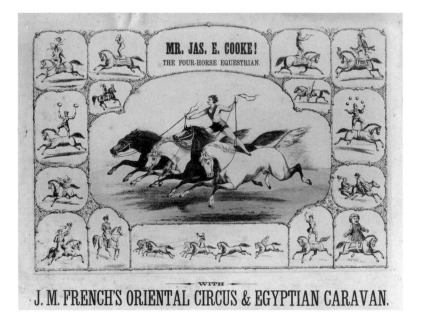

In 1815 Boston's *Columbian Centinel* noted, "The taste for Equestrian Exhibitions has much increased and crowds of fashionable and respectable families assemble at the Circus. The applause given to the riders calls forth their best feats, and gives that encouragement which fosters merit."[18] While not all Americans were convinced of the legitimacy of this form of popular entertainment, by around 1820 the general contours of the circus were firmly in place. The use of the canvas tent starting around 1825 made traveling even easier and reduced the need to build permanent or semipermanent wooden structures, which were expensive and flammable. (See chapter 8, "The American Circus Tent.") By the 1830s the circus had penetrated the West, bringing its increasingly familiar form and content through vast portions of the United States.

The blend of feats on horseback and comic equestrian acts was noted in the first complete published account of a circus in *The Knickerbocker* in 1839:

> The horses, beautifully marked and caparisoned, are obedient to the slightest will of the rider, and yet by their proud looks and haughty bearing, seem conscious of their lineage; while the

equestrians vie with each other in rich costume, and their plumes dropping softly over their painted faces, make them as bright as Lucifer, in the eyes of the crowd. They ride gracefully, displaying to advantage their elastic forms, swollen into full proportion by exercise and training. As soon as the audience is sufficiently recovered to particularize the different members of the troop, they are attracted by the grotesque behavior of the clown, who has got upon his horse the wrong way, and sits preposterously facing the tail. In this manner he slips on and off, encouraged with immense laughter. Next the remarks go round, and everyone praises to his neighbor the remarkable lightness and agility of a juvenile equestrian. He has not yet completed his eleventh summer, and not a horseman in the troop can vie with him in daring. . . . So light and agile is he, that he appears not human, but, as he flies round the ring with a daring rapidity, and his snow-white trowsers and gemmed vest mingle their colors and become indistinct, he seems like an apple-blossom floating on the air. But look! look! What the devil is that fellow at, disrobing himself? He has kicked himself out of his pantaloons, and thrown away his coat, his horse flying all the while. 'Angels and ministers of grace defend us!' he is plucking off his very—shirt! Nay, nay, do not be so alarmed, nor turn away your heads, ye fair ones, timidly blushing. Look again, and behold a metamorphosis more wonderful than any in Ovid; for lo! he pursues his swift career in the flowing robes of a woman! And now the pony is to perform a no less wonderful exploit, and leap through a balloon on fire. . . . Last of all, comes Billy Button, or the Hunted Tailor. I forget the plot of this piece, exactly, which is yearly enacted with much

Fig. 10.3. "Mr. Jas. E. Cooke! The Four-Horse Equestrian with, J. M. French's Oriental Circus & Egyptian Caravan," ca. 1870. Poster. Collection of the New-York Historical Society

Fig. 10.4. "James Robinson the Champion Bareback Rider of the World," 1882. Poster, printed by the Courier Company, Buffalo. Circus World Museum, CWi-2334

acceptation in every considerable village in the country. There are some very good points about it, that never come amiss to a rural audience, as when the perverse pony shakes off the cabbaging tailor from his back, not allowing him to mount, or, dangerously acting on the offensive, chases him around the ring.[19]

Acrobatic feats on the backs of horses speeding around the ring were at the core of the circus. These tricks were either performed on a pad or carpet used to cushion the horse's back, or, in bareback or rosinback acts (named for the use of rosin to keep the human performers' feet from slipping). Levi North, an American rider in the 1820s and 1830s, is said to be the first to achieve a forward somersault on a moving horse. Bareback riding was pioneered by James Hunter in 1822 but popularized by James Robinson in the 1850s (*fig. 10.4*).[20] Performing in 1856 with Spalding & Rogers Circus, Robinson turned twenty-three consecutive forward and backward somersaults over four-foot-wide banners on the back of his horse named Bull. Robinson was famous for his backward somersault, which began facing the horse's tail and ended with him facing forward on the back of his horse.[21]

In addition to vaulting and other forms of trick riding, circuses also featured a host of comedic acts, which included flying wardrobe acts (in which numerous costumes were discarded while a rider stood on his horse, with the rider often starting as an enormous peasant woman), and many variations of "The Tailor's Ride to Brentford," in which an inept equestrian tries to ride a horse. This performance took

place in many variations, including peasant acts in which a drunk attempts to ride a circus horse after the original performer failed to appear. After staggering toward and onto the horse, as Mark Twain's Huck Finn describes it, "he just stood up there a-sailing around as easy and comfortable as if he warn't ever drunk in his life—and then he begun to pull off his clothes and sling them . . . and finally skipped off, and made his bow and danced off to the dressing-room, and everybody just a-howling with pleasure and astonishment."[22]

Other kinds of horse acts developed as the century progressed. Dancing horse acts first became popular in Europe in the 1830s, although it is not clear how popular these variations of dressage might have been in the United States. In these *haute école* (high-school) animal acts the horse appears to dance, walk sideways, or bow without any apparent directions from the rider. They provided an elite and European style of human–animal performances for

American audiences that lent further continental sophistication to the circus and marked its international refinement, as at the end of the nineteenth century, when Barnum and Bailey advertised a "Grand Equestrian Tournament" featuring *haute école* skills such as show jumping and dressage.[23]

"Liberty" horses performed without a rider, harnesses, or leads, first individually, then in increasingly larger groups. In 1897 Barnum and Bailey presented seventy liberty horses in a single ring. Part of their appeal was the fact that the training of liberty horses seemed invisible, even magical, while the horses themselves, although lavishly decorated in gorgeous trappings, appeared to perform in increasingly natural ways (*fig. 10.5*).

The circus also featured specialist horse acts, which besides the Incombustible Horse included numerous dancing horses, such as one observed by Nathaniel Hawthorne in 1835 that kept "excellent time to the music, with all four feet." (Hearing of the

Fig. 10.5. "Walter L. Main, 63 Performing Horses in One Ring," ca. 1899. Poster, printed by the Courier Company, Buffalo. Courtesy of the Library of Congress Prints and Photographs Division

deaths of two dancing horses, Hawthorne speculated that since "[t]he physical exertion seems very moderate; it must be the mental labor that kills them.")[24] Other notable acts featuring individual horses included the rope-walking pony Blondin (with Forepaugh's Circus, 1787), the horse Eclipse, who would leap from one swinging platform to another and jump through a ring of fire (also with Forepaugh), and Jupiter, who was lifted into the air by a balloon surrounded by fireworks (*fig. 10.6*).

The daily working relationship between the trainer and the horse was obviously central to the creation and successful execution of these animal acts. Most circus riders brought their own horses with them, as horses trained to perform were quite valuable. The circus proprietor W. C. Coup detailed the cost of horses in 1890s:

> The draught horses . . . bought by me averaged $200 each; the usual circus horse, however, costs much less, and so long as it does its work all right [in parades and general haulage] the main purpose is answered. . . . Ring horses, whether for a "pad" or a "bare-back" act, must have a regular gait, as without it the rider is liable to be thrown. They are frequently and generally owned by the performers themselves, and I have known a crack rider to pay as high as $2000 for one whose gait exactly suited him.[25]

While there are few first-hand recollections of this relationship from the early American circus, the bond between rider and horse was undoubtedly a close one, and the proper care of horses a task essential to the very functioning of the circus. An animal's illness or injury could cancel or significantly alter performances. The loss of fourteen horses in a violent storm at sea on January 27, 1826 devastated

Joseph Cowell's troupe, which was headed to Charleston after a successful short season in Baltimore. The Charleston *City Gazette* noted the loss and observed that a stranger offered to lend them as many horses as they needed to get back into business, although those horses would have to undergo additional training for the circus.[26]

The training of circus horses in the nineteenth century was basically a more advanced form of the way that regular horses were broken and trained for working, riding, and racing. In 1799 John Durang "purchased an elegant bay horse . . . trained for the race course" and then "broke this horse into the circus exercise in a few weeks in my own yard. I made a compleat charger of him; he would go on his knees or lay down, leap over the bars, run after the Tailor, and a handsome saddle horse for the street, and work in harness."[27] After the Civil War, one

Fig. 10.6. Jupiter, the Balloon Horse, 1909. Photograph. Circus World Museum, CWi-2326

could find advice on how to train all sorts of animals in popular books like *Haney's Art of Training Animals (fig. 10.7)*, which included "detailed instructions for teaching all circus tricks and many other wonderful feats."[28] Today we would find many of the methods used to train horses for specialty acts to be cruel. Consider this account by Alfred T. Ringling in 1900 on the training of Madame Noble's trick horse Jupiter, which walked around the ring on his two hind legs in a "vertical position."

> [He] was taught the feat while a colt by being fed apples from a point high above his head, which he could reach only by raising himself to the position for which he has since become famous. The tender muscles of the colt were thus developed to sustain him in a position unnatural to the horse of everyday life; and the task of afterward making him perform this work in a place where apples could not be fed to him from a derrick, was solved by rewarding him immediately after he passed from the big tent into the passage-way to the stables.[29]

BREAKING HORSE FOR THE " CIRCLE."

The training of horses to do ever more exciting and complicated tricks answered the need to make an increasingly familiar entertainment more novel. Equestrian acts were such a staple of the American circus that these performances were, paradoxically, simultaneously remarkable and unremarkable. Circus equestrians were still celebrated for their skill and daring, as in a short illustrated poem that appeared in the periodical *The Bachelor (fig. 10.8)* in 1841, in which a "young rider" says "The Ring is the place for me. Well mounted there on my coal-black steed, I ride with ease and grace, And receive applause for each daring deed, From every smiling face."[30] Yet printed accounts of the circus increasingly failed to describe horsemanship in detail, noting, as did an author for the *Southern Literary Gazette* in 1852, that "we shall not pretend to describe a spectacle with which everybody is more or less familiar."[31] As horse acts became more difficult to make truly spectacular, traditional equestrian feats appeared less frequently in circus advertising over time. Instead, circus horses were marketed for their individual talents, or in terms of their tremendous quantity, as when Barnum and Bailey featured four hundred horses in their circus parade in 1891.[32]

The long-standing appeal of the human–horse partnership in the American circus testifies to the intensity and significance of this relationship in American culture as a whole, especially in the age before these living machines were replaced by actual machines. The circus enabled many performers to continue lives on horseback begun years before their careers in the ring commenced. Astley, for example, was able to continue his military horsemanship in riding academies and circus, just as Buffalo Bill and the members of his Wild West show did at the end of the nineteenth century. Audiences took pleasure in watching these animals and the humans who ex-

Fig. 10.7. "Breaking Horse for the Circle," illustration from *Haney's Art of Training Animals* (New York: Jesse Haney & Co. 1869), 53. Courtesy American Antiquarian Society

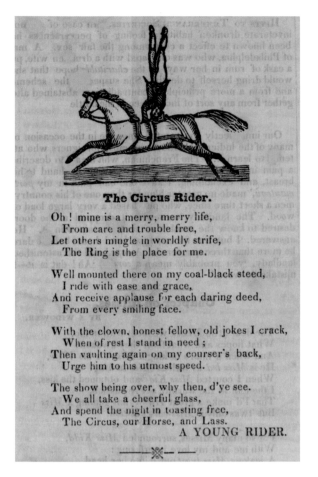

The Circus Rider.

Oh ! mine is a merry, merry life,
    From care and trouble free,
Let others mingle in worldly strife,
    The Ring is the place for me.

Well mounted there on my coal-black steed,
    I ride with ease and grace,
And receive applause for each daring deed,
    From every smiling face.

With the clown, honest fellow, old jokes I crack,
    When of rest I stand in need ;
Then vaulting again on my courser's back,
    Urge him to his utmost speed.

The show being over, why then, d'ye see,
    We all take a cheerful glass,
And spend the night in toasting free,
    The Circus, our Horse, and Lass.
                    A YOUNG RIDER.

ercised dominance over them. Walt Whitman expressed the appeal of the equestrian portion of the American circus when writing in 1856 of the value of "the sight of such beautiful and sagacious horses as he [Dan Rice's Circus] has. . . . His riders, too, and strong men, and dancers, are all perfect in their several ways, and afford a lively evidence of what *practice* will enable men to do."[33]

Elaine Walker has recently observed in her history of the horse: "Humans love to see the horse leap and run, but also to know it can be controlled. The vicarious danger of watching someone else risk their life on the back of a half-tamed creature offers a satisfying spectacle for the audience, while enabling this second-hand experience of speed and danger validates the risks of the rider."[34] Animal acts featuring humans and their horses were a staple of

the American circus and a bridge between the natural and the cultural at a moment that saw the start of the gradual removal of horses from everyday life.

The Menagerie, Van Amburgh, and Cat Acts

Paralleling the development of the circus and its varied equestrian acts in antebellum America was the growth of animal exhibitions, which included both shows of individual animals and menageries. Animal exhibitions began in British North America in the 1720s, with the announcement of the exhibition of a "Lyon, being the King of Beasts" at the house of a Mrs. Adams in Boston.[35] Lions sporadically appeared before American audiences throughout the eighteenth century, taking on new meaning amid the revolutionary conflict with Britain, when seeing a lion in a cage or captured tigers on an English frigate took on nationalistic flavor.

By the 1790s, all kinds of exotic animals could be seen in American cities, including menageries featuring several different animal species, such as the Menage of Living Animals connected to the Columbian Museum in Boston, which in 1798 contained a "very tame, harmless, docile and playful" bear, a porcupine, baboon, and owls.[36] Menageries similar to this one started traveling in the second decade of the nineteenth century, but always presented more of a challenge because exotic, wild animals had to be caged and transported on wagons, unlike the horses that were at the center of the early circus. The two forms of entertainment clearly influenced each other, however, both in terms of logistics and marketing and in the movement of many men between these related forms of popular entertainment.[37]

Two aspects of the pre–Civil War history of the display of animals in menageries are worth noting:

Fig. 10.8. "The Circus Rider," *The Bachelor* (1841), 4. Courtesy American Antiquarian Society

the constant effort to attract audiences to new curiosities, and the consolidation of the business over time. From the arrival of the first elephant in 1796, pachyderms were the single most desirable attraction in American menageries and circuses. Their size, intelligence, and partial trainability accounted for much of their appeal, as did stories of their "magnanimity" toward some humans, as in a lithograph depicting an elephant saving his trainer from other wild animals that had broken loose in the menagerie (*fig. 10.9*). After enough Americans had "seen the elephant," to use the contemporary expression, other animals, including the rhinoceros and giraffe, first imported to the U.S. in the 1830s, garnered their share of attention (*fig. 10.10*). While early exhibitions of exotic animals had often fea-

tured just a single animal, the trend over time was for ever-larger groupings of animals in fixed or itinerant menageries, which before the formal establishment of zoological parks after the Civil War (New York, 1864; Philadelphia, 1870) were the only way Americans could see and think about such an ever-expanding variety of exotic animals (*fig. 10.11*). From the 1790s through the Panic of 1837 there was a gradual pattern of consolidation in the animal exhibition business, one that resulted in the Zoological Institute, a short-lived (1835–37) menagerie holding company created by speculators. As circus historian Richard Flint has argued, "whether the novelty was wearing off for the public or the cost of importing and providing daily feed and care for the beasts was too burdensome, the

Fig. 10.9. J. Martin. "Magnanimity of the Elephant Displayed in the Preservation of His Keeper J. Martin, in the Bowery Menagerie, New York," 1835. Etching and aquatint. Somers Historical Society

number, size, and variety of animal caravans shrank considerably" after 1840.[38]

In fact, the only large-scale menagerie to tour the United States before the Civil War was the Van Amburgh Menagerie, which returned to the states in 1846 and traveled for almost four decades. This show was named after the great animal trainer Isaac Van Amburgh, and a closer look at his career highlights the history of lion taming, an act that would become

a staple of the circus and that emphasized man's dominance over the natural world (*fig. 10.12*).

Isaac Van Amburgh was born in Fishkill, New York, in 1808 and first developed his experience working with wild animals as a cage boy. Although he was not the first animal trainer to enter a cage full of wild animals, he became the most famous after his performances in New York in the winter of 1833–34.[39] Van Amburgh apparently replaced a Mr. Roberts

THE MAJESTIC AND GRACEFUL GIRAFFES, OR CAMELEOPARDS

▲ *Fig. 10.10.* "The Majestic and Graceful Giraffes or Camelopards," 1838. Chromolithograph, printed by H. R. Robinson, New York. © Shelburne Museum, Shelburne, Vermont, 1959-67.80

as the lion tamer in the June, Titus, Angevine & Co. menagerie, after Roberts was mauled by a tiger in Haverhill, Connecticut. Van Amburgh was first advertised by name in January 1834 in performances as Constantius in the play *The Lion Lord* at the Bowery Theatre in New York; this drama was written to capitalize on his performances in the cage with two lions. Van Amburgh toured with June, Titus, Angevine & Co. from the summer of 1834 through 1837, when he left on a European tour that lasted for seven successful years (*fig. 10.13*). Capitalizing on

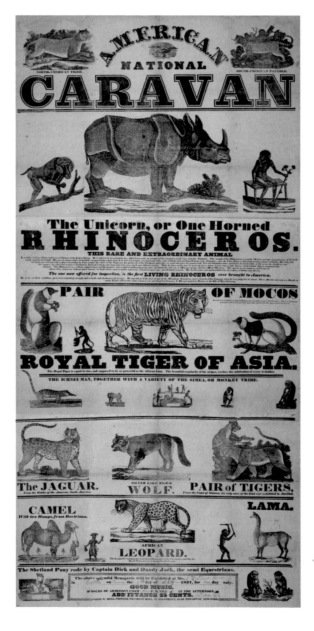

Van Amburgh's return to America as a global celebrity in 1845, Titus and the Junes renamed their menagerie the Van Amburgh Menagerie and performed at the Bowery Amphitheatre in New York in the winter of 1845–46, before extensive touring. Isaac Van Amburgh was the only human performer in this menagerie, although he only rarely entered the cage after 1847 and retired permanently in 1856.[40]

Van Amburgh's significance lies in the way he reshaped both the performances of keepers in their interactions with big cats and the broader perceptions of lions and tigers. Although the voluminous literature about lions and tigers tended to emphasize the nobility of the former and the treacherousness of the latter, audiences that saw these species often observed docile or sleepy animals in small cages carted around by wagons, hardly exciting their imaginations of savage creatures. Although newspapers and periodicals stressed the latent savagery of these animals in captivity through lurid stories of animal attacks and escapes, early cat acts were often playful in nature (*fig. 10.14*).[41] As the *Painesville* (*Ohio*) *Telegraph* observed in 1832, "It is truly astonishing to witness with what patience and good humor this [lion] suffers himself to be played with; the keeper opening his mouth, putting his hand in his tremendous jaws, pulling out his tongue and even wantonly whipping him, fearless and safe."[42] Another newspaper account from 1833 noted: "It is very interesting to witness the fondness of the leopard for his keeper during these visits."[43]

Van Amburgh's presence in New York City, talent for publicity, and, more importantly, a change in the character of the act inside the cage, led to his worldwide fame. His performances emphasizing the savagery of lions, tigers, and leopards and his exhibitions were marked by violence toward these animals, who were often beaten into submission. An account

Fig. 10.11. "American National Caravan," 1831. Poster, printed by Jared W. Bell, New York. Courtesy, American Antiquarian Society

MR VAN AMBURGH
as he appears at Drury Lane Theatre.
Presented with Nº 66 of the STAR, Nov.ʳ 17ᵗʰ 1838.

▲ *Fig. 10.12.* T. C. Wilson. "Mr. Van Amburgh as he appears at Drury Lane
Theatre," 1838. Lithograph. © National Portrait Gallery, London, D4554

was provided by the London *Times*: "On one occasion the tiger became ferocious. Van Amburgh coolly took his crow bar and gave him a tremendous blow over the head. He then said to him, in good English, as if he were a human creature, 'You big scoundrel, if you show any more of your tricks, I'll knock your brains out.'"[44] Van Amburgh's physical displays of mastery over wild and ferocious animals while dressed in a gladiator's chest plate and toga proved much more popular than the more gentle interactions across species lines seen in the earlier animal acts.[45]

Today this distinction is described as being between taming and training, or as performers put it, between two different styles of performance: *en ferocite* (dominance over aggressive animals) and *en douceur* or *en pelotage* (quieter acts with apparently docile animals).[46] In practice, however, the distinction between the two could be hard to assess. Accounts of Van Amburgh using brute force to beat animals into submission were fairly common, so much so that they were satirized in an 1838 British pamphlet by R. H. Horne, entitled *The Life of Mr. Van Amburgh, the Brute-Tamer* (1838), which suggested that Van Amburgh could train any animal once he "introduced himself with his crow-bar."[47] This association of Van Amburgh with violence persisted after his death. In 1869 the *Times* of London described the "subduing of wild beasts, as men have learned from Van Amburgh," as "merely the result of merciless thrashing when they are young. The application of the heavy cudgel, the iron bar or the red-hot ramrod on the tender limbs gives an impression which the threatening glance of him who wields these weapons keeps for ever fresh in the brute's memory."[48]

Yet other accounts described Van Amburgh's kindness to his animals, drawing a contrast between his skill and the brutal violence used by lesser trainers. When Van Amburgh returned to the United States

Fig. 10.13. "Van Amburgh's Royal Collection of Trained Animals!," July 26–27, 1841. Broadside, printed by Frederick Turner, Birmingham. Collection of the John and Mable Ringling Museum of Art, Tibbals Collection, ht2000734

after his success in Europe, press accounts started describing him as a true original, noting "all the rest who have undertaken to go into the 'wild beast's den' have been mere imitators." They also argued that these lesser performers "could only control the animals by beating them on the head with a bar of iron or billet of wood; while Mr. Van Amburgh maintains his perfect mastery over the most ferocious by a single glance of his eye."[49] The supposed power of Van Amburgh's gaze was also emphasized in the many promotional materials that helped burnish the animal trainer's legend, including John Tryon's *An Illustrated History and Full and Accurate Description of the Wild Beasts, and Other* *Interesting Specimens of Animated Nature Contained in the Grand Caravan of Van Amburgh & Co.* (1846), which argued that "until the exhibitions made by Mr. Van Amburgh, it was never credited that man could hold absolute supremacy over the wild tenants of the desert and the forest."[50]

This emphasis on Van Amburgh's dominance over wild nature is crucial in explaining his success in America and Europe in the 1830s and 1840s. As an account in a New York newspaper put it, "His fearless acts of placing his bare arm moist with blood, in the lion's mouth and thrusting his head into the distended jaws of the tiger—the playful tender-

A YOUNG LADY ATTACKED AND FRIGHTFULLY LACERATED BY A BENGAL TIGER, AT PHILADELPHIA.

Fig. 10.14. "A young lady attacked and frightfully lacerated by a Bengal tiger, at Philadelphia." 1859. Unidentified clipping. Picture Collection, The New York Public Library, Astor, Lenox and Tilden Foundations

ness of the lion and the tiger toward the infant and the pet lamb, who are put into the same cage with them—are all attended with the most thrilling and dramatic interest."[51] The mastery over wild animals displayed by Van Amburgh served to naturalize the dominance of Euro-Americans over nature, bringing explorers' accounts of encounters with savage big cats in adventure stories and travel literature vividly to life. They could also emphasize the prospect of peace on earth, as when a lamb, or a human infant, was exhibited amid these lions and tigers.

Attitudes toward wild animals in Van Amburgh's exhibitions in London vacillated "between notions of dominion and redemption." These displays of control demonstrated "the supremacy of the human will" while providing a "vicarious thrill of danger" to spectators, one that we shall see was appropriate given the animals' agency.[52] Van Amburgh's royal patronage (Queen Victoria attended at least six performances) and use of the Bible and stories from ancient history to frame his show as a "Great Moral Exhibition" helped counter criticism and legitimize and elevate his performances, as did Van Amburgh's appearance in several paintings by Sir Edwin Henry Landseer, which provided a high-culture version of the many popular prints and lithographs of the lion

Fig. 10.15. Sir Edwin Henry Landseer. *Portrait of Mr. Van Amburgh, as He Appeared with His Animals at the London Theatres*, 1846–47. Oil on canvas. Yale Center for British Art, B1977.14.61

tamer standing in triumph over his lions, tigers, and jaguars or wrestling with or lying among them. [53]

This mastery over exotic animals and the lands and people they represented was implied in Landseer's images of Van Amburgh. The point of view of Landseer's 1839 *Isaac Van Amburgh and His Animals* (Royal Collection, Windsor Castle) (*see fig. 2.7*) is from within the cage, with a recumbent Van Amburgh surrounded by wild animals and looking out at the spectators, prompting, as Kurt Koenigsburger has observed, "mediation on the relation of exotica to English subjects with a carefully cultivated separation and distance."[54] A later Landseer painting, *Portrait of Mr. Van Amburgh as He Appeared with His Animals at the London Theater* (1847, Yale Center for British Art, New Haven, Connecticut), emphasizes his command over the animals as the viewer looks into the cage at the fierce tiger and cowering lions (*fig. 10.15*). Contemporary British critics noted the contrast between the brutality used in training and performance and the staging of Landseer's paintings, however; one wrote that the artist conveyed "no idea of the moral power exercised by man over the brute race. This is no lord of the creation."[55]

Concern about the treatment of these animals and disdain for what one critic called "the tawdry indications of stage and salon sentiment that surrounded" Van Amburgh were largely, if not exclusively, expressed in England, reflecting the differences in the ways audiences in the two countries thought about both nonhuman animals and popular culture.[56] On both sides of the Atlantic, however, readers seemed constantly interested in the risks involved in lion taming. Newspapers in Europe and the United States reprinted stories about Van Amburgh's performances, especially when they went awry. While rehearsing for his performance with lions, tigers, and leopards as the "Lion Conqueror of Pompeii" at Astley's Royal Amphitheatre in London in 1838, for example, a tiger that "was utterly unable or unwilling to accomplish" the tricks that Van Amburgh wanted him to perform was chastised "with a large horsewhip." "Smarting under the pain of the lash, the animal became incensed, and suddenly sprang upon Mr. Van Amburgh, who instantly was hurled with violence to the ground." Van Amburgh eventually "got the better of his foe … striking the prostrate animal with his clinched fist, the blows following in quick succession, over the head, face and particularly the nose, until the blood flowed from the subdued animal, who here quivered under the grasp of his conqueror."[57]

Stories such as this one testified to the life-threatening danger faced by those working with big cats while simultaneously serving as useful publicity for attracting audiences to daredevil performances during which anything could happen. In 1840 American papers noted that while performing in Paris, where "after recovering from a wound in his leg caused by a tiger, [Van Amburgh] has been again bitten in the arm by a lion, and will be unable for some time to perform at Rouen."[58] Rumors of Van Amburgh's death in the cage spread several times in the 1840s: in 1844 he was reputed to have been torn to pieces by a lion, and in 1846 he was thought to have been "killed by one of his animals, somewhere in Rhode Island." Van Amburgh was indeed, according to the promotional biography sold at exhibitions of his menagerie, "seriously injured in both places referred to," but "he escaped in the end with life, and a self-assurance that he had conquered the whole animal kingdom."[59]

Entering the cage was life-threatening, of course. Animal trainer Matthew Ferguson was killed in 1844, found "in the den of the male leopard,

MISS E. CALHOUN. The celebrated LION QUEEN, as she appears with her Group of 9 Lions.
Tigers & Leopards, now attached to VAN AMBURGH & C⁰ˢ Magnificent Collection of living wild Animals.

quite dead and dreadfully mangled" in Bolton, England. Although he had a whip in his hand, it had been ineffective. "It is supposed that he had ventured into the den for the purpose of training the animal, a la Carter or Van Amburgh."[60] Van Amburgh's success spawned numerous imitators, many of whom adopted the same act and promotional strategies (even borrowing the iconic imagery of Van Amburgh in the cage) in their own performances, as seen in a lithograph advertising the pioneering female lion tamer Miss E. Calhoun (*fig. 10.16*). Largely because of Isaac Van Amburgh, performances with big cats became a staple of the American circus, one that persists thanks to the desire to see exotic animals and witness human derring-do. In many ways, the appeal of these shows has not changed much since Nathaniel Hawthorne saw a keeper enter the cage in 1838: "A man put his arm and head into the lion's mouth,—all the spectators looking on, so attentively that a breath could

Fig. 10.16. Eliphalet M. Brown. "Miss E. Calhoun, the Celebrated Lion Queen, as She Appears with Her Group of 9 Lions, Tigers & Leopards, Now Attached to Van Amburgh & Co's. Magnificent Collection of Living Wild Animals," 1848. Lithograph, E. Brown, Jr. lithographer; printed by Sarony & Major, New York. Courtesy American Antiquarian Society

not be heard. That was impressive—its effect on a thousand people, more than the thing itself."[61]

Both wild animals and horses had to be tamed and trained for the circus, raising questions about the possible cruelty involved in doing so that produced sporadic and generally unsuccessful opposition to the circus. These concerns, which first emerged in the nineteenth century, have tremendous implications for the modern circus, which is increasingly condemned for its use of animal performers.

Menagerie Good, Circus Bad

An anonymous pamphlet promoting Van Amburgh's menagerie argued that "the principal object of Van Amburgh & Co. has been to excite a taste for the study of Natural History in those persons who have not hitherto attended to the subject; and more particularly in the impression of moral and religious feelings."[62] This emphasis on education and morality was used to contrast the menagerie from the circus, which in an age of religious enthusiasm and the cheap print available to disseminate those ideas, was increasingly under attack. In response, proprietors of circuses emphasized their displays of exotic animals, making combinations of circuses and menageries not only wise from a practical business perspective, but from a public relations one as well.

In the early nineteenth century, injunctions against the cruelty involved in the training of animals promoted the development of distinctions between the menagerie and the circus. In *The Circus*, an American Sunday School Union chapbook for children, young Alfred and Silas Brown encounter a man pasting up broadsides featuring "pictures of men and horses." This man urges the boys not to tell their father about the show, but to "come after school, and be sure to bring your money, and I will show you something worth seeing." These good children return to their father, prompting Mr. Brown into thinking that "this was a good time to tell them what he thought of the circus." Their father then described how "the poor animals . . . have to be whipped very hard and treated very cruelly before they can be taught these things." After describing the cruel and foolish acts of the circus and its bad influence on the young, he provided an example from his own childhood of how one boy attempted to mimic the circus riders and wound up breaking his arm. Mr. Brown informed his sons, "I shall not take you to the circus, but in a short time there is to be a show of wild beasts; and then I will take you to see it."[63]

Menageries provided an educational and morally instructive alternative to the circus, and these collections of exotic animals were described as "a very popular entertainment, unexceptionable on the score of morals, and visited by the 'most straitest sects' of the people."[64] For some Christian moralizers, the circus was not entirely terrible, with performances with horses often exempted from reasons not to support this popular entertainment. In the lengthy anti-circus dialogue "Are You Going to the Circus?" (1847), a girl named Mary suggests, "I cannot see what harm there is in men riding beautiful horses" and her uncle replies, "Oh, there is no harm in that, but it is only part of the performance." This adult goes on to register the only major criticism against horse acts: the riding of women, noting, "I have seen women doing so, standing on the saddle, gaily, or indeed gaudily dressed, with very short dresses, and throwing themselves about in an unbecoming manner." These female performances thus "encourages young women to be fond of gay dress, and to be bold and immodest in manner, and all this in opposition to the word of God."[65] This concern about female immodesty explained why Carolyn Cowles Richards was prohibited from attending the circus as a child in the late 1850s. She recalled that her grandmother "said it was all right to look at the creatures God had made, but she did not think He ever intended that women should go only half dressed and stand up and ride on horses

Fig. 10.17. "Adam Forepaugh's New and Greatest All-Feature Show Performing Animals," 1888. Poster, printed by the Central Litho & Eng. Co. of N.Y. Collection of the New-York Historical Society

bare back, or jump through hoops in the air."[66] The Raymond, Waring and Company circus excluded women from its equestrian acts in an 1840 advertisement in Philadelphia, asserting that "the introduction of Females into an Equestrian Establishment is not calculated to advance our interests, while they not infrequently mar the harmony of the entertainments, and bring the whole exhibition into disrepute. It never was ordained by Nature that woman should degrade the representatives of her sex which are not calculated for any other than the stalwart male."[67] Here larger concerns about gender, religion, and propriety in the antebellum period shaped both ideas about and actual audience attendance at the circus.

"Are You Going to the Circus?" nicely enumerated anticircus themes that were developed in greater depth and vehemence in antebellum America. The Salem, Massachusetts *Asteroid*, for example, asserted in 1844 that modern circus performers are "an idle, ill-behaved, low-bred, immoral, dissipated, debauched, vicious, Sabbath-breaking, blasphemous gang, creating disturbances, inculcating vile desires, destroying the harmony and polluting the morality of every peaceful town they enter."[68] Other texts continued to lament the money wasted on circuses that could have been put to better use on charity, schooling, and missionary work.[69] Some of this hostility was deserved, for as P. T. Barnum recalled:

> In those days the circus was very justly the object of the Church's animadversions. In afterpiece, "The Tailor of Tamworth" or "Pete Jenkins" . . . drunken characters were represented and broad jokes, suited to the groundlings, were given. Its fun consisted in the clown's vulgar jests, emphasized with the still more vulgar and suggestive gestures, lest providentially the point may be lost. Educational features the circus of

that day had none. Its employees were mostly of the rowdy element, and it had a following of card-shapers, pickpockets and swindlers generally, who were countenanced by some of the circus proprietors, with whom they shared their ill-gotten gains. Its advent was dreaded by all law abiding people, who knew that with it would inevitably come disorder, drunkenness, and riot.[70]

The instructive amusement of the "show of wild beasts" contrasted favorably with the general immorality and uselessness of the circus. In addition, concern over the ways nonhuman animals were trained also helped to distinguish between worthy and debased looking, drawing distinctions between different ways of seeing animals that reflected a larger segmentation of antebellum popular culture.[71]

The inclusion of wild animals in the American circus, a process largely complete by the period now known as the "golden age of the circus," helped to legitimize this cultural institution, even as audiences drew a wide range of lessons about race, gender, nation, and modernity from the circus's human and animal performances.[72] All of the animals used in the circus were, in some way, tamed or trained. Even behaviors that seemed "wild" were often taught or exaggerated. In this sense the circus—and the menagerie and zoological park—can provide only limited lessons about the natural world, and to be less charitable, they only really mark human dominion over nature (*fig. 10.17*).

As Americans' attitudes about animals have changed, so has their understanding of the appropriate display of animals in the circus and the zoo. As the "domestic ethic of kindness" to animals has expanded, many Americans see the use of captive wild animals in the circus as exploitative, an unnecessary limit upon the animals' freedom, even in

comparison to the zoo, where the training of animals is not generally designed for public consumption, only to help keepers manage the animals.[73] Growing sentiment that captive wild and performing animals largely serve human intellectual and emotional needs, telling us very little about the lives and needs of the animals themselves, has promoted a trend away from the use of animals in the circus. Starting in the 1970s a new kind of circus combined traditional circus arts with theatrical techniques while moving away from the use of animal acts. The most famous of these new circuses is Montreal's Cirque du Soleil (founded in 1984), which is marked by the absence of both the ring and the exploitation of animals.

The founders of the *nouveau cirque* felt that the traditional circus was unable to offer anything new, just different versions of the same experience that viewers had by the end of the nineteenth century. They also realized they could charge much more for a mix of traditional circus acts and theatrical spectacle. Given the costs of purchasing and maintaining living animals and the growing public concern for ethical treatment and exhibition of circus animals, these new circuses have tended to do away with animal acts.[74] As Cirque du Soleil's Guy Laliberté has been quoted, "I would rather give jobs to three artists than feed one elephant."[75]

1 For a discussion of the cultural work of exhibitions, both serious and comic, of monkeys and apes in post-revolutionary America, see Brett Mizelle, "Man Cannot Behold It without Contemplating Himself: Monkeys, Apes, and Human Identity in the Early American Republic," *Explorations in Early American Culture: A Supplemental Issue of Pennsylvania History* 66 (1999), 144–73.

2 Important studies of the early American circus, often more concerned with chronology and "firsts" than analysis, include R. W. G. Vail, *Random Notes on the History of the Early American Circus* (Worcester: American Antiquarian Society, 1933); Stuart Thayer, *Annals of the American Circus, 1793–1860* (Seattle: Dauven and Thayer, 2000).

3 American circus proprietors constantly sought new novelties, importing new animal and human performers from abroad and modifying older acts to attract new audiences. This continuous evolution can make the circus hard to pin down, hence my focus on two staple animal acts featuring horses and big cats.

4 Howard Loxton, *The Golden Age of the Circus* (London: Grange Books, 1997), 10–14.

5 *Essex Gazette* (Salem, MA), Nov. 12–19, 1771, 67; Isaac Greenwood, *The Circus: Its Origins and Growth Prior to 1835* (New York: The Dunlap Society, 1898), 60–63; "Horsemanship, by Mr. Bates," broadside (Boston: n.p., 1773); Early American Imprints, first series, no. 42405.

6 See Ann Fairfax Withington, *Toward a More Perfect Union: Virtue and the Formation of American Republics* (New York and Oxford: Oxford University Press, 1991).

7 *Pennsylvania Packet*, Aug. 15, 1785; John Culhane, *The American Circus: An Illustrated History* (New York: Holt, 1990), 2–3.

8 (Philadelphia) *Aurora. General Advertiser*, Oct. 27, 1792; Nov. 5, 1796; James S. Moy, "Entertainments at John Bill Ricketts's Circus, 1793–1800," *Educational Theatre Journal* 30, no. 2 (May 1978), 186–202. For an astute analysis of early national Philadelphia's culture, see David R. Brigham, *Public Culture in the Early Republic: Peale's Museum and Its Audience* (Washington, D.C.: Smithsonian Institution Press, 1995).

9 *Federal Gazette and Philadelphia Daily Advertiser*, May 17, 1793. For a detailed account of Ricketts's performances and career, see Moy, "Entertainments at John Bill Ricketts's Circus," 186–202.

10 Cited in Thayer, *Annals*, 13.

11 Culhane, *American Circus*, 4–5. Horses mentioned in broadsides, newspaper advertisements, and programs were, in effect, celebrity animals, although the names of the majority of circus animals, particularly common species such as horses, were known only to their owners and trainers.

12 John Durang, *The Memoir of John Durang, American Actor, 1785–1816* (Pittsburgh: Published for The Historical Society of York County and for the American Society for Theatre Research by the University of Pittsburgh Press, 1966), 45; Moy, "Entertainments at John Bill Ricketts's Circus," 199.

13 Thayer, *Annals*, 20.

14 According to Stuart Thayer, this marks the first time that elephants were part of the circus (*Annals*, 27, note 41).

15 Charles Durang, "The Philadelphia Stage," published serially in the *Sunday Dispatch* beginning May 7, 1854, cited in Thayer, *Annals*, 40.

16 Renée Sentilles, *Performing Menken: Adah Isaacs Menken and the Birth of American Celebrity* (Cambridge and New York: Cambridge University Press, 2003). For the wild west show, see Joy S. Kasson, *Buffalo Bill's Wild West: Celebrity, Memory, and Popular History* (New York: Hill and Wang, 2001).

17 "Crack! Bang! The Bill Show's Open," New York City, n.d., cited in Janet Davis, *The Circus Age: Culture and Society under the American Big Top* (Chapel Hill: University of North Carolina Press, 2002), 154.

18 *Columbian Centinel* (Boston), Nov. 15, 1815, cited in Thayer, *Annals*, 36. This praise was directed at the company of Robert Davis, which performed in Boston from Oct. 1815 to March 1816.

19 "Circus," *Knickerbocker* 13, no. 1 (Jan. 1839), 74–76.

20 Thayer, *Annals*, esp. 22, 86, 98–99.

21 Tom Ogden, *Two Hundred Years of the American Circus: From Aba-Daba to the Zoppe-Zavatta Troupe* (New York: Facts on File, 1993), 301.

22 Mark Twain, *The Adventures of Huckleberry Finn* (New York: Harper and Brothers, 1935), 547.

23 Grand Equestrian Tournament, poster, Barnum & Bailey, 1894, reproduced in Davis, *Circus Age*, 94.

24 Nathaniel Hawthorne, *Hawthorne's Lost Notebook, 1835–1841*, ed. Barbara S. Mouffe (University Park: Pennsylvania State University Press, 1978), 3.

25 W. C. Coup, *Sawdust and Spangles: Stories and Secrets of the Circus* (Chicago: H. S. Stone & Co., 1901), cited in Robert M. Lewis, *From Traveling Show to Vaudeville: Theatrical Spectacle in America, 1830–1910* (Baltimore and London: Johns Hopkins University Press, 2003), 132.

26 Thayer, *Annals*, 78. The Charleston city council even voted to waive the regular license fee for the company's engagement.

27 Durang, *Memoir*, 104–5.

28 *Haney's Art of Training Animals: A Practical Guide for Amateur or Professional Trainers* (New York: Jesse Haney & Co., 1869). The author of this book thanked the proprietors of the Van Amburgh and "Yankee" Robinson "collections of trained and wild animals" for their assistance in the sections on circus and menagerie animal training (preface).

29 Alfred T. Ringling, "What the Public Does Not See at a Circus," *National Magazine* 12 (1900), 189–92, quoted in Lewis, *From Traveling Show to Vaudeville*, 139. Today, of course, circus proprietors would never publish an article that described animal training.

30 "The Circus Rider," *Bachelor* 4 (1841), unpaginated.

31 "A Flare-up in the Circus," *Southern Literary Gazette* 1, no. 35 (June 19, 1852), 291–93. This account concerned a near riot that broke out after a circus clown humiliated a local resident: "Horses, pied and spotted, and of all colours, made their appearance. Children rode, women rode, the clown rode, and it was all sorts of riding…. Journeys to Brentford, Gilpin's race, and several other pieces, were enacted. The equestrians had their share of applause; but, after all, the glory of the spectacle was in that comical fellow, the clown."

32 "Barnum and Bailey Parade Tonight," *New York Daily Tribune*, March 25, 1891, cited in Davis, *Circus Age*, 3.

33 "The Circus," *Life Illustrated*, Aug. 30, 1856, cited in Lewis, *From Traveling Show to Vaudeville*, 124–26.

34 Elaine Walker, *Horse* (London: Reaktion Books, 2008), 164. Two recent reminders of the significance of horses in nineteenth-century America are Ann Norton Greene, *Horses at Work: Harnessing Power in Industrial America* (Cambridge, MA: Harvard University Press, 2008) and Clay McShane and Joel Tarr, *The Horse in the City: Living Machines in the Nineteenth Century* (Baltimore: Johns Hopkins University Press, 2007).

35 *Boston Gazette*, Sept. 19–26, 1720, [2]; this lion died in 1732, having "travelled all over North America by Sea and Land," *Pennsylvania Gazette*, Jan. 25, 1732, [2].

36 *Massachusetts Mercury*, Jan. 26, 1798, [3].

37 See Richard W. Flint, "Entrepreneurial and Cultural Aspects of the Early-Nineteenth-Century Circus and Menagerie Business," in *Itinerancy in New England and New York*, ed. Peter Benes, Dublin Seminar for New England Folklife (Boston: Boston University, 1986), 131–49. Thayer has argued that the first nonperforming animal to appear with a circus troupe was a sloth that was exhibited with the Lafayette Company circus in 1827 (Thayer, *Annals*, 89). He also argued that the first circus and menagerie combination left winter quarters in Charleston, South Carolina to tour to the north in 1828 (Thayer, *Annals*, 99).

38 For an overview, see Stuart Thayer, "A History of the Traveling Menagerie in America," *Bandwagon*, Nov.–Dec. 1991, 64–71 and Jan.–Feb. 1992, 31–36; and Richard W. Flint, "American Showman and European Dealers: Commerce in Wild Animals in Nineteenth-Century America," in *New Worlds, New Animals: From Menagerie to Zoological Park in the Nineteenth Century*, ed. R. J. Hoage and William A. Deiss (Baltimore and London: Johns Hopkins University Press, 1996), 97–108.

39 In November 1829, for example, an advertisement in the *Pensacola* (Florida) *Gazette* noted, "the keeper will enter the respective cages of the lion and lioness." Most of these trainers were unnamed in advertisements and have therefore remained unrecognized. See Thayer, "'The Keeper Will Enter the Cage': Early American Wild Animal Trainers," *Bandwagon* 26, no. 6 (Nov.–Dec. 1982), 38–40.

40 Henry D. B. Bailey provides a first-person history and reminiscence of Isaac Van Amburgh in *Local Tales and Historical Sketches* (Fishkill, NY: John. W. Spaight, 1874), 399–406. Van Amburgh died of a heart attack on Nov. 29, 1865, at the age of fifty-seven.

41 See, for example, an account of a boy "shockingly mangled by a tyger . . . having approached too near the cage," *Essex Register* (Salem, MA), Aug. 7, 1816 and "Frightful Scene with a Leopard," *New World* 8, no. 11 (March 16, 1844), 349. In both cases, the authors urged the intervention of the authorities to address the risk of exhibitions of exotic animals. In the 1844 instance, the animal trainer Jacob Dreisbach "was committed to prison for trial" for assault after a tiger said to be under his control badly mauled a twelve-year-old boy.

42 *Painesville* (Ohio) *Telegraph*, Aug. 23, 1832, cited in Thayer, "The Keeper Will Enter the Cage," 39.

43 (St. Thomas, Ontario) *Liberal*, July 25, 1833, cited in Thayer, "The Keeper Will Enter the Cage," 39.

44 *The* (London) *Times*, Sept. 10, 1838, cited in Thayer, "The Keeper Will Enter the Cage," 40.

45 Americans clearly preferred to see animals doing something and lamented their lack of activity in their accounts of visits to animal exhibitions and menageries. See for example the many entries in the diary of the Reverend William Bentley of Salem, Massachusetts, cited in Brett Mizelle, "Contested Exhibitions: The Debate over Proper Animal Sights in Post-Revolutionary America," *Worldviews* 9, no. 2 (2005), 223–26.

46 Howard Loxton noted that American wild animal acts tend to emphasize the power of the animal in attack while in Europe greater emphasis was placed on the skill of the trainer; Loxton, *Golden Age of the Circus*, 86. Clyde Beatty's great "fighting act" in the early twentieth century exemplified performance *en ferocité*. For a critical history of cat acts, see John Stokes, "'Lion Griefs': The Wild Animal Act as Theatre," *New Theatre Quarterly* 20, no. 2 (May 2004), 138–54.

47 [Richard H. Horne], *The Life of Van Amburgh: The Brute-Tamer! With Anecdotes of His Extraordinary Pupils. By Ephraim Watts, Citizen of New York* (London: Robert Tyas, 1838).

48 (London) *Times*, Aug. 24, 1869, cited in E. S. Turner, *All Heaven in a Rage* (London: Michael Joseph, 1964), 267.

49 (New London, CT) *Morning News*, May 21, 1846, [2].

50 John Tryon, *An Illustrated History and Full and Accurate Description of the Wild Beasts, and Other Interesting Specimens of Animated Nature Contained in the Grand Caravan of Van Amburgh & Co.: Together with a Particular Account of Mr. Van Amburgh's Performances in the Caverns of Trained Animals, as Exhibited by Him in Europe and America, before the Highest Classes of Citizens, Gentry and Nobility . . .* (New York: Jonas Booth, 1846), 5.

51 "Animal Subjugation," *New-York Mirror*, July 7, 1838, 15.

52 Diana Donald, *Picturing Animals in Britain, 1750–1850* (New Haven: Yale University Press for the Paul Mellon Centre for Studies in British Art, 2007), 191–92.

53 Queen Victoria visited Drury Lane Theatre on Jan. 24, 1839, "going personally upon the stage and witnessing the feeding of Van Amburgh's lions." See "Later from Europe" in *Portsmouth Journal of Literature and Politics*, Feb. 23, 1839, [2].

54 Kurt Koenigsberger, *The Novel and the Menagerie: Totality, Englishness, and Empire* (Columbus: Ohio State University Press, 2007), 41–42.

55 *Athenaeum*, May 8, 1847, 495, cited in Donald, *Picturing Animals in Britain*, 195.

56 *The Examiner*, May 8, 1847, 293, cited in Donald, *Picturing Animals in Britain*, 195.

57 "Furious Attack on Mr. Van Amburgh, of Astley's Amphitheatre, by One of His Tigers," *Farmer's Cabinet* 8, no. 2 (Oct. 19, 1838), 2.

58 *Portsmouth Journal of Literature and Politics*, March 14, 1840. This account also mentioned "Van Amburgh's courage in hitting the lion on the nose to make him lose his hold."

59 "A Brief Biographical Sketch of I. A. Van Amburgh, Now Travelling with His Menagerie throughout the New England States," (broadside, with no publisher or place of publication, ca. 1840, Harvard Theatre Collection "Menageries" folder). The (New London, CT) *Morning News* noted Van Amburgh was not dead on June 19, 1846.

60 "A Dreadful Death," *New Hampshire Patriot*, April 11, 1844, [1].

61 Nathaniel Hawthorne, *The American Notebooks*, ed. Randall Stewart (New Haven and London: Yale University Press, 1932), 64–65.

62 Hyatt Frost, *A Brief Biographical Sketch of I. A. Van Amburgh, and an Illustrated and Descriptive History of the Animals Contained in this Mammoth Menagerie and Great Moral Exhibition, Comprising More in Number and a Greater Variety Than All Other Shows in the United States Combined* (New York: Printed by Samuel Booth, 1862).

63 *The Circus* (Philadelphia, American Sunday School Union [between 1827 and 1853]), 11–14. The contents of this tract also appeared in the periodical *Youth's Companion* 16, no. 35 (Jan. 6, 1843), 139. See also

64 "Circus," *The Knickerbocker, or New-York Monthly Magazine* 13, no. 1 (Jan. 1839), 69.

65 "Are You Going to the Circus? A Dialogue," *Well-Spring* (Boston), 4, no. 45 (Nov. 12, 1847), 181–82. This anti-circus dialogue was a reprint of a British tract originally produced by the London Religious Tract Society, reminding us that opposition to the circus was as transnational as the institution itself.

66 Carolyn Cowles Richards, quoted in Davis, *Circus Age*, 86.

67 Advertisement for Raymond, Waring and Co. Circus, Chestnut Street Amphitheatre, Philadelphia, June 20, 1840, cited in Davis, *Circus Age*, 87.

68 "Circus," *Asteroid* 1, no. 3 (Oct. 1848), 10.

69 See, for example "Circus," *Common School Journal* 9.17 (Oct. 15, 1847), 317 and the (Lowell, MA) *Daystar* 1.9 (July 6, 1850), 2, which argued that two traveling circuses "carried away hundreds of dollars which should have been expended by the attendants in paying their honest debts."

70 P. T. Barnum, *Life of P. T. Barnum: Written by Himself* (Buffalo: Courier Company, 1888), 348.

71 See Mizelle, "Contested Exhibitions," 231–33.

72 See Davis, *Circus Age*, esp. xii–xiiii, 10–18, 144–47.

73 Catherine C. Grier, *Pets in America: A History* (Chapel Hill: University of North Carolina Press, 2006).

74 The first local ban on animals in the circus was approved in Hollywood, Florida, in 1991. See the chapter "Must There Be Animals?" in Ernest Albrecht, *The New American Circus* (Gainesville: University Press of Florida, 1995). See also, for example, "Call For Wild Animals to Be Banned from the Circus," *New Scientist* 202, no. 2709 (May 23, 2009), 5, which summarizes a global animal welfare study on circus elephants and tigers.

75 Michael Small, The Arts, *People*, May 2, 1988, quoted in Albrecht, *New American Circus*, 79. Laliberté today says the exclusion of animals was an "artistic decision," albeit one that also gave Cirque du Soleil excellent publicity.

chapter 14 in this volume, "The Circus in Nineteenth-Century American Children's Literature."

"BONAVITA."

⑪

PERFORMED IDENTITIES
ᴬˢ CIRCUS ILLUSIONS

PETA TAIT

Captain Jack Bonavita calmly and quietly presented his circus act with a record-breaking twenty-seven lions in 1901.[1] He was reportedly called a "hero" by Theodore Roosevelt, who was impressed by this new style of wild-animal act.[2] Since the danger facing Bonavita was posed by a nonhuman animal species, he was being praised for his capacity as a human to withstand such a threat. But Bonavita wore a military-style costume and doubtless the fabricated performance identity of the trainer contributed to an impression of heroic action (*fig. 11.1*). The animal act implicitly presented humanness inflected with cultural identity. Within a broader socio-political context, however, a costume that also evoked ideas of aggressive confrontation complicated an act that displayed the results of methodical training and claimed to be scientific.

Trainer identity in big-cat acts was typical of the illusions created by performative identity in cir-cus and sideshow by the turn of the twentieth century. By then, the exotic animal act provided a demonstration of control that was indicative of the conquest of nature in modernity.[3] It can be argued that the trained wild-animal acts accorded with populist notions of evolution that were deemed to represent progress in a simplified interpretation of Darwin's science and the subsequent arguments that challenged notions of human separateness from animals.[4] Therefore were modernist trainer identities pointing to nineteenth-century military triumph or twentieth-century scientific advancement? This chapter approaches the circus from the perspective of performance studies and therefore the discussion of its cultural meaning is performer and act specific. It considers how military and scientific concepts played out in the performance identities presented by wild animal trainers, Jack Bonavita and Louis Roth (*fig. 11.2*).[5] These are contrasted briefly with the way in which Roth performed across nationality and gender, and with the safari hunter identity of Peter

◄ *Detail of fig. 11.1.* Captain Jack Bonavita with his lions, ca. 1900. Photograph. Circus World Museum, CWi-2303

wild animal trainers learned from each other in a closely connected grouping.

Trainer identity responded to social expectations, and acts often acquired a standard costume style in the modern circus. Modernist values with regard to animals were evident by the beginning of the twentieth century in Western culture, and manifest through anti-cruelty laws, the sentimentalization of animals, and "civilized behaviour to animals."[7] The trained wild act complied with these new modernist imperatives whereby the trainer's self-control became indicative of "civilized behaviour," and increased knowledge and care accompanying the training that conditioned animal responses also reflected progress from older-style menagerie cage acts and was therefore deemed scientific by the trainers.

The aesthetic effects of circus bodies were created by interweaving social dress with innovative and unconventional elements and these delivered a complex mix of cultural signs. In her analysis of fashion and social change in relation to physical bodies, sociologist Joanne Entwistle concludes, "[d]ress is tied up to social life in more than one way: it is produced out of economic, political, technological conditions as well as shaped by social, cultural, and aesthetic ideas."[8] Costuming that suited the artistic and athletic circus act utilized clothing modes and identities as it, in turn, influenced social fashions.[9] For example, in 1859 the inventor of trapeze action, aerialist Jules Leotard, also invented the leotard costume worn with tights, and this combination was subsequently worn in trapeze acts by male and female acrobats. Since the body-fitting costume revealed the muscularity of both male and female aerial bodies, gender identity difference was physically challenged during the act.[10] As an indirect consequence, aerialists with gender-bending muscular bodies confirmed the instability of cultural identity. These

Taylor. The work of these two trainers was foundational in twentieth-century big-cat performance as Bonavita instructed Roth, who subsequently taught the two most famous trainers, Clyde Beatty and Mabel Stark, although it was Taylor who shaped Beatty's performance identity.[6] The trained big-cat act was a cultural invention that regularly appeared in the circus ring from the 1890s, and it came to typify the traditional circus in modernity. The two trainers discussed here were seminal and indicative of how

Fig. 11.1. Captain Jack Bonavita with his lions, ca. 1900. Photograph. Circus World Museum, CWi-2303

Fig. 11.2. Louis Roth with lions. Photograph from Dave Robeson, *Louis Roth, Forty Years with Jungle Killers* (Caldwell, Idaho: Caxton Printers, 1941). Illinois State University's Special Collections, Milner Library

costumes were well in advance of the late-modernist social shifts whereby such gymnastic attire became ubiquitous. The circus delivered theatrical social identities as part of the act but the performance of gender and ethnic or racial identity might not necessarily correspond with a performer's off stage identity. Identity was performed as a circus illusion.

Aerial acts and trained big-cat acts were regularly integrated into circus tent programs by the 1890s, although Bonavita and Roth worked for the leading animal trainer, Frank Bostock (*fig. 11.3*), who was more associated with menagerie and sideshow companies. In keeping with social Darwinism, Bostock reiterated that "the trained animal is a product of science."[11] It was assumed that the methodical training of wild animals was scientific because animal instinctive behavior was being controlled and that this developed their mental capacity and thus benefited them. But the science of wild animals was paradoxical in relation to their survival. Roosevelt, who was keenly interested in "sciences connected with geography," went on African safari after his presidency, and in 1909 acquired a large number of preserved animal specimens for museum collections to benefit the public.[12] Circus, too, claimed to be educational, especially since its specimens were brought live from remote geographical regions. Circus animal performance reflected the prevailing belief system in culture whereby wild animals were regarded as embodying nature, which was available to be exploited and improved.

The human in the animal act underscored beliefs about nature. Bonavita and Roth contributed to the convention of the big-cat trainer in quasi-military-style costuming with elaborate braiding, and a safari hunter identity was soon added to military identities of the circus. Captain Bonavita's title reinforced the costumed performance identity of the American John Gentner.[13] Bonavita's 1901 act set

a record for the largest number of lions displayed together in one act and he managed the lion group with minimal speaking. The audience reaction to the beginning of Bonavita's act was quantifiable. Bostock described how "his entrance with the twenty-seven lions was so impressive that for a few seconds after the first flare of the band the silence was intense."[14] Outnumbered by lions, it seemed that a lone human figure could not escape or properly defend himself should they decide to attack. Bonavita

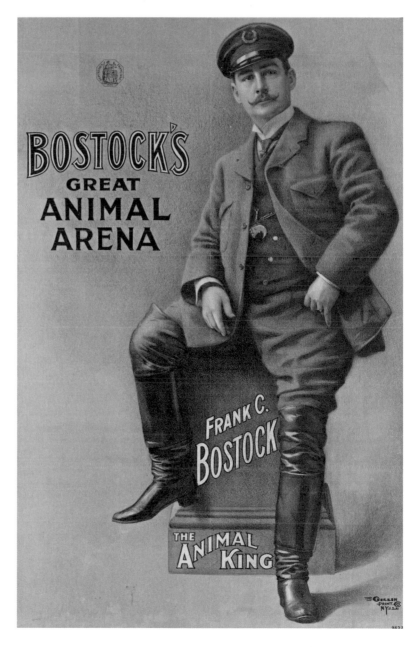

Fig. 11.3. "Bostock's Great Animal Arena: Frank C. Bostock, the Animal King," ca. 1899. Poster, printed by Gillin Print Co., New York. Collection of the John and Mable Ringling Museum of Art, Tibbals Collection, ht2004234

tary metaphor could be useful to explain the motivation of the animal trainer.

While a military uniform suggested physical training and self-control, it also carried an unmistakable inference of heightened masculinity. Yet the ideal of the soldier in social situations required suppression of any masculine potential for aggression. In close proximity with the lions, Bonavita's stoicism exemplified a manly ideal that corresponded with that of military hero but it could also be aligned with the impression of a disinterested man of science. This manly reserve was interpreted as complete mastery over anxiety and nervousness, and certainly Bonavita revealed perseverance to stay in this work over years since he had at least fifty accidents in the ring, eventually losing an arm.[17] Perhaps unsurprisingly, animal performance proved popular for decades with military spectators. After Roth performed in Austin, Texas, in 1939, he was awarded an "attached commission" as a Colonel Aide-de-Camp by the American army.[18]

Because Bonavita was viewed as regularly risking his life with potentially hostile animals even when they were made compliant, this was interpreted as a triumph over human instincts to flee and ultimately the fear of death. His species identity was being admired so that the male trainer had become a hero of the human species.

appeared to control them through his presence, although it is likely that they were following his gestures and body positions. General Miles, from the War Office, who was "particularly impressed," wrote to Bostock commending Bonavita's control "of these noble creatures" as "truly remarkable," and Bostock agreed, commenting that Bonavita gave the impression of a "peculiarly reserved" gentleman offstage (*fig. 11.4*).[15] By implication, such masculine qualities contributed to his control. Bonavita was esteemed for his bravery by the men considered courageous in society, which aligned his trainer identity with that of a soldier. In reference to his injuries from lion attacks, Bonavita explained: "A man does not refuse to go into battle because he has been hurt."[16] A mili-

Uniform Acts

A military uniform carried connotations of military-like training and discipline. As Michel Foucault explained, from the eighteenth century a soldier in Europe was physically trained to appear straight and alert through increasingly regimented practices that disciplined the appearance of the body.[19]

Fig. 11.4. Captain Jack Bonavita. Photograph from Frank Charles Bostock, *The Training of Wild Animals* (New York: Century, 1903), 211. Illinois State University's Special Collections, Milner Library

Fig. 11.5. "P. T. Barnum's Greatest Show on Earth . . . The Grand United Barnum and London Double Brigade Brass & Reed Band," 1882. Poster, printed by the Strobridge Lithographing Company, Cincinnati. Cincinnati Art Museum, Gift of the Strobridge Lithographing Company, 1965.686.28

Foucault wrote that "discipline produces subjected and practiced bodies, 'docile' bodies."[20] The appearance of conformity and obedience achieved by disciplining the soldier's body served the purpose of authority while it also removed individuality and suppressed reactions. Standardized clothing further advanced the idea of a disciplined body. The use of uniforms in circus costuming connected with an impression of emotional impassivity and docility sought from military identity.

Uniforms were derived from the dress of the military or the church and adopted to represent order and civility, and the design and use of military uniforms were greatly expanded in nineteenth-century Europe.[21] Countries adopted a specific color, so that red was used in England, blue in Prussia, and white by other countries. A naval or infantry outfit was standardized through the decoration of the jacket with prominent buttons, braid, epaulets, and chest pockets with flaps, although the lower half still varied from short to long pants and horse-riding attire. During the Napoleonic era the focus on regulating the jacket accorded attention to the upper body and encouraged an idea of an overtly sexualized muscularity.[22] The subsequent proliferation of military look-alike uniforms to identify all types of social activity extended to men's white or khaki safari suits.[23] This type of dress was associated with tropical regions of European colonies and provided the basis of the safari suit and its subsequent adaptation as a circus costume. Clothes and uniforms in particular had an important function as symbols of authority and social power in the nineteenth century.[24]

Posters of circus bands attest that quasi-

military-style uniforms were used in circus-band costuming in the second half of the nineteenth century (*fig. 11.5*).[25] Individuals provided direct links between the circus and the military from the outset, as circus in the ring owes its origins to an ex-soldier, Philip Astley, and his equestrian shows after 1768.[26] But a performer would also co-opt a social identity. Bostock, who grew up in the Wombwell menagerie business and took over its management in 1881, appeared as Captain Bostock in his own act with eight trained lions during the 1880s. Big cats were only reliably trained for the circus from that time, to supersede menagerie acts started earlier, in the mid-1820s. These involved a handler who entered a small

cage of lions often in a confrontational encounter. Bostock promoted the way that training created well-controlled displays through improved knowledge derived from the study of animals in captivity and husbandry. As trained big-cat acts flourished and nineteenth-century menagerie cage entertainments with presenters in Romanesque shifts disappeared, the trainer's costume became a central part of the impression of a new style of animal act. Bostock's military attire confirmed an idea that the trainer would instill order and disciplined behavior in other species, and his costume set a precedent.

Trained wild-animal acts in the circus after the 1880s were dominated by two family businesses in particular, the Hagenbeck's and Bostock's, and notably brothers, Carl and Wilhelm Hagenbeck and Frank and Edward Bostock. A Hagenbeck act with trainer Henrich Mehrmann, who married into the Hagenbeck family, traveled from Germany to the Chicago World's Fair in 1893, around the same time that acts managed by Frank Bostock reached the United States (*fig. 11.6*).[27] Hagenbeck trainers like Mehrmann, however, were more likely to be costumed in everyday wear. This choice of costume was socially meaningful because the wearing of an evening suit gave an impression of formality and implied that an animal act might correspond with socially esteemed artistic events such as concerts. Hagenbeck's were more concerned with offsetting any impression of harsh treatment than maximizing an idea of control. Costumed as a gentleman, the trainer conveyed notions of genial masculine self-restraint to allay concerns about how the animals were treated and at the same time supported the Hagenbeck training rhetoric proclaiming the absence of cruelty and tricks achieved through gentle training with rewards.[28] By 1900, however, prominent Hagenbeck trainers were also wearing military costumes.

▲ *Fig. 11.6.* Napoleon Sarony. Heinrech Mehrmann with a tiger and a lion, 1893. Photograph. Collection of the New-York Historical Society

Performers' costumes were central to the ideas delivered in circus performance. At the turn of the twentieth century, a military costume predominated among the male trainers working for Bostock. Certainly it reassured nervous spectators that the trainer was in control, but military identity conveyed social status, which could enhance the standing of an act, although the choice of color had more to do with aesthetic effect than nationalism. Since ex-soldiers did join the circus, a uniform could indicate an authentic military background, although at the same time it usefully depersonalized the identity of the trainer. There were practical reasons for uniform costuming in trained animal acts because a performer could be more easily replaced without disruption to the act. This was crucial because wild animal training and compliance relied on minimal change in the practiced routine and environment including that of the trainer's appearance. To some extent, thick fabric such as that used for military-style uniforms also gave some protection from the incidental scratches of the animal performer claws, and camouflaged the scars on the skin from such scratches. Crucially, a standardized costume informed the audience about the type of act as it met their expectations.

The social meanings conveyed by quasi-military-style uniforms in the animal act also encompassed geographical conquest. The acquisition and exploitation of exotic animals followed the nineteenth-century expansion of colonial empires.[29] The viewing of animals was framed by this background of imperialist conquest. Zoos reflected a voyeuristic consumption of imperialism by the public—which she states was achieved through the enslavement of animals for consumption.[30] Wild animals came from geographical areas in Africa, Asia, and South America that were subsumed as colonies and occupied by the military of respective European countries. The colonial possession of land carried a presumption of the ownership of the animals, and animals were hunted and transported in increasingly large numbers back to Europe, England, and the United States. Wild animals, dead or alive, provided tangible evidence of geographical conquest to a curious public.

Lions proved particularly trainable and provided an ideal embodiment of late-nineteenth-century ideas of Africa and empire. A male lion was deemed the king of animals on the basis of the mane's regal appearance and a patriarchic family structure. The hierarchical world of the lions corresponded to human ideas of social order, so a lion seemed a suitable foe for a colonial hero.

While groups of lions could be trained to do feats, animal training was not quite as reliable as the label of science inferred. An impression that the trainer engaged in military-like encounters may have been more apt. Ellen Velvin, a writer of animal stories, gave an extended account of a rehearsal of Bonavita's lion act at Coney Island on the occasion of a fight involving all twenty-seven lions after some new lions had been in the same space.

> Instead of getting on their pedestals in their usual way, the lions, with one exception, a big, muscular fellow, began to sniff at the corners of the arena, where the newcomers had been exercising, . . . the big lion with an ugly snarl leaped from his pedestal into the thick of the fray, and in an instant twenty-seven lions were fighting with teeth and claws . . . Bonavita vainly tried to regain mastery over the fighting beasts. The lions were no longer the puppets of a show; they were the monarchs of the forest, wild, and savage.[31]

Bonavita only narrowly escaped the brawl and serious injury by jumping over some of the lions and Bostock had recounted a similar incident previously. Methodical training could not forestall an unexpected interruption to the routine. After 1901, Bonavita's act expanded to include tigers and other animals as he created a different style of trained act and his performance demeanor changed accordingly. Tragically, Bonavita died from an attack by a polar bear while working with the film company Selig's Menagerie in Los Angeles in 1918.[32]

By the early twentieth century, the stereotypical animal trainer was a male performer in a quasi-Hussar uniform. By the late 1880s, French writer Hugues Le Roux noted that presenters of animal acts either wore "the red uniform of the Horse Guards" or "gentlemen's evening dress."[33] As happens in the circus, the act itself had acquired a costume tradi-

tion, and a particular one. A military-like figure conveyed human dignity and discipline combined with dominance of others. But it was the animals who were increasingly trained through repetitious practice; it was animal natures that were subjected to military discipline.

Scientific Confusions

While Bonavita described his work in military metaphors, the younger Roth claimed that he was interested in "comparing scientific findings with his own observations."[34] Roth sought to increase his knowledge of animal behavior and explained his own approach as scientific because it was based on close, careful observation. Accordingly, animal training for the circus was regarded as a scientific practice in the

Louis Roth & Big Lion Group

Fig. 11.7. "Louis Roth & Big Lion Group." Photograph. Circus World Museum, CWi-2341

early decades of the twentieth century. But Roth also described how the conditioning of the physical action of the animal performers produced military-like precision. For a new act with a female presenter, he trained with twelve mountain lions or pumas (also called cougars or panthers) and explained: "[t]he cats took their seats after reaching the arena from the tunnel, then went through a full routine act, to finish by walking on their hind feet, obeying military commands, and drilling with the precision of soldiers."[35] The big cats had acquired a military identity.

When Louis Roth first performed as an adolescent, he wore the costume of a French army general.[36] Roth was born in Hungary and at thirteen migrated to the United States to work, and personally wanted to avoid serving in the Hungarian military draft as a soldier.[37] One further identity illusion throughout the circus internationally was that of a performer's nationality in performance, which was not necessarily his or her personal one. A fake military identity and rank accorded with a borrowed nationality. One implication of performing identity in animal acts, however, was that the science of animal performance was also part of the illusion.

Roth showed his capacity early when he trained a Hagenbeck conditioned lion, Leo, to wrestle with him, and Bonavita sent him a congratulatory telegram for this new feat.[38] Roth took over some animals trained by Bonavita about 1905, although Roth's friendship with Bonavita had begun when young Roth attempted to save a lion, Sultan, after he attacked Captain Weiss and Roth claimed that he tried unsuccessfully to save Weiss before he was killed.[39] Sultan was to be taken away until Roth intervened. Bonavita took into his act several young lions that the adolescent Roth trained. Roth first gained work at thirteen as a cage boy looking after the animals for Captain Koenigsdorfer at Louis

Ruhe's Wild Animal Farm and he worked for Bostock's animal acts some time after 1901, when Bostock had four separate touring shows, and subsequently for George W. Rawlins Trained Wild Animal Show, before eventually joining the Al G. Barnes Circus in 1909 (*fig. 11.7*). The adolescent Roth worked for Bostock's superintendent Herman Weedon, and Roth's first act involved playful young lions that he trained to mount pedestals in a pyramid formation. This provided a curtain-raiser to the main act, presented by so-named Captain Weedon. Then, transferred to Rochester, Roth provided a curtain-raiser to another Bostock show in which Captain Weiss worked with lions and tigers. This is where Roth developed an affinity for the lion Sultan, and also for the tiger Lady.[40]

The Weiss show included Mademoiselle Vivant, a middle-aged performer described as a "girl," who made toys of four heavily maned lions that looked ferocious but remained as docile as dogs."[41] In contrast to the enhanced social and masculine status accorded male counterparts by a military title, the promotion of Vivant denoted social subservience. An expectation of a young female may have contributed to an act's appeal and the application of the label *girl* to a mature female carried connotations of sexual availability while also suggesting someone who was not in full control. By the turn of the twentieth century, Bostock managed several experienced female trainers and in photographs these performers wear everyday clothing for costumes.[42] Female social roles were believed to reflect woman's innate nature (which precluded aggression), so feminized nomenclature and feminine costuming offset social resistance to the female trainer's usurpation of the masculine activity of taking risks with big wild animals. Vivant seemed to confirm feminine identity although she physi-

Tait

cally transgressed the limits of gender roles. Roth's description of the lions as being like "toys" and "dogs" is revealing. Wild-animal performers deemed to behave like toys and pet dogs became aligned with the domestic sphere and the female trainer, with sympathetic nurturing and mothering, so that feminine care made wild animals docile. Female social roles were removed from the public

sphere and, by implication, scientific progress. Interestingly though, an idea of femininity could still convey nervousness and fearfulness. Arguably then, a female trainer was accorded less prestige because her feminine identity evoked the possibility of an intuitive understanding of animals and how to calm them. A female performer was nominally closer to the domain of nature and thus animal identity. Accordingly, in the hierarchies of species and gender, triumphant human identity was the preserve of a hero.

The legendary Mabel Stark, taught by Roth and working with Roth-trained animals from 1911, would, however, mostly wear the protective, decoratively braided male costume that accompanied the big-cat act (*fig. 11.8*). Early in her career, she even

Fig. 11.8. Harry A. Atwell. Mabel Stark with the Ringling Bros. and Barnum & Bailey Circus at Chicago, 1922. Photograph. Circus World Museum ,CWi-46

Fig. 11.9. "Al. G. Barnes Wild Animal Circus: Miss Mabel Stark and Her Ferocious Giant Jungle Tigers," ca. 1930–35. Poster, printed by the Erie Lithograph Company, Erie, Pennsylvania. Collection of the John and Mable Ringling Museum of Art, Tibbals Collection, ht2001088

Fig. 11.10. Louis Roth. Photograph from Dave Robeson, *Louis Roth, Forty Years with Jungle Killers* (Caldwell, Idaho: Caxton Printers, 1941). Illinois State University's Special Collections, Milner Library

wore a female version of a safari military costume (*fig. 11.9*). A fascinating twist in gender identity arose once Stark and female trainers regularly appeared in these uniforms. If a female trainer was unavailable, a male substitute might have to cross-dress to fulfill promotional and audience expectations, while continuing to wear a militarized costume. A photograph of a cross-dressed Roth shows him in his costume but wearing a wig and makeup under a hat (*fig. 11.10*). Here the military-style costume signed masculinity as the performing body faked femininity, so that trainer identity was doubly gendered in the animal act.

The adolescent Roth advanced quickly as a professional trainer as he rejected the offer to return to Europe with the Bostock show and went to work with Rawlins for two years until the group disbanded, and to train some big cats that included the aforementioned Leo, who had been imported from Hagenbecks. Leo was trained to respond to a hand signal and voice commands and to wrestle. He would "rise to his hind feet, throw his front legs about his master, and wrestle in a realistic fashion, until Louis dropped to the ground and the lion stood over him."[43] This feat enacted a lion attack and the trainer's capacity to physically defeat a lion made the human appear superior.

After he joined the Barnes Circus, Roth became the pre-eminent trainer of his day. He worked there for the next two decades, building the circus up into one of the largest touring shows with animal acts. In the heyday of the five-ring Barnes Circus during the 1920s, with over 1,000 employees, Roth worked two acts and supervised seven other presenter/trainers working with big cats, elephants, and bears that he had trained.[44] He had as many as thirteen acts to supervise and he taught a number of well-known trainers.[45] Two of America's leading trainers, Stark and Beatty, first learned from Roth.[46] When Al G. Barnes sold the circus to John Ringling in 1931, Roth went to work for the film company Selig's Zoological Gardens. He subsequently trained animals for films and for Selig's live shows. As well as working with bears, Roth's major training feats included the wrestling lion, a wrestling tiger, three lions riding horses, a tiger riding an elephant, a leopard riding a zebra, a roaring lion on a horse, and a number of other mixed-species acts (*fig. 11.11*).[47] He also trained eight leopards for an act.[48]

It was the conditioning of an animal's physical movement through repetition and the suppression of self-willed behavior and instincts that was comparable to military discipline. The offstage care of the animal performers also required a regular rou-

▲　*Fig. 11.11.* Louis Roth with a bear cub, ca. 1928. Photograph. Circus World Museum, CWi-2345

tine, especially because the time and effort of training increased their value and this necessitated adequate care to ensure survival. Military motifs for animal acts confirmed that nature could be made to conform to human discipline and this was assumed to be scientific.

Safari Natures

While proclaiming scientific benefit, Roosevelt's safari adventure in the first decade of the twentieth century was indicative of expeditions to hunt wild animals in their habitat. Exotic animals exhibited in foreign places inspired excursions back to their geographical lands. Roosevelt led a scientific expedition to British East Africa in 1909–10 that collected 14,000 specimens of skeletons for the Smithsonian Institution (*fig. 11.12*).[49] Regardless of the educational purpose of natural history museums, their collections required the accumulation of a diverse range of specimens in a process that blurred the distinction between a scientific excursion and big game trophy hunt. Roosevelt was called a hunter-naturalist and explained that with his group of scientists, "I felt as if I had all the fun, I would kill the rhinoceros or whatever it was, and then they would go out and do the solid, hard work of preparing it."[50] This was the preparation for the transportation of a salted carcass. Roosevelt also wrote that "it is not a very hard thing to go off into the wilderness and kill an elephant, or a white rhino."[51] Presumably it was more difficult to capture and transport back the live specimens seen in the circus.

Unsurprisingly, the safari hunter identity appeared in trained wild big-cat acts to imply that the trainer was a hunter who had brought the animals back with him from a safari. Big game hunting "was predicted on heroic confrontation between hunter and prey."[52] Peter Taylor, from Birmingham, England, promoted himself in the American circus by about 1913 and claimed a background as a big game hunter in Africa and South America.[53] Taylor presented what is called a fighting or hurrah style of animal act, which involves the trainer appearing to be in confrontation with angry wild animals and he

Fig. 11.12. Warrington Dawson. Theodore Roosevelt on horseback, March 14, 1910. Photograph. Courtesy of the Library of Congress, Prints and Photographs Division

Fig. 11.13. "Sells Floto Circus: Peter Taylor and the Most Thrilling Death-Defying Animal Act in World," ca. 1928. Poster, printed by the Erie Lithograph Company, Erie, Pennsylvania. Collection of the John and Mable Ringling Museum of Art, Tibbals Collection, ht2000639

taught one to simulate an attack (*fig. 11.13*). A photograph of Taylor shows him dressed in a light-colored military jacket with brass buttons and a high neckline and wide jodhpurs narrowing at the knee to boots (*fig. 11.14*).[54] He carries a whip and gloves in an emulation of an English officer in colonial Africa; the costume often involved a pith helmet. While Roth seemed to wrestle Leo, Taylor appeared to adapt an older menagerie-cage escape trick. He presented a confrontational act that can be contrasted with the reception of Bonavita's 1901 controlled act so that spectators could not be blamed for believing that an animal was attacking Taylor. The costumed identity of a colonial safari hunter no doubt reinforced an impression that the animals had been brought directly from their habitat. In escaping from hostile animals, Taylor confirmed the prowess of the human species.

The idea that the animals had been taught to perform these attacks was not credible to onlookers and this style of act made famous by Clyde Beatty aroused opposition and became controversial with some accusations that it was cruel. Under scrutiny from a society for the humane treatment of animals, Taylor defended the performance by explaining that this hostility in performance was not indicative of how trainers treated their animals, and that they respected and understood the animal performers and did not need to mistreat them.[55] Instead they could communicate clearly and kindly and use good discipline, although this involved whip cracking. Beatty, who dominated twentieth-century big-cat acts through his live shows and films, started out as Taylor's assistant and took over Taylor's animal performers and safari costume when Taylor suddenly retired in 1925.[56] Beatty continued with the safari theme until the 1960s and used a military style for his attendants with "twelve armed men who stood outside the arena in military-looking uniforms and

PETER TAYLOR.

brightly polished steel helmets looked smart and soldierly."[57] Beatty made this safari confrontation with an underlying military motif into the most famous twentieth-century big-cat act (*fig. 11.15*).

A safari hunter identity emerged out of a military one to provide a direct connection between a trained animal act in the circus and animal hunting in remote geographical regions. Acts in which the animals were trained in feats of aggressive action further suggested that the animals were newly acquired from the wild. They conveyed ideas of the threat and danger from nature for humans and the trainer's escape confirmed the superiority of the

Fig. 11.14. Harry A. Atwell. Peter Taylor, ca. 1923. Photograph. Circus World Museum, CWi-2310

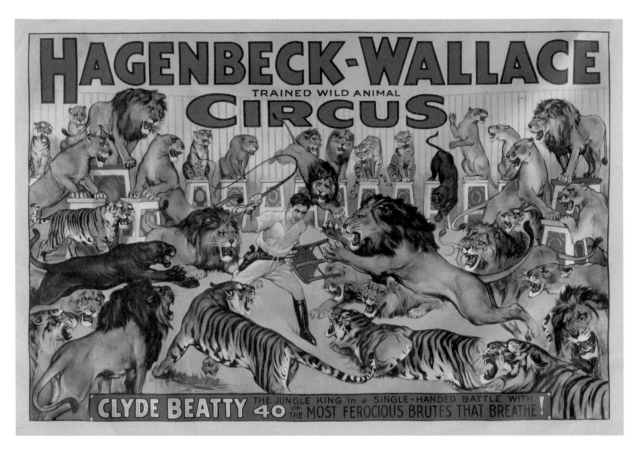

human species. While such an act accorded with social Darwinism, it eschewed scientific precepts.

The militarized trainer identity prevailed in performance in the first half of the twentieth century, a compounded nineteenth-century identity that continued regardless of whether training could be considered scientific. Circus identity illusions reflected older social values about nature. In the training of big cats, Bonavita and Roth set precedents that influenced twentieth-century animal performance in the circus and their quasi-military uniforms and safari suits continued to be worn by male and female trainers as standard costuming accompanying the modernist animal act. Trained animal acts developed in the context of late nineteenth-century beliefs that

animals were emblematic of nature's wildness and costumes suggest that these ideas remained acceptable for most of the twentieth century in confirmation of a wider modernist project of conquest and exploitation. Costumes contributed to ideas of human separateness from animals. The performance identity of the male trainer in animal acts contributed to cultural belief in the hierarchical dominance of the human species throughout modernism.

Fig. 11.15. "Hagenbeck-Wallace Trained Wild Animal Circus: Clyde Beatty the Jungle King in a Single-Handed Battle with 40 of the Most Ferocious Brutes that Breathe," ca. 1934. Poster, printed by the Erie Lithograph Company, Erie, Pennsylvania. Collection of the John and Mable Ringling Museum of Art, Tibbals Collection, ht2000830

1 Frank Bostock's acts were presented at the midway carnival at the Pan-American Exhibition. For descriptions of Bonavita's act, see Frank Bostock, *The Training of Wild Animals* (New York: Century Co., 1903), 37–40, 43–44, 78, 136, 198, 238; Joanne Carol Joys, *The Wild Animal Trainer in America* (Boulder, CO: Pruett Publishing, 1983), 30, 28–32. For a history of turn-of-the-twentieth-century American circus and cultural analysis, see Janet Davis, *The Circus Age* (Chapel Hill: University of North Carolina Press, 2002).

2 Bostock, *The Training of Wild Animals*, 218.

3 For a general discussion of nature, animals and modernity, see Adrian Franklin, *Animals and Modern Cultures: A Sociology of Human–Animal Relations in Modernity* (London: Sage, 1999).

4 See Peter Singer, *Animal Liberation,* 2nd ed. (London: Random House, 1995), 205–12; Keith Tester, *Animals and Society* (London: Routledge, 1991), 152.

5 This interpretation draws on contemporary commentaries, biographies, secondary sources, and photographs.

6 Also see Peta Tait, *Wild and Dangerous Performances: Animals, Emotions, Circus* (Basingstoke, England: Palgrave Macmillan, 2012). This book contains an extended analysis of acts by Clyde Beatty and Mabel Stark and other trainers.

7 Franklin, *Animals and Modern Cultures*, 34.

8 Joanne Entwistle, *The Fashioned Body* (Cambridge: Polity Press, 2000), 111.

9 See Veronica Kelly, *The Empire Actors: Stars of Australasian Costume Drama 1890s–1920s* (Sydney: Currency House, 2010), 10, for a discussion of the interconnections between performance and costume, and social fashion and cultural meaning.

10 Peta Tait, *Circus Bodies: Cultural Identity in Aerial Performance* (London: Routledge, 2005), 20–22.

11 Bostock, *The Training of Wild Animals*, 185. See Tait, *Circus Bodies*, 15, 23, for discussion of social Darwinism and the circus.

12 Theodore Roosevelt, "Wild Man and Wild Beast in Africa," *National Geographic* 22, no. 1 (Jan. 1911), 1; Iain McCalman, "Teddy Roosevelt's Trophy: History and Nostalgia," in *Memory, Monuments and Museums*, ed. Marilyn Lake (Melbourne: Melbourne University Press, 2006).

13 John Turner, *Victorian Arena: The Performers. A Dictionary of British Circus Biography. Volume Two* (Formby, England: Lingdales Press, 2000), 12. To date, it is unclear if Bonavita had a military background, and Bonavita's photographs show him with medals pinned to his jacket; see Bostock, *The Training of Wild Animals*.

14 Ibid., 217.

15 Ibid., 218.

16 Ibid., 220 quoted by Bostock.

17 Ibid., 220; A. H. Kober, *Circus Nights and Circus Days*, trans. by C. W. Sykes (London: Sampson Low, Marston, 1931): 125; Davis, *Circus Age*, 160, quoting Cleveland Moffett about Bonavita's "steady nerve" during an attack in 1900.

18 Dave Robeson, *Louis Roth, Forty Years with Jungle Killers* (Caldwell, ID: Caxton Printers, 1941), 240.

19 Michel Foucault, *Discipline and Punish*, trans. Alan Sheridan (New York: Vintage Books, 1979), 135.

20 Ibid., 138.

21 Jennifer Craik, *Uniforms Exposed: From Conformity to Transgression* (Oxford: Berg, 2005).

22 Ibid., 34.

23 Ibid., 21–22.

24 Ibid., 41, citing Cohn.

25 For examples of circus-band uniforms on posters from the mid-nineteenth century, see Peter Verney, *Here Comes the Circus* (London: Paddington Press, 1978), 31, 67, 69.

26 For a history of Astley's, see A. H. Saxon, *Enter Foot and Horse* (New Haven: Yale University Press, 1968), 10, 18.

27 Joys, *The Wild Animal Trainer in America*, 296–97, provides a timeline "Wild Animal Acts in America."

28 Carl Hagenbeck, *Beasts and Men*, trans. and abridged by Hugh S. R. Elliot, and A. G. Thacker (New York: Longmans, Green, and Company, 1909); Nigel Rothfels, *Savages and Beasts: The Birth of the Zoo* (Baltimore: The Johns Hopkins University, 2002).

29 Harriet Ritvo, *The Animal Estate. The English and Other Creatures in The Victorian Age* (Cambridge: Harvard University Press, 1987).

30 Linda Kalof, *Looking at Animals in Human History* (London: Reaktion Books, 2007), 153.

31 Ellen Velvin, *Behind the Scenes with Wild Animals* (New York: Moffat, Yard and Co., 1906), 50–2.

32 Robeson, *Louis Roth, Forty Years with Jungle Killers*, 164. For the list of Bonavita's films, see http://www.imdb.com/name/nm0093844/.

33 Hugues Le Roux, *Acrobats and Mountebanks*, illus. Jules Garnier and trans. A. P. Morton (London: Chapman and Hall, 1890), 136. For most of the twentieth century, trainer costumes included quasi-military outfits and tropical safari suits with knee-high boots and also equestrian and sporting outfits.

34 Robeson, *Louis Roth, Forty Years with Jungle Killers*, 74.

35 Ibid., 199–200.

36 Ibid., 56.

37 Ibid., 75.

38 Ibid., 92.

39 Ibid., 61–62.

40 Ibid., 68.

41 Ibid., 59.

42 Bostock, *The Training of Wild Animals*.

43 Robeson, *Louis Roth, Forty Years with Jungle Killers*, 91.

44 Ibid., 128.

45 Ibid., 199.

46 See Joys, *The Wild Animal Trainer in America*, 73–77; Tait, *Wild and Dangerous Performances* (forthcoming).

47 Robeson, *Louis Roth, Forty Years with Jungle Killers*, 140–41.

48 Ibid., 189.

49 Roosevelt, "Wild Man and Wild Beast in Africa," 4.

50 Ibid., 3.

51 Ibid., 4–5.

52 Kalof, *Looking at Animals in Human History*, 151.

53 Joys, *The Wild Animal Trainer in America*, 92–93.

54 Ibid., 93.

55 Peter Taylor, "Training Wild Animals for Circus and Stage Not Cruel," *Billboard*, June 30, 1925, 62.

56 Joys, *The Wild Animal Trainer in America*, 100–101. Taylor either suffered a head injury or a phobic response or left for other reasons.

57 Clyde Beatty with Edward Anthony, *Facing the Big Cats* (London: Heinemann, 1965), 42.

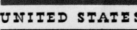

⑫

THE AMERICANIZATION OF THE CIRCUS CLOWN

RODNEY HUEY

The origins of the modern American circus clown are neither modern nor American. Clowns and clowning of one sort or another are ancient and widespread human cultural activities. Historians of Western cultural traditions trace rudimentary clown performances at least as far back as the seventh century B.C. Evidence of various manifestations of clowning have been found in most cultures and eras ever since. During the fourth century B.C., for example, comedic Phylax plays were commonplace in Greek colonies in Italy; scenes from those plays are recorded on red-figure ceramics of the period. In the later Middle Ages, mountebanks and charlatans entertained with traveling troubadours throughout Europe while carnival fools and court jesters ridiculed the seats of highest power. Clownish characters fit comfortably into both secular *sotties* and religious mystery plays of the fifteenth and sixteenth centuries, while Shakespearian wise fools were some of literature's most illustrious clowns ever brought to the stage. The prevailing historical narrative credits the half-masked, costumed characters of Italy's *commedia dell'arte* with paving the way for the fully developed clown personae that emerged in nineteenth-century England and France.[1]

Anthropology and folklore studies expand the historical record, revealing that clowning is a ubiquitous phenomenon that has appeared in all parts of the world from the distant past to the present. It may, indeed, be a human universal. While names, costumes, and contexts for clowning vary from one society to the next, the general function of clowns, broadly understood, appears to be shared around the globe. In her cross-cultural study of clowns' performed functions, Lucille Hoerr Charles found several prevailing tendencies. For one, "a clown is concerned always with something which is not quite proper; with something embarrassing, astonishing, shocking." For another, clowns typically employ exag-

◀ *Detail of fig. 12.14.* Edward Klauck Todhunter, designer; C. A. Brooks, engraver. United States Postal Service circus stamp commemorating the centennial of the birth of John Ringling, 1966. Scott #1309. Collection of Matthew Wittmann

Mr. GRIMALDI, as *CLOWN*

in the Popular Pantomine of *HARLEQUIN & ASMODEUS*, now Performing at the Theatre Royal Covent Garden, Setting to with a Grotesque
Figure which he makes up of a series of Vegetables, Fruit &c. and which becoming Animated beats him off the Stage.

geration and rely on humor for effect—but humor is no simple matter. Charles quotes Ralph Piddlington's conclusion that "the ludicrous is always anti-social and serves as compensation for conscious attitudes that are socially correct." Finally, Charles observes that representations of "earthiness, poverty, renegade irresponsibility, irreverence and license of all sorts" are constants in clowning.[2]

If clowns of one variety or another have been found in most societies over the centuries, then clowning has a history. On the other hand, the near-universal appearance of this type of cultural performer also suggests that clowning, at least sometimes, might be less a learned role than a sociocultural imperative. In other words, the question of why there are clowns at all may be a variation on the old conundrum of nature versus culture. Yes, clowns in any society arguably have antecedents. But clowns also continually seem to be created anew, taking forms not necessarily patterned on the past.

One constant of clowns, however, is their cultural specificity. The many different names given to clownlike performers in Western Europe alone should be enough to indicate that the content of clowning is linked to its framing culture and evolves in concert with that culture. And that brings us back to our original question about the origins of circus

clowning in America. We might also wonder about what particular forms of clowning became prominent during the great age of the American circus and in the years of slow decline that followed. In theory at least, there should be something identifiably American about American circus clowning.

The story, of course, is muddled by the insistent internationality of the circus, a trait intensified once American circuses begin to travel around the globe. And that means that the American clown story cannot be narrowly national. British and continental antecedents are arguably relevant. Actor Joseph Grimaldi (1778–1837) introduced Clown as a new stage figure in London's Covent Garden in 1800. Grimaldi's Clown was grotesquely dressed and sported exaggerated makeup with large red triangles on both cheeks, bushy eyebrows, puffy trousers, and a cockspur wig (*fig. 12.1*). With his wild dances, frenzied gyrations, and persistent banter with the audience, Clown struck at least one observer as "half-rascal, half-fool … [a] criminal and innocent at once, an ancient of days and a guttersnipe."[3] Sometimes described as the "father of modern clowning," Grimaldi's look, demeanor, and behavior created the mold for what was later referred to as the "auguste" style of clowning, characterized by discordant costuming, exaggerated makeup, and haphazard actions reminiscent of a country bumpkin or social misfit. In performances, the auguste clown is often the butt of the joke who eventually wins through innocence, simple reasoning, and purity of heart. The stereotypical clown of circuses, advertisements, and posters is usually an auguste clown, recognizable by natural flesh tones, oversized eyes and mouth, and red bulbous nose.

Across the English Channel, French actor Jean-Gaspard Deburau (1776–1846) premiered Pierrot in 1825, a French adaptation of the *commedia*

Fig. 12.1. R. Norman. *Mr. Grimaldi as Clown*, 1811. Print on wove paper, etching with aquatint, colored; published by R. Ackermann, London. The Lewis Walpole Library, Yale University, 811.02.08.01+

dell'arte's Pedrolino, as a sophisticated clown dressed in a white costume with oversized sleeves, ruffed collar, and all-white facial makeup. In contrast to Grimaldi's Clown, Pierrot was a hopeless romantic who used wit, sarcasm, and subtle gestures as his comical narrative.[4] Pierrot became the prototype for the sophisticated whiteface clown; today we see whiteface clowns as street mimes or as contemporary versions of the sophisticated, well-mannered circus clown, such as Europe's Pipo.

A third type of clown, developed somewhat later, is the "character" clown, who incorporates various elements of the auguste or the whiteface, but whose overall persona is a caricature of a specific cultural role, such as policeman, doctor, athlete, usher, or even grumpy senior citizen. Big Apple Circus's Barry "Grandma" Lubin, with minimal auguste facial features, was a contemporary character clown who spoofs a feisty grandmother who always gets her way (*fig. 12.2*). One of the more popular character clowns in the United States is the "tramp" clown—a sympathetic representation of the down-on-his-luck or out-of-work drifter. With tattered clothes, unshaven makeup, and a downturned mouth, the tramp clown was popularized from the early 1930s through midcentury by circus clowns Otto Griebling and Emmett Kelly. Clowning types are determined by facial makeup, costuming, and behavior. While most contemporary clowns fall into one of these three dominant types, many young, creative clowns mix and mingle various elements to produce hybrids adaptable to today's diversified audiences.

Although both clowns and circuses can be traced to antiquity, the two have only been systematically paired since the late eighteenth century. The first modern-era circus was born out of former British cavalryman Philip Astley's (1742–1814)

equestrian exhibition on the outskirts of London in 1768. Originally a trick-riding show in a forty-two-foot circular riding ring, Astley later added strongman feats, acrobats, human-pyramid building, and a comical rope-dancer named Fortunelly as interludes between riding displays. Thus, Astley brought together the three essential elements that have since defined the circus within a ring—performing animals, acrobatic feats, and clowning. Astley expanded the clown's role to include a comedy riding routine (emulated throughout the industry for decades afterwards) and promoted the clown from rope-dancer and comedy rider to verbal sparring partner with the equestrian director. The latter evolved into the position known as ringmaster, costumed with top hat, red tailcoat, jodhpurs, and high-topped boots. Astley's innovations provided a new performance format for the clown, which would play a prominent role for the next one hundred years.[5]

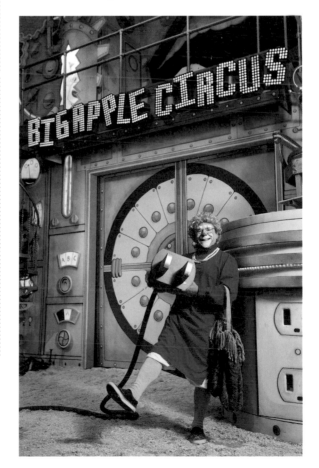

Fig. 12.2. Maike Schulz. Barry Lubin as Grandma in the Big Apple Circus, 2011. Photograph. Big Apple Circus

Like many other cultural products of the era, the English circus was imported to the United States, where it swiftly took root. On April 3, 1793, a Scot named John Bill Ricketts (1760–ca. 1800) gave America's first circus performance in Philadelphia. An adaptation of Astley's show, Ricketts presented an equestrian display accompanied by acrobatic feats and a clown named McDonald. Ricketts's circus apparently enjoyed considerable success; George Washington visited the show during its first month and sold his famed white steed, Jack, to Ricketts.[6] McDonald was later replaced by a riding comedy duo, evidence of the continuing centrality of equestrian displays and clowning to the early circus. In 1795 Ricketts hired actor John Durang (1768–1822), purportedly America's first native-born clown, who honed his riding skills to perform comedy acts on horseback. Durang also performed with Ricketts in theatrical skits, such as playing Pantaloon to Ricketts's Harlequin in the "Harlequin in Philadelphia," evidence of the long shadow of the *commedia dell'arte*.[7]

The introduction of the tent gave circus performances a new degree of control and predictability. Not only did the tent mean that the show would go on whether rain or shine, it also meant there was no guessing about the size or configuration of the next venue. It would be always the same—until the circus acquired a new tent. At first the touring tent was relatively small, at least compared to what it would later become, and that modest scale enabled certain types of performance. Singing clowns, for example, were popular circus features from the 1830s on and they began to receive the type of top billing that had usually been reserved for equestrians (*fig. 12.3*). Some of the better singing clowns included Joe Pentland (*fig. 12.4*), "an accomplished ventriloquist, balancer, comic singer, and performer of legerde-

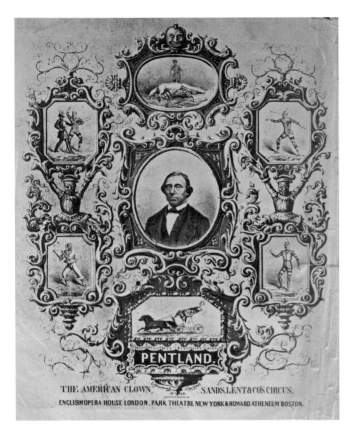

main;"[8] Irishman Johnny Patterson, who also sangmain;"[8] Irishman Johnny Patterson, who also sang on Tony Pastor's stage in New York City;[9] Thomas Barry, the "Hibernian Jester;"[10] and Peter Conklin, described by one historian as "one of the greatest singing clowns that the world of sawdust and spangles has ever produced."[11] In addition to their wages, singing clowns earned money selling songbooks, or "songsters," after each performance (*fig. 12.5*). For the most successful, the additional revenues sometimes exceeded their salaries. Circus owners soon recognized the money-making potential of songsters and began to take their cut by selling "songster privileges" to singing clowns.[12] In his memoirs, Conklin boasted about employing a shill to pose as a wounded Civil War soldier to gain patrons' sympathy, and through this gimmick purportedly sold 100,000 songsters in one season.[13]

That singing constituted a prominent part of clown performance in nineteenth-century America suggests that clowning was less susceptible to the internationalism that flavored other aspects of the circus. To be successful, singers sang in English, whereas language was largely irrelevant to equestrian or acrobatic presentations. Clowning that depended on song or speech was less mobile than other classes of performance. Clowns, singing or otherwise, also differed from most of their contemporaries in the theater. Although there were some exceptions, most stage actors were required to be versatile in order to remain financially solvent; the ability to play many different roles is often considered the hallmark of a distinguished actor or actress. Clowns, on the other hand, typically invented a single character that they re-inhabited at every performance, often throughout an entire career. Over time, that character evolved as its actor honed new skills and new routines. The critical point is that the enactor and the character became inseparable. In the most notable instances, a fully developed clown persona evolved into a life-long role that blurred the distinction between character and cultural figure. Put another way, over time there might be several score Hamlets or Romeos, but

▲ *Fig. 12.4.* "Pentland, The American Clown: Sands, Lent & Co.'s Circus," 1848. Lithograph, printed by E. Brown Jr., New York. Collection of the John and Mable Ringling Museum of Art, Tibbals Collection, ht2001239

▲ *Fig. 12.5.* "Pete Conklin, The Great Clown," 1868. Songster. Inquirer Print, Lancaster, Pennsylvania. John Hay Library, Brown University Library

most popular blackface performer of his time and creator of the black caricature Jim Crow. The newly christened Rice performed in his early years with a number of blackface minstrels, among them Dan Emmett, alleged composer of "Dixie." Rice's greatest impact came as a speaking clown in the circus. He would typically "exchange quips with the crowd and ringmaster, spout doggerel, dance jigs and offer a variety of songs."[15] Outfitted in his red, white, and blue costume, tall stovepipe hat, and signature goatee, Rice was a "talking clown, quipping spontaneously, booming out Shakespeare, singing about bloomers (and) feuding with Horace Greeley."[16] Some have called him "democracy's first jester"[17] and "the closest thing America has had to an embodiment of Uncle Sam."[18]

All of that noted, however, it is not at all clear that audiences familiar with more recent clowns would identify Rice as an example of the genre. For one thing, he wore no makeup. For another, much of his act required an audience able to hear him. He spoke, orated, sang, mocked, and mimicked, and all of it was audible. Furthermore, his performance often included political content and satire, now more typically associated with stand-up (and a few sit-down) comedians. Rice's embodiment of the clown was succeeded by another and different variant, as changes in the circus forced redefinition of the nature and activities of the clown. Not all were welcome.

Change in the circus industry intensified toward the end of the nineteenth century. A handful of aggressive entrepreneurs transformed the circus from a loose collection of traveling troupes into tightly managed business units. Most notable among them—or at least the most famous today—was Phineas T. Barnum, the "father of ballyhoo," who earned a reputation as America's greatest showman well before his entry into the circus business in 1871.

of a particular clown character only one, always performed and embodied by the same person.

A British chronicler of clowning noted that "America produced some interesting and completely new clown types which owed little to European tradition."[14] One who might have fit that description was Dan Rice (1823–1900), a versatile performer of multiple talents and careers (*fig. 12.6*). Rice is so little known today that biographer David Carlyon called him "the most famous person you never heard of," but he enjoyed exceptional prominence in the nineteenth century. Rice was a quick-witted political satirist who often spoke in verse and responded to audience questions in a colloquial-language parody of Shakespeare. Born Dan McLaren, Rice adopted his stage name from white minstrel Thomas D. Rice (1808–1860), a New Yorker who became the

Fig. 12.6. Dan Rice, ca. 1860. Lithograph. Harvard Theatre Collection, Houghton Library, Harvard University

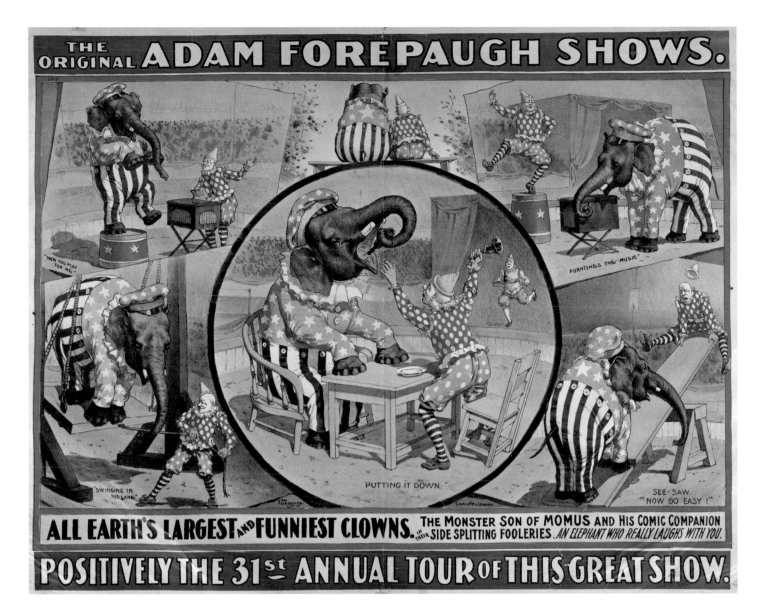

The size and efficiency of Barnum's operation reflected the surely increasing prominence of the business mentality within the industry and the subordination of all parts to the smooth and profitable working of the whole. Fierce competition in the 1870s and 1880s among the largest shows spawned ongoing innovation. The circus was put on rails, new marketing techniques were introduced and refined, and the performance space itself was radically altered. In 1873, Barnum added a second ring in his circus, followed by a third ring in 1881, a move that vastly increased seating capacity. These and other refine-ments ushered what is known as the golden age of the circus, roughly a four-decade period beginning in the early 1880s and lasting up until about 1920.[19]

The shift from one ring to three had a significant impact on the performance of the clown. Because the expanded performance space severely diminished the intimacy between performer and audience, clowns were increasingly forced to rely on visual gags, spelling the end of the singing and talking clown (*fig. 12.7*). No longer could Dan Rice or any of his imitators and emulators speak from the circus ring and be heard in the last row of the bleach-

Fig. 12.7. "The Original Adam Forepaugh Shows: All Earth's Largest and Funniest Clowns," 1894. Poster, printed by the Strobridge Lithographing Company, Cincinnati. Collection of the John and Mable Ringling Museum of Art, Tibbals Collection, ht2000428

ers. Assessing the changed landscape, a pair of recent commentators argued that the three-ring railroad circus introduced a "whole new style of uniquely American clowning based on flamboyant costumes, loud noises, oversized props, and aggressively violent routines."[20] Whatever elements of verbal wit or cultural commentary clowns had once offered were effectively banished from the circus. Put otherwise, yet another class of American artisan had been deskilled and demoted in the interests of corporate profit and was poised to become downwardly mobile.

In a concurrent development, shortly after Ringling Bros. Circus purchased the Barnum & Bailey Circus in 1907, co-owner Al Ringling issued an edict that "there would be no principal clown" in the show other than himself.[21] Ringling might have reacted to the popularity and overhead expense of Frank "Slivers" Oakley (1871–1916), a clown as well known at the turn of the century as Charlie Chaplin would become two decades later (*fig. 12.8*). Oakley

is reported to have earned up to 750 dollars a week working for Barnum & Bailey, an impressive sum when compared to the 35 dollars per week earned by other members of clown alley.

An enormously talented performer, Oakley's sole routine required the entire hippodrome track, which he took over to play a one-man game of baseball in which he played all nine positions, plus the umpire. One observer claimed that Oakley's act "stopped the show" and that his argument with the umpire "caused cases of audience hysteria which required medical attention."[22] It is highly doubtful that doctors were actually called in to quell uncontrollable fits of laughter, but Oakley was an obvious hit with his all-American baseball routine. He left Barnum & Bailey in 1907 and took his act to England but quickly discovered the limits of cultural exportation. British audiences knew little about baseball and cared even less; cricket was their sport. Oakley unsuccessfully attempted to play his one-man game on the vaudeville stage before asking for his old job back at the circus. Otto Ringling agreed to hire him back but only as a "walk-around" clown at 50 dollars per week.

▲ Fig. 12.8. Frederick Whitman Glasier. Frank "Slivers" Oakley on horse, ca. 1903. Photograph. Collection of the John and Mable Ringling Museum of Art, Glasier Glass Plate Negative Collection, 1132

▲ Fig. 12.9. "Ringling Bros. and Barnum & Bailey Combined Shows, The Children's Favorite Clown," 1917. Poster, printed by the Strobridge Lithographing Company, Cincinnati. Billy Rose Theatre Division, The New York Public Library for the Performing Arts, Astor, Lenox and Tilden Foundations

Despondent over what he considered Ringling's insulting offer, Oakley later committed suicide.[23]

Then as now, corporations liked to present a positive image of themselves to the public and clowns served as ambassadors for the circus. George Hartzell, a handsomely costumed whiteface clown who performed with Ringling Bros. Circus and later the combined Ringling Bros. and Barnum & Bailey Circus was a good example. Hartzell was aggressively promoted as the "Millionaire Clown" because, according to press reports, he and his seamstress wife "earned good salaries, saved their money, and invested it wisely."[24] One newspaper report pointed to his "extensive real estate holdings" as proof of his financial well-being, claiming that his considerable wealth allowed him to assemble "an exquisite and costly wardrobe which he uses."[25] Not surprisingly Hartzell became a marketing vehicle for the show and an early instance of clown as mascot.

During the 1917 season, a likeness of him with children gathered around appeared on a poster bearing the caption "The Children's Favorite Clown" and press accounts frequently noted that his "specialty is devoted to making children laugh" (*fig. 12.9*).[26] The nature of Hartzell's performance in the ring is not entirely clear; he may have been most useful as symbol—safe, docile, unthreatening. Whatever of clowns' performances might once have been unpredictable and aimed at adults only had disappeared. This clown, at least, seems to have been complicit in the project of sanitizing, trivializing, and infantilizing the role of a once potentially subversive cultural actor.

With few exceptions, by about 1920 circus clowns had been effectively transferred from the spotlight to the footlights to become what one observer described as "colorful brigades of loony pranksters and suave misfits that cluttered hippodrome tracks with infectious merriment."[27] Perhaps that is accurate but it could also be described as a process that pushed formerly prominent players downward into a clown proletariat of sorts (*fig. 12.10*). The relegation to the hippodrome track enforced the image of the clown as a common laborer

▲ *Fig. 12.10*. Edward J. Kelty. Ringling Bros. and Barnum & Bailey (Combined) Circus. April, 1924. Photograph. Collection of the John and Mable Ringling Museum of Art, Tibbals Collection, ht0004827

who put in his hours and collected a paycheck. Clown routines took note of that new image, reflecting everyday deeds and frustrations of working men and women. Among standard group routines were a firehouse gag in which fireman funsters rescue a baby from a burning house; several police gags reminiscent of the Keystone Kops, in which the police always, remarkably enough, manage to get their man; and a variety of parodies of military life. One might say that the clown figure had become the unheralded, interchangeable, and standardized cog in the larger circus machine that kept the show running smoothly for the stars and profitably for the owners. Their clowning on the hippodrome track became a metaphor for the factory workers who struggled to make

ends meet but who seldom reaped the fruits of their labors. Charlie Chaplin had captured the inhumanity of the assembly line in his 1936 film *Modern Times*; something of the same Depression-era perspective appeared in clown routines as well. But mention of the Keystone Kops and Chaplin suggests that much of the traditional clown function was migrating to the emerging and dynamic medium of the motion picture. The circus was being displaced as a leading entertainment, its various components either ossified or increasingly derivative of innovations generated in other industries.

P. T. Barnum is purported to have said that clowns are the pegs on which to hang a circus. The adage was never more applicable than to the

Fig 12.11. "Ringling Bros. and Barnum & Bailey: 100 Clowns," ca. 1928. Poster, printed by the Erie Lithograph Company, Erie, Pennsylvania. Collection of the John and Mable Ringling Museum of Art, Tibbals Collection, ht2001520

twentieth-century ensemble clowns who were "being used only to fill stage waits while cages are being set, props arranged, or nets spread for more glamorous numbers" or as "fill-in supers in the lavish production displays" (*fig. 12.11*).[28] Within this fairly dismal scenario, however, a handful of individual performing clowns were able to rise above the hordes through their talent, appealing routines, and imaginative gags. They were self-taught, having developed their clowning skills from close observation of other clowns, adopting and adapting to craft their own personas, routines, and individual clowning styles. They fashioned costumes, props, and routines from the substance of everyday life and, by the middle of the 1950s, even as the circus declined around them, several had attained considerable recognition. It was in this era that today's image of the typical American clown was formulated and the clown became the instantly recognizable symbol of the circus.

Felix Adler (1898–1960) became a consummate performer, beginning his career with Ringling Bros. in 1914. His distinctive pear-shaped body (created with the aid of inflated beach balls to expand his derriere) and fancy costume were complemented by a miniature hat and tiny umbrella. Adler also embedded the appropriate birthstone for each month on the tip of his putty nose, and trained young piglets to drink milk from an oversized baby bottle. When each piglet inevitably grew too big for the gag, Adler traded it to a farmer for a new piglet (*fig. 12.12*).

It has been estimated that Adler trained more than 350 piglets during his clowning career. A whiteface clown, Adler was billed as "King of the Clowns" and also as "White House Clown," in recognition of his performances before three U.S. presidents. Adler may also have been the first circus clown to appear on television.[29]

Several performing clowns had European origins but tended to downplay their foreign backgrounds for American audiences. Johann Jacob Ludwig (1903–1992) anglicized his name to Lou Jacobs when he emigrated from Germany in 1923. He worked as a contortionist and acrobat before landing a clowning spot with Ringling Bros. and Barnum & Bailey in 1925, a job he held for more than half a century (*fig. 12.13*). Jacobs developed a number of clown gags that became classics.[30] One was a hunting routine that he performed with a pet Chihuahua; another involved zipping around the hippodrome track on self-propelled water skis. He created a motorized bathtub that, in the words of one chronicler, "managed to sum up the old American spirit of invention and innovation that put a country on wheels and gave it the best plumbing in the world."[31]

Jacobs's signature prop was his two-by-three-foot miniaturized car, into which he managed to fold his six-foot frame. When Jacobs prematurely intro-

Fig. 12.12. Felix Adler with pig, late 1930s–early 1940s. Photograph. Circus World Museum, CWi-2295

Fig. 12.13. Sverre O. Braathen. Lou Jacobs, August 12, 1941. Photograph, Kodachrome. Illinois State University's Special Collections, Milner Library, BSP0022

duced his midget car gag in 1946, the vehicle stalled, forcing him to get out and push it around the track. The audience, thinking that the breakdown was part of the act, laughed at the frustrated clown pushing the car. And so, until he was able to perfect the motorized prop, he faked the breakdown and never failed to get a laugh.[32] In 1952 Jacobs mentored Hollywood actor Jimmy Stewart for his role as Buttons the Clown in Cecile B. DeMille's Academy Award–winning film *The Greatest Show on Earth*, and even made a cameo appearance in the film himself. Jacobs's facial makeup was originally inspired by that of famed European clown Albert Fratellini; Jacobs later added a cone-head prop to create what many consider the ultimate American expression of the auguste clown tradition.

Jacobs's image appeared on posters and in countless advertisements but his greatest exposure came when it was printed on a five-cent U.S. postage stamp in 1966 (*fig. 12.14*). Juxtaposing a slightly schematized depiction of Jacobs's face and the word "circus," the stamp formalized the equation clown = circus. Jacobs continued to perform with Ringling until he retired in 1987 at the age of eighty-four.

Another native of Germany, Otto Griebling (1896–1972) immigrated to the United States as a bareback rider but after a nasty fall ended his riding career in 1930, he turned to clowning. Griebling performed as a tramp clown, working with Hagenbeck-Wallace, Clyde Beatty and Cole Brothers, and finally Ringling Bros. and Barnum & Bailey.[33] Griebling perfected the tramp role, signaled by "ragged clothes stubby beard, flattened hat and downcast expression" and persistence in the face of repeated rejection

(*fig. 12.15*).[34] He was known for running gags that evolved throughout an evening's performance: watering a small plant that grew into a gigantic tree by the end of the show; attempting to deliver a block of ice that melted before he could find the recipient; and, in a parody of a mailman, trying to hand off the same parcel year after year without ever locating the correct addressee. Griebling's clowning presence was so powerful that, in contrast to the experience of some of his predecessors, he was given free rein to perform solo anywhere on the circus floor or in the seats, which at times meant injecting himself into another artist's display. Griebling's style has been described as neither straight comedy nor pathos but a "blending of the two so that the line between them could not be discerned."[35] His distinctive style of clowning has never been successfully replicated by any other clown.

Emmett Kelly (1899–1979) performed with Griebling for Clyde Beatty and Cole Brothers before joining Ringling Bros. and Barnum & Bailey in 1942, then went on to become one of the most recognizable circus clowns in American history. When he first began clowning in 1924 he performed as a whiteface clown who experimented with a tramp character but was told that he looked too "dirty and unkempt" for whiteface. Instead of cleaning up his costume, he simply changed his facial makeup to match his tattered attire, adding an unshaven look and downturned mouth (*fig. 12.16*). And thus Weary Willie was born.[36] Kelly's signature routine was attempting to sweep a pool of light into his hat—a simple yet classic routine easily adaptable to any setting. He was a standout in the Ringling show until 1956, when he left to become mascot for the Brooklyn Dodgers. He later enjoyed a lucrative film and television career. Kelly continued to perform as Weary Willie until he died in 1979 at the age of eighty.

Fig. 12.14. Edward Klauck Todhunter, designer; C. A. Brooks, engraver. United States Postal Service circus stamp commemorating the centennial of the birth of John Ringling, 1966. Scott #1309. Collection of Matthew Wittmann

What is worth pondering is that two of America's most famous twentieth-century clowns made their marks performing tramp roles. Although both refined their characters during the Great Depression, their careers spanned the period of economic expansion that lasted from the end of World War II until about 1980. During those years the majority of Americans were financially better off than before or since. Most experienced a continually rising standard of living and expected their children to do even better than they had. Whether tramp clowns were reminders of the bad old days, cautionary exemplars, modern manifestations of the universal clown as impoverished outsider, or something else altogether is not clear. But it does seem telling that clowns in the richest nation on earth in a period of relative economic well-being remained popular portraying society's losers.[37]

In addition to high-visibility figures like Adler, Jacobs, Griebling, and Kelly, there were a number of other, lesser-known clowns who left their mark on the industry. Bobby Kaye (1908–1983) began his clowning career in 1923, working with several circuses before joining the Ringling show. There he later served as an advance clown after leaving clown alley. Master prop builder Mark Anthony (1915–1990) performed as a tramp clown; his makeup "featured a bald pate surrounded by red stringy hair and a bulbous nose topped with a fly."[38] Frankie Saluto (1906–1982) was a dwarf clown who made a career as a miniature impression of Charlie Chaplin.[39] Paul "Prince" Albert (1914–1987), also a dwarf clown, devoted himself to parodying royalty during his fifty years of working for Ringling. Duane "Uncle Soapy" Thorpe (1924–1995) clowned with Ringling for over forty years and was the last of the self-actuated veteran clowns to perform with The Greatest Show on Earth before retiring at the end of the 1990 season.

On July 16, 1956, Ringling Bros. and Barnum & Bailey folded its big top for the last time, effectively announcing the death of the American tented circus. Earlier that year, several smaller circuses had been forced to close, falling victim to the suburbanization that was pushing circus grounds farther away from urban centers and to the new medium of television that was bringing entertainment directly into American homes. But the eulogy proved premature. Rock and roll promoter Irvin Feld stepped in to take over the booking and marketing of The Greatest Show on Earth. The mammoth show was drastically downsized by eliminating the 2,000-man tent crew, reducing the number of acts, booking the circus into the modern sports arenas that were springing up around the country, and temporarily transporting the show by truck rather than rail. A leaner, more efficient circus was back in business for the start of the 1957 season.

Feld promoted and marketed Ringling Bros. and Barnum & Bailey for a decade before he and two partners purchased it on November 19, 1967, mark-

▲ *Fig. 12.15.* Otto Griebling, 1961. Photograph. Circus World Museum, CWi-2296-1

Huey

Thorpe joined other veteran and retired clowns as instructors. At the end of the first session, Clown College graduated twenty-eight novice clowns, half of them joining one unit and the other half assigned to the new second show. Feld also split up the veteran clowns between the two shows, thus guaranteeing that rookie clowns could continue to get on-the-job training under the tutelage of these seasoned masters. In thirty consecutive annual sessions, Clown College graduated almost 1,300 male and female fledgling clowns, created an institution that could hope to guarantee that the art of clowning would continue to be passed on to future generations, and provided a springboard for clowning to flourish in a variety of formats and performance art forms.[41]

Today, a new generation of performing clowns entertains millions of children and adults not only in circuses, but also theme parks, cruise ships, Las Vegas showrooms, television programs, and movies. Although only a handful of contemporary clowns had the privilege of studying under the veteran clowns, each is indebted to the lineage of those self-taught masters who imported the idea of circus clowning from Europe and transformed it into an American popular culture icon.

The archetypical American clown today, in whatever character, style or format, represents the masses, not the classes. Each stands shoulder-to-shoulder with ordinary people to rock the boat, question the accepted, flaunt human foibles, and defy common sense to assure us that when all bets are down, the little guy still has a fighting chance to win.

ing the first time that the legendary circus was owned by anyone other than a Ringling, Barnum, or Bailey. Feld's first action was to purchase the German Circus Williams to gain the talents of the young animal trainer Gunther Gebel for the 1969 season. Using Gebel as the centerpiece, Feld then built a second traveling unit equal in size and scope to the existing show. However, since European circuses still relied on only two or three clown performers rather than the clowning ensembles that had become typical of American circuses, Feld needed clowns; and he needed them quickly.

As owner of The Greatest Show on Earth, Feld already employed a majority of the performing clowns in the United States. Most of them were at least sixty years old. He is purported to have quipped: "I know they can fall down, but can they get up again?" Feld promptly founded Clown College in 1968 as a training facility for novice clowns and was able to persuade the best of the veteran clowns to teach at his "school for fools," a move designed to preserve and perpetuate the aging art of American circus clowning.[40] Lou Jacobs, Otto Griebling, and Duane

Fig. 12.16. Sverre O. Braathen. Emmett Kelly and Angela Reynolds, September 9, 1944. Photograph, Kodachrome. Illinois State University's Special Collections, Milner Library, BSP0177

1 A brief historical overview of clowns before the emergence of the American circus appears in John H. Towsen, *Clowns* (New York: Hawthorn Books, 1976), 3–82.

2 Lucile Hoerr Charles, "The Clown's Function," *Journal of American Folklore* 58, no. 227 (Jan.–March 1945), 25–34.

3 Richard Findlater, *Grimaldi: King of Clowns* (London: MacGibbon & Kee, 1955), 10.

4 Towsen, *Clowns*, esp. 79–82.

5 Ibid., 85–89.

6 John Culhane, *The American Circus: An Illustrated History* (New York: Henry Holt and Co., 1990), 1.

7 *The Constitutional Diary and Philadelphia Evening Advertiser*, Dec. 12, 1799, 2.

8 Robert J. Loeffler, "Two Clowns of Yesterday," *Bandwagon* 18, no. 5 (Sept.–Oct. 1974), 20.

9 Ibid., 19.

10 Robert J. Loeffler, "Thomas Barry Hibernian Jester," *Bandwagon* 51, no. 4 (July–Aug. 2007), 33.

11 Robert J. Loeffler, "Biographies of Some of the Early Singing Clowns," *Bandwagon* 13, no. 5 (Sept.–Oct. 1969), 20.

12 Loeffler, "Thomas Barry," 34.

13 Loeffler, "Biographies," 19.

14 Beryl Hugill, *Bring on the Clowns* (London: David & Charles, 1980), 142.

15 John Durant and Alice Durant, *Pictorial History of the American Circus* (New York: Castle Books, 1957), 43.

16 David Carlyon, *Dan Rice: The Most Famous Man You've Never Heard Of* (New York: Public Affairs, 2001), xiii.

17 Culhane, *American Circus*, 49.

18 Carlyon, *Dan Rice*, 411.

19 Janet M. Davis, *The Circus Age: Culture & Society under the American Big Top* (Chapel Hill: University of North Carolina Press, 2002).

20 LaVahn G. Hoh and William H. Rough, *Step Right Up! The Adventures of Circus in America* (White Hall, VA: Betterway Publications, 1990), 198.

21 Arthur Borella, "Why Circus Clowning Lags," *Billboard*, Dec. 1, 1934, 35.

22 Fred Bradna as told to Hartzell Spence, *The Big Top: My Forty Years with The Greatest Show on Earth* (New York: Simon and Schuster, 1952), 216.

23 Towsen, *Clowns*, 259–60, 266–68, 270–71.

24 "Lure of 'White Tops' Claims Richest Clown," *Rockford* (Illinois) *Republic*, Aug. 14, 1920, 3.

25 "Head Circus Jester is Native of Phila," *Philadelphia Inquirer*, May 2, 1919, 24.

26 "Here's an Act Not on the Big Show Program." *Salt Lake Telegram*, Aug. 5, 1917, 30.

27 David Hammarstrom, *Behind the Big Top* (South Brunswick, NJ. A. S. Barnes and Co., 1980), 218.

28 Bill Ballantine, "The Art of Clowning—By an Ex-Clown," *New York Times Magazine*, March 28, 1954, 67.

29 Towsen, *Clowns*, 280–81.

30 Ibid., esp. 268–69.

31 John Culhane, "School for Clowns," *New York Times Magazine*, Dec. 30, 1973, 18.

32 Bruce "Charlie" Johnson, "Lou Jacobs' Miniature Car," *The Clown in Times* 4, no. 3 (Spring 1998), 60.

33 Towsen, *Clowns*, 299–305.

34 *Famous Clowns*, unsigned and undated biographical sketch, Ringling Bros. and Barnum & Bailey Circus publicity files, unpag.

35 John McCandlish Phillips, *City Notebook: A Reporter's Portrait of a Vanishing New York* (New York: Liveright Publishing, 1974), 315.

36 Towsen, *Clowns*, 294–99; *Famous Clowns*, unpag.

37 George Speaight, *A History of the Circus* (London: Tantivy Press, 1980), 96, notes that hobo or tramp clowns were "mainly an American specialty" that spread from the vaudeville stage to the circus but offers no explanation for their popularity in the United States.

38 Tom Ogden, *Two Hundred Years of the American Circus* (New York: Facts on File, 1993), 15.

39 Ibid., 310–11.

40 Paul Bouissac, *Circus & Culture: A Semiotic Approach* (Bloomington: Indiana University Press, 1976), 151–75, demonstrates that many clown routines are formulaic, presumably meaning that they are also teachable.

41 Female clowns are evidence of changing mores. Although women had occasionally performed in European clowning contexts, they had rarely, if ever, appeared as clowns in earlier American circuses. Speaight, *History of the Circus*, 96, says that female clowns were never common in circuses of the nineteenth or twentieth century.

13

^{THE} AMERICAN CIRCUS SPECTACLE

JENNIFER LEMMER POSEY

When Circus Day came to Fort Worth, Texas on September 30, 1912, schools and offices were closed so the population could turn out to experience all of the sights and sounds of the Barnum & Bailey Circus.[1] The day began with a street parade and the setup of a city of canvas tents, with its midway filled with strange attractions, inexpensive souvenirs, and rich aromas. But the transformative magic of the circus truly began as the audience took their seats inside the massive big top. The show started on a large stage integrated into the seating at one side of the tent as a curtain raised on a scene depicting Egyptian priests in the streets of Alexandria. This was the opening of the grand spectacle, or "spec," as they were called in circus parlance, *Cleopatra*. The track around the big top slowly filled with multitudes of performers garbed in lavish Egyptian costumes and accessories (*fig. 13.1*). This initial display was soon disrupted by the raucous entrance of hundreds of horses carrying

the Roman legion, led by a chariot bearing Mark Antony. When the energy of this initial charge subsided, a dramatically pantomimed scene played out on the stage as Cleopatra offered herself and half of her kingdom to the Roman general. Cleopatra then entertained Antony with a festive celebration that filled the big top with motion, color, and sound. Egyptian citizens reveled as the riches and strengths of the kingdom, and the circus itself, were displayed through races, musical performances, and a parade of exotic animals. After a performance by a troupe of three hundred dancers, the curtain descended on a scene showing Antony falling for the wily and enchanting Cleopatra.

The scene then shifted to their palace ten years later, as the couple and the audience enjoyed a festival of courtly dancing and other exotic performances. The celebrations were soon interrupted by a charge from Julius Caesar's army, who was met by Antony and his men in a dramatic battle. The show concluded as Antony was returned to the palace

Detail of fig. 13.11. "Ringling Bros., *Magnificent Spectacular Introductory Tournament,*" 1907. Poster, printed by the Strobridge Lithographing Company, Cincinnati. Collection of the John and Mable Ringling Museum of Art, Tibbals Collection, ht2001298

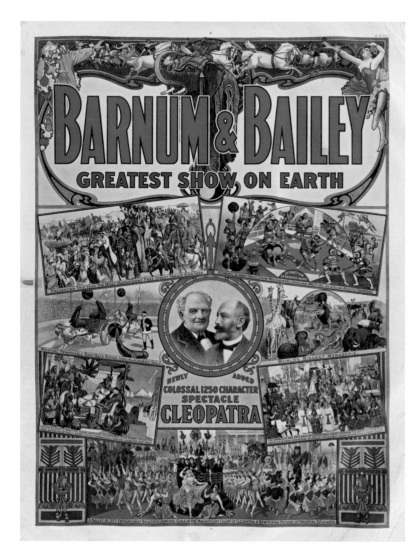

recreated "the sensational meeting" of Antony and Cleopatra, the "period of revelry and abandonment" that ensued, and their tragic end. The *Fort Worth Star-Telegram* described *Cleopatra* as a "Shakespear-ean production" and the program made it known that the episodes seen under the canvas paralleled those in Shakespeare's play.[3]

The American circus spectacles that were popular in the late nineteenth and early twentieth centuries were real-time theatrical experiences of familiar stories from history and literature. As the century progressed and other outlets such as film proved better able to portray such tales, the form and content of circus spectacles correspondingly changed. The evolution of these grand displays demonstrates how the American circus incorporated other forms of entertainment and responded to larger trends in American culture. An examination of their history offers a window into the evolution of the circus in the United States and the shifting expectations of audiences from the late eighteenth century to today.

Since the mid-twentieth century, circus performances have largely consisted of a series of short presentations of unique and generally unrelated acts. Audiences expect to be entertained by the antics of clowns, the amazing stunts of performers on horseback or flying through the air, and assorted animal acts. In their heyday at the turn of the twentieth century however, American circuses also featured theatrical and processional displays, called spectacles, or specs. Specs allowed circuses to showcase the size and splendor of their organizations, employing eye-catching props and magnificent costumes for seeming multitudes of animals and performers (*fig. 13.2*). Although the precise form of the specs varied, they were essentially lavish pantomimes that exploited the readily available resources

to die in his lover's arms and the despairing Cleopatra grabbed a serpent from the basket of one of her court performers and met her own end. As the curtain descended and the performers and trappings of *Cleopatra* proceeded out of the big top, the ringmaster blew his whistle to usher three herds of elephants into the rings as the more customary circus acts commenced.[2]

The program for the 1912 performance described Egypt as "the oldest theatre upon which the drama of mankind was played" and detailed how the stories of Moses, the ancient Greeks, and the Egyptian pharaohs continued to captivate people's imaginations. The introduction explained how the spectacle

▲ *Fig. 13.1.* "Barnum & Bailey Greatest Show on Earth, Colossal 1250 Character Spectacle *Cleopatra*," 1912. Poster, printed by the Strobridge Lithographing Company, Cincinnati. Collection of the John and Mable Ringling Museum of Art, Tibbals Collection, ht2000318

of the circus in an exotic or historical setting. While their most obvious purpose was to entertain, many specs also seemed to reach for the loftier goal of edifying their audiences with presentations of biblical, historical, or literary themes (*table 13.1*).[4] The publicity for circus spectacles thus promoted the idea that they imparted some knowledge or experience that could be taken away when audiences emerged from the big top. This extended a long tradition of American circuses presenting their entertainments as educational, which was meant to nullify opposition from those who questioned the respectability of traveling shows.

The history of American circus specs begins with John Bill Ricketts, who opened the first proper circus in the United States in 1793. Ricketts's shows included both equestrian displays and lavish pantomimes such as *The Death of Captain Cook*, which featured exotic costumes and props as well as original music and dance.[5] These displays were called pantomimes, although some did include scripted dialogue. They were generally tied to current events or popular tales. Ricketts and other early circuses rotated productions frequently to attract additional and repeat patrons as they were less mobile than later shows, frequently spending weeks or even months in a single location.

By the middle of the nineteenth century, American circuses were traveling under canvas, moving from one location to another within a few

Fig. 13.2. Frederick Whitman Glasier. Barnum & Bailey's *Tribute of Balkis* cast, 1903. Photograph. Collection of the John and Mable Ringling Museum of Art, Glasier Glass Plate Negative Collection, 0492

days. This change had the benefit of allowing a circus production to be planned at the beginning of a season. There was little need to make change, since the audience was new at each stop on a show's route. The inspirations for spec performances varied from widely recognized tales such as "Jack and the Beanstalk" to historical figures such as Revolutionary War hero Major General Israel Putnam (*fig. 13.3*).[6] As the nineteenth century progressed, changes to the physical structure of the circus and shifting cultural boundaries led to corresponding changes in the production of specs. The increasing popularity of the street parade in the 1860s and the growth of the more prominent tented shows into the enormous multi-ring railroad circuses of the 1880s were particularly important developments. The parades demonstrated that lavish displays could be accomplished without specific narratives. The large size of the tent made complicated dialogue impossible, leading to an emphasis on impressing audiences with increasingly grand visual spectacles. At the same time, as historian Lawrence Levine has noted, there was a "growing chasm between 'serious' and 'popular' culture" that American circuses were forced to negotiate.[7]

Circus specs of the 1870s and 1880s were often strictly processional, generally serving as grand entrées to the performance (*fig. 13.4*). In this format, specs framed the overall production and the entrée provided an opportunity to fill the tent with all of the people and animals that traveled with the show. As seen in the Sells Brothers poster, even menagerie stock such as giraffes and camels could make an appearance, while costumed circus workers often bolstered the ranks of performers. The resulting mass of movement sought to overwhelm and transport the audience from the everyday into a world where men fly and elephants dance.

Fig. 13.3. "The Grand Opening Fete of Spaulding & Rodgers' Two Circuses, Monday, September 11, 1848." Broadside. Collection of the John and Mable Ringling Museum of Art, Tibbals Collection, ht4000898

While the processional format was effective, the larger circuses focused on increasing the size and scope of their specs as a way to distinguish themselves from their competitors. In 1881 what might best be described as the golden age of the circus spectacle was inaugurated with Adam Forepaugh's production *Lalla Rookh and the Departure from Delhi*, a grand entrée spec.[8] While in truth this spec was still little more than an extravagant procession, the scale of the overall production was far larger than anything that had come before. In addition to the grandeur of the display itself, Forepaugh publicized the new spec by announcing a 10,000-dollar contest to find the "Handsomest Woman in the World" to serve as its centerpiece.[9] The prearranged winner was the actress Louise Montague (*fig. 13.5*) and buoyed by her beauty

Fig. 13.4. "Sells Brothers' Interior Pageant and Oriental Entree!" 1882. Poster, printed by the Strobridge Lithographing Company, Cincinnati. Cincinnati Art Museum, Gift of the Strobridge Lithographing Company, 1965.683.25

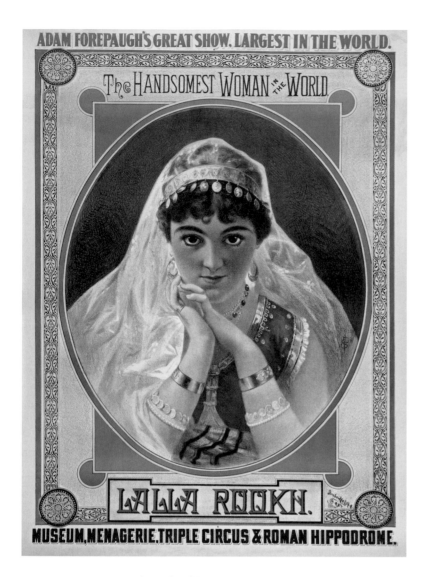

ADAM FOREPAUGH'S GREAT SHOW, LARGEST IN THE WORLD.

The HANDSOMEST WOMAN IN THE WORLD.

LALLA ROOKH.

MUSEUM, MENAGERIE, TRIPLE CIRCUS & ROMAN HIPPODROME.

and good publicity, *Lalla Rookh* contributed much to the show's successful 1881 season.[10]

Lalla Rookh was inspired by a Thomas Moore poem, an Orientalist romance first published in 1817. Although Levine points to an emergent division between highbrow and lowbrow entertainments in the latter half of the nineteenth century, the turn to literary source material by the Forepaugh circus points to how cloudy such distinctions could be in practice.[11] In a sense, circuses sought to split the difference by portraying their presentations and most notably their specs, as a kind of entertainment that appealed to audiences from all stations. For citizens in most towns and cities across America, circus spectacles

were the largest theatrical productions they would have the opportunity to see in a given year. At this time, a growing enthusiasm for civic pageantry was sweeping across urban centers of America and should be viewed as a significant parallel to the massive circus specs.

In advance of the centennial celebrations of 1876, communities began to plan for large-scale celebrations that included pageants and parades. These events were generally organized by religious or civic groups and, in many cities, annual celebrations for specific holidays became popular. Mardi Gras festivities in New Orleans and Cincinnati's Order of Cincinnatus' pageants were both examples of the more formally organized public celebrations that took shape in the 1870s.[12] These pageants and celebrations were observed by entire communities and blurred social boundaries in something of the same spirit as circus day festivities. They were intended to appeal widely and to convey lessons in morality and civic responsibility. In many respects the production and promotion of circus specs followed their lead.

One of these new public celebrations was the Veiled Prophet Fair, which was held in St. Louis for the first time in October 1878. Attracting over 50,000 spectators, it consisted of an elaborate procession and ball organized by a secret society of prominent citizens. The festivities were intended to be both a commercial stimulus for the city and a way to reestablish the social unity that had been shattered by labor battles of the previous year.[13] The initial Veiled Prophet parade not coincidentally took place the same week that the Forepaugh show was ending its season in St. Louis.[14] Indeed, there were many parallels between Forepaugh's *Lalla Rookh* spec and the new public celebration, not the least of which was that the invented mythology of the Veiled Prophet

▲ *Fig. 13.5.* "Adam Forepaugh's Great Show, Largest in the World, *Lalla Rookh*," 1882. Poster, printed by the Strobridge Lithographing Company, Cincinnati. Collection of the John and Mable Ringling Museum of Art, Tibbals Collection, ht2000413

organization was also loosely based on a poem by Thomas Moore. Moreover, the Queen of Love and Beauty, who was crowned at the Veiled Prophet Ball, certainly echoed the beauty contest that the Forepaugh circus used to promote its spec just a few years later. If such an event could resonate in one community, it made sense for a savvy impresario to capitalize on it and take it to audiences nationwide. Forepaugh went so far as to have himself depicted on a poster in the guise of the Veiled Prophet of Khorassan, a title that was given to the member chosen to preside over the celebrations (*fig. 13.6*). Just as the Veiled Prophet parade was intended to establish the importance of St. Louis, Forepaugh meant to demonstrate his success against competitors, like P. T. Barnum, who is uncharitably depicted lagging behind in the background.

Forepaugh first staged *Lalla Rookh* in 1881 and it was so successful that it served as the major pro-

duction of his circus through 1887. There was no immediate response from his competitors, including the Barnum & Bailey Circus, which was the largest traveling show of the era. With three rings of action and famous attractions like the elephant Jumbo, the show did not seem to have a strong need for a spectacle. But when they did finally enter into the realm of large-scale specs, Barnum & Bailey did so in grand fashion by hiring famed producer and choreographer Imre Kiralfy to concoct something that would be unlike anything ever before presented under the big top. The result was a spec that blurred the lines between the worlds of high art and popular performance. *Nero, or the Destruction of Rome*, mounted on a scale that was rare even for permanent theatrical venues, brought the historic tale to life for audiences. Publicity for the 1890 season puffed the spec as "the most stupendous, glorious, overwhelming spectacle in all human annals."[15] The production was actually a recycled version of a spectacle that Kiralfy had staged, first, on Staten Island for several weeks in the summer of 1888 and then for Barnum & Bailey's short 1889–90 winter season in London. By drawing from productions that had been successful in metropolitan areas, the show brought a new kind of experience to rural audiences. Indeed, the spec itself was likely prompted by a popular run of Anton Rubenstein's *Nero* at the Metropolitan Opera House in 1887 and was an indication of how circuses reworked ostensibly highbrow material and delivered it to a much larger audience.[16]

Printed advertisements for the Barnum & Bailey production claimed that the spec took place on a stage five hundred feet wide and two hundred feet deep and included twelve hundred characters. It was billed as the embodiment of "Rome rebuilt" (*fig. 13.7*). *Nero* could have been a stand-alone show perceived by audiences as an opportunity to

Fig. 13.6. "The Veiled Prophet and King of Showmen, Adam Forepaugh," ca. 1880. Poster, printed by the Courier Comapny, Buffalo. Collection of the John and Mable Ringling Museum of Art, SN1547.208.10

experience an urban pageant. In combination with a circus, it was an almost irresistible attraction. The publicity also called attention to the spec's elevated origins. For example, the cover to the libretto, which was available for purchase at the performances, featured a reproduction of the French artist Jean-Léon Gérôme's famous 1872 painting *Pollice Verso*.[17] The spec thus added value both in the quality of the circus performance and served as an example of the edifying quality of the otherwise common entertainment.

In contracting Imre Kiralfy, Barnum & Bailey raised circus productions to a new level by taking on the road what traditionally had been possible only in permanent venues. Born in Hungary, Imre Kiralfy began his career as a dancer, but he found his calling as a director and producer of lavish stage spectacles. He made his way to the United States in 1869 and had his initial success with a sensationally popular version of the musical *The Black Crook* at Niblo's Garden in New York. Kiralfy went on to stage massive spectacle productions for the Staten Island Amusement Company and he achieved enough renown to ensure that each of his circus productions

was branded so that the public would know the creative individual behind them. Kiralfy benefited as much as the circus from the working relationship, as he was able to stage shows that would have been impossible in the theaters of the time and thereby expand his audience nationwide.[18]

Following the success of *Nero*, Kiralfy created the spec *Columbus and the Discovery of America*, which surpassed all prior efforts in its scale and grandeur. *Columbus* was staged during the 1892 and 1893 seasons of the Barnum & Bailey Circus, coinciding with the quadricentennial of the explorer's landing in the New World. Conceived as an awe-inspiring spectacle as well as an educational reenactment of the landmark event, Kiralfy claimed it to be "a faithful, authentic, and complete reproduction of the chief historic incidents in the life of that great mariner."[19] With a cast of twelve hundred, including some three hundred dancers, the production was arranged in four acts that included processions, battles, and ballets (*fig. 13.8*). It ran for more than an hour at the conclusion of the circus performance and was so well received that other circus shows were forced to take notice.[20]

Fig. 13.7. "Imre Kiralfy's Grand Spectacle of *Nero, or the Destruction of Rome*," May 22, 1891. Herald, printed by Richard K. Fox Show Printing, New York. Collection of the John and Mable Ringling Museum of Art, Tibbals Collection, ht4000100

In 1893 the Adam Forepaugh circus, which was also under the management of James Bailey and several partners, produced *The American Revolution*. Scripted by William Gillette, an American actor and playwright best known for his role as Sherlock Holmes, the spec was intended to capitalize on the nationalism surrounding the Columbian Exposition. The performance opened with Paul Revere's ride and the scenes that followed traced the course of the Revolutionary War, from the signing of the Declaration of Independence to the inauguration of George Washington (*fig. 13.9, see fig. 4.15*).[21] The posters and wardrobe were designed by H. A. Ogden, an important artist at Strobridge Lithographing Company, the major show printer of the day. Ogden was also recognized as an illustrator specializing in the history of American military garb. Its patriotic appeal and association with Gillette and Ogden ensured good press and raised the quality of the production.

The winning strategy of employing recognizable and respected talents was one that James Bailey would use throughout his career. In 1898,

Fig. 13.8. "The Barnum & Bailey Greatest Show on Earth, Imre Kiralfy's *Columbus and the Discovery of America*," 1892–93. Poster, printed by the Strobridge Lithographing Company, Cincinnati. Collection of the John and Mable Ringling Museum of Art, Tibbals Collection, ht2000143

while showing at London's Olympia Theatre, the Barnum & Bailey show closed with the military spec *The Mahdi, or for the Victoria Cross*, based on contemporary news coming out of the Sudan, where the Mahdi sought to gain control of their region from the Egyptian administration, overseen by the British Empire (*fig. 13.10*). The show was "prepared" by Bennett Burleigh, a British war correspondent who himself had served in the conflict.[22] Use of such current material was unusual, but since the British forces were within months of ending the long conflict at the time of the production, an opportunity to see the action in the safety of a performance hall would have been appealing to British audiences. The spectacle included caravans, battle scenes, a gunboat, and even an Arab funeral procession, among other exotic features. The subject resonated with a Western fascination with orientalist themes, which Bailey's shows began to incorporate around the turn of the century.

Bailey clearly valued the artistic input of dramatic producers and he hired Imre's brother Bolossy Kiralfy, to create specs for the Barnum & Bailey show upon its 1903 return from Europe. At the time, the Ringling Bros. were their principal rivals and the five brothers pursued a different philosophy by dividing the work to make use of each one's unique talents. Although all of the brothers contributed ideas for specs, the final staging and direction seems to have fallen primarily to Alfred T. (Alf T), Albert (Al), and later Charles Ringling.[23]

The Ringling Bros. broke from their formula in 1903 when they hired John Rettig to mount the lavish *Jerusalem and the Crusades*. The move was most certainly in response to the return of Barnum & Bailey from Europe. Rettig began his career producing pageants for the Order of Cincinnatus. In 1886 he staged *The Fall of Babylon* at a baseball field in Cincinnati and in the following year *Rome under Nero*. Interestingly enough, each of these productions took place one year before Kiralfy staged similar production with the Staten Island Amusement Company. Rettig, who was credited with scenic design for the Kiralfy spectacles, maintained that the concepts for both Staten Island pageants were derived directly from the Cincinnati productions.[24] Subsequent successful specs for both the Adam Forepaugh and the John Robinson circuses, made Rettig enticing to the Ringlings.

Jerusalem and the Crusades was described as being "on a scale of magnificence and grandeur never before attempted" and newspapers noted how it was "arranged by artists of note and ability in the amusement field."[25] While Rettig was credited in the program, his name did not appear in the show's press for the season and in the years that followed Al and Alf T. Ringling resumed their roles in conceiving and producing the spec. In 1905, the show presented *Field of the Cloth of Gold*, which was based on the historic 1520 meeting of King Henry VIII of England and King Francis I of France. In describing his method for conceiving of a new spec, Alf T. Ringling stated that "the first essential is a simple, striking story... and the second essential is that the story must permit of a lavish

Fig. 13.9. Harry Ogden. "Adam Forepaugh Shows: Historical Scenes and Battles of the American Revolution 4th of July 1776 Signing the Declaration of Independence for American Liberty," 1893. Poster, printed by the Strobridge Lithographing Company, Cincinnati. Collection of the John and Mable Ringling Museum of Art, Tibbals Collection, ht2000418

display of color in the way of costumes and trappings and properties."[26] This philosophy clearly derived from the success of the Kiralfy specs, yet the brothers did not necessarily wish to emulate the size of those productions. While the Ringling Bros.' specs did include corps of ballerinas and staged tableaus, they never attempted to match the scale of Barnum & Bailey's *Columbus*. This was also undoubtedly in part a business decision, as the cost of productions with hundred of performers was obviously high and the space required for the stages meant one long side of the big top was not available for ticketed seats.

After taking control of Barnum & Bailey Circus in 1907, it took the Ringling brothers some time to fully master the management of two large circuses simultaneously. For both shows, spectacles were sharply scaled back for several years, with the Barnum & Bailey presenting *Grand Tournament* which opened its next four seasons (*fig. 13.11*). Described as a "unique and transcendentally beautiful introduction to the regular performances," the

Fig. 13.10. "The Barnum & Bailey Greatest Show on Earth, *The Mahdi, or for the Victoria Cross*," 1897. Poster, printed by the Strobridge Lithographing Company, Cincinnati. Cincinnati Art Museum, Gift of the Strobridge Lithographing Company, Cincinnati, 1965.816

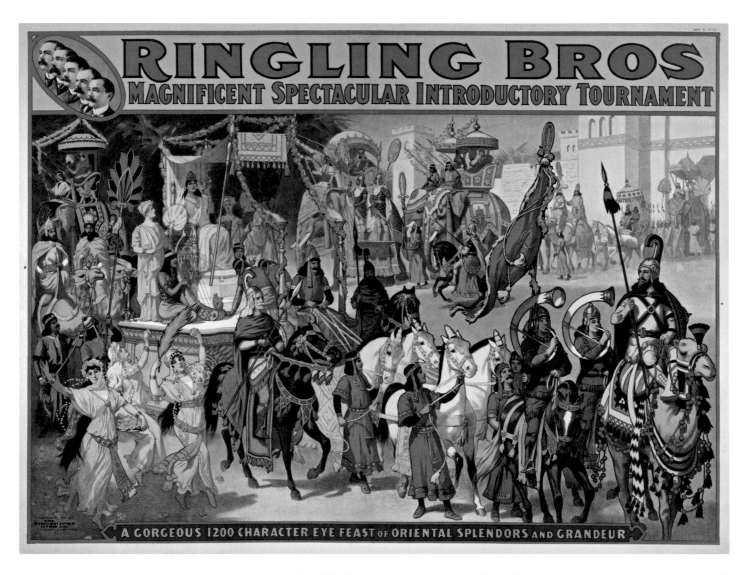

tournament was a procession that filled the big top with characters intended to represent "every known human and animal accompaniment in vogue."[27]

It was not until 1912 that the Ringling Bros. once again mounted specs for both circuses. That season the Ringling Bros. Circus offered *Joan of Arc* while the Barnum & Bailey Circus produced *May Cleopatra*. In typical fashion, printed advertisements for the Barnum & Bailey production pro-

nounced it "the greatest amusement event in all history," replete with "1250 characters, 300 dancing girls" and a "chorus of 400."[28] Although exaggerated, these numbers do suggest that the Ringlings were at least attempting to recreate a display akin to Kiralfy's specs two decades earlier. The exotic costuming of the cast, elaborate sets, and the melodramatic performance of circus star Jennie Silbon as Cleopatra captivated audiences (*fig. 13.12*).

Fig. 13.11. "Ringling Bros., Magnificent Spectacular Introductory Tournament," 1907. Poster, printed by the Strobridge Lithographing Company, Cincinnati. Collection of the John and Mable Ringling Museum of Art, Tibbals Collection, ht2001298

The Ringlings also began to draw on outside talents for their 1912 specs. Ottokar Bartik was the ballet master of the Metropolitan Opera House and choreographed both shows. The music for *May Cleopatra* was arranged by Faltis Effendi, who was purported to be the one-time bandmaster of the Khedive of Egypt.[29] The inspiration for *Joan of Arc* came after John Ringling attended a similar show at the Hippodrome in Paris (*fig. 13.13*).[30] In all of this, the Ringlings demonstrated how circus specs brought aspects of highbrow culture to a broader public.

From 1914 through 1918, the Ringling brothers alternated production of new specs for the two circuses. In general, the specs presented by the Barnum & Bailey show were dominated by Oriental themes, as seen in *The Wizard Prince of Arabia* in 1914 (*fig. 13.14*) and *Aladdin and His Wonderful Lamp* in 1917 and 1918. The Ringling show in turn offered specs based on chivalric subjects such as *Cinderella* in 1916 and 1917 and *The Days of Old* in 1918. By employing similar themes, the circuses were able to recycle props and wardrobe from season to season (*fig. 13.15*). When

Fig. 13.12. Frederick Whitman Glasier. Jennie Silbon and the cast of *Cleopatra*, 1912. Photograph. Collection of the John and Mable Ringling Museum of Art, Glasier Glass Plate Negative Collection, 0709

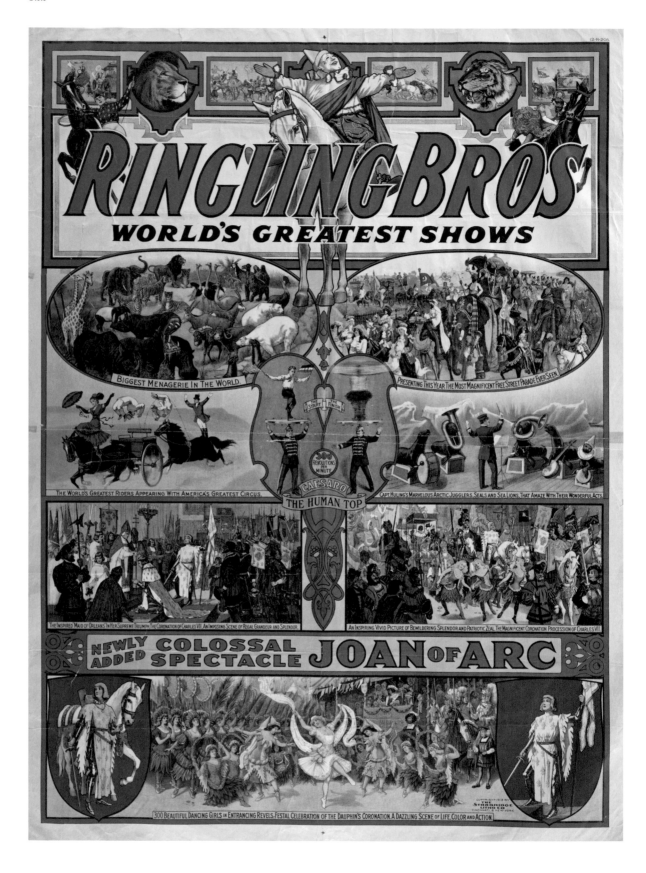

Fig. 13.13. "Ringling Bros.' Newly Added Colossal Spectacle *Joan of Arc*," 1912. Poster, printed by the Strobridge Lithographing Company, Cincinnati. Collection of the John and Mable Ringling Museum of Art, Tibbals Collection, ht2001331

the Ringling Bros. and Barnum & Bailey Combined Shows premiered in 1919, the extravagant pageants were a thing of the past. Of the five original brothers who went into the circus business, only three remained and their resources had diminished throughout the war years. The combined circus opened with a rather simple tournament-style procession, which made it clear that the age of the grandiose circus spectacle had passed. It was not just the prohibitive theatrical costs, but competition from the motion picture industry that brought about its decline.

Despite all of this, a few extravagant specs such as *The Durbar of Delhi* and *Nepal*, featuring Frank Buck, would be produced in the 1930s (*fig. 13.16*). It was not until John and Henry Ringling North took over management of their uncles' circus in 1938 that the Ringling Bros. and Barnum & Bailey show would again make a significant effort to stage an elaborate production. What emerged was a new kind of spec, one that was influenced by the musical productions of music halls like the Folies Bergère, popular through the 1920s, and nightclubs like the Copacabana which had its heyday in the 1940s. Once again, the circus producers looked to develop specs that reflected entertainments that were not readily available to the American public. This modernized cultural pedigree

Fig. 13.14. "The Barnum & Bailey New Big Indo-Arabic Spectacle, *The Wizard Prince of Arabia*," 1914. Poster, printed by the Strobridge Lithographing Company, Cincinnati. Collection of the John and Mable Ringling Museum of Art, Tibbals Collection, ht2000329

Posey

Fig. 13.15. Ringling Bros. Circus, the cast of *Cinderella*, May 1916. Photograph. Collection of the John and Mable Ringling Museum of Art, Tibbals Collection, ht0005298

Fig. 13.16. Edward J. Kelty. Ringling Bros. and Barnum & Bailey Combined Circus, Madison Square Garden, 1938. Photograph. Collection of the John and Mable Ringling Museum of Art, Tibbals Collection, ht0004786

Fig. 13.17. Max Weldy. Design for a spectacle parade, *The Return of Marco Polo*, Indian section, 1940. Ink, paint on paper. Collection of the John and Mable Ringling Museum of Art, Tibbals Collection, ht3003536_017

came with a new generation of artists creating displays filled with movement, brilliantly colored wardrobes, and beautiful showgirls.

The circus was no longer a primary source of entertainment in America; more than ever it was dependent on its novelty. John Ringling North focused on keeping the show fresh. For the 1940 season, North recruited Max Weldy, an American designer working in Paris, to produce a lavish spectacle. Weldy had worked with the Moulin Rouge and the Folies Bergère to create shows during the 1920s for which he designed and constructed costumes, props, and scenery (*fig. 13.17*).[31] *The Return of Marco Polo* was a nod to the specs of the past, illustrating the epic narrative of the explorer's travels in a procession organized with distinct units representing various exotic lands that Marco Polo visited. In the *New York Times* article "New Trimmings Color Old Show," the reviewer described the mix of "tootling weird jungle music, bewitching dancing girls, wild animals" as "fine stuff."[32]

To prepare for the 1941 season, North hired industrial designer Norman Bel Geddes, whose famous Futurama pavilion at the 1939 New York World's Fair had set a new direction for American design. Brought in to modernize the look of the circus from front lot to performance, Bel Geddes brought a talented team, which included John Murray Anderson, a choreographer and director noted for his productions with the Ziegfeld Follies, and the young costume designer Miles White, already a great success with his designs for revues such as those of the Copacabana. The team conceived a spec story based on traditional nursery rhymes. *Old King Cole and Mother Goose* occured about halfway through the show and was hailed as a "rollicking, frolicking, happy, clean and colorful spectacle" (*fig. 13.18*).[33]

Although Bel Geddes left the circus after the 1942 season, the Ringling Bros. and Barnum & Bailey Circus continued to mount innovatively designed circus performances and parade-style specs in the 1940s and 1950s.[34] As an integrated part of the actual circus performance, there was less need to have a narrative; instead of worrying about plot development, the production team aimed to use the spec as an interlude from the physically challenging circus acts, filled with color, music, excitement, and gaiety.

White, who left with Bel Geddes, returned to the Ringling show in 1947 to design costumes for *The Wedding of Cinderella* under the direction of John Murray Anderson. White's contributions to the spec displays and costumes were unmatched in the 1950s. He turned elephants into butterflies, horses into chickens, men into fish, and show girls into queens (*figs. 13.19, 13.20*). His aesthetic sensibilities and unrivaled creativity brought a new, whimsical, otherworldly style of spec production. White designed for the circus until 1955 and is still recognized as one of the most innovative designer of circus costumes of the twentieth century.[35]

Perhaps White's departure was in some way related to the struggles that the Ringling management

Fig. 13.18. Ringling Bros. and Barnum & Bailey Circus, entry of *Old King Cole*, portrayed by Felix Adler, 1941. Photograph. Collection of the John and Mable Ringling Museum of Art, Tibbals Collection, ht0003652

Fig. 13.19. Sverre O. Braathen. Elephants pulling a *Cinderella* spectacle float. Ringling Bros. and Barnum & Bailey lot, Freeport, Illinois, August 14, 1947. Photograph, Kodachrome. Illinois State University Special Collections, Milner Library, BSP1156

Fig. 13.20. Miles White. *Cinderella* spectacle float, 1947. Ink and watercolor on paper. Collection of the John and Mable Ringling Museum of Art, Tibbals Collection, ht3000290

was facing in keeping alive the traveling tented show in the 1950s. There was an abbreviated season in 1956, which was also the last year the Ringling show traveled under the big top. John Ringling North, however, was still enamored with bringing in artists to improve the circus and commissioned French Impressionist artist Marcel Vertès to conceive and design the spec procession for that season. *Say It with Flowers* was filled with beautiful showgirls costumed as flowers, but fell short of the whimsy and color of White's productions. A review in the *New York Times* praised the spec for using the majority of the show's performers and animals, but in reality, Vertès costumed only about eight hundred people and animals for the whole circus production, including two production numbers, a far cry from the thousand or so that were used in a single spec in the early twentieth-century productions.[36] The review in *Billboard* noted its "apparent economy in staging," which consisted of only five floats and used just thirteen of the show's fifty elephants.[37]

Positioned eighth in a three-and-a-half-hour performance composed of twenty-four different displays, *Say It with Flowers* was performed right before the intermission. The five floats, themed variously with flower gardens, frogs, and harvests, proceeded around the track accompanied by mounted and walking units of men and women dressed as flowers, animals, and insects (*fig. 13.21*). As a relatively minor part of the overall circus performance, the spec played almost no role in defining the show. This new template would spread to smaller shows as American circuses renewed their focus on the skills and feats of the human and animal performers rather than attempting to compete with theatrical productions, bringing to a final close the age of the grand spectacular. In its heyday, though, the American circus spectacle was an integral part of the performance, one that not only entertained but also edified its audience with its combination of historical and cultural influences presented in a most magnificent manner.

Fig. 13.21. Marcel Vertès. *Say It with Flowers*, spectacle float, 1956. Gouache on paper. Collection of the John and Mable Ringling Museum of Art, Tibbals Collection, ht3003340

CIRCUS SPECTACLES

Year	Circus	Display or Spectacle	Design and Production
1881–86	Forepaugh	*Lalla Rookh and the Departure from Delhi*	
1887–91	Forepaugh	*Custer's Last Battle*	
1889–91	BB	*Nero, or the Destruction of Rome*	Imre Kiralfy
1891–92	Ringling Bros.	*Caesar's Triumphal Entry to Rome*	
1892	Forepaugh	*Fall of Ninevah*	John Rettig
1892–93	BB	*Columbus and The Discovery of America*	Imre Kiralfy
1893	Forepaugh	*The American Revolution & Scenes & Battles of 1776*	William Gillette
1894	BB	*Grand Pageant of Nations*	
1895	BB	*Grand Water Circus*	
1896	BB	*Oriental India*	
1897	BB	*Columbus and The Discovery of America*	Richard Barker
1897–98	BB	*The Mahdi, or for the Victoria Cross*	Bennet Burleigh
1899	Ringling Bros.	*Last Days of the Century, or the Light of Liberty*	
1899	BB	*Chinese Gordon's Advance, Capture in the Sudan*	
1901–2	Ringling Bros.	*Grand Fetes of Ancient Rome*	
1902	BB	*Le Voyage de Balkis*	Bolossy Kiralfy, Alfred Edel
1903	BB	*A Tribute of Balkis*	Bolossy Kiralfy, Alfred Edel
1903–4	Ringling Bros.	*Jerusalem and the Crusades*	John Rettig
1904–5	BB	*The Durbar of Delhi*	Bolossy Kiralfy
1905–6	Ringling Bros.	*Field of the Cloth of Gold*	Albert Ringling
1906–7	BB	*Peace, America's Immortal Triumph*	Bolossy Kiralfy
1907–8	Ringling Bros.	*A Magnificent Spectacular Introductory Tournament*	
1908–11	BB	*The Grand Tournament*	
1909–11	Ringling Bros.	*The Pomp and Splendor of Ancient Egyptians*	
1912–13	Ringling Bros.	*Joan of Arc*	Ottokar Bartick
1912–13	BB	*Cleopatra*	Ottokar Bartick
1914	BB	*The Wizard Prince of Arabia*	Alf T Ringling
1915	BB	*Lalla Rookh and the Departure from Delhi*	
1914–15	Ringling Bros.	*Solomon and the Queen of Sheba*	Albert Ringling, Ottokar Bartick
1916	BB	*Persia or the Thousand and One Nights*	
1916–17	Ringling Bros.	*Cinderella*	Charles Ringling, Ottokar Bartick
1917–18	BB	*Aladdin and His Wonderful Lamp*	
1918	Ringling Bros.	*In Days of Old or When Knighthood Was in Flower*	Charles Ringling, Ottokar Bartick
1919–24	RBBB	*Tournament*	
1925	RBBB	*Fete of the Garlands*	
1926–29	RBBB	*Tournament and Garland Entry*	
1931–32	RBBB	*Tournament and Garland Entry*	
1933–36	RBBB	*Durbar of Delhi*	
1937	RBBB	*India*	
1938	RBBB	*Nepal*	Charles LeMaire
1939	RBBB	*The World Comes to the World's Fair*	Charles LeMaire
1940	RBBB	*The Return of Marco Polo*	Max Weldy
1941	RBBB	*Old King Cole and Mother Goose*	Norman Belle Geddes
1942	RBBB	*Holidays*	John Murray Anderson, Norman Belle Geddes
1943	RBBB	*Let Freedom Ring*	John Murray Anderson, Billy Livingston, Max Weldy
1944	RBBB	*Panto's Paradise*	Billy Livingston
1945	RBBB	*Alice in Circus Wonderland*	Billy Livingston
1946	RBBB	*Toyland*	Billy Livingston
1947	RBBB	*The Wedding of Cinderella*	John Murray Anderson, Miles White
1948	RBBB	*Night Before Christmas*	John Murray Anderson, Miles White
1949	RBBB	*Birthdays*	John Murray Anderson, Miles White
1950	RBBB	*When Dreams Come True*	John Murray Anderson, Richard Barstow, Miles White
1951	RBBB	*Circus Serenade*	John Murray Anderson, Richard Barstow, Miles White
1952	RBBB	*The Good Old Times*	Richard Barstow, Miles White
1953	RBBB	*Candyland*	Richard Barstow, Miles White
1954	RBBB	*Dreamland*	Richard Barstow, Miles White
1955	RBBB	*Holidays*	Richard Barstow, Miles White
1956	RBBB	*Say It with Flowers*	Richard Barstow, Marcel Vertès

1 "Everybody Works Again: Circus Day over, School Open," *Fort Worth Star-Telegram*, Oct. 1, 1912, 9.

2 W. P. Dodge, "Rehearsing the Circus," *Theatre Magazine* 15 (May 1912), 146, 148–49, xi, xvii.

3 *The Barnum & Bailey Greatest Show on Earth Magazine and Daily Review* (Buffalo: Courier Co., 1912) n.p.

4 Robert Barbour Johnson, "The Old Time Spec," *White Tops* 28, no. 5 (Sept.–Oct. 1955), 8.

5 James S. Moy, "Entertainments at John B. Ricketts's Circus, 1793–1800," *Educational Theatre Journal* 30, no. 2 (May 1978), 187–202.

6 For a comprehensive list of documented specs performed by American circuses from the days of Ricketts up to the 1956 Ringling Bros. and Barnum & Bailey spec *Say It with Flowers*, see Fred Pfening, Jr., "Spec-ology of the Circus, Part One," *Bandwagon* 47, no. 6 (Nov.–Dec. 2003), 4–20; "Spec-ology of the Circus, Part Two," *Bandwagon* 48, no. 1 (Jan.–Feb. 2004), 3–21.

7 Lawrence Levine, *Highbrow Lowbrow: The Emergence of Cultural Hierarchy in America* (Cambridge, MA: Harvard University Press, 1988), 68.

8 Pfening, "Spec-ology, Part One," 5.

9 "Mr. Adam Forepaugh," *Macon Telegraph*, March 19, 1881, 2; the scheme actually originated with Forepaugh's capable press agent, Charles H. Day: *New York Clipper*, Dec. 17, 1881, 2.

10 "Forepaugh's Circus," *Indianapolis Sentinel* 30, no. 117 (April 27, 1881), 5.

11 Levine, *Highbrow Lowbrow*, 57–61.

12 The New Orleans Mardi Gras carnival crowned its first Rex in 1872 and began using ride-on floats in 1877. The Order of the Veiled Prophet held its first parade in 1878. Cincinnati's pageant traditions began with parades in 1882. David Glassberg, *American Historical Pageantry: The Uses of Tradition in the Early Twentieth Century* (Chapel Hill: University of North Carolina Press, 1990), 25–27.

13 Thomas M. Spencer, *The St. Louis Veiled Prophet Celebration Power on Parade, 1877–1995* (Columbia: University of Missouri Press, 2000).

14 *Route of Adam Forepaugh's Museum, Menagerie and Circus. Season of 1878.*

15 Barnum & Bailey Herald, July 17, 1890, Courier Co., Buffalo. Tibbals Collection ht4000095, the John and Mable Ringling Museum of Art.

16 "Amusements," *New York Times*, March 17, 1887, 5.

17 The painting depicts a victorious gladiator standing on the throat of an enemy as the Colosseum crowd cheers him on. The title, *Pollice Verso*, means "with a turned thumb," and reference to the hand gesture that crowds made to indicate the fate of a defeated gladiator. Emily Beeny, "Blood Spectacle: Gérôme in the Arena," in *Reconsidering Gérôme*, ed. Scott Allan and Mary Morton (Los Angeles: J. Paul Getty Museum, 2010), 50.

18 Barbara Barker, "Imre Kiralfy's Patriotic Spectacles: 'Columbus, and the Discovery of America' (1892–93) and 'America' (1893)," *Dance Chronicle* 17, no. 2 (Jan. 1, 1994), 149–78.

19 Imre Kiralfy, "A Word from the Author" in *Imre Kiralfy's Columbus and the Discovery of America* (New York: J. A. Bailey, 1892), n.p.

20 Kiralfy took the Columbus production, added additional scenes and performers, and produced it as a feature of the Columbian Exposition in Chicago in 1893.

21 Great Forepaugh Show program, *The American Revolution and the Scenes and Battles of 1776* (Buffalo: Courier Co., 1893).

22 "Barnum's in London," *New York Times*, Jan. 16, 1898, A3.

23 Jerold W. Apps, *Ringlingville USA: The Stupendous Story of Seven Siblings and Their Stunning Circus Success* (Madison: Wisconsin Historical Society, 2005).

24 "Fall of Babylon. Cincinnati Gives New York a New Sensation," *Cincinnati Commercial Tribune* 47, no. 278 (July 7, 1887), 1; "Rettig to Kiralfy. The Cincinnatus Artist Replies to Charges of Plagiary," *Cincinnati Commercial Tribune* 47, no. 356 (Sept. 27, 1888), 6.

25 "Crusades Pictured in Big Spectacular Gorgeous Production Presented by Ringling Bros. in Connection with Circus," *Salt Lake Telegram*, July 15, 1903, 5; "The Ringling Brothers," *Omaha World Herald* 41, no. 282 (July 19, 1903), 8.

26 George McAdam, "What It Costs in Money and Effort to Devise a Circus Spectacle," *New York Times*, April 8, 1917, SM4.

27 *The Barnum & Bailey Greatest Show on Earth Magazine and Daily Review* (Buffalo: Courier Co., 1911), n.p.

28 "Barnum & Bailey: August 19, 1912," herald, Central Printing. Tibbals Collection ht4000116, the John and Mable Ringling Museum of Art.

29 Dodge, "Rehearsing the Circus," xi.

30 Pfening, "Spec-ology, Part One," 12.

31 "Sarasotan to Close Shop after 50 Years in Trade," *Sarasota Herald Tribune*, Jan. 30, 1972.

32 "New Trimmings Color Old Show," *New York Times*, April 6, 1940, 22.

33 "Dash of Nostalgia Spices 1941 Circus," *New York Times*, April 8, 1941, 27.

34 The Bel Geddes team was able to bring acclaimed dancer and choreographer George Balanchine in to help arrange the famous elephant ballet for the 1942 season. See the essay on circus music by Leon Botstein in this volume.

35 Ernest Albrecht, "Miles White, the Little Eccentric with the Big Talent," *Bandwagon* 37, no. 6 (Nov.–Dec. 1993), 50–60.

36 Michael James, "Circus Opens Run in Old-Time Style," *The New York Times*, April 5, 1956, 16; Michael

C. Bussacco, *Heritage Press Sandglass Companion Book: 1960-1983* (Archibald, PA: Tribute Books, 2009), 62.

37 Jim McHugh, "Big One: From Troubled Seas a Great Show," *Billboard*, April 14, 1956, 64.

Table 13.1. Circus spectacles, 1881–1956
BB–Barnum & Bailey
RBBB—Ringling Bros. and Barnum & Bailey
Table compiled from Fred D. Pfening, Jr., "Spec-ology of the Circus, Parts One and Two," with additions by the author.

14

THE CIRCUS IN NINETEENTH-CENTURY AMERICAN CHILDREN'S LITERATURE

ELLEN BUTLER DONOVAN

"The circus is coming!" is a familiar exclamation in children's literature of the nineteenth century. In many novels and stories for children written between 1870 and 1910, the arrival of the circus is a highlight of the summer. Just as regularly, children's magazines featured an article or story about the circus at least once in summer issues, and information about the circus periodically appeared at other times of the year. However, though circuses changed over the time period as they took advantage of new technologies and modes of transportation, the fictional circus that appears in stories for children is forever the wagon-drawn "mud show" that pauses at the town line just long enough to spruce up into a parade, offers a one-ring show in the afternoon and again in the evening, and then travels overnight to the next village or town. The fictional circus in children's literature may feature gorgeous circus wagons, but it almost never travels by rail. Bareback riding is the most celebrated event of the circus performance; animal acts and clowns, if mentioned at all, are reduced to the background hubbub of the circus grounds. And the fictional children who visit the circus rarely live in the city; instead their surroundings are suburban if not rural, featuring open space rather than the confines of an urban neighborhood. Furthermore, fictional children never attend an evening circus performance. They may attend the circus accompanied by their parents or an older sibling, or they may attend with their friends, with or without parental permission. But they always attend the afternoon show. These characteristics are not surprising in that nineteenth-century children's literature was both produced and consumed by the middle class. Consequently, it is dominated by a middle-class perspective that defined childhood as a protected space, characterized by an intact nuclear family and a rural environment.

The assumption that children would have been familiar with the circus and visited it routinely

Detail of fig. 14.1. "The Barnum & Bailey Greatest Show on Earth, A Child's Dream," 1896. Poster, printed by the Strobridge Lithographing Company, Cincinnati. Circus World Museum, CWi-2324

is supported by advertising that portrayed the circus as particularly appropriate for children. Though circus posters were often sensational, featuring wild animals leaping toward the viewer or death-defying acrobatic, trapeze, or bareback riding acts or magnificent historical extravaganzas, circus owners also knew how to appeal to middle-class parents. Barnum and Bailey depicted delightful circus acts as the stuff of a child's dream (*fig. 14.1*). In addition to the happy (rather than death-defying) acts depicted on the

circus poster, it is significant that the dreaming child is lovely, androgynous, and well cared for. The lace on the child's garments, the colorful counterpane (in keeping with the costumes of the performers), and the snowy pillow convey a safe and comfortable image of childhood. Similarly, Barnum and his partners advertised Jumbo the elephant as the "children's giant pet" and pictured Jumbo being ridden by a score of youngsters as a distracted nurse strolls an infant disconcertingly close to Jumbo's big feet (*fig. 14.2*). The well-dressed children in the posters are clearly members of the middle-class audience that circus owners sought to entice.

Some of the most familiar texts describing childhood in the nineteenth century treat the circus as a child's entertainment. In *A Boy's Town* (1890), William Dean Howells's autobiographical account of his boyhood in the small town of Hamilton, Ohio, he devoted an entire chapter to the delights of circuses and menageries. Howells recounted a time in the 1840s when one-ring circuses featured acrobats, slack-rope walkers, bareback riders, and sideshow curiosities, while the menagerie featured wild animal acts. In his accounting of the merits of each kind of show, Howells noted that circuses were far more attractive for their sheer gaudiness, their fearsome and heart-stopping performances, the opportunities they provided for proving a boy's prowess in "hooking" into the show (sliding in under the tent without paying the entrance fee), and the hours of subsequent entertainment after the circus had moved on as neighborhood boys got up their own circuses.

As is characteristic of *A Boy's Town*, Howells's account of the circus visit adopts an ironic stance toward his younger self, thereby suffusing the narration with nostalgia while winking slyly but benignly over the heads of children at adult readers. The delight the boy and his pals experience at the circus is

Fig. 14.1. "The Barnum & Bailey Greatest Show on Earth, A Child's Dream," 1896. Poster, printed by the Strobridge Lithographing Company, Cincinnati. Circus World Museum, CWi-2324

lovingly detailed: their anticipation of the show once the circus posters appear, their anxiety over scraping together the price of the ticket, their early rising to meet the circus procession at the town limits and to trot alongside it to the circus site, and, not least, their enjoyment of the performance. Even entering the tent is a moment of wonder for the young Howells and his friends: "Inside the tent, they found it dark and cool, and their hearts thumped in their throats with the wild joy of being there; they recognized one another with amaze, as if they had not met for years, and the excitement kept growing, as other fellows came in."[1]

Furthermore, the young Howells does not see the circus as labor. The roustabouts are described

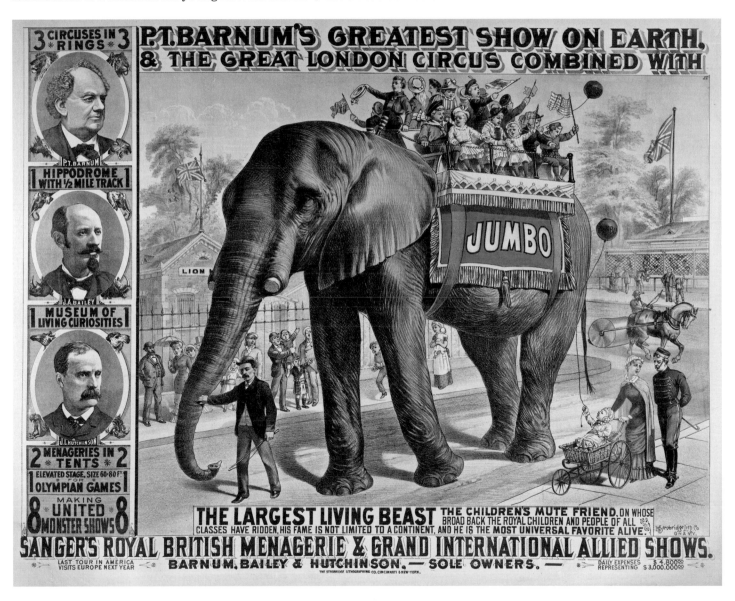

▲ *Fig. 14.2.* "P. T. Barnum's Greatest Show on Earth, The Largest Living Beast," 1883. Poster, printed by the Strobridge Lithographing Company, Cincinnati. Collection of the John and Mable Ringling Museum of Art, Tibbals Collection, ht2004522

as "mighty men" or "massive." And those boys lucky enough to haul water in exchange for a half-price entrance ticket have the advantage over boys who have enough pocket money to buy their admission: "fellows who had money to go in would have been glad to carry water just for the glory of coming close to the circus-men."[2]

IN THE RING.

Staying true to the boy's priorities, Howells summarized most of the circus performance and focused on the routine of the tipsy country jake invited to ride a recalcitrant horse, a version of the "Pete Jenkins from Mud Corners" routine that Mark Twain used to good effect in *The Adventures of Huckleberry Finn* (*fig. 14.3*). This trick is almost as old as the circus itself.[3] For the boys attending the circus, being familiar with the performance distinguished the worldlier boys from the naive youngster: "When they [the ringmaster and the clown] bring him up to the horse, he falls against it; and the little fellows think he will certainly get killed. But the big boys tell the little fellows to shut up and watch out."[4]

Howells may have included this routine because it was his favorite part of the circus, but he also uses the incident to celebrate a quintessentially American identity. Though the rider starts out as a tipsy country jake who descends from "one of the top-seats" (i.e., less desirable) to the ring and clambers on to the skittish horse, through the performance he is transformed by shedding his layers of costume from country-jake to Irish immigrant to British soldier to American sailor to "James Rivers, the greatest three-horse rider in the world."[5] The sequence suggests a rise in social status, culminating in the final transformation that offers a personal identity and status. In the eyes of the boys, the country jake's transformation into James Rivers, the ideal American, is achieved through the circus performance.

Howells extends his commentary on American identity and status through another motif associated with the circus—running away. Maintaining the ironic stance he uses throughout the book, Howells introduces his chapter on the circus with remarks regarding a boy's desire to run away. Howells lists several reasons why boys considered running away, including being required to

Fig. 14.3. H. F. Farney. "In the Ring," illustration for William Dean Howells, *A Boy's Town* (Boston: Harper & Brothers, 1890). Courtesy American Antiquarian Society

do chores or denied permission to go swimming. In these obviously thin excuses, readers recognize that the boys were not abused or justified in their desire to escape from home. Howells remarks that none of the boys did run off, except one who was "found, homesick and crying in Cincinnati, and was glad to come back."[6] This boy's unsuccessful attempt to run away is blamed on the fact that he did not run away with the circus: "If he made any mistake, it was in not running off with a circus, for that was the true way of running off. Then, if you were ever seen away from home, you were seen tumbling through a hoop and alighting on the crupper of a bare-backed pie-bald and if you ever came home you came home in a gilded chariot, and you flashed upon the domestic circle in flesh-colored tights and spangled breech-cloth."[7] Boys could not achieve their full potential by splitting wood or pulling weeds; however, if a boy ran away with the circus, he was sure to return to his home in glory.

Howells's account of the circus is characteristic of the way that the nineteenth-century circus is remembered in the popular imagination—as a quintessentially American entertainment. As such, it was appropriate for children, particularly boys, who not only appreciated the spectacle of the show but also used the show to heighten their aspirations, albeit naively. Howells's account conveys a nostalgic and benign view that played to Americans' own ideas about childhood: that it was essentially rural, male, protected by the structure of the nuclear family, and optimistic. However, this representation of the circus is by no means the dominant depiction in the novels and periodicals explicitly marketed for children. Instead of the nostalgia and good-humored irony characteristic of *A Boy's Town*, the stories and novels express a deep ambivalence about the circus. Repeatedly, children's literature teeters unsteadily between depictions of the fascination and glamour of the circus and portrayals of deception, evil, and abuse on the grounds of the circus. In *The Circus Age*, historian Janet M. Davis argues, "the railroad circus collapsed the world under canvas—right at home—for urban and rural consumers across the United States."[8] In her analysis of the vast array of spectacles and acts in the three-ring railroad circus, Davis concluded, "As a corporation on wheels, the circus's labor performances of the new industrial order, its variegated exhibitions of human and animal relationships, and its spectacles of America's growing power in world affairs heralded the arrival of a new modern age."[9] Similarly, in children's literature, the circus also "collapsed the world under canvas" but instead of bringing the wide world to children, it brought the adult world. In stories and novels for children, the traveling show becomes a trope or metaphor for the temporary incursion of the adult world into the pastoral world of childhood.

Scholars such as Anne Scott MacLeod have convincingly argued that by the mid-nineteenth century, American culture had shifted its understanding of childhood as rational training ground for adulthood to childhood as a romantic phase that needed protection from the rough-and-tumble world of the expanding country.[10] Children were frequently depicted as idealized—innocent, spiritual, intuitively good (for example, Little Eva of *Uncle Tom's Cabin*)—and were protected from the dangers of society by strong nuclear families and the isolation of villages or towns that featured agrarian or other natural landscapes. Though, of course, real children often lived in much more diverse (and sometimes far more dire) circumstances, the cultural idea of children as conveyed in literature and the visual arts reinforced a protected pastoral experience as the ideal.

Because the circus was a traveling show, not a local permanent institution, it could not be integrated into the village life important to the culture's understanding of childhood. In addition, as a complex business and social organization, the circus included some disreputable elements considered inappropriate for children. Both of these features of the circus allowed authors to use it as a vehicle to represent a variety of social conditions or cultural transformations that threatened a pastoral ideal of childhood. The variety of issues authors associated with the circus suggests the fragility of that pastoral ideal.

Beginning with Sunday-school tracts, the circus was roundly condemned as an entertainment. For example, in *The Circus*, a tract published by the American Sunday-School Union in 1827 and reissued into the 1850s, young Alfred and Silas Brown are curious as they watch a man pasting up circus posters. The man encourages the boys to attend the circus, but cautions them not to tell their parents where they are going if they think their parents will disapprove. Alfred and Silas, as models of good behavior, do ask their parents if they can attend the circus. Their father sets forth a reasoned argument critical of the circus. His condemnation includes both expected and surprising reasons: the animals (particularly horses) are "whipped and very cruelly treated" in order to make them perform their tricks; the circus employees are "idle and worthless people," who do not stay in one place and take the money of people who can ill afford to spend it on foolishness; the circus is the site of gambling and drinking; and boys who see the circus want to "do just as those men do" and join the circus as soon as they are able, or go home to try the circus tricks and end up getting seriously injured.[11]

Almost two decades later, the New England Sabbath School Union offered a similar argument in *A Peep at the Circus, or a Business for Life* (1844). In this case the child, Ellen, has questioned the adult narrator about the presence of the beautiful horses and the men who are riding them. The narrator explains that they belong to a circus and explains to Ellen how a circus operates. The narrator also points out that women as well as men ride in the circus, though they come in for just as much, if not more, opprobrium:

> There are not only men and boys who become circus-riders, but sometimes women too; who, instead of living quietly and soberly, staying much at home, and wearing the ornaments of meek and quiet spirits, as the Bible commands them, spend their time in dressing gaudily, and riding about from place to place, to exhibit themselves in the circus. Perhaps you can hardly believe that any woman could love such business as this; but I assure you there are those who do follow it, for I myself have seen five or six ladies at a time riding in the streets, with other circus-riders, and have been told by those who witnessed the evening performance that they rode there.[12]

Once the narrator describes the circus, Ellen disappears from the narrative and the narrator addresses an unnamed child reader (referred to as "you") and asks, rhetorically, if the child desires to be a circus rider. In response, the narrator presents a closely reasoned argument about the value of honest respectable work and then just as closely measures the occupation of circus riding against those principles. Once the reader is convinced that circus riding is not noble work, the narrator goes on to enumerate another set of reasons against attending the circus: the circus is a frivolous waste of time in a world where life is short; if children need entertainment, they should participate in an activity that exercises their bodies and their minds; the circus is a waste of money when a child can use that money to buy a good book or, even better, to buy a Testament to send to "some poor hungry child" or "some heathen"; and, finally, by going to the circus, children encourage the circus performers in their ignoble work.[13]

In another tract published by the American Sunday-School Union, *Freddy the Runaway; or The Lost One Found* (1850), discursive reasoning is replaced by only slightly more subtle literary elements. The writer portrays the circus environment as rife with stealing and bad language and through the events of the plot associates it with gypsies and white slavers, thereby creating a much more fearsome portrayal than the systematic reasoning Mr. Brown presented to his sons.

Though the tracts are explicitly critical of the circus, it is worth remembering that they also, inadvertently, document the pleasures of the circus, for the tracts acknowledge the beautiful animals, exciting spectacle, and accomplished performers that are so attractive to the children in the stories. Several decades will pass before children are cautioned that the circus is deceptive—false in its advertising and masking with a veneer of beauty and grace the brutal labor of circus life. At midcentury, however, authors sought to safeguard children's moral and spiritual innocence as well as to dismiss the very physicality of circus labor. Explicit injunctions against the circus similar to those found in the Sunday-school tracts appeared throughout the nineteenth century, particularly in relation to comic portrayals of overly fastidious adults. But literature for children never really shook its ambivalence about the circus, substituting for explicit warnings events and characters that evoke fearsome conse-

quences for children's participation in or attendance at the circus.

Though the Sunday-school tracts express the most critical view of the circus for children, they participate in the dominant pattern in children's literature: the use of the circus to express anxieties about childhood and the social forces that transformed American society in the nineteenth century. This ambivalence is clearly evident in the work of one of the famous nineteenth-century writers for children, Louisa May Alcott. Her novel *Under the Lilacs* was serialized in the 1877–78 volume of *St. Nicholas*, one of the premier children's magazines of the period, and published by Roberts Brothers in 1878.[14] *Under the Lilacs* depicts the fortunes of Ben Brown and his trained circus dog, Sancho. Ben has run away from the circus to search for his father, who had also been a circus performer but who had left Ben in the care of the circus manager's wife while he sought a new position. Ben's travels take him to a rural New England village, where he falls into the care of the widow Mrs. Moss and then is informally adopted by Miss Celia, the owner of the property that Mrs. Moss oversees. By the end of the novel Ben is reunited with his father, who takes a job in the village and marries Mrs. Moss.

Within this narrative of families lost, found, and remade are Ben's narratives of circus life, descriptions of circus play, and adventures that take advantage of Ben's skills as a former circus bareback rider. When Ben gives an account of himself to the Moss family early in the novel, he emphasizes the glory of his circus career: "You jest oughter have seen me when I was a little feller all in white tights, and a gold belt, and pink riggin', standin' on father's shoulder, or hangin' on to old General's tail, and him gallopin' full pelt; or father ridin' three horses with me on *his* head wavin' flags, and everyone clappin' like fun."[15] However, the narrator allows readers only a brief opportunity to romanticize circus life before turning to Ben's account of his life after his father has gone to seek a new job and Amelia, the circus manager's wife and Ben's guardian, dies. Instead of emphasizing his thrilling and skillful tricks, Ben relates that he was forced to drink gin to slow his growth and to perform, despite a fall that injured his back and left him dizzy and weak.[16] With no adult to protect him, his only recourse to escape this abuse was to run away.

Despite the trauma and danger associated with the circus, Ben's experiences and character, a result of his time with the circus, are celebrated in the narrative. Repeatedly Ben's acrobatic skills charm children and adults alike. His "lively tales of circus life" entertain fretful Thorny, Miss Celia's invalid brother, and later he is entrusted with the task of teaching Thorny to ride. When Miss Celia falls while riding and her horse returns without her, Ben intuits what has happened and his knowledge of horse behavior (gained at the circus) allows him to find and revive her. When Ben is enrolled in school, the narrator praises the patience and determination he uses to master his school tasks and explicitly links those qualities to his circus experience.

At the heart of the novel Alcott includes a visit to the circus, which draws on many of the same conventions as Howells's account in *A Boy's Town*. Alcott titles the chapter "Someone Runs Away," alluding both to the literary trope and to contemporary fears regarding boys running away from home to join the circus. In this instance, however, Ben and his friends are not running away but attending the performance without permission, and the "someone" who runs away turns out to be the stolen Sancho. When the children arrive at the circus, Ben is clearly in his element, able to authoritatively guide his friends around the menagerie and into the circus performance. The circus evokes "excitement," "astonishment," "delight," "raptures," and "awe" from the children, and the narrator reports that with each performance the children plan how they might replicate the feat at home.[17]

Nevertheless, Alcott manifests fears about the circus when she reiterates Ben's prior abusive circus experience by displacing it onto Sancho. The dog is stolen from Ben at the circus. Subsequent chapters develop Sancho's plight, including having his coat shorn and dyed black and his tail bobbed, and being beaten by the man who is making him perform. In short, Sancho's natural identity has been deformed—his name and appearance changed—ostensibly in order to hide the theft, but analogously to reinforce the grotesque manipulation that Ben suffered as an unprotected circus performer. When Sancho returns to Ben, his spirit is changed: "his once sweet temper was a trifle soured; and, with a few exceptions, he had lost his faith in mankind.... [N]ow he eyed all strangers suspiciously, and the sight of a shabby man made him growl and bristle up, as if the memory of his wrongs still burned hotly within him."[18] Though Howells would later use the circus to fashion a putatively authentic national identity, Alcott here associates the circus with deformed identities that harm the natural goodness of the individual.

If Alcott's novel closed with the return of the damaged Sancho, we could easily interpret the story as a cautionary tale to warn children of the dark underside of circus life. Instead, Alcott avoids wholesale condemnation of the circus by relying on circus imagery and metaphors throughout the rest of the novel. In several other incidents toward the close of the novel, Ben's association with the circus provides valuable experience and skill. Furthermore, Ben's birthday celebration is compared to a circus ("the quiet place look[ed] as lively as a circus tent") and includes circus activity. At the end of a series of tableaus offered as part of the birthday entertainment, Ben appears as a circus rider in order to prove to the village boys that "he had not boasted vainly of past splendors." When Ben completes his trick riding before the "excited audience," the narrator comments, "[Ben] found this riding in the fresh air with only his mates for an audience pleasanter than the crowded tent, the tired horses, profane men, and painted women, friendly as some of them had been to him."[19] In short, Ben repudiates his life as a circus performer for that of a school boy in the rural village. His choice is underscored by the title of the novel, *Under the Lilacs*, which asserts the domestic and pastoral over the cosmopolitan circus.

Alcott's contradictory representation of the circus experience—including Sancho's abuse and Ben's repudiation of the circus life as well as her consistent use of circus imagery as natural, lively, and celebratory—suggests that the circus as a setting and as a metaphor touches on deeply held beliefs or ideals. Alcott uses the circus to illustrate historical aspects of childhood that disrupted the bucolic ideal of childhood. For example, the circus highlights Ben's unprotected status as an orphan. The plight of working orphans and child performers was fresh on Alcott's mind, for the composition of *Under the Lilacs* was likely prompted by her reading of the highly publicized case of a rescue by the Society for the Prevention of Cruelty to Children of a young child performer from New York City's Tivoli Garden Theater in 1875 and her visit to the Newsboys' Home during the same month.[20] The rescue of the child slack-rope walker Prince Leo by the Society for the Prevention of Cruelty to Children was featured in a front-page story in the *New York Times* on November 8, 1875. Other articles or related notices appeared

on November 9, 11, 13, 17, and 24 and December 16, 1875. The incident sparked attention about the plight of child performers, and the following year the State of New York enacted strict legislation forbidding child performers. In fact, some of the children in Alcott's novel refer to a law that makes children's performance illegal: "I've heard some men say that it's against the law to have small boys now; it's so dangerous and not good for them."[21]

By depicting the circus as an intrusion of the adult world into the bucolic world of childhood, Alcott's story pits the benefits of family, village life, and, particularly, an education against the deceptive glories of the circus. For Alcott, there are no good alternatives to the rural, domestic, middle-class life she sets forth for her characters. However, her insistence suggests that these values needed to be reinforced for her child readers, that they could not be assumed. In using the circus, she acknowledges it as an attractive alternative, from the child's perspective, to the supposedly sedate protected life within the family. But by having Ben repudiate his circus life and happily live with his father and Mrs. Moss in the village, Alcott reinforces rural domestic life as the appropriate environment for a child.

Stories that appear in juvenile periodicals during this period repeatedly emphasize the merits of a sheltered middle-class life to young readers. One of the aspects of the circus that is commented on regularly is the lack of middle-class domesticity in the living conditions of the circus performers. In the case of Rob, the central figure in Amanda Douglas's story "How Rob Ran Away," which appeared in *Oliver Optic's Magazine* (1868), lack of cleanliness as well as other absent domestic practices, such as his mother's tucking him into bed and saying his prayers with him, prompt him to give up circus life after a week and return home.[22] The story implies

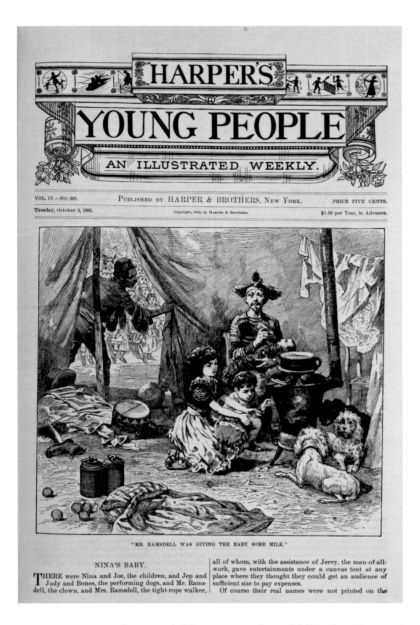

HARPER'S

YOUNG PEOPLE

AN ILLUSTRATED WEEKLY.

VOL. IV.—NO. 205.   PUBLISHED BY HARPER & BROTHERS, NEW YORK.   PRICE FIVE CENTS.

Tuesday, October 2, 1883.   Copyright, 1883, by HARPER & BROTHERS. $1.50 per Year, in Advance.

"MR. RAMSDELL WAS GIVING THE BABY SOME MILK."

NINA'S BABY.

THERE were Nina and Joe, the children, and Jep and Judy and Bones, the performing dogs, and Mr. Ramsdell, the clown, and Mrs. Ramsdell, the tight-rope walker, all of whom, with the assistance of Jerry, the man-of-all-work, gave entertainments under a canvas tent at any place where they thought they could get an audience of sufficient size to pay expenses.

Of course their real names were not printed on the

mary of what is, admittedly, a thin plot, does not do justice to the impact of the story, for the editors featured the story by placing it first in the issue and the subject of the cover illustration (*fig. 14.4*). Though Mr. and Mrs. Ramsdell are loving parents, their topsy-turvey domestic arrangements are conveyed in the unsigned illustration. The disorder of the scene suggested by the strewn garments and fruit on the ground, the haphazard placement of circus props such as the drum, and the comical Mr. Ramsdell in his clown costume feeding the baby, will likely be remedied when the family lives in a "real house."

Just as reinforcement of middle-class domesticity is a repeated element in circus literature for children, anxiety about abusive child labor conditions weaves through stories depicting the circus. In "Philemon's Circus" by Mary Densel (*Harper's Young People*, 1880) Densel's description of the child trapezist makes clear that his father and uncle treat him as an object rather than a son or nephew: "[T]hen small Bill was sent spinning through the air, sixty-five feet from the ground, to be caught by his uncle, tossed back to his father, now seized by an arm, now by a leg, now almost missed, now twirled round and round like a ball."[24] The narrator follows with a description of the agony felt by Bill's mother (a circus performer herself) as she watches the performance. In William Everett's *Thine, Not Mine,* young Diego, a bareback rider, is forced to jump through a series of closed (paper) hoops that disorient and frighten him. After several falls, the last of which seems to knock him unconscious, "Proprietor Kendall [the ringmaster] ran to the boy, dragged him up, shook him like a leaf, struck him three or four cruel blows on the head, and bade him go on."[25] In Laura C. Lillie's *Rolf House,* a young girl must stand on the top of a cannon when it is fired and serve as the target for a knife-throwing exhibition.[26] She is visibly terrified by her forced par-

that any child accustomed to middle-class domesticity will find circus life distasteful.

In the anonymous story "Nina's Baby," which appeared in *Harper's Young People* (1883), the Ramsdell family operates a small circus that is barely surviving financially.[23] On the way to the next show location, the daughter Nina discovers a baby in the road. When the happy parents are reunited with the baby, they offer the Ramsdell family a cottage for use in the off-season, which will allow the Ramsdell children to go to school for the first time. This brief sum-

▲ *Fig. 14.4.* "Mr. Ramsdell was Giving the Baby Some Milk," unsigned illustration for *Harper's Young People*, Oct. 2, 1883. Courtesy American Antiquarian Society

ticipation in the performance. These portrayals of fearful child performers are not balanced by any depictions of child performers who enjoy their work. Aside from the children in "Nina's Baby" and Mademoiselle Jeannette, whom we will meet in *Toby Tyler*, no child circus performer enjoys his or her work. The authors did not or could not imagine a healthy environment for a child aside from the bucolic childhood we see in *Under the Lilacs*.

By far the most famous circus in nineteenth-century children's literature is that in James Otis [Kaler]'s *Toby Tyler, or Ten Weeks with a Circus*, serialized in *Harper's Young People* in 1880 and published as a novel by Harper & Brothers the following year.[27] Though the author went on to write several more novels about the circus, *Toby Tyler*, was his most successful, appearing in over thirty editions and adapted for two film versions.[28] One of the causes of its popularity is its focus on circus life. While other stories for children use a circus setting or include a visit to the circus, *Toby Tyler* is one of the few novels focused almost entirely on life in the circus. Even the two novels that Horatio Alger, Jr. produced about circus life, *The Young Acrobat, or The Great North American Circus* (1887) and *The Young Circus Rider, or, The Mystery of Robert Rudd* (1883) frequently direct the readers' attention away from the protagonist's temporary occupation with the circus to the larger narrative of the protagonist's rise in status to wealth and middle-class stability.[29] To be sure, Alger does portray the occupation of a talented circus performer as better than no job at all, but characters in both novels aspire to more than a circus life, and that aspiration diminishes the role the circus plays in the overall narrative.

Toby Tyler, in contrast, is about life in the circus and full of behind-the-scene details rather than cursory descriptions of performances. Otis depicts Toby's tasks as a lemonade and candy seller as well as his training as a bareback rider, and thoroughly develops the friendships between Toby and members of all levels of the circus hierarchy—from gruff Ben, the wagon driver, to Mr. and Mrs. Treat, the Fat Lady and Skelton Man of the sideshow, to Mademoiselle Jeannette, the young bareback rider who is his riding partner in the show. Each of these friendships allows Otis to provide realistic details about circus life. Readers found his representation of the circus so convincing that rumors developed that Otis must have been with the circus at some point in his life. Details about James Otis Kaler's early life are sparse, but David Russell, in his biographical sketch of the author, states that he worked for a time as a publicity man for a circus.[30] However, a more recent biographical sketch by Otis's grandson John Kaler explains that his grandfather received an assignment while working for *Frank Leslie's Boys and Girls Weekly* "to accompany the P. T. Barnum circus on its travels and prepare articles on his experiences" during the last year that Barnum traveled by wagon rather than by rail (1872) and that this experience served as the foundation for the story.[31]

Aside from simply including details about the workaday world of the circus, Otis chose to present sympathetically Toby's decision to run away to the circus. While many authors for children frame the protagonist's decision to run away as naive or ungrateful, Otis suggests that Toby's decision improves his situation.[32] Toby is an orphan, and his stated reason for running away from Uncle Daniel's farm is related to his desire to eat more than Uncle Daniel provides. At the beginning, readers are free to imagine Toby as an adopted orphan mistreated as cheap labor, a serious social situation during the time period. Consequently, Toby's running away to the circus would not be condemned automatically as it would be if he ran away from his biological family. Although Toby's employer at the circus, the lemonade seller Mr. Lord, turns out to be even more exploitive, Toby's innate goodness makes him the object of kindness among the circus performers and workers. The unconventional surrogate family that develops in the first few chapters—including Mr. Stubbs the monkey, Ben, and the Treats—provides the affection and care missing from Toby's experience on Uncle Daniel's farm.

Furthermore, even though quite early in the novel Toby regrets his decision to run away and determines to save money to return to Uncle Daniel, that desire subsides into the background as readers watch Toby's developing relationships with the circus performers. The return is delayed when Mr. Stubbs throws away Toby's savings as he sleeps. However, this hurdle in Toby's affairs is fortunate in that it forces him to remain with the circus where, shortly thereafter, he is trained to become a bareback rider, in effect achieving a rise in status and a salary that will far exceed that of Ben and the Treats. By being a bareback performer, Toby attains the pinnacle of circus performers.

Despite the way the circus permeates the novel and seems to offer Toby both financial and emotional stability and support, Otis's novel does not escape the ambivalences regarding childhood circulating in the culture, particularly the role of child labor and, by extension, the value of the child. As noted earlier in the discussion of *Under the Lilacs*, contemporary concerns about child performers and child labor were prompting the establishment of rescue organizations and legislation protecting children. In *Toby Tyler*, Otis presents a more highly charged argument by linking Toby's labor with slavery. Though Toby's change of status to bareback rider is hailed by his friends in eco-

nomic terms (Toby will be his "own boss," a "brilliant success," and "started in the business"), Otis also describes his experience using conventions and metaphors associated with slavery, for Toby's labor is compelled. Toby must escape—must run away *from* the circus—to gain a measure of control over his life. The description of Toby's escape echoes the descriptions used in slave narratives and novels that include an escape from a brutal master. Otis also underscores the brutality of Mr. Castle as "master": though Toby suffered from Mr. Lord's cuffs and kicks, Mr. Castle wields a whip as he trains Toby in bareback riding: when Toby "failed in any little particular the long lash of the whip would go curling around his legs or arms, until the little fellow's body and limbs were nearly covered with blue-and-black stripes."[33] Moreover, Toby's identity as a person is degraded to a simple economic exchange: Mr. Castle, the ringmaster, negotiates with Mr. Lord, the lemonade seller, for Toby's time, promising Mr. Lord a percentage of Toby's earnings. When Toby's progress as a bareback rider is assured, Mr. Lord and Mr. Castle view Toby as a source of income. Even Ella Mason, the girl who is advertised as Mademoiselle Jeannette, urges Toby before their first performance to do well so that they will each receive the dollar that her mother has offered them if they succeed in their performance. According to John Seelye, the subtitle of the novel, "Ten Weeks with a Circus" echoes Richard Dana's *Two Years before the Mast*. Seelye argues that both books "dispel boyish dreams of a runaway life."[34] In addition, both books reveal oppressive labor practices by using language or tropes associated with slavery.[35]

Though these labor and economic issues are central to Toby's experience in the circus, Otis ultimately resolves them by asserting a different value system based on sentiment and affection. Viviana

Zelizer has presented that after the Civil War, American society struggled to define the value of a child. Examining court cases, legislation, newspaper articles, and other documents, Zelizer contends that nineteenth-century society recognized the economic or labor value of the child as well as the sentimental value. Consequently, child labor was not always condemned. In fact, farm labor or domestic labor was considered not only appropriate but beneficial to the child.[36] However, Otis sidesteps the role of economics in the value of a child. Instead of resolving Toby's conflict by offering a more appropriate labor within a more conventional family unit (as Alcott does in *Under the Lilacs*), Otis emphasizes the affective relationships that Toby develops. In effect, Toby's value as a circus performer and ultimately his value as a laborer is outweighed by his sentimental value.

Otis underscores Toby's sentimental value in several ways. First, Toby's innate goodness and his naïveté draw together a number of well-intentioned people employed at the circus who create a family with Toby at the center. This family will be temporarily reunited in the sequel, *Mr. Stubbs's Brother*, and again in *Old Ben*. Toby's most important relationship, however, is with Mr. Stubbs the monkey. Toby's conversations with and care of Mr. Stubbs prove that his value inheres in his relationships rather than in his labor, for his rise to success is based on that relationship. Toby's ability to round up the monkeys when they escape their cage is due to the attention he has already paid Mr. Stubbs and results in not only getting to keep Mr. Stubbs as his own but also his being trained as a bareback rider.

Mr. Stubbs dies at the end of the novel, shot accidentally by a hunter when Toby and Mr. Stubbs are running away from the circus. In *Audacious Kids: Coming of Age in America's Classic Children's Books*,

Jerry Griswold argues that Mr. Stubbs's death represents the death of Toby's childhood, a necessary step in Toby's growth into a self-sufficient young man.[37] However, Otis's readers, both adults and children, were not as philosophical. Letters to Otis repeatedly bemoaned the fact that Mr. Stubbs died, asking why it was necessary, or asserting that Toby should have stayed with the circus so that Mr. Stubbs could live. Correspondents commented on the death of Mr. Stubbs more often than any other element of the story.[38] While it would be easy enough to dismiss their responses as maudlin, their consistent reference to that event underscores Toby's sentimental value over his economic value. Furthermore, Mr. Stubbs's death also signals that circus life cannot be integrated into the childhood that Toby returns to on Uncle Daniel's farm.

Just as important is Uncle Daniel's conversion at the end of the novel. Rather than presenting a tearful Toby who regrets running away, the narrator focuses on Uncle Daniel's regret: "My poor boy . . . my love for you was greater than I knew, and when you left me I cried aloud to the Lord as if it had been my own flesh and blood that had gone afar from me. Stay here, Toby, my son, and help to support this poor old body as it goes down into the dark valley of the shadow of death."[39] Whereas early in the novel Uncle Daniel complains that Toby does not do enough work around the farm to justify the amount of food he eats, in the conclusion Uncle Daniel makes no comment about the value of Toby's labor. Instead, Toby's status has changed—Uncle Daniel calls him "my son" and compares him to "my own flesh and blood," thereby establishing a new paternal relationship. In addition, Toby's work at the end of the novel is spiritual rather than physical. Though Uncle Daniel describes his death in terms of his "old body," the thrust of the passage is not on physical care or the ways in which Toby will help Uncle Daniel on the farm, but on the spiritual preparation necessary to attain heaven, for Uncle Daniel goes on to say, "in the bright light of that glorious future, Uncle Daniel will wait to go with you into the presence of Him who is ever a father to the fatherless." Though the novel portrays Toby's regret that he ran away, the conclusion of the novel is far less interested in Toby's change of heart than his change of status, a change that emphasizes his sentimental value as a son rather than his economic value as a worker. By emphasizing Toby's sentimental value over his economic value, the novel seems to anticipate ideas about childhood that Zelizer argues will come to prominence decades later. However, it would be a mistake to see Otis as breaking new ground. Instead, Otis harks back to an older romantic version of childhood that emphasized the child as agent of spiritual renewal or transformation. The circus, as a traveling secular entertainment, offers no possibility for Toby's role, and by extension, no possibilities for children.

Of the number of Otis's other novels featuring circuses, *Mr. Stubbs's Brother* offers the most interesting and complex ideas. As mentioned earlier, in *Mr. Stubbs's Brother* Otis tries to depict a possible integration of the circus world with the quotidian world of village life. When the novel opens, Toby has been home for several months and his friends have finally convinced him to help them organize a circus of their own. No sooner do they begin practicing their acts than the posters of the very circus Toby ran away with appear on fences and barns. With Uncle Daniel and Aunt Olive's permission, Toby invites the Treats and Old Ben for dinner between the afternoon and evening performances. Otis makes much of the visual discrepancy of the performers, in costume, socializing with Uncle Daniel and Aunt Olive in their parlor, but the occasion is a success, including Ben's decision to use his savings to help support a young crippled orphan boy whom Toby has befriended. The integration inadvertently turns into an invasion when the performers give Toby another monkey, whom Toby calls Mr. Stubbs's brother. Having a monkey on the farm leads to a series of comically frustrating situations. However, Otis ultimately fails in his attempt to integrate Toby's unconventional circus family with his conventional family on the farm. Abner, Toby's crippled friend, is severely injured by an accident at the circus and eventually dies of that injury. Mr. Stubbs's brother destroys the boys' efforts to perform their own circus and at the end of the novel is caged in a shed so that he will not harass the farm poultry or do other property damage.

As we have seen in Alcott's novel, Otis's novels about the circus are torn by tensions and contradictory values. On the one hand, Otis seems to offer a possibility of a safe childhood in the unconventional life of the circus, by means of the surrogate families and social networks constructed by the generous and well-meaning circus folk. However, ultimately the circus world and the quotidian world of the farm must remain separate, with the farm world defined as the appropriate life of the child. In effect, Otis reinforces the pastoral ideal of childhood.

Despite the conflicted representations of the circus found in the fiction for children, nonfiction articles tended to represent the circus more sympathetically, possibly because both the readers and the writers assumed a shared experience of particular circus performances. In most volumes over the course of its twenty-year history, the editors of *Harper's Young People* included an article that reported circus news, such as announcements that Barnum's circus had moved into winter quarters.

Similarly, in 1901 *St. Nicholas* offered readers a multipart series entitled "Careers of Danger and Daring" by Cleveland Moffett, which included one installment that featured "the aerial athlete," or trapeze artist, and another that profiled wild animal trainers. However, the most extensive nonfiction account of the circus for children is William O. Stoddard's two-part essay "Men–and–Animal Shows, and How They Are Moved About," which appeared in *St. Nicholas* in 1882.[40]

Stoddard's topic is the "modern American show" rather than the small mud-show circuses that are featured in fictional accounts. Although he does not profile a specific circus company, he does refer to "Mr. Barnum's circus" occasionally to illustrate his points. The complex movement of the circus was often celebrated as a "disciplined *pageant* of labor," according to Janet Davis (my emphasis).[41] Stoddard's informative account, in contrast, demystifies the circus operation. In the first installment, he provides a brief history of the circus and then turns his attention to the menagerie exhibit. He explains how circuses acquire exotic animals, even including the costs of purchasing animals such as zebras, tigers, and gnus. He interviews liontamers who emphasize that patience, rather than cruelty, is the key to successful animal training. He explains the care necessary to keep menagerie animals healthy, both on tour and in winter quarters. When he turns his attention to the human circus performers, he explains the off-season work of managers and others who must keep in contact with the performers and make judgments at the beginning of each season as to which acts will be employed. Stoddard explains that the skills of performers must be constantly exercised rather than allowed to fall dormant and that employees who "acquire bad habits" (intemperance seems to be the condition of most concern) will not be hired.

Stoddard goes on to describe the planning that makes the circus "city" move smoothly. He explains that the circus hires, trains, and carries with it every person who will perform a task, and that every piece of equipment or material has a specific place on the train that transports the circus from location to location. In addition, Stoddard explains the network of employees who must arrive before the circus reaches its next engagement in order to advertise the upcoming show and to purchase materials such as food for the animals. He also informs his readers that only a small percentage of circus employees perform in the ring and that the vast majority of employees are behind the scenes. They unload the trains, raise both the big top and the secondary tents, care for animals, and care for other employees. He explains how the hundreds of people who work for a circus are fed each day on the circus grounds. Once the basics of the tent city are established, Stoddard then turns to the performance space and emphasizes to readers the necessity of building a proper ring to avoid injury to riders and horses and the care needed for the machinery of the acrobats. Even the performance itself is labor: "When at last all things are finished, and the hour has arrived for the band to strike up, and the guests of the tent-city have gathered to witness the results of all this outlay and care and toil, there comes an hour of excitement and amusement,—to everybody who does not belong to the circus menagerie. The show people are busy with the hard, anxious work of making fun for the visitors."[42] Stoddard concludes the essay with a description of the striking of the tent.

Stoddard's demystification of the circus erases the romantic and exotic and substitutes efficient domestic practice as the attraction of the show. The tasks of feeding hundreds of employees, maintaining the health of animals, keeping costumes and other performance materials in good order, and construct-

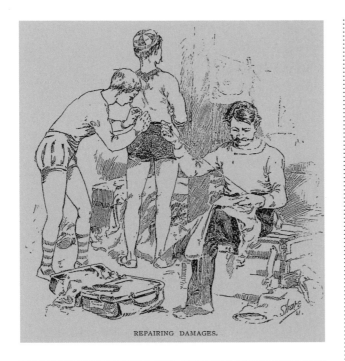

REPAIRING DAMAGES.

THE LAUNDRY.

ing the circus site dominate the article. In fact, Stoddard ignores the performance almost completely. The illustrations in the article support the portrayal of the circus as a version of domestic labor, for they depict scenes that readers would associate with domestic life: performers mending their costumes, the interior of a dining tent, a man washing clothing in a washtub (*figs. 14.5, 14.6*). Even in the pictures of animals practicing their tricks, the captions either domesticate their behavior or emphasize practice and hard work rather than performance (*figs. 14.7, 14.8*). In closing his account, Stoddard warns his readers that boys are not wanted at the circus (other than as paying audience members):

> [The circus manager] would not have them at any price, although hundreds are sure to offer, continually, with their heads full of dime-novel ideas of circus life, its "adventures," and its "glories." They know nothing at all of the hard work, the patient training beforehand, neither do they think of the experience and thorough knowledge of at least some one trade required by every member of the manager's army of helpers.... boys with circus-fever are after something which will enable them to wear tights and spangles. They seldom if ever think of the hard work, severe training, wearying repetitions, and terrible risks of injury and life-long maiming that must be undergone before a manager will allow a performer to appear in public.[43]

Stoddard's advice at the end of his essay is double-edged. On the one hand, he sounds the same note heard regularly in children's literature of the period—boys who run away with the circus rue their decision. On the other hand, by deromanticizing the circus he highlights the labor of the circus, thereby

Fig. 14.5. "Repairing Damages," illustration for "Men-and-Animal Shows, and How They Are Moved About," *St. Nicholas, an Illustrated Magazine for Young Folks* 9, no. 5 (March 1882). Baldwin Library of Historical Children's Literature, University of Florida

Fig. 14.6. "The Laundry," illustration for "Men-and-Animal Shows, and How They Are Moved About," *St. Nicholas, an Illustrated Magazine for Young Folks* 9, no. 5 (March 1882). Baldwin Library of Historical Children's Literature, University of Florida

THE ELEPHANT'S TOILET.

ELEPHANTS PRACTICING DURING THE TEACHER'S ABSENCE.

Fig. 14.7. "The Elephant's Toilet," illustration for "Men–and–Animal Shows, and How They Are Moved About," *St. Nicholas, an Illustrated Magazine for Young Folks* 9, no. 5 (March 1882). Baldwin Library of Historical Children's Literature, University of Florida

Fig. 14.8. "Elephants Practicing during the Teacher's Absence," illustration for "Men–and–Animal Shows, and How They Are Moved About," *St. Nicholas, an Illustrated Magazine for Young Folks* 9, no. 4 (Feb. 1882). Baldwin Library of Historical Children's Literature, University of Florida

validating the entertainment as skillful work.

In one other way Stoddard is critical—not so much of the circus as of the audience. As mentioned above, he begins his essay with a brief history: "There probably was never a time when people were not fond of staring at 'shows'" and he goes on to describe the violence of both Roman and medieval "shows."[44] He returns to this idea again toward the end of the essay when he discusses the circus acts themselves: "There still lurks among us, in spite of all our civilization, a relic of the coarse and morbid appetite which made the heathenish, savage populace of Rome clamor for the bloody shows of the arena. We are still uncivilized enough, many of us, to be drawn to gaze upon a performance which seems to be full of danger. It is a disgraceful appetite, but every manager caters to it, more or less."[45] According to Stoddard, circus managers aim for a middle way between such appetites and "the kindlier sensibilities" of those members of the public who refuse to buy tickets for such events.

Stoddard concludes that many of the members of the audience have their appetite for danger satiated in the menagerie display, the feats of horsemanship in the ring, and the "perilous and . . . impossible" tricks of the acrobats.[46]

Stoddard's account provides a useful contrast to the fictional depictions of the circus. Whether the difference is due to the requirements of writing non-fiction which prevented Stoddard from using the circus to convey ideology about childhood or to an alternative view of childhood is difficult to determine. Nonetheless, Stoddard's language in this passage is directed not toward the child readers or the idea of childhood; rather, his language suggests an inchoate sense of circus performances as existential acts, as activities that acknowledge and test what it means to be human.[47] In the context of nineteenth-century American culture, when philosophers had not yet developed an elegant vocabulary to articulate these ideas, Stoddard uses the expressions and values available to him to convey his reaction. His focus on the skillful labor that permeates the circus recuperates the circus from the charge of frivolous entertainment, thereby lending dignity to the performers. Furthermore, that same physicality central to the labor described in the article is removed from the brutish violence he attributes to the Roman circus and instead expresses grace and courage in the face of human limitation.

The ambivalence and complexity of written accounts of the circus are also evident in the illustrations that accompany stories about the circus. Despite the regular appearance of the circus in children's literature, very rarely were images of the circus included with the stories or articles. With the notable exceptions of Stoddard's articles and W. A. Rogers's illustrations for *Toby Tyler* and *Mr. Stubbs's Brother*, most writing for children did not

THE MANAGERS OF THE CIRCUS LOOKING AT THE POSTERS OF THEIR RIVAL.

▲ *Fig. 14.9.* William A. Rogers, "The Managers of the Circus Looking at the Posters of Their Rival," illustration for James Otis, *Mr. Stubbs's Brother* (New York: Harper, 1882). Illinois State University's Special Collections, Milner Library

include images of the circus. For example, Alcott's *Under the Lilacs* was serialized in *St. Nicholas*, a lavishly illustrated magazine in its day, and despite the rich circus content, no illustrations depict the performance or the other celebrated circus-associated behavior. Mary Mapes Dodge, the first editor of *St. Nicholas*, famously announced that the pictures in the magazine would be of especially high quality, suggesting verisimilitude and energy as important qualities: "They should be heartily conceived and well executed; and they must be suggestive, attractive and epigrammatic. If it be only the picture of a cat, it must be so like a cat that it will do its own purring, and not sit a dead, stuffed thing, requiring the editor to purr for it."[48] Despite these high aesthetic standards, editors or illustrators (or both) may have been motivated by a conservative desire to present to children only the seemly and uplifting and thereby avoided depicting performers in (relatively) scantily clad costumes, even though the text of articles and stories often expressed the assumption that children had been to the circus and would be familiar with such sights.

Similarly, one of the regular features of circus literature is a comment about the duplicity of circus advertising. Invariably, either the narrator or a more experienced character comments on the truth value of the circus poster, noting that the posters disguise true identity or exaggerate the performance. In James Otis's *Mr. Stubbs's Brother*, the illustrator William. A. Rogers subtly suggested as much in his illustration of Toby and his friends viewing the circus posters that papered his small village (*fig. 14.9*). The caption for the illustration "The Managers of the Circus Looking at the Posters of Their Rival," alludes to the boys' desire to get up their own circus as well as the common occurrence of competitive papering by rival circuses. Toby, as the boy who

Fig. 14.10. "Roman Chariot Race Four-to-Hand," illustration from *A Peep at the Circus* (New York: McLoughlin Brothers, 1887). Chromolithograph. Baldwin Library of Historical Children's Literature, University of Florida

Fig. 14.11. "Acrobats and Jugglers and Their Wonderful Feats," illustration from *A Peep at the Circus* (New York: McLoughlin Brothers, 1887). Chromolithograph. Baldwin Library of Historical Children's Literature, University of Florida

THE CIRCUS PROCESSION.

Open the gates, and draw the curtain,
Here comes something fine, that's certain;
Louder the band begins to play,
Open the gates, and clear the way!

Enters a Queen with a King beside her;
Every horse is proud of his rider;
Two by two they march to the tune,
And head the procession that will follow soon.

Here is something very funny,
Surely worth the entrance money;
At the sight what laughter peals!—
'Tis an Elephant on wheels!

Close behind him a relation,
In a state of perspiration,
Dons his specs, and wields his fan
Just like any gentleman.

Here is Jumbo, gentle creature,
Kindness shown in every feature;
On his back the children are,
Safe as in a jaunting car.

Shetland ponies—small and stocky—
Each one mounted by a jockey—
March 'twixt Elephants and Giraffes;
'Tis no wonder Towser laughs.

Here's a funny turnout, surely,
With an Ostrich lashed securely
To a coach, Zenobia shares!
And well the bird the burden bears!

Goats upon the mountains ramble,
And in harness sometimes amble;
But a tandem-team like this,
Is a sight you should not miss.

Through the desert Camels travel,
Speeding o'er the sand and gravel,
Bearing heavy burdens too,

Here the roads are rough and stony;
And the Camel's back's so bony,
None but Clowns would dare to go

Fig. 14.12. The Circus Procession (New York: McLoughlin Brothers, 1888). Chromolithograph. Courtesy American Antiquarian Society

Now a Clown in line appearing
With a tandem, swells the cheering;
Standing on his Horse's back
Thus he guides them round the track.

On a Donkey rides another,
Quite as funny as his brother,
Blowing bugle notes so loud,
He astonishes the crowd.

Now a Clown in line appearing
With a tandem, swells the cheering;
Standing on his Horse's back
Thus he guides them round the track.

On a Donkey rides another,
Quite as funny as his brother,
Blowing bugle notes so loud,
He astonishes the crowd.

Hark, the trumpet loudly pealing
Knocks the plaster from the ceiling,
As there marches on the course
The Jumbos of the police-force.

Clowns, and Dogs with queer expression
Have their place in this procession;
And 'tis hard for dogs, I know,
On their two hind legs to go.

Who are these with courtly manners
Bearing lofty poles and banners?
Faithfully they represent
Followers of the tournament.

Next a line of pretty pages
Our attention close engages;
The Chinese Giant in the rear
Making them like dwarfs appear.

Goodness gracious! Did you ever?
Here are harnessed up quite clever
Two Giraffes! The whip they heed;
Nor venture at a break-neck speed.

A Soldier comes! On stilts he's stalking!
Back of him a Dude is walking,
Either side of him a friend
As you can see;—AND THAT'S THE END!

THE CIRCUS PROCESSION

Copyrighted 1888 by McLOUGHLIN BROS. N.Y.

spent ten weeks with the circus, is depicted in the posture of a teacher, pointing out to his young friend Abner various details; meanwhile, the other boys in the image appear to absorb the posters without any critical filter.

Fig. 14.13. *E. Elephant, Esq., Showman* (New York: McLoughlin Brothers, 1896). Chromolithograph. Collection of The New-York Historical Society

However, outside of the literary marketplace, images of the circus were available to children. Beginning in the 1880s as commercial use of chromolithography developed, McLoughlin Brothers published illustrated books about the circus for children. The New York publishing house produced illustrated books, toy books, Mother Goose books, and primers as well as paper dolls and sets of playing cards for children, in addition to ephemera for the adult market. While the publishing house made no effort to break into the literary marketplace, it pursued innovation in color printing, adopting chromolithography early and paying particular attention to the design elements of books. The resulting books remain some of the most beautiful images of the circus in the Gilded Age.[49]

Surviving business records of McLoughlin Brothers are spotty, but according to the publisher's catalogues available at the American Antiquarian Society (AAS), by 1886 the firm was producing the Circus Stories Series, which included books ranging in price from fifteen cents to one dollar.[50] Titles such as *A Peep at the Circus*, *Visit to the Circus*, *Wonders of the Circus*, and *Circus Sights* depict moments of circus performance (*fig. 14.10*).[51] The books feature full-page illustrations approximately ten by six inches. Some editions are printed in two colors and some in four colors. In addition, the books include well-designed pages of composite illustrations, composed of isolated details of a performance (*fig. 14.11*). Some of the pictures are accompanied by a short verse describing the scene.

All of these books share some illustrations in common, suggesting that the McLoughlin Brothers were cleverly using their pre-existing plates to create additional products. The common images, as well as the similarities in the backgrounds of the images, suggest that the illustrator (likely Charles

Kendrick, according to AAS records[52]) was using the circus performances in Madison Square Garden as the model for his pictures; the acts depicted in the books match specific acts that Barnum advertised during the 1880s. For example, the McLoughlin Brothers book *The Menagerie and Arab Show* (1890) depicts trick cattle and trick bears, both acts that were featured in Barnum's 1889 show according to a Barnum & Bailey advertising magazine in the AAS holdings.[53]

The McLoughlin Brothers books' attention to design was quite innovative. *The Circus Procession* (1888) is printed on paper that has been glued to boards and then accordion bound so that it can stand on edge and open to represent the entirety of a circus procession, either as a parade or as the Grand Entry or Pageant that signaled the opening of the performance (*fig. 14.12*). *E. Elephant, Esq., Showman* (1896), in a nod to Barnum's persona, is cut in the shape of an elephant walking upright and tipping his hat (*fig. 14.13*). The sixteen pictures in the book alternate between color and black-and-white and have been recycled by reducing or cropping previously used images.

The depiction of the circus in the books published by McLoughlin Brothers contrasts sharply with the depiction in the more literary children's books and periodicals. Instead of the one-ring tent show traveling from village to village, the circus in the Circus Stories Series is performed in an interior space, likely Madison Square Garden. Just as significantly, the tone of McLoughlin Brothers books is far less cautionary and more celebratory. A comparison of illustrations can illuminate this difference.

The single illustration of a circus performance in *Toby Tyler* is Toby's first and only performance as a bareback rider (*fig. 14.14*). Rogers depicts a tense Toby with clenched fists, rather

MADEMOISELLE JEANNETTE AND MONSIEUR AJAX.

awkwardly squatting in preparation for his jump through a paper hoop that Mademoiselle Jeannette has already burst. Toby's posture reveals his discomfort and fear and, by extension, that he does not belong at the circus. The illustration reinforces the book's theme that the circus was no place for children. In *Circus Sights* (1890) the figure jumping through the paper hoop shows far more control and grace (*fig. 14.15*). In addition, the color and design elements of the picture underscore the desirability of viewing the performance, as well as being the performer who is the object of the concern and delight expressed on the faces of the audience members in the background.

Why are circus tricks celebrated in *Circus Sights* but not in *Toby Tyler*? One possible answer is

Fig. 14.14. William A. Rogers, "Mademoiselle Jeannette and Monsieur Ajax," illustration for James Otis, *Toby Tyler, or Ten Weeks with the Circus* (New York: Harper, 1881). Illinois State University's Special Collections, Milner Library

Donovan

▲ *Fig. 14.15.* "Leaping from a Horse's Back through a Paper Hoop,"
illustration from *Circus Sights* (New York: McLoughlin Brothers, 1890).
Chromolithograph. Courtesy American Antiquarian Society

that *Circus Sights* does not require the child to enter into the world of the circus as *Toby Tyler* does. Children can view the pictures in *Circus Sights* safely ensconced in their homes. By their very presentation, McLoughlin Brothers books encourage an appreciation of the circus from a distance and as a performance. However, Toby Tyler's story demands that Toby (and by extension the child reader) enter the world of the circus, a world that American authors did not view as safe and would not sanction.

I have argued in this essay that representations of the circus in nineteenth-century children's literature reveal the gaps and fissures in that society's ideas about childhood: what children should experience, what they should be, and how they should be treated. The circus, in its currency and ubiquity, offered a contemporary institution on which authors could bank—readers would be familiar with the circus as well as find it alluring. However, despite the circus's obvious popularity and the efforts to advertise the circus as especially suitable for children (*fig. 14.16*), many writers for children avoided using the circus as a textural element, as one of many details that reflected children's experience back to them in the pages of their books. Instead, the contradictions and ambivalences evident in the stories suggest that authors were depending on the circus to carry their ideological baggage. As a traveling show, the circus invaded the bucolic space authors desired for childhood and brought elements of the adult world that children would eventually face: a world filled with difficult, dreary, or dangerous labor, oppressive managers, duplicitous messages, insubstantial and ephemeral satisfactions or recompense, and devoid of play or enjoyment. For the most part, the stories and novels I've discussed caution readers to postpone an engagement with that adult world, to remain as long

as possible in the sheltered world of an idealized childhood. So while the circus may have been a particularly appropriate entertainment for a child, it was also, according to authors, an appropriate way to inform children about the adult world, a world of work rather than play.

Fig. 14.16. P. T. Barnum and Sarah J. Burke. *P. T. Barnum's Circus, Museum and Menagerie* (New York: White & Allen, 1888). Illinois State University's Special Collections, Milner Library

This essay could not have been written without the expertise and generous help of the staff of the American Antiquarian Society, particularly Laura E. Wasowicz, Curator of Children's Literature, and Lauren Hewes, Andrew W. Mellon Curator of Graphic Arts. I owe a debt of thanks to Kevin J. Donovan and Bobbie Solley, who graciously read earlier versions of this essay.

1 William D. Howells, *A Boy's Town* (New York: Harper & Brothers, 1890), 97–98.

2 Ibid., 97.

3 For a brief history of this equestrian gag, see John Culhane, *The American Circus: An Illustrated History* (New York: Henry Holt & Co., 1990), 47–49. Later in this same chapter, when Howells records the pleasures of circuses over menageries, he comments, "The boys would really rather have seen a bare-back rider, like James Rivers, turn a back somersault and light on his horse's crupper, any time" (107). The description of the stunt suggests that James Rivers may be based on James Robinson, who was, according to many, the preeminent acrobatic bareback rider of his time. See Culhane, *The American Circus,* 58–59.

4 Howells, *A Boy's Town,* 100.

5 Ibid., 101.

6 Ibid., 95.

7 Ibid.

8 Janet M. Davis, *The Circus Age: Culture & Society under the American Big Top* (Chapel Hill: University of North Carolina Press, 2002), 227.

9 Ibid.

10 Anne Scott MacLeod, *American Childhood: Essays on Children's Literature of the Nineteenth and Twentieth Centuries* (Athens: University of Georgia Press, 1994), esp. 143–56.

11 *The Circus.* Written for the American Sunday-School Union and Revised by the Committee of Publication (Philadelphia: American Sunday-School Union, 1827), 10–13.

12 *A Peep at the Circus, or A Business for Life.,* 2nd ed. (Boston: New England Sabbath School Union, 1844), 9.

13 Ibid., 28–30.

14 Louisa May Alcott, *Under the Lilacs,* serialized in *St. Nicholas Magazine* 5 (Dec. 1877–Oct. 1878) and published separately (Boston: Roberts Brothers, 1878).

15 Louisa May Alcott, *Under the Lilacs* (1878; rpt., Boston: Little, Brown and Co., 1928), 25. Further references are to this edition.

16 Ibid., 27.

17 Ibid., 125.

18 Ibid., 187.

19 Ibid., 227–28.

20 Alcott arrived in New York City in November 1875 and recounted her visit to the Newsboys' Home to her nephews Frederick and John Pratt in a letter dated Dec. 4, 1875.

21 Alcott, *Under the Lilacs,* 128.

22 Amanda M. Douglas, "How Rob Ran Away," *Oliver Optic's Magazine: Our Boys and Girls* 4, no. 94 (Oct. 17, 1868), 662–65.

23 "Nina's Baby," *Harper's Young People: An Illustrated Magazine* 4, no. 205 (Oct. 2, 1883), 753–55.

24 Mary Densel, "Philemon's Circus," *Harper's Young People: An Illustrated Magazine* 1 (July 13, 1880), 531.

25 William Everett, *Thine, Not Mine* (Boston: Roberts Brothers, 1891), 28.

26 Laura C. Lillie, *Rolf House* (New York: Harper & Brothers, 1886).

27 James Otis, *Toby Tyler, or Ten Weeks with a Circus,* serialized in *Harper's Young People* 2 (Dec. 1880–April 1881) and published separately (New York: Roberts Brothers, 1881).

28 Otis's other circus novels are *Mr. Stubbs's Brother* (1882), *The Clown's Protégé* (1883), *Andy's Ward, A Story of Circus People* (1895), *The Wreck of the Circus* (1897), and *Found by the Circus* (1909). In 1923 Jackie Coogan starred as Toby Tyler in *Circus Days,* the first motion picture adaptation of *Toby Tyler,* and the story was reintroduced to the baby-boom generation through Disney's 1960 movie version starring Kevin Corcoran as Toby. The Disney adaptation softens much of the brutality in Otis's novel, omitting the beatings Toby endures in the novel; Mr. Stubbs dies in the novel but recovers from his gunshot wound in the movie; Toby's attempt at running away from the circus succeeds in the novel, but does not in the movie. However, the movie closes with Uncle Daniel and Aunt Olive retrieving him from the circus, but only after they celebrate his new skill as a bareback rider by staying for a performance and owning him to strangers as "our boy."

29 Horatio Alger, Jr., *The Young Circus Rider, or, The Mystery of Robert Rudd* (Philadelphia: Porter & Coates, 1883) and *The Young Acrobat of the Great North American Circus* (1887, rpt. New York: The Federal Book Company, 1900).

30 David L. Russell, "James Otis Kaler," *Dictionary of Literary Biography,* vol. 42: *American Writers for Children before 1900* (Detroit: Gale, 1985).

31 John Kaler, "James Otis Kaler, A Biographical Sketch," *Dime Novel Round-Up* 69, no. 6 (Dec. 2000), 187.

32 Jerry Griswold, author of *Audacious Kids: Coming of Age in America's Classic Children's Books* (New York: Oxford University Press, 1992), noted the consistent references to Toby's eating in the novel and argues that Toby's "oral greed" must be tamed in order for him to attain maturity (170). However, the absence of a female figure in Uncle Daniel's household, the relationship between work and eating that Toby describes, and Toby's own naive charm suggest that Uncle Daniel's farm is not the kind of family situation preferred for children.

33 James Otis, *Toby Tyler, or Ten Weeks with a Circus* (New York: Harper & Brothers, 1881), 177.

34 John R. Seelye, preface, *Toby Tyler, or Ten Weeks with a Circus* (New York: Garland, 1977), vi.

35 David R. Roediger, *The Wages of Whiteness: Race and the Making of the American Working Class* (New York: Verso, 1991), 68.

36 Viviana A. Zelizer, *Pricing the Priceless Child: The Changing Social Value of Children* (New York: Basic Books, 1985), 73–112.

37 Griswold, *Audacious Kids,* 184.

38 Notebook of correspondence regarding *Toby Tyler,* James Otis Kaler Collection, South Portland Public Library, South Portland, Maine.

39 Otis, *Toby Tyler,* 262.

40 William O. Stoddard, "Men-and-Animal Shows, and How They Are Moved About," *St. Nicholas; An Illustrated Magazine for Young Folks* 9, no. 4 (Feb. 1882), 314–23; and no. 5 (March 1882), 366–76.

41 Davis, *Circus Age,* 43.

42 Stoddard, "Men-and-Animal Shows," no. 5, 372.

43 Ibid., 376.

44 Stoddard, "Men-and-Animal Shows," no. 4, 314.

45 Stoddard, "Men-and-Animal Shows," no. 5, 372–73.

46 Ibid., 374.

47 A number of circus historians and scholars have argued that a significant appeal of the circus is the way circus acts test our commonplace understanding of human capacity. For example, Helen Stoddart, *Rings of Desire: Circus History and Representation* (Manchester: Manchester University Press, 2000): "Circus is, above all, a vehicle for the demonstration and taunting of danger and this remains its most telling and defining feature. Physical risk-taking has always been at its heart; the recognition that to explore the limitations of the human body is to walk a line between triumphant exhilaration and, on the other side of this limit, pain, injury or death. The body in the circus is utterly self-reliant; it is preserved by skill and strength only, never by faith, fate or magic" (4). See also Davis, *Circus Age,* 236–37.

48 Mary Mapes Dodge, "Children's Magazines," *Scribner's Monthly,* July 1873; rpt. in *St. Nicholas and Mary Mapes Dodge: The Legacy of a Children's Magazine Editor, 1873–1905,* ed. Susan R. Gannon, Suzanne Rahn, and Ruth Anne Thompson (Jefferson, NC: McFarland, 2004), 17.

49 Laura Wasowicz, "Brief History of the McLoughlin Bros." Available at the website of the American Antiquarian Society, http://www.americanantiquarian.org/mcloughlin.htm (accessed Feb. 8, 2012).

50 McLoughlin Brothers titles about the circus appear as early as 1883 in the American Antiquarian Society holdings. However, no evidence exists that the firm established the circus books as a series until 1886.

51 I cannot help but surmise that someone on editorial staff at McLoughlin Brothers was familiar with the Sunday-School tract discussed earlier, *A Peep at the Circus, or a Business for Life,* and ironically resurrected the title for the company's own book.

52 Though several of the McLoughlin Brothers books included illustrations signed by Charles Kendrick, a number include illustrations only signed C. K., and some have no identifying mark.

53 *The Barnum & Bailey 15 United Shows* (Buffalo: Courier Co., 1889). Uncatalogued collection of broadsides. Available at the American Antiquarian Society (Worcester, Entertainment BDSDS, Circuses and Menageries, after 1880).

15

CIRCUS TOYS
IN THE GILDED AGE

EUGENE W. METCALF

The year 1903 was a landmark in the history of the American circus. During that year, more circuses were on the road than at any other time in U.S. history. Traveling by wagon and railroad, these circuses crisscrossed the nation, some playing coast to coast.[1] They ranged from small mud shows, with a single tent and a few performers, to spectacular three-ring extravaganzas featuring sprawling tent cities, herds of exotic animals, crowded midways, titillating sideshows, and armies of performers, roustabouts, advance men, candy butchers, and other circus workers. Between roughly 1880 and 1920, the circus was perhaps the most prominent, widely experienced, and influential form of American popular entertainment. This was the golden age of the American circus.

The year 1903 was important in the history of the circus for another reason as well. That year, the A. Schoenhut Company of Philadelphia introduced what would become one of the most popular toys in America—the Humpty Dumpty Circus (*fig. 15.1*). Originally consisting of only three wooden pieces—a clown, a chair and a ladder—the roster of Schoenhut characters grew quickly. By 1904 a donkey, elephant, white horse, poodle, and hobo had been added to the troupe (*fig. 15.2*). In an advertisement in *Ladies' Home Journal* of the same year, Schoenhut announced that its circus toys were also being sold in England, Germany, France, Austria, Italy, Spain, South Africa, and Australia.[2] Sales were so strong that by 1906, twelve more animals had been added to the menagerie, as well as a lion tamer, three kinds of acrobats, a tent, a wild animal cage, and a tightrope. Within six years of its introduction, this toy circus was virtually complete, featuring a total of over thirty animals and twenty performers. In addition to the Schoenhut pieces, numerous other popular circus toys were introduced by other East Coast toy manufacturers during this period—from miniature trains and wagons to puzzles, blocks, pull toys, paper dolls, articulated figures, and mechanical banks.

Detail of fig. 15.1. Humpty Dumpty Circus, 1903. A. Schoenhut Company, Philadelphia. Wood, cloth, paper, nails, enamel paint, elastic cords, metal, wood composition material, papier-mâché. Andy Yaffee Collection

Mirroring the Social World

••

As in all cultures, the use and meaning of toys reflect the larger social world from which they come. This is especially true for the proliferation of toys with circus themes popularized during America's Gilded Age. From the late nineteenth to the early twentieth century, America experienced profound change in virtually every aspect of daily life. One of the most significant transformations was the country's rapidly evolving capitalist enterprise and the development of the modern system of industry and business that cultural historian Alan Trachtenberg has dubbed the "incorporation" of America. This process of incorporation substantially altered the character of American capitalism, changing it from an economic system dominated by family businesses and simple partnerships to one increasingly character-

ized by large corporate entities. The development of the corporate system shaped other structures of culture as well, fundamentally influencing "values and outlooks" and resulting in a "remaking of cultural perceptions" that affected Americans' notions about their society and themselves. [3]

With the advent of corporate society, a new, urban middle class emerged in which the husband's labor removed him from home, while his wife assumed the responsibility of raising children no longer needed as workers in the family business or fields. The result was not only a shift in the nature of the family and gender relationships, but also a change in the perception of childhood: children came to be valued as emotional rather than economic capital. Now removed from the world of adults, they were romanticized as inhabitants of a special, almost prelapsarian world and cherished as

▲ *Fig. 15.1.* Humpty Dumpty Circus, 1903. A. Schoenhut Company, Philadelphia. Wood, cloth, paper, nails, enamel paint, elastic cords, metal, wood composition material, papier-mâché. Andy Yaffee Collection

icons of purity and innocence. And as the nature of childhood was reconceived, so were the activities and objects of children, particularly play and toys.

In the midst of these profound changes, American life became rife with contradiction and conflict as traditional ways of being were often confronted and overwhelmed by new structures of experience. Both the circus and circus toys can be seen as key symbolic markers of this new world, cultural productions that mirror the changing and unpredictable society out of which they arose. The gigantic three-ring circus presented—and often overwhelmed—its viewers with a conglomeration of conflicting and spectacular impressions. Presenting feats of breathtaking skill and daring, genuine curiosities, and outrageous fakes, the circus conflated and confused the real with the imaginary in ways that dazzled rather than clarified experience.

According to Trachtenberg, the circus represented a paradigm of Gilded Age culture in America, "in scale, in the management of illusion, [and] in roles prepared for seated audiences." Americans responded to the circus as passive spectators rather than active participants, as consumers rather than actors in the spectacle of events and activities that unfolded before their eyes.[4] At a time when Americans were becoming consumers of not only goods but experience, the circus represented a site for the consumption of culture.

Circus toys engaged the young in the same paradigm. Removed from the world of adult work, middle-class children became consumers of goods and experience rather than producers of them. And in a culture where traditional values, activities, and identities were increasingly obfuscated by new structures of understanding and experience, the type of toys consumed by children began to change. No longer only traditional representations of the adult world or small versions of real-world adult tools, playthings became, like the spectacle of the circus, instruments of escape, fantasy, and play. The Humpty Dumpty Circus was a perfect example. Advertised as the "Toy Wonder," Schoenhut's "Marvelous Toy Circus" presented a dazzling spectacle designed to "call forth exclamations of wonder from grown folks as well as children." Catalogues portrayed animals and performers doing "10,001 astonishing tricks."[5] Much more than the simple toy menagerie wagons with animals that had become popular in the late nineteenth century, the Schoenhut circus created an enormous fantasy world that encouraged children to escape the every day and explore fantastic new realms of the imagination.

Transportation, Technology, and Circus Toys

It was not long after the popularization of traveling circuses that manufacturers of toys were producing playthings that replicated circus activities and personnel. A favorite toy was the horseman. Often

Fig. 15.2. Humpty Dumpty Circus clown figures, 1903. A. Schoenhut Company, Philadelphia. Wood, cloth, paper, nails, enamel paint, elastic cords, metal, wood composition material, papier-mâché. Andy Yaffee Collection

featuring a figure on horseback who moved up and down on his mount, this toy was made in numerous versions. One of the most interesting examples was the Lively Horseman, made before 1879 by Charles M. Crandall of Pennsylvania and New York. It featured a clown figure who bounced up and down astride a horse that bucked as it was pulled across the floor (*fig. 15.3*). A variation on the theme of the horseman was a horse pulling a figure, often a clown, in a chariot or wagon. A favorite form of pull toy, these playthings often featured some kind of action, like a bell ringing, as the toy moved forward. One of the most spectacular examples of the horse and rider toy was made around 1890 by W. S. Reed Company of Leominster, Massachusetts. Called the Gigantic Circus and Mammoth Hippodrome, the toy contained four articulated, mounted riders who performed tricks as they spun around a central hand-cranked spoke while two acrobats performed on trapezes overhead. Made of wooden cutouts with images rubber-stamped onto them, this colorful and fanciful creation was one of the most ambitious and active early renderings of the circus on horseback (*fig. 15.4*).

Another type of popular circus toy was the circus wagon. Hundreds of these toys were made in wood, paper, tin, and cast iron. Many were created in the form of menagerie or animal wagons and came with a variety of beasts that could be posed, both inside and outside the cage. An interesting early example was Crandall's Performing Animals wagon, which featured an animal trainer and a number of ferocious creatures, including a lion and tiger. The ornate wooden toy was featured in "Crandall's Wholesale Price List for 1879–80," which whimsically announced: "It will be noticed that the exhibition is under the special charge of the famous clown, Mr. Merryman, the trainer of these wild animals, whose astonishing power

Fig. 15.3. Lively Horseman, ca. 1870s. Charles M. Crandall, Waverly, New York. Lithographed wood, nails. Andy Yaffee Collection

Fig. 15.4. Gigantic Circus and Mammoth Hippodrome, ca. 1890. W. S. Reed Company, Leominster, Massachusetts. Wood, string, metal eyelets. Courtesy of Jim Sneed, All About Wood Toys

over these ferocious beasts, and whose fearless management of them, electrify the beholder . . . This unparalleled combination of talent . . . is now making the TOUR OF THE WORLD, and it is proposed to give every man, woman and child in this, and in every other country, the opportunity to enjoy it."[6]

One circus wagon toy that came as a set was called the American and European Menagerie, produced by R. Bliss Manufacturing Company of Pawtucket, Rhode Island, around 1890 (*fig. 15.5*). Composed of four wooden wagons pulled by a zebra, horse, elephant, and camel, the lithographed creation was available in two sizes—one that was two-and-a half feet long and sold for 25 cents and the other five feet long that sold for a dollar. "Every boy likes a caravan or menagerie," said the 1895 Bliss catalogue in which these toys appeared.[7] Some of the largest and most spectacular circus wagons were made of cast iron by the Hubley Manufacturing Company of Lancaster, Pennsylvania, in 1922 as a part of its Royal Circus. Composed of numerous brightly painted wagons pulled by teams of horses, the Hubley circus included a bandwagon with ten musicians, a chariot, a calliope wagon, and other wagons containing giraffes, lions, monkeys, rhinos, eagles, tigers, and bears (*fig. 15.6*). A 1922 Hubley advertisement trumpeted: "The Hubley Circus Has Arrived. Twenty-five Circus Toys Cast in Iron."

Fig. 15.5. Circus wagons from the American and European Menagerie, ca. 1890s. R. Bliss Manufacturing Company, Pawtucket, Rhode Island. Lithographed paper on wood. Richard Mueller Collection

Although much of the early toy imagery of the circus focused on its fanciful wagons, history would soon prove that the real future of the circus was not horse-drawn; it lay with the railroad, a major symbol of the modern era and a product of continuing technological development. Advances in air brakes, automatic couplers, and standard-gauge tracks allowed railroads to utilize more powerful locomotives and to manage greater loads. American circuses took advantage of these improvements and a few shows took to the rails in the late 1850s. By 1880, all of the largest shows were railroad circuses. Trains encouraged the growth of the size and spectacle of the circus, and soon many circus shows included simultaneous acts in three rings, surrounded by a hippodrome track for chariot and horse races.[8] In addition to the railroad, the arrival of other technologies further assisted the expansion and mechanization of the American circus. The introduction of the power stake driver in the early twentieth century, followed by the use of devices such as a mechanized apparatus for loading and unloading canvas, greatly facilitated the mounting of shows. The addition of electric lightbulbs, tractors, and automobiles soon made the circus a paradigm of mechanical and industrial efficiency.

Not surprisingly, the same industrial processes that supported the development of the circus also underlay the creation of circus toys. Before the last decades of the nineteenth century, few industrially manufactured toys were produced in the United States. This changed around the turn of the twentieth century as new industrial technologies, and the mass production that followed, made toys cheaper and more readily available. While at the beginning of the twentieth century 50 percent of the toys sold in the United States were imported, mostly from Germany, by 1920 90 percent of the toys sold in America were made in the United States, and many of these toys were industrially produced.[9] Like most manufacturers at the time, toy makers were quick to utilize a variety of new materials and manufacturing techniques. For example, in the 1890s, pressed steel and offset lithography largely replaced tinplate and labor-intensive hand painting on toys. Shortly afterward, steel, instead of the more expensive brass, was used to make clockwork mechanisms.[10]

The R. Bliss Manufacturing Company was one of many toymakers to use new technologies. Founded in 1832, the company originally made wooden screws and clamps for pianos and cabinet making and was known for its innovative industrial

Fig. 15.6. Bandwagon from the Royal Circus, 1922. Hubley Manufacturing Company, Lancaster, Pennsylvania. Cast iron. Courtesy of The Strong, Rochester, New York, 77.2233

Fig. 15.7. Circus blocks, ca. 1890s. R. Bliss Manufacturing Company, Pawtucket, Rhode Island. Lithographed paper on wood. Richard Mueller Collection

practices, including the invention a machine to cut wood screws more rapidly and accurately. Bliss began making wooden toys sometime in the early 1870s, and by the 1880s and 1890s, it was producing a number of circus toys, including colorful blocks with lithographed circus scenes (*fig. 15.7*). Bliss was especially well known as a maker of numerous wooden toy trains, including a variety of circus trains. Two such trains, with engines pulling menagerie cars, appeared in their 1895 catalogue. One of them, called Barnum's Circus Train, was advertised as "lithographed in bright and attractive colors to represent 'America's greatest railroad circus.'"[11] Included with each train were circus and menagerie figures made of fiberboard and mounted on bases.

Bliss was only one of many American toy companies manufacturing circus trains. The Morton E.

Converse Company, of Winchendon, Massachusetts, made a variety of wooden and metal toys, among them circus trains. Two of their toy trains sought to catch customers' attention by associating themselves with well-known circuses. One of their wooden menagerie cars was called the Barney and Bailum's Circus, while the other also was named after a twist on the famous slogan: The World's Greatest Shows (*fig. 15.8*).

The wooden, cast iron, and clockwork trains produced in the latter decades of the nineteenth century were among that era's most exciting toys, but it was the development of the electric train that truly captured the technological imagination of children, particularly boys, in the early years of the twentieth century. The first electric toy train was created by Joshua Lionel Cowen in 1901. And soon, with the

invention of the electric transformer a few years later, many other American companies began making electric trains, a few with circus themes. Certainly the most spectacular of the circus trains was an electric version made in 1928 by the E. R. Ives & Company of Bridgeport, Connecticut. Like the real railroad circuses on which it was modeled, the Ives Railway Circus made a spectacular presentation, which included a locomotive, tender, three flatcars (each carrying two menagerie wagons with animals), an animal car (often carrying the most ferocious beasts), an equipment car, a performer's car, and a large tent, numerous flags, a cardboard sideshow backdrop, animal cages, wagon ramps to load and offload the wildlife, and a dozen exotic animals. "Ladies and gentlemen," announced the Ives catalogue, "Right this way for the wonder of circus land. The one and only original Ives Railway Circus, with all equipment of the biggest show on earth. See the marvelous Ives train loaded with circus paraphernalia and contraptions . . . Be there bright and early to see the circus unloaded . . . . Every day is a circus day right in your own home with the Ives Railway Circus—action—fun—excitement (*fig. 15.9*)."[12]

Circus Toys and the New Consumerism

As important as technology and new manufacturing techniques were in the proliferation of new types of toys, it was revolutionary changes in marketing that finally brought these toys into American homes. Although increasing industrialization gradually resulted in the production of more toys following the Civil War, there was little effort to market them. As American historian Gary Cross has noted, most manufacturers made toys as a sideline, and often sold them like dry goods. Grouped in wholesale catalogues by type, along with other kinds of miscellaneous hardware merchandise, toys were often sold from barrels or stacked in piles on store shelves. The brand names of toys were unimportant and there was little, if any attempt made to promote toys by emphasizing their special qualities.[13] Indeed, what advertising there was tended to be aimed not at children but at parents, who were generally concerned with how well the toy might teach practical skills or stand up to hard use. Perhaps for this reason, mechanical banks became very popular in the latter decades of the nineteenth century.

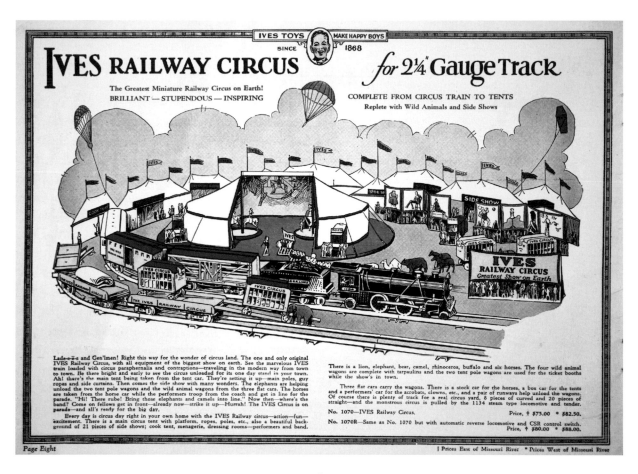

Made of virtually indestructible cast iron, toy banks were favored by parents because they taught the habits of thrift and saving. Among the many circus-themed banks were those made by the J. & E. Stevens Co. of Cromwell, Connecticut, which often incorporated motifs like performing clowns, cantering bareback riders, or acrobats who swung and did somersaults when a coin was inserted. Stevens' Funny Clown Bank, produced in 1890, took the form of a clown sitting on top of a globe. When a coin was inserted in the bank, the clown and globe spun, and then the clown flipped into a handstand (*fig. 15.10*). Another bank even rewarded children according to the amount they saved. Made by J. Barton Smith

Company of Philadelphia around 1890, this toy featured a boy sitting on a trapeze. When a penny was inserted in the boy's head, he spun once. A quarter resulted in three spins, and for a half dollar, the boy spun six times.

Numerous board games with circus themes and images aimed to teach children necessary attitudes and skills. One of these, made by McLoughlin Brothers of New York in 1898 and called Fun at the Circus, featured circus figures who advanced across the squares of the board or up and down ladders and poles, depending on the twirl of a spinner (*fig. 15.11*). Another game, made by Milton Bradley Company of Springfield, Massachusetts around 1900, was called

Fig. 15.8. Menagerie car, Barney & Bailum's Circus, ca. 1910. Morton E. Converse Company, Winchendon, Massachusetts. Lithographed wood. Richard Mueller Collection

Fig. 15.9. Ives Railway Circus, 1930. E. R. Ives & Company, Bridgeport, Connecticut. Advertisement. Toy Train Reference Library of the Train Collectors Association

Game of Walking the Tight Rope. In this game, players assumed the roles of circus figures who competed with each other to walk across a precarious tight rope strung over a river. The winner gained the other side of the river. Losers fell off the rope into the water. Although games like these presented opportunities to play, they were also cautionary tales for children in an increasingly competitive, mobile, and corporate society, where life was rife with periodic economic downturns and depressions; where

success, often achieved at the expense of others, might well depend on factors beyond the control of the individual, and where economic missteps could lead to a disastrous outcome.

Toward the end of the century, the ways toys were sold began to change. By this time, the development of the child-centered family and the emergence of play as a primary occupation of the young, combined with increases in production began to revolutionize the way toys were merchandised. Perhaps one of the earliest signs of this change occurred in 1875, when Macy's organized the first toy section in a department store. Department stores emerged in the 1870s and 1880s as a new form of retailing. Offering an astonishing array of goods never before gathered together under one roof, department stores specialized not only in selling merchandise, but in creating and expanding its meaning in ways that both attracted buyers and taught them new roles as consumers. In department stores, goods became more than objects to satisfy practical needs; they assumed larger meanings associated with status and desire. This expanded sense of merchandise, and the activity of consuming it, was reified in the physical setting of the department store. Department stores were huge multifloored emporiums with sparkling cut-glass chandeliers, glimmering mirrors, burnished wood trim, and polished marble floors that enticed shoppers into their sumptuous world with spectacular window displays. The department store's only real competition, in terms of sheer spectacle, was the circus.

Circus toys fit comfortably into the new world of the department store. No longer jumbled together on store shelves with other types of general-sales merchandise, they were now offered as part of a coherent group of consumables in a setting that enhanced their marketability. And it was not long

Fig. 15.10. Clown on globe mechanical bank, 1890. James H. Bowen for J. & E. Stevens Co., Cromwell, Connecticut. Painted cast iron. Courtesy of The Strong, Rochester, New York, 73.1517

before Macy's competitors, as well as other newly developed merchandising institutions such as variety stores and mail-order catalogues, were also selling toys and presenting them so that they stood out from other goods.

A. Schoenhut, producer of the Humpty Dumpty Circus, took particular advantage of this revolution in marketing. Schoenhut utilized not only up-to-date manufacturing methods to make its toys, but also a variety of innovative new marketing techniques. Recognizing the importance of presentation, Schoenhut developed a group of point-of-purchase figures, many in the shape of its circus toys, to call attention to its products. Over three feet tall, these articulated wooden figures included clowns in colorful suits, donkeys, and elephants, as well as various barrels, chairs, and ladders on which these figures could perform. Set up in venues where the circus toys were sold, the figures were backed with large banners proclaiming "Schoenhut's Humpty Dumpty Circus." Schoenhut also created "fancy boxes" for its circus toys that could be used in point-of-purchase displays by sellers. The tops of these boxes were covered with colorful lithographed pictures illustrating the wonders of the circus inside. When the box tops were folded back, they served as backdrops for the Schoenhut toys.

In its merchandising, Schoenhut took advantage of other developments in advertising and popular media. The company presented its toys in national and international newspapers, magazines, and trade catalogues. Directing its message not only to parents, but beginning to address children as well, the company's advertisements went beyond the mere presenting of information. They also sought to teach children how to play with their articulated circus figures and to entice parents to purchase them. Catalogues featuring the circus toys presented scores

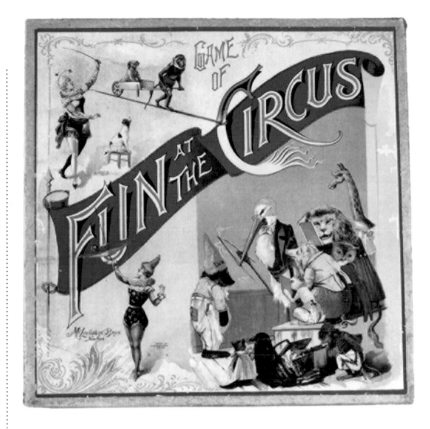

of pictures showing how to use the toys by balancing them on each other and by posing them to create fanciful performances (*fig. 15.12*). They also emphasized, for the benefit of parents, the toys' educational value, high quality, and solid construction. "In order to do successfully all the tricks illustrated in the following pages, be sure to first set the limbs and head of each figure in the proper position before setting them up and balancing them," the catalogue advised children. And parents were told "Mothers say these toys are the best toys they ever knew … They commend themselves to parents as the only good toy made that will stand rough handling for years."[14]

Schoenhut used other innovative merchandising techniques of the era. Offering its circus toys in different-size sets ranging in price from one dollar to 35 dollars, Schoenhut encouraged purchasers to "start a circus with a few pieces then keep adding until your Greatest Show on Earth is complete."[15]

Fig. 15.11. Fun at the Circus, 1889. McLoughlin Brothers, New York. Courtesy of The Strong, Rochester, New York, 107.3861

370

Moreover, by frequently adding new figures to the circus, Schoenhut promoted continued interest in their line (*fig. 15.13*). Finally, using a sales technique that had become popular in the promotion of numerous other types of products, Schoenhut firmly associated its circus with a variety of well-known public personalities. The first was George Washing-

ton Lafayette Fox, a famous pantomime actor who, in the late 1860s, created and starred in a fanciful stage play entitled *Humpty Dumpty*. The longest running production of its time, this show made Fox one of the highest-paid actors of his generation and turned his character into a well-known advertising symbol. When Albert Schoenhut created his circus toys some forty years later, Fox's character gave the new toys a popular and recognizable association. Another well-known figure, Foxy Grandpa, a popular comic strip character who later became the central figure in a number of books and Broadway productions, was incorporated by Schoenhut into the circus as a sideshow performer. Max and Maurice, well-known characters in an 1875 book by Wilhelm Busch, also became Schoenhut circus figures. Finally, in 1909, Schoenhut inducted one of the most popular and widely admired figures of the day into its circus when it created a play set featuring Teddy Roosevelt on his 1909 African safari. "Teddy's Adventures in Africa," read the advertising copy, "performed by new additions to Schoenhut's Humpty Dumpty Circus Toys."[16]

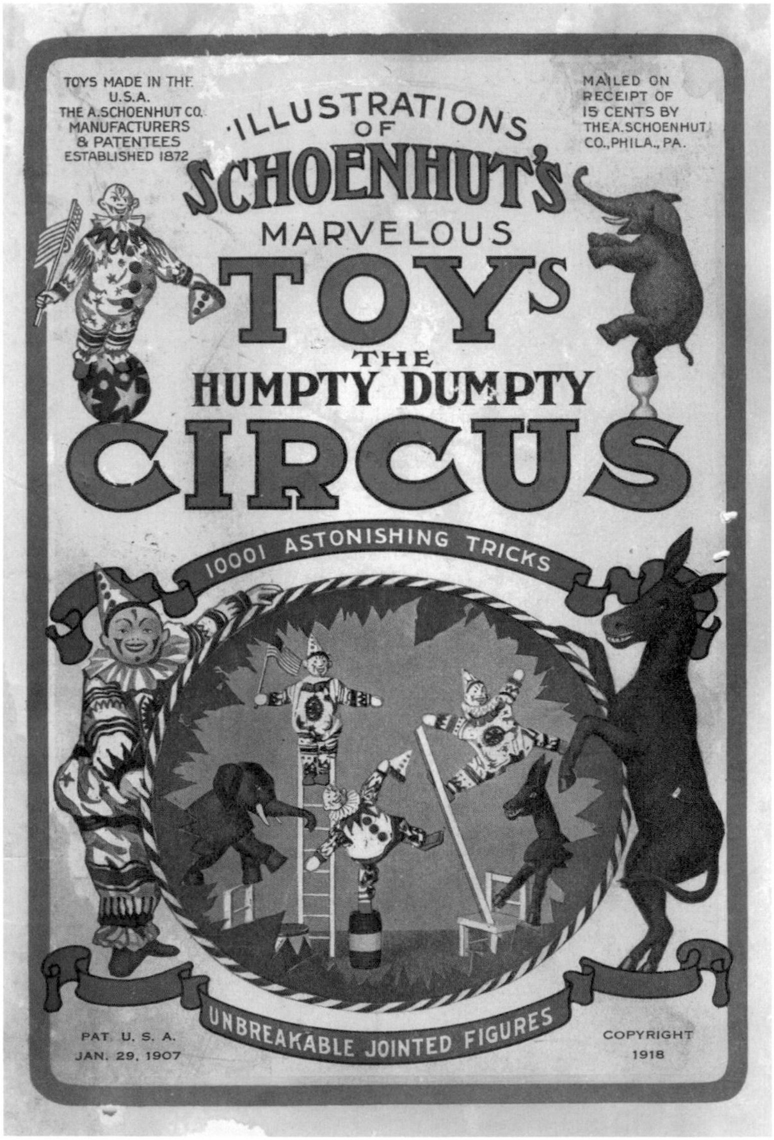

Circus Toys, Colonialist Spectacles, and the Other

Teddy Roosevelt embarked on his African adventure shortly after retiring from the American presidency, and, with the support of the Smithsonian Institution, he set sail for Africa in April of 1909. Roosevelt's trip was to be a scientific expedition, and so it included a photographer (Roosevelt's son), field naturalists, taxidermists, and guides. Known as an intrepid hunter and adventurer, Roosevelt's adventures were followed with interest, and reports of his activities were regularly presented in the American press.

Fig. 15.12. Page from "Illustrations of Schoenhut's Marvelous Toys, the Humpty Dumpty Circus." A. Schoenhut Company, 1918. Courtesy of The Strong, Rochester, New York

Recognizing a merchandizing opportunity, Schoenhut rushed to produce its Roosevelt toys and had them on the shelves in time for Christmas. In order to take advantage of circus figures already in production, Schoenhut used a number of its existing circus animals for the Roosevelt series, but also created some new ones, including a rhino, deer, zebu, hyena, gorilla and gazelle (*fig. 15.14*). In addition, it also offered figures of "Teddy," a guide, photographer, taxidermist, naturalist, and doctor. To make the set authentic, Schoenhut fabricated a group of "African Negroes." Two of these, the African Negro Chief and the Arab Chief, were made using the head molds from the Schoenhut circus clown except that their faces were painted brown and they were dressed in different costumes. Another group of natives produced for the set was completely new to the Schoenhut line. Created with entirely different

heads than previous Schoenhut characters, these figures were equipped with spears, knives, and a drum. They wore loincloths and had Afro-textured hair or wore head-cloths (*fig. 15.15*).

It is not surprising that Schoenhut presented Roosevelt's African safari as a performance in their toy circus. At the turn of the century, one of the most popular shows presented at the circus and the Wild West show was what Janet Davis has called the "foreign relations spectacle."[17] Featuring dramatic and colorful reenactments of American historical and foreign relations events, these "specs" sometimes included hundreds of performers and promoted a view of American history and foreign policy that supported American expansionist and colonialist activities. For many circusgoers, these presentations became a significant way to experience and learn about American history and international relations.

Fig. 15.13. Humpty Dumpty Circus ringmaster figure, 1903. A. Schoenhut Company, Philadelphia. Wood, cloth, paper, nails, enamel paint, elastic cords, metal, wood composition material, papier-mâché. Andy Yaffee Collection

Fig. 15.14. Price list for Teddy's Adventures in Africa, 1909. A. Schoenhut Company, Philadelphia. Advertisement. Courtesy of The Strong, Rochester, New York

Fig. 15.15. Teddy's Adventures in Africa, 1909. A. Schoenhut Company, Philadelphia. Wood, cloth, paper, nails, enamel paint, elastic cords, metal, wood composition material, papier-mâché. Courtesy of Jim Sneed, All About Wood Toys

Particularly popular were dramas portraying famous Native American battles, like the Battle of the Little Big Horn, which presented the westward movement as a struggle between savagery and civilization, as well as scenes as and battles from popularly supported colonialist ventures such as the Spanish-American War, which was portrayed as a war to spread democracy and freedom. The character of Roosevelt had already become a popular figure in these circus reenactments, since shortly after the end of the Spanish-American conflict, Buffalo Bill's production of the "Battle of San Juan Hill" had presented Roosevelt as a heroic figure leading the Rough Riders to victory.

Yet it was not just the fact that Roosevelt's expedition fit comfortably into a model of colonialist spectacle that made it appropriate as a toy in the Humpty Dumpty Circus. Partly as a consequence of the imperialist ventures of the times, Americans were anxious to see the inhabitants of newly annexed and controlled territories, a desire that circuses were quick to exploit. Indeed, at the turn of the century, "the importation and presentation of nonwesterners was big business. . . . Major circuses had full-time agents who combed the globe for cultural curiosities."[18] Shown together with the animals inside the menagerie tent, "primitives" were presented by many large circuses in an "Ethnological Congress." Recognizing that exotic and "primitive" people were as much an oddity to most Americans as rare and unusual animals, circus proprietors presented them together as an "educational" experience. And not only were peoples from foreign lands displayed as oddities. Often native-born Americans were misrepresented as foreigners and dressed up in outrageous and bizarre costumes to play the part. In addition, by the 1870s many circuses also presented their ethnological exhibits as part of their sideshows that also featured freaks or people with physical deformities, or those with the ability to contort or present their bodies in unusual ways. "Through costuming, staging, advertising pictures, and 'true life' booklets, showmen fabricated a conception of 'natives' that accurately captured—or rather reflected—what they were to U.S. citizens. The presentations reinforced pictures already in the American mind."[19]

Schoenhut's African Negroes were easily understood by children to be the primitives presented in the Ethnological Congress, and this encouraged children, like their parents, to wonder about the nature of primitive life. However, Schoenhut's Africans were not the only "others" represented in its toy circus. Performers included a black minstrel and Chinese acrobat. Minstrels have a long history in the American circus, where white clowns in blackface performed as Negroes, caricaturing African Americans for the amusement of the white audience. Schoenhut's minstrel—called the Negro Dude—is an accurate representation of this tradition. Dressed in a fancy tailcoat and top hat, the Negro Dude was made with the same carved head and Caucasian features as the clowns, and thus could not be confused with the African Negroes in the Teddy Roosevelt set. The Chinese acrobat was also a faithful reproduction of a contemporary circus performer. With hair braided in a long queue, the acrobat delighted children by reminding them of strange and exotic Chinese circus performers who could hang by their hair. Finally, the Schoenhut circus also contained a sideshow. Featuring three grotesques whose large heads were out of proportion to their bodies, the show was presented on a special circus wagon with a flat platform on which the figures could be displayed. Schoenhut also produced two canvas backdrops for their circus that depicted various sideshow tents. "See the beautiful snake charmer," proclaimed the sign on one tent. "Tips the scales at 550 pounds," touted another outside the tent of the fat lady. "The only bearded lady on earth," said still another.

Schoenhut toys were not the only playthings that represented "primitives" as circus performers. In 1892, the W. S. Reed Company created a game of dexterity called the Tip Tip Marble Game in which marbles were rolled into pivoting wooden cups held by clowns. As a decoration, on the base of the game, an image was printed of an Asian circus performer in a multicolored kimono dexterously holding a fan and precariously balancing on a tipping chair. Another circus toy that incorporated numerous images of the "other" was the Cut-Out Circus for the Children created in 1913 by the Curtis Publishing Co. of Philadelphia (*fig. 15.16*). This five-page paper circus, drawn by C. Duran Chapman, included numerous performers, animals, and vehicles that could be cut out and attached to cardboard stands. Part five of the Cut-Out Circus, called "The Side Show," featured a giant, fat lady, Chinese twins, Tom Thumb's wedding party, a snake charmer, and four minstrels. "When you exhibit the minstrels," advised the text on the paper toy, "if you have a phonograph, it could play ragtime or sing funny songs or make a speech."[20] Such stereotypical representations, or worse, were common fare for toys of the time. Many popular playthings featured "coons" and "darkies" in derogatory postures and situations, and similarly belittling characterizations were used to signify other groups.

It was not only the humans presented in the menagerie tent who were used by turn-of-the-century Americans as a gauge against which to measure themselves and their civilization. It was the animals as well. By the 1890s, the country had become

sufficiently urbanized to change most American's reaction to the wilderness and its inhabitants.[21] No longer threatened by the forest or "wild Indians," Americans now often saw the city, rather than the wilds, as a place of peril and danger. Associated with the foreign-born, urban slums, and political corruption, it was the city that threatened national democracy. In this state of mind, Americans turned to the wilderness as a symbol of hope and possibility. The creation of the national parks was one response to this change in attitude, and early accounts of the territory to be incorporated into the parks displayed a developing reverence and romanticism about the natural landscape. Connected to this change in attitude about the landscape was a change in how Americans viewed wild animals. As people moved to the city, seeing undomesticated animals became a rarer experience, and more of a spectacle. In the increasingly popular zoos and circuses of the 1800s, seemingly strange and exotic animals were offered up to the wonder and amazement of the public.

Exotic animals such as lions, camels, and polar bears had been exhibited in menageries as early as the middle of the eighteenth century, and in 1796, the first elephant was exhibited in the United States. But early menageries displayed their animals rather than performing with them. In the late 1820s, as menageries started to combine with circuses, this began to change. By the end of the century, the circus animal act was well established and provided an entertaining venue for Western society's new vision of the wild. No longer dangerous denizens of the jungle, animals had become exotic creatures understood primarily in terms of human needs and projections.[22]

Although circus promoters were fond of presenting many performing circus beasts as wild and ferocious, virtually all of these animals had been trained, and taught to mimic or respond to human

OCT 1913
A Cut-Out Circus for the Children
Part V—The Side Show: By C. Durand Chapman
TO MAKE the stage cut out two sections and mount on heavy paper or on cardboard. Cut slits in floor where indicated. Bend on dotted lines and paste number 2 to number 1. The stage will now look like the little outline drawing of finished stage shown on the right.
NUMBER 1. PASTE NUMBER 2 ALONG THIS STRIP
CUT platform and tight-rope posts from stiff cardboard, sizes indicated. Set up posts in platform, stretch a string tight over tops and fasten in the notches. Mount balance base on heavy paper for tight-rope performers, bend on dotted line and hang on tight rope.
NUMBER 2. BEND DOWN ON DOTTED LINE AND PASTE OR GLUE TO NUMBER 1
500 Lbs
Two posts like this for tight-rope
6 inches
Trapeze
6 inches
Platform, tight-rope and trapeze
Trapeze
Tight-rope Balance
Number 1.
Finished Stage
Number 2.
8 inches
Space for Stage
Platform
12 inches
SET the stage on the platform in space indicated by dotted lines.
ATLAS
1000 LBS
THE Fat Lady, the Giant, the Chinese Twins, General Tom Thumb and Wedding Party, the Quartet of Minstrels, the Trumpeter and the Bass Drum Man, also the Snake Charmer and the Boa Constrictor—all are exhibited on the stage, one after the other, in many combinations. The Showman stands down in front and announces each act. When you exhibit the Minstrels, if you have a phonograph, it could play ragtime or sing funny songs or make a speech. Cut slits in the dumb-bell and the big weight. Atlas, the strong man, holds up the big dumb-bell, the 1000-lb. weight and then the big world. Cut slits in the world for his hands at the bottom, and the slit at the top is for any of the other performers. The Clown can stand on his head up there. The strip with fine slits in it is for Atlas to hold on his hands, and the Clown stands on his hands on that, or on one foot, as you please. The Dog and the Cat may take turns on the trapeze. Cut slits in the trapeze bar, and put the hands or feet of the acrobats in the slits. There are many more combinations. The Fat Woman might stand on top of the world and Atlas hold it all up. This can be done by pasting a short flap on back of globe to extend over back of Atlas; also an extra flap on Fat Woman to extend over back of globe, and an extra thickness on flap of Atlas.

Fig. 15.16. "A Cut-Out Circus for the Children, Part V: The Side Show," 1913. Curtis Publishing Co., Philadelphia. Paper. Courtesy of The Strong, Rochester, New York, 76.3571

behavior.[23] From the monkeys who rode on horseback, to bears who roller-skated and lions who snarled ferociously from atop platforms, circus animals were trained to titillate, amuse, and engage humans. While paradoxically serving as symbols of pure and untrammeled wilderness, animals were now anthropomorphized, inducted into human society, and portrayed with human characteristics.

An early and important example of this representation of animals in toys can be recognized in the Happy Family menagerie wagon produced by Charles M. Crandall in the 1880s (*fig. 15.17*). This toy was modeled on an early exhibit created by P. T. Barnum that housed a lion, tiger, panther, and lamb in one cage in order to reference the biblical phrase "the lion shall lie down with the lamb." Crandall's version contained an ornate wooden cage wagon and fifteen animals together with their keeper. Representing the idea that predatory animals who were natural enemies might learn to dwell together as one happy family, the toy served as an ethical model for the young. According to "Crandall's Wholesale Price List for 1879–1880," when the wagon was set up properly and the animals added, "the effect is stupendous.... A toy so complete or so comprehensive of the wants and tastes of childhood as this has never been offered. It is not only a 'Happy Family' itself, but carries the spirit of happiness into every family where it goes."[24] Crandall's Happy Family set the tone for a legion of circus menagerie toys that would follow, all portraying nonthreatening, and eventually cute, animals coexisting happily together in a mock-human world where nature has been tamed and peaceful coexistence reigned.

Performing animals were one of the most common types of circus toy produced. Thousands of

Fig. 15.17. Happy Family, ca. 1880s. Charles M. Crandall, Waverly, New York. Wood, metal eyelets. Courtesy of The Strong, Rochester, New York, 76.1097

these kinds of toys were made, featuring virtually every circus animal. Yet of all the animals portrayed in toys, the bear may have the most interesting history. According to popular culture historian Gary Cross, bears appeared only infrequently in nineteenth-century toy catalogues, and when they did, they were a bit frightening and not very appealing to children.[25] All this changed in the first years of the twentieth century, with the invention of the teddy bear. Although there is disagreement about who made the first teddy bear, it was almost immediately identified with Teddy Roosevelt and, by 1906, it had become an international fad. Unlike earlier toy bears, the teddy bear, which was soft, cuddly, and stood on two legs, once again exemplified the imposition of human qualities and desires onto the animal world. With the popularity of the teddy bear, circuses soon developed more elaborate bear acts, and scores of circus toys were made featuring performing teddy bears. One of the most interesting of these, made by Watrous Manufacturing Company (East Hampton, Connecticut) in 1907, was a pull toy that featured a dancing bear on a moving platform.

Standing upright and wearing a green sweater with purple trim, the bear danced as the toy was pulled (fig. 15.18).

Another popular performing animal was the monkey. Closely linked to humans through evolutionary theory and its popularizations, monkeys were frequently presented in human guise when they performed in the circus, and they were sometimes presented as the "missing links" in human evolution within the Ethnological Congress. Monkeys appeared ubiquitously as circus toys, often dressed like people or performing human activities. In a 1900 cast-iron pull toy made by Gong Bell (of Connecticut), a monkey dressed in red pants, a blue jacket, and a red hat sits on a platform behind a galloping horse. As the toy is pulled, the horse jumps forward and causes the monkey to rock up and down. Schoenhut's monkey, introduced into the Humpty Dumpty Circus in 1906, was dressed in virtually the same costume as the Schoenhut acrobats. Wearing a pointed cap similar to those worn by the clowns, he was capable of performing the same acrobatics and tricks undertaken by the human characters.

Fig. 15.18. Dancing teddy bear, clown, monkey and bear, 1907. Watrous Manufacturing. Company, East Hampton, Connecticut. Stamped metal. Richard Mueller Collection

Of all the performing animals in the circus, the most popular was the elephant. (See chapter 9, "Elephants and the American Circus.") A symbol of the circus itself, elephants were a mainstay of any circus performance and understandably one of the most common subjects of circus toys. Always emblematic of the circus, elephant images can be found in virtually all types of toys, from paper dolls to pull toys and plush toys to mechanical banks. Of the multitude of elephants that have performed in the circus, there is, of course, one who became the most famous—Jumbo. One of the greatest spectacles in American circus history, Jumbo was purchased by P. T. Barnum from the London Zoological Society in 1882. The largest animal in captivity, he weighed over six-and-a-half tons and stood twelve feet tall at the shoulders. On his departure from London, Jumbo lay down in the street, patriotically refusing, according to many Englishmen who decried his sale, to leave the country. English newspapers also reported that among the most troubled by Jumbo's departure was his "wife," an elephant named Alice who was reported to "mourn" and bellow for hours after he departed.

Once in the United States, Jumbo became a renowned celebrity, a featured act who traveled in his own private railroad car with a special keeper. This continued for three and a half seasons, until one evening, while going from the circus tent to his boxcar, Jumbo was hit and killed by a westbound express freight train. Jumbo's death was reported across the world.[26] It was claimed by P. T. Barnum that he died heroically while trying to save the life of a smaller elephant, his friend, who had also been on the railroad track. Moreover, after Jumbo's death, his bereaved "widow," Alice, was brought to America where she was exhibited alongside Jumbo's preserved carcass while other elephants in the ring wiped their eyes with giant black-bordered handkerchiefs. Although much of this remarkable spectacle was engineered by Barnum, it nevertheless points out how circus animals were often embraced for their human activities and meanings. Not surprisingly, such sentimentalized tributes made the Jumbo elephant toy, which has been produced for over a century in every conceivable form, one of the most popular circus toys ever made.

Among the Jumbo toys that were made during the animal's life and shortly after its death were numerous cast-iron banks, some on wheels and others free standing. Many of these wore blankets that said Jumbo and either nodded their heads or moved their trunks when a coin was inserted. Another popular Jumbo toy was made by the Gibbs Manufacturing Company of Canton, Ohio. Advertised in their 1911 catalog as "The Wonderful Trick Elephant," the two-dimensional lithographed toy had a wooden body, head, and trunk and legs cut out of sheet metal. When the toy was pulled, the elephant reared up on

Fig. 15.19. Performing Jumbo, ca. 1911. No. 23, Gibbs Manufacturing Company, Canton, Ohio. Lithographed wood, sheet metal, nails, paper. Richard Mueller Collection

its hind legs. "Performing Jumbo," said a tag on the base of the toy, "Does all the tricks you ever saw at a circus and many others besides" (*fig. 15.19*).

Circus Toys and the Imaginary World of Childhood

As the nineteenth-century awakening of belief in children's special qualities joined with the capacity of manufacturers to produce more goods, a significant market for children's products developed. Removed from the world of work, children became, in fact, quintessential consumers. Nascent participants in an expanding market system where goods were now valued as much for their psychological qualities as their utilitarian use, children were taught to appreciate the intangible meanings of consumables through their whimsical toys. As citizens in a developing consumer society, children were weaned into an expanded sense of the significance of goods, based as much on desire as utility.

But in this market, children not only became the object of marketing as consumers, they also became the subject. As social historian Stephen Kline has pointed out, by the latter years of the nineteenth century, the new sensibility of innocence and purity associated with childhood became a staple of advertising. Images featuring the cherubic and innocent faces of children and appeals to purchase goods in the name of what children represented became standard fare in product promotions. Within the emerging idea of childhood, innocence, wonder, and hope became compatible with industrial progress and economic expansion. In turn, the advertising images of happy children full of wonder and imagination helped to further define the experience of children and the expectations of their parents.[27]

With its magical and imaginative gestalt, the circus became the perfect realm to transport into the childhood world of toys. Playing with miniature acrobats, clowns, and elephants, children could reenact and embellish narratives they had seen at the circus. Whether with one or two toys, or a complete circus set, youngsters were able to act out the wondrous fantasies of youth for themselves and their parents. It was commonplace in the period for advertisers to show parents observing the playful activities of their children with approval and delight. One example of this is a full-page picture on the back of the 1904 and 1918 Schoenhut catalogues depicting two smiling parents watching their children, one of whom appears decked out in a fanciful paper hat, playing with Humpty Dumpty Circus toys (*fig. 15.20*).

While all circus toys could be utilized in childlike imaginative play, some of them lent themselves even more effectively to the creation of whimsy and fantasy. One of the earliest, made by Charles M. Crandall in the 1870s and called Crandall's Menagerie, included six two-dimensional circus animals whose body parts were held together with tongue-and-groove construction so that they could be disassembled and remade into remarkably whimsical and fantastic configurations. Attaching an elephant's head to a giraffe's neck on a zebra body, children could reimagine and reconstruct the natural world. "One of the most wonderful and amusing things ever brought out for the entertainment of children," touted the catalog. "The six animals composing the Menagerie are beautifully painted, and so arranged into 56 pieces in each box that *tens of thousands* of most laughter-provoking figures can be made up with them."[28] Another toy, called the Pull-Apart Animal Circus, was made in 1916 by Reeve and Mitchell and then in 1921 by Playthings Manufacturing Company, both in Philadelphia (*fig. 15.21*). Like Crandall's

Menagerie, the animals and performers in this toy could also be disassembled and reassembled in fanciful and unusual shapes and forms. "Get the idea," said the advertising copy. "The animals, performers, etc., all pull apart and the parts are all interchangeable. A never-ending variety of set-ups can be built or the funniest animals put together. A zoo, a circus and a building game all in one!" In this way, the Pull-Apart Animal Circus allowed the creation of an entire, virtually limitless fantasy world.[29]

The fanciful and imaginary world of circus toys was an important site of cultural meaning and practice for both children and their parents in the Gilded Age. As youngsters played with these toys, they participated in the new mythology of childhood and began to learn many of the necessary attitudes and skills of a consumer society as well. More than any other group of toys, circus playthings encouraged children to inhabit an imaginary world apart from that of their parents, a place where sweater-wearing bears danced upright on two legs and trapeze artists accomplished the impossible feat of six flips over a bar if you put a half dollar in their head. Parents also benefitted from their children's play with circus toys. For parents, who now sought emotional connection rather than economic gain from their children and who valued the qualities of childhood as a sign of cultural renewal, giving toys to their youngsters was an important way to demonstrate their affection as well as cultivate the qualities they most desired in their children. In a developing consumer economy where people and relationships were increasingly defined through market transactions, adults' promotion of childhood, as well as their relationships with their children, were reified through consumer spending—and what better object to represent the new burgeoning relationship between parents and children than the wondrous circus toy.

Fig. 15.21. Pull-Apart Animal Circus, 1921. Playthings Manufacturing Company, Philadelphia. Wood, enamel paint. Collection of Judith Lile

Fig. 15.20. Back page of "Illustrations of Schoenhut's Marvelous Toys, the Humpty Dumpty Circus," 1918. Courtesy of The Strong, Rochester, New York

Many people were very helpful in the preparation of this essay. At the Strong Museum of Play I was assisted by: Chris Bensch, vice president for collections; Patricia Hogan, curator; Nicolas Ricketts, curator; and Carol Sandler, director of Libraries and Archives. Jan Athey, librarian at the National Toy Train Museum, helped me find information on numerous toy trains and other early playthings. Richard Mueller offered information on pull toys, and Jim Sneed and Joanne Cubbs read early versions this essay and made numerous helpful suggestions.

1 Janet M. Davis, *The Circus Age: Culture and Society under the Big Top* (Chapel Hill: University of North Carolina Press, 2002), 7.

2 Evelyn Akerman, *Under the Bigtop with Schoenhut's Humpty Dumpty Circus* (Annapolis, MD: Gold Horse Publishing, 1996), 3.

3 Alan Trachtenberg, *The Incorporation of America: Culture and Society in the Gilded Age* (New York: Hill and Wang, 1982), 3–4.

4 Ibid., 122–23.

5 "Illustrations of Schoenhut's Marvelous Toys: The Humpty Dumpty Circus" (Philadelphia: A. Schoenhut Company, 1906).

6 "Crandall's Wholesale Price List for 1879–80" (Montrose, PA: Charles M. Crandall, 1880).

7 R. Bliss Manufacturing Company, "Fall Catalogue," 1895 (Pawtucket, RI: R. Bliss Manufacturing Company, 1895).

8 Tom Parkinson and Charles Philip Fox, *The Circus Moves by Rail* (Boulder, CO: Pruett Publishing Co., 1978).

9 Stephen Kline, *Out of the Garden: Toys, TV, and Children's Culture in the Age of Marketing* (New York: Verso, 1993), 145.

10 Gary Cross, *Kids' Stuff: Toys and the Changing World of American Childhood* (Cambridge: Harvard University Press, 1977), 29.

11 R. Bliss Manufacturing Company, "Fall Catalogue."

12 "Ives Manufacturing Company 1930 Catalog" (Bridgeport, CT: Ives Manufacturing Company, 1930).

13 Cross, *Kids' Stuff*, 22–23.

14 "Illustrations of Schoenhut's Marvelous Toys."

15 Ibid.

16 Advertisement for Teddy's Adventures in Africa from unknown publication in Akerman, *Under the Bigtop*, 110.

17 Davis, *The Circus Age*, 143.

18 Robert Bogdan, *Freak Show: Presenting Human Oddities for Amusement and Profit* (Chicago: University of Chicago Press, 1988), 198.

19 Ibid.

20 *The Cut-Out Circus for the Children, Part V: The Side Show* (Philadelphia: Curtis Publishing Co., 1913).

21 Roderick Nash, *Wilderness and the American Mind* (New Haven: Yale University Press, 1967), 143–45.

22 Stuart Thayer, *Annals of the American Circus, 1793–1860* (Seattle: Dauven and Thayer, 2000); Joanne Joys, *The Wild Animal Trainer in America* (Boulder, CO: Pruett, 1983).

23 Davis, *The Circus Age*, 149.

24 "Crandall's Wholesale Price List for 1879–80."

25 Cross, *Kids' Stuff*, 94.

26 John Culhane, *The American Circus: An Illustrated History* (New York: Holt, 1990), 127–35.

27 Kline, *Out of the Garden*, 52–53.

28 "Crandall's Wholesale Price List for 1879–80."

29 Advertisement for Pull-Apart Animal Circus in *Playthings Magazine*, Aug. 1925.

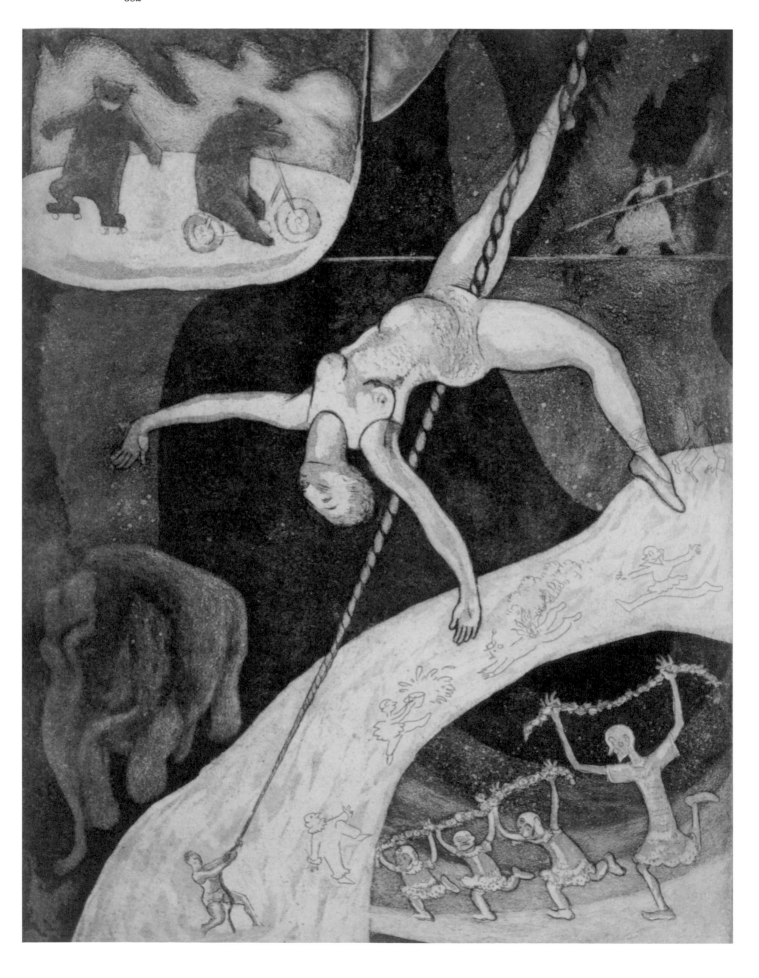

16

THE WPA CIRCUS IN NEW YORK

SUSAN WEBER

The Works Progress Administration (WPA) Circus, established under the Federal Theatre Project in 1935, was the only instance in United States history in which the federal government sponsored circus performances.[1] The main unit was located in New York City with smaller shows operating as stage productions in Reading, Pennsylvania; Buffalo; Boston; and other cities.[2] The goal of the WPA Circus was to "rehabilitate unemployed circus performers" and to provide a professional-level circus to Americans struggling amid the Great Depression.[3] The largest unit of the WPA Circus was active in New York City from the fall of 1935 through the summer of 1939. Over its four-year existence, the WPA Circus performed for millions of children and others in need of the cheering influence of the circus (*fig. 16.1*).[4] As a symbol of America's past, this "worthy institution" brought innocent pleasure to a city whose residents were beset by economic crisis and an uncertain future.[5] The history of the WPA Circus, however, has largely been overlooked. But rich contemporary sources—newspapers, trade magazines, and government records—document its contribution to the arts and life in New York during the tough years of the Depression.

One of the most significant aspects of the WPA Circus and the Federal Theatre Project more generally was the recognition that popular entertainment was an industry that warranted government help like any other. The Works Progress Administration was an ambitious New Deal program established by President Franklin Roosevelt in 1935 to create jobs for American workers suffering through economic troubles. At its peak, the WPA employed over three million people and supported four major arts-related projects. Although the Federal Theatre Project was but a small part of this massive program, government sponsorship of what American historian Michael Denning has aptly described as "cultural workers" made a lasting impact on American culture.[6]

Fig. 16.1. William Hicks. "WPA Circus," ca. 1937. Etching aquatint. Spencer Museum of Art, The University of Kansas, Gift of the WPA Arts Project, 0000.0365. Avonne Gardener is depicted on her Spanish web (middle); two of the George Stanley bears roller-skate and bicycle (upper left); the elephant Japino (lower left) and; four cross-dressed male clowns perform a comedic ballet (bottom right)

The fact that the WPA saw fit to organize a circus attested to the devastating impact that the Depression had on the circus business in the United States. When John Ringling took over the American Circus Corporation in 1929, he held title to six major circuses and *Billboard* intoned that the move presaged "a new era of prestige and prosperity for the circus."[7] After three years of poor receipts, cutbacks, and consolidation, however, Ringling's dire financial situation forced him to accede control of the Ringling Bros. and Barnum & Bailey show and its remaining subsidiaries to his creditors. Despite belt-tightening across the board, the principal independent circuses likewise suffered as the Depression deepened.[8] The Cole Bros. and Christy Bros. shows folded in 1930, and the Miller Bros. 101 Ranch Wild West Show and Robbins Bros. Circus went under in dramatic fashion early the following season. Although the situation improved somewhat as the decade progressed, the prolonged downturn left thousands of circus workers and performers jobless. The circus was also unable to escape from the labor struggles engulfing the nation, as a variety of different unions pressured circus management for improved wages and working conditions. The 1938 season of the Ringling Bros. and Barnum & Bailey Circus was abruptly ended by a bitter battle between

the AFL-affiliated American Federation of Actors and John Ringling North, who demanded an immediate 25 percent pay cut in light of the show's slow business.[9] When the union refused, North simply folded up the tents and returned the circus to its winter quarters in Sarasota while the public lamented its closing and disputed who was right.

The circus in the 1930s thus reflected the larger social and cultural currents that were sweeping the nation. An increasing preoccupation with class divisions and concerns about joblessness, combined with what one historian has described as the "problem of leisure," were the driving force behind such programs as the Federal Theatre Project.[10] The WPA Circus was seen as ameliorative in that it promised to both employ and entertain Americans struggling amid the Depression. It was thus part and parcel of a broader New Deal agenda that was focused on getting Americans back to work and fortifying and uplifting the nation through a variety of cultural programs. As many commentators have noted, popular culture offers a window into the desperation and contradictions that characterized the era and the WPA Circus was a very public example of how the government, artists, performers, and audiences dealt with the tumultuous times.[11]

Armories, Arenas, and Tents

The WPA Circus began its performances in the armories, arenas, and stadiums around the metropolitan New York City region. Madison Square Garden, the usual venue for visiting circuses, was out of the question due to its high rental fees, so more affordable spaces were sought. Armory drill sheds, with their large, unobstructed floor space and monumental ceiling heights, met requirements necessary for the

Fig. 16.2. Armory interior during circus performance, ca. 1935. Photograph. Federal Theatre Project Collection, Special Collections & Archives, George Mason University Libraries, Circus 59-5-3

Fig. 16.3. WPA Circus tent with auxiliary tent, 1936. Photograph. Franklin D. Roosevelt Presidential Library

aerial acts and the large audiences of a full-blown circus production.[12] The first performance was held at the Second Naval Battalion Armory in Brooklyn on October 17, 1935. Conditions there were not perfect. The lighting was makeshift and there were no safety nets for the high-wire acts.[13] Melvin D. Hildreth, president of the Circus Fans of America, described in a review for *White Tops* the minimally adorned performance area with "no ring curbs; apparatus . . . scattered from one end to the other, aerial rigging . . . hung from the rafters, and . . .decidedly a lack of actual circus atmosphere."[14] Two years later conditions were still not ideal and *Billboard* remarked that "acts work under difficulties . . . because of the fact that the Coliseum floor has not been covered with a soft base. The cement pavement necessarily curtails some of the ground acts and prevents proper guying for aerial riggings" (*fig. 16.2*).[15] Despite such logistical problems, reviewers found that "the spirit of the circus was there in abundance."[16]

In order to reach audiences in less-populated areas of the boroughs, where there were no arenas or stadiums, in May of 1936 the WPA Circus purchased a tent. This 4,000-seat enclosure was a 100-foot-round top with three 40-foot middle pieces.[17] It had a marquee, dressing rooms, and electric equipment.[18] There was stabling for animals and a cookhouse in adjoining tents (*fig. 16.3*). A hippodrome area for parades and races enclosed two rings and a central platform. With the acquisition of this tent, the circus now could have an indoor and outdoor season, and it went on to perform twenty-one one-week stands through all of the boroughs. The indoor season began in early November and continued into March. The outdoor season started in May and ended in early October.

The tents were not without problems. On September 18, 1936, the main tent and the others blew down during a storm. The big top was lowered in time to save those beneath it. Although there were

no casualties, the tent was so damaged that it had to replaced, but the circus was up and running again by September 22.[19] In June 1938 a severe rainstorm blew down the tent in Elmhurst, Queens.[20] There was no damage but a little more than two months later the tent had to be restored, for on August 28, 1938, the replacement tent caught fire after a performance at Tremont Avenue and East 177th Street in the Bronx.[21] Still, there were no casualties and the cause of the fire was never discovered and the show went on under a new tent just days later.[22]

The WPA Circus typically stayed in one location for three days, usually Thursdays to Saturdays, with a Saturday matinee and occasionally one on Sunday as well. During the late spring and summer season, a tent would go up on Monday to allow for rehearsals before the show opened later in the week. Occasionally, shows were held over when there was great demand and the schedule allowed. When the circus played in Ridgewood Grove Stadium at the end of April 1937 there was such a rush of ticket sales that the show was extended an additional week into the month of May.[23] The city provided all utilities (water, gas, electric) free of charge. Local civic organizations like the American Legion co-sponsored the show and received part of the proceeds.

The WPA circus was a modest operation compared to the large railroad circuses of the era, but it still required over forty trucks to operate, as its properties included animal cages, a light plant, a calliope, and an array of tents.[24] Much of the specialized circus equipment had been purchased from defunct circus organizations. The seats were rented from the firm of John Martin and the grandstand concessions were controlled by a certain Ed Kelman.[25] The transport of the circus by truck was not unusual, for most midsize circuses had abandoned the railroads for the more mobile and cost-effective motor vehicle.

In addition to the usual large-scale productions, smaller units of the circus played at hospitals and other human service organizations in and around the city. A visit by the clowns, trained dogs, and the strong woman Madame Sandwina to the pediatric department at Bellevue Hospital was reported in the *New York Times* on November 9, 1935.[26] One hundred and fifty children, mostly suffering from polio and tuberculosis, were entertained in the hospital's auditorium. During the same month a troupe of performers from the WPA Circus amused children at St. John's Home for Boys in Brooklyn and at Greenwich House, which served the immigrant population in Greenwich Village, one of the most congested neighborhoods in New York. Even the elite Union League Club on Park Avenue hosted a WPA Circus unit at its annual Christmas party on December 25, 1935, for the benefit of the patients of the Hospital for the Ruptured and Crippled and for wards of the Salvation Army. The reporter for the *New York Times* recounted, "Besides clowns, there was a trained dog act, a contortionist, a ventriloquist and acrobats. The WPA band played Christmas songs and the children sang."[27] On June 10, 1936 a unit of the circus again regaled pediatric and other patients at Bellevue Hospital in the courtyard at the foot of East 27th Street. The *New York Times* documented "about 400 children watched the performance from the 'Day Camp Boat' for tubercular patients, tied up at a nearby-pier."[28] A year later WPA performers were still visiting children in local hospitals.[29]

The Federal Theatre Project also mounted a smaller stage production called the Tom Thumb Circus, which visited schools, churches, and organizations throughout the metropolitan New York area from winter to spring 1937. It was "a miniature indoor circus consisting of 'sight' acts for children."[30] The *Brooklyn Citizen* described it as "one of the faster and

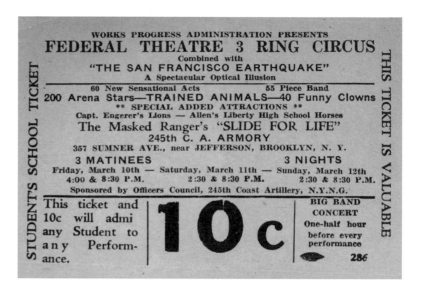

more extravagant of the WPA presentations dealing in the old time New York Variety stage" when it performed at the Bay Ridge Methodist Church, Ovington Avenue, in March 1937.[31] The following week the show played at the East New York Community Center, New Jersey Avenue, Brooklyn and the reviewer for *Brooklyn Citizen* informed its readership "the presentation consists of nineteen circus and vaudeville acts excellently blended into a fast-moving production. The cast is headed by Arthur Shaw, premier juggler; Tower and Howard, comedians; Captain David Powers, ventriloquist, [and] Richard Kenny, master magician."[32] Further Tom Thumb presentations occurred through April and May.[33]

Initially, admission to the WPA Circus was free. Federal Theater Project officials later instituted modest admission fees. Children paid 10 cents, adults 25 cents, while reserved seating cost 40 cents. The monies raised helped to defray production costs. In time, prices rose. Children paid 15 cents in 1937 and 25 cents in 1939. Hundreds of children from orphanages, settlement houses, clubs, and foundations, however, were admitted free during each performance. Fourteen thousand children—purportedly the largest number ever to attend a circus show—were accommodated around a three-ring set-up at the 258th Field Artillery in the Bronx in January of 1936.[34] Eight thousand of these children were bused to the performance through the WPA Recreation Department from settlement houses throughout the city.[35] Children attending public schools were eligible for discounted tickets at 10 cents (*fig. 16.4*).

Although children were the primary target audience, the Federal Theatre Project conducted an audience survey of adults in April 1937.[36] It revealed that people who attended the circus represented all occupations, socioeconomic backgrounds, and ages. The largest number of adults attending were either manual workers or housewives. Many (28 percent) had little or no experience with a live performance in the commercial theater or vaudeville. They enjoyed the circus performances and thought that this arm of the Federal Theatre Project was doing an admirable job of reaching people who were not theater-goers. This mostly new audience endorsed a permanent Federal Theatre.

Promotion and Advertising

Posters were an effective way to advertise upcoming circus performances.[37] Days before the circus arrived, bright posters in primary colors with black lettering were typically pasted throughout a neighborhood and placed in store windows, libraries, and post offices. These were not the large-scale lithographed pictorial posters that had been used by the major commercial circuses, but modest-sized notices communicating essential information such as show, date, place, time, ticket price, and listing some of the acts. The most typical image was a white-faced clown (*fig. 16.5*).

Press releases and photographs were sent to local papers for advance publicity. Reporters were invited to visit the show grounds. Special interest stories and reviews of the circus acts often appeared

Fig. 16.4. Federal Theatre 3 Ring Circus, student ticket, for Brooklyn performance, February 5–6, 1938. Collection of the author

four-year run. Described as a "demon press agent who has kept certain adjectives a secret from Webster," he wrote as many as twelve press releases in a day.[40]

In addition to city newspapers, advertisements also ran in the specialty circus periodical *White Tops*. Articles about WPA Circus performers often appeared in its pages, where other circus personnel and performers, circus aficionados, and general interest groups learned of WPA Circus events and developments. Goodwin developed a special relationship with its sponsoring organization, the Circus Fans' Association, a circus enthusiast club established in 1926 and comprised of about one hundred industrialists and professionals. Their motto was "We fight anything that fights the circus." Goodwin dedicated the first show of every season to the group, calling it "Circus Fans' Association Night" and arranged for its members to attend free. Additional ticket sales from this show were donated to the association. Goodwin also dedicated his written program each season to them. The association, in turn, passed a resolution at its annual convention in 1938 commending Goodwin's support and "heartily endorsing the aims and programs of the WPA circus in providing employment for unemployed and needy circus folk and at the same time providing an opportunity for thousands of children to see a real circus act at a moderate admission fee."[41]

Sponsoring clubs and community groups also placed advertisements in local newspapers. When the WPA Circus appeared in the 14th Regiment Armory in Brooklyn for their three-night run in March 1937, a small black-and-white ad was placed in the *Brooklyn Citizen*.[42] In May the Canarsie Scouters Council, in cooperation with the Federal WPA Theatre, advertised the upcoming circus performances in the *Canarsie Courier*.[43]

the following days. The first issue of *Federal Theatre Magazine* reported that the show was the subject of a movie newsreel.[38] The WPA Circus had its own full-time press agent, Wendell J. Goodwin, who had been with circuses his entire career. Goodwin performed as a circus clown, then worked as an advance agent and press agent for a number of American circuses. Burlesque, minstrel, and vaudeville shows also employed him, and he even managed a prison show for a time.[39] Goodwin was a skilled press agent who kept the WPA Circus in the news throughout its

Fig. 16.5. "Federal Theatre for New York City Presents the World's Greatest Circus," February 11–13, 1939. Poster. Federal Theatre Project Collection, Special Collections & Archives, George Mason University, F6-15A-1 display

Another mode of advertising was to drive a van posted with circus advertising and equipped with speakers announcing the circus's arrival throughout appropriate neighborhoods (*fig. 16.6*). Finally, local civic groups were contacted, and large banners were raised on site (*fig. 16.7*).

Although most established circuses had discontinued the circus parade due to the increased difficulty of navigating the congested city streets (see chapter 6, "The Circus Parade"), the WPA Circus incorporated the traditional parade as part of its marketing strategy. The band, an elephant decked with advertising, a circus car with clowns sitting atop it and adorned with posters, circus wagons with animals, and the entire company would march through the main street (*fig. 16.8*). The excitement generated by the three-dimensional advertisement through the center of the community often brought audiences to the circus grounds. A smaller fifteen-minute parade was often staged before the circus tent opened. Local marching bands sometimes headed this smaller parade. A fife, drum, and bugle corps from the Mount St. Michael's Home, Greenridge led the parade in West Brighton, Staten Island in September 1937.[44] In Canarsie, Brooklyn, the Boy Scouts of the Canarsie troops headed the parade.[45]

Free acts were often staged on the circus lot to attract people to encourage them to buy tickets for a later performance. The *Brooklyn Citizen* reported on one unusual outdoor exhibition at which "the strong man of the circus, known as 'The Great Paris,' attempted to hold sixteen dappling Grey's [*sic*] belonging to a milk company. Two eight horse teams p[u]lling in opposite directions will challenge the strength and endurance of the strong man."[46] Three hundred boys from the Police Athletic League and the Flatbush Boy's Club were invited to watch this historic act. The Great Paris, however, did not

Fig. 16.6. Advertising car, 1935. Photograph. Franklin D. Roosevelt Presidential Library

Fig. 16.7. Federal Theatre Presents the World's Greatest Circus, 1935–36. Photograph. Library of Congress Federal Theatre Project Collection

Fig. 16.8. Japino the elephant decked with advertising, Skillman Avenue, 46th Street, Sunnyside, Queens, May 2, 1938. Photograph. Library of Congress Federal Theatre Project Collection

live up to the expectations of the children, since he only pitted his strength against two teams of two horses and not eight as advertised to break the record of the Mighty Nicholas. In fact, the scheme did not go as planned. The *New York Times* recounted that the children booed "when the mighty man looked up expectantly for applause after an exhibition of grimaces and shouts."[47]

The circus band usually gave thirty-minute performances before the main show began. This custom was part of a strategy to attract people inside the tent to hear the music. The WPA Circus had the largest circus band on record. It began with thirty pieces and expanded by the 1937 season into a fifty-five-piece ensemble, musicians courtesy of the Federal Music Project. In addition to these thirty-minute concerts before each show, the band played throughout the two-and-a-half-hour program. At first the band lacked uniforms but as the season evolved they were provided.[48] At times the band wore black tuxedos. During several seasons they donned traditional marching-band costumes, entering the circus tent in brilliant red with gold braid, the conductor dressed in a complementary white costume with extra gold braid and hat (*fig. 16.9*). In warmer weather the band wore lightweight costumes with red jackets and white pants with orange side stripes. Performances began with the national anthem, followed by a program of march-es and popular numbers familiar to the audience. The conductor had to select music to accompany each act. A reviewer described a typical concert:

> Following the national anthem, which brings them to their feet, the band goes into a familiar piece. The audience starts singing the words and keeping time with their feet. The leader directs them in the singing, with a prancing clown to help them. In a few minutes the house is full of song and rhythm. A little girl steps into the arena and starts dancing. One number, especially, always brings their ten thousand voices together into a riot of mirth, song and applause. It is *The Music Goes' Round and Around*.[49]

For its first two years Max Tilkin, previously in the orchestra of the Palace Theatre, conducted the band. When he suddenly died in the summer of 1937, pianist and band member William Cutty took over as conductor until the circus's demise in 1939.[50]

Children were intentionally a large part of the audience for the WPA circus. The motto of the circus in its first year was "400,000 children can't be wrong." The numbers were updated as more children attended the show. By the 1938 spring season, the slogan was "two and a half million children can't be wrong" (*fig 16.10*). This motto remained part of the circus's marketing strategy until it closed in the summer of 1939.[51] The circus sometimes held contests as part of its marketing strategy for children. A hi-lo contest was held on the circus lot in Kew Gardens, Queens, in June of 1937. The first one hundred children to register were eligible for the contest. Eliminations took place at the circus lot the coming Thursday afternoon and the six winners competed on the elevated platform in the circus tent.[52]

Most popular was the Typical American Boy

Fig. 16.9. Circus band, conducted by William Cutty, ca. 1937. Photograph. Federal Theatre Project Collection, Special Collections & Archives, George Mason University

contest, in which "a representative youth symbolizing the love of the small boy for the circus" was chosen.[53] To be considered, a boy filled out an application and sent it with an accompanying photograph to the executive staff of the circus. The winner would be the guest of Burns O'Sullivan, the managing director, and sit with the members of the Circus Fans' Association on their next Save the Circus night. In early 1939, 795 boys applied and Francis J. Connolly, a fourteen-year-old from the Bronx, won the contest.[54] A photograph of Connolly appeared in *White Tops*; it showed him being congratulated by clown Frank Walter.[55]

Personnel and Performers

The WPA Circus began with an experienced team to organize and direct its activities. Burns O'Sullivan was managing director and general contracting agent. He had started with the Barnum and Bailey Circus as a stagehand and rose to become assistant equestrian director and then stage director of spectacle in 1914, a position he filled until 1921. He then became general manager of the Walter L. Main show, general agent for the Gorman Brothers circus, general manager of the Berry Brothers circus, and manager of the Keith-Albee regime, among other positions.[56] When the Depression hit, he was with the Barton Brothers circus, which he had to close. In fact, O'Sullivan bought much of the abandoned paraphernalia of the Gorman circus for the WPA Circus, including the Gorman light plant when that company went out of business in 1936.[57] Staff included Wendell J. Goodwin, special press representative; Harold Sullivan, exploitationist; Joseph McDevitt, special agent; Edward Sullivan, general manager with show; James Toms, director of personnel with

show; Ben Probst, ring-master; and Billy Walsh, announcer, whose "dignified introduction of feature acts and numbers lend no little color and austerity to the ceremonies."[58] James Meaney was circus rigger and Joseph Wall, superintendent of properties.[59]

The WPA Circus began with a roster of 143 people, including 50 performers. It was originally to have comprised five small units but logistical problems led to the decision to have one large outfit and a miniature indoor group called the Tom Thumb Circus.[60] The performers of the large unit included:

> two dog acts; eight clowns including a midget; iron-jaw single, single trapeze, two-girl web act, mixed balancing team, acrobatic male, mixed hand-to-hand balancing team, male tumbler and contortionist, table and chair mixed team, bounding rope act, slack wire, man-woman bike novelty, three stiltwalkers (clowns); strong woman (assisted by her husband, who is not on salary) . . . iron-jaw fem, a spread array of 14 comedy acrobats and male gymnast working on triple bar; double trapeze, three people [on] tight wire and nine pyramid builders and tumblers

Fig. 16.10. Dick Rose. Clown with children at WPA festival in Sheep Meadow, Central Park, May 2, 1936. Photograph. Library of Congress, Federal Theatre Project Collection

of which a couple are Arabs and the rest drafted from the other acrobatic acts with Arab wardrobing and makeup.[61]

In addition, there were "30 musicians, 15 watchmen, 23 attendants, 14 maintenance workers, 6 stage helpers, 3 stagehands and 2 junior project supervisors."[62]

By 1937 the WPA employed around 300 people from the relief rolls of New York (fig. 16.11). About two-thirds of its members were performers while the other third was made up of ushers, stagehands, tent men, costume designers, managers, supervisors, agents, and twenty-four-hour men, who were responsible for the site twenty-four hours before the circus decamped. Some of the ushers and stagehands were performers who had worked in the circus or vaudeville previously. Joe Ring, who toured all over North and South America with his boxing kangaroo, was the head usher and Frankie Grace, who used to be a dancer at the Palace Theater and with Kitty Doner in Al Jolson's shows at the Winter Garden, was also an usher, while Hazel Gardener and her husband Dan, former acrobats, were in charge of the cook tent.[63] The WPA Circus expanded to 375 people and by 1938 was billing itself as "Now the largest Circus in the World."[64]

The performers were a combination of seasoned professionals too old to be the featured stars in the few remaining circuses in the United States or very young performers who had not found jobs in the tight employment market. Whether old or young, experienced or green, they were all paid the same low wage of $23.86 per week, a much-reduced salary for many of the features who were used to receiving 1,000 dollars per week. According to an article in the *New York Times*, "Everyone gets the same, roustabouts and star acts, the director of the whole show and the slowest of the stage hands."[65] The government regulations did not permit more than one member of the same family to be on the WPA payroll, so many members of a family act, a common practice in the circus, had to live on one salary. These conditions made some reviewers criticize the quality of a circus composed of performers on relief. *Billboard*, for example, reported in 1937 that the WPA Circus was "sadly lacking in legitimate circus talent."[66] Most reviewers, however, wrote positively about the circus and lauded the performers for their "spirit, originality, and enthusiasm."[67] In 1937 the circus added a sideshow that consisted of vaudeville acts from the Federal Variety Unit of the WPA.[68] We know that a man named Mack Casso headed it; little else is known of its personnel and their attributes.

The omission of large animal acts was another criticism leveled against the circus in its early years. *Billboard* commented that the only real weakness in the performance was its lack of "trained animal turns. Current circumstances make it impossible for such an act to obtain work under the WPA banner."[69] The reporter was referring to the fact that the circus would not pay for animals directly. Small animals were part of some of the displays, such as the dog acts, but their owners received no money for them. Hallie Flanagan, the national director of the Federal

Fig. 16.11. The performers and staff of the WPA Circus, Astoria, Queens, ca. 1936. Photograph. Federal Theatre Project Collection, Special Collections & Archives, George Mason University

Theatre Project, explained the lack of large-scale animals: "There were no elephants on relief."[70] As criticism persisted, FTP officials tried to work out a solution to "feed and care for animals so that big animal acts may be included in units." A compromise was reached wherein the WPA would provide food, transport, and shelter for the animals but their owners would receive no additional wages. To meet this criticism, the WPA slowly began to employ animal acts: an elephant was added in 1936 and some performing bears were brought on a year later.

The program for winter 1937, published in *Billboard*, reveals that out of twenty-one displays, two were now devoted to animals.[71] One of them still included dogs but there was the addition of a troupe of bears. The elephant hired six months previously did not have its own act, but participated in the opening pageant.[72] Dog performances continued to be a central part of the activities of the WPA circus during the 1937 tenting season. Three different dog acts with the addition of a pony venture now appeared simultaneously in the first display after the opening tournament in which all of the circus performers and animals paraded around the stage. In ring 1 appeared Fred Rex and his dog and pony act, billed as Professor Rex and his "reinless, rearing and jumping ponies" (*fig. 16.12*). In ring 2 was William Rhode and his dogs and monkeys, described as his "educated canines featuring 'Spot,' the dog with the human brain"; in ring 3 was Harry De Dio and his trained dogs (*figs. 16.13*).[73] Billy Rhode's exploit was commented on in the *New York Times*, especially his "high-diving pup, Blackberry—fifteen feet into a fireman's net."[74] Another reviewer for the *New York Times* described Harry De Dio's triumph in which "a dog stood on its master's head, balancing on its forepaws."[75] He also had monkeys as part of his enterprise. Another dog act, which appeared in the

Fig. 16.12. Professor Rex's Dog and Pony Act, May 1936. Photograph. National Archives and Records Administration

Fig. 16.13. William Rhode, animal trainer, and three of his canines, ca. 1937. Photograph. Federal Theatre Project Collection, Special Collections & Archives, George Mason University, Circus 478-2-5

circus at different seasons, was the Frank Brother's dogs, known as the "only troupe of performing Chinese canines in show business."[76] There was also a bucking mule called Dynamite, the Kicking Mule, which was one of the staples of the WPA Circus, and later there were trained camels.[77]

An elephant was finally located for the circus.[78] She was apparently looked after terribly, as owner Ed Rowland had let her roam free in a wooded area near Patterson, New Jersey. The *Federal Theatre Magazine* reported: "Her skin hung in folds like the set for the Dakota farm in *Native Ground*; her stomach draped under her like the backdrop of a one-night stand company; her ears were frost bitten; her scaly sides looked like slides in a cancer clinic."[79] She was rehabilitated by circus personnel and gained two hundred pounds in six days; several gallons of linseed oil cured her skin problems.[80] Rosie the Elephant was one of the most publicized animals in the WPA Circus. She was billed as the World's Smartest Elephant. She had been part of the Ringling Bros. and Barnum & Bailey Circus for many years and also appeared in Billy Rose's *Jumbo*.[81] When she was added to the show in November 1936 she was outfitted with red velvet headgear, gold jewelry, and gilded toenails. As part of her act she bowled and played ten pins.[82] Her handler and trainer was Joe Chokemallski. Rosie had several names: she was also called Young Jumbo, and, at other times Japino, and publicized as "the sacred black elephant from the twenty-third temple of his most exalted highness, the Rajah of Tinkakay." Japino was the cause of many notices in the press, since she escaped from the various circus lots seven times and was always returned by the police with the help of her handler. The most publicized of her dramatic escapes was when Japino was discovered wandering the streets of Queens en route to visit the Ringling Bros. and Barnum & Bailey Circus lot a few blocks away to visit her old friends.[83]

Japino was featured in many circus announcements. When the circus came to Elmsford, Queens, for example, she was the headlined act. The *Long Island Star* declared that "Former Battle Elephant for Indian Rajah Among Features of WPA Circus."[84] She also constantly made the headlines. In the circus parade before the show in Canarsie, Brooklyn, she jolted four people off her back when her howdah slipped and its four riders fell to the ground.[85] When she had a toothache, the press followed her dental work by the circus veterinarian.[86] She made many of the metropolitan papers when she sat down for five hours and refused to be transported to her next location until a young girl with a handful of turnips lured her into the van.[87] Finally, she was used as a picket in Times Square when there was a protest against cuts in the WPA Circus budget in June 1937.[88] She wore a sign that read: "The WPA cuts are coming. I'm on my way to the glue works." Children throughout the metropolitan area wrote letters to circus officials to protest her removal and a clever reporter for the *Long Island Star* wrote the headline "Pupils Want Japino to Stick on WPA, Not Envelopes."[89]

Fig. 16.14. Stanley George and His Performing Bears, ca. 1936. Photograph. Federal Theatre Project Collection, Special Collections & Archives, George Mason University, Circus 595-4

The elephant was so much trouble that circus officials decided to retire her in the fall of 1937. When children of the New York area heard the news they flooded the White House with letters and petitions about the future of their old friend. President Roosevelt issued an executive order decreeing that "Japino should remain in Winter quarters and receive not less than three bales of hay a day." Japino made the headlines again and rejoined the circus in spring of 1938. In ads in *White Tops* for the spring season she was again a star feature, advertised as "The Largest and Oldest Elephant in Captivity. Bigger than Jumbo. Japino Has Passed More than 100 Summers and Winters. The Same Big Fellow Your Granddad Fed Peanuts to a Half Century Ago. Still Hale and Hearty."[90] She continued performing with the WPA Circus until it closed. [91]

Stanley George and his performing bears were a popular animal act in the WPA Circus. George was hired in October 1936 and worked with his brother. Previously, the feature was known as the George Brothers.[92] The bears were known for their ability to ride a bicycle, roller-skate, walk a tightrope, turn somersaults, and other feats (*fig 16.14*). The Stanley brothers were of Roma descent and came from a family that had trained bears for almost two hundred years. They had performed with circuses in South America, Europe, and the United States.[93] Stanley George would wear the traditional Roma costume of full linen shirt, striped sash, breeches with embroidered side stripes, and high leather boots. The bears also had costumes designed for them. When Minnie first entered the ring she wore a satin cape like many of the human aerialists. Two of the bears even had costumes for the opening spectacle in a red, white, and blue scheme. For her tightrope act Minnie sported a rhinestone collar with a matching rhinestone belt above her white tulle skirt with blue edging (*fig.*

16.15). Bill had a red and white costume comprising a pom-pom hat with striped edging and a corresponding scarf. He held a hockey stick and wore roller skates. Red and white cuffs completed the costume for his roller-skating stunt. White rhinestones adorned the muzzles of both bears.

The act was described in detail in the *Canarsie Courier* when the WPA Circus performed for the first time in Canarsie, Brooklyn in May of 1937:

▲ *Fig. 16.15.* Robert Byrne. Costume design for performing bears, Minnie and Bill, ca. 1937. Drawing with fabric swatches. Library of Congress, Federal Theatre Project Collection

Two of the big bears participate in a game of seesaw, one rides a tricycle with a mate furnishing pushing power. A comedy conceit introduces one bear playing horse, hitched to a cart and driven by the trainer, with another big monster by his side. Protesting against the bulky load, the harnessed bear stops, turns around and deliberately unhitches himself. The bear in the cart then gently tosses the trainer over the dashboard as a gentle hint that he shall become the beast of burden, which he does, pulling the bear around the ring. Another stunt depicts the trainer and two bears at lunch. A bottle is opened and the trainer proceeds to fill small glasses. He is interrupted by one of the bears, who takes the bottle between his paws, falls on his back and drinks in great glee. Another bottle meets a somewhat similar fate. Both bears and the trainer simulate intoxication, lock arms in a very human sort of way and stagger about the ring while the band plays, "We Won't Go Home, Until Morning".... This amazing Rocky Mountain exhibition concludes with a desperate wrestling match between man and monster, in which skill and science is pitted against brute strength in a contest so terrific that the very atmosphere seems to tingle with the tenseness of the strain.[94]

The same review of the performance, lifted from the show's press agent, was printed in the *New York Post* when the show appeared in October of that year at the Jamaica Arena. The reporter titled his article "Seven Bears to Head Cast of WPA Circus."[95] Stanley George and his bears made it again into the press in June of 1937 when someone stole one of the bear's skates and muzzle when the circus was in Stapleton, Staten Island. The *Staten Island Advance* headline read "Bruin's Skates Swiped an'

Now He's Very Sad."[96] When the circus traveled to White Plains in February of 1938 a photograph of one of Stanley's black bears appeared in the *White Plains Reporter*.[97]

In an article on the WPA Circus in *White Tops* in 1938, George outlined how he trained his bears over a period of six years.[98] He considered Russian brown bears the best for circus work. "They are almost intelligent. Sometimes they express a feeling which corresponds to the feeling humans have, when they raise an eyebrow." It was important for a trainer to know how to bridge the gap between his desire and the animal's understanding of that task. George believed that the whip was not an effective training device. Instead he stressed the importance of patience. He noted that brown bears are slow learners. This was not because they lacked intelligence but because they are slow developers who live long lives, often fifty years and more. "We start training the little cubs at six months. We get them used to a soft shoe, as the first step in teaching them to roller skate. This, altogether, requires about two years. In another two years they will walk a wire. We teach our bears to hug us, to ride a bicycle, to turn somersaults, to wheel a baby carriage. Six years, and they are educated. My bears, now nine years old, have traveled with me on circus journeys through South America, Europe and our own country."

Part of the same account had already run in a 1937 article in *Star Weekly* called "Circus for the Jobless." Reporter Hazel Canning described the large appetites of two of the brown bears, Minnie and Bill. She quoted George who noted, "they like the best in carrots, cooked meats, thick soup, spinach (they never argue about spinach) and milk, of which they drink a gallon a day. Good appetites and a good conscience keep them sensitive to my praise, and sorry at my reproof."[99] Ironically, these bears

probably ate a lot better than much of the WPA Circus audience.

Stanley George was outshone, however, by Captain Ernest Engerer and his lion act, which joined the circus in 1938. Billed as "The Lion King," Engerer performed with his two lions Leo and Peter (*fig. 16.16*). According to press agent Goodwin, Engerer "puts these sinuous, slinking, snarling haters of man through their paces."[100] They were two full-grown "savage-backed maned Nubian lions" that, according to circus press, were "captured alive in the fetid jungles of Africa."[101]

Ernest Engerer was born into a Bavarian family with a long history of training wild animals. He was educated at the Hagenbeck Training School in Hamburg and was employed as a wild animal trapper for the Hagenbeck Zoo. He served in the Imperial German Army and did a stint in southwest Africa in 1910. Engerer immigrated to the United States in about 1914 and made his livelihood as an animal trainer and performer.[102] In addition to wild cats, he worked with ponies and police dogs. He ran a small dog-training academy and kennel in Long Island and had his own small family circus called Captain Engerer's Society Circus.

Fig. 16.16. Captain Ernest Engerer, ca. 1937. Photograph. Library of Congress, Federal Theatre Project Collection

Engerer became famous in America when he won the title of "World's Greatest Lion Tamer" at a competition sponsored by the National Convention of Lion Tamers at the Cleveland Exposition in 1930. Each contestant was required to tame an unbroken wild animal and teach it one trick. This was a difficult enough feat under any circumstances but even more so for Engerer, who lost an arm when he was attacked by one of his lions in 1918.[103] This was not to be his only serious encounter with his lions. On February 26, 1939 he was attacked by one of his lions as he approached their cage to feed them. Leo thrust his paw through the bars of the cage and grabbed Engerer's leg. Then Peter, the other lion, grabbed his second leg and the two began to claw him and drag him into their cage. Engerer's son Ernest, upon hearing his father's cries, saved him by beating the lions with a stick until they released their grasp. Engerer was immediately rushed to the hospital.

His eighteen-year-old son, who often performed with his father, then took his place. He introduced his act by telling the audience the story of the attack and then proceeded to do tricks with these same lions. He continued the act until his father

Fig. 16.17. Liberty horse act, ca. 1937. Photograph. Library of Congress, Federal Theatre Project Collection

recovered and returned a month later. This incident generated articles in the *New York Times,* the *Long Island Daily Press*, and other papers.[104] Not one to give up, Engerer continued to work as a lion tamer for another fifteen years until he was killed by another one of his lions in 1964 at a performance in Winston-Salem, North Carolina.

In the final years of the circus, splashier animal acts were added. The Masked Ranger along with "his marvelous horse Pronto that jumps over the moon," a take-off of the popular "Lone Ranger" radio show that began in 1933, was hired in 1939. M. H. Allen and his performing "liberty" horses had become part of the program the previous year (*fig 16.17*). Liberty horses were trained to perform without harnesses, leads, or riders. They responded to the crack of a whip or verbal commands. These horses were all of one color in this case, all white and aesthetically stunning. They were a major feature of the show.[105]

Strong Woman and Strong Man

Kate Brumbach Heymann, known professionally as Madame Sandwina, had been out of work for six years when she was hired for the WPA Circus (*fig. 16.18*). Her strong-woman performance included holding aloft her husband, Max, and doing tricks with him. She was best known for her ability to bend seven-foot-long iron bars into double spirals and to break chains. Lying on a bed of nails while two clowns beat an anvil resting on her stomach was another part of her act. The *New York Daily Star* wrote of her as "a huge person who performs several feats that appear to be quite difficult, including tossing a man around."[106]

Sandwina had been a major headliner with the Barnum & Bailey circus back in 1911. In 1912 she

was the central feature of an advertising poster, where she was described inaccurately as 6 feet 1 inch tall, 220 pounds, and 23 years old.[107] With typical circus hyperbole, she was billed as "Germany's Most Herculean Venus Possessing The Most Perfect Female Figure . . . Strongest Woman that Ever Lived." Sandwina was a major circus star and was included in an article in *Harper's Weekly* that described her as having "as pretty a face, as sweet a smile and as fine a head of silky brown curls as a man could ask to see . . . but she [also] had the muscles of Thor. Those shoulders! And the arms on her a pair of thick, white graceful, rippling pythons! A condition not a theory confronts us. The New Woman is not threatening; she is here. She is modestly billed as Katie Sandwina, Europe's Queen of

Fig. 16.18. Madame Sandwina, Strongest Woman, May 1936. Photograph. National Archives and Records Administration

Strength, Beauty and Dexterity."[108] By the time she was performing in the WPA Circus she was a middle-aged, gray-haired woman. Her femininity was enhanced by her velvet tunic with jeweled-edged lappets; tight, laced-up leather boots with two-inch heels; and her hair piled high on top of her head.

Born into a circus family in Germany, her parents were strength athletes and her fifteen siblings performed in the family's circus.[109] Katie began working in the circus at age two and took on wrestlers in the audience when she was a teenager. She married Max Heymann, a handbalancer and acrobat, and together they worked up an act in which Sandwina demonstrated her great strength by lifting Max above her head and then doing the manual of arms with him as if he were a rifle. The venture was a success and Keith's Orpheum Vaudeville cir-

cuit hired the couple in 1909. In 1910 they joined the Ringling Circus.[110]

The Great Paris, billed as the "Strongest Man of This or Any Age," replaced her in August 1937 (*fig. 16.19*).[111] He had formerly been a wrestler called Ivan the Terrible.[112] He dressed in a Roman gladiator's costume with helmet, tunic, and sandals. He weighed 246 pounds and the girth of his arms was billed as equaling that of a normal man's body. His act included twisting iron bars into knots and bending a coin between the palm of his hand and his thumb.[113] The Great Paris made it into the papers for the wrong reason when he was arrested after a show in Newark, New Jersey in April 1938 for abandoning his wife.[114]

Chief White Cloud

Chief White Cloud, billed as a full-blooded Mohawk Indian from upstate New York near the Canadian border, was a famous roper and trick rider. He had won many rodeos and championships and appeared in the numerous Wild West shows popular in America in the first decade of the twentieth century, including Tompkins Wild West Show and also in such established circus organizations as Al G. Barnes and the Ringling Bros. and Barnum & Bailey.[115]

In 1937 the "Chief" was part of a two-person roping feature with the star performer Eva Berducci. They were billed as "White Cloud and Eva, trick and fancy ropers." She had been part of Miller Brothers' 101 Ranch Circus and the Buffalo Bill's Wild West Circus.[116] Berducci was credited with originating the walkover somersault while bareback riding. She performed her rope trick of spinning five separate ropes before the abdicated Edward VIII, at the Calgary Stampede.[117]

Fig. 16.19. Meyer Paris, "Strongest man of this or any other age," ca. 1937. Photograph. Library of Congress, Federal Theatre Project Collection

Fig. 16.20. Chief White Cloud, *The Last Frontier*, 1939. Photograph. Library of Congress, Federal Theatre Project Collection

Due to the popularity of this genre of performance, it was expanded into a ten-minute Wild West display composed of a "congress of full-blooded Mohawk Braves, cowboys and cowgirls" in 1938.[118] The ten-minute spectacle was called *The Last Frontier* and "recreated the sports and pastimes of the romantic far West" (*fig. 16.20*). Usually the last act in the show, it was part of the 1938[118] and 1939 seasons and was advertised in the WPA posters and press releases for those two years. The *Orange Courier* described the act: "The circus is featuring its Wild West troupe, with such noted performers as the Roberts Duo of whip crackers and trick fancy ropers; Chief White Cloud, a full-blooded Mohawk Indian who twirls, controls, and manipulates three separate ropes at one time; Princess Sylvia, noted Indian War dancer. This excellent company gives a ten-minute exhibition of the sports and pastimes of the far West that was."[119]

Photographs of the spectacle reveal that the performers were costumed in full Plains Indian dress while the cowboys and cowgirls were outfitted in Western attire. Horsemanship was a good part of the show and many photographs record the entertainers seated on horses. Chief White Cloud was identified with a white horse called White Beauty and a painted horse called Spot.

Press releases concentrated on White Cloud, and ignored the other Wild West performers. He was portrayed as a very Westernized, Americanized

Fig. 16.21. "Clown Alley," ca. 1937. Photograph. Library of Congress,
Federal Theatre Project Collection

Native American. His upbringing included education at the Carlisle Indian school in Pennsylvania and membership in the Catholic Church.[120] Publicity also mentioned that he led a good Christian life and never smoked or drank. He married Love Star in a Catholic ceremony. White Cloud was a licensed pilot as well as a talented musician who played a number of instruments. In addition, he was a compiler of cowboy songs and stories many that he thought were in danger of being lost.[121]

Clowns

Clowns figured prominently in the WPA Circus, announcing the beginning of the show, amusing the audience with their gags while equipment was being changed, and injecting a general level of comedy into the enterprise. Although clowns did not receive top billing, with their grotesque painted faces and colorful, outrageous costumes they were the most identifiable members of a circus troupe. The image of a

clown appeared in promotional photos and in the majority of the WPA Circus posters.

At the beginning of the first season there were eight clowns, including a dwarf known as Shorty, at 4 feet 3 inches, and a giant clown, known as Slim, who was 6 feet 6 inches.[122] Clowns of even more extreme heights eventually replaced them: 30-inch George Thornton and the 7-foot, 8-inch Forest "Slim" Glenn.[123] Other early clowns were Lollipop, who "played his slide trombone in a series of diminishing minors" and Frank Ward, "who extracted melody from a pair of wooden spoons and played a tune on a baby's bottle punched full of holes."[124] George Herman, known as Salt Pork, was a clown tumbler who climbed up on a rickety chair atop a rickety table pretending to almost lose his balance.[125]

As many as fifty clowns took part in WPA Circus performances between 1935 to 1939 (*fig. 16.21*). This unusually large number of clowns was related to the shortage of wild animals in the show. Many of these clowns had been featured stars in major circuses in the United States and abroad. During the 1937 season more than one-third of the displays were dedicated to clown acts. All of the four standard clown types were represented in the WPA Circus's "Clown Alley": the white-face clown, the auguste clown, the character clown, and the tramp or hobo clown. Lew A. Ward, Tommy Bell, Artie Mongan, Alec Campbell, Frank Walter, Jack Riano, Bill Stanley, Oscar Lowande, Charles Ledegar, Jimmy Hughes, Jack Kennedy, Max Rosenberg, Mike Alvin, Billy Ritchie, and Charlie Fortuna were some of the clowns mentioned in the press and or photographed for press use.[126] Additional clowns were Rocco, Dodo, and Dippo.[127]

Lew A. Ward was known as the "bozo of the white top" (*fig. 16.22*).[128] He was the producing clown, which meant that he was responsible for acts, cos-

tumes, and props and also performed.[129] He usually wore a baggy suit with a small polka-dotted shirt with white collar, a thin bowtie, and large leather shoes. He started as a lightweight prizefighter, then he joined vaudeville, where he had a tramp act with a performing dog.[130]

Charlie Fortuna was the most famous of the WPA clowns. The *Daily News* described him as the clown "that put the punch in the WPA Federal Theatre Project's three-ring circus."[131] Billed as La La, he had a totally silent act. He dressed in a baggy black suit with white starched shirt and bow tie and wore large white gloves and a tall tophat (*fig. 16.23*). He played pool with baseballs and burlesqued the act of star aerialist Avonne Gardener with the elephant Japino. Fortuna also cracked peanuts with a large sledgehammer and stared for a long period of time at a person in the audience "for the fun of contemplation."[132] He was often compared to Charlie Chaplin and when a reviewer for the *Standard Star* wrote on his act for the WPA Circus he titled his review "WPA Circus Will Feature Chaplin-esque Clowning." He was also known as "the happy poet of pantomime."[133] A member of a Spanish circus family, The Flying Fortunas, he had performed in the Circus Diaz for five years on the horizontal bars

▲ *Fig. 16.22.* Lew A. Ward, ca. 1937. Photograph. Library of Congress, Federal Theatre Project Collection

but preferred being a clown.[134] When *Billboard* staged a "Favorite outdoor performer" contest in 1939, he was a popular entry.[135]

One popular clown routine was when a group of rowdy clowns came out juggling all sorts of items including balls, pots, and chinaware. One of these clowns had a tall pole on which was piled a tray full of cups and saucers. The other mischief-making clowns then tried to make him spill his tray. The tray begins to fall on the audience but nothing happens because the china is attached to the pole.[136] Another act involved a clown ballet with thirteen cross-dressed dancers, beautifully costumed in tutu and white sneakers (*fig 16.24*). Dance master Jack Mason choreographed the performance.[137]

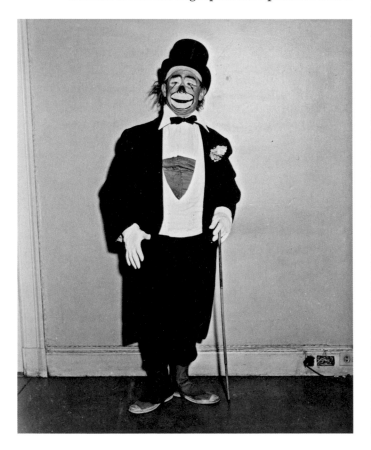

Although the reviewer for *Billboard* was not sure that this escapade belonged in a circus for children, he found the "burlesque ballet routine reminder of the joey's [clown's] work should be eligible for any man's show."[138]

The opening clown adventure was immensely popular with the children. A clown policeman (Hymie Gordon) chased a red-haired clown tramp around the arena and through the audience. The tramp would elude the policeman and run back into the center of the middle ring to continue his pantomime act. Carrying a large truncheon the policeman would sneak up behind him as the children tried to warn him of the policeman's impending attack. The children screamed louder and louder but the clown would pretend not to hear them. Finally, the policeman appeared behind the tramp and then struck him with the truncheon and the audience went "into an uproar of mirth."[139]

Arthur Mongan was known as Milo the Clown. He made it into the pages of *Billboard* and *Brooklyn Citizen* with his walk around specialties in March of 1937. The reporter for *Billboard* wrote: "Milo the clown has had pictures of his brick-layer walk-a-round taken so that he 'can hand them down to posterity.'"[140] The reviewer for *Brooklyn Citizen* described his act as "Funnier than ever...his bricklayer, golfer and football walk-a-rounds brought screams of laughter from both old and young."[141]

Other comic acts included Billy Ritchie, the tramp cyclist and his company of assistants. This genre of clowning originated in vaudeville so it is not surprising that Ritchie had appeared with the Ziegfeld Follies of 1917–18 with W. C. Fields and Will Rogers.[142] Ritchie started performing in 1893 and worked in Australia, the United States, South America, and Europe.[143] In 1913 he did his trick-riding feature at the Casino in Monte Carlo, where

▲ *Fig. 16.23.* Charlie Fortuna, La-La, ca. 1937. Photograph. Library of Congress, Federal Theatre Project Collection

he reputedly received ten thousand francs for one day's work.[144] He performed before many crowned heads of Europe, including the former king of Spain, Alfonso XII; King Edward VII of the United Kingdom; and Kaiser Emperor Wilhelm of Germany.[145]

Charles Ledegar was billed as "the clown on the bounding rope." Burt Wells did a comedy slack-wire act. Frank Walter was paired up with a trained giraffe named Jargo. In addition, Jack Riano, a comedy tumbler, did a Popeye the Sailor clown number adapted from the popular cartoon strips and animated films of the 1930s. Riano had appeared in some of the cartooning for Fleischer Studios on the Popeye animated film. Riano wore a blue sailor suit with red collar and belt, had the disproportionately muscular forearm with two anchor tattoos, and held a corncob pipe in his mouth. As part of his role he carried around with him the can of spinach that gave him his superhuman strength (*fig. 16.25*). Riano had once trouped with Beatrice Lillie in the 3rd Little Show at the Music Box Theater.[146] Six years earlier he was with a troupe called the Folies Bergère, and before then as a chandelier jumping "monkey" with the Four Rianos, who played the major circuits.[147]

According to the press, one of the children's favorites was Alec Campbell, a clown tumbler. The *Brooklyn Eagle* reported that Campbell was one of the favorite clowns with the WPA and two weeks later The *Daily Advocate* highlighted a photograph of Alec Campbell with the caption "Alec Campbell (above) reputed to be the children's favorite clown performs his antics and capers at every performance of the WPA circus."[148] Another clown was played by Artie Morgan, who walked on stilts and wore a traditional striped clown costume with ruffles around his neck. A troupe of comedy acrobats called the Gaik Troupe performed with the circus in 1939.

Fig. 16.24. Clown ballet, May 1936. Photograph. National Archive and Records Administration

Fig. 16.25. Jack Riano as Popeye, ca. 1938. Photograph. Library of Congress, Federal Theatre Project Collection

Spectacles

SAVAGE AFRICA

In the week of May 22, 1937 the spectacle *Savage Africa* was added to the show. It was a reworking of an African dance drama, *Bassa Moona* (The Land I Love), presented by the Negro Theatre Project in New York City.[149] Created by Momadu Johnson and Norman Coker, it had played at the Lafayette, Ritz, Daly, and Majestic theaters for forty-three performances from December 8, 1936, to February 1, 1937.[150] Barry Farnel designed the costumes and scenery, and it was reported that he "spent months in research to give *Bassa Moona* an authentic production."[151] Approximately sixteen thousand people had viewed the show. Burns O'Sullivan revised the

dance drama for the circus, making it more suitable for an audience mostly of children. He billed it as a stupendous display of the darkest continent. The fifteen-minute presentation contained all of the ingredients of a stereotyped African production for a low-level, mostly white and uninformed American audience. It featured "King Alake and his consorts in their native jungle haunts, 100 witch, voodoo and native dancers," the executioner in action, the death of the slave dancer, the human sacrifice, the missionary in the stew pot, and the wedding of the prince and princess.[152] The spectacle included an appearance by the elephant Japino, here billed as the sacred black elephant in the scene of the death of the slave dancer.[153] Nine native drummers kept up an incessant tom-tom beat (*fig. 16.26*). When Japino swiped Compina with his hind foot over her left eye and she required three stitches, it made headlines in the metropolitan papers. An African village was built on the lot at Throggs Neck, Queens to accompany the spectacle. Five straw huts were erected in the front yard of the site and the cast of the spectacle dressed in tribal costumes was scattered about. In the report for the 1937 season, press agent Goodwin reported that the erection of the African Village "had helped business a great deal."[154]

In 1937 a discrimination case was launched against the WPA when thirty-one performers borrowed for the WPA Circus spectacle, including Momodu Johnson from the company of *Bassa Moona*, were dismissed. Willis Morgan, president of the City Projects Council, brought the case before the appeals board. The hearing was reported in the *New York Times*. The suit alleged unfair dismissal and charged Willis Diggs with acting prejudicially. He was accused of ordering "the members of the Negro company not to mingle or fraternize in any way with any of the whites."[155] The actors were reinstated a week later.

Fig. 16.26. Compina, specialty dancer with the spectacle *Savage Africa*, 1937. Photograph. Library of Congress, Federal Theatre Project Collection

CIRCUS CONTINENTAL

Another spectacle created for the WPA Circus was *Circus Continental* in May 1938. It was described as "the magnificent inaugural pageant and grand tournament that opens every performance."[156] A Goodwin press release described it in some detail:

> With the true hand of a big-time showman, he mixed people, trappings, costumes, howdahs, palanquins, all sorts of circus paraphernalia, marvelous educated canines, ponies, the hues of the rainbow in silk, satins, velvets, Japino, the sacred black elephant in her enormous tassel of colored cellophane, beautiful girls, handsome gypsies, monkeys and Oriental brown bears, pendants, plumes and gigantic European fans into one glittering, vividly colored, moving mass—a processional of European pomp and splendor—and over the whole he showered rhinestones by the thousands.
>
> O'Sullivan, the super-showman, did this with the cyc of a great artist. The color scheme of the huge and magnificent tournament is worthy of a Ziegfeld. Its lighting is breath-takingly beautiful. It is the last word, this "Circus Continental," and, as its 200 people and animals move in mighty ranks into its enactment, it seemingly resolves into a rainbow marching—a rainbow studded with gold and silver and precious jewels, lighting up in auras of sunrise and sunset hues here and there in its dazzling entity castles and towers out of a child's fairyland of Prince Charmings and Princesses Beautiful.[157]

AMERICA WITH A PARADE OF THE STATES AND SNOW WHITE

One of the spectacles organized for the opening of the circus in 1939 was *America with a Parade of the*

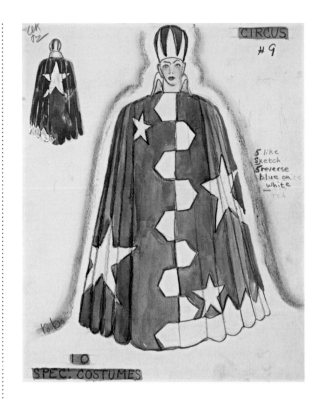

States.[158] All of the circus performers, including the animals, were dressed in specially designed red, white, and blue costumes. Giant red or blue stars were the predominant decoration of the floor-length capes that many of the performers wore in this spectacle (*fig. 16.27*). The spectacle in the show's final season was *Snow White and the Seven Dwarfs*. Based on the fairy tale by the Brothers Grimm and the Disney animated film (1937), the first to be in color, it must have been a popular addition to the program.

Aerial Acts

Aerial acts were often the most thrilling and exciting features of a circus performance. The WPA Circus had quite a list of featured aerialists who appeared in different seasons. Ernie Sharron did an aerial broom

▲ *Fig. 16.27.* Robert Byrne. Costume design for *America, Parade of Stars*, 1939. Drawing. Library of Congress, Federal Theatre Project Collection

Lady Grace, aerialist, Addie Kay with her neck swivel, and Mademoiselle Doreena, the Czarina of the Clouds, who performed a contortion act on a rope swing suspended high above the circus floor.[161] The Masked Marvel of Mongolia also known as "Mister ? the Mystery Man from Siam" slid from the top height of the arena down to the ground doing an extremely dangerous "back slide."[162]

Burt Lancaster and Nick Cravat performed a comedic triple bar act for two years. The act involved swinging between three horizontally set bars above the floor in a series of "fly-overs and daring conjunctive giant swings from bar to bar" (*fig. 16.28*).[163] The strangely balanced pair, the stately Burt Lancaster and the 5-foot-2-inch Cravat, whose real name was Nicholas Crussia, first met at the Union Settlement House, where they learned acrobatics from Curly Brent.[164] They worked for the King Brothers Circus and the Cole Brothers before the WPA Circus hired them. The *New York Amsterdam News* described them as "America's foremost triple bar experts, who offer an exhibition of humorous acrobatic stunts a la pantomime that is absolutely amazing."[165] Cravat often fell and got injured; such wipeouts were noted in the newspapers. Cravat was injured twice in five weeks and ended up both times in the hospital.[166] Cravat left the WPA Circus to join the aerial bar act of Walter Guice, appearing with the Ringling Bros. and Barnum & Bailey Circus. Lancaster had already left the WPA Circus and joined the Newton Brothers Circus.[167] Both went on to become Hollywood actors.

One of the most publicized performers was Avonne Gardener, billed as the Spanish web aerialist. She climbed a rope with foot and hand loops hung from an attached aerial point and did acrobatics from it (*fig 16.29*). The audience would "crane necks and keeps mouths open" to see her perform.[168] She was often written about as "Avonne Gardener, the abso-

act; Virginia Diaz performed a tight-wire act; Nick Kenny did Roman rings; Metzler and Neuman were Roman ring experts as well; the Russell Brothers were aerial thrillers who did a double trapeze act, as did Eddie Geer and Stasia. Trapeze artist June Loya was billed as "the daring young girl on the flying trapeze." New York's *Daily News* announced that "June Loya . . . will offer a new sensational half-twist to a heel catch sixty feet in the air."[159] Other performers included Alvin and Kenny on swivel bar, Sylvia Reckless on trapeze, the Joe Bell Trio, tightrope dancers, and Shots O'Brien, billed as the only man in the world to accomplish the extremely dangerous back walk over to a triple standing somersault, part of a troupe called the Twelve Desert Whirlwinds.[160] There were also

Fig. 16.28. Burt Lancaster and Nick Cravat on the triple horizontal bars, ca. 1936. Photograph. Library of Congress, Federal Theatre Project Collection

lutely fearless little Miss whose thrilling exploits have made two continents gasp: the inimitable Avonne assisted by Hazel Gardener." Hazel was Avonne's mother, herself a featured member of vaudeville shows, who performed an acrobatic act with her husband. She doubled in the WPA Circus as assistant to her daughter and as a cook with her husband in the circus food tent. Avonne herself had already appeared in the Gorman Brothers circus in 1934.[169] She continued to expand her feature and was reported to be busy learning new tricks to her act and, as "queen of the air" was "busy learning a new giant swing from the top of the perilous Spanish web."[170] Avonne also did acrobatics on the back of a trained horse, a Crematolian stallion named Skippy. In 1938 she resigned from the WPA Circus to join a commercial circus.

Misses Powers and Price formed one of the featured acts of the circus (*fig 16.30*). Working one hundred feet in the air, they were billed as "World Renowned Welsh Wire Artists." According to press agent Goodwin, Welsh-born Price and Powers were "the greatest and most daring tight wire act in America today." They were born into circus families. Their parents toured with the Davy Taylor circus in North Wales. Advertisements invited the public to see them perform "the rhumba on the silver cable,

walk two abreast on the narrow strands, and climax their thrilling act when Alice Powers walks the tight rope in her bare feet. She is the only little girl in the world to accomplish this feat."[171] They worked in circuses all over the United States in separate productions before being paired together in the WPA Circus. Alice Powers had done a high-wire act with her husband for a great many years. Her husband fell from the ropes during a show in Fall River, Massachusetts, and seriously injured his back. Pauline Price, an older circus performer, had traveled to Japan in 1919 as part of the Julian Eltingo troupe.[172] The two performers were one of the first features hired by the WPA Circus and continued to be part of the troupe for all four years of the circus's existence.

There was also an iron-jaw act performed by Marie Mung. The aerialist was suspended at the end of rope held in place by a mouthpiece. She did a series of spins and twists. When interviewed she stated that she "played all over . . . Only recently I played the Canadian National Exhibition at Toronto." She started to work in circuses at the age of sixteen and joined

Fig. 16.29. Avonne Gardener on the Spanish web, 1935. Photograph. Franklin D. Roosevelt Presidential Library

Fig. 16.30. Price and Powers, "The Famous Welsh Wire Artists," ca. 1935. Photograph. Library of Congress, Federal Theatre Project Collection

Weber

▲   *Fig. 16.31.* Hamed Mohamed and his troupe of Arabian acrobats, ca. 1936.
Photograph. Federal Theatre Project Collection, Special Collections &
Archives, George Mason University

Sells-Floto and Ringlings.[173] The WPA Circus employed another iron-jaw performer, Anne Howe.[174] Her exploit was described as the "iron jawed girl who climaxes the show with a slide for life by her teeth."[175]

Another group of performers did acrobatic stunts on the ground. This group included Artie Herbert, billed as "the highest stilt walker in the world," the perch act of Jack McCarthy and Harry Sills, which was noteworthy because "Sill's 200 pounds makes him the heaviest top-mounter in any circus."[176] There were three Risley acts in which members lying on their backs juggled fellow acrobats with their feet: the Martian troupe of Risely acrobats, the Virginia Melford trio, and the Royal Wizards. The Brachards were a troupe of comedy acrobats and the Brutal Brothers were hand balancers, as were Joe Allen and Emery Swartwood. Arnold and Kress were skaters. Garnat and Duhring were a comedy balancing act, Ling Tey was a Chinese gymnast, and the Bedell family were ground tumblers.

The best-publicized of these acts was Moroccan-born Hamed Mohamed and his troupe of Arabian somersault acrobats, who built a human pyramid (*fig. 16.31*). Sometimes called the International Twelve, they were known for their stunt in which Hamed would "support forty men arranging themselves like branching candelabro from his sides and shoulders." In an excerpt from an interview published in *White Tops,* he boasted, I can carry nine men," he says, "a weight of about 1,500 pounds."[177] Mohamed was picked up as a small boy by an American circus man who watched him play on a playground in his childhood, "saw me, and hired me on the spot."[178]

Another pyramid building group hired in 1939 was called MacGregor's' Scotch Highlanders, known as "unparalleled builders of picturesque pyramids."[179] They would dress in orange flannel shirts

with alternating red and blue pleated skirts, imitation brick leggings to match the angled caps, and black-and-white spats (*fig 16.32*). Albert Arden, known as the Human Frog, appeared with Marie Genaro as contortionists. There were also illusionists at times, including Emmy Barbier. She previously appeared with her own act on the old-time Keith Albee and Orpheum circuits.[180]

Circus Controversy

The WPA Circus was not without its share of controversy during its four-year run. During a performance in Central Park, parents contacted the New York Parks' Department complaining that they found the circus performance to contain "vulgar and suggestive sequences (*fig. 16.33*).[181] Ralph Whitehead, head of the

Fig. 16.32. Robert Byrne. Costume design for the "Scotch Highlanders," ca. 1938. Drawing with fabric swatches. Library of Congress, Federal Theatre Project Collection

Federal Theatre's Vaudeville, Musical Comedy and Circus Division, launched an investigation. He concluded that there were only two acts, both clown acts, that could be considered possibly containing anything "vulgar:" one in which a clown wore two balloons on his chest, and the second in which a clown had a string of firecrackers attached to his trousers; when they went off he ran across the stage losing them. Newspapers reported that "Whitehead did not bar the balloons but ordered the clown to wear a coat over them," and in the second, "the clown could keep [wearing] his trousers."[182] The controversy, however, led to the cancellation of the Parks Department tour of the WPA Circus in the city parks.

In 1938 there were reports of thievery by circus personnel from tickets sales in Canarsie, Brooklyn, and in Hollis, Queens. A Federal grand jury in Brooklyn indicted three circus employees on counts of "conspiracy and embezzlement."[183] The *New York Times* reported that the prosecution charged that "Joseph Harris, standing at the gate of the circus ... palmed tickets and gave patrons parts of previously used tickets ... Abe Halle retained the whole tickets and delivered them to Julius Specter for resale." The case was tried and the three defendants were found not guilty.[184]

Conclusion

The WPA Circus continued to play the boroughs of New York and its outlying suburbs until the end of June 1939, when Congress discontinued the Federal Theatre Project.[185] On June 30, 1939, the WPA Circus played its last performance at the Rockville Center in Nassau County, Long Island. Staff were given a month to close down the enterprise. A month after the last show a group of performers, headed by Oscar

Lowande and canvas and seat supplier John Martin, joined together to form a cooperative venture.[186] It was a small, one-ring circus with a 100-foot tent that could accommodate 2,200 people. The admission was 25 cents for adults and 15 cents for children. There was a concert band and a sideshow for an additional 10 cents apiece. The main feature was Captain Ernest Engerer and his lions and other domestic animal acts but the endeavor failed after three weeks.[187]

The demise of the Federal Theatre Project was largely due to Congressional objections about the leftist politics that inflected many of its varied productions. Though it was but a small part of the overall project, the WPA Circus seems to have been a very successful program that employed and entertained Americans during the troubled years of the Depression. In her memoirs, published twenty-six years after the close of the circus, Hallie Flanagan gave due respect to the artistry and importance of the endeavor:

> Above all, there was the Federal Theatre circus. I saw the circus in the 258th Field Artillery Armory where 14,000 children were guests of W.P.A. and the Police Department, and in East Harlem at the Star Casino, with children swarming in from a radius of fifty blocks; and always I learned something from it .... These aerialists, cyclists, balancers, these tightrope walkers, strong men, and clowns, those cloggers, hoofers, and tappers, had a tradition and a technique.... In the apparently effortless grace of a trapeze flier, I have heard reiterated the fact that all performance demands virtuosity. And in the faces of our clowns, many of them former big-top headliners, I have seen the tragic-comic mask which was in a special way the symbol of Federal Theatre."[188]

Fig. 16.33. Dick Rose. Children at WPA festival in Sheep Meadow, Central
Park, May 2, 1936. Photograph. Library of Congress, Federal Theatre Project
Collection

1 The best overview of the Federal Theatre Project is Jane Sherron De Hart, *The Federal Theatre, 1935–1939; Plays, Relief, and Politics* (Princeton: Princeton University Press, 1967). Also see Susan Quinn, *Furious Improvisation: How the WPA and a Cast of Thousands Made High Art out of Desperate Times* (New York: Walker & Co., 2008); and Barry Witham, *The Federal Theatre Project: A Case Study* (New York: Cambridge University Press, 2003). For a complete history of the formation and administration of the WPA Circus, see John-Stuart Fauquet, "Elephants on Relief? Circus and the WPA (1935–1939)," (MA thesis, University of Wisconsin–Madison, 2007), chap. 1, "The Circus and Its Administration," 7–22.

2 "Philadelphia Region Gets Going," *Federal Theatre Magazine* 21 (Feb. 1936), 8.

3 "N.Y. WPA Show Hits High Mark in Attendance; Admish Plans Success," *Billboard* 48 (July 25, 1936), 38.

4 Anthony Buttitta, "There Were No Elephants on Relief," *Federal Theatre Magazine* 1 (Jan. 26, 1936), 23–26. Millions of people attended the WPA Circus during its four-year existence. According to Hallie Flanagan, during the first six months of the project from 1935 to 1936, "86,625 persons . . . saw our New York Federal Theatre Circus at 57 performances between October 17 and February 1": "A Report on the First Six Months," *Federal Theatre* 1 (March 1936), 10. By May 1, 1936 "well over half a million" people had attended its performances and by the end of that year it had showed before "approximately 790,000 customers": "WPA Unit Plays to 790,000 in N.Y.," *Billboard* 48 (Oct. 3, 1936), 36. In February 1937 the *New York Times* reported that 415,000 customers had attended the WPA Circus for that year: "WPA Actors Play to 5,500,000 in City," *New York Times*, Feb. 14, 1937, 43.

5 *The Long Island Advocate*, quoted in Frederic Denver Pfening III, "The American Circus and the Great Depression: 1929–1939" (MA thesis, Ohio State University, 1976), 42.

6 Michael Denning, *The Cultural Front: The Laboring of American Culture in the Twentieth Century* (New York and London: Verso, 1997).

7 "The Circus Mergers," *Billboard* 41 (Oct. 12, 1929), 89; quoted in Pfening, "The American Circus and the Great Depression," 9.

8 Charles P. Fox and Tom Parkinson note that the relatively modest motorized circuses weathered the tough times far better than the much larger and more expensive railroad shows: Charles P. Fox and Tom Parkinson, *Circus in America* (Waukesha, WI: Country Beautiful, 1969), 105. For the best study of the circus during the Depression years, see Pfening, "The American Circus and the Great Depression."

9 Among the many unions that had a hand in organizing circus workers, the most prominent were the International Alliance of Billposters, the International Brotherhood of Teamsters, the American Federation of Musicians, and the American Federation of Actors. For an account of the Ringling Bros. and Barnum & Bailey's labor troubles in the 1930s, see David Lewis Hammarstrom, *Big Top Boss: John Ringling North and the Circus* (Urbana: University of Illinois Press, 1992), 44–55.

10 In Susan Currell's formulation, the "problem of leisure" in the 1930s emerged as the question of what Americans were doing with their free time and became a preoccupation of economists, reformers, and government officials. The recreational and cultural programs associated with the New Deal were formulated in part to address concerns about how "improper" leisure contributed to society's ills: Susan Currell, *The March of Spare Time: The Problem and Promise of Leisure in the Great Depression* (Philadelphia: University of Pennsylvania Press, 2005), 19–28.

11 Warren Susman famously contended that Mickey Mouse was more crucial to understanding the 1930s than Franklin D. Roosevelt: Warren Susman, *Culture as History: The Transformation of American Society in the Twentieth Century* (New York: Pantheon Books, 1984), 103. Also see Lawrence Levine, "The Folklore of Industrial Society: Popular Culture and Its Audiences," *American Historical Review* 97 (Dec. 1992), 1369–99.

12 For more information on New York's Armories, see Nancy L. Todd, *New York's Historic Armories: An Illustrated History* (Albany: State University of New York Press, 2006).

13 "WPA Circus Ready for Uptown Debut," *New York Times*, Nov. 3, 1936, N1.

14 Melvin D. Hildreth, "The Works Progress Circus," *White Tops* 9 (Dec. 1935–Jan. 1936), 35.

15 "WPA Show Playing Week-End Dates," *Billboard* 49 (Feb. 6, 1937), 40.

16 Hildreth, "The Works Progress Circus," 35.

17 "WPA Circus to Open in Kings Wednesday," *New York Times*, Aug. 26, 1937. Hallie Flanagan Papers, Billy Rose Theatre Division, The New York Public Library for the Performing Arts, *T-MSS 1964-002 (hereafter HFP), box 40.

18 "N.Y. WPA Show Hits High Mark in Attendance; Admish Plan Success," 38.

19 "WPA Unit Plays to 790,000 in N.Y.," *Billboard* 48 (Oct. 3, 1936), 36, 49.

20 Wendell J. Goodwin, *WPA Circus*, National Service Bureau Federal Theatre Project, Works Progress Administration, 1938, 17. Copy in George Mason University Library.

21 "Circus Tent Burns after 2,200 Depart," *New York Times*, Aug. 28, 1938, 29.

22 "New Tent For WPA Circus," *New York Times*, Aug. 29, 1938, 10.

23 "WPA Circus Extends Stay in Ridgewood," *Brooklyn Citizen*, April 20, 1937, HFP, box 38.

24 "Circus to Open Here Tomorrow with Large Cast," *Daily Star, L.I.* Oct. 6, 1937, HFP, box 40.

25 "Infant Park up Fast, Strong," *Billboard*, June 28, 1952, 76.

26 "WPA Circus Performance Given for 150 Children at Bellevue," *New York Times*, Nov. 9, 1935, 17.

27 "Union League Club Host to Children," *New York Times*, Dec. 25, 1935, 20.

28 "WPA Circus at Hospital," *New York Times*, June 10, 1936, 5.

29 *The New York Times* reported that circus performers from the WPA Circus staged a show in the children's ward at Greenpoint Hospital in Brooklyn. See "Child Patients See Circus," *New York Times*, Sept. 19, 1937, HFP, box 40.

30 "Facts and Figures: New York," *Federal Theatre Magazine* 2 (March 1937), 9, 18, HFP, box 9.

31 "Four WPA Brooklyn Shows Slated for Close of Week," *Brooklyn Citizen*, March 4, 1937, HFP, box 38.

32 "WPA 'Tom Thumb Circus'" to Play in East New York," *Brooklyn Citizen*, March 13, 1937, HFP, box 38.

33 On May 21, 1937 the circus appeared at Public School No. 220, 48th Street and Ninth Avenue, Brooklyn. The *Brooklyn Citizen* reported that the "two and a half hour program . . . was picked from the top ranks of the Variety unit of the WPA Theater." On May 26, 1937, the Tom Thumb Circus played at the Borough Park Young Men's Hebrew Association at 14th Street, Brooklyn. This was the last mention of its existence in the press. On April 9, 1937, the parent's association staged a presentation at Public School 128 at 21st Avenue, Brooklyn "Tom Thumb Circus At P.S. 128 Tomorrow, "*Brooklyn Eagle*, April 9, 1937, HFP, box 38.

34 Goodwin, *WPA Circus*, 6.

35 Ibid.

36 "Circus, Audience Survey Report, New York City," June 2, 1937, National Play Bureau, Federal Theatre Project, WPA, National Archives, College Park, MD (hereafter FTP, NA), record group 69.4.4, stack 530, box 254.

37 For more information on the marketing of the circus in America, see Charles Philip Fox and Tom Parkinson, *Billers, Banners and Bombast* (Boulder: Pruett Publishing, 1982).

38 *Federal Theatre Magazine* 1 (Nov. 25, 1935), 6.

39 "Personal Glimpses and Comments on Canvaseers," *Forest Hills Post*, July 2, 1937, HFP, box 39.

40 "Bruin's Skates Swiped an' Now He's Very Sad," *Staten Island Advance*, June 11, 1937, HFP, box 39; "WPA Press Agent Thinks His Sacred Elephant's Very Cute," *Long Island Daily Advocate*, Dec. 31, 1937, HFP, box 40.

41 "Circus Fans Association Endorses WPA Circus Program," Goodwin press release, Aug. 1, 1938, FTP, NA,

record group 69.2.2, stack 530, box 145; "Circus Fans Association, Resolution Sent to the President," statement prepared by Ed Maulsby in refutation of Congressional accusations, July 1939, the Federal Theatre Project Collection, Music Division, Library of Congress, Washington, D.C., container 6.

42 Advertisement for WPA Circus, "14th Regiment Armory," *Brooklyn Citizen,* March 12, 1937, HFP, box 38.

43 "Canarsie's First Circus Next Week May 25," *Canarsie Courier,* May 21, 1937, HFP, box 39.

44 "Island Mother Leads Circus Parade on Horse," *Staten Island Advance,* Sept. 23, 1937, HFP, box 40.

45 "Big Tent Will Be at Remsen and Flatlands," *Canarsie Courier,* May 2, 1937, HFP, box 39.

46 "WPA 3-Ring Circus Opens Here Tonight," *Brooklyn Citizen,* Sept. 2, 1937, HFP, box 40.

47 "4-Horse Strong Man Booed by Youngsters," *New York Times,* Sept. 2, 1937, 16.

48 Hildreth, "The Works Progress Circus," 35.

49 Anthony Buttitta, "There Were No Elephants on Relief," 24.

50 Wendell J. Goodwin, "WPA Circus, Official Route Book for the 1937 Tenting Season," 9. A Goodwin press release on the circus band revealed that Cutty planned to revive such nostalgic circus music as "The Barnum Gallop," "The Ringmasters March," and "Here Comes Walter L. Main." See "New Federal Theatre Features Band Concert," Goodwin press release, FTP, NA, record group 69.2.2, stack 530, box 145.

51 "Why this Federal Theatre Circus," WPA Circus poster, May 23, 1938, FTP, NA, record group 69.2.2, stack 530, box 145.

52 "World's Top Attraction Here July 1–3," *F. H. Kew Gardens,* June 25, 1937, HFP, box 39.

53 "Circus Fans' Night at the WPA Circus," *White Tops* 12 (Feb.–March 1939), 15.

54 "WPA Show Stages Circus Fans' Night," *Billboard,* Feb. 11, 1939, 39.

55 Photograph of Francis Connolly, winner of the Typical American Boy contest, being congratulated by clown Frank Walter, *White Tops* 12 (Feb.–March 1939), back cover.

56 Goodwin, *WPA Circus,* 4.

57 Joseph T. Bradbury, "Gorman Bros. Circus Seasons of 1934–36," *Bandwagon,* March–April 1992, 4, 16–17.

58 "Thousands Visit Big Tent First Three Nights," *Canarsie Courier,* May 28, 1937, 1.

59 Goodwin, *WPA Circus,* 27.

60 "50 Artists, 93 Others Get Work At NY, Bow of First WPA Circus," *Billboard,* Oct. 26, 1935, 3, 69.

61 Ibid.

62 Ibid.

63 Walter Winchell, "Old Favorites with WPA Circus," *White Tops* 11 (April–May 1939), 8.

64 Advertisement, *White Tops* 12 (Dec. 1938), 32.

65 "WPA Circus Ready For Uptown Debut," *New York Times,* Nov. 3, 1935, N1.

66 "WPA Show Playing, Week-end Dates," 40.

67 Hildreth, "The Works Progress Circus," 35.

68 Goodwin, *WPA Circus,* 10.

69 Ibid.

70 "N.Y. WPA Show Hits High Mark in Attendance; Admish Plans Success," 38.

71 The circus is divided into sections known as displays. A display is an act or acts that perform in one or all of the three rings simultaneously. When the act or acts are finished, new acts perform as part of a new display.

72 The program in its entirety was as follows: Grand entry and opening pageant, WPA dogs, William Rhode, Harry Di Dio, Bruno Radke, clown number, acrobats Pantzer and Arden, Four Nelsons Comique, Garant and Duhring, clown walkaround, on slack wire, Burt Wells and Scotty, Charles Ledegar, James Flanagan, clown baseball game, Spanish web, Edna Martell, the Beckmans, Avonne Gardener, Price and Powers, Welsh wire artists, Chief White Cloud, in an exhibition of the sports and costumes of the Far West; White Cloud, Emory Swartwood, Ernest Arnold; McCarthy and Sills, high perch; clown number, aerialists, Eddie Gear, Neuman and Metzler, Joli Coleman, clown walkaround, Kress and Corns, skaters, acrobatic novelties, Vintour and Winston, Joe Allan, the Franklins; Sandwina, strong woman, clown walkaround; triple troupe, Four Royal Wizards; Billy Ritchie troupe, comedy cyclists; Iron jaw, Marie Mang, Ann Howe, clown number, Stanley Georges' performing bears, clown ballet; 12 Desert Whirlwind acrobats. "N.Y. WPA Show Playing Week-End Dates," 40.

73 Wendell J. Goodwin, "A Circus Thrills Crowd Opening of Winter Tour," *White Tops* 12 (Christmas 1938), 10.

74 "WPA Circus Plays to Absent Mayor," *New York Times,* Nov. 1, 1935, 23.

75 "WPA Circus Performance Given for 150 Children at Bellevue," *New York Times,* Nov. 9, 1935, 17.

76 Circus, FTP, NA, record group 69.2.2, stack 530, box 145.

77 "WPA Unit Plays to 7,900 in N.Y.," *Billboard,* Oct. 3, 1936, 36.

78 The official program for the 1937 tenting season published by Goodwin reveals that an elephant now appeared with its own act; the program reads: "Display #13—Japino, the sacred black elephant, presented by his keeper and trainer, the most honorable Sir Joseph Chokenallski." The other acts in the 1937 program were:

Display #1—Grand Tournament. Display #2— Ring 1—Rex's ponies. Ring 2—De [sic] Dio's dogs. Ring 3—Rhode's dogs. Display #3—Clowns. Display #4—Wire acts. Ring 1—Bert Wells. Ring 2—Charles Ledegar. Ring 3—James Flanagan.

Display #5—Clowns. Display #6—Ring 1—Brutal Brothers, Hand Balancers. Ring 2—Arnold & Kress, Skaters. Ring 3—Melford, Jackson & Russell, Risley Act. Display #7—Clowns. Display #8—Meyer Paris, Strongman. Display #9—The Clowns, featuring Charles Fortune [sic]. Display #10—Horizontal Bar Act, Nick Cravat & Burt Lancaster. Display #11—Clowns. Display #12—An Aerial Fantasy. Ring 1—Edna Martell & Buddy Taylor. Ring 2—Fred & Dora Beckman. Ring 3— Avonne Gardener, the absolutely fearless little Miss whose thrilling exploits have made two continents gasp; the inimitable Avonne assisted by Hazel Gardener. . . . Display #14—Price & Powers, Tight wire act. Display #15—Clowns. Display #16—Iron Jaw, Marie Mang. Display #17—The WPA Federal Theatre Project's Mighty Three Ring Circus takes great pride in presenting for the first time in America the superspectacle "Savage Africa"; a Burns O'Sullivan production. Display #18—Ring 1—Joe Allen & Emory Swartwood, hand balancers. Ring 2—Albert Arden & Marie Genaro, contortionists. Ring 3— The Brachard Troupe, contortionist. Display #19—Clowns. Display #20—Ring 1—Ernie Sharron, trapeze. Ring 2—Russell Brothers, double traps. Ring 3—Eddie Geer & Stasia, trapeze. Display #21—Ring 1—White Cloud & Eva, trick & fancy ropers. Ring 2—The Martian troupe, Risley act. Ring 3—Vintour & Winston. Display #22—Funny Billy Ritchie, the original tramp cyclist & his co. of excellent assistants. Display #23—Clowns. Display #24—Ring 1—The Nelson Troupe, comedy tumblers. Ring 2—Alvin & Kenny, swivel bar. Ring 3—"Tumble In." Display #25—Clowns. Display #26—Stanley George's performing bears. Display #27—Clowns. Display #28—Ring 1—Sylvia Reckless, Trapeze. Ring 2— Metzler & Neuman, Roman rings. Ring 3—June Loya, Trapeze. Display #29—Pyramid Builders.

Goodwin, *WPA Circus,* 15. For an analysis of this program see Alan Kreizenbeck, "The Theatre Nobody Knows: Forgotten Productions of the Federal Theatre Project, 1935–1939" (PhD diss., Graduate School of Arts and Sciences, New York University, 1979), chap. 3, "The Circus," 90–119.

79 Frank Merlin, "Circus Notes," *Federal Theatre Magazine* 2 (June 1937), 23.

80 Ibid.

81 "WPA Show Briefs," *Billboard* 49 (March 6, 1937), HFP, box 38.

82 Willson Whitman, "Job for Jumbo," *The Stage* 14 (March 1937), 98–99.

83 "Elephant Escapes From WPA Circus," *New York Times,* May 15, 1937, 21. "Elephant's Love Is Circus Riot,"

Daily News, May 16, 1937, HFP, box 39; "Its Spring and Young Jumbo Is Just Like Everyone Else," *New York Post,* May 15, 1937, HFP, box 39; "Cop Safari Captures Elephant," *World Telegram,* May 15, 1937; "Elephant Goes Native and Troops to Circus," *Brooklyn Eagle,* May 15, 1937; "Circus Elephant Quits Relief Rolls," *Evening Journal,* May 15, 1937, HFP, box 39; "WPA Elephant, Heeding Circus Call Bolts and Wins His Way to Big Top," *Times Union,* May 15, 1937 HFP, box 39.

84 "Former Battle Elephant for Indian Rajah among Features of WPA Circus," *Long Island Star,* June 14, 1937, HFP, box 39.

85 "Elephant Jolts 4 Women off Back," *Times Union,* May 26, 1937; "4 Local Women Fall from Elephant," *Canarsie Courier,* May 28, 1937, HFP, box 39.

86 "Japino Acted Like a Trouper when Big Cavity was Filled," *N.R. Standard Star,* Oct. 26, 1937, HFP, box 40.

87 "WPA Elephant on 5 Hour Strike," *New York American,* May 31, 1937, HFP, box 39; "Elephant Stages a 5-Hour Sit-Down Strike; Girl, 6, Ends It after Efforts of 50 Men Fail," *New York Times,* May 31, 1937, 32; "Biggest Sit-Down, WPA Elephant on 5-Hour Strike," *New York American,* May 31, 1937, HFP, box 39; "Relief Elephant Sits and Defies All Kings' Men," *Tribune,* May 31, 1937, HFP, box 39; "Elephant Sits Five Hours But Rises for Girl," *Citizen,* May 31, 1937, HFP, box 39.

88 "Elephant Acts as Picket Used to Protest WPA Circus Cut," *New York American,* June 15, 1937, HFP, box 39.

89 "P.S. 89 Pupils Want Japino to Stick on WPA, Not Envelopes," *Long Island Star,* June 16, 1937, HFP, box 39.

90 Advertisement, "The Federal Theatre Circus," *White Tops* 11 (April–May 1938), 32 (June–July 1938), 16 (Oct.–Nov. 1938), 12.

91 "Elephant President Roosevelt Saved Returns to WPA Circus," Goodwin press release, April 27, 1939, National Archives. FTP, NA, record group 69.2.2, stack 530, box 145.

92 "WPA Unit Plays to 790,000 in N.Y.," *Billboard* 48 (Oct. 3, 1936), 36.

93 Goodwin, "WPA 3 Ring Circus," 21.

94 "Brainy Bears Full of Tricks at the Circus," *Canarsie Courier,* May 21, 1937, HFP, box 39.

95 "Seven Bears To Head Cast of WPA Circus," *New York Post,* Oct. 29, 1937, HFP, box 40.

96 John Deacon, "Bruin's Skates Swiped an' Now He's Very Sad," *Staten Island Advance,* June 11, 1937, HFP, box 39.

97 "Circus Star," *White Plains Reporter,* Feb. 18, 1938, HFP, box 41.

98 Goodwin, "WPA 3 Ring Circus," 21.

99 Hazel Canning, "Circus for the Jobless," (Toronto) *Star Weekly,* Jan. 30, 1937, HFP, box 43.

100 Goodwin press release, April 27, 1939, HFP, cited in Kreizenbeck, "Theatre Nobody Knows," 116.

101 Goodwin press release, Feb. 6, 1939, HFP, cited in Kreizenbeck, "Theatre Nobody Knows," 116.

102 Biographical Sketch, Engerer Family Papers ca. 1920–1964, 2008 Special Collections Department / Long Island Studies Institute, Axinn Library, Hofstra University, New York.

103 Capt. Ernest Engerer, "Among Wild Beasts," *The Community Journal* 2 (Aug. 8, 1930), 1, Engerer Family Papers ca. 1920–1964, 2008 Special Collections Department / Long Island Studies Institute, Axinn Library, Hofstra University, New York.

104 "Two Lions Attack Trainer in Queens," *New York Times,* Feb. 25, 1939, 17; "Trainer Clawed, Son "Tames" Lion," *New York Times,* Feb. 26, 1939, 32; "Two Old Favorites Back in Circus Lineup," *Long Island Daily Press,* May 2, 1939, Engerer Family Papers ca. 1920–1964, 2008 Special Collections Department / Long Island Studies Institute, Axinn Library, Hofstra University, New York.

105 This act was advertised in the promotional posters as Allen's Liberty High School Horses and in circus ads as M. H. Allen and His Liberty Horses Including Blue, "World's greatest high school horse" and Arizona Arietta, "America's foremost equestrienne whose equal does not exist—in an exceptional exhibition of dressage." Advertisement, "Federal Theatre Project for New York City Brings You WPA Great 3 Ring Circus," *White Tops* 11 (April–May 1938), 20.

106 George Burton, "Circus Arrives Its Colossal—(Swell to Us!)," *New York Daily Star,* May 19, 1937, HFP, box 39.

107 An image of the Katie Sandwina chromolithograph poster for Barnum & Bailey from 1911 can be found in the Howard Tibbals Poster Collection, Ringling Museum ref no. ht200317.

108 William Ingliss, "Here's The Circus," *Harper's Weekly,* April 1911, 18. Todd-Sandwina File, Stark Center for Physical Culture and Sports, University of Texas at Austin.

109 Joanna Frueh, Laurie Fiersten, and Judith Steins, eds., *Picturing the Modern Amazon* (New York: Rizzoli, 2000), 54.

110 For more information on Katie Sandwina, see John D. Fair, "Kati Sandwina: Hercules Can Be a Lady," *Iron Game History* 9 (Dec. 2005), 4–7; Jan Todd, "Center Ring: Katie Sandwina and the Construction of Celebrity," *Iron Game History* 10 (Nov. 2007), 4–13.

111 Goodwin, *WPA Circus,* 20.

112 Winchell, "Old Favorites with WPA Circus," 8.

113 "WPA Circus Is Showing Here for A. L. Posts," (Brooklyn) *Record,* June 8, 1939, FTP, NA, record group 69.2.2, stack 530, box 145.

114 "Woe for WPA Circus," *New York Sun,* April 22, 1938, HFP, box 41.

115 Joseph T. Bradbury, "Tompkins Wild West Show, Supplement II," *Bandwagon* 15 (Nov.–Dec. 1971), 27;

Chang Reynolds, "The Al G. Barnes Wild Animal Circus 1923," *Bandwagon* 29 (May–June 1985), 17. He had also given three command performances before the Duke of Windsor. Winchell, "Old Favorites With WPA Circus," 8.

116 "WPA Three-Ring Circus Due Tomorrow for Week," *Staten Island Advance,* June 7, 1937, HFP, box 39.

117 Ibid.

118 On the Wild West shows, see Joy S. Kasson, *Buffalo Bill's Wild West: Celebrity, Memory, and Popular History* (New York: Hill and Wang, 2001); Paul Reddin, *Wild West Shows* (Urbana: University of Illinois Press, 1999); Michael Wallis, *The Real Wild West: The 101 Ranch and the Creation of the American West* (New York: St. Martin's Press, 2000).

119 "Federal Theater Circus Will Be Presented at Armory Here," *Orange Courier,* Feb. 19, 1938, HFP, box 41.

120 "Famous Indian Heads WPA Circus Wild West Display," Goodwin press release, May 12, 1939, FTP, NA, record group 69.2.2, stack 530, box 145; "Famous Indian Heads Cast of WPA Circus in New York," *Hartford Times,* May 16, 1939, 10.

121 Ibid. He believed that many of these songs came from the folk songs of immigrants and were adapted to the words of the cowboy songs. Some of these songs could be heard over the radio.

122 "50 Artists, 93 Others Get Work At N.Y. Bow of First WPA Circus," *Billboard* 47 (Oct. 26, 1935), 3, 69.

123 "Circus," Goodwin press release, n.d., FTP, NA, record group 69.2.2, stack 530, box 145.

124 "WPA Circus Performance Given for 150 Children at Bellevue," *New York Times,* Nov. 9, 1935, 17.

125 Ibid.

126 "WPA Circus to Return on Tuesday," *Staten Island Advance,* Sept. 17, 1937, HFP, box 40.

127 "Announcement was made today by the . . ." Goodwin press release, n.d., FTP, NA, record group 69.2.2, stack 530, box 145. Rocco was featured in a two-part article in *White Tops* 12 (April–May 1939), 5–6, and (June–July 1939), 23–24, which followed his previous adventures in circuses in America, Mexico, Cuba, South America, Continental Europe, Australia and Asia. During this time he starred with Publinos in Cuba, Trevinos and Orin in Mexico, Frank Brown in South America, the Wirths in Australia, and Harmston's show in Asia.

128 "WPA Circus To Open in King's Wednesday," *New York Times,* Aug. 25, 1937, HFP, box 40.

129 "Boss Clown of WPA Show," *Daily Advocate,* May 11, 1937, HFP, box 38.

130 Hazel Canning, "Circus for the Jobless," (Toronto) *Star Weekly,* Jan. 30, 1937, HFP, box 43.

131 "Circus Coming," (New York) *Daily News,* June 5, 1938, HFP, box 42.

132 "WPA Circus Will Feature Chaplin-esque Clowning," *N.R. Standard Star,* Nov. 17, 1937, HFP, box 40.

133 Ibid.

134 Goodwin press release, "WPA Circus Will Feature 'Chaplin-esque Clowning,'" 1937, FTP, NA, record group 69.2.2, stack 530, box 145, 1–2.

135 Goodwin press release, "WPA Performers Gain More Votes in Contest," Feb. 6, 1939. FTP, NA, record group 69.2.2, stack 530, box 145.

136 Buttitta, "There Were No Elephants on Relief," 25.

137 "Circus," Goodwin press release, n.d., FTP, NA, record group 69.2.2, stack 530, box 145.

138 "WPA Show Playing Week-end Dates," HFP, box 38.

139 Buttitta, "There Were No Elephants on Relief," 23–24.

140 "WPA Show Briefs," Billboard, March 6, 1937, HFP, box 38.

141 "Big Rosie Gives Audience at WPA Circus Cause for Laughs and Cheers," Brooklyn Citizen, March 12, 1937, HFP, box 38.

142 Winchell, "Old Broadway," HFP, box 41.

143 "'Tramp Bicyclist' Cheered by Kings, is in WPA Circus," Brooklyn Daily Eagle, July 26, 1936, 4A.

144 "WPA Press Agent Calls on His Very Finest Adjectives but Reporter Finds Real Thrills are Behind the Scenes," Staten Island Advance, June 9, 1937, HFP, box 39.

145 Winchell, "Old Favorites with WPA Circus," 8; "Tramp Bicyclist," 4A.

146 Winchell, "Old Favorites with WPA. Circus," 8.

147 Goodwin, "WPA Circus, Official Route Book of the 1937 Season," 10.

148 "Children's Favorite," Daily Advocate, April 30, 1937, HFP, box 38; "Future Star," Brooklyn Eagle, April 16, 1937, HFP, box 38.

149 On African Americans in the Federal Theatre Project, see Rena Fraden, Blueprints for a Black Federal Theatre, 1935–1939 (New York: Cambridge University Press, 1994); Ronal Ross, "The Role of Blacks in the Federal Theatre, 1935–1939" in The Theatre of Black Americans: A Collection of Critical Essays, ed. Errol Hill (New York: Applause Books, 2000), 231–46. On race relations in the Federal Theatre Project, see Nathan Irvin Higgins, Harlem Renaissance (New York: Oxford University Press, 1973); Stephanie Leigh Batiste, Darkening Mirrors: Imperial Representation in Depression-Era African American Performance (Durham, NC: Duke University Press, 2012).

150 "Facts and Figures," New York Federal Theatre 2 (March 21, 1937), 22.

151 "African Dance," Daily Worker, Dec. 6, 1936, HFP, box 34.

152 "WPA Circus Extends Stay in Ridgewood," Brooklyn Citizen, April 20, 1937, HFP, box 38.

153 "WPA Circus in Winter Quarters to Re-open Oct. 30th," Goodwin press release, Oct. 1937, FTP, NA, record group 69.2.2, stack 530, box 145. Some of the performers in this production were "Joe Hardy, James Adams, Oyebucha Cole, Alice Ramsay the Amazon; Leola Crosby, the slave dancer; Compina, a specialty

dancer; Minnie Nylton, John Antiga, Sobi Tori, James McLean, and Rose McLenoire." "WPA Circus to Pitch Tent in Stapleton Next Week," Staten Island Advance, June 2, 1937, HFP, box 39; "F. H. V. Sponsors Big Top, World's Top Attraction Jul. 1–3," Forest Hills Kew Garden Post, June 25, 1937, HFP, box 39.

154 Goodwin, WPA Circus, 20.

155 St. Clair Bourne, "WPA Dismissals 'Done With Bias,'" The New York Amsterdam News, July 17, 1937, 1.

156 "O'Sullivan Shows Hand of the Master Producer," Goodwin press release, May 1, 1938, FTP, NA, record group 69.2.2, stack 530, box 145.

157 Ibid.

158 "Circus Fans' Night at the WPA Circus," White Tops 12 (Feb.–March 1939), 15.

159 "WPA Circus Opens in Jamaica Arena Oct. 30," Daily News, Oct. 18, 1937, HFP, box 40.

160 "WPA Circus Coming To Brooklyn Friday," Brooklyn Citizen, March 30, 1938, HFP, box 41.

161 Brooklyn Citizen, March 30, 1938, quoted in Kreizenbeck, "Theatre Nobody Knows," 116.

162 "Mystery Man from Siam Joins WPA Circus," Goodwin press release, n.d., FTP, NA, record group 69.2.2, stack 530, box 145.

163 "WPA Circus Star Joins Ringling," Goodwin press release, May 1, 1938, FTP, NA record group 69.2.2, stack 530, box 145.

164 Kate Buford, Burt Lancaster: An American Life (Cambridge, MA: Da Capo Press, 2008).

165 "Circus Coming In All Its Glory," New York Amsterdam News (March 13, 1937), 10.

166 "Performer Injured at WPA Circus," Staten Island Advance, Sept. 25, 1937, HFP, box 40.

167 "WPA Circus Star Joins Ringling," Goodwin press release, May 1, 1938; Buford, Burt Lancaster, 42.

168 "WPA Press Agent Calls on His Very Finest Adjectives," HFP, box 39.

169 "Personal Glimpses and Comments on Canvassers," Forest Hills Post, July 2, 1937, HFP, box 39.

170 "WPA Circus Opens in Jamaica Arena Oct. 30," Daily News, Oct. 18, 1937, HFP, box 40.

171 Goodwin, "WPA 3 Ring Circus," 21; "WPA Press Agent Thinks His Sacred Elephant's Very Cute," Long Island Daily Advance, Dec. 31, 1937, HFP, box 40.

172 "Personal Glimpses and Comments on Canvaseers," Forest Hills Post, July 2, 1937, HFP, box 39.

173 Canning, "Circus for the Jobless," HFP, box 43.

174 "Circus Division of the Variety Theatre," 5.

175 "Circus," press release, FTP, NA, record group 69.2.2, stack 530, box 145.

176 Ibid.

177 Goodwin, "WPA 3 Ring Circus," 21.

178 Ibid.

179 "Elephant President Roosevelt Saved Returns To WPA Circus," Goodwin press release, April 27, FTP, NA, record group 69.2.2, stack 530, box 145.

180 "WPA Three-Ring Circus Due Tomorrow for Week," Staten Island Advance, June 7, 1937, HFP, box 39.

181 "Order Cleanup for WPA Circus," New York News, May 6, 1936, quoted in Fauquet, "Elephants on Relief? Circus and the WPA (1935–1939)," 54.

182 "Orders Probe of WPA Ouster," New York Morning Telegraph, May 7, 1936, quoted in Fauquet, 54.

183 "WPA Circus Fraud Charged to Three," New York Times, Aug. 31, 1938, 36; "3 Are Held In WPA Fraud," New York Times, Sept. 1, 1938, 2.

184 "3 Freed on Charges of Robbing the WPA," New York Times, Dec. 14, 1938, 4.

185 Hallie Flanagan, "Congress Takes the Stage," New York Times, Aug. 20, 1939, 1.

186 "N.Y. WPAers Taking out Own One-Ringer on Co-op Plan," Billboard, July 29, 1939, 30.

187 "Circus Again Takes It on Chin," Billboard, Dec. 30, 1939, 93. "Oscar Lowande Circus Commonwealth Venture Made up of FTP Circus Blew up August 21 at Canarsie, L.I., after Being out Three Weeks," Billboard, Dec. 30, 1939, 93.

188 Hallie Flanagan, Arena: The History of the Federal Theatre (New York: Benjamin Blom, 1965), 79.

⓱

DISABILITY AND THE·········· CIRCUS

RACHEL ADAMS

The bus runs on used cooking oil that has to be scavenged from restaurant dumpsters. It keeps breaking down, until finally it dies completely. There is garbage everywhere and arguments erupt over who should clean up. The giant tries to talk and people keep interrupting him. The Elephant Man has been left behind. The clown has lost his dog, who is also his best friend. The Human Tripod has a vicious hangover and spends all day lying on the couch. The giant gets fed up and catches a plane back to Oregon. Lobster Girl pulls a black hair from her chin and worries that she's getting fat. These scenes from a film called *The Last American Freak Show* illustrate how far we've come from the romantic ideal of running away to join the circus. It is 2006, and the performers in The 999 Eyes of Endless Dream have missed the heyday of the freak show by about one hundred years (*fig. 17.1*).

For six weeks, filmmaker Richard Butchins accompanied this traveling freak show as it drove from Oregon to Austin, stopping to perform at bars, nightclubs, parties, and a wedding along the way. His documentary *The Last American Freak Show* is a road narrative in the vein of Jack Kerouac's *On the Road* or Ken Kesey's *The Electric Kool-Aid Acid Test* in that it details the allure and the disillusionment of vehicular travel across the American continent. Like these precursors, it recognizes the road as a place where rebels and outcasts seek escape from the pressures of mainstream society. It appreciates the impulse toward nonconformity, while also recognizing the loneliness and discomfort that come with self-imposed marginality. What distinguishes Butchins's story is that the majority of his travelers have significant congenital disabilities. They are "freaks" not only in their rejection of social norms but because of their deviance from bodily norms. As in Katherine Dunn's 1986 road novel *Geek Love*, the performers in The 999 Eyes make a living by exhibiting themselves—flaunting their differences rather than attempting to hide or normalize them. But this isn't

CONGRESS OF FREAKS AT RINGLING BROTHERS AND BARNUM & BAILEY (COMBINED) CIRCUS.

fiction; it's real life. Some use wheelchairs or prostheses, and some require consistent medical attention.[1] *The Last American Freak Show* asks why people with disabilities would chose to exhibit themselves as freaks after the 1990 Americans with Disabilities Act (ADA) America, and what it meant for Butchins—who is himself disabled—to undertake this journey.

The Last American Freak Show was controversial. In 2008 it was banned from the BAFTA (British Academy of Film and Television Arts) Disability Arts Film Festival after the head of events declared that "the aesthetic of the film was wrong, that it was too explicit, raised too many questions and was too demanding for the event in question."[2] Butchins has never been able to find a distributor. And yet, the film has screened to considerable acclaim at festivals around the world, where it has received enthusiastic reviews. What makes *The Last American Freak Show* provocative is that, unlike other recent documentaries about contemporary circus life such as *American Carny: True Tales from the Circus Sideshow* (Nick Basile, 2008), *Sideshow: Alive on the Inside* (Lynne Doughtery, 2003), or *Sideshow: The New Sideshow* (Tim Miller, 2003), this film bluntly tackles questions about the meaning of disability at the freak show. Given that people with disabilities were often cruelly exploited by circus managers and showmen, it questions what place people with disabilities might occupy within the modern circus and what their performances can tell us about being disabled in twenty-first century America.

Disability and the Freak Show

The circus has long been a gathering place for people with exceptional talents. It was P. T. Barnum who first realized the potential for combining the exhibition of human oddities with more traditional circus fare such as trained animals, clowns, acrobats, and dancers.[3] Barnum got his start as a showman by capitalizing on disability. He purchased an elderly black woman named Joice Heth, whom he advertised as the 161-year-old mammy of George Washington (*fig. 17.2*). Heth was not congenitally disabled, but her body was bent and twisted with age and decades of hard work. Under Barnum's management, this unremarkable old woman became a sensation. When

Fig. 17.1. Edward J. Kelty. Congress of Freaks at Ringling Bros. and Barnum & Bailey Combined Circus, 1924. Photograph. The Collection of the John and Mable Ringling Museum of Art, Tibbals Collection, ht0004824

public interest in Heth waned, he rekindled it by spreading the rumor that she was not a living person, but an automaton. Barnum exhibited Heth until the day she died, when he garnered further publicity by arranging for a public autopsy to verify her age.[4] Over the course of his career, Barnum was responsible for introducing some of the most famous human curiosities of his time: the conjoined twins Chang and Eng; the diminutive Tom Thumb; Lavinia Warren; Commodore Nutt; William Henry Johnson, the "What Is It?"; the giants Anna Swan and Colonel Routh Goshen; Maximo and Bartola, the Aztec children; and Charles Tripp, the no-armed boy (*fig. 17.3*).[5] These performers' unusual bodies provided the raw material for the creation of freaks. Barnum's genius lay in understanding how to use narrative and props to turn bodily impairment into a spectacle people would pay to see. He soon had many imitators, and the freak show became a regular feature of the American circus.

Sometimes human oddities were incorporated into the circus ring, but more commonly they were part of a sideshow (*fig. 17.4*). Located in its own tent and requiring an extra fee for admission, the sideshow was among the most popular and profitable attractions at the circus. Freaks were defined by bodily features spectacular enough to make audiences want to stare, however the sideshow always contained an element of performance. Costumes, props, the showcasing of unique abilities and talents, and extensive advertising turned people with disabilities into freaks. Not every freak was disabled. Sideshows also included people with extremely long hair or nails, tattoos, and women in pants, as well as non-Western people, and those with unusual talents like sword swallowing, fire eating, and contorting. Sideshow acts could also be inspired by current events. "I am speaking of America—the land of real

humor, of ingenuity, or resource," reported journalist William Fitzgerald in 1897, "When some important political or other event agitates that great country, topical sideshows spring up with amazing promptness."[6] Thus, at various points in the nineteenth century, suffragettes, Philippinos, Native American chiefs, and Africans were exhibited as freaks.

Born freaks—those with congenital disabilities—were the aristocrats of the sideshow world. The more unusual their bodies, the better chance they had to control their salaries and working conditions. Chang and Eng Bunker, the famous conjoined twins, set their own terms when they toured with P. T. Barnum. They made enough money to settle in

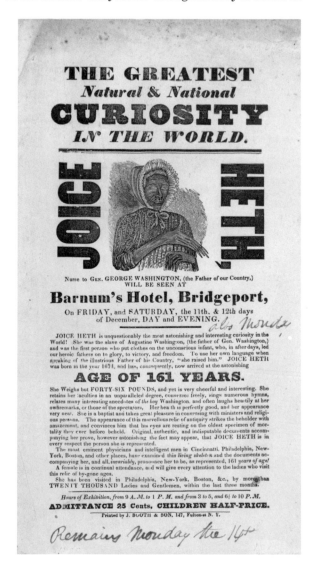

Fig. 17.2. "Joice Heth, The Greatest Natural & National Curiosity in the World," 1835. Handbill, printed by J. Booth & Son, New York. Somers Historical Society

North Carolina, where they married sisters and fathered twenty-one children.[7] Few freaks were this fortunate. The conjoined twins Daisy and Violet Hilton never achieved the enduring success of their precursors. After a lonely and abusive childhood, they seemed poised to embark on a glamorous career as film and vaudeville stars (*fig. 17.5*). But they were exploited by managers and agents, who abandoned them once their public appeal declined. They ended their lives in obscurity, working at a grocery store and dying alone in their small apartment.[8] Joseph Merrick, who was exhibited as the Elephant Man in the late nineteenth century, fared no better. After touring Europe, he was robbed and abandoned by his manager. So severe were his disabilities that it was dangerous for him to appear in public alone

(*fig. 17.6*). He finally made his way to London, where he was rescued by Dr. Frederick Treves. He spent the rest of his life in Treves's London hospital, where he died of asphyxia while sleeping.[9] The life of Julia Pastrana, The Bearded and Hairy Lady, was also filled with hardship and betrayal (*fig. 17.7*). Her parents sold her to a showman who taught her to dance and play music, and eventually married her. She gave birth to a baby with features much like her own, who lived for only two days. Pastrana died soon after from complications of childbirth. But that was not the end of her career. After having both wife and baby mummified, Pastrana's husband continued to exhibit them in a glass case.[10]

In the era before the welfare state, many people with severe disabilities turned to freak shows for economic support. Some parents sold children born with disabilities to showmen, having no other means to care for them. American cities passed "ugly laws" banning persons with "unsightly or disgusting" disabilities from appearing in public.[11] These ordinances made the possibility of gainful employment, or even begging, more difficult. A souvenir carte-de-visite sold at a freak show makes the case for a man whose hands were disabled after being struck by lightning at age six: "He would gladly undertake any labor that would furnish him a livelihood, but how can he? Yielding, therefore, to the suggestions of friends he offers for sale his photograph, hoping that the small profit derived therefrom will contribute to his maintenance and support."[12] His plea represents exhibitionism as a form of work that allows a man who has no other means of income to earn a living. It allows spectators to conceive of staring as a charitable act. Any squeamishness they might feel about gawking can be assuaged by buying a photo.

Freak shows could provide a livelihood for people with disabilities, but they were also a source

Fig. 17.3. P. T. Barnum and General Tom Thumb (Charles S. Stratton), ca. 1850. Photograph. © Bettmann/Corbis

Fig. 17.4. Frederick Whitman Glasier. Sideshow banner and entrance, Zip, the Pinhead (William Henry Johnson) playing violin at center, 1906. Photograph. The Collection of the John and Mable Ringling Museum of Art, Glasier Glass Plate Negative Collection, 0033

of community, a place where their differences were accepted and even affirmed. While the show was on the road, the circus or carnival was a total environment where work and life ran seamlessly into one another. When not performing, circus folk were eating, sleeping, and spending their spare time together, creating a subculture insulated from the outside world with its own vocabulary, customs, and values. Onstage, freak shows exploited the continuity between life and performance by having people with disabilities perform everyday tasks: a person with no arms and legs lighting a cigarette; conjoined twins dancing, singing, and turning cartwheels; Lobster Boy tying knots. A familiar spectacle was the wedding of two unlikely performers, such as a midget and a giant or a fat lady and a human skeleton, who then could be advertised as "The World's Strangest Couple." Many of these weddings were simple publicity stunts, however, some disabled performers— such as Jeanie The Half-Girl and the giant Al Tomaini, and Percilla The Monkey Girl and Emmitt Bejano, The Aligator-Skinned Man—also found enduring love backstage at the sideshow, where unusual bodies were the norm (*figs. 17.8, 17.9*).[13] Both of these couples met while touring with the freak show, eventually retiring and remaining together to the end of their lives. Those who did not find romance often appreciated the friendship and camaraderie of circus life. Beginning in the 1940s, many circus performers spent their winters in Gibsonton, Florida (aka Showtown USA), where the fire chief was a giant, the sheriff a dwarf, and unique zoning laws allowed them to keep elephants and carnival rides on their front lawns.[14]

With the rise of scientific understandings of disability, freak shows became less socially acceptable. Advances in medical knowledge and treatment made it possible to cure some conditions that once would have led to disabilities. Doctors began to provide scientific reasons for disabling conditions, framing them as pathology rather than sources of wonder. Increasingly, public sentiment turned away from the freak show, which had never been a completely respectable form of entertainment in the first place. It was no longer tolerable for people with disabilities to exhibit themselves for paying customers to gawk at. Rather, it was believed that they should receive treatment, and the incurable should be concealed from view in hospitals and institutions. In later decades, similar complaints would be leveled about the exploitation of trained animals.[15] As a result, many of today's circuses—such as Cirque du Soleil, the Jim Rose Circus, the Bindlestiff Family Circus, Circus Smirkus, The Flying High Circus, and Circus Chimera—consist entirely of able-bodied performers, featuring no animals or people with disabilities.

Although changing times sent freak shows into decline, they never disappeared entirely.[16] Instead, they moved to the social margins, where they continued to court less prosperous and respectable clientele. By the mid-twentieth century, freak shows were no longer part of the circus, surviving instead at county fairs, traveling carnivals, and New York's

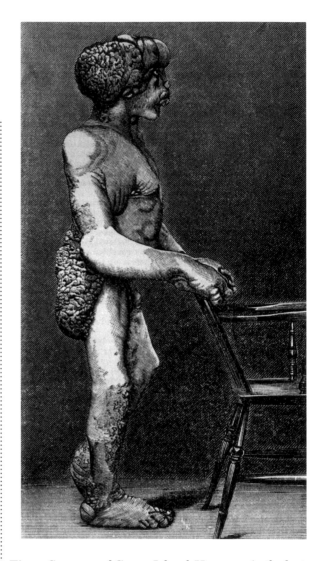

Times Square and Coney Island. However, in the last twenty years live freak shows have seen something of a revival among young hipsters and bohemians, who have brought them back under the aegis of circus performance. In *Freaks and Fire*, J. Dee Hill claims that the contemporary circus functions along the lines of a tribe, attracting the same populations as alternative cultural gatherings like the Burning Man festival and Rainbow Family.[17] Participants tend to be young and white, with backgrounds in dance, theater, music, and fine arts. Whereas once the families of circus folk passed their acts from one generation to the next, few participants in the contemporary sideshow are connected to earlier generations of circus performers.

◀ *Fig. 17.5.* Violet and Daisy Hilton, upon their return from performing in England, October 6, 1933. Photograph. © Bettmann/Corbis

▲ *Fig. 17.6.* Joseph Merrick, the Elephant Man, illustrating the deformities caused by neurofibromatosis, 1886. Engraving from British Medical Journal 2, no. 1354, 1188. © Corbis

Most of what passes as a freak show today is vaudeville-style performance involving musicians, artists, and people with unusual abilities such as acrobatics and contortion, fire eating, sword swallowing, pounding nails into various parts of the body, walking on glass or burning coals, and escaping. It is rare to find people with congenital disabilities in troupes such as The Jim Rose Circus, The Bindlestiff Family Circus, Circus Contraption, and Yard Dogs Road Show, where often the performers are extremely fit and able-bodied (*fig. 17.10*). When people with disabilities are included, there is less of a divide between the born and the made, since they are also performing. For example, Jennifer Miller is a woman with a beard who has worked with the Bindlestiffs, at Coney Island, and her own troupe, Circus Amok. Some venues showcase her beard more than others, however she is also a skilled acrobat who dances, chews light bulbs, and delivers monologues that combine comedy and social criticism (*fig. 17.11*). Tony Torres was a dwarf who exhibited himself at Coney Island's Sideshows by the Seashore. But he did so in the guise of Koko the Killer Clown, an act that involved wearing heavy makeup, dancing, cracking jokes, and making balloon animals. Born freaks are thus no longer the sideshow's elite, nor are they considered necessary to its success since the contemporary circus relies almost entirely on working acts, and performers with sensational talents, skills, or bodily adornments such as piercings, dreadlocks, and tattoos.

What makes The 999 Eyes of Endless Dream stand out among contemporary freak shows is that so many of its performers are disabled, and disability is at the forefront of their acts: a dwarf chews on light bulbs and walks on crushed glass; a woman with no legs turns cartwheels and sings; the Lobster Girl ties knots with her unusual hands; Lobster Boy does

magic; and all of them tell stories, both funny and sad, about living with a disability in America (*fig. 17.12*). In *The Last American Freak Show*, filmmaker Richard Butchins explores how The 999 Eyes recalls and rescripts the traditional place of disability within the freak show. He asks what it means for a contemporary person with a disability to exhibit herself as a freak, and what he, as a person who is himself disabled, learns from his encounter with the freak show.

Performing Disability

Early in *The Last American Freak Show*, Butchins describes the genre as "a truly American art form." In making this claim, he alludes to the fact that, although circuses and freak shows have a long his-

tory in Europe and other parts of the world, it was the American P. T. Barnum who first recognized their potential as a mode of commercialized mass entertainment, developing them into a form that has become known throughout the world. Given that the freak show came into its own in the United States, it makes sense that Butchins would travel there to investigate how it is faring in the new millennium. As the British Butchins observes the troupe, he participates in a long-standing European fascination with America that can be traced back to the writings of Hector St. John de Crèvecoeur, Alexis de Tocqueville, Charles Dickens, and many others. During their tour, The 999 Eyes drive from Oregon to Texas, stopping to perform in small cities and towns along the West Coast and southwestern U.S. As he films the troupe, Butchins also documents the American landscape. Like his characters, his establishing shots also tend to capture places that are unsightly and marginal: highways, roadsides, parking lots and rest stops, motels, diners, dumpsters, and bars.

Promoting itself as "the last genuine traveling freak show in the United States," The 999 Eyes claims to be bringing the freak show back from the past, repackaged for the twenty-first century. Much as it recalls its precursors, this freak show is also decidedly modern (*fig. 17.13*). When we first meet them, many of the performers travel in a 1988 International Bluebird school bus owned by Laurent Martin, aka Lowrent the Clown. The motor has been converted to run on used vegetable oil scavenged from the back of restaurants and anywhere else it can be found. Butchins uses infrared lights to film several late-night scenes in which the performers—still dressed from the evening's show—search dumpsters for fuel. In his blog, he describes oil as an abundant national resource "which in the U.S.A. is everywhere because they fry everything they eat."[18] Whereas Barnum was the first to transport his circus by train, The 999 Eyes are pioneers in the technology of enviofuel. Taking advantage of others' waste, the converted bus also provides a modern twist on the classic circus caravan, reflect-

Fig. 17.8. Bernice "Jeanie" Smith and Al Tomaini, ca. 1950–55. Photograph. Circus World Museum, CWi-2298

Fig. 17.9. Emmitt Bejano and Percilla Roman, ca. 1940s. Photograph. Circus World Museum, CWi-2297

ing a contemporary awareness about the environmental impact of burning fossil fuel. In terms of personal style, the freaks are modern as well, adorned with dreadlocks, multicolored hair, piercings, tattoos, and heavy makeup. While technology is not a significant aspect of their performances, where a low-budget homemade aesthetic prevails, it is central to life offstage, where the troupe members communicate by email, quarrel over cell phone minutes, fly in by plane, shop at the mall, and watch CNN in their motel rooms.

While The 999 Eyes enjoys the conveniences of the modern world, the troupe also calls itself "the last" of its kind, a phrase that gestures backward to a waning tradition. It may be closer to its nineteenth-century forerunners than any other contemporary sideshow in that it privileges the "born freak" over all other performers. Indeed, its claim to distinction is that it includes more born freaks than its competitors. During the 2006 tour, these include H. E. A. Burns, aka The Lobster Girl; Ken, The Elephant Man; a dwarf named Dierdre (aka Dame Demure, The Dancing Dwarf); Jackie, The Human Tripod; Erik, The Gentle Giant; and Jason Black, The Lobster Boy. On their website, the group defines a freak as "a human oddity that has chosen to share, celebrate and exploit his/her own genetic anomaly through performance."[19] Here they uphold the carnies' traditional reverence for born freaks, while adding a modern recognition of genetics as the cause of some of their disabilities.

The performers' online biographies are filled with exaggeration and pure humbug, knowingly evoking the rhetorical tradition of sideshow pamphlets. For example, it presents the story of Ken (aka the Elephant Man or Pegleg) as "an inspirational triumph over adversity":

Born in 1895, inflicted with the genetic disorder NF to the point of having one leg removed, Pegleg traveled the freakshow circuit. He stayed on until 1935 when scientists, whose goal it was to kill the freakshow for social control, stole him from the midway to experiment on and study him to prove that his condition was that of a sick human and not of a Fabulous Freak ... because funding for the project was cut they decided to freeze him until more funds could be obtained. The funding never came and Poor Pegleg was forgotten.

Until one day a kindly showman snuck into the basement of a medical anomalies laboratory. Her initial goal was to obtain a two-headed baby for her show, but it was there that she then discovered the man frozen. After defrosting Pegleg she set out to help him in his mission of revenge on the scientists who are still trying to destroy the freakshow Museum of Mutant-strosities by institutionalizing, exploiting and abusing freaks for medical answers and experimentation.[20]

Fig. 17.10. Roy Volkmann. Bindlestiff Cirkus Magic Hat Troupe, 2007. Photograph. ©Bindlestiff Family Cirkus

Ken's biography leaves no question about its veracity. However, its tale of evil scientists and kind show people alludes to an underlying historical truth, the long-standing conflict between the freak show's investment in wonder and sensation (Fabulous Freak), and medicalized understandings of disability (a sick human). Show people have long been disdainful of the scientists' cultural prestige at the same time that they sought to appropriate it by seeking experts who could validate the freak's authenticity, and by calling themselves doctors, professors, and scientists. The 999 Eyes website expresses a similar ambivalence toward medical professionals in that it denigrates the treatment of people with disabilities as specimens to be studied and classified while at the same time giving Ken's condition a medical name and providing a link to the Wikipedia article on neurofibromatosis.

As was true of previous generations, the performers in *The Last American Freak Show* see The 999 Eyes as a source of community and affirmative self-expression. Butchins explains that the freak

show gives them the means to come "out of the institution and the welfare office," where people with disabilities have been relegated for generations. In the wake of the Americans with Disabilities Act, opportunities for inclusion in schools and the workplace have increased. But it is still true that most people with disabilities are poor and have difficulty finding employment. They continue to face social prejudice, challenges of transportation and access, and discrimination in hiring.[21] The performers in Butchins's film resist becoming a part of the disability underclass by seizing control of their own representation. A disabled body is a hypervisible body, one that cannot escape being laden with an excess of meaning. In his classic study of stigma, Erving Goffman described how the stigmatized person must constantly manage his or her identity to avoid causing discomfort to others.[22] The performers in The 999 Eyes are all too familiar with the burden of other people's pity, condescension, and disgust. They see the freak show as an opportunity to showcase their talents rather than their limitations, rescripting the identities available for people with disabilities.

Much as *The Last American Freak Show* emphasizes The 999 Eyes' confrontational and explicit presentation of disability, it also makes considerable effort to show that freaks are just like everyone else. In this, it recalls Tod Browning's 1932 film *Freaks*, which featured some of the best-known congenitally disabled circus performers of its time. Many of the scenes in the first half of *Freaks* show the disabled actors engaged in ordinary activities like doing housework, socializing, rolling a cigarette, or getting dressed. These scenes aimed to normalize the characters by demonstrating that in spite of their unusual bodies, they are much like everybody else. The problem with *Freaks* was that as the story developed, it turned into a horror film, trafficking in more cli-

Fig. 17.11. Andrew Lichtenstein. Jennifer Miller denouncing Mayor Giuliani's policies in one of her circus shows, July 1999. Photograph. Corbis, © Andrew Lichtenstein / Sygma / Corbis

chéd associations between disability and malfeasance. Like Browning, Butchins expends a certain amount of footage to show his disabled characters engaged in everyday life tasks that normalize their disabilities. All the while, they talk about their feelings, showing their very human capacities for loneliness, pain, friendship, and humor. We see them lounging on a motel bed watching CNN, quarreling over who has to clean up, shopping at the mall, and nursing hangovers. Butchins interviews H. E. A., The Lobster Girl, in a kitchen where she is cleaning up and preparing a drink. We watch Ken washing dishes and getting lost on the highway. Dierdre takes out the garbage, dressed in jeans and a t-shirt. At the same time, the film constantly reminds us of the freaks' differences from ordinary people, pointing out the ways they are denied opportunities for full social integration.

While nobody is getting rich, the members of The 999 Eyes have chosen bohemian scarcity as an alternative to the poverty and social marginality endured by many people with deforming disabilities.[23] When asked if she is worried about being exploited, Jackie, who is a musician and songwriter, claims that all forms of entertainment involve some degree of exploitation. "I love performing," she remarks decisively, explaining that because of her disability, "there is no other arena for me to do what I want to do." Dierdre is more ambivalent about her persona, the Dancing Dwarf. Her act includes dancing, walking on glass, eating light bulbs, and making jokes about her short stature (*fig. 17.11*). Onstage, she pushes the audience to confront their preconceptions about little people, while offstage she expresses concern that she is simply playing into stereotypes. "I'm sure if I were in touch with the dwarf community they would hate me for sending off such a bad image," she confesses. Many of the

acts play with stereotypes. Ken describes being teased as a child and bares his tumor-covered body, demanding that the spectators acknowledge their disgust, but also their desire to look. Jackie sings about being half a woman. Erik the giant claims that during tangles with the law he has avoided arrest because of his great height.

That the freaks willingly flirt with self-exploitation is evident in an episode where they perform as extras in a self-financed horror film by Andrew Getty, grandson of billionaire John Paul Getty. The troupe takes a break from the tour to work with Getty, who explains that he has hired them to add an aura of menacing strangeness to the mis-en-scène. "I'm trying to show this town full of strangers," he tells them. "I was thinking the only way to do that is to make them physically abnormal.... That's the only way an audience will get it." Butchins, who frequently uses voiceover to reflect on the meaning of the events he has filmed, has little to say during this scene. Perhaps he believed that it would be more powerful if Getty's ridiculous comments simply spoke for themselves. The film rarely ventures beyond the intimate circle formed by the troupe and their closest friends. Getty provides a view from the outside, confirming that disability still functions as an easy signifier of trouble and social disorder. The freaks themselves, accustomed to using their unusual bodies for profit and attention, seem unfazed by Getty's uncritical reliance on such tired clichés. As long as they are paid, they seem to have no problem

Fig. 17.12. Dierdre the Dancing Dwarf. Still from *The Last American Freak Show*, 2008

acting the part of sinister strangers. But even without comment, it is hard to believe they do not enjoy profiting from Getty's foolishness. As in The 999 Eyes performances, these self-styled freaks are unconcerned with promoting the respectable, uplifting images of people with disabilities favored by the able-bodied. They are quite willing to entertain stereotypes as long as they feel that they have something to gain from the situation.

In deciding to film this troupe, Butchins was aware that he would need to confront his own assumptions about how people with disabilities can best negotiate the cultural meanings of stigma. He represents *The Last American Freak Show* as a journey from skepticism to insight. His initial impressions of the troupe are not entirely positive. Their performances seem chaotic and amateurish, and he worries that the show is little more than self-exploitation. As time goes on, he comes to appreciate what the troupe is accomplishing, finding an inspiring sense of purpose beneath their raucous and lighthearted performances that resonates with his own understanding as a person with a disability.

At every turn, The 999 Eyes reject polite, socially acceptable approaches to their differences. Butchins comes to understand their show as a refusal of able-bodied ideas about how the disabled should behave. Against critics who charge that The 999 Eyes, and his film, present negative stereotypes of disability, he affirms their commitment to self-expression, however crude and confrontational. "Go figure," he writes sarcastically on his blog.

> A bunch of freaks decide to celebrate diversity in a way of their own choosing, why that will never do. It would seem that they are only allowed to act in ways deemed appropriate by the able bodied, they after all know whats best. . . . Well, not surprisingly, I and the members of the freak show would seek to disagree. It's largely the only time that some members of the troupe get any kind of positive reaction from people. . . . It's not the disability that stops them functioning successfully in society but the barriers and prejudices that society places in front of them that causes the problems. Don't blame the freaks for being freaks, look at yourselves and realise we are all freaks. Perhaps this freak show and my film about them, will give people an opportunity to examine their attitudes to the disabled. That would be good. So, why don't you go and spend a week in a wheelchair, see how it feels.[24]

Butchins's anger is palpable as he decries efforts by the able-bodied to set the terms for how people with disabilities should comport themselves. He presents disability less as a problem of bodily impairment than a social problem, having to do with an unaccommodating and prejudicial environment. On the one hand, in saying "we are all freaks," he asks his audience to think about the

Fig. 17.13. Cast members from *The Last American Freak Show*, top: Erik the Gentle Giant, H. E. A. Burns, aka The Lobster Girl, Jason the Lobster Boy, Ken the Elephant Man; bottom: Dierdre the Dancing Dwarf, Jackie the Half Girl. Still from *The Last American Freak Show*, 2008

extent to which normalcy depends on context. But on the other, his suggestion that they "spend a week in a wheelchair" suggests the difficulties of grasping the realities of life with a disability. This is a reminder that people with disabilities are not the same as freaks, that "freak" is not an unshakeable essence but an identity adopted for the purpose of performance. The 999 Eyes invite spectators to explore their own freakishness without allowing them to forget that people with disabilities face exceptional challenges.

As he gains understanding about the troupe, Butchins also acquires insight about his own disability. "Making this film put me in touch with my disability in a way I hadn't been before," he said in one film review. "I felt looked-at, whereas I'd always taken great pains to hide my disability."[25] Butchins claims that seeing how this unusual group of people treat their disabilities made him more comfortable about identifying himself as disabled. And, in confronting the resistance of the cinematic establishment to screening his film, he became more outspoken about the right of people with disabilities to represent themselves, even when those representa-

tions conflict with able-bodied assumptions about how disability should be seen.

Although he concludes his film on a positive note, Butchins does not shy away from depicting the suffering endured by the disabled members of The 999 Eyes. Some of their discomfort comes from the predictable challenges of life on the road. They often travel in uncomfortable, squalid conditions. The bus is dirty and decrepit. After it breaks down, they exchange it for an RV that is even dirtier. They spend the nights camping in tents, sleeping on borrowed floors or in cheap motel rooms. They take drugs, drink too much, and don't get enough sleep. But Butchins also emphasizes that the disabled performers' experiences differ from those of their able-bodied compatriots. Most of them confess to having been taunted as children. Erik says that, as a child, people "thought I was retarded" because his height made him look twice his age. H. E. A. The Lobster Girl admits that she was ashamed of her disability, particularly during high school. In one scene, Jason speaks candidly with Butchins. His surroundings are depressing: a room with paint peeling from the walls, dirt in the corners, cluttered with cheap bric-a-brac.

Fig. 17.14. Dierdre the Dancing Dwarf. Still from *The Last American Freak Show*, 2008

He explains that before joining the freak show, he had avoided people with disabilities. He would try to hide by putting his hands in his pockets. Then he bursts into tears. When Butchins asks Jason why he is crying, he responds: "I just really love my life. And I love my dog, pathetic as that sounds. When you're alone, she's been my best friend." Watching this scene, one can't help but feel that these are not just tears of happiness. Becoming a part of this troupe has clearly caused Jason to think more deeply about the consequences of his disability and, perhaps, about the inadequacy of the social support he has waiting for him at home.

The most disturbing figure is Ken, who is the oldest member of the troupe and the one whose disability most evidently causes persistent suffering. One of his legs has been amputated, he has a speech impediment, and tumors cover his body. Billing himself as Peg Leg or The Elephant Man, Ken exposes himself from the waist up, while explaining what it is like to live in a body that evokes fear and loathing in other people (*fig. 17.15*). When he removes his prosthesis, the camera repeatedly zooms in on a stump that is reddened, scarred, and covered in tumors. If his performance is designed to give people a chance to stare at his body in a way that would otherwise be impolite, the camera takes this voyeurism one step further, allowing the film viewer an even more intimate and unsparing look at his disability. At one point, Ken's stump becomes inflamed, a recurring problem Laurent attributes to a crude amputation that left it vulnerable to infection. In another scene, the camera follows Ken into a mall where shoppers and clerks stare at him in open disgust, one man visibly flinching and turning away. As the tour nears its end, the film focuses on the bickering and dissention that breaks out among the performers. One night, Butchins finds Ken limping alone through darkened streets looking for the performance venue, after having been left behind by the rest of the group. In the next scene, he argues with Sam, who has borrowed his cell phone. She shouts that she is fed up, and throws it at him. Afterward, Ken tells Butchins that he often considers leaving the group, but he seems to have nowhere else to go. By devoting a significant amount of screen time to Ken, the film thus complicates its more affirmative message about the empowering self-expression enabled by the freak show. For Ken in particular, that opportunity comes at a cost, forcing him to endure the animosity of fellow performers and to further expose his body to the stares of other people.

The Last American Freak Show ends six months after the troupe arrives in Austin, Texas. When Butchins returns to the U.S., he discovers that strained friendships and hurt feelings seem to have been mended. The group is preparing for a new round of performances. Many of them live together in a big house, presided over by one of their two managers, the strong and temperamental Samantha X. As he reflects back on his experience, Butchins claims that his initial doubts about The 999 Eyes have given way to appreciation. "These performers are trying to bring an awareness of their 'normality' to peoples [*sic*] attention through entertainment (it is, after all a 'show'), and that's a valid and worthwhile, if sometimes, challenging thing to watch," he writes on his blog. "They deserve support not denigration for what they are doing. This film documents this and as a result is funny, entertaining and sometimes difficult, it makes you feel uncomfortable on occasion and encourages you to examine your preconceptions about disability and that's the point."[26] Butchins argues that the freaks' achievement is admirable, even if—or perhaps because—it sometimes makes us squirm. The fact that the viewer feels uncomfortable should not be a reason to reject the

Fig. 17.15. Ken, The Elephant Man. Still from *The Last American Freak Show*, 2008

film, but rather to further probe her own attitudes toward disability.

The Last American Freak Show raises timely questions about disability, popular culture, and history in contemporary America. Most of these performers came of age after the ADA, which guaranteed the civil rights of people with disabilities. The decades since its passage have seen significant advancement toward accommodation in schools, the workplace, public space, and transportation.[27] However, the freaks' stories point to a lingering social intolerance. As children, all of them endured the cruelty of their peers. All continue to face prejudice and lack of access to the full opportunities for work and pleasure enjoyed by their non-disabled counterparts. They perform in a freak show because they believe there is no other venue to showcase their talents. They are fully aware that freak shows of the past often exploited people with disabilities. But they have appropriated the form for the present, turning it into a medium for edgy, alternative self-expression. Performing as freaks gives them an opportunity to talk about their experiences and to show off what they can do, emphasizing ability and accomplishment rather than limita-

tion. In these shows the freaks confront, and then explicitly reject, able-bodied assumptions about how people with disabilities should behave, with the goal of forcing spectators to interrogate their own preconceptions (*fig. 17.16*). They do so while surrounded by a tolerant and accepting community. The tour and the group home enable the same kind of continuity between life and work that has always been an aspect of circus culture. It is not simply about doing your act and going home, but a kind of total environment in which life and art are mutually reinforcing.

To put all of this on film is to give it a somewhat different meaning. To approve of what the freaks are doing onstage is not necessarily to like watching them in *The Last American Freak Show*. Unlike a freak show, film enables the viewer to appease her desire to stare without concern that her gaze will be returned. There is an element of voyeurism about *The Last American Freak Show*. Its intimate documentary style allows viewers to look without consequences and in some cases—like the revelation of Ken's stump or Jason's tears—to show things that the performers, no matter how confessional, would never reveal onstage. The story is constructed to create a parallel

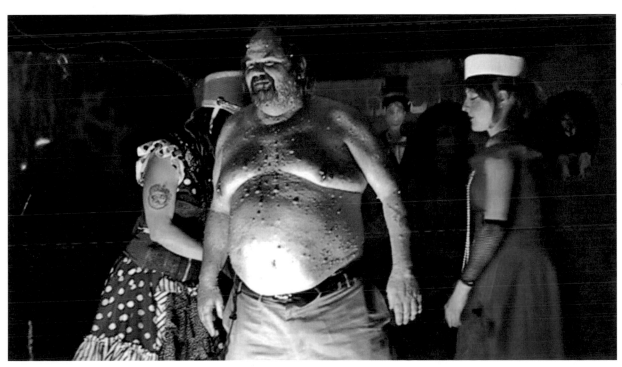

between Butchins's growing appreciation of the freaks' project, and deepening insight about his own disability. He repeats this message several times over the course of the narrative, without ever speaking openly about the nature of his disability or showing it on film. It is true that within his own logic, there should be a place for privacy as well as disclosure of one's disabilities. But it allows for an uncomfortable dynamic in which the filmmaker remains invisible as a disabled person while his subjects are exposed.

In prompting reflection on the disparity between film and live performance, *The Last American Freak Show* further underscores the significance of The 999 Eyes project. Part of what makes freak shows work is the fact that they are live, relying on a direct confrontation between spectator and performer. The thrill of the freak show is in its promise of a close and unmediated encounter with otherness. Live performance also gives the freak the possibility of agency.

However much she is objectified, the freak maintains her capacity to look back, challenging the audience to recognize her humanity and to be mindful of the impulse behind the urge to stare. These conditions cannot be replicated in electronically reproduced forms of media. It is easy to congratulate ourselves on the fact that we no longer tolerate the exploitation of people and animals that once was a routine aspect of circuses past. However, many of the spectacles that were once found at the circus can now be seen on television and the internet, where we can watch them over and over again, from multiple angles and in close-up, with no obligation to acknowledge the fact that we are staring. Without leaving home, we can see a person too fat to get out of bed, a family of little people, a plastic surgery gone horribly wrong, unchecked by anxiety that our gaze may be returned. Like other alternative circuses, The 999 Eyes restores the sideshow tradition of live performance and the elements of reciprocity, spontaneity, and unpredictability it entailed. However, it is unique in putting disability at the center of its performances. In challenging the audience to confront their own prejudices, it turns the encounter between freak and normal into something quite different than it was for earlier generations. This is a freak show that asks spectators to think about why they are looking. Here they are invited to confront the contradictions between a culture that claims to accept and include people with disabilities, while it continues to treat the disabled body as pathological, loathsome, and sensational. Living with bodies that cannot escape notice, the participants in The 999 Eyes expose themselves, attempting to seize control over how they will be viewed by others. When we flinch at what they're doing, we must ask ourselves whether our dismay might be better directed at a society where integration of people with disabilities is still far more an ideal than a reality (*fig. 17.17*).

Fig. 17.16. H. E. A. The Lobster Girl. Still from *The Last American Freak Show*, 2008

Fig. 17.17. Still from *The Last American Freak Show*, 2008

1 While Butchins downplays this aspect of the performers' lives in the film, see Jack Ruby Murray, "999 Eyes," for an account of the challenges of traveling with a troupe of people with disabilities, in *Bizarre Life*, Aug. 2009, http://www.bizarremag.com/weird-news/bizarre-life/7972/999_eyes.html (accessed July 14, 2010).

2 James Macintyre, "BAFTA faces backlash over withdrawal of disability film," *The Independent*, Feb. 8, 2008, http://www.independent.co.uk/news/media/bafta-faces-backlash-over-withdrawal-of-disability-film-779884.html (accessed July 20, 2010).

3 John Culhane, *The American Circus: An Illustrated History* (New York: Holt, 1990).

4 Benjamin Reiss, *The Showman and the Slave: Race, Death, and Memory in Barnum's America* (Cambridge, MA: Harvard University Press, 2001).

5 Bluford Adams, *E. Pluribus Barnum: The Great Showman and the Making of U.S. Popular Culture* (Minneapolis: University of Minnesota Press, 1997); P. T. Barnum, *Struggles and Triumphs, or Forty Years' Recollections of P. T. Barnum Written by Himself* (New York: Penguin, 1981); A. H. Saxon, *P. T. Barnum: The Legend and the Man* (New York: Columbia University Press, 1989).

6 Quoted in Rachel Adams, *Sideshow U.S.A.: Freaks and the American Cultural Imagination* (Chicago: University of Chicago Press, 2001), 11.

7 Robert Bogdan, *Freak Show: Presenting Human Oddities for Amusement and Profit* (Chicago: University of Chicago Press, 1988), 200–203.

8 Ibid., 166–73.

9 Ashley Montagu, *Elephant Man: A Study in Human Dignity* (New York: Outerbridge and Dienstfrey, 1971); Peter W. Graham and Fritz H. Oehlschlager, *Articulating the Elephant Man: Joseph Merrick and His Interpreters* (Baltimore: Johns Hopkins University Press, 1992).

10 Rosemarie Garland Thomson, *Extraordinary Bodies: Figuring Physical Disability in American Literature and Culture* (New York: Columbia University Press, 1997), 70–77.

11 Sue Schweik, *The Ugly Laws: Disability in Public* (New York: NYU Press, 2009).

12 In Adams, *Sideshow U.S.A.*, 14.

13 *Alive on the Inside* features interviews with Jeanie and Percilla, both widowed, who talk at length about married life.

14 See the film *Gibtown*, directed by Melissa Shachat and Roger Schulte (Decoy Film Properties, Inc., 2001) and Hanspeter Schneider, *The Last Sideshow* (London: Dazed Books, 2004).

15 See for example http://www.circusco.com/ (accessed July 15, 2010).

16 Adams, *Sideshow U.S.A.*, 210–28.

17 J. Dee Hill, *Freaks and Fire: The Underground Reinvention of Circus* (New York: Soft Skull Press, 2009).

18 Richard Butchins blog post, http://angelsstandcorrected.com/, February 19, 2008 (accessed May 1, 2012).

19 See http://www.999eyes.com/biopage.html (accessed July 22, 2010).

20 www.999eyes.com/elephantman.html (accessed May 1, 2012).

21 Joseph Shapiro, *No Pity: People with Disabilities Forging a New Civil Rights Movement* (New York: Three Rivers Press, 1994).

22 Erving Goffman, *Stigma: Notes on the Management of Spoiled Identity* (New York: Touchstone, 1986), 91–102.

23 When they aren't on the road, some of the performers have more conventional employment: Dierdre works as a research scientist investigating brain damage in veterans of the Iraq war and Jason has to leave the tour to return to an unspecified job.

24 See http://angelsstandcorrected.com/, Jan. 29, 2008 (accessed July 31, 2010).

25 Ryan Gilbey, "How the 'Freaks' Got Their Freak On," *Guardian*, March 27, 2009, http://www.guardian.co.uk/film/2009/mar/27/last-american-freak-show-disability (accessed July 31, 2010).

26 http://angelsstandcorrected.com/, January 31, 2008 (accessed May 1, 2012).

27 Shapiro, *No Pity*.

▲ Frederick Whitman Glasier. Clown with 3 equestrians, ca. 1903.
Photograph.Collection of the John and Mable Ringling Museum of Art,
Glasier Glass Plate Negative Collection, 1194.

Bibliography

Archives

● ●

A. H. Coxe Collection, Blythe House, Olympia, V&A Theatre Museum Collections, London, UK.

American Antiquarian Society, Worcester, MA. Uncatalogued collection of broadsides. Entertainment BDSDS, Circuses and Menageries, after 1880.

Archival Collections, Work Contracts, Circus World Museum, Baraboo, WI.

Benjamin F. Brown Collection, William L. Clements Library, The University of Michigan, Ann Arbor, MI.

Broadside Collection, M–485, Hawai'i State Archives, Honolulu, HI.

Circus Friends Association, Liverpool, UK.

Circus Scrapbook Collection, Billy Rose Theatre Collection, New York Public Library for the Performing Arts, New York, NY.

Department of Rare Books and Special Collections, Princeton University Library, NJ.

Dolph Briscoe Center for American History, University of Texas at Austin, TX.

George Mason University Libraries, Fairfax, VA.

Harry Ransom Center for the Humanities, Austin, TX.

Harvard Theatre Collection, Houghton Library, Harvard University, Cambridge, MA.

Hertzberg Collection, Witte Museum, San Antonio, TX.

Howard Tibbals Collection, John and Mable Ringling Museum of Art, Sarasota, FL.

James Otis Kaler Collection, South Portland Public Library, South Portland, ME.

Joseph T. McCaddon Collection, Bridgeport Public Library, Bridgeport, CT.

Joseph T. McCaddon Collection, Princeton University Library, Princeton, NJ.

Laura Howe Nelson Collection, Somers Historical Society, Somers, NY.

Leonidas Westervelt Circus Collection, New-York Historical Society, New York, NY.

Mander and Mitchenson Collection, Bristol, UK.

National Archives, College Park, MD.

Newspaper Collection, Circus World Museum, Baraboo, WI.

Program Collection, Robert Parkinson Research Library, Circus World Museum, Baraboo, WI.

Route Book Collection, Circus World Museum, Baraboo, WI.

Special Collections Department / Long Island Studies Institute, Axinn Library, Hofstra University, Hempstead, NY.

Tyne and Wear Archive, Newcastle, UK.

Printed and Digital Sources

● ●

"Abandonment of the Parade." *Billboard*, June 23, 1906, 18.

"The Adam Forepaugh Shows Program." Buffalo: Courier, 1893.

Adams, Bluford. *E. Pluribus Barnum: The Great Showman and the Making of U.S. Popular Culture*. Minneapolis: University of Minnesota Press, 1997.

Adams, Rachel. *Sideshow U.S.A.: Freaks and the American Cultural Imagination*. Chicago: University of Chicago Press, 2001.

"African Dance." *Daily Worker*, December 6, 1936.

Akerman, Evelyn. *Under the Bigtop with Schoenhut's Humpty Dumpty Circus*. Annapolis, MD: Gold Horse, 1996.

Albrecht, Ernest. "Miles White, the Little Eccentric with the Big Talent." *Bandwagon* 37, no. 6 (November–December 1993), 50–60.

———. "Must There Be Animals?" In *The New American Circus*, ed. Ernest Albrecht, 201–23. Gainesville: University Press of Florida, 1995.

Alcott, Louisa May. *Under the Lilacs*. Boston: Roberts Brothers, 1878. Serialized in *St. Nicholas Magazine* 5 (December 1877–October 1878).

———. *Under the Lilacs*. 1878. Reprint, Boston: Little, Brown, 1928.

Alexander, Shana. *The Astonishing Elephant*. New York: Random House, 2000.

Alger, Horatio, Jr. *The Young Circus Rider; or, The Mystery of Robert Rudd*. Philadelphia: Porter & Coates, 1883.

———. *The Young Acrobat of the Great North American Circus*. 1887. Reprint, New York: Federal Book Company, 1900.

Allen, Mike. "These Days, the Circus Animals Sneak into Town." *New York Times*, February 19, 1995.

Allen, Robert C. *Horrible Prettiness: Burlesque and American Culture*. Chapel Hill: University of North Carolina Press, 1991.

Altman, Rick. "The Silence of the Silents." *Musical Quarterly* 80, no. 4 (1998), 648–718.

Ambrose, Stephen. *Nothing Like It in the World: The Men Who Built the Transcontinental Railroad, 1863–1869*. New York: Simon and Schuster, 2000.

Amidon, C. H. "From Where Came Our Circus Music." *White Tops* 48, no. 2 (March–April 1975), 25–29.

Amidon, Charles, and Stuart Thayer. "Early Parades, Early Bandwagons." *Bandwagon* 21, no. 6 (November–December 1977), 32–34.

"Among Wild Beasts." *The Community Journal* 2, August 8, 1930.

"Amusements." *New York Times*, March 17, 1887.

Anastasi, Rachel N. "Forty Horse Hitch a Kinetic Sculpture." *Milwaukee Sentinel*, July 10, 1989.

"Ancestor of Clowns, Old Dan Castello Talks of His Experiences of Long Ago." *Syracuse Standard*, undated clipping, Circus World Museum, Baraboo, WI.

Anderson, Stuart. *Race and Rapprochement: Anglo-Saxonism and Anglo-American Relations, 1895–1904*. Rutherford, NJ: Fairleigh Dickinson University Press, 1981.

Andress, Charles. *Day by Day with Barnum & Bailey*. Buffalo: Courier, [1904].

"Animal Subjugation." *New-York Mirror*, July 7, 1838.

Apps, Jerry. *Ringlingville USA: The Stupendous Story of Seven Siblings and Their Stunning Circus Success*. Madison: Wisconsin Historical Society Press, 2005.

"Are You Going to the Circus? A Dialogue." *Well-Spring* (Boston) 4, no. 45 (November 12, 1847), 181–82.

Ariano, Terry. "Beasts and Ballyhoo, the Menagerie Men of Somers." *Bandwagon* 49, no. 1 (January–February 2005), 23–30.

Assael, Brenda. *The Circus and Victorian Society*. Charlottesville: University of Virginia Press, 2005.

Associated Press. "Circus Parade Returning, But Funds Still Needed." *WISN—Milwaukee*, March 13, 2008; http://www.wisn.com/entertainment/15589403 /detail.html.

"Bailey and Co." *Columbus* (Georgia) *Times*, December 28, 1858.

Bailey, Henry D. B. *Local Tales and Historical Sketches*. Fishkill, NY: John W. Spaight, 1874.

"Bailey's Circus." *Columbus* (Georgia) *Daily Sun*, December 29, 1858.

Bain, David Haward. *Empire Express: Building the First Transcontinental Railroad*. New York: Viking Press, 1999.

Bakhtin, Mikhail. *Rabelais and His World*. Bloomington: Indiana University Press, 1984.

Baldwin, Thomas, and J. Thomas. *A New and Complete Gazetteer of the United States: Giving a Full and Comprehensive Review of the Present Condition, Industry, and Resources of the American Confederacy*. Philadelphia: Lippincott, Grambo, 1854.

Ballantine, Bill. "The Art of Clowning—By an Ex-Clown." *New York Times Magazine*, March 28, 1954.

"Banquet to Mr. Barnum." *Times* (London), November 9, 1889.

Barker, Barbara. "Imre Kiralfy's Patriotic Spectacles: 'Columbus, and the Discovery of America' (1892–93) and 'America' (1893)." *Dance Chronicle* 17, no. 2 (January 1, 1994), 149–78.

Barkin, Ben. "Size of Crowd at Circus Parade Not as Important as Response." *Milwaukee Sentinel*, August 30, 1989.

"Barnum and Bailey." *Newcastle Daily Journal*, July 25, 1898.

The Barnum & Baily 15 United Shows. Buffalo: Courier, 1889.

The Barnum & Bailey Greatest Show on Earth Magazine and Daily Review. Buffalo: Courier, 1912.

"The Barnum & Bailey Official Route Book," season of 1893. Buffalo: Harvey L. Watkins, 1893. Route Book Collection, Circus World Museum, Baraboo, WI.

"The Barnum & Bailey Show." *Times* (London), December 24, 1897.

"Barnum and Bailey's." *Sheffield Weekly Independent*, June 18, 1898.

"Barnum and Bailey's." *Leeds Evening Express*, June 20, 1898.

"Barnum and Bailey's Show." *The Era* (London), May 7, 1898.

"Barnum and Bailey's Show." *Birmingham Daily Mail*, May 31, 1898.

"Barnum and Bailey in Nottingham." *Nottingham Daily Express*, June 10, 1898.

"Barnum and Bailey Parade Tonight." *New York Daily Tribune*, March 25, 1891.

"Barnum at Olympia." *The Era* (London), November 9, 1889.

"The Barnum Banquet." *The Era* (London), November 16, 1889.

"Barnum in Burton." *Burton Evening Gazette*, October 17, 1898.

"Barnum Opens in Brooklyn." *New York Times*, April 26, 1887.

Barnum, P. T. *Life of Barnum*. New York: Redfield, 1855.

——. *Struggles and Triumphs, or Forty Years' Recollections of P. T. Barnum*. Hartford: J. B. Burr, 1869.

——. *Life of P. T. Barnum: Written by Himself*. Buffalo: Courier, 1888.

——. *Thirty Years of Hustling: Or, How to Get On*. Rutland, IL: C. C. Thompson, 1890.

"Barnum's Annual Debut." *New York Times*, April 12, 1890.

"Barnum's Female Dressers." *The Era* (London), December 7, 1898.

"Barnum's Great Parade." *New York Times*, March 11, 1884.

"Barnum's in London." *New York Times*, January 16, 1898.

"Barnum's Parade." *New York Times*, March 24, 1883.

"Barnum's Show." *Saturday Review*, November 16, 1889, 558.

"Barnum's Show at Olympia." *The Era* (London), November 16, 1889.

Beatty, Clyde, and Edward Anthony. *Facing the Big Cats*. London: Heinemann, 1965.

Beeny, Emily. "Blood Spectacle: Gérôme in the Arena." In *Reconsidering Gérôme*, ed. Scott Allan and Mary Morton, 40–53. Los Angeles: J. Paul Getty Museum, 2010.

"Behind the Scenes at Barnum and Bailey's." *Evening Dispatch*, July 20, 1898.

Beisel, Nicola. *Imperiled Innocents: Anthony Comstock and Family Reproduction in Victorian America*. Princeton: Princeton University Press, 1997.

Bell, Duncan. *The Idea of Greater Britain: Empire and the Future of World Order, 1860–1900*. Princeton: Princeton University Press, 2007.

"Beneath White Tents, A Route Book of Ringling Bros.' World's Greatest Shows, Season 1894." 1894. Program Collection, Robert Parkinson Research Library, Circus World Museum, Baraboo, WI.

Benes, Peter. "Itinerant Entertainers in New England and New York, 1687–1830." In *Itinerancy in New England and New York*, edited by Peter Benes, 112–30. Boston: Boston University, 1986.

——. "To the Curious: Bird and Animal Exhibitions in New England, 1716–1825." In *New England's Creatures, 1400–1900*. The Dublin Seminar for New England Folklife, 147–63. Boston: Boston University, 1995.

Bentley, Rensselaer. *The Pictorial Reader: Containing a Variety of Useful and Instructive Lessons upon Familiar Subjects: With Illustrations to Render Them Interesting and Attractive*. New York: George F. Cooledge & Brother, 1847.

Berger, Meyer. *Meyer Berger's New York: A Great Reporter's Love Affair with a City*. New York: Fordham University Press, 2004.

"The Best Parade on Television." *Lodi* (California) *News-Sentinel*, November 24, 1988.

"Big Day To-Morrow." *Arkansas Democrat*, October 17, 1898.

"Big Rosie Gives Audience at WPA Circus Cause for Laughs." *Brooklyn Citizen*, March 12, 1937.

"Big Show on Parade Today." *Milwaukee Sentinel*, October 21, 1969.

"The Big Show." *St. Louis Daily Globe-Democrat*, May 29, 1877.

"Big Tent Will Be at Remsen and Flatlands." *Canarsie Courier*, May 2, 1937.

"Biggest Sit-Down, WPA Elephant on 5-Hour Strike." *New York American*, May 31, 1937.

"Billing Like a Circus." *Billboard Advertising*, September 1, 1896.

Bingham, Mrs. H. A. *The Ladies Repository, A Universalist Monthly Magazine for the Home Circle* 39 (1867), 204.

Biographical Sketch, Engerer Family Papers, ca. 1920–64, 2008. Special Collections Department / Long Island Studies Institute, Axinn Library, Hofstra University, Hempstead, NY.

"Blaze at Big Circus." *Washington Post*, May 22, 1910.

Bliss, R. Manufacturing Company. *Fall Catalogue, 1895*. Pawtucket, RI: R. Bliss Mfg. Co., 1895.

Block, Geoffrey. "Bigger Than a Show—Better Than a Circus: The Broadway Musical, Radio, and Billy Rose's *Jumbo*." *Musical Quarterly* 89, nos. 2–3 (2007), 164–98.

Blodgett, Geoffrey. "Father Finney's Church." *Timeline* (January–February 1997), 21–33.

Bogdan, Robert. *Freak Show: Presenting Human Oddities for Amusement and Profit*. Chicago: University of Chicago Press, 1988.

Bonin, Jean M. "Music from the 'Splendidest Sight': The American Circus Songster." *Notes* 45, no. 4 (June 1989), 699–713.

Borella, Arthur. "Why Circus Clowning Lags." *Billboard*, December 1, 1934, 35.

"Boss Clown of WPA Show." *Daily Advocate*, May 11, 1937.

Bostock, E. H. *Menageries, Circuses and Theatres*. New York: Frederick A. Stokes, 1928.

Bostock, Frank. *The Training of Wild Animals*. New York: Century, 1903.

Bouissac, Paul. *Circus & Culture: A Semiotic Approach*. Bloomington: Indiana University Press, 1976.

Bourne, St. Clair. "WPA Dismissals 'Done with Bias.'" *New York Times*, July 17, 1937.

Braathen, Sverre O. "Circus Bands: Their Rise and Fall . . ." Self-published pamphlet, n.d.

——. "How Do You Like Your Circus Music?" *Bandwagon* 1, no. 3 (August 1957), 5.

——. "Recorded Circus Music." *White Tops* 39, no. 2 (March–April 1966), 27–28.

——. "Circus Windjammers." *Bandwagon* 15, no. 3 (May–June 1971), 12–23.

——. "Chords and Cues." *Bandwagon* 15, no. 5 (September–October 1971), 4–15.

Braathen, Sverre O., and Faye O. Braathen. "The Parallel Development of Circuses and Bands in America." *Bandwagon* 16, no. 6 (November–December 1972), 4–8.

Bradbury, Joseph T. "The Historian's Column." *White Tops* 41, no. 3 (May–June 1968), 28–30.

——. "Tompkins Wild West Show, Supplement II." *Bandwagon* 15, no. 6 (November–December 1971), 27.

——. "Gorman Bros. Circus Seasons of 1934–36." *Bandwagon* 36, no. 2 (March–April 1992), 4–17.

"Brainy Bears Full of Tricks at the Circus." *Canarsie Courier*, May 21, 1937.

"A 'Bran[d] New Circus in Town." *Milwaukee Journal*, July 18, 1892.

Bratton, J. S. "British Heroism and the Structure of Melodrama." In *Acts of Supremacy: The British Empire and Stage, 1790–1930*, edited by J. M. MacKenzie, 18–61. Manchester: Manchester University Press, 1991.

Briarmead, Chess L. "The American Circus." *New York Clipper* (Supplement), April 17, 1875.

Brigham, David R. *Public Culture in the Early Republic: Peale's Museum and Its Audience*. Washington, DC: Smithsonian Institution Press, 1995.

"Broadway Cable Cars in Tangle." *Chicago Daily Tribune*, April 2, 1896.

Brown, Janine L., Nadja Wielebnowski, and Jacob V. Cheeran. "Pain, Stress and Suffering in Elephants." In *Elephants and Ethics: Toward a Morality of Coexistence*, edited by Christen Wemmer and Catherine A. Christen, 125–26. Baltimore: Johns Hopkins University Press, 2008.

Brown, T. Alston. "A Complete History of the Amphitheatre and Circus from Its Earliest Date to 1861." *New York Clipper*, December 20, 1860, and February 9, 1861.

Brugmann, Bruce B. "Circus Parade Stirs Baraboo with Activities of Yesteryear." *Milwaukee Journal*, March 25, 1963.

——. "Horses Will Power Circus Parade Units." *Milwaukee Journal*, April 24, 1963.

Buford, Kate. *Burt Lancaster: An American Life*. Cambridge, MA: Da Capo Press, 2008.

Burkholder, J. Peter. *All Made of Tunes: Charles Ives and the Uses of Musical Borrowing*. New Haven: Yale University Press, 1995.

Burton, George. "Circus Arrives Its Colossal—(Swell to Us!)." *New York Daily Star*, May 19, 1937.

Bushnell, George, Jr. "Milwaukee Recreates Old-Time Circus Parade." *Chicago Tribune*, June 18, 1967.

Bussacco, Michael C. *Heritage Press Sandglass Companion Book: 1960–1983*. Archibald, PA: Tribute Books, 2009.

Buttitta, Anthony. "There Were No Elephants on Relief." *Federal Theatre Magazine* 1 (January 26, 1936), 23–26.

"Call For Wild Animals to Be Banned from the Circus." *New Scientist* 202, no. 2709 (May 23, 2009), 5.

Canning, Hazel. "Circus for the Jobless." (Toronto) *Star Weekly*, January 30, 1937.

"The Career of George W. Hall, Jr., an Old-Timer in the Show Business." *Billboard*, June 24, 1922, 49.

Carlyon, David. *Dan Rice: The Most Famous Man You've Never Heard Of*. New York: Public Affairs, 2001.

Carmeli, Yoram S. "The Invention of Circus and Bourgeois Hegemony: A Glance at British Circus Books." *Journal of Popular Culture* 29, no. 1 (Summer 1995), 213–21.

Castagnino, Raúl H. *El Circo Criollo: Datos Y Documentos Para Su Historia, 1757–1924*. Buenos Aires: Lajouane, 1953.

Catalogue of the Great Sale of the Property Belonging to the 2d Section of the Zoological Institute . . . Nov. 13, 1837, Howard Tibbals Collection, John and Mable Ringling Museum of Art, Sarasota, FL.

"Centre Piece." *New York Clipper*, June 1, 1867.

Chandler, Alfred Dupont, ed. *The Railroads: The Nation's First Big Business Sources and Readings*. New York: Harcourt, 1965.

———. *The Visible Hand: The Managerial Revolution in American Business*. Cambridge, MA: Belknap Press, 1977.

Chandler, Ernest. *Awnings and Tents, Construction and Design*. New York: Ernest Chandler, 1914.

Charles, Lucile Hoerr. "The Clown's Function." *Journal of American Folklore* 58, no. 227 (January–March 1945), 25–34.

"Charms of Circus Draws Big Crowd," unidentified newspaper clipping, Monroe, WI, August 18, 1899. Newspaper Collection, Circus World Museum, Baraboo, WI.

"Chicago Too Crowded for Circus Parade." *Chicago Daily Tribune*, August 15, 1924.

"Child Patients See Circus." *New York Times*, September 19, 1937.

"Children's Favorite." *Daily Advocate*, April 30, 1937.

Chwast, Seymour, and Steven Heller. *The Push Pin Graphic: A Quarter Century of Innovative Design and Illustration*. San Francisco: Chronicle Books, 2004.

The Circus. Written for the American Sunday-School Union and Revised by the Committee of Publication. Philadelphia: American Sunday-School Union, 1827.

"Circus." *Asteroid* 1, no. 3 (October 1848), 10.

"The Circus." *Bainbridge* (Georgia) *Democrat*, October 23, 1890.

"The Circus." *Burlington Daily Free Press & Times*, July 26, 1883.

"The Circus." *Columbus* (Georgia) *Daily Sun*, November 17, 1868.

"Circus." *Common School Journal* 9, no. 17 (October 15, 1847), 317.

"Circus." *Knickerbocker, or New-York Monthly Magazine* 13, no. 1 (January 1839), 69, 74–76.

"The Circus." *Life Illustrated*, August 30, 1856.

"The Circus." *Waxahachie Daily Light*, (Texas) November 2, 1898. Dolph Briscoe Center for American History, University of Texas, Austin.

"Circus Again Takes It on Chin." *Billboard*, December 30, 1939, 93.

"Circus Animals Aboard." *New York Times*, November 12, 1897.

"The Circus Annual, A Route Book of Ringling Bros. World's Greatest Shows," season 1901. Chicago: Central Printing and Engraving Co. 1901. Route Book Collection, Circus World Museum, Baraboo, WI.

"Circus Comes to Town on Tiptoe." *Richmond Times-Dispatch*, February 14, 1995.

"Circus Coming." (New York) *Daily News*, July 5, 1938.

"Circus Coming in All Its Glory." *New York Amsterdam News*, March 13, 1937.

"The Circus Does Not Seem the Same, Somehow." *Hartford Courant*, June 10, 1917.

"Circus Elephant Quits Relief Rolls." *Evening Journal*, May 15, 1937.

"Circus Elephants Parade into Town." *New York Times*, April 8, 1935.

"Circus Fans' Night at the WPA Circus." *White Tops* 12, nos. 4–5 (February–March 1939), 15.

"The Circus is Coming to Town." *New York Times*, March 29, 1896.

"The Circus is Here." *Fayetteville* (Arkansas) *Observer*, October 5, 1899.

"The Circus is Here." *Columbus* (Georgia) *Daily Sun*, November 19, 1867.

"The Circus Parade." *North American* (Philadelphia), April 18, 1891.

"Circus Parade Dismal Failure." *Lewiston* (Maine) *Daily Sun*, July 1, 1948.

"Circus Parade is Cut Out." *New York Times*, October 12, 1902.

"Circus Parade Thrills Crowd." (St. Petersburg, Florida) *Evening Independent*, September 25, 1926.

"Circus Parade Today." *Palm Beach Post*, January 17, 1974.

"Circus Parades." *Billboard*, April 10, 1926, 48.

"Circus Ponies Run Away with a Cage Filled with Monkeys." *Chicago Daily Tribune*, June 23, 1900.

"The Circus Rider." *Bachelor* 4 (1841), n.p.

"Circus Star." *White Plains Reporter*, February 18, 1938.

"Circus Tent Burns, 15,000 March Out." *New York Times*, May 22, 1910.

"Circus Tent Burns After 2,200 Depart." *New York Times*, August 28, 1938.

"Circus to Open Here Tomorrow, With Large Cast." *Daily Star, LI*, October 6, 1937.

"Circus Star." *White Plains Reporter*, February 18, 1938.

"The Circus Mergers." *Billboard*, October 12, 1929, 89.

"Circuses Barred from Peachtree and Whitehall." *Atlanta Constitution*, November 17, 1914.

Clausen, Connie. *I Love You Honey, But the Season's Over*. New York: Holt, Rinehart and Winston, 1961.

Cline, Bob. *America's Elephants!* North Las Vegas: T'Belle LLC Publications, 2009.

"The Clown Business." *Eldora* (Iowa) *Weekly Ledger*, June 2, 1887.

Clubb, Ros, et al. "Compromised Survivorship in Zoo Elephants." *Science* 322, no. 5908 (December 12, 2008), 1649.

Cockrell, Dale, ed. *Excelsior: Journals of the Hutchinson Family Singers*. Stuyvesant, NY: Pendragon Press, 1989.

Cohen, Hennig, and Tristram Peter Coffin. *America Celebrates!: A Patchwork of Weird & Wonderful Holiday Lore*. Detroit: Visible Ink Press, 1991.

Collins, Glenn. "Running Away to the Circus: In Anxious Times Get Thrills and Catharsis." *New York Times*, March 19, 2003.

———. "Circus Flies o'er Troubles with Greatest of Ease." *New York Times*, March 24, 2009.

"Come to the Circus." *Enquirer-Sun* (Columbus), November 29, 1877.

Conklin, George. *The Ways of the Circus*. New York: Harper Brothers, 1921.

Conover, Richard E. "The European Influence on the American Circus Parade." *Bandwagon* 5, no. 4 (July–August 1961), 3–9.

———. *The Fielding Bandchariots: Reflections on the Golden Age between Rome and Ringling*. Xenia, OH: Richard E. Conover, 1969.

———. "Pictorial Encyclopedia of Parade Wagons." *Bandwagon* 13, no. 6 (November–December 1969), 14–27.

The Constitutional Diary and Philadelphia Evening Advertiser, December 12, 1799.

Consuegra, David. *American Type Design and Designers*. New York: Allworth Press, 2004.

Cook, James W. *The Colossal P. T. Barnum Reader*. Urbana: University of Illinois Press, 2005.

———. "The Return of the Culture Industry." In *The Cultural Turn in U.S. History: Past, Present, and Future*, edited by James W. Cook, Lawrence B. Glickman, and Michael O'Malley, 291–317. Chicago: University of Chicago Press, 2008.

Cooke, Louis E. "Reminiscences of a Showman." *Newark Evening Star*, July 1, 1915.

———. "Reminiscences of a Showman." *Newark Evening Star*, October 28, 1915.

———. "Charles H. McConnell." *Newark Evening Star*, December 2, 1915.

———. "Reminiscences of a Showman." *Newark Evening Star*, December 2, 1915.

Coombes, Annie E. *Reinventing Africa: Museums, Material Culture and Popular Imagination in Late Victorian and Edwardian England*. New Haven: Yale University Press, 1997.

Cooper, F. C. "The Oldest Showman Active." *Billboard*, June 22, 1912, 23.

"Cop Safari Captures Elephant." *World Telegram,* May 15, 1937.

Corliss, Richard. "That Old Feeling IV: A Tale of Two Circuses." *Time,* April 20, 2001.

"Cost and Construction of Tents." *Ohio Cultivator* 8 (February 1, 1852), 40.

Coup, W. C. "A Novelty, A Portable Opera House is the Last Great Scheme." *Jersey County* (Jerseyville, IL) *Democrat,* October 26, 1882.

———. *Sawdust & Spangles: Stories and Secrets of the Circus.* Chicago: Hubert S. Stone, 1901.

Cowell, Joe. *Thirty Years Passed Among the Players in England and America.* New York: Harper & Brothers, 1844.

Craik, Jennifer. *Uniforms Exposed: From Conformity to Transgression.* Oxford: Berg, 2005.

"Crandall's Wholesale Price List for 1879–80." Montrose, PA: Charles M. Crandall, 1880.

Cravat, Nick. [Obituary], *The Independent,* March 24, 1994, 1–3; http://www.independent-co.uk/news/ people/ obituary-nick cravat-1431014.html (April 14, 2011).

Crawford, Richard. *America's Musical Life: A History.* New York: W. W. Norton, 2001.

Cross, Gary. *Kids' Stuff: Toys and the Changing World of American Childhood.* Cambridge, MA: Harvard University Press, 1977.

Crowley, W. G. *Route of Cooper, Bailey & Co's Great International, Ten Allied Shows in One, During the Season of 1876.* San Francisco: Francis & Valentine, Printers, 1876.

———. *The Australian Tour of Cooper, Bailey & Co's Great International Allied Shows.* Brisbane: Thorne & Greenwell, 1877.

"Crusades Pictured in Big Spectacular Gorgeous Production Presented by Ringling Bros. in Connection with Circus." *Salt Lake Telegram,* July 15, 1903.

Culhane, John. "School for Clowns." *New York Times Magazine,* December 30, 1973.

———. *The American Circus: An Illustrated History.* New York: Henry Holt, 1990.

Currell, Susan. *The March of Spare Time: The Problem and Promise of Leisure in the Great Depression.* Philadelphia: University of Pennsylvania Press, 2005.

The Cut-Out Circus for the Children, Part V: The Side Show. Philadelphia: Curtis Publishing, 1913.

Dahlinger, Fred, Jr. "Steam Calliopes in the Billboard." *Bandwagon* 13, no. 5 (September–October 1969), 24–27.

———. "The Origins of Early Circus Calliope Instruments." *Bandwagon* 25, no. 4 (July–August 1981), 18–19.

———. "The Barnum & London New York Tableaus." *Bandwagon* 30, no. 1 (January–February 1986), 26–28.

———. *Show Trains of the 20th Century.* Hudson, WI: Iconografix, 2000.

Dahlinger, Fred, Jr., and Stuart Thayer. *Badger State Showmen: A History of Wisconsin's Circus Heritage.* Madison: Grote Publishing, 1998.

"Dash of Nostalgia Spices 1941 Circus." *New York Times,* April 8, 1941.

Davies, Hugh. "Una-Fon." In *New Grove Dictionary of Musical Instruments.* Vol. 3, ed. Stanley Sadie, 700. London: Macmillan, 1984.

Davis, Janet M. *The Circus Age: Culture and Society under the American Big Top.* Chapel Hill: University of North Carolina Press, 2002.

Davis, Susan G. *Parades and Power: Street Theater in Nineteenth-Century Philadelphia.* Philadelphia: Temple University Press, 1986.

Daws, Gavan. *Shoal of Time: A History of the Hawaiian Islands.* New York: Macmillan, 1968.

Day, Charles H. "Barnum on the Tented Field." *New York Clipper,* July 6, 1872.

———. "The Eventful Career of Levi J. North." *New York Clipper,* March 6, 1880.

———. "The Elephant as Advertisement." *Billboard,* March 23, 1901.

———. "Making Much of Music." *Billboard,* May 11, 1901, 7.

———. *Ink from a Circus Press Agent.* San Bernadino, CA: Borgo Press, 1995.

Deacon, John. "Bruin's Skates Swiped an' Now He's Very Sad." *Staten Island Advance,* June 11, 1937.

De Grazia, Victoria. *Irresistible Empire: America's Advance through Twentieth-Century Europe.* Cambridge, MA: Harvard University Press, 2005.

De Hart, Jane Sherron. *The Federal Theatre, 1935–1939; Plays, Relief, and Politics.* Princeton: Princeton University Press, 1967.

Denier, Tony. *How to Join the Circus and Gymnasium.* New York: Dick & Fitzgerald Publishers, 1877.

Denning, Michael. *The Cultural Front: The Laboring of American Culture in the Twentieth Century.* New York and London: Verso, 1998.

Densel, Mary. "Philemon's Circus." *Harper's Young People: An Illustrated Magazine* 1 (July 13, 1880), 531.

Dodge, W. P. "Rehearsing the Circus." *Theatre Magazine* 15 (May 1912), 146, 148–49, xi, xvii.

Donald, Diana. *Picturing Animals in Britain, 1750–1850.* New Haven: Yale University Press for the Paul Mellon Centre for Studies in British Art, 2007.

Douglas, Amanda M. "How Rob Ran Away." *Oliver Optic's Magazine. Our Boys and Girls* 4, no. 94 (October 17, 1868), 662–65.

"A Dreadful Death." *New Hampshire Patriot,* April 11, 1844.

Dressler, Albert, ed. *California's Pioneer Circus: Memoirs and Personal Correspondence Relative to the Circus Business through the Gold Country in the 50's.* San Francisco: H. S. Crocker, 1926.

Duce, Herbert Cecil. *Poster Advertising.* Chicago: Blakely Printing Co., 1912.

Dupavillon, Christian. *Architectures du cirque, des origins à nos jours.* Paris: Éditions du Moniteur, 2001.

———. *La tente et le chapiteau.* Paris: Éditions Norma, 2004.

Durang, John. *The Memoir of John Durang, American Actor, 1785–1816.* Edited by Alan Seymour. Pittsburgh: University of Pittsburgh Press for The Historical Society of York County and the American Society for Theatre Research, 1966.

Durant, John, and Alice Durant. *Pictorial History of the American Circus.* New York: Castle Books, 1957.

"Editor's Easy Chair." *Harper's New Monthly Magazine* 41 (June–November 1870), 779–81.

"Eight Elephants Arrive." *New York Times,* March 11, 1887.

"The Elephant." *Farmer's Cabinet,* April 24, 1835.

"Elephant Acts as Picket Used to Protest WPA Circus Cut." *New York American,* June 15, 1937.

"Elephant Escapes From WPA Circus." *New York Times,* May 15, 1937.

"Elephant Goes Native and Troops to Circus." *Brooklyn Eagle,* May 15, 1937.

"Elephant Jolts 4 Women off Back." *Times Union,* May 26, 1937.

"Elephant Sits Five Hours But Rises for Girl." *Citizen,* May 31, 1937.

"Elephant Stages a 5-Hour Sit-Down Strike; Girl, 6, Ends It after Efforts of 50 Men Fail." *New York Times,* May 31, 1937.

"Elephant's Love Is Circus Riot," (New York) *Daily News,* May 16, 1937.

Engerer, Capt. Ernest. "Among Wild Beasts." *The Community Journal* 2 (August 8, 1930), 1. Engerer Family Papers, ca. 1920–64, 2008. Special Collections Department / Long Island Studies Institute, Axinn Library, Hofstra University, Hempstead, NY

Entwistle, Joanne. *The Fashioned Body.* Cambridge: Polity Press, 2000.

Estevan, Lawrence, ed. *San Francisco Theatre Research* 1 (1938), 85–86.

"Everybody Works Again: Circus Day over, School Open." *Fort Worth Star-Telegram,* October 1, 1912.

"The Event of the Week." *Daylight,* September 10, 1898.

Everett, William. *Thine, Not Mine.* Boston: Roberts Brothers, 1891.

"F. H. V. Sponsors Big Top, World's Top Attraction Jul. 1–3." *Forest Hills Kew Garden Post,* June 25, 1937.

"Facts and Figures: New York." *Federal Theatre Magazine* 2, no. 4 (March 1937), 9, 18.

Fair, John D., and Katie Sandwina. "Hercules Can Be a Lady." *Iron Game History* 9 (December 2005), 4–7.

"Fall of Babylon. Cincinnati Gives New York a New Sensation." *Cincinnati Commercial Tribune* 47, no. 278 (July 7, 1887), 1.

"Famous Indian Heads Cast of WPA Circus in New York." *Hartford Times,* May 16, 1939.

Fauquet, John-Stuart. "Elephants on Relief? Circus and the WPA (1935–1939)." MA thesis, University of Wisconsin, Madison, 2007.

Featherstone, Simon. "The Blackface Atlantic: Interpreting British Minstrelsy." *Journal of Victorian Culture* 3, no.

2 (1998), 234–51.

Federal Gazette and Philadelphia Daily Advertiser, May 17, 1793.

Feder, Stuart. *Charles Ives: "My Father's Song" A Psychoanalytic Biography*. New Haven: Yale University Press, 1992.

———. *The Life of Charles Ives*. Cambridge: Cambridge University Press, 1999.

"Federal Theater Circus Will Be Presented at Armory Here." *Orange Courier*, February 19, 1938.

Feuer, Stephanie. "Tunnel Visions." *New York Times*, March 16, 2008.

Field, Al G. *Watch Yourself Go By*. Columbus, OH: Spohr and Green, 1912.

"50 Artists, 93 Others Get Work At NY, Bow of First WPA Circus." *Billboard*, October 26, 1935, 3, 69.

Findlater, Richard. *Grimaldi: King of Clowns*. London: MacGibbon & Kee, 1955.

Fitzroy, David. *Myers' American Circus*. Prestwich, UK: D. Fitzroy, 2002.

Flagg, Harriet S. "Applying Art to the Circus Poster." *The Poster* 6 (February 1915), 37.

Flanagan, Hallie. "A Report on the First Six Months." *Federal Theatre* 1 (March 1936), 10.

———. "Congress Takes the Stage." *New York Times*, August 20, 1939.

———. *Arena, The History of the Federal Theatre*. New York: Benjamin Blom, 1965.

"A Flare-up in the Circus." *Southern Literary Gazette* 1, no. 35 (June 19, 1852), 291–93.

Flint, Richard W. "Rufus Welch: America's Pioneer Circus Showman." *Bandwagon* 50, no. 5 (September–October 1970), 4–11.

———. "Entrepreneurial and Cultural Aspects of the Early-Nineteenth-Century Circus and Menagerie Business." In *Itinerancy in New England and New York*, edited by Peter Benes, 131–49. Boston: Boston University, 1986.

———. "American Showmen and European Dealers: Commerce in Wild Animals in Nineteenth-Century America." In *New Worlds, New Animals: From Menagerie to Zoological Park in the Nineteenth Century*, edited by R. J. Hoage and William A. Deiss, 97–108. Baltimore: Johns Hopkins University Press, 1996.

———. "A Great Industrial Art: Circus Posters, Business Risks, and the Origins of Color Letterpress Printing in America." *Printing History* 25, no. 2 (2009), 18–43.

Foner, Eric. *Reconstruction: America's Unfinished Revolution, 1863–1877*. New York: Harper and Row, 1988.

Forbes, Derek. *Illustrated Playbills*. London: Society for Theatre Research, 2002.

"Forepaugh in Vermont." *Burlington Daily Free Press & Times*, June 21, 1883.

"Forepaugh's Circus." *Indianapolis Sentinel* 30, no. 117, (April 27, 1881), 5.

"Former Battle Elephant for Indian Rajah among Features of WPA Circus." *Long Island Star*, June 14, 1937.

"Forty Old Cars to Pace July 4th Circus Parade." *Milwaukee Journal*, June 22, 1963.

"4-Horse Strong Man Booed by Youngsters." *New York Times*, September 2, 1937.

"4 Local Women Fall From Elephant." *Canarsie Courier*, May 28, 1937.

"Four WPA Brooklyn Shows Slated for Close of Week." *Brooklyn Citizen*, March 4, 1937.

"400,000 See Circus Parade in Milwaukee." *Chicago Tribune*, July 5, 1964.

Fox, Charles Philip, ed. *A Ticket to the Circus*. Seattle: Superior, 1959.

———. *Old-Time Circus Cuts*. New York: Dover Publications, 1979.

———. *America's Great Circus Parade: Its Roots . . . Its Revival... Its Revelry*. Greendale, WI: Country Books, 1993.

Fox, Charles Philip, and F. Beverley Kelley. *The Great Circus Street Parade in Pictures*. New York: Dover Publications, 1978.

Fox, Charles P., and Tom Parkinson. *Billers, Banners and Bombast: The Story of Circus Advertising*. Boulder, CO: Pruett, 1985.

Fraden, Rena. *Blueprints for a Black Federal Theatre, 1935–1939*. New York: Cambridge University Press, 1994.

Franklin, Adrian. *Animals and Modern Cultures: A Sociology of Human–Animal Relations in Modernity*. London: Sage, 1999.

Franzen, Ernst-Ulrich. "Drums, Sweat, and Cheers Endure." *Milwaukee Sentinel*, July 10, 1989.

Friend, Ted H. "Behavior of Picketed Circus Elephants." *Applied Animal Behaviour Science* 62 (1999), 73–88.

Friend, Ted H., and Melissa L. Parker. "The Effect of Penning Versus Picketing on Stereotypic Behavior of Circus Elephants." *Applied Animal Behaviour Science* 64 (1999), 213–55.

Friedman, Andrea. *Prurient Interests: Gender, Democracy, and Obscenity in New York City, 1909–1945*. New York: Columbia University Press, 2000.

"Frightful Scene with a Leopard." *New World* 8, no. 11 (March 16, 1844), 349.

"From California." *New York Times*, July 31, 1860.

Frost, Hyatt. *A Biographical Sketch of I. A. Van Amburgh: And an Illustrated and Descriptive History of the Animals Contained in this Mammoth Menagerie and Great Moral Exhibition*. New York: Samuel Booth, 1862.

Frost, Thomas. *Circus Life and Circus Celebrities*. London: Tinsley Bros., 1876.

Frueh, Joanna et al., eds. *Picturing the Modern Amazon*. New York: Rizzoli, 2000.

"Full of Interest, Reminiscences of a Veteran Amusement Manager. An Interview with Mr. G. R. Spalding." *St. Louis Republic*, February 1, 1880.

"Furious Attack on Mr. Van Amburgh, of Astley's Amphitheatre, by One of His Tigers." *Farmer's Cabinet* 8, no. 2 (October 19, 1838), 2.

"Future Star." *Brooklyn Eagle*, April 16, 1937.

Gannon, Susan R., Suzanne Rahn, and Ruth Anne Thompson, eds. *St. Nicholas and Mary Mapes Dodge: The Legacy of a Children's Magazine Editor, 1873–1905*. Jefferson, NC: McFarland, 2004.

Geggis, Anne. "Amazing Human Feat." *Burlington Daily Free Press & Times*, June 5, 1991.

Geraghty, Christine. "Re-examining Stardom: Questions of Texts, Bodies and Performance." In *Stardom and Celebrity: A Reader*, ed. Sean Redmond and Su Holmes, 98–110. London: Sage, 2007.

Gilbey, Ryan. "How the 'Freaks' Got Their Freak On." *Guardian*, March 27, 2009. http://www.guardian.co.uk/film/2009/mar/27/last-american-freak-show-disability.

Girardi, Tamara Simpson. "2 Teachers to be Balloon Handlers in Macy's Parade." (Pennsylvania) *Valley News Dispatch*, November 23, 2008.

Glassberg, David. *American Historical Pageantry: The Uses of Tradition in the Early Twentieth Century*. Chapel Hill: University of North Carolina Press, 1990.

Glenroy, John H. *Ins and Outs of Circus Life, or, Forty-Two Years Travel of John H. Glenroy, Bareback Rider, through United States, Canada, South America and Cuba*. Compiled by Stephen Stanley Stanford. Boston: M. M. Wing, 1885.

Goffman, Erving. *Stigma: Notes on the Management of Spoiled Identity*. New York: Touchstone, 1986.

Goldmark, Daniel. *Tunes for 'Toons: Music and the Hollywood Cartoon*. Berkeley: University of California Press, 2005.

Good, Robert. "Route Book, Season of 1877, P. T. Barnum's New and Greatest Show on Earth." Philadelphia: Spangler and Davis, 1877.

Goodwin, Wendell J. "Circus." Press release, n.d. Federal Theatre Project, National Archives, record group 69.2.2, stack 530, box 145.

———. "Mystery Man from Siam Joins WPA Circus." Press release, n.d. Federal Theatre Project, National Archives, record group 69.2.2, stack 530, box 145.

———. "WPA Circus, Official Route Book for the 1937 Tenting Season." Press release, n.d. Federal Theatre Project, National Archives, record group 69.2.2, stack 530, box 145.

———. "WPA Circus Will Feature 'Chaplin-esque Clowning.'" Press release, 1937. Federal Theatre Project, National Archives, record group 69.2.2, stack 530, box 145.

———. "WPA Circus in Winter Quarters to Re-open Oct. 30th." Press release, October 1937. Federal Theatre Project, National Archives, record group 69.2.2, stack 530, box 145.

———. WPA *Circus*. National Service Bureau Federal Theatre Project Works Progress Administration, 1938. Copy in George Mason University Library.

———. "WPA 3 Ring Circus." *White Tops* 11, nos. 6–7 (April–May, 1938), 21.

———. "O'Sullivan Shows Hand of the Master Producer." Press release, May 1, 1938. Federal Theatre Project, National Archives, record group 69.2.2, stack 530, box 145.

———. "WPA Circus Star Joins Ringling." Press release, May 1, 1938. Federal Theatre Project, National Archives, record group 69.2.2, stack 530, box 145.

———. "Circus Fans Association Endorses WPA Circus Program." Press release, Aug. 1, 1938. Federal Theatre Project, National Archives, record group 69.2.2, stack 530, box 145.

———. "A Circus Thrills Crowd Opening of Winter Tour." *White Tops* 12, nos. 2–3 (December 1938–January 1939), 10.

———. "WPA Performers Gain More Votes in Contest." Press release, February 6, 1939. Federal Theatre Project, National Archives, record group 69.2.2, stack 530, box 145.

———. "Elephant President Roosevelt Saved Returns to WPA Circus," Press release, April 27, 1939. Federal Theatre Project, National Archives, record group 69.2.2, stack 530, box 145.

———. Press release, April 27, 1939. Lincoln Center for the Performing Arts.

———. Press release, May 12, 1939. Federal Theatre Project, National Archives, record group 69.2.2, stack 530, box 145.

Gossard, Steven. "Frank Gardner and the Great Leapers." *Bandwagon* 34, no. 4 (July–August 1990), 12–25.

Graham, Peter W., and Fritz H. Oehlschlager. *Articulating the Elephant Man: Joseph Merrick and His Interpreters*. Baltimore: Johns Hopkins University Press, 1992.

"Grand Entrance of the Asiatic Caravan, Museum and Menagerie of P. T. Barnum." *Farmer's Cabinet*, July 31, 1851.

"The Great Circus." *Boston Daily Advertiser*, June 7, 1880.

"The Great Circus." *Savannah Morning News*, November 24, 1868.

"Great Circus Parade Returns to Milwaukee after Six Years." *USA Today*, June 29, 2009.

Great Forepaugh Show program. *The American Revolution and the Scenes and Battles of 1776*. Buffalo: Courier, 1893.

"The Great Show at St. Helen's." *St. Helen's Reporter*, Oct. 11, 1898.

"The Great United States Circus." *Illustrated London News*, September 12, 1857.

"The Greatest Show." *New York Times*, March 11, 1888.

"The Greatest Show." *Nottingham Daily Express*, June 19, 1898.

"Greatest Show to Return." *New York Times*, December 22, 1901.

Green, Harvey. *Fit for America: Health, Fitness, Sport and American Society*. Baltimore: Johns Hopkins University Press, 1986.

Greene, Ann Norton. *Horses at Work: Harnessing Power in Industrial America*. Cambridge, MA: Harvard University Press, 2008.

Greenwood, Isaac J. *The Circus, Its Origin and Growth Prior to 1835*. New York: Dunlap Society, 1898.

"Greet Santa Claus as King of Kiddies." *New York Times*, November 28, 1924.

Grier, Catherine C. *Pets in America: A History*. Chapel Hill: University of North Carolina Press, 2006.

Grippo, Robert, and Christopher Hoskins. *Macy's Thanksgiving Day Parade*. Charleston, SC: Arcadia, 2004.

Griswold, Jerry. *Audacious Kids: Coming of Age in America's Classic Children's Books*. New York: Oxford University Press, 1992.

Gura, Philip F., and James F. Bollman. *America's Instrument: The Banjo in the Nineteenth Century*. Chapel Hill: University of North Carolina Press, 1999.

Haberman, Clyde. "A Public Street Turned Private on Macy Day." *New York Times*, December 1, 2009.

Hagenbeck, Carl. *Beasts and Men*. Translated and abridged by Hugh S. R. Elliot, and A. G. Thacker. New York: Longmans, Green, 1909.

Hamm, Charles. *Music in the New World*. New York: W. W. Norton, 1983.

Hammarstrom, David Lewis. *Behind the Big Top*. South Brunswick, NJ: A. S. Barnes, 1980.

———. *Big Top Boss: John Ringling North and the Circus*. Urbana: University of Illinois Press, 1992.

Haney's Art of Training Animals: A Practical Guide for Amateur or Professional Trainers. New York: Jesse Haney, 1869.

Harris, George Washington. "A Sleep Walking Incident." *Spirit of the Times*, September 12, 1846.

Harris, Neil. *Humbug: The Art of P. T. Barnum*. Chicago and London: University of Chicago Press, 1973.

Hawthorne, Nathaniel. *The American Notebooks*. Edited by Randall Stewart. New Haven and London: Yale University Press, 1932.

———. *Hawthorne's Lost Notebook, 1835–1841*. Edited by Barbara S. Mouffe. University Park: Pennsylvania State University Press, 1978.

"Head Circus Jester is Native of Phila." *Philadelphia Inquirer*, May 2, 1919.

Healy, Patrick. "At 64 Degrees, with 59 Balloons, One Perfect Thanksgiving Day Parade." *New York Times*, November 26, 2004.

Helfer, Ralph. *Modoc: The Story of the Greatest Elephant that Ever Lived*. New York: Harper, 1998.

"Helium Monsters Invade Broadway." *New York Times*, Dec. 1, 1933.

Henderson, J. Y. *Circus Doctor; as Told to Richard Taplinger*. New York: Bantam Books, 1952.

Hendricks, W. Quinett. *Stranger Than Fiction*. n.p.: W. Quinett Hendricks, 1928.

"Here's an Act Not on the Big Show Program." *Salt Lake Telegram*, August 5, 1917.

Hildreth, Melvin D. "The Works Progress Circus." *White Tops* 9, nos. 2–3 (December 1935–January 1936), 11.

Hill, J. Dee. *Freaks and Fire: The Underground Reinvention of Circus*. New York: Soft Skull Press, 2009.

Hoh, LaVahn G. and William H. Rough. *Step Right Up! The Adventures of Circus in America*. White Hall, VA: Betterway Publications, 1990.

Hoover, Will. "Slain Elephant Left Tenuous Legacy in Animal Rights." *Honolulu Advertiser*, Aug. 20, 2004. http://the.honoluluadvertiser.com/article/2004/Aug/20/ln/ln19a.html.

[Horne, Richard H.]. *The Life of Van Amburgh: The Brute-Tamer! With Anecdotes of His Extraordinary Pupils. By Ephraim Watts, Citizen of New York*. London: Robert Tyas, 1838.

Horowitz, Helen Lefkowitz. *Rereading Sex: Battles over Sexual Knowledge and Suppression in Nineteenth-Century America*. New York: Knopf, 2002.

"Howe's Great Circus in Brooklyn." *New York Times*, November 7, 1865.

Howells, William Dean. *A Boy's Town*. New York: Harper & Brothers, 1890.

———. *Literature and Life*. New York: Harper & Brothers, 1902.

Hoyt, Helen P. "Theatre in Hawaii–1778–1840." *Annual Report of the Hawaiian Historical Society* (1960), 7–18.

"Huge Circus Encamps on Lewiston Soil." *Lewiston Evening Journal*, June 27, 1918.

Hugill, Beryl. *Bring on the Clowns*. London: David & Charles, 1980.

Hutchinson, F. B. "Official Route Book of the Adam Forepaugh Shows," season 1894. Buffalo: Courier, 1894 Route Book Collection, Circus World Museum, Baraboo, WI.

"I Love a Parade." *St. Petersburg Times*, June 23, 1963.

"Illustrations of Schoenhut's Marvelous Toys: The Humpty Dumpty Circus." Philadelphia: A. Schoenhut Company, 1906.

"In Our Busiest Streets at the Busiest Hour." *Chicago Tribune*, April 14, 1920.

"Infant Park Up Fast, Strong." *Billboard*, June 28, 1952.

"Infernal Transaction—Death of the Elephant." *Boston Gazette*, July 29, 1816.

Ingliss, William. "Here's the Circus." *Harper's Weekly*, April 1911.

"Island Mother Leads Circus Parade on Horse." *Staten Island Advance*, September 23, 1937.

"It Couldn't Be They Weren't at Home." *Billboard*, April 26, 1952.

"It's Spring and Young Jumbo Is Just Like Everyone Else." *New York Post*, May 15, 1937.

"Ives Manufacturing Company 1930 Catalog." Bridgeport, CT: Ives Manufacturing Company, 1930.

James, Michael. "Circus Opens Run in Old-Time Style." *New York Times*, April 5, 1956.

"Japino Acted Like a Trouper when Big Cavity was Filled." *N. R. Standard Star,* October 26, 1937.

Jay, Ricky. *Learned Pigs & Fireproof Women: Unique, Eccentric and Amazing Entertainers.* New York: Villard Books, 1986.

Jennings, John J. *Theatrical and Circus Life.* St. Louis: Dan Linahan, 1882.

Johnson, Bruce "Charlie." "Lou Jacobs' Miniature Car." *The Clown in Times* 4, no. 3 (Spring 1998), 60.

Johnson, Robert Barbour. "The Old Time Spec." *White Tops* 28, no. 5 (September–October 1955), 8.

Jones, Charles Henry. "Transporting the Greatest Show on Earth." *Ludgate Illustrated* 6 n.s. (September 1898), 399–408.

Jones, Kathy. "I Love a Parade: A Diary of the Macy's Thanksgiving Day Parade, Ground-Zero." *Newsweek,* Nov. 24, 2000. http://www.thedailybeast.com/newsweek/2000/11/24/i-love-a-parade.html.

Joseph, Charles M. *Stravinsky and Balanchine: A Journey of Invention.* New Haven: Yale University Press, 2002.

Joys, Joanne. *The Wild Animal Trainer in America.* Boulder, CO: Pruett, 1983.

———. "The Wild Things." PhD diss., Bowling Green University, 2011.

Kaler, John. "James Otis Kaler, A Biographical Sketch." *Dime Novel Round-Up* 69, no. 6 (December 2000), 187.

Kalof, Linda. *Looking at Animals in Human History.* London: Reaktion Books, 2007.

Kasson, Joy S. *Buffalo Bill's Wild West: Celebrity, Memory, and Popular History.* New York: Hill and Wang, 2001.

"Katti Lanner's Pupils." *The Era* (London), November 30, 1889.

Kaufman, Michael T. "Heavy Tread of Elephants Makes Hearts Lighter." *New York Times,* March 24, 1995.

Kelley, Francis Beverley. "Toscanini of the Big Top." *Saturday Evening Post,* August 21, 1943.

Kelly, Veronica. *The Empire Actors: Stars of Australasian Costume Drama 1890s–1920s.* Sydney: Currency House, 2010.

Ketcham, Diane. "Herd in the Tunnel." *New York Times,* April 4, 1993.

Kipling, Rudyard. "The White Man's Burden." *McClure's Magazine* 5.7, no. 4 (February 1899), 363.

Kiralfy, Imre. "A Word from the Author." In *Imre Kiralfy's Columbus and the Discovery of America.* New York: J. A. Bailey, 1892.

Kirkpatrick, John, ed. *Charles E. Ives: Memos.* New York: W. W. Norton, 1972.

Kitchen, Robert. "Edward Kendall: America's First Circus Bandmaster." *Bandwagon* 21, no. 4 (July–August 1977), 25–27.

———. "19th-Century Circus Bands and Music." *Bandwagon* 29, no. 5 (September–October 1985), 14–17.

Kline, Stephen. *Out of the Garden: Toys, TV, and Children's Culture in the Age of Marketing.* New York: Verso, 1993.

Kline, Tiny. *Circus Queen and Tinker Bell: The Memoir of Tiny Kline.* Edited by Janet Davis. Urbana and Chicago: University of Illinois Press, 2008.

Kober, A. H. *Circus Nights and Circus Days.* Translated by C. W. Sykes. London: Sampson Low, Marston, 1931.

Koenigsberger, Kurt. *The Novel and the Menagerie: Totality, Englishness, and Empire.* Columbus: Ohio State University Press, 2007.

Kolodin, Irving. *The Metropolitan Opera, 1883–1935.* Oxford: Oxford University Press, 1936.

Koon, Helene. *Gold Rush Performers: A Biographical Dictionary of Actors, Singers, Dancers, Musicians, Circus Performers and Minstrel Players in America's Far West, 1848 to 1869.* Jefferson, NC: McFarland, 1994.

Kreizenbeck, Alan. "The Theatre Nobody Knows: Forgotten Productions of the Federal Theatre Project, 1935–1939." PhD diss., Graduate School of Arts and Sciences, New York University, 1979.

Kunhardt, Philip B., Jr., et al. *P. T. Barnum, America's Greatest Showman.* New York: Knopf, 1995.

Kwint, Marius. "The Legitimization of the Circus in Late Georgian England." *Past and Present* 174 (2002), 72–115.

Landrum, Carl. "George Gauweiler, Band Master." *Bandwagon* 25, no. 1 (January–February 1981), 17–20.

"Later from Europe." *Portsmouth Journal of Literature and Politics,* February 23, 1839.

Lay, M. G. *Ways of the World: A History of the World's Roads and of the Vehicles that Used Them.* New Brunswick, NJ: Rutgers University Press, 1999.

Leach, William. *Land of Desire: Merchants, Power, and the Rise of a New American Culture.* New York: Vintage Books, 1993.

"Legal Holidays." *The Tribune Almanac and Political Register* 17 (January 1905), 233.

Lehnhardt, John, and Marie Galloway. "Carrots and Sticks, People and Elephants: Rank, Domination, and Training." In *Elephants and Ethics: Toward a Morality of Coexistence,* edited by Christen Wemmer and Catherine A. Christen, 167–84. Baltimore: Johns Hopkins University Press, 2008.

Leipzig, Robert N. "425,000 Cheer Parade." *Milwaukee Sentinel,* July 5, 1963.

Lent, L. B. *New York Clipper,* January 6, 1866, 311.

Le Roux, Hugues. *Acrobats and Mountebanks.* Illustrated by Jules Garnier and translated by A.P. Morton. London: Chapman and Hall, 1890.

"Lessons Make Way for the Parade." *Reading Eagle,* May 9, 1917.

"Letter to the Editor: De Francesco v. Barnum." *The Era* (London), Dec. 7, 1889.

Levine, Lawrence. *Highbrow Lowbrow: The Emergence of Cultural Hierarchy in America.* Cambridge, MA: Harvard University Press, 1988.

———. "The Folklore of Industrial Society: Popular Culture and Its Audiences." *American Historical Review* 97 (December 1992), 1369–99.

Lewis, George "Slim." *I Loved Rogues.* Seattle: Superior, 1978.

Lewis, Robert M. *From Traveling Show to Vaudeville: Theatrical Spectacle in America, 1830–1910.* Baltimore and London: Johns Hopkins University Press, 2003.

Lhamon, W. T. *Jump Jim Crow: Lost Plays, Lyrics, and Street Prose of the First Atlantic Popular Culture.* Cambridge, MA: Harvard University Press, 2003.

Library of Congress. "Thanksgiving Timeline, 1541–2001." *Thanksgiving—For Teachers (Library of Congress);* http://www.loc.gov/teachers/classroommaterials/presentationsandactivities/presentations/thanksgiving/timeline/1541.html.

Lillie, Laura C. *Rolf House.* New York: Harper & Brothers, 1886.

Lindsay, Col. Hugh. *History of the Life, Travels and Incidents of Col. Hugh Lindsay.* Philadelphia: n.p., 1859.

"Line up Told for Ringling N.Y. Telecast." *Billboard,* April 2, 1955.

Loeffler, Robert J. "A Critical Re-Examination of the History of the Steam Calliope, Part 1." *White Tops* 28, no. 6 (November–December 1955), 17–21.

———. "A Critical Re-Examination of the History of the Steam Calliope, Part 2." *White Tops* 29, no. 1 (January–February 1956), 17–21.

———. "Biographies of Some of the Early Singing Clowns." *Bandwagon* 13, no. 5 (September–October 1969), 20.

———. "Two Clowns of Yesterday." *Bandwagon* 18, no. 5 (September–October 1974), 19–22.

———. "Thomas Barry Hibernian Jester." *Bandwagon* 51, no. 4 (July–August 2007), 33.

Logan, Olive. *Before the Footlights and Behind the Scenes.* Philadelphia: Parmelee, 1870.

"A London Correspondent." *The Era* (London), August 4, 1878.

Loxton, Howard. *The Golden Age of the Circus.* London: Grange Books, 1997.

"Lure of 'White Tops' Claims Richest Clown." *Rockford* (Illinois) *Republic,* August 14, 1920.

Macintyre, James. "Bafta Faces Backlash Over Withdrawal of Disability Film." *The Independent,* February 8, 2008; http://www.independent.co.uk/news/media/bafta-faces-backlash-over-withdrawal-of-disability-film-779884.html.

MacKenzie, John M., ed. *Imperialism and Popular Culture.* Manchester: Manchester University Press, 1986.

Mackie, Charles. *Norfolk Annals.* Norwich, UK: Norfolk Chronicle, 1901.

MacLeod, Anne Scott. *American Childhood: Essays on Children's Literature of the Nineteenth and Twentieth Centuries.* Athens: University of Georgia Press, 1994.

MacMinn, George Rupert. *The Theater of the Golden Era in California.* Caldwell, ID: Caxton, 1941.

"Macy Parade." *New York Times,* November 25, 1954.

"The Mahdi: or, for the Victoria Cross." Barnum & Bailey's Greatest Show on Earth, show program. London:

Walter Hill, 1898. Program Collection, Robert Parkinson Research Library, Circus World Museum, Baraboo, WI.

Malamud, Randy. "Famous Animals in American Culture." In *A Cultural History of Animals in the Modern Age*. Vol. 6, edited by Randy Malamud, 1–26. Oxford and New York: Berg Publishers, 2007.

"Mammoth National Circus." *Pittsfield Sun*, May 7, 1846.

"Many Sightseers." *New York Times*, April 1, 1897.

Maretzek, Max. *Revelations of Opera Manager in 19th-Century America: Crotchets and Quavers and Sharps and Flats*. Vol. 1 (1855), Vol. 2 (1890). Reprint, edited by Charles Haywood. New York: Dover Publications, 1968.

Martell, Joanne. *Millie-Christine: Fearfully and Wonderfully Made*. Winston-Salem, NC: John F. Blair, 1999.

Martin, Jonathan D. "The Grandest and Most Cosmopolitan Object Teacher: Buffalo Bill's Wild West and the Politics of American Identity, 1833–1899." *Radical History Review* 66 (1996), 92–123.

Massachusetts Mercury, January 26, 1798.

Matthews, Brander. "The Pictorial Poster." *Century Magazine* 44 (September 1892), 748–56.

May, Earl Chapin. *The Circus from Rome to Ringling*. New York: Duffield & Green, 1932.

McAdam, George. "What It Costs in Money and Effort to Devise a Circus Spectacle." *New York Times*, April 8, 1917.

McCabe, John H. "Historical Essay on the Drama in California." In *First Annual of the Territorial Pioneers*, 73–76. San Francisco: W. M. Hinton, 1877.

McCalman, Iain. "Teddy Roosevelt's Trophy: History and Nostalgia." In *Memory, Monuments and Museums*, ed. Marilyn Lake, 58–75. Melbourne: Melbourne University Press, 2006.

McConachie, Bruce A. *Melodramatic Formations: American Theatre and Society, 1820–1870*. Iowa City: University of Iowa Press, 1992.

McCoy, Millie-Christine. *History and Medical Description of the Two-Headed Girl*. Buffalo: Warren Johnson, 1869.

McHugh, Jim. "Word Must Be 'Greatester' on Ringling Show." *Billboard*, April 9, 1955.

———. "Big One: From Troubled Seas a Great Show." *Billboard*, April 14, 1956.

McShane, Clay, and Joel Tarr. *The Horse in the City: Living Machines in the Nineteenth Century*. Baltimore: Johns Hopkins University Press, 2007.

Meer, Sarah. *Uncle Tom Mania: Slavery, Minstrelsy, and Transatlantic Culture in the 1850s*. Athens: University of Georgia Press, 2005.

Meggs, Philip B. *A History of Graphic Design*. New York: Van Nostrand Reinhold, 1992.

Merlin, Frank. "Circus Notes." *Federal Theatre Magazine* 2 (June 1937), 23.

Middleton, George. *Circus Memoirs: Reminiscences of George Middleton as Told to and Written by His Wife*. Los Angeles: G. Rice & Sons, 1913.

Mihara, Aya, and Stuart Thayer. "Richard Risley Carlisle, Man in Motion." *Bandwagon* 41, no. 1 (January–February 1997), 12–14.

"Milwaukee Salutes 4th with a Parade." *New York Times*, July 5, 1963.

Mizelle, Brett. "Man Cannot Behold It without Contemplating Himself: Monkeys, Apes, and Human Identity in the Early American Republic." *Explorations in Early American Culture: A Supplemental Issue of Pennsylvania History* 66 (1999), 144–73.

———. "Contested Exhibitions: The Debate over Proper Animal Sights in Post-Revolutionary America." *Worldviews* 9, no. 2 (2005), 223–26.

———. "'I Have Brought My Pig to a Fine Market': Animals, Their Exhibitors, and Market Culture in the Early Republic." In *Cultural Change and the Market Revolution in America, 1789–1860*, ed. Scott C. Martin, 181–216. Lanham, MD: Rowan & Littlefield, 2005.

Moffett, Cleveland. "How the Circus Is Put Up and Taken Down." *McClure's* 5 (June 1895), 49–61.

Montagu, Ashley. *Elephant Man: A Study in Human Dignity*. New York: Outerbridge and Dienstfrey, 1971.

Morier, James Justinian. *The Adventures of Hajii Baba of Ispahan in England*. London: John Murray, 1828.

Moss, Roger W. *Century of Color: Exterior Decoration for American Buildings, 1820–1920*. Watkins Glen, NY: American Life Foundation, 1981.

"Move to Punish Duluth Lynchers." *New York Times*, June 17, 1920.

"Moving the Circus Animals." *New York Times*, March 24, 1895.

Moy, James S. "Entertainments at John B. Ricketts's Circus, 1793–1800." *Educational Theatre Journal* 30, no. 2 (May 1978), 186–202.

"Mr. Adam Forepaugh." *Macon Telegraph*, March 19, 1881.

Murphy, T. E. "The Day the Clowns Cried." *Reader's Digest* (June 1953), 59–62.

Murray, Charles Theodore. "In Advance of the Circus." *McClure's Magazine* (August 1894), 253. Circus Scrapbook Collection, MWEZ+N.C.6312, Billy Rose Theatre Collection, New York Public Library for the Performing Arts.

———. *A Modern Gypsy, A Romance of Circus Life*. New York: American Technical Book, 1897.

Murray, Jack Ruby. "999 Eyes." *Bizarre Life* (August 2009); http://www.bizarremag.com/weird-news/bizarre-life/7972/999_eyes.html.

"N.Y. WPA Show Hits High Mark in Attendance; Admish Plans Success." *Billboard*, July 25, 1936, 38.

"N.Y. WPAers Taking Out Own One-Ringer on Co-Op Plan." *Billboard*, July 29, 1939.

Nash, Roderick. *Wilderness and the American Mind*. New Haven: Yale University Press, 1967.

"New Tent for WPA Circus." *New York Times*, August 29, 1938.

"New Trimmings Color Old Show." *New York Times*, April 6, 1940.

Newman, Simon P. *Parades and the Politics of the Street: Festive Culture in the Early American Republic*. Philadelphia: University of Pennsylvania Press, 1997.

"Nina's Baby." *Harper's Young People: An Illustrated Magazine* 4, no. 205 (October 2, 1883), 753–55.

999 Eyes Freakshow. "99 Eyes Freakshow"; www.999eyes.com.

"No Circus Parade This Year." *New York Times*, March 8, 1903.

"No More Circus Parades." *New York Times*, April 15, 1905.

"A Novelty, A Portable Opera House is the Last Great Scheme." *Jersey County* (Jerseyville, IL) *Democrat*, October 26, 1882.

O'Connell, James F. *A Residence of Eleven Years in New Holland and the Caroline Islands: Being the Adventures of James F. O'Connell, Edited from His Verbal Narration*. Boston: B. B. Mussey, 1836.

Ogden, Tom. *Two Hundred Years of the American Circus: From Aba-Daba to the Zoppe-Zavatta Troupe*. New York: Facts on File, 1993.

"Old Adam and New Noah." *New York Times*, June 19, 1887.

"Old John's Circus." *Rocky Mountain News*, August 12, 1873.

"Old-Time Circus Opens at Garden." *New York Times*, March 31, 1955.

"The Oldest of Showmen." *New York Sun*, July 6, 1879.

"On Cultural Markets." *New Left Review* 17 (September–October 2002), 114.

"On Strike at Olympia." *The Era* (London), November 30, 1889.

"100,000 Children See Store Pageant." *New York Times*, November 30, 1928.

"Order Cleanup for WPA Circus." *New York News*, May 6, 1936.

"Orders Probe of WPA Ouster." *New York Morning Telegraph*, May 7, 1936.

"Orders to Run Cars." *Milwaukee Journal*, June 11, 1894.

"Oscar Lowande Circus Commonwealth Venture Made up of FTP Circus Blew up Aug. 21 at Canarsie, L.I., after Being out Three Weeks." *Billboard*, December 30, 1939, 93.

Osterhout, Jacob E. "Ringling Bros. Circus Elephant Prepare for a Safari through NYC." (New York) *Daily News*, March 22, 2009.

Otis, James. *Toby Tyler or Ten Weeks with a Circus*. New York: Roberts Brothers, 1881. Serialized in *Harper's Young People* 2 (December 1880–April 1881).

———. *Mr. Stubbs' Brother: A Sequel to Toby Tyler*. New York: Harper & Brothers, Franklin Square, 1882.

———. *The Clown's Protégé: A Story of a Circus*. New York: A. L. Burt, 1883.

———. *Andy's Ward, A Story of Circus People*. Philadelphia: Penn Publishing, 1895.

———. *The Wreck of the Circus*, New York: Thomas Y. Crowell, 1897.

———. *Found by the Circus*. New York: Thomas Y. Crowell, 1909.

Owen, Barbara. "Calliope." In *New Grove Dictionary of Musical Instruments*. Vol. 1, edited by Stanley Sadie, 301–2. London: Macmillan, 1984.

"Pair of Midget Cattle (Male and Female) from Upolu or Samoa." Adam Forepaugh Shows. n.d. Howard C. Tibbals Collection, John and Mable Ringling Museum of Art, Sarasota.

Parkinson, Bob. "Circus Balloon Ascensions." *Bandwagon* 5, no. 2 (September–October 1964), 3–6.

Parkinson, Robert L. "Merle Evans." Introduction to *A Tribute to Merle Evans: An Anthology of Circus Music*. Boston: New England Conservatory of Music, distributed by Golden Crest Records, 1971; reissued on compact disc by Athens, GA: Windjammers Unlimited, 1997.

———. *Directory of American Circuses, 1793–2000*. Baraboo, WI: Circus World Museum, 2002.

Parkinson, Tom, and Charles Philip Fox. *The Circus Moves by Rail*. Boulder, CO: Pruett, 1978.

A Peep at the Circus, or A Business for Life. 2nd ed. Boston: New England Sabbath School Union, 1844.

People for the Ethical Treatment of Animals. "Circuses." 2012; www.circuses.com.

"Performer Injured at WPA Circus." *Staten Island Advance*, September 25, 1937.

"Personal Glimpses and Comments on Canvaseers." *Forest Hills Post*, July 2, 1937.

Pfening, Fred D., Jr. "Circus Songsters." *Bandwagon* 1, no. 6 (November–December 1963), 10–12.

———. "The American Circus and the Great Depression: 1929–1939." MA thesis, Ohio State University, 1976.

———. "Spec-ology of the Circus, Part One." *Bandwagon* 47, no. 6 (November–December 2003), 4–20.

———. "Spec-ology of the Circus, Part Two." *Bandwagon* 48, no. 1 (January–February 2004), 3–21.

———. "A Documentary History of the Barnum and London Circus in 1881." *Bandwagon* 52, no. 6 (November–December 2008), 5–70.

———. "The Strobridge Lithographing Company, the Ringling Brothers, and Their Circuses." In Spangenberg and Walk, 36–42.

Pfening III, Frederic Denver. "The American Circus and the Great Depression: 1929–1939." MA thesis. Ohio State University, 1976.

"Philadelphia Region Gets Going." *Federal Theatre Magazine* 25 (February 1936), 8.

Phillips, Fred H. "Centennial of the Calliope." *White Tops* 28, no. 2 (January–February 1955), 2–4.

Phillips, John McCandlish. *City Notebook: A Reporter's Portrait of a Vanishing New York*. New York: Liveright, 1974.

Pickering, Michael. "Mock Blacks and Racial Mockery: The 'Nigger' Minstrel and British Imperialism." In *Acts of Supremacy: The British Empire and Stage, 1790–1930*, edited by J. M. MacKenzie, et al., 179–236. Manchester: Manchester University Press, 1991.

———. "John Bull in Blackface." *Popular Music* 16, no. 2 (May 1997), 181–201.

———. *Blackface Minstrelsy in Britain*. Aldershot, UK, and Burlington, VT: Ashgate, 2008.

"A Pickpocket Comes to Grief." *Burlington Daily Free Press & Times*, July 26, 1883.

Plowden, Gene. *Merle Evans: Maestro of the Circus*. Miami: Seeman, 1971.

Poda, Paula A. "Crowd's Glee Spurs Forty Horse Hitch, 10 Ton Wagon." *Milwaukee Sentinel*, July 17, 1989.

Pollak, Michael. "Hoofing it to Midtown." *New York Times*, February 29, 2004.

Posey, Jake. *Last of the 40-Horse Drivers, The Autobiography of Jake Posey*. New York: Vantage Press, 1959.

Potts, E. Daniel, and Annette Potts. *Young America and Australian Gold: Americans and the Gold Rush of the 1850s*. St. Lucia: University of Queensland Press, 1974.

Preston, Katherine K. "Art Music from 1800–1860." In *The Cambridge History of American Music*, edited by David Nicholls, 203–4. Cambridge: Cambridge University Press, 1998.

Prince, Richard E. "Victor H. Robbins, American Bandmaster." *Circus Fanfare* 18, no. 5 (1988).

"Professor Risley and Japanese Acrobats: Selections from the Diary of Hirohachi Takana." *Nineteenth Century Theatre* 18, nos. 1–2 (1990), 62–74.

"P. S. 89 Pupils Want Japino to Stick on WPA, Not Envelopes." *Long Island Star*, June 16, 1937.

"P. T. Barnum's Grand Colossal Museum and Menagerie." *Daily Quincy* (Illinois) *Whig*, August 19, 1853.

"Pushing Holiday Trade." *New York Times*, November 14, 1926.

Quinn, Susan. *Furious Improvisation: How the WPA and a Cast of Thousands Made High Art out of Desperate Times*. New York: Walker, 2008.

Rankin, Hugh F. *The Theater in Colonial America*. Chapel Hill: University of North Carolina Press, 1965.

"Rapid Transit." *Boston Daily Advertiser*, May 15, 1897.

Reiss, Benjamin. *The Showman and the Slave: Race, Death, and Memory in Barnum's America*. Cambridge, MA: Harvard University Press, 2001.

"Relief Elephant Sits and Defies All Kings' Men." *Tribune*, May 31, 1937.

Rennert, Jack. *100 Years of Circus Posters*. New York: Darien House, 1974.

———. *American Circus Posters*. Baraboo, WI: Circus World Museum, 1984.

Renoff, Gregory J. *The Big Tent: The Traveling Circus in Georgia, 1820–1930*. Athens: University of Georgia Press, 2008.

Rosenberg, Manuel. "Billing the Greatest Show on Earth." Interview with Nelson Strobridge in *The Artist and Advertiser* 2, no. 2 (February 1931), 5.

"Rettig to Kiralfy. The Cincinnatus Artist Replies to Charges of Plagiary." *Cincinnati Commercial Tribune*

47, no. 356 (September 27, 1888), 6.

"Revival of Circus Parade to Feature Pageant Program." *Sarasota Herald*, February 20, 1937.

Reynolds, Chang. "The Al G. Barnes Wild Animal Circus 1923." *Bandwagon* 29, no. 3 (May–June, 1985), 12–19.

Ribbens, Tom. "March in the Rain." *Milwaukee Journal Sentinel*, January 3, 2000.

Ringling, Alfred T. *Life Story of the Ringling Brothers*. Chicago: R. R. Donnelley & Sons, 1900.

———. "What the Public Does Not See at a Circus." *National Magazine* 12 (1900), 189–92.

Ringling, Charles E. "Minus the Circus Parade." *Billboard*, December 13, 1924, 6.

"Ringling Bros's Circus Parade." *Pittsburgh Press*, July 3, 1901.

"The Ringling Brothers." *Omaha World Herald*, July 19, 1903.

Ringling Brothers and Barnum & Bailey Circus. "Pachyderm Parade on Capitol Hill Celebrates St. Patrick's Day and Marks the Arrival of Ringling Bros. and Barnum & Bailey to Washington, D.C." marketwire. com (March 12, 2009); www.marketwire.com/ press-release/Pachyderm-Parade-on-Capitol-Hill-Celebrates-St-Patricks-Day-Marks-Arrival-Ringling-Bros-960493.htm.

"The Ringling's Big Show." *Savannah Morning News*, November 7, 1896.

Ritvo, Harriet. *The Animal Estate: The English and Other Creatures in the Victorian Age*. Cambridge, MA: Harvard University Press, 1987.

Robeson, Dave. *Louis Roth, Forty Years with Jungle Killers*. Caldwell, ID: Caxton Printers, 1941.

Robinson, Gil. *Old Wagon Show Days*. Cincinnati: Brockwell, 1925.

"Robinson and Elred's Great Southern Circus." *Columbus* (Georgia) *Enquirer*, December 24, 1850.

Rockwell, David, and Bruce Mau. *Spectacle*. New York: Phaidon, 2006.

Roediger, David R. *The Wages of Whiteness: Race and the Making of the American Working Class*. New York: Verso, 1991.

Roe, Jill. *Marvellous Melbourne: The Emergence of an Australian City*. Sydney: Hicks Smith & Sons, 1974.

Rogers, Kory. *Shelburne Museum's Circus Collection*. Shelburne, VT: Shelburne Museum, 2010.

Roosevelt, Theodore. "Wild Man and Wild Beast in Africa." *National Geographic* 22, no. 1 (January 1911), 1.

Root, Harvey W. *The Ways of the Circus, Being the Memories and Adventures of George Conklin, Tamer of Lions*. New York: Harper & Brothers, 1921.

Rosenberg, Gail S., and Angela Patten. "1883 Forepaugh Posters Discovered in Vermont." *Bandwagon* 35, no. 4 (July–August 1991), 34–5.

Ross, Gary. *At Large: The Fugitive Odyssey of Murray Hill and His Elephants*. New York: Random House, 1992.

Ross, Ronal. "The Role of Blacks in the Federal Theatre,

1935–1939." In *The Theatre of Black Americans: A Collection of Critical Essays,* edited by Errol Hill, 231–46. New York: Applause Books, 2000.

Rothfels, Nigel. *Savages and Beasts: The Birth of the Zoo.* Baltimore: Johns Hopkins University, 2002.

———. "Why Look at Elephants." *Worldviews: Environment, Culture, Religion* 9, no. 2 (Summer 2005), 166–72.

Rourke, Constance. *American Humor: A Study of the National Character.* New York: Harcourt, Brace, 1931.

———. *Roots of American Culture, and Other Essays.* New York: Harcourt, Brace, and World, 1942.

Rowell, George. *Queen Victoria Goes to the Theatre.* London: P. Elek, 1978.

Roy, Matthew. "A Change in Tradition." *Virginian-Pilot,* February 22, 2006.

Ryan, Mary P. "The American Parade: Representations of the Nineteenth-Century Social Order." In *The New Cultural History,* edited by Lynn Hunt, 131–53. Berkeley: University of California Press, 1989.

Rydell, Robert W., and Rob Kroes. *Buffalo Bill in Bologna: The Americanization of the World, 1869–1922.* Chicago: University of Chicago Press, 2005.

"Sand's, Nathan's, & Co.'s." *Tioga County Agitator,* September 2, 1858.

Sanger, "Lord" George. *Seventy Years a Showman.* 1910 Reprint, London: J. M. Dent & Sons, 1926.

"Sarasotan to Close Shop after 50 Years in Trade." *Sarasota Herald Tribune,* January 30, 1972.

Saxon, A. H. *Enter Foot and Horse: A History of Hippodrama in England and France.* New Haven: Yale University Press, 1968.

———. *The Life and Art of Andrew Ducrow & the Romantic Age of the English Circus.* Hamden, CT: Archon Books, 1978.

———. *Selected Letters of P. T. Barnum.* New York: Columbia University Press, 1983.

———. *P. T. Barnum: The Legend and the Man.* New York: Columbia University Press, 1989.

"Schlitz Cancels Parade in Milw." *New Pittsburgh Courier,* May 4, 1968.

Schneider, Hanspeter. *The Last Sideshow.* London: Dazed Books, 2004.

Schweik, Susan. *The Ugly Laws: Disability in Public.* New York: New York University Press, 2009.

"Seen in a New Light." *Daily Inter-Ocean* (Chicago), April 9, 1896.

Sellers, Charles Grier. *The Market Revolution: Jacksonian America, 1815–1846.* New York: Oxford University Press, 1991.

Sentilles, Renée. *Performing Menken: Adah Isaacs Menken and the Birth of American Celebrity.* Cambridge and New York: Cambridge University Press, 2003.

"Seven Bears To Head Cast of WPA Circus." *New York Post,* October 29, 1937.

Shachat, Melissa and Roger Schulte, directors. *Gibtown.* Decoy Film Properties, Inc., 2001.

Shanley, J. P. "Circus on Video: Improvements Noted in Coverage of Big Show After Seven-Year Lapse." *New York Times,* April 3, 1955.

Shapiro, Joseph. *No Pity: People with Disabilities Forging a New Civil Rights Movement.* New York: Three Rivers Press, 1994.

Shelburne Museum Newsletter, Summer 1991.

Sheriff, Carol. *The Artificial River: The Erie Canal and the Paradox of Progress, 1817–1862.* New York: Hill and Wang, 1996.

"Shocking Calamity!" *New Hampshire Sentinel* (Keene), September 23, 1820.

Shrock, Joel. *The Gilded Age.* Westport, CT: Greenwood Press, 2004.

Singer, Peter. *Animal Liberation.* 1975. 2nd ed. London: Random House, 1995.

Sissons, David C. "Japanese Acrobatic Troupes Touring Australasia, 1867–1900." *Australasian Drama Studies* 35 (October 1999), 73–107.

"Six Giant Balloons in Store's Pageant." *New York Times,* November 21, 1948.

Slout, William L. *Joe Blackburn's A Clown's Log.* San Bernardino, CA: Borgo Press, 1993.

———. *Amphitheatres and Circuses: A History from Their Earliest Date to 1861, with Sketches of Some of the Principal Performers.* San Bernardino, CA: Borgo Press, 1994.

———. *Ink from a Circus Press Agent.* San Bernardino, CA: Borgo Press, 1995.

———. *Clowns and Cannons: The American Circus during the Civil War.* San Bernardino, CA: Borgo Press, 1997.

———. *Olympians of the Sawdust Circle: A Biographical Dictionary of the Nineteenth-Century American Circus.* San Bernardino, CA: Borgo Press, 1998.

———. "The Recycling of the Dan Rice Paris Pavilion Circus." *Bandwagon* 42, no. 3 (May–June 1998), 13–21; no. 4 (July–August 1998), 13–14, 16–21.

———. *A Royal Coupling: The Historic Marriage of Barnum and Bailey.* San Bernardino, CA: Borgo Press, 2000.

———. *Theatre in a Tent.* San Bernardino, CA: William L. Slout, 2000.

———. "Two Rings and a Hippodrome Track." *Bandwagon* 44, no. 6 (November–December 2000), 18–21.

———. "Chicken or the Egg; A Double Ring Controversy." *Bandwagon* 51, no. 1 (January–February 2007), 29–36.

Small, Michael. "The Arts," *People,* May 2, 1988.

Smith, Mark M. *Listening to Nineteenth-Century America.* Chapel Hill: University of North Carolina Press, 2001.

Solly, Circus. "Under the Marquee." *Billboard,* December 12, 1914, 23.

Spangenberg, Kristin L. "The Strobridge Lithographing Company: The Tiffany of Printers." In Spangenberg and Walk, 20–27.

Spangenberg, Kristin L., and Deborah W. Walk, eds. *The Amazing American Circus Poster: The Strobridge Lithographing Company.* Cincinnati and Sarasota: Cincinnati Art Museum and John and Mable Ringling Museum of Art, 2011.

"Sparks Circus to Give Parade." (St. Petersburg) *Evening Independent,* October 24, 1929.

Speaight, George. "The Origin of the Circus Parade Wagon." *Bandwagon* 21, no. 6 (November–December 1977), 37–39.

———. *History of the Circus.* London: Tantivy Press, 1980.

Spence, Hartzell. *The Big Top: My Forty Years with The Greatest Show on Earth.* New York: Simon and Schuster, 1952.

Spencer, Thomas, M. *The St. Louis Veiled Prophet Celebration Power on Parade, 1877–1995.* Columbia: University of Missouri Press, 2000.

St. Leon, Mark. *Spangles & Sawdust: The Circus in Australia.* Richmond, VIC: Greenhouse Publications, 1983.

———. "Cooper, Bailey & Co. Great International Allied Shows: The Australian Tours, 1876–78," 2 parts. *Bandwagon* 36, nos. 5–6 (September–October and November–December 1992), 17–30; 36–47.

———. *The Circus in Australia: Its Origins and Development to 1856.* Vol. 1 of *The Circus in Australia.* Penshurst, NSW: Mark St. Leon, 2005.

———. "Circus & Nation: A Critical Inquiry into Circus in Its Australian Setting, 1847–2006, from the Perspectives of Society, Enterprise, and Culture." PhD diss., University of Sydney, Australia, 2006.

———. *The American Century, 1851–1950.* Vol. 3 of *The Circus in Australia.* Penshurst, NSW: Mark St. Leon, 2007.

———. *Circus: The Australian Story.* Melbourne: Melbourne Books, 2011.

———. Staff Reports. "Circus Animal Walk Planned for Tuesday." News-Record.com, February 8, 2010. http://www.news-record.com/content/2010/02/08/article/circus_animal_walk_planned_for_tuesday.

Starr, S. Frederick. *Bamboula! The Life and Times of Louis Moreau Gottschalk.* Oxford: Oxford University Press, 2000.

Stewart, Alvaro Betancourt, comp. "My Dairy, or, Route book of P. T. Barnum's Greatest Show on Earth and the Great London Circus for the season 1882." 1882. Miscellaneous Materials, "Route Books," box 47, JMP, McCaddon Collection of the Barnum and Bailey Circus, Rare Books and Special Collections, Princeton University.

Stoddard, William O. "Men-and-Animal Shows, and How They Are Moved About." *St. Nicholas: An Illustrated Magazine for Young Folks* 9, no. 4 (February 1882), 314–23; no. 5 (March 1882), 366–76.

Stoddart, Helen. *Rings of Desire: Circus History and Representation.* Manchester: Manchester University Press, 2000.

Stokes, John. "'Lion Griefs': The Wild Animal Act as Theatre." *New Theatre Quarterly* 20, no. 2 (May 2004), 138–54.

"The Street Pageant To-Night." *New York Times*, March 27, 1895.

Studwell, William E, Charles P. Conrad, and Bruce R. Schueneman, eds. *Circus Songs: An Annotated Anthology*. New York: Haworth, 1999.

Sturtevant, C. G. "Getting It Up and Down." *Billboard*, March 24, 1928, 187.

———. "When the American Circus Went Abroad." *White Tops* 12 (November–December 1939), 3.

———. "My Friend, Jimmy Whalen." *White Tops* 15 (December 1941–January 1942), 5–7.

———. "Who's Who in the American Circus." *White Tops* 36 (January–February 1963), 5–8.

Sukumar, Raman. *The Living Elephants: Evolutionary Ecology, Behavior and Conservation*. New York: Oxford University Press, 2003.

Susman, Warren I. *Culture as History: The Transformation of American Society in the Twentieth Century*. New York: Pantheon Books, 1985.

Tait, Peta. *Circus Bodies: Cultural Identity in Aerial Performance*. London: Routledge, 2005.

———. *Wild and Dangerous Performances: Animals, Emotions, Circus*. Backingstroke, UK: Palgrave Macmillan, 2012.

"Talk with a Showman." *Lebanon* (Ohio) *Patriot*, June 26, 1879.

"Tanbark Odds—and—Ends." *New York Clipper*, November 24, 1884.

Taylor, Peter. "Training Wild Animals for Circus and Stage Not Cruel." *Billboard*, June 30, 1925.

Teel, Jay. *The Crime and Execution of Black Diamond, The Insane Elephant*. Ansted, WV: Petland Press, 1930.

"Ten Thousand Saw It." *Savannah Morning News*, November 9, 1895.

Tester, Keith. *Animals and Society*. London: Routledge, 1991.

"Thanksgiving Day Parade in Color." *Southeast Missourian* (Cape Girardeau), November 17, 1961.

"Thanksgiving Parades Draw Large Throngs." *Billboard*, December 4, 1948, 49.

"Thanksgiving TV Spotlight." *Sunday Herald* (Bridgeport, CT), November 20, 1955.

Thayer, Stuart. "Stuart Thayer's American Circus Anthology" (compendium of his articles published in *Bandwagon*); http://www.circushistory.org/Thayer/Thayer.htm.

———. "Joseph E. Warner—Pioneer of the Three-Tent Circus." *Bandwagon* 14, no. 1 (January–February 1970), 20–23.

———. "One Sheet." *Bandwagon*, 18, no. 5 (September–October 1974), 23.

———. "The Anti-Circus Laws in Connecticut, 1773–1840." *Bandwagon* 20, no. 1 (January–February 1976), 18–20.

———. "One Sheet: The Development of Tents." *Bandwagon* 20, no. 3 (May–June 1976), 3, 27.

———. "Legislating the Shows: Vermont, 1824–1933." *Bandwagon* 25, no. 4 (July–August 1981), 20.

———. "'The Keeper Will Enter the Cage': Early American Wild Animal Trainers." *Bandwagon* 26, no. 6 (November–December 1982), 38–40.

———. "Notes on the History of Circus Tents." *Bandwagon* 30, no. 5 (September–October 1986), 28–30.

———. "Rufus Welch's Worst Season." *Bandwagon* 34, no. 6 (November–December 1990), 66–68.

———. "Carl Robinson, Bandleader." *Bandwagon* 35, no. 4 (July–August 1991), 16–19.

———. "A History of the Traveling Menagerie in America." *Bandwagon* 35, no. 6 (November–December 1991), 64–71, and 36, no. 1, (January–February 1992), 31–36.

———. "The Out-Side Shows." *Bandwagon* 36, no. 2 (March–April 1992), 24–26.

———. "Victor Pepin's Genealogy." *Bandwagon* 36, no. 3 (May–June 1992), 31.

———. "The First Cookhouse." *Bandwagon* 36, no. 4 (July–August 1992), 25.

———. "The Circus Roots of Negro Minstrelsy." *Bandwagon* 40, no. 6 (November–December 1996), 43–45.

———. *Traveling Showmen: The American Circus before the Civil War*. Detroit: Astley and Ricketts, 1997.

———. "Parade Wagons 1847." *Bandwagon* 42, no. 2 (March–April 1998), 2–3.

———. *Annals of the American Circus, 1793–1860*. Seattle: Dauven and Thayer, 2000.

———. *The Performers: A History of Circus Acts*. Seattle: Dauven and Thayer, 2005.

———. "The Oldest of Showmen: The Career of Benjamin F. Brown of Somers, New York." *Bandwagon* 50, no. 5 (September–October 2006), 10–16.

———. "The Steamboat, the Circus, and Cincinnati." In Spangenberg and Walk, 11–13.

Thayer, Stuart, and William L. Slout. *Grand Entrée: The Birth of the Greatest Show on Earth, 1870–1875*. San Bernardino, CA: Borgo Press, 1998.

Thomson, Rosemarie Garland. *Extraordinary Bodies: Figuring Physical Disability in American Literature and Culture*. New York: Columbia University Press, 1997.

"Thousands Visit Big Tent First Three Nights." *Canarsie Courier*, May 28, 1937.

"3 Are Held in WPA Fraud." *New York Times*, September 1, 1938.

"3 Freed on Charges of Robbing the WPA." *New York Times*, December 14, 1938.

"The Three Ring Business." *The Era* (London), January 13, 1894.

Tipper, Harry, and George Burton Hotchkiss. *Advertising, Modern Business*, vol. 4. New York: Alexander Hamilton Institute, 1914.

Todd, Jan. "Center Ring: Katie Sandwina and the Construction of Celebrity." *Iron Game History* 10 (November 2007), 4–13.

Todd, Nancy L. *New York's Historic Armories: An Illustrated History*. Albany: State University of New York, 2006.

"Tom Thumb Circus at P.S. 128 Tomorrow." *Brooklyn Eagle*, April 9, 1937.

"Too Big to Parade." *Reading Eagle*, April 13, 1907.

Towsen, John H. *Clowns*. New York: Hawthorn Books, 1976.

Trachtenberg, Alan. *The Incorporation of America: Culture and Society in the Gilded Age*. New York: Hill and Wang, 1982.

"Trainer Clawed, Son 'Tames' Lion." *New York Times*, February 26, 1939.

"'Tramp Bicyclist' Cheered by Kings, is in WPA Circus." *Sunday Eagle*, July 26, 1936.

"Travel in New York." *Baltimore Sun*, July 9, 1905.

Truzzi, Marcello. "The Decline of the American Circus: The Shrinkage of an Institution." In *Sociology and Everyday Life*, edited by Marcello Truzzi, 312–22. Englewood Cliffs, NJ: Prentice-Hall, 1968.

Tryon, John. *An Illustrated History and Full and Accurate Description of the Wild Beasts, and Other Interesting Specimens of Animated Nature Contained in the Grand Caravan of Van Amburgh & Co.: Together with a Particular Account of Mr. Van Amburgh's Performances in the Caverns of Trained Animals, as Exhibited by Him in Europe and America, before the Highest Classes of Citizens, Gentry and Nobility . . .* New York: Jonas Booth, 1846.

Turner, E. S. *All Heaven in a Rage*. London: Michael Joseph, 1964.

Turner, Frederick Jackson. "The Significance of the Frontier in American History." *Report of the American Historical Association* (1893), 199–227.

Turner, John. *Victorian Arena: The Performers. A Dictionary of British Circus Biography*, vol. 2. Formby, UK: Lingdales Press, 2000.

Turner, Timothy G. "Old Time Circus Parade Thrills Los Angeles." *Los Angeles Times*, September 22, 1936.

"The Twilight Parade." *Daily Inter-Ocean* (Chicago), June 17, 1879.

"Two Lions Attack Trainer in Queens." *New York Times*, February 25, 1939.

"Two Old Favorites Back in Circus Lineup." *Long Island Daily Press*, May 2, 1939.

Twyman, Michael. *Breaking the Mould: The First Hundred Years of Lithography*. London: British Library, 2001.

"Union League Club Host to Children." *New York Times*, December 25, 1935.

"Urban Population of the United States." *National Geographic* 12 (January 1901), 345.

Vail, R. W. G. *Random Notes on the History of the Early American Circus*. Worcester, MA: American Antiquarian Society, 1933.

"Van Amburgh in Paris." *Spirit of the Times*, September 28, 1839.

Velvin, Ellen. *Behind the Scenes with Wild Animals*. New York: Moffat, Yard, 1906.

Verney, Peter. *Here Comes the Circus*. London: Paddington, 1978.

Walker, Elaine. *Horse*. London: Reaktion Books, 2008.

Wallett, W. F. *The Public Life of W. F. Wallett, The Queen's Jester: An Autobiography*. Edited by John Luntley. London: Bemrose and Sons, 1870.

Walton's Vermont Register and Farmer's Almanac for 1883. White River Junction, VT: White River Paper, 1883.

Warrell, Fred. "The Circus, A Mechanical Wonder Show." *Popular Science* 103, no. 1 (July 1923), 21–23, 83.

Wasowicz, Laura. "Brief History of the McLoughlin Bros"; http://www.americanantiquarian.org/mcloughlin.htm.

Waterbury, Kathleen. "Parade Stirs Volunteer Spirit." *Milwaukee Sentinel*, July 12, 1991.

Watkins, Clifford Edward. *Showman: The Life and Music of Perry George Lowery*. Jackson: University of Mississippi Press, 2003.

———. "The Travels of the Showman Perry G. Lowery." *Bandwagon* 48, no. 2 (March–April, 2004), 22–26.

Watkins, Harvey L. "Barnum and Bailey and the World." 1897–1899 (n.p.), 19.

"Weary Circus Here after a Long Trip." *Milwaukee Sentinel*, March 18, 1909.

Weigley, Russell F. "The Border City in Civil War, 1854–1865." In *Philadelphia: A 300 Year History*, edited by Russell F. Weigley, 363–416. New York: W. W. Norton, 1982.

Weintraub, Stanley. *Victorian Yankees at Queen Victoria's Court: American Encounters with Victoria and Albert*. Newark: University of Delaware Press, 2011.

Wemyss, Francis Courtney. *Twenty-Six Years of the Life of an Actor and Manager*. Glasgow: R. Griffin, 1847.

White, Eric Walter. *Stravinsky: The Composer and His Work*. 2nd ed. Berkeley: University of California Press, 1984.

"Why! Mr. Forepaugh Answers." *Burlington Daily Free Press & Times*, June 14, 1883.

Witham, Barry. *The Federal Theatre Project: A Case Study*. New York: Cambridge University Press, 2003.

Whitman, Willson. "Job for Jumbo." *The Stage* 14 (March 1937), 98–99.

Whitehouse, Beth. "Macy's Parade: Where to Watch on Thanksgiving." *Newsday* (New York), November 24, 1988.

Wilkinson, Howard. "Local Kids Ready to Step Out." *Cincinnati Inquirer*, November 26, 2003.

Williams, Simon. "European Actors and the Star System in the American Theatre, 1752–1870." In *The Cambridge History of American Theatre*. Vol. 1 of *Beginnings to 1870*, edited by Don B. Wilmeth and Christopher Bigsby, 303–37. Cambridge: Cambridge University Press, 1998.

Wilmeth, Don B., and Tice L. Miller. *The Cambridge Guide to American Theatre*. Cambridge: Cambridge University Press, 1996.

Wilmeth, Don B., and Edwin Martin. *Mud Show: American Tent Circus Life*. Albuquerque: University of New Mexico Press, 1988.

Wilmeth, Don B., and C. W. E. Bigsby, eds, *The Cambridge History of American Theatre*, Vol. 1 of *Beginnings to 1870*. Cambridge: Cambridge University Press, 1998.

Wilson, Clarence. "First Steam Calliope Worcester Invention." *White Tops* 17, no. 7–8 (June–July 1944), 17.

Winchell, Walter. "Old Broadway." *New York Daily Mirror*, February 1, 1938.

———. "Old Favorites with WPA Circus." *White Tops* 11 (February–March 1938), 8.

Winegar, Karin. "The Circus is Coming on Wheels." *New York Times*, June 30, 2002.

Winter, Marian Hannah. "Theatre of Marvels." *Dance Index* 7, nos. 1–2 (January–February 1948), 26–28.

Withington, Ann Fairfax. *Toward a More Perfect Union: Virtue and the Formation of American Republics*. Oxford and New York: Oxford University Press, 1991.

Wittmann, Matthew. "Empire of Culture: U.S. Entertainers and the Making of the Pacific Circuit." PhD diss., University of Michigan, 2010.

———. "Menageries and Markets: The Zoological Institute Tours Jacksonian America." *Common-Place* 12, no. 1 (October 2011), n.p.

"Woe for WPA Circus." *New York Sun*, April 22, 1938.

Woo, Michelle. "Gilbert Band Heats up NYC." *Arizona Republic*, November 26, 2004.

"World's Top Attraction Here July 1–3." *F. H. Kew Gardens*, June 25, 1937.

"WPA 3-Ring Circus Opens Here Tonight." *Brooklyn Citizen*, September 2, 1937.

"WPA Actors Play to 5,500,000 in City." *New York Times*, February 14, 1937.

"WPA Agent Thinks His Sacred Elephant Very Cute." *Long Island Daily Advocate*, December 31, 1937.

"WPA Circus at Hospital." *New York Times*, June 10, 1936.

"WPA Circus Coming to Brooklyn Friday." *Brooklyn Citizen*, March 30, 1938.

"WPA Circus Extends Stay in Ridgewood." *Brooklyn Citizen*, April 20, 1937.

"WPA Circus Fraud Charged to Three." *New York Times*, August 31, 1938.

"WPA Circus is Showing Here for A.L. Posts." (Brooklyn) *The Record*, June 8, 1939.

"WPA Circus Opens in Jamaica Arena Oct. 30." (New York) *Daily News*, October 18, 1937.

"WPA Circus Performance Given for 150 Children at Bellevue." *New York Times*, November 9, 1935.

"WPA Circus Plays to Absent Mayor." *New York Times*, November 1, 1935.

"WPA Circus Ready for Uptown Debut." *New York Times*, November 3, 1936.

"WPA Circus to Open in King's Wednesday." *New York Times*, August 26, 1937.

"WPA Circus to Pitch Tent in Stapleton Next Week." *Staten Island Advance*, June 2, 1937.

"WPA Circus to Return on Tuesday." *Staten Island Advance*, September 17, 1937.

"WPA Circus Will Feature Chaplin-esque Clowning." *N. R. Standard Star*, November 17, 1937.

"WPA Elephant on 5 Hour Strike." *New York American*, May 31, 1937.

"WPA Elephant, Heeding Circus Call Bolts and Wins His Way to Big Top." *Times Union*, May 15, 1937.

"WPA Press Agent Calls on His Very Finest Adjectives but Reporter Finds Real Thrills are Behind the Scenes." *Staten Island Advance*, June 9, 1937.

"WPA Show Briefs." *Billboard*, March 6, 1937.

"WPA Show Playing Week-End Dates." *Billboard*, February 6, 1937, 40.

"WPA Show Stages Circus Fans' Night." *Billboard*, February 11, 1939, 39.

"WPA Three-Ring Circus Due Tomorrow for Week." *Staten Island Advance*, June 7, 1937.

"WPA 'Tom Thumb Circus' to Play in East New York." *Brooklyn Citizen*, March 13, 1937.

"WPA Unit Plays to 790,000 in N. Y." *Billboard*, October 3, 1936, 36.

Wright, Richardson. *Hawkers and Walkers in Early America*. Philadelphia: J. B. Lippincott, 1927.

"Young Circus Fans Overwhelm Police." *New York Times*, April 2, 1939.

Zelizer, Viviana A. *Pricing the Priceless Child: The Changing Social Value of Children*. New York: Basic Books, 1985.

Index